Sources of Japanese Tradition

SECOND EDITION

VOLUME 2, ABRIDGED

PART 1

Introduction to Asian Civilizations

WM. THEODORE DE BARY, GENERAL EDITOR

Sources of Japanese Tradition
(1958; vol. 1, 2nd ed., 2001; vol. 2, 2nd ed., 2005; vol. 2, 2nd ed., abr., 2006)

Sources of Indian Tradition
(1958; 2nd ed., 1988)

Sources of Chinese Tradition
(1960; vol. 1, 2nd ed., 1999; vol. 2, 2nd ed., 2000)

Sources of Korean Tradition
(vol. 1, 1997; vol. 2, 2001)

Sources of Japanese Tradition

SECOND EDITION

VOLUME TWO: 1600 TO 2000, ABRIDGED

PART ONE: 1600 TO 1868

Compiled by Wm. Theodore de Bary, Carol Gluck,
and Arthur E. Tiedemann

WITH THE COLLABORATION OF
Willem Boot, J. S. A. Elisonas, Grant Goodman, Donald Keene,
Peter Nosco, Janine Sawada, Barry Steben, John A. Tucker

and contributions by
William Bodiford, Ian James McMullen, Rosemary Mercer,
Tetsuo Najita, Kate Nakai, Mary Evelyn Tucker, Paul Watt

COLUMBIA UNIVERSITY PRESS

NEW YORK

Columbia University Press wishes to express its appreciation for assistance given by the Japan Foundation toward the cost of publishing this book.

Columbia University Press
Publishers Since 1893
New York Chichester, West Sussex

Library of Congress Cataloging-in-Publication Data
Sources of Japanese tradition / compiled by Wm. Theodore de Bary . . . [et al.] ; with the collaboration of Andrew Barshay . . . [et al.] ; and contributions by William Bodiford . . . [et al.]. — 2nd ed.
    p. cm. — (Introduction to Asian civilizations)
    Includes bibliographical references and index.
    Contents: v. 1. From earliest times to 1600
               v. 2. 1600 to 2000
               v. 2, abr., pt. 1. 1600 to 1868
               v. 2, abr., pt. 2. 1868 to 2000
    ISBN 0-231-12138-5 (vol. 1, cloth)   ISBN 0-231-12139-3 (vol. 1, paper)
    ISBN 0-231-12984-X (vol. 2, cloth)
    ISBN 0-231-13916-0 (vol. 2, abr., pt. 1, cloth)   ISBN 978-0-231-13917-5 (vol. 2, abr., pt. 1, paper)
    ISBN 0-231-13918-7 (vol. 2, abr., pt. 2, cloth)   ISBN 0-231-13919-5 (vol. 2, abr., pt. 2, paper)
    1. Japan—Civilization—Sources.   2. Japan—History—Sources.   I. De Bary, William
Theodore, 1919–   II. Bodiford, William M.   III. Series.
    DS821.S68 2001
    952–dc21   00-060181

Acknowledgment is gratefully made for permission to reprint from the following:

Excerpts from Keene, Donald, The Japanese Discovery of Europe, 1720–1830, Revised Edition. Copyright © 1952 and 1969 by Donald Keene. Used with permission of Stanford University Press, www.sup.org.

Dedicated to the memory of
Marius Jansen
(1922–2000)

In appreciation of his distinguished contributions to Japanese studies
and of his early collaboration with this project.

CONTENTS

PREFACE

Sources of Japanese Tradition is part of a series introducing the civilizations of India, China, Korea, and Japan to general education, through source readings that tell us what these peoples have thought about themselves, the world they lived in, and the problems they faced living together.

The original *Sources of Japanese Tradition* (1958) was a single volume covering developments from earliest times to the mid-twentieth century. Later this book was divided into two paperback volumes, one from earliest times through the eighteenth century, and the other from the nineteenth to the twentieth century. This division reflected the one prevailing in American education that distinguished modern from traditional primarily on the basis of the encounter with the West in the nineteenth century. The second edition, however, reflects the increasing recognition in both the West and Asia that major factors in the modernization process stemmed from indigenous, pre-nineteenth-century developments. In other words, modernization was not to be understood simply as Westernization. Hence, in their second editions, the Chinese, Korean, and Japanese *Sources* are divided into two volumes, with the second in each case starting from the seventeenth rather than the nineteenth century.

The substantially enlarged volume 2 of the *Japanese Sources* reflects more than just the extended time span from 1600 to 2000. Rather, in this second edition—in volumes 1 and 2 as well as in the abridged parts 1 and 2 of volume 2—educational works have been given particular attention. Instead of focusing on leading thinkers who represented new trends in intellectual or doctrinal thought, we have included basic instructional texts and curricula that helped establish the common terms of educated discourse. Volume 2 also reflects our greater attention to education in both the Tokugawa and Meiji periods as a major factor in the modernization process. Other new developments, covered in part 2, are found in the so-called new religions bridging the dichotomy between traditional and modern.

Even though the early modern period, the subject of part 1, was dominated by Neo-Confucian scholarship and schooling, the warrior ethic continued to play a major role under the military regime of the Tokugawa shogunate, even while the leadership class was being "civilized" by Neo-Confucianism. Buddhism, too, although rejected on intellectual and moral grounds by the Neo-Confucians, persisted on a religious level in ways represented here by a special chapter on the subject. Finally, women's issues (especially education) are included in both parts of volume 2, as they have been in all volumes of the second edition of the East Asian *Sources*.

Since the original edition of *Sources of Japanese Tradition* was published more than forty years ago, many aspects of Japanese (and, indeed, East Asian) studies have undergone substantial development, and we have tried to draw on new studies and expertise wherever possible. Accordingly, the list of collaborators and contributors has expanded greatly, and the compilers are indebted to many distinguished colleagues for their cooperation with this project, a public-service contribution to general education not often recognized.

Marius Jansen was among those collaborators who helped in the planning of this volume, but his untimely death prevented him from contributing to it. This volume is therefore dedicated to him in recognition of his outstanding leadership in Japanese studies and his generous help with both the first and the second editions.

In the final editing of this volume, we have benefited from the extraordinary competence and generous help of Miwa Kai, former curator of the Japanese collection at Columbia University. Others to whom we are indebted for their assistance in producing this volume include Marianna Stiles, Martin Amster, Josephine Vining, and Yuan Zheng. Among our contributors, Tetsuo Najita wishes to acknowledge the collegial assistance of Katsuya Hirano and Yasuko Satō; and Andrew Gordon wishes to thank John Campbell, Sheldon Garon, Timothy Gordon, Laura Hein, Simon Partner, Robert Pekkanen, Ken Ruoff, Mark Selden, M. William Steele, William Tsutsui, and Professors Nakamura Masanori and Hashizume Daizaburō.

EXPLANATORY NOTE

The consonants of Japanese words or names are read as they are in English (with g always hard) and the vowels as in Italian. There are no silent letters. The name Abe, for instance, is pronounced "Ah-bay." The long vowels ō and ū are indicated except in the names of cities already well known in the West, such as Tokyo and Kyoto, and in the words familiar enough to be included in *Webster's Collegiate Dictionary*. All romanized terms have been standardized according to the Hepburn system. Chinese philosophical terms used in Japanese texts are given in their Japanese readings (e.g., *ri* instead of *li* for "principle," "reason") except where attention is specifically drawn to the Chinese original, in which case the *pin-yin* system is followed. Sanskrit words appearing in italics follow the standard system of transliteration found in Louis Renou's *Grammair sanskrite* (Paris: Adrien-Maisoneuve, 1930), pp. xi–xiii. Sanskrit terms and names appearing in roman letters follow *Webster's New International Dictionary*, second edition unabridged, except that a macron is used to indicate long vowels and the Sanskrit symbols for ś (ç) are uniformly transcribed as *sh* in the text itself. Personal names also are spelled in this manner except when they occur in the titles of works.

Japanese names are given in their Japanese order, with the family name first and the personal name last. The dates given after personal names are those of birth and death except in the case of rulers, whose reign dates are preceded by "r." Generally, the name by which a person was most commonly known in

Japanese tradition is the one used in the text. Since this book is intended for general readers rather than specialists, we have not burdened the text with the alternative names or titles usually accompanying biographical references to a scholar that are found in Chinese or Japanese historical works. For the same reason, the sources of translations given at the end of each selection are as concise as possible. There is a complete bibliography at the end of the book.

The name following the chapter title in the table of contents refers to the writer of all the introductory material in that chapter unless otherwise noted. The initials following the source at the end of each selection are those of the translator or compiler. Excerpts from existing translations have often been adapted and edited to suit our purposes. In particular, we have removed unnecessary brackets and footnotes and have inserted essential commentary in the text whenever possible instead of putting it in a footnote. Those interested in the full text and annotations may, of course, refer to the original translation cited with each excerpt. As sources for our own translations, we have tried to use standard editions that would be available to other scholars.

W. T. de B.

Tokugawa Period (1600–1867)

1600   Ieyasu is victorious at Sekigahara, and the Tokugawa shogunate begins.

1603   Tokugawa shogunate is established.

1608   Hayashi Razan becomes Confucian tutor to the shogun.

1615   Code for the Warrior Households (Buke shohatto) is promulgated. Osaka Castle is destroyed, and Hideyoshi's heirs are defeated.

1616   Ieyasu (1543–1616) dies.

1617   Christians are again persecuted.

1624   Spaniards are expelled.

1637–1638   Shimabara revolt takes place. Japanese are forbidden to leave Japan.

1639   Portuguese are expelled.

1640   Other Europeans are excluded.

1647   Kumazawa Banzan, having studied Ōyōmei philosophy under Nakae Tōju, enters the service of Lord Ikeda of Okayama.

1648   Nakae Tōju (1608–1648) dies.

1657   Great fire breaks out in Edo. *History of Great Japan* (*Dai-Nihonshi*) is begun.

1665   Chinese émigré Zhu Shunshui settles in Mito as an adviser to the Mito school.

1670	*General History of Our State* (*Honchō tsugan*) is completed by the Hayashi school.
1682	Yamazaki Ansai (1618–1682) dies.
1685	Yamaga Sokō (1622–1685), an early proponent of the Way of the warrior (*bushidō*), dies.
1687	Reform program of Kumazawa Banzan (1619–1691) arouses the shogunate's wrath.
1688–1704	Genroku period, during which the novels of Saikaku, the plays of Chikamatsu, the poems of Bashō, and *ukiyo* prints are created.
1691	Hayashi Hōkō is named hereditary head of the state university.
1703	Incident of the forty-seven *rōnin* takes place.
1705	Itō Jinsai (1627–1705), a proponent of "ancient studies," dies.
1709	Arai Hakuseki (1657–1725) becomes Confucian adviser to the shogunate.
1714	Kaibara Ekken (1630–1714) dies.
1715	Yoshimune becomes shogun. Arai Hakuseki is dismissed as Confucian adviser.
1716	Relaxation of edicts against foreign learning gives rise to Dutch studies.
1728	Ogyū Sorai (1666–1728) dies at the high tide of Chinese studies. Kada Azumamaro (1669–1736) petitions the shogunate to establish a school of National Learning.
1732	Great famine devastates the country.
1734	Muro Kyūsō (1658–1734) dies.
1746	Tominaga Nakamoto (1715–1746), a rationalist philosopher, dies.
1769	Kamo Mabuchi (1697–1769), a National Learning scholar, dies.
1783–1786	Serious famines and epidemics plague the country.
1787	Matsudaira Sadanobu institutes various fiscal and social reforms in the shogun's administration.
1789	Miura Baien (1723–1789), a rationalist philosopher, dies.
1790	Shogunate issues an edict suppressing heterodox learning.
1791–1792	American and Russian ships visit Japan, followed by repeated attempts to open relations with Japan.
1801	Motoori Norinaga (1730–1801), a National Learning scholar, dies.
1817	Kaiho Seiryō (1755–1817), a rationalist thinker, dies.
1821	Honda Toshiaki (1744–1821), an economic and political thinker, dies.
1825	Aizawa Seishisai (1792–1863) writes *New Proposals* (*Shinron*).
1842	Opium War ends.
1843	Hirata Atsutane (1776–1843), a National Learning scholar, dies.
1846	James Biddle, commanding American warships at Uraga, requests Japan to open to trade.
1850	Satō Nobuhiro (1769–1850), a political thinker, dies.

1853   Commodore Matthew Perry's "black ships" arrive in Edo Bay.

1854   Perry returns and negotiates the Treaty of Kanagawa. Yoshida
              Shōin, with Sakuma Shōzan's encouragement, tries to stow away
              on a ship to America.

1856   Townsend Harris, the first American minister to Japan, arrives. Ni-
              nomiya Sontoku (1787–1856), an agrarian reformer, dies.

1858   Commercial treaty between Japan and the United States is signed.

1859   Yoshida Shōin (1830–1859) is executed.

1860   First Japanese mission is sent to the United States.

1863   British bomb Kagoshima in retaliation for antiforeign outbursts.

1867   Keiki, the last Tokugawa shogun, resigns, ending the Tokugawa
              shogunate.

CONTRIBUTORS

BS	Barry Steben, National University, Singapore
DK	Donald Keene, Columbia University
IJM	Ian James McMullen, Oxford University
JAT	John A. Tucker, East Carolina University, Greenville
JS	Janine Sawada, University of Iowa
JSAE	Jurgis S. A. Elisonas, Indiana University
KN	Kate Nakai, Sophia University
MET	Mary Evelyn Tucker, Bucknell University
PN	Peter Nosco, University of British Columbia
PW	Paul Watt, Depauw University
RM	Rosemary Mercer, Victoria University of Wellington
RT	Ryusaku Tsunoda
TN	Tetsuo Najita, University of Chicago
WB	Willem Boot, Leiden University
WBd	William Bodiford, University of California, Los Angeles
WTdB	Wm. Theodore de Bary, Columbia University

Sources of Japanese Tradition

SECOND EDITION

VOLUME 2, ABRIDGED

PART 1

PART IV

The Tokugawa Peace

Modern Japan began to take shape in the Tokugawa period (1603–1868), after the military reunification of the country in the late sixteenth century. Accordingly, many historians have been tempted to mark the beginning of the modern era in Japan with the founding of the Tokugawa regime. True, there is some incongruity in calling "modern" a period during which the feudal system and military government inherited from medieval times were perpetuated. We might also ask why, with the drastic changes made after Japan's opening to the West, it still should have needed modernizing. But we would have even more difficulty explaining the country's success in undertaking such a comprehensive reorganization of its national life and assuming an active role in the modern world, if during the preceding centuries Japan had not already been traveling, though perhaps more slowly and unevenly, in the direction of its subsequent rapid progress.

Among the changes in Japanese society that helped prepare it for this role, we may point to significant trends in thought that were already well established in the Tokugawa period—which was known also as the Edo period after the location of the shogunate's capital at Edo (modern Tokyo). The first of these changes was a marked shift in attention from religious questions—from the Buddhist search for release from the bonds of this world—to more mundane problems. This is not to suggest that Buddhism suddenly went into eclipse or that its light ceased to shine among the Japanese people as a whole but that the intellectual world responded almost immediately to the ruling class's need for a secular ideology that, after centuries of violence and disorder, would maintain some semblance of order and stability. Whatever else Buddhism had done for the soul in the anguished medieval period, it did not propose a public philosophy or provide for a civil society. Privatization of religious experience was paralleled by privatization of power and internecine warfare.

The late medieval period had been dominated by the great houses of the daimyō—literally, "great names"—a term that itself betrays the privatization of power and its loss by the imperial court. The court's loss of power had long since been identified with a court aristocracy, known as kuge, a word signifying the privatization of state power (kō) largely by the Fujiwara clan (ge). In his drive to reunify the country, Toyotomi Hideyoshi had arrogated to himself the title of kanpaku, translated as "imperial regent" or "civil dictator," both terms ironically reminiscent of the imperial house's original claim to represent a unified civil state.

By the time of Japan's unification under Tokugawa Ieyasu, the tradition of feudal military rule had become so strongly embedded in Japanese life that Ieyasu's attempt to superimpose a higher authority naturally came about through the enactment of legislation modeled on the medieval house laws. Mostly this confirmed local decentralized rule but also was aimed to prevent any agglomeration of power that could challenge the shogun's control. Even the imperial court was treated by the new regulations as a private household confined within its own courtly rituals.

This was true as well for the principal religious communities, both Buddhist and Shinto. Even the great religious movements in Japanese Mahayana Buddhism, often thought "popular" in the sense that they had broken out of the old Heian mold and, in some cases, formed new lay communities, were seen as essentially sectarian: universalist in theory but competitive in practice. Their "expedient means"—a key feature of Mahayana universalism—had adapted itself so well to the medieval landscape that Oda Nobunaga, Hideyoshi, and Ieyasu (though their tactics differed) regarded Buddhist communities as rival sects, allied when convenient with one or another feudal power and sometimes a potential threat to their own position.

Japanese Buddhism, both early and late, had adhered to the idea of religion and the state as mutually supportive and protective, but implicit in this relationship was respect for their complementary spheres of authority. Power holders generally refrained from interposing themselves in sectarian issues, while Buddhist sects in privatized lineages and those that emphasized personal intuition more than doctrine had almost no public philosophy or program to offer.

True, the Ashikaga shoguns and the leading daimyo had had Zen advisers, but their advice was largely prudential and tactical, not based on any political philosophy or ideology. To justify or dress up their seizure of power, the Ashikaga had legitimized themselves by patronizing Zen temples, landscape gardening, the tea ceremony, and nō drama; that is, they had identified themselves with the contemporary high culture of the capital, just as the rulers of the Heian period had done when they could no longer lay claim to governing a universal state in the name of "all-under-Heaven."

In his turn, Nobunaga had overruled the Ashikaga precisely on the ground that they had forfeited any moral claim to acting on behalf of "all-under-Heaven."[1] Hideyoshi, a foot soldier from out of nowhere with no aristocratic pedigree, tried to legitimize his assumption of supreme authority by assuming the old title of civil dictator (reminiscent of the Fujiwaras), by constructing a new Great Buddha image in Kyoto (in imitation of Shōmu's Daibutsu in Nara), by playing the Ashikaga game as patron of the tea ceremony on a grand scale, and by having himself deified in a new Shinto shrine.

Although such ritual ploys had largely lost their currency by Ieyasu's time, he had no less need of legitimization, especially since he had forsworn his guardianship of Hideyoshi's son and designated successor, Hideyori. Like the Ashikaga and the leading daimyo, Ieyasu had a retinue of Buddhist advisers, but, again, they provided no public philosophy or civil ideology. Their influence in practical matters, therefore, did not prevent Ieyasu and his successors from turning to the new Neo-Confucian secular culture that was developing in East Asia.

In the seventeenth century, what Japan's leaders sought was less peace of mind than the peace of the country, and it was natural that they should turn for this to Confucianism, the philosophy devoted to achieving social peace and order. Hence the new "this-worldliness" of the Tokugawa era did not directly concern the material or physical world so much as the personal world of intellectual and moral cultivation in the context of social relations. It was in this domain that Neo-Confucianism, from its beginnings in China and passage through Korea, made its greatest impact. In addition, other elements of Neo-Confucian culture spread from China and Korea and commanded attention on their own merits apart from any official sponsorship, nourishing and invigorating Japanese life even more widely in the seventeenth and eighteenth centuries.

What was "new" in sixteenth-century Japanese Neo-Confucianism had arisen in eleventh-century China and fourteenth-century Korea as a reaction to an earlier age dominated by the military and by Buddhism. The Song Neo-Confucians' new philosophical formulations were a response to the fundamental challenge of Buddhist philosophy, rejecting Buddhist skepticism of the world in order to provide a positive metaphysical basis for a new humanistic culture and civil society. As the product of a rising civil, scholar-official class, the Neo-Confucian philosophy at first was a challenge to the establishment and later

---

1. See de Bary et al., eds., *Sources of Japanese Tradition*, 2nd ed., vol. 1, chap. 19.

was adopted by dynastic rulers who could not stabilize their rule without that class's support and active involvement. But its adoption by the ruling powers and their subsequent incorporation of Neo-Confucianism into the official ideologies should not obscure the fact that Neo-Confucianism spoke more broadly for a whole new cultural movement that, just as it had first developed independently of the ruling ideology, continued much of its growth in areas beyond official control.

This Neo-Confucian teaching, based mainly on the system of Zhu Xi, had been available to the Japanese earlier when Zen monks, heavily engaged in the China trade, brought Neo-Confucian texts back to the leading Zen monasteries. Zen advisers to the Ashikaga, however, had done little to promote them. Tending to be dismissive of the Neo-Confucian philosophy as simply mundane, they did not recognize its "Learning of the Mind-and-Heart" as a spiritual discipline on the same plane as their own.

With the establishment of a unified military regime under Ieyasu, a new, coherent ideology was needed, along with secular learning that would serve a more centralized system, albeit in many aspects still "feudal." Answering to both purposes, centrality and feudalism, was the key concept of Neo-Confucian teaching: "self-cultivation (i.e., discipline) for the governance of men," based on the cultivation by ruler and ruled alike of man's morally responsible self and socially responsive nature.

Meanwhile, the Neo-Confucian learning itself had developed and spread since Zhu Xi's time. It was no longer just the Song learning of the twelfth century that had been known to Zen monks but a political doctrine that had been adapted first by the Mongols in Yuan China, then by the Ming dynasty (1368–1644), and next by the Chosŏn dynasty in Korea (1398–1910). In late-sixteenth-century Korea, Japanese expeditionary forces returned with the texts and artifacts of a whole new culture, bringing with them libraries covering a range of Neo-Confucian scholarship and secular literature. These were accompanied by Korean scholars, nominally prisoners of war, who quickly became advisers to the Tokugawa and their branch houses.

In its earlier forms, Neo-Confucianism was closely identified with a Chinese-style civil bureaucratic state, the like of which was not found in Tokugawa Japan. Many of Confucianism's meritocratic features, especially those of the civil service examination system, contrasted sharply with the aristocratic, hereditary features of the Tokugawa shogunate. Nevertheless, Neo-Confucianism itself was a broader intellectual and educational movement than the institutional forms adapted to the dynastic state. It had spread through local academies in Song China, and then into Mongol Korea, China, and Chosŏn Korea. Even in Korea, it was sustained by the relatively independent local academies of the Yangban elite. Thus, even allowing for the major differences between Chinese and Korean bureaucracy and Japanese feudalism, it is not surprising that Neo-Confucian culture bridged the two and flourished in both the domain and the private schools of Tokugawa-period Japan, developing diverse forms in the process. Thus we can speak of official schools maintained by the shogunate or its branches and also of relatively independent individual schools. Together they produced a prolific, wide-ranging intellectual life, with orthodoxy a contested issue.

Compared with Buddhism's emphasis on the evanescence of this world, Neo-Confucianism stressed the substantiality, orderliness, and intelligibility of "Heaven-and-earth and all things." In the minds of a significant few Tokugawa thinkers, this attitude eventually helped foster a new interest in the study of both nature and human society. More immediately, however, it was expressed in a typical Confucian concern for the study of human history as revealing the constant laws of human behavior and political morality. As applied to Japan, this study took forms that had no precedent in China's experience. For instance, it focused on the question of legitimate shogunal and imperial rule and on the unbroken succession of the reigning house, which later fed into the imperial restoration movement. This, in turn, abetted the rise of a new nativism: the National Learning movement, which contributed to the study of Japanese literature and the revival of Shinto. In time, both these trends fused into an intense nationalism, which consciously rejected Chinese influences while incorporating essential elements from the great residue of Confucian intellectual and moral cultivation. Perhaps the most striking example of this was the development of *bushidō*, the "Way of the warrior," which joined Japanese feudal traditions and some Buddhist influences with elements adapted from Confucian ethics to form a new military cult.

New developments in the Tokugawa period benefited from the relative stability of Japanese domestic life, the growth of the economy, and the adaptation of Neo-Confucian teachings, especially to the townspeople in the burgeoning urban areas. The "seclusion" policy (*sakoku*), aimed primarily at protecting Japan from foreign intrusion and incursion, kept foreign trade largely under shogunal control but did not isolate the Japanese from all Western learning. Pursuing the Neo-Confucian instinct for "the investigation of things," the Japanese took up Dutch studies, so called because Western learning came through the Dutch at Nagasaki.

Although rapid economic growth and an expanding population in the seventeenth and eighteenth centuries put great pressure on the means of subsistence, on Japan's limited natural resources, and especially on the limited capabilities of the feudal system, the concurrent spread of schooling, both elite and popular, meant that by the nineteenth century, Japan had the human resources needed to meet the challenge of the West.

If Confucianism inadvertently contributed to a growing sense of nationalism, Confucian rationalism, along with some exposure to Western science through the Dutch at Nagasaki, helped keep that nationalism from ignoring Japan's own limitations. We are speaking here of a much less pervasive force in the nation's life: a critical consciousness found mostly in individuals of the educated class. Nonetheless, it was the same class that produced the leaders of Japan's eventual modernization, and we cannot help but be impressed that by the end of the Tokugawa period, many members of the samurai, whose qualifications to rule had once been strictly martial, had become competent in other fields of leadership, intellectual as well as political. The example of Yoshida Shōin—a great hero of the Restoration movement who combined nationalism, Confucian moral discipline, and an intense awareness of the need to learn from the West— was an exception. Even before Yoshida, other educated Japanese, most of them samurai, already had been grappling with some of the greatest problems, mainly economic, of their own society and with some questions that became pressing only when Japan's doors were forcibly opened. Although these thinkers may not have had any direct influence on their own age, they showed that despite the anachronisms of the shogunate itself and the entrenched feudal system, other forces were at work that would better prepare Japan to take its place in the new world.

Chapter 20

IEYASU AND THE FOUNDING OF THE
TOKUGAWA SHOGUNATE

Tokugawa Ieyasu (1543–1616) was the third of Japan's three unifiers and succeeded where his predecessors Oda Nobunaga (1534–1582) and Toyotomi Hideyoshi (1537–1598) had failed. Ieyasu managed to establish a stable regime that gave peace to the Japanese islands for 250 years. The form he chose for his government was that of a warrior regime, a *bakufu* (military headquarters), after the precedents of the earlier Kamakura and Muromachi *bakufu*. Although aware of these precedents, Ieyasu put in place a government that was by no means an exact copy of the earlier warrior regimes. Under his system, the centralization of feudal state and society went much further than it had in either of the earlier periods. The whole of Japan was ruled by the shogun and approximately 260 feudal lords, called *daimyo*, who were appointed by the shogun. As a rule, their positions were hereditary, in the sense that a daimyo would be succeeded by one of his sons or adoptive sons and this succession would be confirmed by the shogun. However, the shogun had the right, which he often used, to assign daimyo to new fiefs, to give them greater or smaller fiefs, or to dismiss them. The shogun himself, the apex of the feudal pyramid, was nominally appointed by the emperor, who thus fulfilled his usual role as the final legitimizing authority in Japan.

In the system that Ieyasu established, however, the emperor had no political influence or administrative responsibility; together with his courtiers, he led a secluded life in an imperial compound in Kyoto. The country, ruled by warriors, can best be conceived as a country under martial law, enforced by a standing army. The daimyo were military commanders, assigned a specific territory in which they had to maintain order and from which they collected income needed to feed and equip their troops. The number of troops they had to maintain was calculated according to the estimated average yield of their domain, expressed in measures of rice (*koku*), the so-called total of rice (*kokudaka*). As long as the daimyos kept their domain quiet and their army operational, they had a more or less free hand in running it. The shogun and his *bakufu* were responsible for overall coordination, for foreign relations, for relations with the imperial court, and for administration of the lands that belonged directly to the shogun, which included such major commercial centers as Osaka, Sakai, and Nagasaki.

It is noteworthy that Ieyasu did not have a blueprint ready at the beginning of his reign in which all these features were spelled out. One of the standard complaints of scholars of the Tokugawa period was that the Tokugawa "did not have a system," by which they meant anything comparable to the Chinese imperial system (or its copy, the ancient Japanese *ritsuryō* system), with its elaborate bureaucracy and all-encompassing law codes and ritual manuals. What came closest to these were two codes that the *bakufu* promulgated in the seventh month of 1615, the Code for the Warrior Households (Buke shohatto) and the Code for the Imperial Court and Court Nobility (Kinchū narabi ni kuge shohatto). These, however, fell far short of what East Asian scholars of Confucianism had come to expect.

It is more realistic to see the Tokugawa system as the result of improvisation in the face of ever-changing political opportunities and internal and external pressures. Of course, it is possible to formulate a number of maxims and guiding concepts at some level of aggregation, but typically such abstractions were never alluded to or invoked when the *bakufu* was formulating its policy. True to its military background, the *bakufu* issued orders: specific ad hoc commands that were intended to settle a certain issue or to attain a concrete objective. It did not reflect on the reasons for choosing a certain policy and did not try to defend its choices in general, moral, or rational terms.

Much of the structure that eventually emerged (indeed all of it, according to the claims of later generations of Tokugawa officials) was due to its founder, Tokugawa Ieyasu, the great ancestor, the deity venerated in the Tōshōgū temple in Nikkō and its branches everywhere in Japan. References to decisions or intentions of the great founder were stock arguments in policy discussions within the *bakufu*, and once an institution had been labeled as "initiated by Ieyasu," it could be changed only with great difficulty. This meant that the life and deeds of the great man were constantly in the minds of later generations of *bakufu* vassals. Not only was Ieyasu's life an important item in Tokugawa propaganda, but it also had precedential value.

Actually, Ieyasu's life did have much to recommend it to his future admirers and hagiographers. He was the only son of a small and struggling warlord in the province of Mikawa, somewhat to the north of present-day Nagoya. From his seventh until his eighteenth year, he lived as a hostage in Sunpu (present-day Shizuoka), as surety for the behavior of his vassals. When at last, in 1560, the daimyo who held him hostage, Imagawa Yoshimoto, was defeated and killed, Ieyasu was free to return home and try to put new life into his flagging band of retainers. He made his peace with Oda Nobunaga in 1561 and became Nobunaga's henchman in eastern Japan, his task being to keep at bay the powerful daimyo Takeda Shingen (1521–1573) and Shingen's successor while Nobunaga was doing battle in the area of the capital and the adjacent areas to the north and west.

Ieyasu narrowly escaped being caught in the chaos that resulted from Nobunaga's murder in 1582. He had been traveling in the Kansai with only a small retinue when Nobunaga's sudden demise forced him to make a difficult journey through the mountains of Iga and Kōga to regain his own domain. The journey itself became a favorite item in later stories and biographies, but in the short run, it prevented Ieyasu from making his mark in avenging Nobunaga's murder. By the time Ieyasu had organized again, Toyotomi Hideyoshi had already killed the assassin, Akechi Mitsuhide, and was in the process of taking over Oda Nobunaga's coalition.

In this process, Ieyasu emerged as Hideyoshi's main opponent. Both were careful to maintain the legality of their cause by backing a member of Nobunaga's family: Hideyoshi, the infant son of Nobunaga's eldest son, and Ieyasu, one of Nobunaga's younger sons, Nobukatsu. On the battlefield, Hideyoshi proved unable to subdue Ieyasu (the battles of Komaki and Nagakute in 1584), but he did manage to persuade Nobukatsu to give up the fight and return to the fold. Finding himself without legitimation, Ieyasu had no choice but to become Hideyoshi's wary but loyal ally (1585).

After the successful conclusion of his campaign against the Hōjō in Odawara (1590), Hideyoshi requested Ieyasu to exchange his present possessions along the eastern seaboard for the Hōjō territory in the Kantō region. Ieyasu accepted, and several months later, still in the same year, he entered the small fishing village of Edo, lying in the marshy coastland of the next bay north of Kamakura, where he decided to build his capital. Thanks to this move, Ieyasu's total *kokudaka* had risen to 2.5 million *koku*, which made him the second largest warlord in Japan, after Hideyoshi himself. As such, he was appointed by Hideyoshi to be the leader of the Council of the Five Elders (Go-tairō), which was composed of Japan's five (in terms of *kokudaka*) strongest warlords. The council was supposed to act as the highest ruling body during the minority of Hideyoshi's son Hideyori (1593–1615). Under the Five Elders, Hideyoshi created a second body, the Five Commissioners (Go-bugyō), whose leading member was Ishida Mitsunari (1560–1600). It was a delicate balance of power that Hideyoshi had instituted, and it did not last; before long, things came to a head, and in the battle of Sekigahara (1600) Ieyasu and his allies prevailed over a coalition put together by Mitsunari.

Although his victory at Sekigahara gave Ieyasu a preponderant position, he still had his allies to consider and a few powerful enemies to deal with. Above all, for the legitimation of his acts he still depended on his position as Hideyori's regent. Most of the warlords who had opposed him at Sekigahara were expropriated and banished or killed, but Ieyasu had to distribute most of the confiscated territories among his allies in order to reward them for their services. Ieyasu did not reign supreme, as is shown, for instance, by the fact that it took more than two years of negotiations to reach an agreement with the ancient and powerful daimyo family Shimazu, who were entrenched in Satsuma at the southern end of Kyushu. Only after this last obstacle to peace had been removed did the court appoint Ieyasu as shogun (Keichō 8/2/12, or 1603).

It is after this turn in his life that Ieyasu's motivation becomes a problem. The sources allow us to confirm what Ieyasu did, but they are silent on his reasons for doing them. It was left to his later biographers and hagiographers to supply these motives, and they were only too glad to jump into the breach. The result is that we have as many Ieyasus as we have biographies, ranging from the dashing and impulsive commander projected in *Mikawa monogatari* (1622), written by his retainer Ōkubo Tadanori, through the wise, warmhearted ruler of Asaka Tanpaku's *Resso seiseki* (1722), to the venerated ancestor of the official chronicle of the Tokugawa *bakufu*, *Tokugawa jikki* (1849). In between are many stories and anecdotes, the best known of which is the anecdote of the nightingale, intended to show the differences in character among Nobunaga, Hideyoshi, and Ieyasu: The three of them sat watching a nightingale, which refused to sing. "If it does not sing, I will kill it," said Nobunaga. "Let us make it sing," said Hideyoshi. "No," said Ieyasu, "let us wait until it starts singing on its own." All Japanese children are told this story, and Ieyasu as the patient planner (or schemer) is still the most popular characterization of him in present-day Japan. It is not necessarily correct, however.

The case most discussed in this connection is Ieyasu's relation to Toyotomi Hideyori, Hideyoshi's heir and Ieyasu's ward. With his appointment as shogun, Ieyasu finally obtained an independent source of legitimacy. Nevertheless, Hideyori still was a power to be reckoned with. This, at least, seems to be the only reasonable explanation of Ieyasu's decision, made a few months after his appointment, to marry his granddaughter, Princess Sen, to Hideyori. Otherwise, an imperial prince would have been a more likely match for her, as indeed happened after the Toyotomi family had finally been eliminated, when in 1620 a second granddaughter of Ieyasu was married to Emperor Go-Mizunoo. The question at issue is whether Ieyasu had been doing his best to accommodate Hideyori and only at the very end had to conclude that accommodation was no longer possible or whether he had laid a trap and was waiting patiently for Hideyori to ensnare himself. Several other questions arise on the same issue: Did Ieyasu consciously defer his final move on the Toyotomi until the old generation of daimyo, who had known Hideyoshi personally, had died out? Did he try to wean the daimyo away from Osaka and make them come to Edo? Did he step down as shogun after less than two years in office and have himself succeeded by his son Hidetada in order to be free to deal with these major issues of policy, or did he do so because he felt that he could afford to retire and that it would be good for Hidetada to make his own mark? The sources can be read in several ways, with none being definitive.

What we do know, however, is what happened. Hideyori and Ieyasu met for the first time in several years on the occasion of Emperor Go-Mizunoo's accession to the throne in 1611. Apparently that interview went well, for Ieyasu returned to Sunpu without taking any measures against Hideyori. Three years later, however, in 1614 Ieyasu raised a number of problems in connection with the dedication of the statue of the Great Buddha in the Hōkōji in Kyoto that Hideyori had decided to restore. But Hideyori refused to comply and took up arms against Ieyasu. In 1615, after a two-stage campaign, Osaka Castle fell and went up in flames, and Hideyori perished with it.

This incident is more than accidental history. Upon its interpretation hinges the debate about the legitimacy of the Tokugawa regime. According to some scholars, the initiative was taken by Ieyasu himself when he decided to settle the matter of Osaka once and for all and wanted to put himself in the clear. Vestiges of this debate can be found in Hayashi Razan's *Bakufu mondō*, and after the Meiji Restoration it came up again. In this way, it became a favorite subject of Japanese historiography.

Another subject, which disappeared in the Meiji period but was much elaborated in Tokugawa sources, was Ieyasu's frugality. Again, this is not merely factual biographical information. Ieyasu may well have been frugal, parsimonious, or even miserly, and it is a fact that he amassed an enormous hoard of gold and silver that kept the *bakufu* solvent for six decades. But this character trait also had an ideological aspect, for some schools of thought considered frugality to be an important virtue in its own right. More specifically, in the context of the Way of Heaven (*tendō*) lore, it was also a virtue related to the length of dynasties, in the sense that the frugality of their founders explained why certain Chinese dynasties lasted as long as they did.

The final and, for Ieyasu, logical step to ensure the continued fortune of his house was to have himself deified. In this he followed a precedent set by Hideyoshi, who had been deified posthumously as Hōkoku daimyojin. The initiative was taken by Ieyasu himself when on his deathbed, two weeks before his death, he declared on several occasions that after his death he would manifest himself as a god. There was some dispute among the ecclesiastics about the rites that should be used to deify Ieyasu. The victory went to the head of the Tendai sect in eastern Japan, Tenkai (d. 1643). It was Tenkai who organized Ieyasu's cult as an avatar of the Yakushi Buddha (Tōshōgū daigongen) and who installed him in his temple in Nikkō. From this temple, the Tōshōgū, Ieyasu continued to watch over the fortunes of the dynasty he had established.

CODE FOR THE WARRIOR HOUSEHOLDS
(BUKE SHOHATTO)

The regulations for warrior households are concerned mainly with military security, the maintenance of a hierarchical order, and the avoidance of material display. Most administration is left to internal, personal "household" management. Note that article 3 asserts that law is not subject to principle, contrary to Neo-Confucian teaching.

1. One must wholly devote oneself to the civil and the military arts and to the Way of the bow and the horse.

To have the civil on the left and the military on the right is the ancient practice. One must be equipped with both. The bow and horse are the most important things for warriors. Weapons are called dismal instruments, but [sometimes] one cannot avoid using them. "In times of order, do not forget turmoil." How could one not exert oneself in training and perfecting oneself [in the use of arms]?

2. Drinking parties and idle, wanton amusements should be restricted.

The rigorous restrictions that codes of law placed [on this behavior] are especially strict. States have been lost because their rulers were infatuated with sex or made gambling their chief occupation.

3. Those who have defied the laws shall not be given sanctuary in any of the provinces.

Law is the root of ritual and decorum. Principle can be violated in the name of the law, but the law cannot be violated in the name of principle. Those who defy the laws will not be punished lightly.

4. The greater and lesser lords of all the provinces and all their stipended officials must speedily expel any soldiers in their service who have been accused of rebellion or murder.

Those who harbor untoward ambitions are the sharp instruments that overturn the state, the dart and sword that cut off people [from their livelihood]. How could one condone them?

5. From now on, no one who is not from that province shall be allowed to live there [freely] among [the inhabitants of that province].

Generally speaking, each province has its own, different customs. If someone either reported abroad the secrets of his own province or reported in his own province the secrets of other provinces, it would be the beginning of fawning and flattering.

6. Any repairs of the castles in the provinces must certainly be reported [to the *bakufu*]—as well as new construction, which is strictly forbidden!

Walls extending more than one hundred *chi* [a measure for city walls: thirty feet long by ten feet high] are a peril to the state. High fortresses and well-dredged moats are the origin of great turmoil.

7. If new [construction] is planned or bands are formed in a neighboring province, you must speedily inform [the *bakufu*].

"All men are given to factionalism, and wise men are few. For this reason they sometimes do not obey their lords or fathers, or they feud with neighboring villages."[1] Why do they plan new things instead of abiding by the old institutions?

8. One must not contract marriages privately.

The bonds of marriage are the way of yin and yang's mutual harmony. One should not enter them lightly. [The explanation of the diagram] *kui* [in the *Yijing*] says: "Marriage should not be contracted out of enmity [against others]. Marriages intended to effect an alliance with enemies [of the state] will turn out badly." The ode "Peach Blossoms" [in the *Shijing*] says: "When men and women behave correctly and marriages are arranged in the proper season, then throughout the land there will be no unmarried men."[2] To use one's marriage relations in order to establish factions is at the root of evil schemes.

9. How the daimyo should report for duty.

Chronicles of Japan, Continued[3] contains a regulation saying: "If one is not engaged in official duties, one should not at will assemble one's clansmen. One cannot move through the capital with a retinue of more than twenty horsemen." Therefore, one should not bring with oneself great masses of soldiers. Daimyo with an estate of 1 million to 200,000 *koku* should not be escorted by more than twenty mounted warriors; those with an estate of less than [1?]100,000 [*sic*] *koku* should reduce their escort proportionally. However, when a daimyo is performing his official tasks, he may be followed by as many men as his rank entitles him to.

10. Restrictions on the type and quality of clothing should not be transgressed.

One should be able to distinguish between lord and retainer, high and low. Ordinary people who have not been authorized to wear them cannot wear white robes with narrow sleeves (*kosode*) of white damask, *kosode* made of glossed unpatterned silk and dyed purple inside, or purple-lined robes (*awase*). It is against all ancient law that nowadays vassals and soldiers are wearing gaudy clothes of damask, gauze, or embroidered silk. This must be strictly regulated.

11. Ordinary people should not ride indiscriminately in palanquins.

In the past, depending on the person, some families rode in palanquins without [the need to obtain a special] permission, and some did so after

---

1. See de Bary et al., eds., *Sources of Japanese Tradition*, 2nd ed., vol. 1, p. 51, article I.

2. Neither the *Yijng* nor the *Shijing* is quoted or interpreted correctly here.

3. *Shoku Nihongi* is the second of the Six National Histories (Rikkokushi). It was finished in 797 and covers the years from 697 to 791.

they had obtained permission. Recently, however, even vassals and soldiers ride in palanquins. This is really the extreme of presumption. Henceforth, a lord of a province and the senior members of his house may ride [in palanquins] without first needing to ask for permission. In addition to them, attendants of nobles, members of the two professions of physicians and astrologers, people sixty years and older, and sick people will be allowed to ride [in a palanquin] after they have applied for permission. The master of vassals and soldiers who willfully ride [in palanquins] should be held to blame.

12. Warriors in the provinces should practice frugality.

The rich will flaunt their wealth more and more, and the poor will be ashamed because they cannot measure up to the average. Nothing is more demoralizing than this. It is something that should be strictly regulated.

13. The lord of a province should select those who have talent and abilities for the tasks of government.

Generally speaking, the way of ruling a state is a matter of getting the [right] men. Merit and faults should be clearly examined, and rewards and punishments should always be appropriate. When a state has good men, that state will flourish more and more; when a state does not, it will certainly perish. This is the clear admonition of the wise men of old.

The preceding [code] must be complied with.

Dated: 7th month of Keichō 20 [1615]

[*Dai Nihon shiryō*, vol. 12, pt. 22, pp. 19–22, WB]

CODE FOR THE IMPERIAL COURT AND COURT NOBILITY
(KINCHŪ NARABI NI KUGE SHOHATTO)

This code does not hesitate to prescribe proper conduct for the emperor and court nobility, and it even censures the emperor's failure to observe court precedents. In addition, the official Buddhist hierarchy is treated as subordinate to the court and is seen as corrupted by it.[4]

1. Of all the emperor's various accomplishments, learning is the most important. If an emperor does not study, he will not clearly know the ancient way; [never yet has such an emperor] been able to establish great peace through his

---

4. Lee A. Butler, "Tokugawa Ieyasu's Regulation for the Court: A Reappraisal," *Harvard Journal of Asian Studies* 54 (1994): 532–36.

rule. *Jōgan seiyō*[5] is a clear text, and although *Kanpyō yuikai*[6] does not plumb the full depth of the classics and histories, it [should be read and memorized, as should] *Gunsho chiyō*.[7] Ever since Emperor Kōkō, [our country has known] a continuous tradition of *waka* (thirty-one-syllable verse) [composition]. Although *waka* are a matter of fine words,[8] composing them is a custom of our country that should not be abandoned. As it says in *Kinpi-shō*,[9] [the emperor] should exclusively concentrate on learning.

2. The three dukes (*sankō*)[10] take precedence over the imperial princes (*shinnō*). The reason is that the great minister of the right, Fujiwara no Fuhito, was ranked above Prince Toneri.[11] Specifically, Prince Toneri and Prince Nakano[12] were posthumously appointed prime minister, and Prince Hozumi[13] was given the same privileges (*jun*) as those of a great minister of the right. All of them already were princes of the first rank and were appointed great minister only afterward. Is this not indisputable [proof] that [imperial princes] rank below the three dukes? After the imperial princes come the former great ministers. The three dukes who are in office rank above the imperial princes, but

---

5. *Jōgan seiyō* (Ch. *Zhenguan zhengyao*), 10 *kan*, was composed during the Tang dynasty by Wu Jing. It purports to contain the discussions that the second emperor of the Tang, Taizong, had with his ministers. These discussions are arranged in forty different categories.

6. *Kanpyō yuikai* is a set of instructions and admonitions written by Emperor Uda for his successor, Emperor Go-Daigo, and given by him to the latter when he abdicated in his favor. The text is in *Gunsho ruijū* 475.

7. *Gunsho chiyō* (Ch. *Chunshu zhiyao*), 50 *kan*, was composed during the Tang dynasty by Wei Zheng and others, on imperial command. It consists of excerpts from the classics and works on government of later writers.

8. Fine, beautiful words but also, in a Buddhist context, "lying words"!

9. *Kinpi-shō*, 3 *kan*, was composed by Emperor Juntoku. The book treats all aspects of the life at court: buildings, utensils, rituals and ceremonies, styles of letter writing, subjects of study, and the like. The text is in *Gunsho ruijū, zatsubu*, and in *Ressei zenshū, Gosenshū* 6.

10. The term *sankō* (Ch. *sangong*) dates back to the kingdom of Zhou and denotes the three highest dignitaries at the royal, later the imperial, court. In Japan, this word denotes the prime minister (*dajō daijin*), the great minister of the left (*sadaijin*), and the great minister of the right (*udaijin*).

11. Toneri-shinnō (675–735), the third son of Emperor Tenmu and a daughter of Emperor Tenji, and the father of Emperor Junnin. He was appointed to oversee the compilation of *Nihon shoki* and, after Fujiwara no Fuhito died (720), was named acting prime minister (*chidajōkanji*). He was appointed as prime minister posthumously (735).

12. Nakano-shinnō (792–867), the twelfth son of Emperor Kanmu. He was appointed as the governor of Dazaifu (Kyushu) in 830. Both his promotion to the first princely rank (*ippon*) and his appointment as prime minister were posthumous, based on the fact that through his daughter he had become the grandfather of Emperor Uda.

13. Hozumi-shinnō (d. 715), the fifth son of Emperor Tenmu. He became acting prime minister (*chidajō kanji*) in 705. He was promoted to the first princely rank (*ippon*) in the first month of 715, half a year before his death.

those who have resigned their office should be seated behind them; they follow after the imperial princes. However, the crown prince is an exception.

When former great ministers or retired regents assume office again, the regent houses (*sekkanke*)[14] may decide on the ranking order among themselves.

3. After a great minister of one of the "Pure and Flowery" houses[15] resigns his office, he should be seated behind the imperial princes.

4. Those who belong to the regent houses but do not possess the requisite talents and abilities—let alone anyone from outside [those houses]—must not be appointed as one of the three dukes or as imperial regent!

5. Those persons who do possess the requisite talents and abilities should not resign their office as one of the three dukes or as imperial regent, even if they have reached a great age. Furthermore, they may be reappointed even after they have resigned their office.

6. Adopted sons continue the family line. However, one must use [i.e., adopt] those of the same clan name. Never has it happened, before or now, that a relative through the female line succeeded as the head of a house.

7. Appointments of warriors (*buke*) in functions and ranks of the imperial bureaucracy must be considered separate from those of the court aristocrats who are actually fulfilling such positions.

8. In case of a change in the era-name, one may select an auspicious one from China's era-names. But the next time, if [we have scholars who are] learned in the rites and know them really well, they should [again] follow the procedure laid down in the old regulations of our court.[16]

9. The emperor's ceremonial robes (*raifuku*) consist of [an outer garment with] wide sleeves (*ōsode*), [an inner garment with] narrow sleeves (*kosode*), and a skirt (*mo*). They are decorated with the twelve symbols.[17] [The ministers' ceremonial robes are different.] Their coats (*hō*) are colored a yellowish green (*kikujin*)[18] or green (*aoiro*); [they are made of] silk. [Or they wear] a coat [whose color] has been decided by the Yin Yang Bureau. Otherwise [they wear] a *nōshi* with a train (*hikinōshi*) or a small *nōshi* (*ko-nōshi*).

---

14. The so-called *sekkanke*, or the houses from whose members the imperial regent (*sesshō* or *kanpaku*) was chosen. In the Tokugawa period, these were the five houses of Konoe, Takatsukasa, Kujō, Ichijō, and Nijō.

15. The so-called *seigake*, or the houses whose members could be promoted up to the office of prime minister. In the Tokugawa period, these were the nine houses of Koga, Saionji, Sanjō, Tokudaiji, Imadegawa, Ōimikado, Kazan'in, Daigo, and Hirohata.

16. This article indicates dissatisfaction with the selection of the era-name Genna. This era-name was used two times in China (in the later Han dynasty [84–87] and in the Tang dynasty [806–820]). It is one of the rare instances in which Japan took over a Chinese era-name.

17. For a diagram and a description, see *Dai Kanwa jiten*, vol. 2, p. 2695, no. 376. According to this dictionary, six of the symbols were pictured on the robe, and six on the skirt.

18. *Kikujin* is the color of mildew. See *Dai Kanwa jiten*, vol. 12, pp. 47818–826.

Article 9 continues with minute details of the prescribed dress for retired emperors, as well as the different ranks of the high nobles.

10. Each of the various houses may propose promotions in rank and office [to the emperor], in keeping with the ancient precedents that apply to that house. However, the emperor should appoint those who are diligently studying the Chinese corpus of courtly lore and precedents or *waka* composition, and also those who have accumulated merit through their exertions for their lord, to higher functions or advance them in rank, even if that would mean a promotion above their [hereditary] rank. Although Shimotsumichi no Mabi [Kibi no Makibi (693–775)] [originally] held [only] the junior eighth rank low, he was appointed great minister of the right because of his talents, wisdom, and reputation; he is an excellent example. The efforts of [studying in the light reflected by the] snow or [projected by] fireflies should not be scorned.

11. Anyone who disobeys orders given by the imperial regent (*kanpaku*) and the military liaison officers (*buke tensō*), and also those given by the intendants (*bugyō*) and private secretaries of the emperor (*shikiji*), must be banished, whether or not he has the status of *tenjōbito*.

12. In determining the gravity of a crime, the ancient law codes should be followed.[19]

13. The abbots of the regent houses (*sekke monzeki*) must be seated behind the imperial abbots (*shinnō monzeki*). But when they are in office as regent or as one of the three dukes, members of the regent houses are higher than the imperial princes, and former great ministers are seated behind them. Since this has been so decided [for imperial princes and members of the regent houses], [the abbots] should be treated correspondingly. However, except for imperial offspring, no *monzeki* should be appointed an imperial prince by edict. The ranking of the retinue of the imperial abbots should be based on the individual background of its members.

Judging by the ancient regulations, it was rare for anyone who had already entered Buddhist orders to be appointed an imperial prince. In recent reigns they have become quite numerous. There is no good reason for this. *Monzeki* other than those born in the regent houses and the imperial family must be treated as honorary abbots (*junmonzeki*).

14. Abbots (*monzeki*) and *inge*[20] may be appointed as high priests [great, regular, and provisional; i.e., *dai-*, *shō-*, and *gonsōjō*] in conformity with the precedents. In those rare cases when someone of the common people (*heimin*) is appointed because of his extraordinary ability, he should be made an honorary

---

19. Actually, the article mentions three categories of ancient Chinese law: the "names" of punishments (*mei*), the "examples" of the application of the punishments (*rei*), and "general rules" (*ritsu*). See *Dai Kanwa jiten*, vol. 2, pp. 3297–331.

20. *Inge* were monks of noble descent who lived in temples subordinate to the *monzeki* temples.

high priest (*jun sōjō*). However, the preceptors (*shihan*) of the emperor and the great ministers are an exception.

15. It goes without saying that *monzeki* may be promoted to assistant high priest [great, regular, and small; i.e., *dai shō* and *shō sōzu*] and to "seal of the law" (*hōin*) and that *inge* may be promoted to assistant high priest [great, regular, small, and provisional] and to Vinaya master (*risshi*), seal of the law, and eye of the law (*hōgen*), according to precedent. However, in the case of a commoner (*heijin*), he will first have to be recommended by his temple. Moreover, when he is selected for his talents, he may be proposed [to the emperor for promotion].

16. The ancient regulations only rarely refer to cases in which abbots of temples were allowed the [privilege of a] purple robe, but in recent years the emperor has granted such permissions indiscriminately. As a result, the order of seniority has been confused, and the official temples have been corrupted. This is not at all as it should be. In future, you will select [candidates for the purple robe] on the basis of their talents and ability and of the number of years they have kept the commandments (*kairō*). [Only those who] have a reputation for wisdom and knowledge may be proposed [to the emperor] for appointment as abbot of a temple.

17. Monks of broad learning (*sekigaku*) who have been selected by their own temple, with a distinction made between regular (*shō*) and provisional (*gon*), and are recommended [to the emperor] may, by imperial permission, be granted the title of "saint" (*shōnin*). However, those who have practiced Buddhism for twenty years or more should be appointed as regular [saint] and those whose years are insufficient, as provisional [saint]. [Those guilty] of disorderly competition and ambitions must be punished by banishment.

The preceding [regulations] must be complied with.

> *Dated: a certain day, 7th month of Keichō 20 [1615]*
> *Signed: Nijō Akizane,*[21] *the shogun [Tokugawa Hidetada],*
> *the retired shogun [ōgosho-sama* (Tokugawa Ieyasu)]

[*Dai Nihon shiryō*, vol. 12, pt. 22, pp. 161–64; WB]

IEYASU'S REVENGE AND COMPASSION

The following anecdote is told in *Tales from Mikawa* (*Mikawa monogatari*), a book written by one of Ieyasu's old retainers, Ōkubo Tadanori. Its historical accuracy may be doubtful, but it vividly shows what was considered acceptable behavior for lords and vassals as well as the extent to which Ieyasu was still smarting from his years in captivity.

---

21. Nijō Akizane (1556–1619). He was *kanpaku* for a few months in 1585 until he stepped down in order to allow Toyotomi Hideyoshi to assume this office. One month after the *kuge shohatto* was signed, he was reappointed as *kanpaku*, which he remained until he died.

TALES FROM MIKAWA
(*MIKAWA MONOGATARI*)

Well then, always be compassionate toward others. Sometimes Ieyasu's falcon would stray into the residence of the Haramiishi *mondo* Motoyasu, and then Ieyasu would go into the woods that lay behind it and make the falcon sit on his hand again. The *mondo* remarked on several occasions that "he was more than fed up with the young lord of Mikawa." Perhaps this had irritated him? After some thirty-seven or thirty-eight years had gone by, Ieyasu attacked the castle of Takatenjin in Tōtōmi that belonged to Takeda Katsuyori of Kai. Ieyasu dug a moat, wove fences, and put up walls and palisades, wanting to subdue the castle by starvation. Haramiishi *mondo* had also sought refuge in this castle. Soon the food ran out, and [Ieyasu's soldiers] caught him alive as he fought his way out of the castle. When they reported this, [Ieyasu said], "The one called Haramiishi is the one who when I was interned in Sunpu, used to say that he was more than fed up with the young lord from Mikawa, whenever I was flying my falcons in Kamihara and one of my falcons strayed into Haramiishi's woods and I went in to retrieve it. I remember him. Haramiishi must also know this. Since he is the Haramiishi who was so completely fed up with me, tell him to cut his belly this instant." Thus he ordered. But Haramiishi's last moments were also fine. "It stands to reason," he said, "and I don't mind." Then he turned to the south and made to cut his belly. One of the bystanders remarked: "Even such an eminent person as Haramiishi apparently does not know about the last hour. Turn to the west and then cut your belly." Haramiishi answered him, saying, "You, you don't know a thing! The Buddha himself taught [in the Lotus Sutra] that 'in the Buddha lands of the ten directions [there is only the Law of the One Vehicle]; there are not two [laws], nor are there three. This does not apply to the teachings of the Buddha on expedient means.'"[22] Do you really think that there is a paradise only in the western direction? How small-minded you are! Why should one prefer one paradise over the other?" With these words, he turned to the south and cut his belly.

[Ōkubo, Mikawa monogatari, in NST, vol. 26, p. 73; WB]

ACCOUNT OF TOKUGAWA
(*TOKUGAWA JIKKI*)

The following anecdote containing Ieyasu's pronouncements on political theory and practice is part of an appendix to the official annals of Ieyasu's reign, based on earlier accounts recorded closer to the events in question.

---

22. Lotus Sutra, chap. 2, *Hōbenbon*. See Watson, trans., *The Lotus Sutra*, p. 35.

In the twelfth month of Keichō 7 [1602] the temple of the Great Buddha in the Eastern Mountains of Kyoto burned down. The former regent, Toyotomi [Hideyoshi], had originally erected [in this temple] a clay statue of the Buddha, but in the first year of the Keichō era [1596] a strong earthquake destroyed it. Hideyoshi then sent for the Buddha of the Zenkōji in Shinano and had it installed, but after his death, his wife, Lady Yodo, saw to it that this Buddha statue was returned to its place of origin. This time, orders were given to the metal casters, and a mold was made in order to cast [the statue of the Great Buddha] in copper. However, when the hot copper was poured into this mold, the woodwork underneath caught fire, and everything up to and including the roof of the temple turned into ashes.

[Several years] later, Lady Yodo secretly contacted the shogun's wife, Lady Sōgen'in, in Edo and told her: "The Great Buddha was constructed by His Excellency. It met with this unfortunate accident, and it would be difficult for Hideyori to restore it by himself. I hope that with help from the Kantō, we will be able to rebuild it. Then His Late Excellency's wishes, too, will not have been in vain. That would be a most joyful event." When Lady Sōgen'in inquired [with Ieyasu] through Honda Sado-no-kami Masanobu, [Ieyasu said]: "Lady Yodo is a woman, and the shogun is still young in years, so probably he will not think [about the request] too deeply. You, however, have worked for many years in senior positions. Why do you bring such a preposterous story to me and expect me to discuss it? This is really going too far."

Since Masanobu appeared to be greatly embarrassed, Ieyasu resumed: "You have heard that the Great Buddha in Nara, which was constructed according to a vow made by Emperor Shōmu, was set on fire by the soldiers of Taira no Shigehira and burned to the ground. Two monks, Shunjō and Saigyō, together collected the money and rebuilt [the temple and the statue]. Although the Tōdaiji was a temple built at the behest of an emperor (chokuganji), [Minamoto no] Yoritomo made no effort to have it rebuilt. By comparison, the Great Buddha in Kyoto was built on a whim of Hideyoshi. If Hideyori wants to use his own means to rebuild it, he may do so, but there is no reason why the shogun should come to his aid. How many temples and shrines do you think there are in Japan? If every time someone claimed that we had some sort of a relation to a temple and we paid to have it repaired, how would we ever defray the expense for the whole empire? Such requests have to be carefully considered. In any case, you may be sure that talk of founding both a new temple and a new shrine is foolish. Please tell this to the shogun and talk it over with your colleagues."

Some time later, members of Ieyasu's personal entourage (godanban), such as Yamaoka Dōami and Maeba Hannyū, happened to be discussing in Ieyasu's presence the notion that the lord of the empire should do something to leave his name to posterity. They noted that Hideyoshi's name would live on because he had erected the Great Buddha in Kyoto. Ieyasu heard this and remarked,

"Hideyoshi loved doing such things, but the only things that I think of constantly are ruling the empire in peace and seeing to it that after several generations, public order and popular customs will be maintained. Aren't those things much more important than constructing a number of Great Buddhas?" His two companions were deeply affected by his penetrating reflections and advice for bringing order to the state. They were ashamed and left his presence, apologizing for their ill-considered remarks.

[*Tokugawa jikki*, vol. 1, pp. 331–32; WB]

LETTER FROM HONDA MASAZUMI AND KONCHIIN SŪDEN TO KATAGIRI KATSUMOTO

As indicated in the previous selection, after the Hōkōji and the statue of the Great Buddha were destroyed by fire, Hideyoshi's son decided to have them rebuilt. Near the time of the dedication ceremony, however, Ieyasu raised a number of problems, which are detailed in a letter that his henchman Honda Masazumi and the Zen monk Konchiin Sūden wrote to Hideyori's guardian, Katagiri Katsumoto (1556–1615). The letter is dated Keichō 19/8/6 (1614).

We bring the following to your attention so that it will be clear [to you]. In regard to the impending inauguration ceremony of the Great Buddha, we disagree with several of the arrangements on which you reported earlier. The other day [when you were here, in Sunpu] Ieyasu happened to see a copy of the inscription of the bell of the Great Buddha in Nara, and he told you that this was how such a text should read. Yet you asked an ignorant country fellow to compose the present inscription, and what he has written is too long and is filled with irrelevant details. More specifically, he has included the taboo name of Ieyasu, which is against the law. Although here, again, ancient custom should be followed, you have written the commemorative ridge plaque in a style of your own devising; moreover, it fails to mention the name of the master builder. Furthermore, we hear that in the dispute between the Tendai and Shingon sects about the seating order, you have decided on equal seating, even though since [the time of] Emperor Kanmu, the Tendai monastery on Mount Hiei has enjoyed special imperial honor. This, too, Ieyasu finds disconcerting. The inscriptions on the bell and the ridge plaque will exist forever. If [in future reigns] they are ever maligned, people will assert that the laws of the person who ruled the empire in those days must have been in confusion and disarray. Ieyasu is not pleased with this. You must fully comply with the above and report it to Hideyori.

We also have sent messengers to the monks of the five Zen monasteries to show them the inscription of the bell and ask them for their opinion.

[*Dai Nihon shiryō*, vol. 12, pt. 14, p. 457; WB]

LETTER FROM TOYOTOMI HIDEYORI TO SHIMAZU IEHISA

A second, much more stringent, set of demands is reported in a letter dated one and a half months later in 1614 (Keicho 19/9/23). It is from Toyotomi Hideyori to Shimazu Iehisa, sealed by Hideyori himself, in which he asks Iehisa to help him against the Tokugawa.

I urgently ask your attention to the following: Suruga [Ieyasu] has become ill disposed toward the impending inauguration ceremony of the Great Buddha. Although I tried to reason with him through messengers, I was told to leave the Great Buddha alone for the time being, and through Ichi-no-kami [Katagiri Katsumoto] I was given these three conditions: to give up Osaka Castle or to take a residence and live in Edo, as all the other daimyo do. If neither [condition] is acceptable, then I should hand over my mother as a hostage. I tried to argue with Ichi-no-kami and told him to resign himself to the situation, but he refused to listen to anything I said. Maybe he is colluding with Suruga? He vehemently insisted that if I did not settle on the basis of these three conditions, it was unlikely that I would be able to hold on to Osaka and therefore would never be able to undo the damage. But consider these conditions yourself! I cannot agree with even one of them. Anyway, we have reached our decision, so I will first send Ichi-no-kami as a messenger to Suruga, as he says that the answer to Suruga is urgent.

I entreat you earnestly to come to my aid. However, the road is long, so it is very important to gather all the information you can. I repeat: it is very important to gather information about the conditions in this area. Therefore I send you this letter under my black seal.

[*Kyūki zatsuroku, kōhen*, vol. 4 of *Kagoshima ken shiryō*, p. 550; WB]

THE REASONS FOR IEYASU'S FRUGALITY

One chapter of the appendix to Ieyasu's annals is devoted to anecdotes and incidental remarks about the extent of and reasons for his frugality.

When he was still very young, he [Ieyasu] was taken away from his own province and was made to live [with the Imagawa] in Suruga and [with the Oda] in Owari. He tasted to the full all the bitterness and hardship of this world of man and gained a deep insight into human character and the nature of the world. His experiences taught him the truth that none of the things that come into being between Heaven and earth are to be treated lightly. Until the end of his days, therefore, he made frugality his guiding principle, cut out unnecessary expenses, and applied himself to achieving solid results. Of course, his own sustenance was correspondingly simple, and he also repeatedly lectured on the topic to his men. As a result, they all imitated his manners, and unlike the warriors in the capital, they did not show any taste for luxury and elegance but lived very simply.

Well now, because of its frugal customs, the Zhou dynasty established a rule that lasted eight hundred years. Ever since then, in both Japan and China, founders of dynasties have invariably created their states and brought order to the empire through frugality and simplicity. [However,] when the great peace had lasted for some time, their descendants grew up in wealth and dignity and completely forgot the hardships their ancestor [had suffered]. Because they indulged their own taste for luxury, in the end they lost the great work of many generations.

Long ago someone asked Gamō Ujisato who would become the lord of the empire when its present ruler, Toyotomi Hideyoshi, had died. Ujisato answered, "Lord Tokugawa is well known and highly regarded these days, but he is a miser by nature and is not made of the stuff that rulers of the empire are made of. After [Hideyoshi's death], the empire will probably go to Maeda Toshiie." Apparently Ujisato had grown accustomed to the extravagance of Oda Nobunaga and Toyotomi Hideyoshi and had mistakenly concluded that this was what rulers of the empire should be like; he did not know that our lord's frugality was ordained by Heaven. It is a pity that Ujisato, great hero though he was, had become stuck in the common vices of his day and had insufficiently reflected on the matter.

[*Tokugawa jikki*, vol. 1, p. 321; WB]

A STORY ILLUSTRATING IEYASU'S FRUGALITY

Another story that illustrates Ieyasu's frugality incidentally mentions the Way of Heaven in this context. Ieyasu's words were reportedly addressed to the women of his court and concerned the importance of washing clothes. It is included in chapter 20 of the appendixes to Ieyasu's annals.

At one time, Okaji-no-tsubone ordered her women to wash a white *kosode* [belonging to Ieyasu] that had become soiled. The women hurt their fingers, and blood flowed from the wounds; she thought it a very cruel task. Since he [Ieyasu] had so many clothes, she asked whether it would be all right if they did not wash them anymore and if he wore only new clothes. Ieyasu answered, "This is not something that you, foolish women, need to understand, but I will explain it to you nevertheless. Come and listen." He called a great number of the women together and said: "The thing about which I have been most careful all my life is not to offend the Way of Heaven. What the Way of Heaven hates most is extravagance. Having seen all the treasure I have amassed here in Sunpu, you no doubt think that it is a lot?" All of them agreed. "This is not my only treasure-house," Ieyasu resumed. "I also have one in the capital, in Osaka, and in Edo, all filled with gold, silver, cloth, and silk. So even if I wore new clothes every day, how could I ever run short? The reason, however, that I have amassed [all this wealth] is to give it, at certain times, to the people of the empire or, by accumulating it for the future generations of my descendants, to prevent the state from ever being short of funds. Therefore, we should not waste even one robe." Although they were women, they all were [impressed by] the wisdom of his holy teaching and did obeisance to him as one does to a Buddha or a god, with the palms of their hands joined together.

[*Tokugawa jikki*, vol. 1, p. 324; WB]

LETTER FROM KONCHIIN SŪDEN

The following letter was written by one of Ieyasu's principal religious advisers, the Zen master Konchiin Sūden, concerning Ieyasu's last days.

Since I have a good messenger going all the way to the Nanzenji, I am sending you this letter. When the liaison officers (*tensō*) returned to Kyoto, I gave them a written report; that will tell you about the situation here in Sunpu. The illness of the minister (*shōkoku-sama* [Ieyasu]) kept him in bed for several days in a row; he was weak, had hiccups and spat out phlegm, and his fever rose. He suffered extreme pain and distress. In view of his condition, everyone from the shogun down to the lowest vassals thronged into the castle. You can imagine how subdued and gloomy everyone was. After the liaison officers left for the capital, his condition greatly worsened.[23] I, old monk that I am, served day after day in the inner quarters and gratefully [listened to] his every instruction, tears streaming [down my face]. One or two days ago, he summoned Honda Kō[zuke-no-suke Masazumi] [1565–1637], Nankōbō [Tenkai (d. 1643)], and me to his bed and instructed us as follows: Immediately after he died, his body should be interred on Mount Kunō; the Zōjōji[24] should be instructed to hold a funeral ceremony (*sōrei*); his ancestral tablet (*ihai*) should be placed in the Daijuji[25] in Mikawa; [and] after a year has gone by, a small hall should be built on Mount Nikkō, where Ieyasu should be invited to reside as a godhead (*kanjō*). He would become the tutelary deity (*chinjushin*) of the eight provinces of the Kantō. At these words, everyone wept. Yesterday, the third, there has been a change from the past few days. He [Ieyasu] is clear and utters one golden word

---

23. The liaison officers had come to Sunpu in order to bring Ieyasu the imperial rescript appointing him prime minister. Ieyasu and Hidetada received them on Genna 2/3/27 (1617) and entertained the officers on the twenty-ninth. In view of Ieyasu's condition, however, on the same day all *kuge* and daimyo were ordered to leave Sunpu and go home. The liaison officers eventually left Sunpu on the fifth day of the fourth month.

24. Zōjōji is a temple of the Pure Land sect in Edo that was patronized by the Tokugawa and where many later Tokugawa shoguns, beginning with Hidetada, were buried.

25. Daijuji is a temple in Mikawa, the province of the origin of the Tokugawa, where Ieyasu's ancestors were buried.

after the other, on all kinds of subjects. All here say that this is no longer a human feat. I hope to send you the joyful tiding that he has recovered even more than this. [Your son] Naizen-[no-kami Shigemasa] [1588–1638] will send you word. In fear and reverence.

Dated: 4th day of the 4th month [of Genna 2]
Signed: Konchiin Sūden
Addressed to: Itakura Iga-no-kami Katsushige [1545–1624]

[*Shintei honkō kokushi nikki*, vol. 3, p. 382a; WB]

THE STORY OF THE MIIKE SWORD

A different aspect of Ieyasu is shown in the story of the Miike sword. Here we see him not as the benevolent lord but as the warrior he was, with blood on his hands. The story tells how one of the heirlooms kept in the Tōshōgū shrine in Sunpu, Ieyasu's Miike sword, was selected. Other versions of the story stress Ieyasu's insistence on trying the sword on a convicted felon as a sign of his humaneness. The story also indicates the private fears and worries that may have inspired his decision to have himself deified.

On the sixteenth of the fourth month, [Ieyasu] summoned his valet Tsuzuki Kyōdaiyu Kagetada and told him to find the Miike sword that he had always secretly treasured and to hand it over to the magistrate [of Sunpu], Hikosaka Kyōbei Mitsumasa. If there was [a prisoner] who had been condemned to death, then [Mitsumasa] had to try this blade; if there was no such person, it would not be necessary to try it. Thus Ieyasu ordered. Mitsumasa and Kyōdaiyu went together to the execution ground, and after some time [Kyōdaiyu] reported back to Ieyasu and said that as instructed, they had tried the blade on a felon and that it had cut through him all the way down to the block without a problem. Ieyasu then told him to exchange it with the sword that was lying at his bedside, [took it out of its scabbard,] swung it two times, three times, and said that with the power of this sword he would protect his descendants of all generations to come. He instructed Sakakibara *naiki* Teruhisa [1584–1643] to preserve it in the [shrine on] Mount Kunō. On the seventeenth, the hour of Ieyasu's death was drawing near. Honda Kōzuke-no-suke Masazumi summoned [a servant] and ordered him to tell the shogun to come over quickly, but Ieyasu said that that would not be necessary. "Tell him," he said, "that after I am gone, he must never forget the Way of the warrior, even in the least." These were his last words before he expired,[26] cradling his head on Teruhisa's knees.

[*Tokugawa jikki*, vol. 1, p. 285; WB]

---

26. The word used is *kakuresasetamaishi*, from *kakureru* (to hide), which is the same word used for gods and emperors.

IEYASU AS HEROIC ANCESTOR

The "accepted version" of Ieyasu's life was the annals and appendixes in the official history of the Tokugawa dynasty, the *Tokugawa jikki*. Ieyasu's annals conclude with a magnificent finale, an elaborate effort of Japanese literary prose by the compilers. It may not be the most correct description of his life, but it indicates what the *bakufu* wanted Ieyasu to be remembered for, two centuries after his death. We take up the story—which begins with the creation of Heaven and earth—with the reign of Emperor Go-Daigo.

In the Genkō and Kenmu eras, Emperor Go-Daigo employed the military power of the Nitta and Ashikaga in order to punish [Hōjō] Takatoki, and as he had planned in his wisdom, he succeeded in executing the Hōjō and restoring imperial rule. However, the imperial family split into south and north, and in the end the Ashikaga unified the empire. Because Takauji, with his deceitful stratagems and devious intellect, had beguiled those above and deluded the masses of the people, his rule was flawed from the outset. Therefore, those below him followed his example, and while the fifteen reigns of the Ashikaga passed, close relatives harmed one another, and fathers, sons, and brothers were at one another's throats. The strong suppressed the weak, and the many molested the few. After the Ōnin War, the empire was shattered to pieces like a roof tile; rebels arose like [swarms of] bees; human relations ordained by the Way of Heaven were discontinued; and for more than a hundred years, myriad people suffered extreme hardship. Hardly had Oda Nobunaga, valorous and sharp, supported Ashikaga Yoshiaki to become shogun than he expelled him. Then he, too, was killed by a rebellious vassal. Then came the time of the regent Toyotomi's grandiose schemes. Although he had come up from the grass roots, had avenged his former lord, and finally unified the empire, he gave himself up to luxury and extravagance and organized foreign campaigns. He paid no attention to the distress of the myriad people and so was unable to pass on his authority to the next generation.

At this time, "a god was sent down from the sacred mountain,"[27] and a true lord was born. He was compassionate and magnanimous; as a military man, he was able to suppress the troubles, and as a civil ruler, he was able to establish order. He finally calmed the waves that for more than a hundred years had raged between the Four Seas and succeeded in unifying the empire. We can forget about the ignorant lords and lying ministers of the Ashikaga, and even the violent Oda and the arrogant Toyotomi both belonged to the kind of people who catch fish for [stocking] their pools and pursue peacocks for [adorning] their shrubbery. It is obvious that for a true lord, Heaven provides all this. We will scrupulously refrain from mentioning even for the briefest moment the

---

27. *Shijing*, ode 259.

merit of having laid the fundament of [the imperial dynasty that will last for] myriad generations without end, but [ever since] the rule of the emperor came under the control of the military, one does not hear of even one lord who truly revered the Way of Yao and Shun and studied the traces of the sages.

Only the heroic ancestor (*resso* [Ieyasu])—who grew to manhood amid the din of arms, who often experienced the misery of drenching rain and tearing winds [when he was on campaign], and who tasted to the full the hardship of [operating in] rough mountain territory—only he, notwithstanding all this bitterness and hardship, knew that there was no other way than the Way of the sages when he began to order the world and bring peace to the realm. He summoned the Confucian scholars of that time—Fujiwara Seika, Hayashi Razan, and others—and listened to them reading the *Great Learning*, the *Analects*, and the *Zhenguan zhengyao*.[28] Besides them, he [Ieyasu] summoned such learned monks as [Saishō] Jōtai, [Konchiin] Sūden, and [Nankōbō] Tenkai and asked them about the annals and biographies of Japan and China. After he had retired to Sunpu, he still had Razan give lectures on the Four Books and Six Classics and the Seven Military Classics, and he kept him with him day and night as his adviser.

After his triumph at Sekigahara, Ieyasu concentrated all the more on the many affairs of state; his only thought was to give the country peace and the people wealth. He began the work [of establishing his dynasty] for the empire and his descendants and passed on his unifying rule to them. Grandly he established great principles and great laws. He handed down his great rule of endless peace to his saintly sons and divine grandsons for many, many generations. Reverently they have accepted his teaching that their spiritual lifeline must exclusively be his godly preference for the civil arts. In this way, the splendor of the sun on Mount Futara [Nikkō] shines everywhere, even farther than Korea and China, and there is no region on Japan's many isles that has not been moistened by the blessings of the dew in the Field of Musashi. Could there be anyone with hair on his head and teeth in his mouth who would not reverently venerate and fearfully worship the virtue and meritorious deeds of this swift-acting god?

[*Tokugawa jikki*, vol. 1, pp. 131–32; WB]

---

28. Concerning the governance of the early Tang dynasty, see de Bary et al., eds., *Sources of Japanese Tradition*, 2nd ed., vol. 1, pp. 84–88.

Chapter 21

CONFUCIANISM IN THE EARLY TOKUGAWA PERIOD

Confucianism first came to Japan along with the importation of Chinese culture sponsored by Prince Shōtoku and the Chinese administrative and political model implemented through the so-called Taika Reforms during the second half of the seventh century. The Confucian classics were taught at the Court Academy (Daigakuryō) from the beginning of the eighth century onward. Basic Confucian ideas, such as the importance of rites and decorum (J. *rei, rai,* Ch. *li*) for the ordering of society, seeped into the common intellectual heritage of the Japanese court, and it was in the same court circles that Neo-Confucianism later became known. Although developments in Japan lagged behind those in China, by the end of the Kamakura period (1185–1333), Japanese court intellectuals were aware that something new had started in Song China. In the following centuries, basic Neo-Confucian texts, such as Zhu Xi's *Collected Commentaries on the Four Books,* were imported and studied.

The most important locus of these studies was the Kiyowara family, who had begun as one of the "families [in charge of] explaining the classics" (*myōgyōke*) in the Court Academy and remained active in the field of Confucian studies until well into the seventeenth century. A second locus of Neo-Confucian studies was the Zen monasteries. Through their frequent contacts with the Chinese, the Zen monks recognized the importance of the Neo-Confucian commentaries for the study of the classics. They therefore studied and taught these commentaries and other texts by Neo-Confucian masters and integrated them into their practice of Chinese literature.

Then, at the beginning of the seventeenth century, things changed. The change may have been less abrupt than the later, Confucian-dominated historiography has often claimed, but in any case, the intellectual atmosphere of the early Tokugawa period was quite different from that of the late Middle Ages. This change was mainly a matter of a new secular attitude: specifically, a denial of the fundamental compatibility of Confucianism and Buddhism, which until then had been commonly accepted.

The change was pioneered by a number of young Kyoto intellectuals, who in the first years of the seventeenth century gathered around Fujiwara Seika (1561–1619).[1] They tried to re-create in Kyoto what they fondly believed was the lifestyle of Chinese literati, and their program can best be characterized as both anticlerical and antimilitary. Although they were loud in their condemnation of Buddhism, as their collected poems and letters show, this did not prevent them from cultivating friendly relations with individual Buddhist monks. These young intellectuals were, of necessity, less open in their condemnation of the Tokugawa *bakufu* or of individual daimyo. Their values differed, however, from those of the warrior class, and if an opportunity presented itself, they did not hesitate to present their dissenting views.

Their central preoccupation was what—for want of a more adequate translation of the Chinese word *wen* (J. *bun*)—may best be rendered as "literary culture or civil culture." This "literature" did not exclude literature written in Japanese but was heavily biased toward literature written in Chinese, Chinese literature, and, above all, the Chinese classics. As Hayashi Razan, looking back on the course that his own studies had taken, wrote,

When I was a child, I sometimes read modern stories [e.g., the *Taiheiki*]. The person who explained them to me [told me that he] thought that such-and-such a word came from Su Dongpo [1037–1101] or from Huang Tingqian [1045–1105] and that such-and-such a phrase came from Li Bo [701–762], Du Fu [712–770], Han Yu [768–824], or Liu Zongyuan [773–819]. When I read the collected works of Li, Du, Han, Liu, Su, and Huang, I noticed that very often what they were based on was the *Wenxuan* (*Literary Anthology*), the *Shiji* (*Records of the Historian*), or the

---

1. Among them we find Hayashi Razan (1583–1657) and his brother Eiki (1585–1638), Hori Kyōan (1585–1642), Kan Tokuan (1581–1628), Matsunaga Sekigo (1592–1657), and Nawa Kassho (1595–1648). This group also had connections with such literary figures as Matsunaga Teitoku (1571–1653) and Kinoshita Katsutoshi (Chōshōshi [1569–1649]) and with the merchant Yoshida (Suminokura) Soan (1571–1632).

Hanshu (*History of the Former Han Dynasty*). When I read the *Shiji* and the *Hanshu*, I saw that they followed the texts of the ancient period. I then read the Five Classics and saw that before them there was nothing from which they derived. Thereupon I clearly realized that these classics constituted the foundation of all later theories, and in this broad perspective I understood what the Way was based on. I cherished only the extra teachings added to the classics by the Chengs and Zhu Xi and looked up to the abundant relics of Confucius and Mencius.[2]

To limit either the ambitions or the historical importance of these intellectuals simply to the study of Confucianism—that is, to the Neo-Confucian commentaries on the Chinese classics— would be doing them an injustice. Their activities included much more, ranging from historiography and medicine to poetry, in both Chinese and Japanese, and the classical Japanese corpus. Hayashi Razan, for one, wrote an extensive commentary on Kenkō's "Essays in Idleness" (Tsurezuregusa). It also would be misleading to identify them simply with the school of Neo-Confucianism that is connected with the Cheng brothers, Mingdao and Yichuan, and with Zhu Xi and that had become the orthodox school in China and Korea. Both Seika and Razan were well aware of later developments during the Ming dynasty, and if Razan opted for the Cheng–Zhu school, he did so for specific reasons and in full awareness that the Confucian tradition had more to offer. The fact that his teacher, Seika, did not make the same choice is in itself proof that the choice for Cheng–Zhu Confucianism was by no means necessary or preordained.

The group around Seika and Razan had no monopoly on Chinese and Confucian studies. Throughout Japan, the basic texts and basic instruction in Chinese were available. No doubt, the capital area was the main center of intellectual activity, but it remained in constant contact with several regional centers. One such center, regarded by Jesuit missionaries for some time as Japan's "university," was the Ashikaga school (established in Ashikaga, in the Kantō region), which was affiliated with the Zen sect and whose curriculum included basic instruction in the Chinese classics. Several of Tokugawa Ieyasu's advisers were Zen monks affiliated with this school.

The flow of information was maintained by monks, who used to study for at least a few years in the principal monasteries in Kyoto, and by samurai, who traveled with their lords to Osaka and Fushimi and spent part of their lives in the capital area. Other contributing factors relevant to the availability of texts were a lively book trade with China, carried on through Nagasaki; the loot from the Korean wars, which included many Neo-Confucian texts by both Chinese and Koreans; and indigenous Japanese efforts at printing. At least some

---

2. Razan, *Shishū*, vol. 2, app. 3, p. 37a.

knowledge was available throughout the country and to all who were interested enough to look for it, as did Neo-Confucians like Nakae Tōju (1608–1648), Yamazaki Ansai (1618–1682), and Kumazawa Banzan (1619–1691), all of whom had been educated in the provinces and had "found the Way" without having been exposed directly to the intellectual milieu of the capital, let alone studied under Seika or any of his disciples.

Not only was this knowledge available, but apparently there also was a new interest in it in all classes of society, ranging from daimyo who went to hear lectures by Seika and who hired his disciples, to the readers of such popular works written in the vernacular as *Gion monogatari*, *Shimizu monogatari*, and the treatises associated with teaching the Way of Heaven.

The skills and knowledge that the Confucian intellectuals offered were their superior command of the Chinese language and the teachings of the Chinese classics. A necessary premise for their activities was, therefore, the general consensus in Japan that some knowledge of Chinese was an asset and that the classics had important things to teach. Whether the Confucian intellectuals subscribed to orthodox or heterodox principles was not an issue in their clients' minds.

In the fluid situation of the seventeenth century, "unattached" intellectuals, who were neither monks nor members of the court aristocracy, were a new breed. They had to live by their wits and to fight for their own niche, their own position in society. For their livelihood, they depended on pupils or patronage, but the market for their skills and knowledge was limited and competition was fierce. They not only had to contend with Zen monks and court nobles, but also had to compete among themselves or form what today would be called networks. The wiser (or less self-assured) among them pursued medicine as a second profession that they could teach as well as practice. Those who did not had to be extraordinarily gifted and lucky (as in the case of Razan) or resign themselves to a life lived in relative poverty (as did Seika and Tōju).

The debates in which these intellectuals engaged did not arise so much from their adherence to different schools as from their attempts to draw attention to their own person and ideas, from their struggle for pupils and patrons. A case in point is Nakae Tōju, who really did not need to wait until he had read Wang Yangming before he could disagree vehemently with Razan. By the same token, the scholarly lineages and affiliations that were recorded so meticulously during the Tokugawa period did not certify doctrinal purity as much as they provided qualifications for employment and patronage. In this period, Japan was an aristocratic, feudal country; purity of ideas may not have been a prime consideration, but purity of lineage, even of scholarly lineage, was. It always was important to know whose son and whose disciple somebody was. Adding to this, as a continuing legacy from the medieval period, was the key role that lineages played in certifying Buddhist monks, especially in Zen.

FUJIWARA SEIKA AND THE RISE OF
NEO-CONFUCIANISM

Fujiwara Seika came from an ancient and noble family, the Reizei branch of the Fujiwara clan, and he was a tenth-generation descendant of the famous poet Fujiwara Teika (1162–1241). Seika was born on the estate of his family in Miki (Harima) and, as a younger son, was destined for an ecclesiastical career. When his father and older brother were killed by a local warlord, Bessho Nagaharu (d. 1580), and the family estate was seized (1578), Seika went to the capital to live with his uncle Jusen Seishuku (dates unknown), who was abbot of the Fukōin, one of the subsidiary temples of the Shōkokuji, a major Zen monastery in Kyoto, and Seika himself became a monk at the Shōkokuji.

During his training, Seika came into contact with Chinese and Confucian studies, and apparently Confucianism appealed to him. Nevertheless, the Koreans with whom he sought contact—that is, the members of the Korean embassy of 1590 and the Korean prisoner of war Kang Hang (1567–1618)—consistently refer to him as a monk (Shun of the Myōjuin). The sources are not clear on this point, but shortly before or after 1600, Seika seems to have renounced Buddhism. Thereafter he lived as a layman and apparently even married and fathered or adopted a son. In any event, the second version of his *Collected Works*, the *Seika sensei bunshū* (preface of 1651; printed in 1717), was compiled by Fujiwara Tametsune, who is described as his great-grandson.

Before 1600, Seika was a great traveler who followed Toyotomi Hidetsugu to the base camp for the first Korean expedition in Nagoya (Kyushu), and in the following year, 1593, he went to Edo to visit Tokugawa Ieyasu, who recently had established his headquarters there. In 1596 he even boarded a ship in order to travel to China, but his attempt failed. After 1600, however, aside from visits to Wakayama, where he stayed with Asano Yoshinaga (1576–1613), he lived in Kyoto in semiretirement, either in his house near the Shōkokuji or in the cottage he built in Ichihara, north of Kyoto, in 1605. Seika was supported by such warrior patrons as Akamatsu Hiromichi (1562–1600), Asano Yoshinaga, and Kinoshita Katsutoshi; by the merchants Suminokura Ryōi and his son Soan; and, no doubt, by his pupils. He also gave occasional lectures to interested daimyo. One such lecture, on the *Great Learning*, was written down and still survives as *Digest of the Great Learning* (*Daigaku yōryaku*).

Seika's main contributions to Confucian and Chinese studies in Japan were his editions of the Four Books and the Five Classics and his ambitious compilation of exemplary Chinese prose and poetry in the various genres, the *Bunshō tattokuroku*. These editions of the classics, and of other Chinese Confucian texts, were made at the request of Akamatsu Hiromichi. The actual writing was by Kang Hang and other Korean captives; Seika's role was restricted to supervision and to the addition of Japanese reading marks. The importance of the exercise was that Seika added these marks according to the Neo-Confucian commentaries. This was a departure from the traditional reading marks used by the Kiyowara, which were based on the older Han commentaries. Seika's collaborator in the literary project was Yoshida Soan, who seems to have done most of the actual work. But this project was never completed. At least, what was printed (in or shortly after 1639) under the name *Bunshō tattokuroku kōryō* was the first six, introductory, chapters, which contained excerpts and quotations relevant to Chinese literary theory.

"THE FOUR LANDSCAPES ARE MINE"

In 1592 Fujiwara Seika traveled to the base camp at Nagoya (Kyushu) as a member of the entourage of Toyotomi Hidetsugu. There he met Ieyasu, who invited him to visit him in Edo. Because Seika had managed to get into Hidetsugu's bad graces, he thought it wise to accept Ieyasu's invitation, and he stayed in Edo for several months. There he lectured to Ieyasu and made a number of friends and useful acquaintances among Ieyasu's vassals, but Seika and Ieyasu themselves apparently did not get along very well. The exposition "The Four Landscapes Are Mine" is a declaration of independence by Seika, and he never tried to get into Ieyasu's good graces again. The basic topoi of the text, that things in nature have no lord and belong to those who enjoy them, have much in common with the first of the "Fu on the Red Cliff" by the Song poet Su Dongpo, but an aesthetic orientation and holism with nature was also a significant aspect of the Neo-Confucian spiritual cultivation of the "humaneness that forms one body with Heaven-and-earth and all things."

Which land does not have mountains? If these mountains have no colors, it is because the mind is lazy. Which land does not have water? If the water is not clear, it is because the heart is busy. These expressions "If the mind is lazy, the mountains have no colors" and "If the heart is busy, the water will not be clear" were used by the ancients, and I also use them. In the sixty provinces of our Japan, you will find the most beautiful places for wandering through and admiring in the eight provinces east of the barrier, and within the eight provinces the crown is held by the four landscapes of Mount Fuji, the Field of Musashi, the Sumida River, and Tsukuba Mountains. Whoever has not seen these has been called less than human. I, too, had long intended to make this trip, for I had once heard that the appreciation of mountains and water inspires you to open your heart to the Way. When Confucius climbed Taishan [mountain] and lingered on the bank of the river, did he not do so for this reason?

In Bunroku 2 [1593] I received a gracious invitation from the lord of the eight provinces, the *asomi* Lord Minamoto, and I visited the castle of Edo in Musashi and remained there until the following year. In my little room of ten feet square in the inn I hung up the two characters *ga-yū* (I have). A guest came by, laughed, and said: "You are lonely and broke. You do not own even one square foot of land, not even the smallest house. You do not own anything! What, then, do you mean by 'I have'?" I answered, "How terribly conventional you are! How boorishly narrow in your views! I possess a spacious house and do not need carpenters, nor do I need to pay for repairs. . . . You cannot say that I do not possess anything! Take the snow in winter: it may be fresh, but that is not enough to make it special. But white, pure snow on a summer morning as it lies high on Mount Fuji's lofty top! Looking up to it, I wear it like a hat from Wu, and it is not at all heavy! Take flowers in spring: they may be beautiful, but that is not enough to make them special. But riotously bloom-ing flowers on an autumn day as they are spread across the several hundreds of *li* of the Field of Musashi! Stooping down to them, I put them on like sandals from Chu, and how good they smell! The water of the swiftly flowing Sumida River, in which the moon is stored, is something you can put into your calabash gourd. The mountains of Tsukuba, which tumble over one another and erase the clouds, are the stuff of poetry. But how could these be the only things? I have the myriad phenomena under my roof. I cannot give them away to others."

The guest replied, "Huh? What you say sounds like Yangzi's egoism. A gentle-man should not subscribe to that creed." I answered, "Correct. All men live under the same roof with me, so I can share everything with them." The guest said, "What you are saying now sounds like Mozi's universal love. A gentleman should not talk that way." I answered, "Right again."

[He said,] "But where does that leave you?" I answered, "All things have a master. How could they not have one? If you want them for yourself, you cannot have them, and if you want to give them to others, that is not possible. All things have a master, and to him they belong." He asked, "Who is this master?" I answered, "The lord of this province [Ieyasu], but when I . . . asked this lord, he did not own them; when I asked the ordinary people, they did not possess them. Alas! What others want I do not possess, and what I possess others do not want. Therefore, my house is empty, but in my heart I travel through heaven. I put the Sumida River into my calabash, fold the mountains of Tsukuba inside a poem. My hat of Mount Fuji, my sandals of the Field of Musashi! My sandals and socks came from here, here I drink from my gourd, and yonder I am inspired to write poetry. Since I live this life of rapture, left to my own devices, it is not only the four landscapes, not only the eight provinces, not only the sixty provinces of Japan—all the beauty one can admire within the four extrem-ities and the eight directions is present in my body. The colors of any mountain under Heaven need not have entered my eye for my eye to be filled with them. I need not have washed myself with the water of any clear stream under Heaven for my ears to become cleansed. I have obtained the highest principles under Heaven in my heart without needing to think. My heart is expansive and my body at ease, and for the first time I have become human. How enjoyable this traveling is! Isn't my land wide? Isn't my house huge? Isn't it well equipped?

Isn't this travel a pleasure? Isn't it enjoyable? In truth, 'military might will not be able to cow me,' nor 'will wealth and rank be able to sweep me off my feet, or poverty, make me budge.'[3] Since I am free of any opinions, obsessions, obstinancy, and ego,[4] how superior I feel, how free to travel! I am sure those things belong to me!"

The guest suddenly rose to his feet, straightened his clothes, and thanked me, saying, "Through your studies you have climbed high and you have come to consider the empire small. 'Looking down, you grieve for others, [enmeshed] in [the cycle] of day and night.'[5] You are no Yang, no Mo."

[Fujiwara Seika, *Seika sensei bunshū*, in NST, vol. 28, pp. 80–82; WB]

LETTER TO THE KOREAN SCHOLAR KANG HANG

Late in 1598 or early in 1599, Seika asked the Korean scholar Kang Hang on behalf of Akamatsu Hiromichi to add a postface to their newly finished edition of the Four Books and the Five Classics, based on the Neo-Confucian commentaries of the Song. Seika's language is typical of the Neo-Confucian depreciation of Han Confucian scholarship as well as of Zhu Xi's claim to repossess the long-lost Way of the sages, as represented by his Four Books. In Seika's view, Japanese Confucianism was still dominated by the old learning of the Han and Tang, introduced in the Nara period, and the new interpretations of the Song philosophers (the "original" teachings of Confucius and Mencius lost in the Han and Tang but now rediscovered) were still largely unknown in Japan. Hence the need for this new edition to proclaim the new dispensation.

Our lord Akamatsu wants me to transmit to you the following: the various houses that in Japan lecture on Confucianism from olden times until now have transmitted only the learning of the Confucians of the Han period and do not yet know the philosophy of principle (*ri*) of the Confucian scholars of the Song. For four hundred years they have not been able to remedy the defects of their inveterate tradition. Quite the contrary: they say that the Confucians of the Han are right and those of the Song are wrong. In truth, one can only smile pityingly on them. . . .

From my youth onward I never had a teacher. I read books on my own and told myself: the Confucians of the Han and Tang never rose above memorizing and reciting words and phrases. They hardly did more than offer explanatory notes on pronunciation and add remarks in the upper margin in order to draw attention to certain facts. They certainly did not have an inkling of the utter

---

3. Reference to *Analects* 8:13.
4. *Analects* 9:14.
5. *Mencius* 7A:24.

truth of the sages' learning. During the Tang dynasty the only one to rise above this level was Han Yu. But he, too, was not without shortcomings. If it were not for the Song Confucians, how could we ever have resumed the broken strands of the sages' learning?

In Japan, however, because the whole country is like this, one man cannot turn back the raging waves that have already toppled or send back the setting sun when it is already falling. I have felt full of pent-up anger and only held the zither and did not play the flute [i.e., I kept my opinions to myself]. For this reason our lord Akamatsu has just now made a new copy of the text of the Four Books and the Five Classics, and he has asked me to add Japanese reading marks to the side of the characters according to the interpretation of the Song Confucians, for the sake of posterity. Whoever in Japan will want to champion the interpretation of the Song Confucians shall have to take these volumes as his basic source. . . .

Please relate these facts, confirm their truth, and write a postface at the end of these works. This has been our lord Akamatsu's long-cherished desire and would please me very much. Do consider it!

[Fujiwara Seika, *Seika sensei bunshū*, in *NST*, vol. 28, pp. 95–96; WB]

FUJIWARA SEIKA'S NEW/OLD LEARNING

Although Seika's critical anthology of Chinese prose and poetry (the *Bunshō tattoku-roku*) was far from finished at the time, Kang Hang wrote a preface for this work, dated 1599, in which he extols Seika's learning and gives insight into the sources of his erudition, which included scholars of the Yuan and Ming who contributed to the later development of Neo-Confucian thought. Kang's point is that Seika is thoroughly up-to-date, compared with the old-fashioned Kiyowara school.

As far as his learning is concerned, Seika is not narrowly confined to one tradition. He did not receive the transmission from a teacher. He has based himself on the classics left over from a thousand years ago and rejoined the strands that had been broken off for a thousand years. He has progressed far, and on his own. Widely he searched, and he resumed the learning from the distant past. From what was represented by the knotted strings, what was borne by the dragon horse and carried by the divine tortoise or stored in the walls of Confucius's [house], up to [the writings of] Zhou Dunyi [1017–1073], the Chengs, Zhang Zai [1020–1077] and Zhu Xi, and Lu Xiangshan [1139–1193], Xu Heng [1209–1281] and Wu Cheng [1249–1333], Xue Xuan [1392–1464], Hu Juren [1434–1484], Chen Xianzhang [1428–1500], and Wang Yangming [1472–1529], and so on, he studied all the books about the philosophy of human nature and principle thoroughly and widely; he has thought them through and analyzed them clearly. In everything he makes it the basis of his learning to extend heavenly principles and to restrain the unruly heart. . . . Japanese scholars everywhere in the country knew only that there existed a learning [that consisted of] memorizing and reciting words and phrases; they did not yet know that the learning of the sages existed: a [Neo-Confucian] learning of human nature and principle, of preserving [one's mind and heart] and of scrutinizing oneself, of knowledge and action being one . . . Seika was born in a country far from China, cut off by the sea, and yet he rescued this one region from its blindness and deafness.

[*Fujiwara Seika shū*, vol. 2, pp. 1–3; WB]

LETTER TO THE HEAD OF ANNAM

On whose behalf Seika wrote this letter is not clear from the letter itself. In the extant printed version(s), both the name of the sender and the date have been suppressed. If the letter can be read in conjunction with the ship's oath that follows it, the sender was Seika's patron, the Kyoto merchant Suminokura (Yoshida) Soan. Each year between 1604 and 1613, the Suminokura sent one officially licensed trading vessel, or "vermilion seal ship," to trade in Southeast Asian waters. Others maintain, however, that it was Tokugawa Ieyasu himself who commissioned the letter. Whatever the case, it undoubtedly dates from 1604 and illustrates to what extent commerce and diplomacy were intertwined and to what extent Chinese culture was the commonly shared frame of reference throughout this whole area. The "poetry and history" mentioned in the letter, are, of course, the two Chinese classics: the *Classic of Odes* and the *Classic of Documents*. Rites and Rightness are two of the Five Constant Virtues.

_____ of Japan addresses this letter to Lord Huang, chief of Annam. In recent years, ships, like pigeons, have come from and gone to your country, from which we may deduce the good state of our mutual relations. This is a source of deep satisfaction. In the sixth month of the year 1604, our ship and crew returned home safely. I was put to shame by your answer to my letter and by the number of exquisite gifts you sent with it. [Six mother-of-pearl shells, five rolls of high-quality white silk, two tusk fans, one flask of aromatic wax, one flask of perfume.] I have no words to describe your generosity.

In your letter you quote from the *Great Learning* and say that it is all a matter of "abiding in trustworthiness." This one word truly expresses the essence of governing one's house and teaching the country. Trust is an inherent part of our human nature. It moves heaven and earth, penetrates metal and stone, and is present everywhere. How could its value be limited only to diplomatic relations and trade between neighboring countries? Is not this why all men everywhere are the same, even though customs may differ when we travel a thousand leagues? If we look at things from this perspective, what is different are secondary things like clothing and language. However, even at a distance of one thousand or ten thousand leagues and even though clothes and speech may differ, there is something that is not far off and does not differ. This is, I think, trust, which is one and universal.

My earlier emissaries behaved badly. As they traveled to and from your country and Japan, their actions belied their words, and often they mistook the situation. Therefore I have punished them according to the law of the land. I assume that in your country you would do the same? As a rule, a ship's crew is recruited from the lads of the market and shop assistants, and when they see even the slightest chance of gain, they forget the shame of the death penalty. They talk too much and in their joy or anger say whatever comes to their mouths; hence, they cannot be trusted. From now on, reliable communications between our two countries will take the form of letters, and the reliability of these letters will be established by their seals. These seals will prove that they are genuine. Therefore I have given the present crew your answering letter of this summer. Please examine it carefully. I also send you a few of our local products as complimentary presents.

In your letter, you say that "our country is a country of poetry and history, of rites and rightness, and not a place of market goods and traders' congregations." Indeed, when one has to handle market goods and trade, if one works only for gain and profit, it is really despicable. However, if one discusses this in more general terms, are not all four classes part of the people (even the despicable merchants)? Are not all eight responsibilities of the state of equal necessity (even trade)? Beyond giving peace to the people and governing them, poetry, history, rites, and rightness make no sense, and without poetry, history, rites, and rightness, it is impossible to give peace to the people or to govern. This also is the fixed, inherent nature of the five quarters: the nature that has trust as one of its principal constituents. What your country is warning against is simply that we might lose this trust, which may bring various unfortunate results. But so long as our two countries have not lost this trust, one single small-minded individual should not be able to cause such an unfortunate outcome. Even so, we should be on our guard. If something like this should happen, both countries have their codes of punishment.

Ship Compact (Soan was sending a ship to Annam; therefore I wrote this at his request)

1. Speaking generally, the purpose of trade is to bring a surplus [in one area] to scarcity [in another] in order to bring profit to both others and oneself. Trade is not harming others while bringing profit to oneself. Even a small profit that is shared by both parties is actually great, and a profit that may seem large but is not shared is in reality small. What one calls profit is the happy result when duties coincide. Therefore it is said that the avaricious merchant gives [only] three, whereas the decent merchant gives five. Keep this in mind.

2. Compared with our country, other countries may differ in customs and speech, but the heavenly endowed principle is always the same. Do not forget what is common; do not be suspicious of what is strange; and do not ever lie or brag. Even if the foreigners are not aware of it, we should be. "Trust reaches even to pigs and fish, and trickery shows itself even to the seagulls." Heaven does not tolerate deception; you should not disgrace the manners of our country. If you meet a humane person or a noble person (*junzi*) in that country, respect him as you would your father or your teacher. Ask about the prohibitions and taboos of that country, and adapt to its customs.

3. Between heaven that covers and earth that bears us up, all peoples are brothers and all things are in common, and all should be seen as one in their right to humane treatment. How much more does this apply to people from the same country? To people of the same ship? If there is trouble, sickness, cold, or hunger, then all should be helped equally; do not even think of wanting to escape alone.

4. Raging waters and angry waves may be dangerous, but one still runs the greatest risk of drowning from human greed. Human greed takes many forms, but the greatest risk of drowning is from liquor and sex. Since you will be traveling together wherever you go, correct one another and admonish one another. The old adage says, "The most dangerous road lies between the bedroom and the dining room." This is quite true. How could one not be careful?

5. Minor matters are treated in the appendices. Keep this [compact] next to your seat day and night, and reflect on it as in a mirror.

In the year Keichō, signed Tei Shigen, officer in charge of trade affairs.

[Fujiwara Seika, *Seika sensei bunshū*, in NST, vol. 28, pp. 88–90; WB]

TEACHINGS OF ZHU XI BROUGHT TO JAPAN

Much of the impression made on seventeenth-century Japanese by Zhu Xi (1130–1200) lay in his remarkable capacity to adapt and enfold in one system of thought the individual contributions of his Song predecessors. For this task he was well equipped by his breadth and subtlety of mind, and by powers of analysis and synthesis which enabled him, while putting ideas together, to articulate each of them with greater clarity and coherence than their originators had done. In this way Zhu defined more precisely such concepts as the Supreme Ultimate (Supreme Pole or Polarity, *taiji*), principle (*li*), material force (*qi*), human nature (*xing*), and the mind-and-heart (*xin*). Of his predecessors it was Cheng Yi upon whose philosophy Zhu mostly built. Consequently his school of thought is often identified as the Cheng–Zhu school, and the doctrine of principle (*li*) is the most characteristic feature of their common teaching.

Zhu Xi likened principle in things to a seed of grain, each seed having its own particularity but also manifesting generic, organic elements of structure, growth pattern, direction, and functional use, whereby each partakes of both unity (commonality) and diversity. Unlike the analogy of the Buddha-nature to the moon and its innumerable reflections in water (in which the latter are understood to be insubstantial, passing phenomena), principle for Zhu was real in both its substantial unity and its functional diversity. Hence he called the study of principle in all things, under both aspects, "real," "solid," "substantial" learning (*shi xue*).

In humankind this principle is one's moral nature, which is fundamentally good. The human mind, moreover, is in essence one with the mind of the universe, capable of entering into all things and understanding their principles. Zhu Xi believed in human perfectibility, in the overcoming of those limitations or weaknesses which arise from an imbalance in one's psychophysical endowment. His method was the "investigation of things" as taught in the *Great Learning*—that is, the study of principles and also self-cultivation to bring one's conduct into conformity with the principles that should govern it.

In this type of self-cultivation, broad learning went hand in hand with moral discipline. The "things" that Zhu Xi had in mind to investigate may be primarily understood as "affairs," including matters of conduct, human relations, political problems, etc. To understand them fully required of the individual both a knowledge of the literature in which such principles are revealed (the classics and histories) and an active cultivation of the Five Human Relationships— parent/child, ruler/minister, husband/wife, older and younger siblings, and friends—through which one could develop to the fullest the virtue of humaneness (*ren*, J. *jin*). It is through humaneness that one overcomes all selfishness and partiality, enters into all things in such a way as to identify oneself fully with them and thus unite oneself with the mind-and-heart of the universe, which is love and creativity itself. *Ren* is the essence of being human, one's "humanity," but it is also the cosmic principle that produces and embraces all things.

At the same time Zhu spoke of this teaching as "real" or "practical" learning (*shixue*, J. *jitsugaku*) because it was based on natural human sentiments and could be practiced in daily life through normal intellectual and moral faculties. These were to be developed through what Confucius, and now Zhu Xi, called "learning for one's self" (meaning for one's own self-development and self-fulfillment), a learning Zhu Xi urged on all, ruler and subject alike.

In contrast to Buddhism there is in Zhu Xi a kind of positivism that affirms the reality of things and the validity of objective study. His approach is plainly intellectual, reinforcing the traditional Confucian emphasis upon scholarship. Zhu Xi himself is probably the most stupendous example of such scholarly endeavor in the Chinese tradition. He wrote commentaries on almost all the Confucian Classics, conceived and supervised the condensation of Sima

Guang's monumental history of China, and interested himself in rites, governmental affairs, education, and agriculture. Zhu was a dynamic teacher at the Academy of theWhite Deer Grotto and kept up an active correspondence on a wide variety of subjects. He had less interest, however, in pursuing his "investigation of things" into the realms of what we would call natural or social science. To the last his humanism manifested itself in a primary concern for human values and ends. The kind of objective investigation that set these aside or avoided the ultimate problems of human life would have seemed to him at best secondary and possibly dangerous. Nevertheless, his philosophy, which stressed the order and intelligibility of things, could in a general way be considered conducive to the growth of science in a larger sense.

Zhu's later influence was felt chiefly through his commentaries on the Four Books—the *Great Learning*, the *Mean*, the *Analects*, and the *Mencius*—which he first canonized as basic texts of the Confucian school. In subsequent dynasties these texts, with Zhu Xi's commentaries, became the basis of the civil service examinations and thus, in effect, the official orthodoxy of the empire from the fourteenth century down to the turn of the twentieth century. Though subsequent thinkers arose to dispute his metaphysics, few failed to share in his essential spirit of intellectual inquiry, which involved focusing upon the Classics and reinterpreting them to meet the needs of their own time. Moreover, in Japan and Korea Zhu's writings likewise became accepted as the most complete and authoritative exposition of Confucian teaching. As such, these texts exerted a significant influence on the entire cultural development of East Asia well into modern times.

> [de Bary and Bloom, eds., *Sources of Chinese Tradition*,
> 2nd ed., vol. 1, pp. 697–99]

DIGEST OF THE GREAT LEARNING
(*DAIGAKU YŌRYAKU*)

As the first text to be read in Zhu Xi's version of the Four Books, the *Great Learning*, originally just a chapter in the *Record of Rites*, was invested with Zhu's philosophy of education through a preface and commentary reflecting Zhu's teachings in general.[6] By Fujiwara Seika's time, this key work had undergone further interpretation by generations of Neo-Confucian scholars in China and Korea who recognized the pivotal character of Zhu's text but worked from it in different directions.

The *Digest of the Great Learning* is the single doctrinal treatise that Seika is known to have written. He composed the work in 1619, shortly before his death, at the request of Asano Nagashige, who was the brother of Seika's patron Asano Yoshinaga and, at

---

6. See de Bary and Bloom, eds., *Sources of Chinese Tradition*, 2nd ed., vol. 1, pp. 720–31.

the time, the daimyo of Makabe (Hitachi). Most of the text is written in Japanese, in a simple classical style with a few vernacular forms, and was printed once, in 1630. In the first part, Seika discusses the Three Guidelines: to manifest luminous virtue (*ming mingde*), to renew (love) the people (*qin min*), and to rest in the utmost good (*zhi yu zhishan*), and, very briefly, the rest of Confucius's words that constitute the first part of the *Great Learning*. Then, as a kind of appendix, there follow a number of quotations and paraphrases from the works of the maverick Chinese thinker Lin Zhaoen (1517–1598) on the topics of *gewu* (the "investigation of things," but not according to Seika) and "manifesting luminous virtue." The second and third parts of the treatise form a continuous commentary on the whole of the *Great Learning*.

The text that Seika uses is not the new text established by the Cheng brothers and Zhu Xi, but the text as it appears in the *Record of Rites* and was made fashionable again by Wang Yangming. Seika's explanations, too, differ from Zhu Xi's and generally follow those of Lin Zhaoen in his *Sibu biaozhai zhengyi* and *Daxue zhengyi*.

Halfway through the first part of the treatise, after he has finished his explanation of the Three Guidelines, Seika makes the following claim on behalf of the *Great Learning*:

> If one has learned this one book by heart, one will need no other volumes, whether a hundred, a thousand or ten thousand. There is no Confucianism outside this work. Lectures exclusively treating the literary arts, which are so popular nowadays, are of no use to a ruler of men. Anyone who is a ruler of men need practice only the disciplining of his own heart and try to apply the teaching of the *Great Learning*." (p. 44)

Seika's interpretation of the Three Guidelines, too, is hardly what we would expect from a follower of Zhu Xi. Seika's main inspiration is again Lin Zhaoen, whose interpretation generally follows Wang Yangming's, which emphasizes "loving the people" rather than "renewing the people" through self-cultivation (as in Zhu Xi).

The meaning of the word "great" in "the Way of the *Great Learning*" is that others and I are one and that the outer and inner coincide. The first two of the Three Guidelines, "to manifest one's luminous virtue" and "to love the people," show that there is no discrimination between others and me; hence, others and I are one. The first two of the Three Guidelines refer to things external, but the third one, "to rest in the utmost good," refers to something internal; hence, outside and inside coincide. Thus when you no longer distinguish between others and yourself and between inner and outer, you will be able to know the meaning of the word "great." [That is,] the word "learning" should not be interpreted exclusively as book learning.

"Luminous virtue," in the first of the Three Guidelines, refers to the Five Human Relationships. When human relationships are not correct, nothing else will be of any use. Therefore we regard it as crucial that the Way of human relationships be made manifest. As the *Classic of Documents* declares: "Heaven has enjoined the luminous courses of duty, of which the several requirements are quite plain."

"Loving the people," in the second of the Three Guidelines, means that high and low are friendly and harmonious now that the human relationships have been made correct. Therefore Mencius said that when those above clarify human relationships, the people below will be affectionate. The word has the meaning of "loving and caring," in other words, the meaning of "to nurture."

To instruct the people in this way and to nurture them is the prime meaning of governing others through self-control. The character *qin* (to be kind) should certainly not be interpreted only in the sense of to be "close and intimate." Lin quotes Mencius to this effect. However, as the character is used in Mencius in the compound *qinmin*, it has the meaning of "to make them become friendly." *Qin* is something that inheres in human relationships, and it has the same meaning as "manifesting virtue." My personal opinion is that while "manifesting [or clarifying] virtue" has the meaning "to instruct," "loving the people" should have the sense of "to nurture the people." This must be why one speaks of "to love and to nurture." Whether later generations condemn me or agree with me, they should do so on this basis.

"The utmost good," in the third of the Three Guidelines ["to rest in the utmost good"], means "the supreme place." The character "to rest" is used in reference to the supreme place in my heart. When I rest in the utmost good, which is the supreme place in my heart, and do not move from there, it will be completely self-evident that according to the *Great Learning* there is no distinction between others and myself, between inner and outer. These three clauses—"to manifest the luminous virtue," " to love the people," and "to rest in the utmost good"—explain the substance starting from the functions. It is not [to be taken as] the order in which one should study. . . .

When you ask to which of the three, "luminous virtue," "loving the people," or "the utmost good," you should apply yourself first, my answer is that our Confucian teaching is a teaching of the "complete substance and great functioning." Therefore, when the substance—that is, the "the utmost good,"—is there, the functions—that is, "luminous virtue" and "loving the people"—will necessarily also be present. You rest in "the utmost good," and the transforming and nurturing of the people will spontaneously be achieved; this is how you "manifest the luminous virtue." The clarification of human relationships, which are the "luminous virtue," begins with "loving the people." Yao's merit reached all bordered by the Four Seas, but that was because he started from "loving the people." In his case, however, we are talking about a sage. Even though an ordinary scholar may do everything he can, he will not be able to enter by practicing this discipline. For ordinary scholars, *gewu* is the discipline to which they should apply themselves and by which means they can enter. [pp. 51–52]

Besides Seika's differences of opinion with Zhu Xi, another striking feature of Digest of
the Great Learning *is the* shingaku *that he proposes—that is, his method of disciplining
the mind-and-heart. The substance of this method appears most clearly in Seika's idiosyncratic interpretation of* gewu *(the "investigation of things"), one of the central terms
in the* Great Learning. *Seika knows that he is out of line, and, as in the rest of the text,
he makes sure he is quoting the right authorities to support his thesis, but the result, if
not unique, is certainly not standard.*

Gewu: Master Lin says: "Here the word *wu* does not mean 'things,' as in the
compound 'affairs and things' (*shiwu*); it is the *wu* that is used in the *Liji* in
the passage 'where a man's likings are not subject to regulation [from within],
he is changed into the nature of things as they come before him.' And the word
ge does not mean 'to impede,' 'to resist' (*gange*); it is the *ge* that is used in the
Shujing in the phrase 'to expel the evil heart.' The heart has changed into a
thing; if one does not call that an evil heart, what then? Therefore, when one
expels this evil heart, at the same time one 'expels a thing.' *Ge* has the meaning
of 'to remove.'" [p. 44]

If you apply yourself consciously to "removing things," this application itself
also is a thing. If there is only one speck of darkness and turbidity in the heart,
all kinds of thoughts will arise. If these thoughts were not there, the heart itself
would be empty and spiritual, and clear knowledge would be born. Then the
functioning of the mind-and-heart in response to the myriad things would be
effortless and appropriate. To think not to have thought, that is thought. It is
not that the *Great Learning* dislikes thought; what it says is that thoughts should
be clear of themselves. This is called the "complete substance and great functioning." If there were only substance and no functioning, or only functioning
and no substance, then we would be uttering heterodox teachings. . . . Some
people also think that the real point is to make the heart empty and that emptiness is the same as being completely free from all distracting thoughts, but
these are dumb, benighted people. . . .

The character *zhi* in *zhizhi* [usually interpreted as "to extend," as in "when
knowledge has been extended"] has the meaning of "to arrive at," as in
the case of someone who has traveled to another province and today, for the
first time, arrives in my village. . . . But those who make an effort to attain
knowledge will not find it, because instead of knowledge, they are distracted
by the effort "to attain it" itself. . . . When you remove things, you thereby
attain knowledge instantly, without having even tried to attain it naturally.
[pp. 55–56]

*The same insistence that the initial step is in itself sufficient and that all the following
stages are already contained in the first one, Seika also spells out elsewhere in this*

treatise. In view of the mirror metaphor that he uses, it is a logical deduction, but the result is different from Zhu Xi's interpretation and closer to Wang Yangming's.

Strictly speaking, the discipline prescribed in this work is fully expressed in the third of the Three Guidelines, "to rest in the utmost good." In that case, however, people whose talents are average or below average would find it difficult to start, so for that reason the *Great Learning* says that we must apply ourselves closely to the practice of *gewu* and clarify our mind-and-heart well. When our mind-and-heart is no longer dark and muddy but clear and limpid, and when, after that, objects arise spontaneously in our mind-and-heart, we should nurture this clear and limpid mind-and-heart and try not to lose it. When we do this for a long time, the "complete substance and great functioning" (*quanti dayong*) will reveal itself. . . . From this level upward it is no good being taught by others. You have to reach it on your own while finding out for yourself the meaning of the six characters "to know," "to settle," "to be quiet," "to be at ease," "to think," and "to obtain." In this way, by applying yourself to the practice of *gewu*, you will at the same time understand the [meaning of] the eight characters "to remove," "to extend," "to make sincere," "to rectify," "to cultivate," "to regulate," "to govern," and "to pacify." [pp. 43–44]

[Fujiwara Seika, *Daigaku yōryaku*, in NST, vol. 28, pp. 43–44, 51–52, 55–57; WB]

HAYASHI RAZAN

Hayashi Razan's career in the service of the *bakufu* began with an interview with Ieyasu. On this occasion, he showed an erudition far surpassing that of the erudites in attendance. As the story is usually told, there was only one interview. However, Razan's *Life Chronology* (*Nenpu*) mentions another audience, which preceded the one described here by Razan himself. The first audience probably took place on the twelfth day, but in any case, it was between the eighth and the fifteenth day of the fourth month of Keichō 10 (between May 25 and June 1, 1605), when Ieyasu had temporarily moved from the castle in Fushimi to Nijō Castle on account of the transfer of the office of shogun to Hidetada. The second audience must have taken place between the twenty-first of the seventh month (September 4, 1605) and the twenty-second of the eighth month (October 4, 1605) of the same year, when Ieyasu was again staying in Nijō Castle. According to a letter from Seika to Razan, a third audience had probably taken place between the other two, at the castle in Fushimi, during the fifth month. In his Commentary on "Tsurezuregusa" (Nozuchi), Razan describes only one interview in such a way that even his own youthful learning is made to show up the Zen monks' virtual illiteracy in Confucian culture.

ON MEETING WITH IEYASU

When I was still young and the prime minister (*daishōkoku* [Ieyasu]) was still the great minister of the center (*naidaijin*) (i.e., *before* Keichō 8/2/12, or March 24, 1603), I had an audience with him at his Nijō palace. The Zen fathers Shōtai and Sanyō Gankichi and Funabashi (Kiyohara) Hidekata also were in attendance at the time. Ieyasu asked how many generations there had been between Han Gaozu and Emperor Guangwu. Because nobody could remember, he asked me whether I knew. I answered that in the annals of the *History of the Latter Han* (*Hou-Han shu*) it was written that Emperor Guangwu was a descendant of Gaozu in the ninth generation. When again he asked in which book something was written about the "spirit-recalling incense," all said that they were not sure, and I answered that the "spirit-recalling incense" does not appear in the main text of the *Records of the Historian* (*Shiji*) or the *History of the Former Han Dynasty* (*Hanshu*) but that in the "Yuefu of Lady Li" in the *Collected Works of Bo Juyi* and in the notes to the poems of Su Dongpo, it was written that Emperor Wu burned such incense and summoned the spirit of his wife. Again Ieyasu asked, "What is meant by 'the orchids of Qu Yuan'?" I answered: "According to the notes to the *Chuci* of Zhu Xi, it was the marsh orchid." The prime minister looked left and right and expressed his amazement, saying, "This youngster knows a lot." This was in Keichō 10 [1605].

[*Hayashi Razan bunshū*, vol. 1, pp. 25f–28a; WB]

THE INVESTIGATION OF THINGS

The following colloquy between Hayashi Razan and Fujiwara Seika (as recorded by Razan) explains the two senses in which the "investigation of things" is to be understood—that is, the recognition of tangible objects and the deeper understanding of the intangible values attached to them. Fathoming these principles requires the full employment of the capacities of the mind-and-heart for entering into things empathetically.

I [Razan] asked, "The expressions 'the extension of knowledge' (*zhizhi*) and 'the investigation of things' (*gewu*) were first commented on by Zheng Xuan and later explained by Sima Guang. When we come to the Cheng brothers and Zhu Xi, they also gave explanations of these phrases that were brilliant and clear. But Wang Yangming again offered a different opinion. What do you think of that?"

The Master said, "It is not easy as yet to tell you that. You must first read more closely and get the taste of it, immerse yourself in it, and take your time with it. The important thing is to understand it in silence. When you have reached the stage [spoken of by Zhu Xi as] 'all at once achieving integral comprehension,' in which you penetrate it suddenly and clearly, then the similarities and differences among the Confucians will be resolved, and they all will be [seen as] essentially one." [p. 201]

Dōshun [Razan] once asked the meaning of "the investigation of things." Master Seika answered, "The Cheng brothers and Zhu Xi explained it as 'to fathom principle exhaustively' (*qiongli*). Let us take it from there. What is the reason that heaven and earth are heaven and earth? What is above and consists of piled-up *qi* is heaven; what is below and in massive form is earth. What makes fire into fire and water into water? Even though someone may be a thousand, ten thousand miles, or more away, if something blazes and flares up, it is surely fire even if it is not called fire. Even though a thousand, ten thousand, or more years ago, if something was liquid and flowed down, that was surely water even if it was not called water. With cold, heat, day, and night, it is the same. Every plant and every tree, the smallest birds and insects, each has its principle (*li*). How much more [this is true of] man! In regard to the human body, if we enumerate those principles (*li*) that man possesses, then we will call the *li* of the eye 'sight and clearness,' those of the ear 'hearing and acuteness,' those of the mouth 'speech and reverence,' and those of the mind-and-heart 'thought and sagacity.' Therefore it is said, 'Man is the most spiritual part of heaven and earth.'[7] The day that one suddenly penetrates this heart, these *li*, and understands them clearly is called 'the investigation of things.'"

I [Razan] said: "'Things' (*wu*) means 'affairs' (*shi*). Now, if there is a 'thing,' there is also an 'affair' (something that matters). When one talks of 'affairs,' however, one is talking about something intangible, and when one talks about 'things,' one is talking about something solid. Parent and child, lord and retainer, all are 'things.' The existence of parental love or of rightness are 'affairs.' Principle is what makes them such [i.e., makes love, love, and fathers, fathers]. Proceeding analogically in all similar cases and thus reaching the inner meaning exhausts the full capacity [for understanding] of the mind-and-heart. Doesn't what one calls 'the investigation of things' (*gewu*) mean reaching things?" Seika replied, "Yes."

Again I [Razan] asked, "In the *Shuogua*, the fifth appendix of the *Yijing*, it says 'to fathom principle exhaustively' (*qiongli*),[8] and in the *Daxue* it says go to things (*gewu*). Why do they phrase it differently?"

Seika answered, "With their thousands of words and myriads of utterances the sages and worthies wanted people to recognize principle. How they express it is not the same, but what they enter into is [the same]. Moreover, all the men

---

7. *Shujing*, "T'ai-shih"; Legge translated this as "Heaven and earth is the parent of all creatures; and of all creatures man is the most highly endowed" (*The Shoo king*, p. 113). *Liji*, "Li yun": "Man is made of the most refined parts of the five elements"; Legge translated this as "The finest subtle matter of the five elements" (*Li Chi*, vol. 1, p. 381).

8. Legge translates this as "They (thus) made an exhaustive discrimination of what was right, and effected the complete development of (every) nature, till they arrived" (*I ching*, p. 442).

of former times had their own method of entry. Zhou Dunyi had his 'giving primacy to quiescence' (*zhujing*); the Chengs had their 'holding to reverent seriousness' (*zhijing*); Zhu Xi his 'fathoming of principle' (*qiongli*); Lu Xiangshan had his 'easy simplicity' (*yijian*); Chen Bosha [had] his 'tranquillity and completeness' (*jingyan*); and Wang Yangming [had] his 'innate knowledge' (*liangzhi*). Their words may seem to differ, but what they enter into is the same."

I said, "If one talks only of principle and not of 'things,' one gallops through a void, and if one talks of 'things' and not of principle, one remains stuck in the phenomenal world. This phenomenal world has form; [whereas] principles are formless. Loyalty and filial piety cannot be discarded unilaterally, depending on whether one's lord or father still lives or has died. 'Things' and principle are naturally one; the Way and the phenomenal world in which the principles are embedded are not two. This is called 'investigating things and fathoming their principles' (*gewu qiongli*)." Seika declared, "So it is."

Master Seika once asked, "What is the most important point of the *Great Learning*?" Dōshun answered, "To make one's intentions sincere (*chengyi*)?" Seika remarked, "Although 'to make one's intentions sincere' is an important point of the *Great Learning*, nevertheless for those who pursue learning 'to go to things and exhaustively fathom their principles' comes first. This is the most urgent task." [p. 204]

[Hayashi Razan, *Razan sensei bunshū*, in *NST*, vol. 28, pp. 201, 204; WB]

THE SAGELY IDEAL VERSUS PRACTICAL COMPROMISE

The following excerpts are from a letter written in June or July 1611 by Razan, then at Ieyasu's headquarters in Sunpu, to his teacher Fujiwara Seika in Kyoto. It reveals the conflict that Razan felt between his commitment to pursue the Neo-Confucian ideal of sagehood and the realities of his service to his military lord. Expressed in a multitude of literary and philosophical allusions, the main points may be summed up as follows:

> Although as to outward circumstance, I have no cause for complaint (who, at my age has seen so much of the world and has such an excellent library at his disposal?), yet I feel lonely and misunderstood. I am urged to conform to people who have no understanding of my skills and aspirations; what is worse, I do conform. Great literary figures of former times maybe felt the same and perhaps turned Daoist precisely for that reason. However, I do not want to follow their path. I want to follow the Confucian sages. But that course implies an obligation to act according to my convictions, and that I find myself unable to do. The strain caused by this conflict is showing in me and affecting even my literary talents.

In other words, Razan felt that the work and atmosphere in Sunpu were not congenial and that the life he was being forced to live there endangered his personal commitment to sagely purity and led him to compromise his Confucian aspirations.

When I was about twenty years old, I read the books by the Cheng brothers, Zhu Xi, and other Confucians. This was the first time I knew that the learning of human nature and principle existed. And when I was twenty-two, I arranged a meeting with you. I heard your arguments and luxuriated in your bountiful kindness. And then I thought that all the virtue and literature of our country lay in you.

The following year I met our lord in Kyoto. In this connection I went to Edo in Musashi. . . . And now I am in Suruga. Every morning and every night, when I look up, I see Mount Fuji rising above the clouds. How can this not be happiness? . . .

However, I am now twenty-nine years old. When I want to tell someone what I am studying all day, I feel useless, like somebody who is skilled in carving up dragons, like someone who is selling ceremonial caps to the people of Yue [where the people cut off their hair and tattoo their bodies].

I "agree with the current customs and consent with an impure age"[9] and pretend that I do this for the sake of harmony. How could I pretend that I learned this from Hui of Liuxia, who "was wanting in self-respect"[10] and "the most accommodating one under the sages?"[11] My present self is not my former self, and yet I am like that man. How could I say that I try to emulate Qu Boyu, who was in office when good government prevailed and who could roll up his principles and keep them to himself when the government was bad?[12] My spirit is wilting, and the same thing is happening to my literary talents. . . .

Confucius said, "Your good, careful people of the villages are the thieves of virtue."[13] Acting the way I do, if I were to say that I am not one of these good, careful persons of the villages, it would be as if I were holding a net, had waded into a river or lake, and were saying to others, "I am not a fisherman." Would it not be better to throw away the net and have people believe me of their own accord?

I have read the books by the sages and worthies. I know that such is their intent; it is something I cannot endure. My ambition, however, to provide for my parents, and the obligations I have to my friends and brothers, do not leave me any choice. To this state things have come. . . .

One more thing I will add. You exhorted me to write *waka* (poetry). Since this is our national custom, you were sure that I would have such an inclination. . . . I have written five rustic poems like the following. My only reason for adding this poem at the end of this letter is to give you something to laugh at. I hope you will not read it to strangers. Twice bowing, I have spoken respectfully

---

9. *Mencius* 7B:37.
10. *Mencius* 2A:9.
11. *Mencius* 5B:1.
12. *Analects* 15:7.
13. *Analects* 17:11.

ikuchiyo to   Feeling like wishing
iwau kokoro o   You many thousands of years
Suruga naru   I want to search Mount Fuji
Fuji no kusuri o   That lies in Suruga
motomemakuhoshi   For immortality's drug.

[*Hayashi Razan bunshū*, vol. 1, pp. 25b–28a; WB]

RESPONSES TO QUESTIONS BY IEYASU

The following excerpts are from *Bakufu mondō* (*Answers to Questions by the Bakufu* [Ieyasu]). These deal with key issues of Neo-Confucian doctrine—for example, the underlying unity of Confucian teaching and the age-old question of whether it is legitimate to overthrow a ruler.

Razan is referred to here by his original Buddhist name, Dōshun, because his position as adviser to the shogun had, by long shogunal custom, been filled by Zen monks. Since Razan had already renounced Buddhism, he was accused by some scholars of insincerity and expediency in accepting such a role. Thus it was not surprising that the question arose of what legitimate discretion was and what mere expediency was in the practical implementation of the Way. Indeed, is the Confucian Way practicable at all without compromising it? Razan asserted that it was and offered a somewhat idealized Ming China as a model.

Ieyasu asked Dōshun [Razan]: "Is the Way still practiced in Ming China? What do you think?" I said that it was. "Although I have not yet seen it with my own eyes, I know it from books. Now, the Way is not something obscure and secluded; it exists between ruler and minister, father and son, man and wife, old and young, and in the intercourse between friends. At this time there are schools in China in each and every place, from the villages and country districts up to the prefectural capitals. All of them teach human relations. Their main objective is to correct the hearts of men and to improve the customs of the people. Do they not then indeed practice the Way?" Thereupon the *bakufu* changed his countenance and spoke of other things. Dōshun, too, did not talk about it anymore.

Ieyasu said to Dōshun: "The Way has never been practiced, neither now nor earlier. Therefore, [in the *Zhongyong* it says] 'The course of the Mean cannot be attained' and 'The path of the Mean is untrodden.' What do you think of this?" Dōshun answered, "The Way can be practiced. What the *Zhongyong* says is, I think, something that Confucius said when he was complaining that the Way was not being practiced. This does not mean that the Way cannot actually be practiced. In the Six Classics there are many lamentations like this. It is not only in the *Zhongyong*."

Ieyasu asked what was meant by "the Mean" (J. *chū*, Ch. *zhong*). I answered, "The Mean [or Middle] is difficult to grasp. The middle of one foot is not the middle of one *jō* [ten feet]. The middle of a room is not the middle of a house. The middle of a province is not the middle of the empire. All things have their own middle. Only when you have found their principle can you say that you have found their middle [mean]. However much they want to know the Mean, those who have only just begun their studies never find it, precisely because they do not know the principles. For this reason we have the maxim, valid now and earlier, that 'the Mean is nothing but principle.'"

In the following passage, Ieyasu proposes a relativistic standard of good and evil, citing the Madhyamika Buddhist doctrine that the Middle Way of Supreme Wisdom lies in adhering to neither good nor evil.[14] Razan responds that the Confucian Mean, in contrast to the Buddhist Middle Way of nondiscrimination, consists of making value judgments and acting on behalf of the common good, by which one achieves unity with the Way. Ieyasu cites the historic examples of Cheng Tang overthrowing the last king of Xia, and King Wu of Zhou overthrowing the last ruler of Shang, as cases comparable to the "expedient means" of Mahayana Buddhism. Razan views these as cases of legitimate discretion in acting for the Way. Thus the argument here hinges on the double meaning of the term (J. ken, Ch. quan), understood by Ieyasu as "expediency" and by Razan as the legitimate exercise of discretion. The former emphasizes moral ambiguity; the latter, the need to resolve the ambiguity by judgments on behalf of the common good.

Ieyasu said, "In both the Middle [Path] and Expediency there can be good or bad. Tang [in overthrowing the last king of Xia] and Wu [in overthrowing the last king of Shang] were vassals who overthrew their lords. Their actions, though bad, were good. As the phrase goes, 'In taking the empire they went against the Way, and in keeping it, they followed the Way.' Therefore, 'neither good nor bad' is the ultimate truth of the Middle [Way]." I answered, "My opinion is different from this. May I be allowed to speak my mind? I think that the Mean is good, that it does not have one speck of evil. The Mean means that you grasp the principles of all things and that your every action accords with the standard of rightness [fitness]. If you regard the good as good and use it and regard evil as evil and shun it, that is also the Mean. If you know what is correct and incorrect and distinguish between what is heterodox and orthodox, this is also the Mean. Tang and Wu followed Heaven and reacted to the wishes of mankind. They never had one particle of egoistic desires. On behalf of the people of the empire, they removed a great evil. How can that be 'good, though bad'? The actions of Tang and Wu were in accord with the Mean; they are instances of [legitimate] discretion.". . .

On the twenty-fifth day of the sixth month the *bakufu* said to Dōshun, . . . "What is that so-called unity that pervades all?" Dōshun answered, "The heart

---

14. See de Bary et al., eds., *Sources of Japanese Tradition*, 2nd ed., vol. 1, chaps. 3, 5.

of the sage is nothing but principle. Now, always and everywhere, principle runs through all things and all actions in the world; the sage reacts to them and acts on them according to this one principle. Therefore it never happens that he goes and does not obtain his proper place. To give an example, it is like the movement of spring, summer, fall, and winter, of warm and cold, day and night: though they are not identical, yet they are a cyclical stream of one and the same original matter that is not disrupted for a single moment. For that reason, actions in the world may be [repeated] ten-, hundred-, thousand- or ten-myriad-fold, but that with which the heart reacts to them is only the one, uniting, principle. With one's lord it is loyalty; with one's father, filial piety; with one's friends, trust; but none of these principles is different in origin." . . .

The *bakufu* again asked, "Were the wars of Tang and Wu instances of discretion or expedience?" Dōshun answered, ". . . The purpose of the actions of Tang and Wu was not to acquire the empire for themselves but only to save the people. . . . If those above are not a [wicked] Jie or Zhou and those below [are] not a [virtuous] Tang or Wu, then one will commit the great sin of regicide; Heaven and earth will not condone this. . . . It is only a matter of the hearts of the people of the empire. If they turn to him, he will become a ruler, and if not, he will be a 'mere fellow' [and killing him will not be regicide]."

[Hayashi Razan, *Razan sensei bunshū*, in NST, vol. 28, pp. 205–8; WB]

"THE THREE VIRTUES"
(SANTOKUSHŌ)

This essay, attributed to Hayashi Razan by his son Gahō, is a concise and coherent summation of the principles of Neo-Confucian self-cultivation, drawn mostly from Zhu Xi's version of the *Great Learning* (*Daigaku*). The text, however, superimposes on that structure a concept of the Three Virtues taken from the *Mean* (*Chūyō*): wisdom, humaneness, and courage. For Razan, these constituted a triad of irreducible, interdependent values governing all human affairs, but with some priority given to intellectual virtue over moral sentiment.

The actual title, "Selections Concerning the Three Virtues" (Santokushō), refers to passages from authoritative texts, with commentary, under subheadings, that is mostly from the *Great Learning*. The contents draw heavily on earlier Neo-Confucians, frequent references to whom—especially the Cheng brothers, Zhu Xi, Chen Chun, Lo Qinshun, and the Korean Yi T'oegye—help locate Razan in one line of "orthodox" Neo-Confucian thinkers. Although Razan is critical of Lu Xiangshan, in this work he quotes Wang Yangming without critical comment.

1. The Three Virtues

1.1. Wisdom means having no doubts in one's mind. Humaneness refers to having no regrets after making judgments or decisions. Being of firm mind and strong determination refers to courage. Wisdom, humaneness, and courage are the sages' three virtues.[15] Referring to these three virtues, Confucius states in the *Analects* that "the wise have no perplexities; the humane have no worries; the courageous have no fears.[16] . . .

Although distinguishable as three virtues, the three are present in man's mind, and thus wisdom embraces humaneness and courage. Without humaneness and courage, great wisdom would be impossible to achieve. Similarly, humaneness includes both wisdom and courage.[17] Without the latter two virtues, perfect humaneness would not be possible. Thus when analyzed, they are three; yet when synthesized, they constitute a unified moral mind. . . .

If today one principle is investigated, and tomorrow one more principle is inquired into,[18] soon one will be free of doubts. If one can thoroughly penetrate one principle, all principles will be clear, even though one has not investigated a great many matters. Within a single principle, one can progress from one matter to ten others. When these are investigated so that one completely comprehends both the internal and external, as well as the beginning and end of the matter, then one's understanding will actually apply to many principles. . . .

2. The Five Relationships (*Gorin*)

2.1. Throughout history the Five Relationships—those between ruler and minister [lord and retainer], parent and child, husband and wife, older and younger brother, and friends—have existed. Since the five Ways have continued unaltered, they are called "universal Ways" (J. *tatsudō*, Ch. *dadao*). . . .

Rulers should love their people; ministers should serve their rulers; fathers should be compassionate toward their sons; husbands should manage external matters, while wives should handle the family's internal affairs; elder brothers should teach their younger brothers, and younger brothers should follow their elder brother's instructions; friends should associate with one another on the basis of rites and justice. Such behavior is entirely within the sphere of wisdom, humaneness, and courage. . . .

2.2. Wisdom refers to understanding the principles of things. . . .

2.3. Humaneness refers to loving things. If one does this as one would if thinking of oneself, then one's humaneness will necessarily be genuine and sincere, devoid of selfishness. . . . Humaneness is, furthermore, life-giving.[19]

---

15. *Mean* 20: "Wisdom, humanity and courage, these three are the universal virtues. The Way by which they are practiced is one" (Chan, *Source Book in Chinese Philosophy*, p. 105).

16. *Analects* 9:27: "One who knows [not "the wise"] is not perplexed."

17. Zhu Xi, *Zhuzi yulei*, chap. 6, p. 172.

18. Zhu Xi, *Daxue huowen*.

19. Zhu Xi, *Ren shuo*, chap. 67, pp. 20a–21b.

Eliminating evil is rightness (J. *gi*, Ch. *yi*). Deliberations as to whether one should kill a thing or help it should address matters of humaneness and rightness. If one eliminates evil by killing, then there is humaneness within the right act of killing. If that is so, killing a rat is humane. If one kills thieves to admonish others against doing evil, that too expresses this same mind. To think that humaneness consists only of compassion is to think simply of "small humaneness." To admonish one evil person and thus provide for the goodness of several others is "great humaneness." Thus, while humaneness is love, one is not being humane by loving evil persons. Rather, humaneness is loving what is good and detesting what is evil. If one acts in this way, how could one be selfish?

2.4. Courage refers to stoutheartedness that conforms to rightness. Acting immediately when one perceives what is morally good is courage. Being hesitant, lazy, or unsure whether or not one should do something, even when one knows what is right, is not courage. . . . Wisdom is understanding humaneness and courage. Humaneness consists of not casting off wisdom and of preserving courage. Courage is practicing both wisdom and humaneness. Of the three virtues—wisdom, humaneness, and courage—not one should be omitted! From the beginning, they have constituted the sincerity of man's whole mind.

3. A Discussion of Principle and Material Force

Razan's discussion of this topic and, later, of the related one of the Four Beginnings and Seven Emotions reflects his familiarity with the views of Lo Qinshun and Yi T'oegye.

3.1. The successive alternation of yin and yang is called the Way. What issues from the Way is morally good, and what completes the Way is called the nature.[20]

Both before and after Heaven and earth opened up, principle always denoted the great Supreme Ultimate. When the Supreme Ultimate moves, it produces yang; when it is still, it produces yin. Together, yin and yang make up the "one, originating material force." Once they have divided, they become two. When they have divided again, they become the five processes (J. *gogyō*, Ch. *wuxing*). The five processes are (1) wood, (2) fire, (3) earth, (4) metal, and (5) water. These five processes create everything.

When they combine and form things, man is one of their products. Skin comes from earth; hair comes from wood; the vital fluids come from water; man's skeleton and muscles come from metal; and man's energy comes from fire. In regard to man's five organs, the essence of fire, wood, earth, metal, and

---

20. *Classic of Changes (Yijing, Xici zhuan); Concordance to Yi ching [Yijing]*, p. 40; Legge, trans., *I ching*, pp. 355–56.

water form, respectively, his heart, liver, spleen, lungs, and kidneys. Thus do the five processes join to create the human body. The active, animated aspect of man is referred to as "material force." Principle refers to what is naturally replete with material force. This principle is the Supreme Ultimate. It is called the Way.

The master of the physical form created by the intermingling of principle and material force is called the "mind."[21] Since this mind contains the original principles of the great ultimate, it is empty and open (J. *kokū*, Ch. *xukung*) like Heaven. Lacking both shape and sound,[22] it consists simply of moral goodness and is devoid of any evil.

Yet in material force, both purity and pollutants, good and evil, coexist. Because of the heterogeneous nature of material force, when people are created, selfishness, excessive desires, and evil emerge as well. For example, when the eyes see beautiful forms, the mind might think of evil. Or when the mouth says something or the hands and feet touch something, it is much the same. Always, selfishness and excessive desires arise from material force. . . .

3.2. The four beginnings come out of our principle, whereas the seven emotions come from material force.[23]

The four beginnings are the first manifestations of humaneness, rightness, ritual decorum, and wisdom. The seven emotions refer to the feelings of pleasure, anger, sorrow, joy, love, hate, and desires. Since man's mind-and-heart is simply moral principle (*dōri*), humaneness, rightness, ritual decorum, and wisdom emerge from it. Because material force consists of both good and evil, the seven emotions emerge from them. Thus the seven emotions are both good and evil, but the four beginnings are purely good, without any evil. If the seven emotions arise in conformity with moral principles, then they are consistent with humaneness and rightness. When influenced by one's ever fluctuating material endowment, the seven emotions arise in accord with selfish desires and may violate moral principles. Because of this evil tendency, one must discern the manner in which they arise. If the seven emotions violate moral principle, they will inevitably lead to evil.

By itself, moral principle could hardly produce activity. If it is combined with material force to form the mind-and-heart, principle is capable of motion and activity. . . .

Although moral principle and material force are two aspects of being, whenever material force exists, moral principle also exists. Since moral principle in itself is formless, it has no place to dwell unless material force exists. Moral principles do not exist apart from material force. It is not that today material

---

21. Zhu Xi, *Zhuzi quanshu*, in SBBY 45:4a–b; Chan, *Source Book in Chinese Philosophy*, p. 631.

22. *Mean* 33.

23. Yi T'oegye, *Chŏn-myŏngdo*, in *Ritaikei zenshū*, vol. 2, p. 233; Yi T'oegye, "Diagram of the Supreme Ultimate," in *To Become a Sage*, trans. Kalton, pp. 37–50.

force exists and tomorrow moral principle comes into being. When either exists, the other exists simultaneously. Material force is what capably moves moral principle, and moral principle is what preserves the order within material force. When one understands that the mind-and-heart is formed from these two, one can manage one's material force with one's mind.

3A.3. It would not be enough to talk about the nature of man and things without including material force. Similarly, it would be inconceivable to talk about material force without including nature. It is a mistake to consider them as two different things.[24]

Accounting for the endowment of moral principle in man is problematic if one discusses moral principle without discerning its relation to material force. Conversely, the myriad things will be hardly discernible if one simply discusses material force without acknowledging moral principle. Nature is principle.[25] Nature should be discussed in conjunction with material force. It is a mistake to divide them.

Man's nature is originally good. In reply to the question of where evil comes from, one should reply that human nature is like water.[26] It is clear. . . .

Material force is also comparable to water. Although originally calm, water forms waves when blown by the wind. Depending on an area's topography, water can turn into a flood. Although it originally tends to flow downward, water can be lifted upward by water carts. Although originally clear, when water flows into mud and mire, it becomes dirty. And although water is able to support boats, it can also sink them. Despite all this, when it returns to its original state, water's fundamental nature is to be clean and calm.

Thus there are disparities in material force. "Disposition of the material force" (J. kishitsu, Ch. qishi) refers to that part of the omnipresent material force that people receive as their physical form. There are disparities among "dispositions of material force," too. . . .

By studying and learning, however, one can reform one's disposition of the material force and change it from evil to good.[27] While the disposition of the material force with which one is born is fixed, one should not abandon it, leaving it as it is. Rather, if one studies, even the foul parts will become clear, just as water returns to its original nature. Likewise in man, dullness becomes bright, ignorance becomes wisdom, weakness becomes strength, and evil becomes good, all through learning. . . .

---

24. Cheng Hao and Cheng Yi, Er Cheng yishu, in Er Cheng quanshu, in SBBY 6:2a; Chan, Source Book in Chinese Philosophy, p. 536, n. 92.

25. Zhu Xi, Mengzi jizhu, in Shushigaku taikei, vol. 8, p. 339 (528).

26. Zhu Xi, Zhuzi quanshu, in SBBY 43:7a–b; Chan, Source Book in Chinese Philosophy, p. 625.

27. Cheng Yi, Yichuan wenji, in Er Cheng quanshu, in SBBY 4:1a; Chan, Source Book in Chinese Philosophy, p. 550.

3.8. The human mind is precarious, but the mind of the Way is subtle. Be discriminating, be unified, and hold fast to the Mean.[28]

These are words from "The Counsels of Great Yu." While the mind is essentially one, its active, moving aspect is called "the human mind" (*jin no kokoro*), and its moral aspect is called "the mind of the Way" (*dō no kokoro*). When cold, one thinks of warm clothing; when hungry, one thinks of food. Eyes long to see beauty; ears long to hear interesting sounds; noses long to smell pleasant odors. All desires are produced by "the mind of man." "The mind of man" has many selfish tendencies yet harbors few concerned for the common good (*ōyake*). Since it easily tends toward evil, the preceding passage states that "the human mind is precarious." "Precarious" refers to the real insecurities that confront the mind when faced with choices between good and evil, right and wrong.

When moral principles prevail in the mind, even though one may think of food and warm clothing, one might still be willing to endure hunger and cold and refuse food and clothing if they are not obtained in a moral way. . . .

"Being discriminating" means discerning and manifesting "the mind of the Way" so that selfishness is not mixed in at all. "Being unified" means preserving and correcting the mind at all times. If by being discriminating and unified, one can make "the mind of the Way" the master and make "the mind of man" follow it, then even precarious situations will become simple, subtleties will become manifest, and all matters will naturally accord with moral principle. Preserving and not losing "the mind of the Way" refers to "holding fast to the Mean." The "Mean" is another term denoting the moral principles that are provided in both the substance and functioning of man's original mind. . . .

4. The *Great Learning*

The following, based on Zhu Xi's preface, emphasizes the importance of universal schooling.[29]

4.1. In the past, during the flourishing of the Tang dynasty [618–907], "great learning" and "elementary learning" (J. *shōgaku*, Ch. *xiaoxue*) referred to two places for education, one for adults and the other for children. From age eight until fifteen, children attended to elementary learning, learning to sweep and clean, ask and answer questions, discipline themselves, read and write, calculate, shoot a bow, ride a horse, and perform rites and music. Such was the method of elementary learning.

---

28. Legge, trans., *Book of Documents*, "Counsels of the Great Yü," p. 125; Legge, *The Shoo king*, pp. 62–63.

29. Zhu Xi, *Daxue zhangju*, in *Shushigaku taikei*, vol. 7, p. 351 (443).

At age fifteen, students entered higher school (*daigaku*) and began to study the Way of the sages and worthies. Places for "elementary learning" and "higher learning" existed in the capital city, as well as in the counties, towns, and villages of the countryside. Depending on what was appropriate to each area, similar schools with similar curricula were established to give instruction to people. . . .

If things are done in this way, people will do good and refrain from evil; they will be correct, not wicked. They will be conscientious toward their ruler, and they will be filial toward their parents. Naturally they will avoid partiality. The state will thus be governed, and the world will be at peace. . . .

6. The Five Constants

6.1. Regarding humaneness, rightness, ritual decorum, and trustworthiness, humaneness is the virtue innate in man's mind-and-heart and the principle of its love for things.[30] . . .

Upon seeing a child about to fall into a well, anyone will feel compassion for him, regardless of whether one knows the child or his parents. . . . In this case, one's mind instantly feels compassion and love for the child, without thought of selfishness.

Also, upon seeing grasses and trees growing luxuriantly, one thinks them interesting; and when finding them withered or broken, one feels sorry. Or seeing birds flying and bustling about, one is amused by them; yet on discovering them dead, one feels grief. This is due to humaneness. By extending this mind-and-heart to all things, one comes to love everything, without exception. . . .

Although the mind itself is not visible, when one sees the birth of everything in the beginning of spring, one can understand the mind of Heaven-and-earth. When man's mind and the mind of Heaven-and-earth become one, their creativity expands, excluding selfishness and greed, so that neither harm nor injury is done to things. This unified mind, then, embodies the way of humaneness (*jin no michi*).

6.2. Rightness (*gi*) is the basis of the mind's decisions. Following the times and circumstances refers to doing what is appropriate. Although life is precious, if our minds do not consent [to what is wrong], we will not accept food and will die. Or we will not accept clothing and die. When deciding whether to accept them and live or refuse them and die—more than just calculating whether one will live by accepting these things—one asks whether if it [is not in] accord with principle one should decline them and die. . . .

Rightness, too, resides in detesting, rejecting, and discarding the evil found in others. Serving one's ruler conscientiously involves rightness as well. . . .

---

30. Zhu Xi, *Lunyu jiju*, in *Shushigaku taikei*, vol. 7, p. 36 (396).

Once this sense of rightness is extended to everyone, all people will do good and refrain from evil. . . .

6.3. Ritual decorum refers to being careful when dealing with others so as not to disorder relationships. Youth should respect the old, and humble persons should revere those of high standing; that is decorum. That various grades of officials wear certain caps and cloaks also is a matter of ritual decorum. Ceremonies for attaining manhood, taking a wife, taking a husband, and manners and etiquette all are matters of ritual decorum. While these examples involve people's actions, their principles emerge from that part of men's minds that preserves order. . . . By extending this mind to all things, one should cause no disorder in relations between ruler and ministers, superior and inferiors, and among people at large. . . .

6.4. While the myriad things are manifold, if they are endowed with principles, one understands that those principles are originally one with the human mind-and-heart. When one comprehends fully the unity of principle, all principles will be understood equally. . . .

6.5. Trustworthiness refers to the fixed principles of man's mind that are wholly without falsehood. While humaneness, rightness, ritual decorum, and wisdom all are genuinely truthful, trustworthiness pertains to being without deception in one's body and mind as one acts. . . .

Is there anywhere in the world that trustworthiness [reliability] does not exist? Three hundred and sixty days make one year. Spring is warm, summer is hot, autumn is cool, and winter is cold. The alternations of the sun and moon, day and night, have not deviated since antiquity. Seeds from grasses and trees produce grasses and trees. Also, birds and beasts give birth to birds and beasts. Humans give birth to humans. Birds fly in the sky; beasts roam in the plains and mountains; fish swim in water. There is no deviance in these things. Examining everything, one sees that none lacks genuine principles (*shinjitsu nori*). These genuine principles are called the "Supreme Ultimate" (Taikyoku). They existed before the beginning of Heaven-and-earth and will exist until the end of Heaven-and-earth. These genuine principles that man receives in his mind and that cannot be lost constitute trustworthiness (reliability).

7. The Seven Feelings

7.1. When distinguishing among pleasure, anger, sorrow, fear, love, hate, and desire, men's minds-and-hearts become limitlessly enlarged. Like Heaven or perhaps the empty sky, the mind can contemplate far into the past, a thousand or even ten thousand years ago. It can imagine a place a thousand or perhaps ten thousand miles away. The mind also can understand the principles of all things. Although it can expand in these ways, the mind exists nowhere outside the body.

Before thoughts arise, the mind is quiet, correct, level, and clear. When something pleasurable appears, the mind is pleased. If something angering arises, it becomes angry. Encountering sorrowful things, the mind is sorrowed.

With frightening things, it is frightened. Confronted with something lovable, the mind loves. Presented with something detestable, the mind detests it. And the mind desires what it experiences as something desirable. These are the mind's activities. . . .

The seven feelings described above are the expressions of the mind. While it is impossible that they be done away with,[31] and while the seven may be seen as one, when one violates principle in the expression of the feelings, the original mind is disturbed, inevitably becoming incorrect. When the mind is incorrect, the self will be disordered, and the country will be ungoverned. When the seven feelings are properly expressed, the original substance of the mind naturally becomes correct and manifest. When the mind is correct, the self is cultivated properly, and the family is ordered. When the family is ordered, the country is well governed. Then the world too will be at peace. Thus the sages' Way makes correcting the mind its foundation. The mind which is corrected and illumined properly is called luminous virtue.

8. Seeing, Hearing, Speech, and Action

8.1. Therefore, the method of the *Great Learning* consists of internally ordering and correcting the mind and its seven feelings. Then externally, one will be minutely respectful in one's appearance, seeing, hearing, speech, and actions. Thus, the learning of the sages and worthies consists of controlling the self, ordering the people, and governing the state.

[Hayashi Razan, "Santokushō," in *NST*, vol. 28, pp. 151–86; JAT]

THE LATER HISTORY OF THE HAYASHI FAMILY SCHOOL

It took father, son, and grandson—three generations of the Hayashi family—to establish its "private school" as the officially recognized school of the Tokugawa shogunate in Edo. Tokugawa Ieyasu was a cautious administrator who, as we have seen, kept in his service Tenkai (1536–1643) of the Tendai sect and Sūden (1569–1633) of the Zen sect. The former became director of the Nikkō shrines, with all esoteric Buddhist temples and syncretic Shinto shrines under his jurisdiction, while the latter was superintendent general of all Zen denominations, with the traditional privilege of drafting government correspondence with foreign countries. Razan objected to the influence of Buddhists in the secular

---

31. Chen Qun, "The Feelings"; Chen Beixi, *Neo-Confucian Terms Explained*, trans. and ed. Chan, p. 62.

affairs of the government, but without much success. Thus in his time, Razan's Neo-Confucianism was far from establishing itself as a state orthodoxy. While still carrying on the old struggle of the Neo-Confucians against the Buddhists — a rivalry already centuries old in China and Korea — Razan found a natural ally in native Shinto.

With a view to strengthening this alliance by showing the essential unity of the Shinto religion and Confucian ethics, and perhaps also to establish himself at court as an authority on Japanese history and Shinto, Razan undertook extensive research into Shinto, which resulted in his *Study of Our Shinto Shrines* (*Honchō jinja-kō*). He also studied the history of Japan and wrote the *General History of Our State* (*Honchō tsugan*), using Zhu Xi's *Outline and Details of the Comprehensive Mirror* (*Tongjian gangmu*) as his model.

Still, Hayashi Razan was unable by himself to overcome Buddhist influence in the government. In fact, to maintain his own position at court, he was forced to comply with an old custom requiring the Buddhist tonsure of all those entrusted with educational duties. It was fortunate, therefore, that he had worthy successors in his own son, known as both Shunsai and Gahō (1618–1680), and his grandson Hōkō (1644–1732). It was Gahō who completed the aforementioned 310-volume *General History of Our State* by 1670. As a consequence of this great scholarly achievement, the academy gained some measure of official recognition, with the title of Kōbunin, and Gahō was named the first doctor of literature (*kōbunin gakushi*). The awarding of the official title, head of the state college (*daigaku-no-kami*), had to wait for another generation.

In 1691, the fifth shogun, Tsunayoshi, himself an ardent Confucian, conferred on Hōkō that eminent title, which became hereditary in the Hayashi family. At the same time, the academy was renamed the School of Prosperous Peace (Shōhei-kō) and moved to a new site in Yushima, where it remained throughout the long Tokugawa rule as the center of official instruction. It also served as a Confucian religious shrine, for images of Confucius and his disciples were installed in a separate temple that was part of the complex.

But official patronage and its ritual functions did not necessarily confer on the school any authority as a definer of orthodoxy. Although some of the shogunate's prestige obviously did rub off on it and it thus became a model for some of the domains to follow, in a relatively decentralized feudal system and diversified intellectual scene, the school remained open to new influences until late in the eighteenth century, when political and ideological pressures brought the issue of orthodoxy more to the fore.

The following is a list of the Hayashi family leaders, all of whom except Razan and Gahō were head of the state university (*daigaku-no-kami*) under the Tokugawa shogunate:

Razan	1583–1657
Gahō	1618–1680
Hōkō	1644–1732

Ryūkō	1681–1758
Hōkoku	1721–1773
Hōtan	1761–1787
Kinpō	1767–1793
Jussai[32]	1768–1841
Teiu	1791–1844
Sōkan	1828–1853
Fukusai	1800–1859
Gakusai	1833–1906

Despite all this, the Hayashi academy remained in many respects a private school closely associated with the Tokugawa ruling house and responsible for training its family retainers, but not a state university in the Chinese or Korean sense, responsible for directing the state's school system or bureaucratically involved with the kind of civil service examination system that existed in China and Korea and that constituted the institutional base for a state orthodoxy. Hence Neo-Confucianism in the Tokugawa period spread mostly through private channels, which allowed for great intellectual diversity and many independent developments.

THE WAY OF HEAVEN

Concurrent with the spread of Neo-Confucianism in the seventeenth century was a new current of thought in East Asia identified as the Way of Heaven (J. *tentō* or *tendō*, Ch. *tiandao*). Many works and many thinkers at this time reflect both trends. *Tendō* is an ancient term found in the Chinese classics, although not in their most ancient parts, and in the *Daodejing* and *Zhuangzi*. Most likely, it is a combination of the concepts *dao* and *tian*, introduced into Daoist circles in the late Zhou period. The two concepts were in some respects incongruous. *Dao* stood for the autonomous, cyclical processes of nature, the constant behind ever-changing phenomena. *Tian*—that is, heaven and the eponymous deity— was anything but unchanging. *Tian* watched, ruled, punished, walked the earth, begot children, and was worshiped by the early kings of Zhou. The combination of *tian* and *dao*, therefore, tended to slough off some of the anthropopathic, volitional aspects of *tian*, apparently because they had become philosophically less respectable. During its semantic development, the word *tiandao* also came to designate one of the three realms in which the Chinese divided the world: the realms of Heaven, Earth, and Man. Later, when Buddhism had spread, *tiandao* was used to translate the Buddhist concept of Heavens, which were,

---

32. Jussai was an heir adopted from the Matsudaira daimyo house of Iwamura (Mino).

after all, one of the six realms of incarnation. As a result, the word also has nuances associated with these Buddhist Heavens and heavenly gods. Two other things are important to remember: *tiandao* regularly alternates with *tian* in the same context, and it retains many of its older meanings and associations.

The word *tiandao* (pronounced both *tentō* and *tendō* in Japanese) was exported to Japan together with the classics in which it was used. It first appears in the Japanese anthology *Kaifūsō* (preface dated 751). After that, however, it had a long but inconspicuous existence until the end of the sixteenth century, when it came to be used as a kind of stopgap: if one could not, or did not want to, designate another cause for a disaster, one could attribute it to "Heaven," and if no one else was likely to punish the miscreant, the Heavenly Way might still do so in the end. A contemporary gloss is given in the Jesuit dictionary *Nippo jisho* (159?), in which the word is translated as "the way, order or providence of Heaven. We already employ this name in order to address God, but the heathens never seem to come further than the first of the above-mentioned meanings." It is true that the Jesuits sometimes used *tendō* to translate the Latin words for "god" (*deus, superi,* Iupiter), but the transliterated form of Deus was preferred in any kind of doctrinal context.

All interpretations of Tendō based on the early texts remain suspect. There is no definite entity to which the word refers. The Chinese emperor made offerings to Heaven (and earth), but he was the only one allowed to do so, and in Japan, no one offered to or worshiped Tendō. There are no shrines, no temples, no rituals, and no scriptures that give a more solid body to this Tendō. Its main use may well have been to allow one to speak about god, luck, destiny, providence, and the like in nondenominational terms.

This changed in the first half of the seventeenth century, when a more or less integrated body of lore was elaborated in which Tendō, the Way of Heaven, was the central concept. This body of lore was fixed in a number of texts, the two most important of which were *The Learning of the Mind-and-Heart and the Five Human Relationships* (*Shingaku gorinsho*) and *The Record of Honda Sado-no-kami Masanobu* (*Honsaroku*). *Shingaku gorinsho* was first printed in 1650 and was reprinted at least six times during the next two hundred years, in a number of versions and under various titles. *Honsaroku*, which was ascribed to Honda Sado-no-kami Masanobu (1538–1616), mostly circulated in manuscript, but it also was printed. About thirty printed copies have survived; the oldest one that can be dated was printed in 1787 (Tenmei 7). To judge by the number of surviving copies, it must have been a very popular text.

Both *Shingaku gorinsho* and *Honsaroku* were also popular texts in the sense that they were reprinted and copied for use by a popular audience. This was made clear in various ways: they were written in Japanese, not in *kanbun* (the preferred medium of the intellectual elite); they were anonymous; and some well-known Confucian scholars tried to distance themselves from vulgar notions expressed in these texts.

The basic ideas were basic Confucian doctrines: the Five Human Relationships and the Five Constant Virtues, with a heavy emphasis on sincerity and frugality. Whoever practices these virtues will enjoy the protection of (the Way of) Heaven, and he and his descendants will prosper. The truth of these statements is proved by examples taken from Chinese and Japanese history. Other schools of thought (Buddhism and, to a lesser extent, Confucianism) are criticized, the central point of the criticism being whether these other schools acknowledged the actual existence of the mind-and-heart. Those that did not were wrong and endangered ethical practice, because ethical practice was based on the concept of posthumous retribution. The hearts of those who had been good would rejoin Tendō, and the hearts of the wicked would roam forever and find no rest. Finally, the text addresses the issue of theodicy: Why do the wicked prosper and the good suffer? The answer is that Tendō may decide to do this according to the merit or demerit accumulated by one's ancestors. That is, the evil they did may more than offset the good you are doing yourself, or the good they did may outweigh the evil you are doing. To this ethical doctrine, *Honsaroku* adds several pages of good advice for the ruler (*Honsaroku* is decidedly more Sinophile and oriented toward the ruling class).

These texts were ascribed to famous Confucians, especially Fujiwara Seika and Kumazawa Banzan. If Seika knew of this body of lore, he never acknowledged it, but Banzan went out of his way to deny authorship. Both had reasons to distance themselves from the texts, for from a Confucian perspective, the flaws were all too evident: this Tendō ("not a god, not a Buddha, and the lord of everything between heaven and earth") had far too much freedom. Whether or not in conscious opposition to this body of lore, Seika defined *tendō* as identical with principle (*li*), which was standard Neo-Confucian doctrine. The Way of Heaven also was obsessively ethical. In this respect, it is closely related to the morality books (J. *zensho*, Ch. *shanshu*) that were popular in East Asia from the sixteenth to the eighteenth century.[33] Both genres have connections to Neo-Confucianism that are at once close and problematic.

Philosophically speaking, the intervention between act and retribution of an anthropopathic entity like Tendō was unnecessary, for every action invited an immediate reaction as part of an automatic, unending chain. Volitional intercession by deities thus had no place here. Since they could do only what was right, it was unnecessary to hypostatize their existence. We can only conclude that the doctrines were aimed at the uneducated, in an attempt to divert them from their mistaken beliefs in gods and magic. Although the doctrines leaned heavily on Confucian notions, they are quite different from the acknowledged vernacular treatises of well-known Confucian scholars.

---

33. See de Bary and Bloom, eds., *Sources of Chinese Tradition*, 2nd ed., vol. 1, p. 899.

First-rate intellectuals never stooped to take issue with Tendō thought. For the most part they ignored it, but a minor journeyman of letters, Takigawa Josui (fl. 1648–1684), went out of his way to publish a detailed criticism of *Shingaku gorinsho*. This book, *The Learning of the Mind-and-Heart According to Takigawa* (*Takigawa shingakuron*), was published in 1660. Along with the appearance of the first printing of *Shingaku gorinsho* in 1650, this is another reason to place the formulation of this body of thought around 1630 to 1640, although Kumazawa Banzan asserts that the book already existed before his birth in 1619. However, the *Kiyomizu monogatari*, which dates from 1638, contains a discussion showing how the subject was debated. The authenticity of *Honsaroku* also was under discussion. Considered opinion, however, eventually settled on Masanobu's authorship. The reasons are explained by Muro Kyūsō (1658–1734), a Confucian scholar who worked for the *bakufu*, in his 1725 preface.

Perhaps because its authorship was judged to be authentic, *Honsaroku* retained its mystique and its reputation of being a "secret" book containing useful knowledge for the rulers. In the second half of the eighteenth century, *Shingaku gorinsho* became a book for children, suitably illustrated to capture their attention.

THE LEARNING OF THE MIND-AND-HEART AND THE FIVE HUMAN RELATIONSHIPS (SHINGAKU GORINSHO)

The Way of Heaven is the lord between heaven and earth. Because it has no form, it is invisible to the eye. It is, however, the work of Heaven's Way that the four seasons follow one another without fail in the order of spring, summer, fall, and winter, that people are born, that flowers blossom and fruits ripen, and that the five grains grow. The human heart, too, has no form, and yet it is the lord of the whole body and reaches everywhere, up to the end of the nails and the very tips of the hairs. This human heart has come down from Heaven and become our heart. Originally, it was one with [the Way of Heaven]. All things that exist between this heaven and earth exist in the belly of Heaven's Way. It is the same as, for instance, the fishes living in the huge sea. The water is everywhere, even inside their fins. Yet the fishes have no idea of getting out of the water and living on the other side of the water. Heaven completely fills the whole of the human heart. For that reason, if you have one compassionate thought, this single thought will communicate itself to Heaven, and if you think ill, this evil will communicate itself to Heaven; for that reason, "the superior man is watchful over himself when alone."

"Luminous virtue" [as in the *Great Learning*] is what has separated itself from Heaven, dwells in our hearts ever so brightly, does not contain even the slightest trace of wicked feelings, and is in accordance with the Way of Heaven. Sages are those in whom this luminous virtue is manifested spontaneously as if they had been born with it from Heaven. Furthermore, after we have been born as humans, we have what is called human desires. Human desires are what we call those deep feelings of greed that are swayed by what we see and hear. If these human desires grow strong, luminous virtue will diminish. Although our appearance will still be human, our hearts will be the same as that of a bird or an animal. Luminous virtue may be compared to the bright body of a mirror, and human desires are what clouds it. If we do not polish this mirror every day and every night, the dirt of human desires will accumulate, and we will lose our original mind-and-heart. Luminous virtue and human desires are our ally and foe, respectively. If human desires are victorious, our ally luminous virtue will not have an easy time of it.

The Five Human Relationships are those between ruler and minister (lord and retainer), parent and child, husband and wife, older and younger brothers, and friends. They are, in other words, what man practices every day and every night. A child serves his parents and does his best to be as filial as possible, and in raising their children, parents teach them the Way and make them learn practical accomplishments. A retainer is single-minded in the service of his lord and does his best to be as loyal as possible, to the extent of offering his life, whereas a lord must feel about his retainers as he feels about his own hands and feet. Since heaven and earth are the beginning of husband and wife, the husband must be compassionate toward her and teach her, and the wife must follow her husband's instructions; the relations between husband and wife should be harmonious, and they should be compassionate and generous toward each other. Younger brothers must respect their elders; they must correct one another's faults and exhort one another to do good. In our dealings with our friends, we must be dependable and careful not to lie. The heart of the Way instructs us to practice these five human relationships. If, however, we do not do this sincerely and with all our heart but only go through the motions, Heaven will know that we are lying, and what we did will have been in vain. Study will help us practice this Way. If you practice this Way, in the end it will help us demonstrate our luminous virtue. If we polish the luminous virtue of our heart and practice the Five Human Relationships with feeling, we will receive the blessings of Heaven, and our children and grandchildren will assuredly flourish, [and we will] after death return to the original realm of Heaven. Heaven, however, will ruin the children and grandchildren of those who rebel, and after their death, their hearts will not return to Heaven but will wander halfway and become one with the birds and the beasts. Because this is the way it is, in Confucianism they fear Heaven and consider it most important to practice the Way.

A feature of the Way of Heaven, as distinct from its basic Confucian ethics, was its attempt to find common ground with Shinto as an aspect of its popular syncretism. Thus Shinto is identified with the virtues of natural simplicity and honesty, rather than with its theism and supernaturalism.

Amaterasu Ō mikami is the mistress of Japan, but her temple is thatched with no more than miscanthus. Her offerings are unhulled rice. By not embellishing her dwelling and by not taking fancy things for food, she expressed her compassion with the people of the realm, and because he followed her decrees and thus practiced the Way, Emperor Jinmu could hand down the empire to his children and grandchildren from generation to generation, and they flourished for I know not how many thousands of years, until the cloistered emperor Go-Shirakawa.

The emperors of old personally took the hoe into their hands and worshiped Heaven; in the new year, they deigned to begin plowing the sacred rice fields and reciprocated the people for their hardship. The emperor of the Engi period [901–923] took off his clothes on a cold night and lamented how cold the people everywhere in the country must feel.

In Shinto, honesty is everything, and commiserating with the people is regarded as its final intention. When at the top one person is honest, the many people below will be honest, too. When at the top one person is greedy, the many people below will be greedy, too. The poem says, "If only the heart / is in accordance with / the Way of sincerity, / then the gods will protect you, / even if you do not pray." By the "Way of sincerity" is meant the sincerity of the Way of Heaven. To pray for oneself, presenting gold and silver to the gods and Buddhas, is most foolish. Even men who possess only a small part of the mind-and-heart of the Way do not accept dishonest presents and bribes. Will then the gods and Buddhas accept them, if you present such gifts to them? When you are personally honest and practice charity toward others and worship Heaven according to ritual decorum and in all sincerity, the gods will protect you, even without your prayers.

Go-Shirakawa broke completely with Amaterasu's decrees, and Yoritomo took the empire. Outwardly he behaved as if he were practicing charity and establishing the Way, but in his heart he seized all-under-Heaven and used it for his own pleasure. In retribution, the place where he died is not known with certainty. Moreover, Yoritomo's son Yoriie was killed by his younger brother Sanetomo, and Sanetomo was killed by his nephew. Thus within forty-two years Yoritomo's children had perished and had lost all-under-Heaven. Such is the punishment of Heaven for those who do not know the Way and do not fear the Way of Heaven, who harass the people and glory in their own splendor.

[*Shingaku gorinsho*, text from Yamamoto, *Shingaku gorinsho no kisoteki kenkyū*, pp. 123–38; NST, vol. 28, pp. 257–64; WB]

THE WAY OF HEAVEN

Understanding the Way of Heaven

The Way of Heaven is not a god, and neither is it a Buddha; it is the lord between Heaven and earth, but it has no body. The mind-and-heart of Heaven fills the myriad things and reaches everywhere. You may compare it to some-one's heart that, though invisible to the eye, becomes the lord of the body, and even the rule of the empire and the state originates in this heart. The original heart of the Way of Heaven has as its main purpose to create peace everywhere between Heaven and earth, to bring quiet to the myriad men, and to cause the myriad things to grow. Again, the one who holds the empire is called the son of Heaven. The Way of Heaven has selected someone whose heart and capacities are sufficient to enable him to govern the realm and has made him the lord of Japan. I have asked questions about the principle of the Way of Heaven as well as I could to all erudites in Japan, but the Shinto scholars have combined Tendai and Shingon Buddhism with the Way of Heaven, and Zen scholars have collected the teachings of Bodhidharma and regard those as its essence. Present-day Japa-nese Confucians denigrate Buddhism, but essentially they have become identical with Zen. In this way I spent several years without understanding the principle of the Way of Heaven any better. When I heard about the government of China, I noticed that in China someone often, without using sword and dagger, brought order to the more than four hundred provinces and passed them on to his sons and grandsons from generation to generation. In Japan, too, from the Age of the Gods onward, the emperors have, from generation to generation, governed the realm and passed it on to their descendants. But I did not understand why during these last years the empire has known no lasting order and the rulers have per-ished after one or two generations, and it remained unclear to me [until now].

[Hayashi Razan, *Honsaroku*, in *NST*, vol. 28, pp. 277–78; WB]

PRINCIPLES OF HUMAN NATURE, IN VERNACULAR JAPANESE (*KANA SHŌRI*)

The author of this work is traditionally thought to be Fujiwara Seika, but it is actually a synthetic work, combining several strains of thought current in sixteenth- and early-seventeenth-century Japan—Neo-Confucian, Buddhist, Shinto, and even Christian—and incorporating much material from earlier texts, like *The Learning of the Mind-and-Heart and the Five Human Relationships* (*Shingaku gorinsho*). One of *Kana shōri*'s main elements is the doctrine of the Way of Heaven (*tendō*), which emphasizes that the ruler and his surrogates are answerable to Heaven, here conceived theistically as a judge upholding the moral order, with the surrogates expressed as principles intrinsic to the mind-and-heart of both the natural order and human nature. In this way, the more theistic conception of the lord of Heaven in Tendō thought contributed a religious element to the moral rationalism of Neo-Confucianism ex-pressed as Heaven's principle (*tenri*). Here it takes the form of personal retribution for one's good and bad deeds, as seen in the morality books that circulated in sixteenth- and seventeenth-century East Asia.[34]

---

34. See de Bary and Bloom, eds., *Sources of Chinese Tradition*, 2nd ed., vol. 1, chap. 24.

The core teaching of the mind-and-heart derives from Zhu Xi's formulation of the sixteen-word method of the mind-and-heart described in his preface to the *Mean* (*Zhongyong zhangzhu*) as a way of governance (legitimate succession) handed down from the sage-kings, Yao and Shun.[35] This "method" had undergone successive adaptations in late Song and Ming China and, as the Way of Heaven, spread to Korea and out through the sea-lanes of East Asia. In sixteenth-century Japan, Zhu's "succession to the Way" coalesced with the Sun Goddess's mandate to the imperial line, emphasized in primal Shinto (*yuiitsu Shintō*).[36]

The Five Human Relationships are those stressed by Zhu Xi as the principal moral obligations (the natural affective response of one's moral nature to the constant universal human relationships) and do not correspond directly to the prevailing political or social relationships in seventeenth- or eighteenth-century Japan. Nevertheless, in different versions and editions, these teachings became widely disseminated during the Tokugawa period, and texts containing them were said to have been found in many peasant households. Moreover, the "learning of the mind-and-heart" later popularized by Ishida Baigan is based on the same Neo-Confucian teaching of Zhu Xi as found here, not on Wang Yangming's teaching (see chap. 22).

Since much of *Kana shōri* is identical to the *Shingaku gorinsho* discussed earlier, the sections dealing with the Way of Heaven, sincerity, the Five Constant Virtues, the Five Human Relationships, and so forth have been omitted. Instead, we have focused on the later portions of the text, mainly the relations among Confucianism, Buddhism, and Shinto and the understanding of the Neo-Confucian learning of the mind-and-heart in the context of Japanese tradition.

13. Emperor Yao

Yao, a sage, was the master of China's four hundred districts. Shun, also a sage, was the son of Heaven. Confucius spread abroad the Way of Yao and Shun. Thus, their Way is also called the Way of the Confucian scholars. Those who study the Confucian Way are called Confucian scholars (*jusha*). . . .

Yao and Shun's Way, however, is not an incredible mystery. Luminous virtue, renewing the people, extending goodness, sincerity, reverent seriousness, the Five Constant Virtues, and the Five [Human] Relationships are their Way's ultimate concerns, their Way's loftiest notions. When one follows their Way in rectifying the mind and being compassionate toward the people, one's rule continues for a long time. If one wields power through intrigue and crafty strategies, in one or two generations one will be destroyed. Even if one's rule lasts for five or six generations, one's power will eventually be terminated in battle. Thus, intrigue and strategies do not produce good rule.

---

35. See de Bary and Bloom, eds., *Sources of Chinese Tradition*, 2nd ed., vol. 1, chap. 21.
36. See de Bary et al., eds., *Sources of Japanese Tradition*, 2nd ed., vol. 1, chap. 15.

them out. One must conclude that this text is one of the perfect gems of later Confucian learning. Consequently, I wrote this postface to it.

1669 (Kanbun 9), Ryūkoku sanjin
9th month, 9th day, Nomen sanchikusho
Published 1691

[Hayashi Razan, *Kana shōri*, in *NST*, vol. 28, pp. 238–55; JAT]

Ieyasu
↓
Yoshinao

Chapter 22

THE SPREAD OF NEO-CONFUCIANISM IN JAPAN

The prestige of Neo-Confucianism as an officially favored teaching arose in part from its support by leading members of the Tokugawa family. Among Ieyasu's many sons who helped promote it, Yoshinao (1600–1650) stands out. Representing one of the three Tokugawa branch families chosen to guard the shogunate's interests in the provinces, with strategic Owari as his domain, Yoshinao was an early convert to Confucianism and a steadfast advocate of Zhu Xi's philosophy. It was this scion of the Tokugawa who erected the Sage's Hall, in which Confucius's image was installed at Ueno in Edo and where Razan had his residence. It was he, too, who induced the third shogun, Iemitsu, to pay personal homage to the image, thus helping make it a center of religious veneration.

Another Tokugawa prince who became especially interested in Confucianism was Tsunayoshi (r. 1680–1709), the fifth shogun. Given as he was to extremes of enthusiasm, Tsunayoshi outdid himself in promoting Confucianism. Through his lavish patronage, a new Paragon Hall was built near the center of Edo, with all the splendor of a state shrine. At the annual commemoration ceremony held there, one of the Hayashis acted as master of ceremonies, and Tsunayoshi himself took great pride in giving a personal lecture on one of the Confucian classics. This was a practice not necessarily appreciated by Confucian scholars themselves, who thought it inappropriate for the ruler to arrogate such a role to himself, instead of deferring to a respected scholar (as in the Classics Mat lectures at the Chinese and Korean courts).

parallel to the first formula) is that reverence and moral seriousness must be exemplified in specific actions appropriate to the situation—that is, to one's own personal responsibilities in life. Thus for Ansai, "rightness" (J. *gi*, Ch. *yi*) meant doing one's specific duty (*meibun*) in accordance with the general Neo-Confucian concept that "principle is one, its particularizations diverse." On this basis, Ansai understood the relationship between ruler and minister (for Zhu Xi, "joined in rightness") to mean in the Japanese context the relationship between lord and vassal, in particular the samurai retainer's duty of loyal service. Thus *gi* was converted from "agreement on what is right (in context)" to an absolute duty of personal loyalty by the retainer to his lord. Ansai further extended this to mean loyalty to the emperor as the specific Japanese instantiation of the rulership principle. Hence, to render these terms as Ansai intended them, we often have to translate *gi/yi* as "duty" or invest it with the more absolute connotations of "righteousness."

4. As a method of personal praxis, Ansai endorsed "quiet sitting" (*seiza*)—for him a form of spiritual/moral self-scrutiny in a meditative posture—as a prelude to right action in daily conduct. This practice (sometimes confused with Zen meditation) was controversial in Neo-Confucian tradition and even among Ansai's disciples. For Ansai (and those disciples who followed him in this, notably Satō Naokata), quiet sitting was one means of personally experiencing the Way. For others, however, it was anathema as too close to "Zen."

In his later years, Ansai became increasingly drawn to the study of Shinto and therefore interpreted this formula in terms strongly suggestive of worship and service of the gods. From one of his Shinto teachers, Kikkawa Koretari (1616–1694), Ansai received the Shinto initiate name Suika, which was derived from a Shinto text that taught people to seek the blessings of the gods through prayer and by keeping one's heart in a state of straightforward sincerity (*massugu*). This expression came to serve as the distinctive mark of Ansai's brand of Confucian Shinto, or Suika Shinto, which combined the ethical maxims and cosmological doctrines of the former teaching with the religious doctrines of the latter.

Actually Ansai went to much greater lengths than this to establish the unity of the two teachings. Not only did he equate Shinto creation legends with Chinese cosmology, and the Shinto pantheon with the metaphysical principles of the Neo-Confucians, but he also identified the key Confucian virtue, reverent seriousness, with the primal stuff of the universe. Despite his attempt to combine these disparate elements in what seemed to him a rationally coherent system, in the end he had to insist that human reason was inadequate to deal with such truths and that much had to be accepted simply on faith. Later Shintoists were glad to dispense with Ansai's tortuous rationalizations while retaining his emphasis on faith, on the moral virtues, and particularly on

reverence for the gods as expressed through devotion to their living embodiment, the emperor. In these respects Ansai was a good example in the seventeenth century of three tendencies that became significant in modern times: the popularization of Confucian ethics in Japan; the revival of Shinto and its development as an articulate creed; and, finally, the intense nationalism that combined Confucian reverence with Shinto tradition to produce emperor worship.

REVERENCE AND RIGHTNESS (DUTY)

It was the pedagogical practice of Confucian scholars to sum up their teachings with a key word or phrase that could easily be fixed in people's minds. Yamazaki Ansai's key virtues of reverence and rightness were taken from a slogan of the Neo-Confucian philosopher Cheng Yi, based on the *Classic of Changes*. As Ansai's Shintoist leanings became more pronounced, he emphasized that aspect of these concepts having to do with worship of the gods and the emperor. Eventually he equated these two virtues with terms found in native texts concerning primitive Shinto mythology: prayer (*negigoto* or *kitō*) and honesty or forthrightness (*massugu* or *shōjiki*). The following is a typical attempt to demonstrate that one's own favorite formula contains the essence of the Confucian classics:

> "By [means of] reverence we straighten ourselves within; by [means of] rightness we square things without." The significance of these eight characters cannot be exhausted by even a lifetime of application.[1] Indeed, Master Zhu was not exaggerating at all in saying this.
>
> In the *Analects* of Confucius, when it says "the superior man cultivates himself with reverent care [J. *kei*, Ch. *jing*], it simply means that by [means of] reverence we straighten [ourselves] within." What is said further in the *Analects*, "To put others at ease by cultivating oneself and thus to put all men at ease" is the same as "By [means of] rightness we square away the [world] without."
>
> "The virtue of sincerity [as taught in the *Mean*] is not merely for perfecting oneself alone; it also is for perfecting things [around us]. Perfection of self is humaneness; perfection of things is knowledge. These are virtues that manifest our nature; this is the Way that joins the inner and the outer [worlds]."[2] Cheng Yi also said: "Reverence and rightness hold each other together and ascend straightway to attain the virtue

---

1. Zhu Xi's comment on a saying by Cheng Yi.
2. *Mean* 25:3.

of Heaven." Thus when Zhu Xi said that these eight characters of Cheng Yi are inexhaustible in their application, he was not exaggerating at all.[3]

LECTURE CONCERNING THE CHAPTERS ON THE DIVINE AGE (IN THE *KOJIKI* AND *NIHON SHOKI*)

When Yamazaki Ansai took up Shinto studies late in life, he developed a cosmology based on early Japanese texts that, despite his own denials, obviously betrays the influence of Chinese models, especially the yin-yang and Five Elements theories incorporated into Neo-Confucian metaphysics. Fundamentally a monist who asserted the identity of the human and divine, Ansai saw all phenomena as produced by fire and regulated by the interaction of two powers: earth and metal. With these powers he identified the supreme virtues of reverence and righteousness.

The equation of reverence (*kei*) here with the native Japanese word *tsutsushimi* depends on the overlapping meanings of the two. *Kei* connotes attentiveness and concentration, whereas *tsutsushimi* connotes reverence, restraint, and, here, "tightening."

The following passage reveals the lengths to which Ansai went to establish the relationship of reverence and earth and metal. We have eliminated some of his complicated philological arguments to smooth the way for the reader but left enough to illustrate Ansai's method and perhaps why some of his own disciples would find it unpersuasive.

There is one important matter to be learned by those beginning to study Shinto. If a student reads the chapters on the Divine Age without first learning this, he will not readily understand the chapters' true significance, but if he has had the proper instruction, he can understand everything in these chapters without further inquiry. This is the key to Shinto, which explains it from beginning to end. This you certainly must know.

I am not sure whether you have heard about it yet, but this is the teaching on earth and metal (*tsuchi-kane*). . . . Do you recall that in the Divine Age text, earth (*tsuchi*) is represented as five (*itsutsu*)? Izanagi cut the fire god Kagu-tsuchi into five, it says.[4] You may not see what that really means, but it indicates the conversion of earth into five. . . .

Earth comes into being only from fire. Fire is mind, and in mind dwells the god (*kami*). This is not discussed in ordinary instruction, and it is only because of my desire to make you understand it thoroughly that I am revealing this to you. Now here is the secret explanation of something very important: why a [Shinto] shrine is called *hokora*. *Hokora* is where the god resides and is

---

3. *Yamazaki Ansai zenshū*, vol. 1, p. 90; Yamakazi, *Suika-sō*, p. 11.
4. Aston, trans., *Nihongi*, vol. 1, p. 29.

equivalent to *hi-kora* (storehouse of fire). *Ho* is an alternative form of *hi* (fire), as seen in the words of *ho-no-o* (fire tail; i.e., flame) and *ho-no-ko* (fire child; i.e., spark). It is interesting that *tsutsushimi* comes only from the mind, which is fire, the abode of the god. Now when the fire god Kagu-tsuchi was cut into five pieces, it led to the existence of earth (*tsuchi*). That can be understood from the theory that fire produces earth.

As for earth, it does not produce anything if it is scattered and dissipated. Only where earth is compacted are things produced. So you can see what is meant by *tsutsushimi* (restraint): it is the tightening of the earth (*tsuchi wo shimuru*). Earth is a solid thing, which is held together firmly (here the master held out his two fists to demonstrate). Water is always running downward, but earth does not run downward; it holds fast. Because it holds fast, it produces things. The mountain that produces metal is particularly hard, as we all know. Metal is formed when the essence of earth is drawn together and concentrated. Metal (*kane*) is joined together (*kane*) with earth. Because of metal, the earth is held firmly together, and because the earth holds together firmly, the metal power is produced. This is going on now right before your eyes.

If there were no earth, nothing would be produced; but even when there is earth, without restraint (*tsutsushimi*), the metal power would not be produced. The restraint is something in man's mind. Just as nothing is produced when the earth is scattered and dissipated, so if man becomes dissipated and loose, the metal power cannot be produced. The metal power is actually nothing other than our attitude in the presence of the god. There is something stern and forbidding about the metal power. When this power reaches the limit of its endurance, we must expect that even men may be killed. So unyielding is it that it allows for no compromise or forgiveness.

As we see every day, only earth can produce metal. That is the principle of earth's begetting metal. But do not confuse it with the Chinese theory that fire produces earth and earth produces metal. Whatever the Confucian texts say does not matter. What I tell you is the Way of the Divine Age, and it is also something that goes on right before your eyes. The sun goddess, you see, was female, but when the storm god got out of hand, she put on warlike attire and took up a sword. Even Izanagi and Izanami ruled the land by using the spade and sword. From earliest times Japan has been under the rule of the metal power. And that is why I have been telling you that Japan is the land of the metal power. Remember that without tightening, the metal power would not come into being, and tightening is a thing of the mind.

There are still more important things to be explained in connection with earth and metal, but these are beyond your capacity now. Without the moral discipline that would prepare you for them, you are not allowed to hear such things.

[*Zoku Yamazaki Ansai zenshū*, vol. 3, pp. 207–12; RT]

ANECDOTES CONCERNING YAMAZAKI ANSAI

A QUESTION OF LOYALTIES

A recurring question among Tokugawa scholars was the dual allegiance seemingly implied by the adherence to Chinese ethics by patriotic Japanese. Ansai's handling of this question suggests the possibility of being both faithful to Confucius and loyal to Japan.

Once Yamazaki Ansai asked his students a question: "In case China came to attack our country, with Confucius as general and Mencius as lieutenant general at the head of thousands of mounted warriors, what do you think we adherents of Confucius and Mencius ought to do?" The students were unable to offer an answer. "We don't know what we should do," they said, "so please let us know what you think about it." "Should that eventuality arise," he replied, "I would put on armor and take up a spear to fight and capture them alive in order to repay my obligations to my country. That would be the Way of Confucius and Mencius."

Later his disciple met [the Confucian] Itō Tōgai and told him about it, adding that his teacher's understanding of Confucius and Mencius was hard to surpass. Tōgai, however, told him smilingly not to worry about the invasion of our country by Confucius and Mencius. "I guarantee that it will never happen."

[*Sentetsu sōdan*, pp. 124–25; RT]

YAMAZAKI ANSAI AND HIS THREE PLEASURES

Although Ansai typifies the fusion of Confucian ethics with the feudal virtues of medieval Japan, this anecdote shows how Confucian insistence on the moral worth of the individual militated against the principle of hereditary aristocracy basic to feudalism. Even while hereditary, aristocratic privilege persisted under the Tokugawa, the meritocratic values of Confucianism increasingly permeated the culture, as will be seen later in many of the writings on education.

The lord of Aizu asked Yamazaki Ansai if he enjoyed any pleasures of his own. Ansai answered:

"Your vassal enjoys three pleasures. Between heaven and earth there are innumerable living creatures, but I am among those who alone possess spiritual consciousness. That is one source of pleasure. Between heaven and earth, peace and war come in defiance of all calculation. Fortunately, however, I was born in a time when peaceful arts were flourishing. Thus I am able to enjoy reading books, studying the Way, and keeping the company of the ancient sages and philosophers as if they were in the same room with me. That is another pleasure."

The lord then said, "Two pleasures you have already told me about; I would like to hear about the third one." Ansai replied, "That is the greatest one, though [it is] difficult to express, since Your Highness may not take it as intended but instead consider it an affront." The lord said, "Ignorant and incapable though I am, I am still the devoted disciple of my teacher. I am always thirsty for his loyal advice and hungry for his undisguised opinions. I cannot see any reason why this time you should stop halfway."

Ansai then declared, "Since you go to such lengths, I cannot hold back, even though it may bring death and disgrace. My third and greatest pleasure is that I was lowborn, not born into the family of an aristocrat." "May I ask you the reason why?" the lord insisted. "If I am not mistaken, aristocrats of the present day, born as they are deep inside a palace and brought up in the hands of women, are lacking in scholarship and wanting in skill, given over to a life of pleasure and indulgence, sexual or otherwise. Their vassals cater to their whims, applaud whatever they applaud, and decry whatever they decry. Thus is spoiled and dissipated the true nature they are born with. Compare them with those who are lowborn and poor, who are brought up from childhood in the school of hardship. They learn to handle practical affairs as they grow up, and with the guidance of teachers or the assistance of friends, their intellect and judgment steadily improve. That is the reason why I consider my low and poor birth the greatest of all my pleasures." The lord was taken aback but said with a sigh, "Indeed, it is as you say."

[*Sentetsu sōdan*, pp. 122–23; RT]

ASAMI KEISAI

Asami Keisai (1652–1711) is known as one of the three eminent disciples of Yamazaki Ansai, the other two being Satō Naokata and Miyake Shōsai. Born in Kyoto the second son of a physician, Keisai began to study medicine as well but soon became interested in Confucianism as a result of a period of study under Itō Jinsai. A friend introduced him to Ansai's academy around 1676, and Keisai's intelligence soon attracted Ansai's attention. But in 1680 Ansai broke off relations with him, apparently because he got entangled in Satō Naokata's "excommunication." In 1687 Keisai completed what became his most famous work, *Immortal Words of Acquiescent Self-Dedication (Seiken igen)*, by which time he was already teaching a large number of students at his own academy in Kyoto. Here Keisai acquired a reputation as an extremely meticulous and thorough teacher with a strong mind for logical consistency but also with a warm and cordial personality. The great concern running through his writings is the relationship between lord and retainer, which he thought should be as deep and unbreakable as that between parents and children. Loyalty, he emphasized, must be made firm and unwavering under all circumstances, so it must not be conditioned on whether one received good treatment from one's lord. Among the Confucian sages, Keisai admired King Wen as the model of this sort of unquestioning loyalty, because when he was imprisoned by King Zhou (the evil last ruler of the Shang dynasty) on the basis of a false accusation, Wen uttered not a word of complaint or judgment against his ruler. The same logic compelled Keisai to reject categorically the Mencian concept of inhumane rulers' inviting their own destruction.

TREATISE ON THE CONCEPT OF THE MIDDLE KINGDOM (CHŪGOKU BEN)

The most difficult problem with using Chinese Confucian concepts to define the meaning of samurai loyalty in the Japanese polity was the Sinocentric nature of the Confucian worldview, which defined Japan as a barbarian land on the periphery of civilization. If taken literally, this worldview was an affront to the honor and pride of the Japanese samurai. Asami Keisai's response to this problem constituted a powerful early statement of Japanese nationalist sentiment, which shows some rather striking similarities in tone to the later National Learning movement. Within the spectrum of teachings concerning Japanese national loyalty, however, Keisai's stance actually represented a middle position between the emotionalist exaltation of Japanese superiority characteristic of Shinto scholars and the rationalistic defense of the Confucian worldview by scholars such as Satō Naokata, Ogyū Sorai, and Dazai Shundai. Keisai's "middle position" strongly influenced the later development of imperial loyalist thought, which similarly combined universalistic Confucian ideals with Japanese uniqueness. Most of the later followers of imperial loyalism, though, in their intoxication with the idea of unconditional loyalty to one's country, seem to have forgotten Keisai's recognition that the people of other countries also have a natural tendency to regard themselves as the center, as "sovereign" states not subject to the imposition of anyone else's concept of world order.

The key terms in the following discussion are *taigi* and *meibun*, both of which are associated in Confucianism with the *Spring and Autumn Annals* (*Chunqiu*). *Taigi* means the "greater righteousness," or supreme duty. *Meibun* combines the concepts of *mei* (names, terms, norms) and *bun* (status distinctions and their differentiated functions). Keisai emphasizes that the highest principle of ethical conduct (righteousness) is universal to all mankind but that its fulfillment takes specific socially and culturally distinct forms, which here is duty to one's own ruler.

The following treatise is based on lectures given by Keisai in 1688/1689 and on an exchange of letters in 1700/1701 with a student of Satō Naokata, who later became a devotee of Suika Shinto.

The terms "Middle Kingdom" (*chūgoku*) and "barbarian" (*iteki*) have been used in Confucian writings for a long time. For that reason, ever since Confucian books came to be widely studied in our country, those who read these books call China (*kara*) the "Middle Kingdom" and call our country "barbarian." In extreme cases, some people lament the fact that they were born in a "barbarian" land. How disgraceful! It is a sad day when people who read Confucian books lose the correct way of reading, failing to understand the true significance of norms and status distinctions (*meibun*) and the real meaning of supreme duty (*taigi*).

Heaven envelops the earth, and there is no place on earth not covered by Heaven. Accordingly, each country's territory and customs constitute a realm-under-Heaven in its own right, with no distinction of noble and base in comparison with other countries. In the land of China, from antiquity, the inhabitants of the nine provinces gradually came to share a single culture (*fū*) and character (*ki*), and since they shared a mutually intelligible language and customs, the region naturally came to constitute a realm-under-Heaven in its own right. The regions surrounding the nine provinces on all sides, whose customs were unlike those of the nine provinces, appeared as so many strange lands, each with its own peculiar ways. Those countries that were near the nine provinces and with which they could communicate through translation naturally seemed from China's point of view to be peripheral lands. Accordingly, the nine provinces came to be called the "Middle Kingdom" (Chūgoku), while the countries on the outer periphery came to be called "barbarian tribes." If one looks at Confucian books without understanding this, when one sees the outside countries referred to as "barbarian," one gets the idea that all countries everywhere are "barbarian" and fails to understand that our country was originally formed together with Heaven-and-earth and had no need to wait for other countries. This is a very serious error.

The questioner replied: "This explanation is certainly clear and correct. Nothing could be better for dispelling the ignorance of a thousand years or for advancing the teaching of norms and duties [status distinctions]. Nevertheless, some matters are still open to doubt, and I would beg to ask you about them one by one. The nine provinces of China are a land where ritual propriety flourishes and morals are highly developed to an extent that other countries cannot achieve. For that reason, it is natural for China to be regarded as the master (*shu*) and for barbarian countries to look up to China."

I answer: In the learning of norms and status distinctions, the first thing is to put aside the idea of evaluating on the basis of moral superiority or inferiority and instead to examine how the basic standards are established. Thus, for example, although Shun's father Gu Sou was wrong, regardless of his morality he was, after all, Shun's father, as no one else in the world could be. There is no principle that justifies despising one's father and regarding him as lower than other fathers in the world just because he is without virtue. Shun simply served him as his own father, in the end winning Gu Sou's pleasure. As a result, Shun and his father became the standard for judging all the fathers and sons in the world. This was a natural result of the dedication to duty (*giri*) that Shun showed in serving his father. Accordingly, for a person born in this country to refer to our country by the contemptuous name "barbarian," feeling that because our country is somehow lacking in virtue it must be ranked below China, forgetting that Heaven also exists above our own country, [and] failing to see that the Way also is flourishing in our own country and that our country can also serve as the standard for other countries is to turn one's back on the supreme duty [greater righteousness (*taigi*)], as would a person who scorned his own father. How much more so inasmuch as in our country the legitimate succession (*seitō*) has continued without break since the beginning of Heaven-and-earth, and the great bond between lord and vassal has remained unchanged for ten thousand generations. This is the greatest of the Three Bonds, and is this not something that no other country has achieved? What is more, our country has a tradition of martial valor and manliness (*masurao*) and a sense of honor and integrity that are rooted in our very nature. These are the points in which our country is superior. Even since the restoration, sagely leaders have appeared several times and ruled our country well, so that the overall level of morality and ritual propriety in our country is not inferior to that of any other country. Those who regard our country right from the start as a kind of deformity, as something on the level of the birds and the beasts, lamenting their fates like hypochondriacs, are certainly a despicable lot. If we look at it in this way, the Way that is taught by Confucian scholars is the Way of Heaven-and-earth and what we in Japan study and develop is also the Way of Heaven-and-earth. In the Way there is no gap between subject (*shu*) and object (*kaku*), between self and other, so that when one studies this Way from the books that reveal the Way, this Way is nothing other than the Way of our own Heaven-and-earth. It is like the fact that fire is hot and water is cold, crows are black and herons are white, parents are beloved, and lords are hard to leave, regardless of whether we speak from the point of view of China, Japan, or India. In such things, there is no basis for saying that there is a special Way of our own country. If a person reads Confucian books and mistakenly thinks that this is the Way of China, so that one has to pull up by the root the whole body of Chinese customs and transplant them to our country, it is because he cannot see the true principle of Heaven-and-earth and is being led astray by the narrowness of what is seen and heard. . . .

The questioner asked: "Well then, is it not the case that Confucius appeared in the world and said all this about China's being the Middle Kingdom and all other countries' being barbarian?"

I answer: If that was Confucius's real intent, then even if it is Confucius, it is a self-centered (*watakushi*) view. If he says it is the Way to say things that besmirch one's own father, then even if these are Confucius's words, they are of no use to us. However, one would not expect Confucius to say such things.

The proof of this is the *Spring and Autumn Annals* itself. . . . Ethical conduct (*giri*) is a matter of knowing what one ought to do at a particular time and in a particular place, and it is that particular time and place that must serve as the primary point of reference (*shu*). This is the essential principle of the Mean. Nevertheless, because the Confucians have preached their concept of the Middle Kingdom versus barbarian lands so effusively for so long, even after all I have said, it is not possible to make the whole thing immediately clear. But this is nothing less than a matter of the supreme duty that men must fulfill in this world, a matter of the great line of legitimate succession, a matter of the Three Bonds and Five Constant Virtues, a matter of the great obligation and great righteousness between lord and vassal. There is nothing in the world that is greater than this. If this principle is not made clear, then even if you read Confucian books, you will all descend to the level of being rebels and traitors against your own country—truly a matter of the most profound regret.

[*Yamazaki Ansai gakuha*, in NST, vol. 31, pp. 416–19; BS]

SATŌ NAOKATA

Satō Naokata (1650–1719) was born in Bingo Province (the eastern part of today's Hiroshima Prefecture) as the son of a retainer of the Fukuyama domain. When he went to study under Ansai in Kyoto in 1670/1671, Ansai rejected him for his lack of fluency in reading Chinese, prompting Naokata to try to master the Neo-Confucian texts. Later, he and Keisai became Ansai's favorite disciples, and it was said that discussing Confucianism with them was the only way to bring Ansai out of his grumpy moods caused by frustration with his students' obtuseness. Thus it is ironic that later disagreements resulting from Ansai's increasing absorption in Shinto led to his breaking off relations with both of them around 1680. Naokata held that the singleness of the Way precluded the possibility that both Confucianism and Shinto were true, and he firmly rejected Ansai's etymologically based attempts to identify the two traditions. Likewise, Naokata's concept of the "correct lineage of ruler and subject," unlike that of Ansai and Keisai, retained the Mencian concept of the legitimacy of removing the ruler in extreme cases of incompetence or misgovernment. Accordingly, Naokata tried to demystify the imperial institution by explaining its genesis in human, rather than divine, terms as a product of nothing more mysterious than human custom. (Needless to say, such passages denying the divine nature of the imperial line were excised from the edition of Naokata's complete works published in 1942.) Naokata spent most of his time teaching and writing in Kyoto until he was invited to Edo in 1694 to serve as guest teacher to the daimyo of Umayabashi domain. He continued teaching in Edo until his death, receiving invitations to serve as lecturer for as many as seven other daimyo.

COLLECTED ARGUMENTS ON THE CONCEPT OF
THE MIDDLE KINGDOM
(CHŪGOKU RONSHŪ)

The following text was compiled by Satō Naokata's disciple, Ono Nobunari, and was first published in 1706.

Master Naokata says in his *A Judgment on the Concepts of Civilization and Barbarism (Ka'i rondan),* "Scholars have all sorts of conflicting views on the argument over the concepts of the Middle Kingdom (Chūgoku) and barbarian lands." All of them start by advocating a single biased theory and end up causing great confusion among beginning students. Originally, the concepts of the Middle Kingdom and barbarian lands were the words of the sages and worthies of China (Chūgoku), and they were put forward with reference to the topography (*tenchi*) of the world as a whole. The method cited in the *Rites of Zhou* for determining the center of the earth using a jade table is clearly referred to in the theoretical writings and recorded conversations of the sages and worthies. This is a matter about which there is no ambiguity, and it is understood even by common scholars. Nevertheless, recently this debate has arisen in our school, centering on whether one should distinguish between the Middle Kingdom and barbarian lands on the basis of the relative condition of the country's morality or whether each country has its own standard of what is the Middle Kingdom and what are "barbarian lands." In the end neither position uses the conception established by the sages and worthies. . . .

Someone asked, "Japan is a small country, but ever since the seven ages of the heavenly gods and the five ages of the earthly gods, it has had the superb teaching called Shinto. Accordingly, those who do not study Shinto lose the benefit of having been born in Japan, and they do not accord with the will (*mikokoro*) of the gods. Thus their descendants will not be able to flourish. From ancient times Japan has been called the country of the gods (*shinkoku*), and it is a superb country that surpasses all other countries."

Master Naokata replied, "What sorts of countries are China, India, and Europe? Who is to determine that only Japan is a land of the gods and that it is an especially wonderful place? Do the gods referred to in the term 'Land of the Gods' not exist in other countries as well? . . .

"If one says recklessly like the Shintoists that one should revere and believe in our country without regard to good or bad or right or wrong, then we do not even need to have any learning. Since one would not expect anyone to be so lacking in discrimination as to say such reckless things, the Shintoists who speak so must have some sort of hidden agenda. This is something I would like to ask the Shintoists about. . . .

"Now further, the statement by Shintoists that Japan is the Middle Kingdom and that it surpasses all other countries is difficult to understand. The concept of the Middle Kingdom is something fixed since ancient times according to geography. Of course, in the Middle Kingdom the Way is clear and the customs are good, and in barbarian countries the customs are inferior. Nevertheless, fundamentally, the meaning of the concepts is fixed on the basis of geography and not on the basis of the goodness or badness of the customs.

"According to the ancient records of Japan, in our country the emperors married women of the same surname to take as their empresses, and everyone in the populace followed this practice. In addition, in some cases people even took their own sisters as their consorts, thereby violating the way of husband and wife taught by the sages. Also, in many cases a minister murdered his ruler and put his younger brother or son in his place. Those whose fathers or older brothers had been killed acceded to the throne of the Son of Heaven on the instructions of the minister who had done the killing, without feeling any shame in the matter and without any idea of taking revenge. When a ruler–vassal relationship exists and the vassal kills the father or older brother and then makes his son or younger brother the ruler, it is difficult to say that the country is superior to all other countries and the righteousness between lord and retainer is correct. Now it is said that Japan has the splendid tradition of one family's ruling the realm continuously and not transferring the right to rule to any other family. But for a brother or cousin of the legitimate heir to become the Son of Heaven by getting rid of the legitimate heir is even worse than for a person of another family to get rid of the legitimate heir. Even though the family line has not changed since Emperor Jinmu, the cases of murder, rebellion, and usurpation of the throne are too many to count. For instance, if a person kills his older brother and takes the throne from him, should we say there is nothing wrong with it because they belong to the same family? If I do not do the killing, but my vassal does and then puts me on the throne, it is shameful. Since this is the case, it seems that in Japan, on the contrary, the Way of the Five [Human] Relations was opened in later times, whereas in antiquity it was not clearly established. For scholars to read the ancient chronicles but not to discover this fact is disgraceful. . . ."

[*Yamazaki Ansai gakuha*, in NST, vol. 31, pp. 420–25; BS]

THE MITO SCHOOL

The interest of Ieyasu's grandson Tokugawa Mitsukuni (1628–1700) in Chinese studies was aroused by the great histories that Chinese writers had produced, rather than by religion or philosophy. This may well be considered one of the distinctive influences of Chinese culture on Japan, in contrast to Indian influence, which was confined to religion, philosophy, and the arts. Mitsukuni inaugurated the project of compiling a national history in 1657 when he established a historiography bureau at his alternative residence at Komagome in Edo.[5] This was four years before he became the second daimyo of the Mito domain. Fortunately, Mitsukuni was able to persuade a Chinese political refugee of wide experience and considerable scholarship to participate as a general adviser in the new undertaking. Zhu Shunsui (1600–1682), a steadfast adherent of the Ming dynasty who had crossed the eastern seas many times in hopes of raising outside help for the Ming cause, was finally forced by the collapse of the Southern Ming Court to seek refuge in Nagasaki in 1659. In 1665, after repeated invitations from Mitsukuni to serve on this historical commission, Shunsui accepted and settled in Mito. To Japanese Confucians, Shunsui symbolized, above all else, unswerving loyalty to his dynasty. This was what Zhu Xi called the "highest duty in fulfillment of one's proper role (*taigi meibun*)" and what had served as a guiding principle in the composition of his *Outline and Details of the Comprehensive Mirror (Tongjian gangmu)*. There is no doubt that the presence of this staunch loyalist made itself felt, for patriotism and loyalty to the throne became the paramount themes of Mitsukuni's history, as well as the cardinal doctrines of those who later carried on the tradition of the Mito school. Through them these ideas exerted a profound influence on the course of Japanese history during the restoration period. Still later, Zhu Shunsui's unceasing resistance to the Manchus served as an inspiration to Chinese students in Japan, who returned home to join in the struggle that brought the Qing dynasty to an end.

The *History of Great Japan (Dai Nihon shi)*, as Mitsukuni's history came to be called, is most famous for its "Three Great Innovations" concerning the history of the imperial line in the Northern and Southern Courts period (1331–1392).[6] The question of legitimacy was, of course, intertwined with the definition of loyalty, since a minister's or vassal's loyalty could be properly directed only to a legitimate ruler or lord (and, conversely, a vassal loyal to a lord defined as illegitimate was normally relegated to the ranks of rebels and traitors). As in the Kimon school, this Neo-Confucian historiographical concern for

---

5. In 1672 Mitsukuni moved the historiography bureau to his main residence at Koishikawa in Edo, naming it the Shōkōkan on the basis of a passage from the preface to the *Zuo zhuan* (a classical commentary on the *Chunqiu*), meaning "illuminate the past in order to ponder [what should be done in] the future." After Mitsukuni's death, a branch of the bureau was established in Mito as well, and in 1829 the two branches of the academy were unified in Mito by Tokugawa Nariaki.

6. The Three Great Innovations were "revisionist" views, maintaining that the ancient empress Jingū was not an "emperor" in her own right but a regent for her son, Emperor Ōjin; that Emperor Tenmu had usurped the throne of Prince Ōtomo; and, as in the case cited here, that the Southern Court represented the legitimate imperial line.

elucidating the relationship between conduct and the moral norms implicit in status-defining titles—that is, in the clarification of *meibun*—derives from the study of the *Spring and Autumn Annals (Chunqiu)*, which was traditionally believed to have been compiled and edited by Confucius. But the moral lessons of history that scholars found in the *Annals* were communicated simply through a bare account of events, not by the addition of evaluative comments by historians. As Zhu Xi put it, "Confucius simply described things as they were, and right and wrong became apparent of themselves."[7]

Thus in Chinese histories the practice developed of keeping the historical accounts themselves free of overt expressions of opinion while striving for the greatest possible accuracy and objectivity, adding a separate section of appraisals (*ronsan*) in which the compiler offered his own evaluations of the personages and events recorded. The Hayashis had decided not to include such evaluative comments in their *General History of Our State (Honchō tsugan)* because of their fear of offending the shogun or powerful *bakufu* leaders by expressing their opinions on sensitive issues. Mitsukuni, however, felt that the purely chronological form of the Hayashis' account failed to make the moral lessons of history sufficiently clear. This led him to adopt the *kiden* (chronological annals plus biographies) style of Sima Qian's *Shiji* and the Chinese dynastic histories, since in the biographies it is possible to consider the implications of a person's actions that are merely recounted in the chronological accounts. A similar desire to clarify the lessons of history led Mitsukuni's successor to instruct Asaka Tanpaku (1656–1737), one of the Mito school's chief historians and a former director of the Shōkōkan, to write appraisals for both the chronological accounts and the biographies. When the first completed portion of the *Dai Nihon shi* was presented to the *bakufu* in 1720, in 250 fascicles, these appraisals were included.

After 1720, work on the *Dai Nihon shi* virtually ceased until 1786, when Tachihara Suiken (1724–1823) became director. Little work had yet been done on two other sections of the history, the essays and tables, as originally planned. The essays were to focus on the history of institutions, rather than on emperors and other individuals, and many Mito scholars, stimulated by the Sorai school's interest in concrete institutions (see chap. 24), were eager to move on to this new stage. Suiken, however, was unwilling to commit the resources for the project, which led to a major factional dispute. Suiken's opponents, led by Fujita Yūkoku (1774–1826) and Komiyama Fūken (1763–1840), also objected to the title *Dai Nihon shi*, on the grounds that Japan had never been called Dai Nihon. Further, they insisted that Tanpaku's appraisals be expurgated, arguing that in China, a country that had dynastic revolutions, it was all right to make retrospective judgments about the merits and demerits of the previous dynasty.

---

7. Zhu Xi, *Zhuzi yulei*, chap. 83.

In Japan, however, with its unbroken imperial line, even when a military leader took over the government, the status distinction between ruler and subject (lord and vassal) was never upset, so a subject was never in a position to judge past rulers freely. Reiterating Zhu Xi's statement just quoted, they argued that the views expressed in the appraisals were only the views of a private individual and not part of Mitsukuni's original intention in initiating the project. Moreover, they said, Tanpaku's appraisals were often harsh in their judgments, verbose, and filled with pedantic allusions to Chinese history. When Hayashi Jussai (1768–1841), then head of the *bakufu* college, was consulted, he agreed that the appraisals might be removed but suggested that they be preserved in a separate form so that Tanpaku's labors would not be lost to future generations. Most of the Mito historians agreed, but a decision was blocked by a few scholars who objected that without the appraisals, the reasons for the Three Great Innovations would become obscured. In 1809 a decision was finally reached, and after some modifications to the Three Great Innovations, twenty-six fascicles of a revised block-printed edition without the appraisals were presented to the *bakufu*. A year later, the same edition was presented to the imperial court. The appraisals were eventually published separately, and they had considerable influence on later loyalist historiography, most notably that of the independent, Kyoto-based historian Rai Sanyō (1780–1832).[8] The *Dai Nihon shi* project was not completed until 1906, a time when Japan's recent victory in the Russo-Japanese War had given rise to a flood of emperor-centered nationalist sentiment.

TOKUGAWA TSUNAEDA

PREFACE TO THE *HISTORY OF GREAT JAPAN* (*DAI NIHON SHI*)

The authenticity of the story related here is suspect because it is not mentioned in any earlier source. However, there is an important parallel between the story of Bo Yi and Shu Qi and Mitsukuni's personal situation, in the fact that Shu Qi, the younger of two brothers, had, like Mitsukuni, been chosen as heir over the older brother. Mitsukuni was quite concerned about this matter (a fact related to his concern with the question of legitimate succession in history), leading him to designate a son of his elder brother as his successor.

This preface was written in 1715 by Tsunaeda, then head of the Mito branch of the Tokugawa family, who recorded the aims of his predecessor Mitsukuni in launching

---

8. Sanyō's histories, particularly *Unofficial History of Japan* (*Nihon gaishi*), were widely read in the late Tokugawa period, greatly influencing the development of imperial loyalist thought. See also chap. 33.

the monumental history project. Two points are emphasized: loyalty to the legitimate imperial house (although not at this time suggesting active rule by the emperor) and the contribution of accurate historiography to the social order. Accuracy, however, did not preclude moral judgment, and objectivity did not mean value free.

My Sire [Mitsukuni] at the age of eighteen once read the biography of Bo Yi[9] and became a staunch admirer of his high character from that time on. Patting the volume containing it, he remarked with emotion, "Only by the existence of this book is the culture of ancient China made available to us, but for the writing of history how could posterity visualize the past?"

Thereupon he resolved to compile a history of Japan. Official chronicles were sought out as sources, and private records were hunted for far and wide. Famous religious centers were visited for rare documents, and eminent personages were approached for their personal memoirs. Thus scores of years have been spent in the work of compiling and editing in order to complete this history.

It was the Sun in person who laid the foundation of this nation more than two thousand years ago. Since then, divine descendants have occupied the throne in legitimate succession; never has an impostor or traitor dared to usurp it. The Sun and the Moon shone bright where the imperial regalia found their abode, splendid and wondrous. The ultimate reason for this can only be traced, I respectfully surmise, to the benevolence and charity of our imperial forebears, which served to keep the people's hearts united in solid support of the country. As for the doings and sayings of the wise ministers and able officials of early times, they may generally be ascertained from ancient records. In the Middle Ages, able sovereigns appeared who preserved the dynasty and maintained its prestige, pursuing policies as beneficial as those of early times. But because there is a dearth of sources for this period, the contributions of individual ministers and advisers are gradually fading into oblivion, to my profound regret. That is the reason why this history is planned.

Having lived close to my lord, [I], Tsunaeda, enjoyed the privilege of listening to his pregnant remark concerning history as a record of the facts. "Write it faithfully on the basis of the facts, and the moral implications will then make themselves manifest. From antiquity to the present time, the customs and manners of the people, whether refined or vulgar, as also the government and administration of successive eras, whether conducive to prosperity or ruin, should

---

9. Bo Yi was a legendary figure of classical China whose biography is in the *Records of the Historian* by Sima Qian. He and his brother were said to have starved themselves in the wilderness rather than live on the bounty of King Wu of Zhou, whom they considered a usurper of the Shang throne. Since King Wu was a great hero to Confucians, many of them condemned the account as fraudulent.

be put down in black and white as clearly as if they were things held in our own hands. Good deeds will serve to inspire men and bad deeds to restrain them, so that rebels and traitors may tremble in fear of history's judgment. The cause of education and the maintenance of social order will thus greatly benefit. In writing one must be true to fact, and the facts must be presented as exhaustively as possible. Arbitrary selection or willful alteration has no place in authentic history. So in this history, all pains have been taken to make it true to fact, even at the expense of literary excellence. An excess of detail is preferable to excessive brevity. As for its final form and arrangement. I shall leave that to some great writer to come." Before the history was completed, my lord died.

[*Dai Nihon shi*, vol. 1, pp. i–ix; RT]

ASAKA TANPAKU

APPRAISAL [APPENDED] TO THE CHRONOLOGY OF EMPEROR GO-DAIGO

In 1221 (Shōkyū 3), the cloistered emperor Go-Toba took advantage of the continuing political struggles in the Kamakura *bakufu* following Minamoto Yoritomo's death to raise troops against the *bakufu*, hoping to assert the authority of the throne. Go-Toba's forces were soundly defeated, and as punishment the *bakufu* banished three cloistered emperors to the Oki Islands, north of Izumo. In 1333 Emperor Go-Daigo escaped from banishment in Oki and began his "Kenmu Restoration" when the Kamakura general Ashikaga Takauji switched sides and seized Kyoto in his name. In the same year, Hōjō Takatoki, the fourteenth Hōjō regent, was driven to commit suicide with his whole family by an attack on Kamakura by Go-Daigo's general, Nitta Yoshisada, bringing an end to Hōjō power.

In Asaka Tanpaku's appraisals, we can see evidence of another principle of historiography corollary to the Confucian rectification of names: the belief that a person's actions will have good or bad repercussions on his descendants (and that the descendants are bound to fulfill the unfulfilled will of their ancestors), a principle important to trying to explain the history of the imperial line. We can also see how the clarification of the past was thought to reveal the course of the future.

The appraisal states: Duke Xiang of Qi carried out revenge against the state of Ji for a wrong it had committed against Qi nine generations earlier, and the *Spring and Autumn Annals* regards this as righteous. The emperor executed Hōjō Takatoki and his whole family in order to wipe out the shame of banishing the three emperors. This was more difficult to accomplish than to avenge Duke Xiang, and it is a meritorious deed of imperial restoration that should be held up as a model for all time. In it we see the expanding fulfillment of cloistered emperor Kameyama's wish.[10] Nevertheless, Ashikaga Takauji nourished a rebellious intent, even relying on the prestige he would gain through betrayal. This was cunning and craftiness even worse than Takatoki's. Why is it, then, that even though Emperor Go-Toba still hoped to return from his tour of inspection in Oki, Go-Daigo's court was left stranded so long in the mountains of Yoshino?

Giving special favor to his ravishing consort, he [Go-Daigo] distributed reward and punishment arbitrarily; the minister[11] who disagreed with him left, and public order was thrown into confusion. Even though loyal ministers and righteous warriors died bloody deaths for his [Go-Daigo's] cause on the battlefield, in the end there was no one who could save him. What is particularly unfortunate is that even though his talent for overcoming disorder was sufficient to bring heroes to his side, his intelligence remained obscured and he was unable to distinguish between loyal followers and flatterers. Even though he hoped to restore the good government of the Engi era [901–923], was it possible for him to succeed?

Since ancient times, initiating the great enterprise [of ruling the empire] has always been difficult, but holding on to it has been even more difficult. With anxiousness and hard work it is possible to restore the fortunes of one's country; with a life of ease and comfort it is possible to forget one's responsibilities. How could the emperor have failed to reflect on this? Nevertheless, the emperor's intrepid spirit would not give up, even if broken a hundred times. His declaration refusing to hand over the regalia to the new king was correct in righteousness and rigorous in its choice of words. His decree dispatching a prince to pacify Mutsu kept the civil and military arts from splitting into two paths.[12] How great they are, these words! This is something that rulers have not been able to achieve since middle antiquity. The thought of

---

10. Go-Daigo was the grandson of Kameyama, who was involved in a succession dispute with his older brother, Go-Fukakusa, beginning in 1272. The dispute was finally resolved by the shogunate, which arranged for the imperial succession to alternate between the two lines. It was Go-Daigo's desire to break this agreement and retain the succession within his own line that led in the first place to his split with the shogunate.

11. Fujiwara no Fujifusa was an aristocratic confidant of Go-Daigo who became one of his chief strategists. In 1334, after Go-Daigo ignored his remonstrances over unfairness in distributing rewards and insufficient attention to government, Fujifusa left him and became a monk in the mountains.

12. Mutsu is a province in the far north of Honshū (modern Aomori Prefecture). Kitabatake Akiie, Chikafusa's son, became governor there in the name of one of Go-Daigo's sons, building up a strong military force that fought on the side of the Southern Court. As a member of a courtier family, he was a representative of civil power who also took on military functions, thus combining civil (*bun*) and military (*bu*), as they were believed to have been combined in ancient times.

restoration only grows more intense when it is frustrated; facing death he [Go-Daigo] took hold of his sword and braced himself for battle. Thus he was able to keep the regalia safe among deep mountain crags and lay down the foundation for a court that lasted for more than fifty years.[13] The place where the legitimate line dwells shines bright like the sun and the moon! Was this not a great accomplishment?

[*Dai Nihon shi sansō*, in NST, vol. 48, pp. 66–67; BS]

KAIBARA EKKEN: HUMAN NATURE AND THE STUDY OF NATURE

Among Japanese Neo-Confucians, perhaps no one combines the cosmological, moral, and rational tendencies of this movement more strikingly than Kaibara Ekken (1630–1714). More than anyone else, he brought Confucian ethics into the homes of ordinary Japanese in language they could understand. Other Neo-Confucians might have taken great pride in demonstrating their command of Chinese-style writing. But Ekken was content to set forth in comparatively simple Japanese the basic moral doctrines that should govern the everyday conduct of the people, their relations with others, their duties within their families and to their feudal lords, their duties in war and peace, and so forth. Although Ekken was addressing the samurai particularly, his writings appealed to all classes and ages, and he gained a reputation for having made Confucian moral teachings "household talk" among the people. To do this, he especially had to reach the women and children. In this way, Ekken did for Confucian ethics what the leaders of the Pure Land sect had done for Buddhism in the medieval period: bringing it down from the realm of doctrinal discussion and to the level of everyday speech.

Raised in a lower-ranking samurai family in Fukuoka, Ekken was educated in Kyoto at the expense of his own domain (*han*) and employed by his own lord (*daimyō*) as an official adviser. This assured him of a career as scholar and writer relatively free of financial concerns. His remarkable productivity was, no doubt, attributable to his moderate but secure income, as well as to the peaceful conditions established by the unification of the country under the Tokugawa shogunate.

For seven years, Ekken studied in Kyoto, still the intellectual capital of that time. There he met many of the most illustrious Confucian scholars in Japan, including Kinoshita Jun'an (1621–1698), Yamazaki Ansai (1618–1682), and Itō

---

13. The exiled Southern Court of Go-Daigo was preserved from 1334 to 1392, when a compromise was reached that led Emperor Go-Kameyama to surrender the regalia to Emperor Go-Komatsu of the Northern Court.

Jinsai (1627–1705). Ekken remained in contact with several of these scholars on successive trips to Kyoto but also occasionally traveled to the political capital, Edo (Tokyo), where he met one of the leading government advisers, the Confucian scholar Hayashi Gahō (1618–1680). In Kyushu he also frequently visited the port city of Nagasaki, where, despite the ban on imported Western books, he bought Chinese and sometimes even Western books. It was there that at age twenty-one he obtained a copy of *Reflections on Things at Hand* (*Jinsilu*), one of the Song Neo-Confucian scholar Zhu Xi's most important works. Some seventeen years later, Ekken wrote the first Japanese commentary on this text (*Kinshiroku bikō*).

Ekken's breadth of concerns reflects his varied life experience, his opportunities for travel, and his contacts with scholars and other groups in the society. Especially impressive is Ekken's range and volume of writings and the unpretentiousness of his learning. From sophisticated Confucian scholarship to popular treatises on Confucian morality, and from botanical and agricultural studies to provincial topographies and genealogies, Ekken demonstrated a range of intellectual and ethical concerns rarely matched in the Tokugawa period. In this, he is said to have been aided in some of his work by his wife, Tōken.

In addition to his commentary on Zhu Xi's *Reflections on Things at Hand*, Ekken's most important philosophical work is the *Record of Great Doubts* (*Taigiroku*), which takes issue with some of Zhu Xi's metaphysics. Here Ekken argues for a philosophy of vitalistic naturalism as a basis for moral self-cultivation and for an active engagement with social and political affairs. He rejects any tendency in Neo-Confucian thought toward transcendentalism, quietism, or self-centered cultivation. Instead, he offers a dynamic philosophy of material force (J. *ki*, Ch. *qi*) as a unifying basis for the interaction of self, society, and nature. He observes that *ki* is the vital spirit present in all life, which should be cultivated both in one's self and in nature.

In describing his monism of *ki*, Ekken is especially indebted to the Ming Confucian Luo Qinshun (1465–1547), who raised questions about Zhu Xi's metaphysics in his important work *Knowledge Painfully Acquired* (*Kunzhiji*). This was first published in China in 1528 and made its way to Japan through Korea. In 1658 there appeared a Japanese woodblock edition, which Ekken— as well as Itō Jinsai, Andō Seian (1622–1701), and others—read shortly afterward. Earlier in Korea, Yi Yulgok (1536–1584) had expressed similar doubts. Thus these three thinkers in succession—Luo, Yi, and Ekken—became central figures in the development of a line of Neo-Confucian thought in East Asia centering on the monism of *ki*, a vitalistic naturalism, and practical or substantive learning (J. *jitsugaku*, Ch. *shixue*, K. *sirhak*).

One of Ekken's intentions was to identify the lingering traces of Buddhism and Daoism in Zhu's thought that he saw as tending toward emptiness and disengagement from worldly affairs. By doing so, he hoped to maintain the important connection between a dynamic cosmology and an active engagement with the world. In other words, Ekken did not want a person's metaphysics to negatively affect his ethical stance in the world.

Ekken did not allow the *Record of Great Doubts* to be published until after his death. Although it came to be highly valued by the revisionist Ogyū Sorai, Ekken did not wish to associate himself with Itō Jinsai's more radical critique and eventual abandonment of Zhu Xi. Even though he disagreed with Zhu Xi on some points, Ekken remained profoundly indebted to his synthesis of Song Neo-Confucianism.

In order to spread Confucian ideas among a wide variety of people, Ekken wrote moral treatises (*kunmono*) in a simplified Japanese style addressed to particular groups, including samurai, families, women, and children. This was part of his deep commitment to Confucian ideas and practices as the foundation for a new moral, sociopolitical order in Japan's emerging period of peace and stability. Ekken's writings and teachings also contributed significantly to Confucianism's rapprochement with Shinto. As naturalistic philosophies emphasizing virtues such as authenticity and sincerity, as well as the vitality of nature, Confucianism and Shinto were regarded by Ekken and other scholars as having shared values.

Ekken's equal concern for moral practicality and rational inquiry, combined in what Zhu Xi called "practical learning" (J. *jitsugaku*, Ch. *shixue*), encompassed fields such as medicine, botany, and agriculture, as well as astronomy, geography, and mathematics. One of Ekken's best-known works is *Plants of Japan (Yamato honzō)*, a classification of plants, herbs, shells, fish, and birds in the style of a natural history, based on a long-established tradition in China of plant taxonomy. In addition, Ekken wrote *Precepts for Health Care (Yōjō kun)*, a practical guide that is still popular, as well as an introduction to Miyazaki Yasusada's agricultural compendium (*Nōgyō zensho*), which was an important exposition of farming techniques (a concern of Zhu Xi's as well). Ekken's practical learning also encompassed local history and topography through his gazetteers of the Kuroda domain and his travel diaries.

ELEMENTARY LEARNING FOR CHILDREN
(SHŌGAKU-KUN)

The opening passage of Kaibara Ekken's *Elementary Learning for Children* sets out with great simplicity his view of the interrelation of humankind and nature through the supreme Confucian virtue of humaneness (J. *jin*, Ch. *ren*). This is precisely what makes human beings truly human and unites Ekken with nature.

In the first paragraph, the compound for "nature" is rendered literally as "Heaven-and-earth" to show the correspondence to "father and mother." Ekken's views echo those in the Neo-Confucian philosopher Zhang Zai's "Western inscription."[14]

---

14. See de Bary and Bloom, eds., *Sources of Chinese Tradition*, 2nd ed., vol. 1, chap. 20.

All human beings may be said to owe their birth to their parents, but a further inquiry into their origins reveals that human beings come into existence because of nature's law of life. Thus all humans in the world are children born of Heaven-and-earth, and Heaven-and-earth are the great parents of us all. The *Book of History* says, "Heaven-and-earth are the father and mother of all things."[15] Our own parents are truly our parents, but Heaven-and-earth are the parents of all in the world. Moreover, even though we are bought up after birth through the care of our own parents and are sustained on the gracious bounty of the ruler, if we go to the root of the matter, we will find that we sustain ourselves using the things produced by nature for food, dress, housing, and implements. Thus not only do all humans at the outset come into being because of nature's law of life, but from birth until the end of life they also are kept in existence by the support of Heaven-and-earth. Humans surpass all other created things in their indebtedness to the limitless bounty of nature. We will see, therefore, that their duty is not only to do their best to serve their parents, which is a matter of course, but also to serve nature throughout their life in order to repay their immense debt. That is one thing all people should constantly keep in mind.

As humans constantly mindful of their obligation to serve nature in repayment of this great debt, they should not forget that just as they manifested filial piety in serving their own parents, so they should manifest to the full their humaneness toward nature. Humaneness means having a sense of sympathy within and bringing blessings to humans and things. For those who have been brought up on the blessings of nature, it is the way to serve nature. It is the basic aim of human life, which they should observe as long as they live, without letting up on it or forgetting it. Humaneness in the service of nature and filial piety are one in principle, a principle that must be known and observed by everyone who is human. There is no [goal] greater than this, none more important. All those living in their parents' home should devote themselves to filial service to their father and mother and, in serving their lord, should demonstrate single-minded loyalty to him. Likewise, living as we do in nature's embrace, we must serve nature and manifest to the full our humaneness. For a human being to be unaware of this important duty, to let the days and years pass idly by and let his life be wasted, is to make himself unworthy of being a human being. Indeed, how can anyone who would be a human being ignore this fact? It is in this that the way of humanity lies. Any way other than this cannot be the true Way.

[First,] to persist in the service of Heaven means that everyone who is human should be mindful that in the morning and evening one is in the presence of Heaven and not far removed from it; that one should fear and reverence the way of Heaven and not be unmindful of it. One should not, even in ignorance,

---

15. *Taishi*, vol. 1.

oppose the way of Heaven or commit any outrage against it. Rather, following the way of Heaven, one should be humble and not arrogant toward others, control one's desires and not be indulgent of one's passions, cherish a profound love for all humankind born of nature's great love, and not abuse or mistreat them. Nor should one waste, just to gratify personal desires, the five grains and other bounties that nature has provided for the sake of the people. Second, no living creatures, like birds, beasts, insects, and fish, should be killed wantonly. Not even grass and trees should be cut down out of season. All are objects of nature's love, having been created and nurtured by it. To cherish and keep them is therefore the way to serve nature in accordance with the great heart of Heaven-and-earth. Among human obligations there is, first, the duty to love their relatives, then to show sympathy for all other human beings, and finally not to mistreat birds and beasts or any other living things. That is the proper order for practicing humaneness in accordance with the great heart of Heaven-and-earth. Loving other people to the neglect of parents, or loving birds and beasts to the neglect of human beings, is to be inhumane.

[Kaibara Ekken, *Ekken zenshū*, vol. 3, pp. 2–3; MET]

RECORD OF GREAT DOUBTS
(*TAIGIROKU*)

In the opening passage, in relation to Zhu Xi's concept of the "succession to (or reconstitution of) the Way," Ekken establishes himself in a manner characteristic of Neo-Confucian discourse. He sees the Way not simply as a system of received authority, subject to some attenuation and loss, but also as subject to successive stages of clarification, revivification, and expansion. That is, even the Song masters can be amended by invoking their own insistence on the need for doubt and questioning and by appealing to the higher ideal and authority of the ancient sages as the ground for reinterpretation.

1. In regard to the Way of the sages, in antiquity although some persons received Heaven's charge and set forth the supreme norm [of human conduct and governance], the method of instruction for the Way had not yet been made known. From the time of Yao and Shun, people received the charge to "be discriminating and become one [with the mind of the Way], and hold fast to the Mean"[16] and also to "reverently spread the teachings of the Five Constant Virtues."[17] This was how teaching first became established. The three periods of the Xia, Shang, and Zhou followed, during which an educational method

---

16. *Shujing*, "Dayumo," as recounted in Zhu Xi, preface to the *Mean*. See de Bary and Bloom, eds., *Sources of Chinese Tradition*, 2nd ed., vol. 1, p. 732.

17. *Shujing*, "Shun dian"; Legge, trans., *The Shoo king*, p. 44.

was gradually provided. But it had not yet been clearly articulated, so Confucius greatly clarified it. The Way of Confucius then found its true heir in Mencius, who clarified it.

From primordial antiquity, the material energies of Heaven-and-earth have gradually changed. Human civilization also has unfolded unceasingly along with these changes. Although even in the enlightened period of Yao and Shun and the three early dynasties, civilization was unable to flower fully, it was only natural that further developments should await later generations. Thus, for the many generations to come, civilization will gradually yet ceaselessly unfold with each age.

After Mencius, from the Han through the Tang periods, the transmission of this Way was nearly cut off. Indeed, it hung by a slender thread. However, in the Song dynasty several exemplary leaders appeared who resuscitated the Way and brought it again to people's attention. Particularly noteworthy were the commentaries and the explanations of the Confucian classics by the Cheng brothers and Zhu Xi. Since the time of Mencius there had been many remarkable scholars, but the Cheng brothers were the most illustrious among those who understood the Way and explicated the teachings. After them came Zhu Xi. Although neither the virtue nor the learning of the Chengs and Zhu quite compared with that attained by the early sages, later generations naturally respected and trusted them. Still, in their manner of expression various points may not have exactly agreed with Confucius and Mencius. Therefore, we must not regard the Song Confucians as equal to Confucius and Mencius. Scholars should have an open mind and be discerning with regard to the similarities and differences and the correctness and mistakes of their teachings. If one reflects deeply, selects carefully, and believes what should be believed and doubts what should be doubted, that will be all right. . . .

2. In their teachings, the Song Confucians regarded the nonfinite (*wuji*) as the basis of the Supreme Ultimate (*taiji*), and Nothingness as the root of the existent. They divided principle (*li*) and material force (*qi*) and regarded them as two things. They did not consider yin and yang as the Way but as physical vessels. They separated the nature of Heaven-and-earth from physical nature, viewing human nature and principle as beyond birth and death [i.e., unchanging]. These ideas are the residue of Buddhist and Daoist thinking and different from the teachings of the early Confucian sages. Scholars must distinguish this precisely and clearly.

In discussing the method of preserving the mind-and-heart, the Song Confucians spoke of making tranquillity central, of quiet sitting, and of apprehending Heavenly principle through silent sitting to purify the mind-and-heart. They regarded quiet sitting to be the everyday method for preserving the mind. This all tends toward quietism rather than toward activity and tranquillity as practices adaptable to circumstances. In other words, this is the same as the Zen practice of meditation to achieve Nirvana. This is not something that true Confucians should approve of. Song Confucians also spoke of the original mind-and-heart as being empty, unobstructed, and transparent and regarded Heaven's principle as limitless and trackless. This is the residue of Buddhist and Daoist thinking, different from the teachings of Confucius and Mencius. Originally the Song Confucians claimed to speak for Confucius and Mencius, but some of their teachings did not originate with Confucius and Mencius but emerged from Buddhism and Daoism. Scholars must be selective. . . . [pp. 12–14]

. . . Although the learning of the Song Confucians is genuine, it still does not match that of the sages. They [the Song Confucians] could not avoid having prejudicial personal viewpoints. Thus teachings frequently appear that are different from the teachings of Confucius and Mencius. These include the following, which are the reasons for my own doubts: (1) taking the nonfinite as the basis of the Supreme Ultimate; (2) separating principle and material force into two separate things; (3) differentiating the nature of Heaven-and-earth from the physical nature; (4) regarding yin and yang not as being the Way but as being concrete things in the world of form; (5) taking the reason for the alternation of yin and yang as the Way; (6) seeing material force and the physical body as subject to life and death; (7) taking principle and the nature as not subject to life and death (changeless); (8) regarding quiet sitting as a method of regular daily practice and taking "holding to tranquillity"[18] as a method for achieving human perfection; (9) using the theories of Confucius and Mencius concerning nature to distinguish between the physical nature and the nature of heaven and earth. [pp. 31–32]

A holistic view is superior to minute analysis, for without being analytical the meaning is clear. If people who teach later generations follow the same line as Confucius and Mencius, they will be correct. If they set forth different teachings departing from Confucius and Mencius, that is unacceptable. The creation of things by Heaven-and-earth begins and gradually evolves. This is a natural principle in accordance with the evolution of material force. . . .

The Song Confucians explain the Supreme Ultimate in terms of the nonfinite (*wuji*); they regard principle and material force as two; they see yin and yang as not being the Way but as concrete things; they think there is a nature of Heaven and earth and a psychophysical nature; they explain innate goodness in terms of "Human nature as principle." Such things do not conform to the original intent of Confucius and Mencius, and they do not follow the same teaching. If scholars examined this matter fairly, without favoring or adulating the various Song teachers, they would perceive the differences. [pp. 25–27]

In Neo-Confucian cultivation, a key question was which virtue, value, or practice should be the guiding principle. Shu, for "master" or, in this case, "guiding principle of the

---

18. *Laozi* 40.

mind," could, depending on the context, also function as a verb: "to give primacy, or first importance, to." Some Neo-Confucians like Yi T'oegye and Yamazaki Ansai who practiced "quiet sitting" stressed "reverence" or "reverent seriousness" as the controlling spiritual principle or as a primary orientation of the mind-and-heart that combined moral awareness with religious consciousness, as opposed to a transrational religiosity (Buddhism and Daoism). Ekken, however, saw this as taking "reverence" too seriously and making too much of it.

72. *Reverence as the Master of the Mind.* Zhu Xi said, "Reverence should be the master of [i.e., should control] the mind-and-heart and be the basis for [dealing with] all matters."[19] He believed that "self-cultivation through reverence" was the ultimate teaching of the sages. Without reverence one could not preserve the mind-and-heart. Thus he advocated reverence as a way to hold the moral mind firmly. . . .

Reverence is all right as a method of self-cultivation. Since [the time of] Yao and Shun, it has been the method of the mind-and-heart (*shinpō*) transmitted by the sages and worthies down through the ages.[20] But because Confucius, Zengzi, Zisi, and Mencius did not speak of giving primacy to reverence, we should know that giving primacy to reverence is not what the ancient sages and worthies regarded as primary. . . .

Those who stress "holding to reverence" today do not understand the Way of reverence. Frequently they become externally solemn but in fact have a false austerity and formality. On the surface they appear self-disciplined and respectful, but actually they are "outwardly strong and inwardly weak."[21] This is because they do not give primacy to loyalty and trustworthiness. Only those who give primacy to loyalty and trustworthiness will be without fault. Indeed, giving them primacy is the foundation of all virtue. [pp. 50–52]

[Kaibara Ekken, *Taigiroku*, in NST, vol. 34, pp. 12–14, 25–27, 31–32, 50–52; MET, WTdB]

THE ŌYŌMEI (WANG YANGMING) SCHOOL IN JAPAN

Deep and lasting as the influence of Zhu Xi's teaching in Tokugawa Japan was, its dominance was far from complete. Indeed, from the vantage point of history, one of the most striking features of Japanese thought in this period was its diversity and vitality. Not only during the waning years of the shogunate when

---

19. Zhu Xi, *Daxue huowen* 5:4.
20. As formulated by Zhu Xi in preface to the *Mean*.
21. *Analects* 17:12.

its control was loosened, but even during the heyday of its power, men of independent mind offered alternatives to the Neo-Confucian schools patronized by the Tokugawa. Among them an important strain of independent thought was represented by Nakae Tōju (1608–1648), regarded as the founder of the Wang Yangming school in Japan, and Kumazawa Banzan (1619–1691), an outstanding example of the personal and political virtues that had already made this school a center of reformist activity in China.

NAKAE TŌJU

Ōyōmei is the Japanese rendering of the name of Wang Yangming, the sixteenth-century Chinese thinker who became the outstanding spokesman for a new learning of the mind in the Ming period that emerged out of Zhu Xi's earlier "learning of the mind-and-heart" based, on the *Great Learning*, and Zhu's preface to and commentary on the *Mean*.[22] Two features of Yangming's teaching appealed especially to Nakae Tōju, who discovered it through the writing of Yangming's disciple Wang Ji[23] after he had spent many years studying the texts and rituals of the Zhu Xi school. One was Yangming's emphasis on people's intuition or moral sense rather than on the intellect and scholarly learning. Not all people have to be scholars, but all people should fulfill their moral nature. For Tōju, the moral sense innate in every man, the inner light that he later called the "Divine Light of Heaven," is man's only sure guide in life.

Tōju was also attracted to Yangming's teaching because of its emphasis on deeds rather than words. The dictates of one's conscience should be carried out directly in action. Yangming explained the unity of knowledge and action by showing that no matter how much a person read and talked about filial piety, he could not be said to have truly learned or understood it until he had put it into practice. Tōju himself gave an example of this. Although it may not have been his only reason for doing so, Tōju resigned a stipended post he held in the service of a feudal lord in Shikoku and returned to his native village in Ōmi Province, near Lake Biwa, in order, he said, to look after his aging mother. This meant taking up the life of a farmer in a region removed from the cultural life of the capital. Nevertheless, his fame spread abroad as a teacher whose precepts were taken to heart by country folk as well as by educated men. That he attracted such able men as Kumazawa Banzan to his school and influenced such great scholars as Arai Hakuseki and Dazai Shundai was due less to his intellectual brilliance than to his gentle-hearted and single-minded pursuit of this way of life, guided only by the Heavenly voice within him.

---

22. See de Bary and Bloom, eds., *Sources of Chinese Tradition*, 2nd ed., vol. 1, chaps. 21, 22, 24.
23. See de Bary and Bloom, eds., *Sources of Chinese Tradition*, 2nd ed., vol. 1, chap. 24.

It is this same single-minded and selfless determination that we find among the followers of Ōyōmei learning in the late Tokugawa, such as the radical rebel Ōshio Chūsai and those zealous patriots, Sakuma Shōzan and Yoshida Shōin, whose example made such an impression on the leaders of the Meiji Restoration. Even in the nineteenth and twentieth centuries, the philosophy that Nakae Tōju espoused was popular (see chap. 32). Sugiura Jūgō, the famous Western-trained preceptor to Emperor Taishō (1912–1926), paid the following tribute to Tōju:

> He was the Sage of Ōmi Province; but is he not also the sage of Japan, the sage of the East, and indeed, the sage of the entire world? For a sage is a sage in the same way in the present as in the past, in the East and in the West. That he was already the sage of Ōmi Province is reason enough for calling him the sage of the entire world.[24]

CONTROL OF THE MIND IS TRUE LEARNING

According to Nakae Tōju, the fundamental truths of life were the same for all human beings, regardless of their station or role in life. Whereas other Confucians generally addressed scholars and officials, Tōju offered guidance to the humblest of men and even to women, whose weaknesses, as commonly viewed, he attributed to their confined life and lack of education.

There are many degrees of learning, but the learning that teaches control of the mind is the true learning. This true learning is of the utmost importance in this world and the chief concern of all mankind. The reason is that it aims at "manifesting luminous virtue,"[25] which is the greatest treasure of mankind. Gold, silver, and jewels are treasures, of course, but they are incapable of severing the root of all human suffering and providing lasting happiness. So they are not man's greatest treasure.

When luminous virtue shines, human suffering of all kinds will cease, and our hearts will be filled with lasting happiness. Everything will be as we want it. Wealth and rank, poverty and lowliness, prosperity and adversity, will have little effect on our enjoyment of life. Moreover, everyone will love and respect us, Heaven itself will help us and the gods will protect us, so that natural calamities and disasters will not harm us, thunder and earthquake will not injure us. Storms may destroy buildings but will leave us untouched. . . . Because of its boundless merits and blessings, this is called "the greatest treasure in the world." It is found in every human being, high or low, old or young,

---

24. Inoue, *Nihon yōmei gakuha no tetsugaku*, p. 18.
25. This phrase is from the opening lines of the *Great Learning*.

male or female, in the inexhaustible treasure-house of the mind-and-heart, but not knowing how to seek it, people in their pitiful ignorance go on searching for treasure in external things, only to sink into a sea of suffering. . . .

Some say that learning seems not to be the business of women. I say that there are many women busy composing poetry in both Chinese and Japanese, and although poetry would seem not to be the business of women, they are not criticized for it. Control of the mind is of the utmost importance to women, and it would be a great mistake to say that it is not their business. The outward manner and temper of women is rooted in the negative (yin) power, and so temperamentally women are apt to be sensitive, petty, narrow, and jaundiced. Because they live confined to their homes day in and day out, theirs is a very private life and their vision is quite limited. Consequently, compassion and honesty are rare indeed among women.

[Nakae Tojū, *Tōju sensei zenshū*, vol. 2, p. 573; RT]

DIALOGUE WITH AN OLD MAN
(OKINA MONDŌ)

Dialogue with an Old Man (1646) is Tōju's most famous work. At a time when Confucianism was struggling to establish itself against the deep-rooted worldview of Buddhism, he presented Confucianism as a religion similar to Buddhism in its concern with the enlightenment of the mind, yet superior to it because it affirms the reality of human nature based on the primacy of the moral sentiments. Filial piety had always formed the core of Confucian arguments against Buddhism, but Tōju, drawing also on the language of Wang Ji, developed this concept into a religious worldview centering on filial piety, seen as the ultimate source of all ethical action and all existing things. Underlying this view is the key Neo-Confucian doctrine concerning the humaneness that forms one body with Heaven, earth, and all things. This Way is compatible with the traditional worship of the Japanese *kami* and is ideally fitted to serve as the Way of the samurai in his life of loyal service in an age of peace.

1. Within all human beings there is a spiritual treasure with which nothing else in the world can compare, known as the supreme virtue and the essential Way. The most important thing in life is to use this treasure, keeping it in our hearts and practicing it with our bodies. Above, this treasure communes with the Way of Heaven; below, its luminosity shines over the Four Seas. For this reason, if we use this treasure and extend it into the Five [Human] Relationships, all our relationships will be harmonious and without malice. If we use it when serving the gods, the gods will accept our offerings. If we use it when ruling the realm, the realm will be at peace. If we use it when ruling our domain, the domain will be in good order. If we use it when regulating our family and clan, our family and clan will be well regulated. If we put it into

practice in our personal life, our personal life will be in order. If we preserve it within our hearts, our hearts will become luminous. If we extend it outward, it will spread beyond heaven and earth. If we draw it inward, it will hide in the innermost reaches of our heart. It is truly a marvelous and supreme spiritual treasure. . . .

Because the Five [Human] Relationships are external, people who do not know the highest principle think that the ways of the Five [Human] Relationships are external and not within one's own heart. This is a delusion. Heaven-and-earth and the ten thousand things all are produced and transformed within the divine radiance (*shinmei reikō*), so that if the filial virtue in my heart is clear, it will commune with the gods (*shinmei*) and shine over the Four Seas. . . . To see the way of the Five [Human] Relationships as external and to abandon them—setting up a dualistic view of inner versus outer, dark versus bright, and being versus nonbeing—is only a delusion that seems to be enlightenment (*satori*). . . . Before all else, it is the child's filial action that is the fountainhead of all human actions and the matter of greatest urgency in human ethics. Therefore, in the sages' five teachings, the principle that was taught first is the need for affection between parent and child.

The following passage is noteworthy for its graphic and very intimate portrayal of the inception of life and the parents' (especially mother's) role in the process.

If one wishes to manifest filial virtue, one should first meditate on the blessings (*ontoku*) received from one's father and mother. During the ten months between conception and birth, the mother endures all the hardships of carrying a child, subjecting herself to countless risks of illness and death. At the same time, the father worries and prays that the fetus will be safe and the pregnancy will proceed smoothly, unable to forget the pains and troubles that his wife is enduring. When the time of birth arrives, the mother has to suffer the pain of having her body ripped open while the father is feverish with anxiety over the safety of both mother and child. If by good fortune both mother and child are all right, he will experience the joy of knowing that the family line will continue.

The mother lies exhausted on her bed drenched with sweat and lays her newborn child on a dry mat. If the child is sleeping, the mother will not even stretch her body for fear of waking it, and even if her body is dirty and stained with blood, she has no time to bathe or wash her hair. Her clothes and makeup are in total disarray, but she gives thought to nothing but whether her child is all right. If the child shows the slightest sign of any sickness, she will anxiously summon the doctor and pray to the gods, wishing only that she could take the place of her child in its pain. During the three years of nursing, the amount of trouble the parents have to endure is incalculable. When the child reaches school age, they will find a teacher to teach the child the Way, arrange for training in the arts, and hope that their child may surpass other children in talent and virtue. When the child reaches marriage age, they will seek an appropriate marriage partner and arrange for an occupation for their child, doing everything they can to ensure that he will prosper. If their child surpasses others in talent and virtue and is happy and prosperous, the parents will feel unlimited joy. If their child falls behind others in talent and virtue and is not happy, they will have no rest from their grieving and worrying.

The father and mother accumulate so much of this love and affection, so much of this care and trouble, in raising and nurturing their child that not one hair on the child's body exists except by virtue of their care. The blessings received from one's parents are higher than the sky and deeper than the sea. Because they are so vast and unparalleled, uncultivated people whose original minds are obscured forget to try to repay them. On the contrary, they seem not even to consider whether such a debt of gratitude really exists. No being in human form—no matter how ignorant or unworthy he may be—should fail to think of repaying the debt of gratitude for every bowl of rice received. Because every person possesses an original mind of filial virtue, in every thought of repaying the blessings (on) he has received, a little bit of that original mind is revealed. If a person forgets to repay this debt despite that original mind, it is because the sunlight of luminous virtue has been obscured by the clouds of human desires and the heart is lost in darkness. By extending every thought of repaying even the tiniest blessing received, one will come to truly understand the depth of the blessings received from one's parents. In this way, the clouds of human desire will disperse, and the sunlight of luminous virtue will become bright. In this way we should strive to extend and develop without limit the original mind's spontaneous filial desire to repay the blessings received from our parents. . . .

81. The birth of human beings seems to be by the action of their parents, but it is not. Actually, they are brought into being by the transforming and nourishing powers of the gods of heaven and earth according to the mandate given them by the August Lord on High of the Great Vacuity. . . . Since the gods of heaven and earth are the parents of the ten thousand things, the August Lord on High of the Great Vacuity is the supreme ancestor of all mankind.[26] If we look from the point of view of this divine principle, the sages and wise men,

---

26. The theistic terms used here come from Wang Ji (de Bary and Bloom, eds., *Sources of Chinese Tradition*, 2nd ed., vol. 1, chap. 24), but the concept of the Great Vacuity derives from the teaching of Zhang Zai (1020–1077), in which the original pre-form state of the elemental force (J. *ki*, Ch. *qi*), which generates matter and life, is called the Great Vacuity (J. *taikyo*, Ch. *taixu*). When the universe first comes into being, "that which is dispersed, differentiated and capable of assuming form becomes material force (*ki*), and that which is pure, penetrating and not capable of assuming form becomes spirit." On the basis of the same distinction between material force and spirit, Tōju claimed that Buddhist *satori* consisted merely of an awakening to "the spiritual awareness (*reikaku*) of the primordial material force (*genki*)," while through the practice of filial piety the Confucian realizes "the spiritual awareness of the primordial spirit (*genshin*)" (question 83).

Shakyamuni and Bodhidharma, the Confucian and the Buddhist, oneself and other people—all in the world who possess human form—all are equally the descendants of the August Lord on High and the gods of heaven and earth. Moreover, since the Confucian way is nothing other than the divine way (*shintō*) of the August Lord on High and the gods of heaven and earth, if a person in human form slanders and disobeys the Way of Confucianism, it is equivalent to slandering the Way of his own ancestors and parents and disobeying their commands. As I explained earlier, to fear and revere the decrees of our great first ancestor, the August Lord on High, and our great parents, the gods of heaven and earth, and to accept and practice their divine way with deep reverence is called filial piety, the supreme virtue. . . .

98. . . . Because the mind of the sage rests permanently in the highest virtue while dealing freely with all the affairs of life (*konpai tekiō*)[27] and has no ego that insists on things being one way or the other,[28] he has no remnant of feelings of preference for high over humble station, wealth over poverty, greatness over insignificance, purity over impurity, or beauty over ugliness. His eye is filled with one thing and one thing only: the divine principles of the Supreme Ultimate (*kōkyoku*). . . . Only when one disobeys the divine principles of the Heavenly Way (*tentō*)[29] is it desire and delusion; to accord with these principles[, however,] is desirelessness and nondelusion. Desire or freedom from desire does not lie in the nature of one's actions but in the quality of the ground of the mind.

[Nakae Tojū, *Okina mondō*, in NST, vol. 29, pp. 222–23, 31–34, 123, 147–48; BS]

THE DIVINE LIGHT IN THE MIND

Tōju's doctrine of innate or intuitive knowledge has strong theistic overtones that reflect his tendency to reinterpret both Confucianism and Shinto in order to show their essential unity.

---

27. *Konpai tekiō* (Ch. *Genbei diying*) refers to *Yi jing*, hexagram 52 (*gen*), called the "double mountain" because it combines two *gen* trigrams associated with mountain. The virtue of mountain is stillness, firmness, and rootedness in the earth. The top and bottom halves of the hexagram are in perfect correspondence, back to back (*diying*). *Gen* is stopping; stopping is becoming settled; when one is settled, one is illuminated. The mind that has come to rest where it should (in perfect goodness) remains tranquil even when the body moves. This concept was greatly popularized by a member of the Wang Yangming school, Lin Zhaoen (1517–1598), whose teaching influenced Fujiwara Seika and Tōju.

28. Allusion to *Analects* 9:4: "Four things that Confucius eschewed: he had no preconceptions, no prejudices, no obduracy, no egotism."

29. In late medieval Japanese, Tentō also means the god of Heaven, so for Tōju it would seem to have the same meaning as Tentei and Kōjōtei. The compound for Tentō also occurs in the *Classic of Documents*, where it is described as having the power to reward good and punish evil in response to the people's pleas to the gods of heaven and earth. The compound for Kōjōtei also is derived from the *Documents*.

The superior man will be watchful over those innermost thoughts known to himself alone. In his everyday thinking, he will not think anything for which he would have to fear if brought into the presence of the Divine. In his everyday actions he will not perform an act of which he might be ashamed if it were known to others. By mistake an evil idea may arise, a wrong deed may present itself; but since there is in the mind a divine awareness illuminating it, what we call "enlightenment" will appear. Once this is realized, rectification will follow; the evil idea and wrong deed will disappear; and the mind will revert to its normal state of purity and divine enlightenment. The ordinary man, unfortunately, continues to think such evil thoughts and goes on doing what he knows is wrong. Nevertheless, since the divine light in the mind makes the man aware [that he is doing wrong], he tries to hide it. In everybody's mind there is this divine light, which is one with the Divinity of Heaven and before which one stands as if in a mirror, with nothing hidden either good or bad.

[Inoue, *Nihon yōmei gakuha no tetsugaku*, p. 81; RT]

THE SUPREME LORD AND GOD OF LIFE

Following Wang Ji in the school of Wang Yangming, Tōju identified the supreme value with the idea of a personal god, which readily harmonized with Shinto belief.

The Great God of Life[30] is called the Supreme Lord Above in the *Classic of Documents*. The Supreme Lord Above is the spirit of the god of life. He is the ruler and parent of all things in the universe; not a single particle of the six directions of the universe or a single second of all time is hidden from the light of his omniscience. But all particular things in the universe are made up of just one virtue and do not combine all the virtues of the Supreme Being. . . . Most miraculous, most spiritual, reaching to where there is no circumference, penetrating to where there is no center, he alone is worthy of devotion and without peer. His virtues are exquisite and unfathomable. Nameless himself, he has been called by the sages the "Supreme Heavenly God of Life," in order to let men know that he is the source of all creation so that they may pay homage to him. [pp. 137–38]

34. A person who is born with a stout spirit and a natural talent for military prowess can master the military arts and achieve merit in battle even without training in the Learning of the Mind. But because he will be lacking virtue, he will become intoxicated with his physical prowess and find killing people enjoyable. He will thus act unrighteously and unjustly, causing much suffering

---

30. A Chinese deity, Daiotsu-Sonshin was incorporated into medieval Shinto as Ōkinoto no Ō-mikoto.

and lamentation among the populace. In the end he will inevitably meet with Heaven's punishment, at the cost of his own life and the destruction of his domain. . . . One has only to look at the history books of both China and Japan. The original purpose of the military arts is to ensure the peace and tranquillity of the state, preserve the good fortune of the warrior class, and bring the blessings of peace to the populace. If instead they become the cause of the misery of the populace, the loss of warriors' lives, and the destruction of the state, then the mastery of military arts and the achievement of military merit are nothing but useless vanity. What is more, if a person knows only of intrigues, trickery, and violence and nothing of the virtues of humaneness and rightness, then even if he has the prowess of a Han Xin or Xiang Yu,[31] he will not be able to hold his shield against an enemy who has self-control. . . . If one really wants to study military arts, why not study the military arts of the man of humaneness against which no man under heaven can stand up? [p. 65]

In a battle situation or at a time when martial prowess is required, those involved must act valiantly. However, this is useless in ordinary times of peace. In times of peace, to devote oneself constantly to acts of valor and bravery on the grounds that one is preparing oneself for battle is an ignorant pursuit and will not be of any use in times of emergency. . . . Those who are fond of proving their fearlessness by unprovoked acts of violence will inevitably end up treating other people with contempt and come to love conflict for its own sake, getting into fights (*kenka*) that end in nothing more than a meaningless death. They will cause anxiety to their parents and steal the fiefs of their lords. Even if they manage to perform "heroic deeds" in the defense of their honor, they are no different from a dog that has a strong bite. A samurai who has a heart should be ashamed of such things. [p. 115]

[Nakae Tojū, Tōju sensei zenshū, vol. 1, pp. 137–38; Nakae Tōju, in NST,
vol. 29, pp. 65, 115; RT]

KUMAZAWA BANZAN: CONFUCIAN PRACTICE IN SEVENTEENTH-CENTURY JAPAN

Nakae Tōju's achievement was to lay the basis for a Japanese Confucian practice that recognized the individual's subjectivity. He taught that human beings were endowed with a faculty akin to conscience, enabling them to determine their own conduct. But Tōju achieved this only after withdrawing from feudal society. Moreover, his later thought was colored by a mystical concern with salvation at the cost of the commitment to social action that is one aspect of

---

31. Han Xin was a famous general who served Liu Bang, the first emperor of the Han. Xiang Yu was the great Chu general who fought Liu Bang for the empire.

the Confucian vision. It thus was left to Tōju's best-known disciple, Kumazawa Banzan (1619–1691), to test his ideas more actively in contemporary feudal society.

Banzan was born in Kyoto, the son of a masterless samurai (*rōnin*). At the age of sixteen, he entered the service of Ikeda Mitsumasa (1609–1682), the Confucian-minded daimyo of the Okayama domain, celebrated as one of the "enlightened rulers" of his generation. But Banzan left Mitsumasa's service four years later and, like Tōju, retired to the countryside. Beginning in the autumn of 1641, he studied for some six months under the direct supervision of Tōju himself. Re-entering Mitsumasa's service in 1645, Banzan attempted—secretly at first—to practice the Confucianism that he had learned under Tōju. His efforts came to Mitsumasa's attention, and he was rapidly promoted to a position of influence in domain affairs. He had two tasks: to exemplify the samurai profession and to disseminate Confucian teaching, particularly Tōju's doctrines, known as Shingaku (Learning of the Mind-and-Heart), in the Okayama domain. For a brief period during the reconstruction following a destructive flood in 1654, Banzan seems to have influenced domain policies in a Confucian direction. The rapid promotion of an outsider, however, aroused hostility from Mitsumasa's hereditary vassals. Furthermore, Banzan's deviant form of the Learning of the Mind-and-Heart was perceived as subversive by a high *bakufu* authority. Banzan himself became ill, and in 1657 he resigned.

His mission to Confucianize the Okayama domain having failed, Banzan now moved to Kyoto, where he began studying Japanese culture, including the court musical tradition and *The Tale of Genji*. He also taught a circle of court nobles and others, but in 1667 he was expelled from the capital. Thereafter, an outsider, he lived a life of exile or semiexile, devoting his time to writing and teaching.

Like Tōju, Banzan was concerned with the problems of Confucian practice in Japanese society. His reflex was evangelical: he wished to see his country adopt Confucian morality and to re-create the arcadian society believed by Confucians to have existed in early antiquity. Like Tōju, Banzan was a relativist. But his approach was broader, more empirical, and, above all, more historical than Tōju's. Banzan explored both the problems of Confucian practice in Japan and the wider problem of political control against the background of cyclical historical evolution, as well as the particularities of the Japanese environment. His positive valuation of Japanese cultural identity did not, however, lead him to chauvinism. At heart, Banzan remained a universalist.

THE WAY AND METHODS

Kumazawa Banzan adopted Nakae Tōju's basic dualistic distinction between the absolute, transcendent, noumenal aspect of morality and its relative, objective manifestations in the phenomena of time and place. He phrased this dichotomy from the point of view of Confucian practice in terms of a transcendent "Way" and its objective manifestations, or "methods," that were relative to and prescriptive for only their particular time and place.

The Way (*michi*) and methods (*hō*) are separate. There is much misunderstanding of this and [much] identification of methods with the Way. Even where the sages of China are concerned, methods vary with successive ages. Still more, when transferred to Japan, many of them are impracticable. The Way consists of the Three Bonds and the Five Constant Virtues.[32] It is correlated with Heaven, earth, and humankind and with the five elements. Even when there was not yet a name for virtue or any of the sages' teachings, this Way was already practiced. Before humankind came into being, it was practiced in Heaven and earth; and before Heaven and earth were parted, it was practiced in the Supreme Void. Even if mankind were exterminated and Heaven and earth returned to nothing, it [the Way] would never perish. Still less [likely it would do so] in [these] latter ages.

As for methods, the sages systematized the good of things in response to time, place, and rank. For this reason methods are correlated with the Way in any one age. But when that age has passed and the human estate has changed, they cannot be employed, even by the sages. When what is incongruent is used, harm is actually done to the Way. What modern scholars practice as the Way is mostly methods. Since they are not congruent with the perfect good of time, place, and rank, it is not the Way.

[Kumazawa Banzan, *Zōtei Banzan zenshū*, vol. 2, pp. 63–64; IJM]

THE TRANSMISSION OF THE WAY TO JAPAN IN EARLY ANTIQUITY

Like many Japanese Confucians, Banzan took a Sinocentric view of the world that acknowledged China's worldwide moral and cultural leadership. He believed also that the Japanese imperial house had been founded by a Chinese sage, Tai Bo, uncle of King Wen, the founder of the Zhou dynasty (1122–206 B.C.E.) in China. Tai Bo performed much the same civilizing role in Japan that the ancient culture heroes of China had performed in that country. He also introduced the universal teachings of Confucian morality. Therefore, although its culture might have its own idiom, Japan was still part of a universal moral and cultural order. At the same time, the Tai Bo legend provided Banzan with a rational and euhemerist account of the origins of the Japanese imperial heritage.

---

32. The Three Bonds are those between ruler and minister, parent and child, and husband and wife. For Banzan, the Five Constant Virtues are the values of "humaneness, righteousness, ritual decorum, wisdom, and trustworthiness."

At this time [early Japanese antiquity], men were like animals. Since they were ignorant of agriculture, they lacked the five cereals; since they were ignorant of cooking, they ate the fruits of plants and trees and consumed raw meat. Since they were without women's work, they used layers of leaves and made furs and skins their apparel. Parents and children possessed the mind of mutual love but were ignorant of respect through ritual decorum.

When Tai Bo crossed [over to] Japan, he established the Way of human relationships, and through love, he taught respect. Transferring the attitude of respect toward parents, he determined the categories of superior and inferior; he instituted ritual decorum; and by acknowledging the sources of things, he informed [people] where they had come from. Finally, there were the rituals of venerating ancestors and Heaven-and-earth. [Tai Bo] systematized the rituals of marriage through go-betweens and emphasized the beginnings of human relationships. He established teachings, using as a basis the nature that men receive from Heaven, and he illuminated the principles endowed in all phenomena.

He taught men how, by cutting wood, to make spades, [and] by bending wood, to make mattocks. . . . Observing the seasons of Heaven and the advantages of earth, they created wet and dry fields; they scattered the five cereals; and in spring and summer they planted and mowed; and in autumn and winter they harvested and stored. . . .

Birds, beasts, serpents, and scorpions approached mankind and inflicted harm. Therefore, he [Tai Bo] had them, by making bows and arrows to repel them, perform the tasks of the hunter. By making nets [and] catching birds and fish, he helped them perform the tasks of fishermen. Had it not been so, birds and beasts would mingle with men, and they would be unable to cultivate. Finally, he made them ward off the wind and rain by making houses. . . . His compassion and beneficence to the realm and to the populace was like Heaven-and-earth giving birth to and nurturing the myriad creatures, with no exception. His knowledge was spiritually intelligent, like a mirror reflecting forms. The people of this land submitted to his virtue like [children] to their father and mother, and in awe of his god-like martial spirit, they made him their lord. . . .

[Kumazawa Banzan, *Zōtei Banzan zenshū*, vol. 6, app., pp. 3–4; IJM]

Banzan believed that Tai Bo's transforming influence had persisted throughout the long period of Japanese history that he called the "royal age" (ōdai), up until the reign of Go-Shirakawa and the beginning of the transition to warrior rule in the twelfth century. He found that the latter stages of this period had been recorded in a great work of literature, The Tale of Genji. *He valued this fictional romance very highly, even comparing it with the Chinese Confucian canonical* Classic of Odes. *This enthusiasm, unusual for a prominent Confucian, inspired Banzan to write a commentary on it. In his introduction to this work, he explained its value together with the historical mission of the imperial court to preserve Japan's ancient moral, cultural, and aesthetic heritage.*

Now the duration of the royal Way of Japan is long because it has not lost rites, music and letters and has not fallen into vulgar practices. Things that are excessively hard and strong do not last long; those that are generous and soft are long enduring. Things, like teeth, that are hard but drop out quickly or, like the tongue, that are soft but last to the end embody the principle of all things. The warrior houses take the power of the realm for a while through the awesomeness of their invincible strength, but like teeth falling out, they do not last long. The kings rest in softness and compliance but do not lose their rank. But when they are soft and have no virtue, the respect of others [toward them] is weak. When [the kings] are not the object of the shame and respect of others, even though they exist, it is as though they do not. In the end, they verge on extinction. What can perpetuate what has become extinct and afford the sight of the rituals, music, and letters of olden times is preserved in this novel [*The Tale of Genji*] alone. Therefore, the first thing to which one should pay attention in this novel is the fine style of remote ages. Rituals were correct and peaceable; their style of music [was] harmonious and elegant; [and] men and women alike were courtly. They constantly played court music, and their attitude was not degraded.

Next, the description of human feelings in the book is detailed. When a person is ignorant of human feelings, he frequently loses the harmony of the human relationships. When they are violated, the state lacks regulation, and the home is not ordered. For this reason, the *Maoshi* (*Classic of Odes*) preserves the debauched airs in order to inculcate familiarity with human feelings, both good and evil. Were the state to consist wholly of superior men, administration and punishments would not have a function. Since the Way of administration exists simply in order to teach ordinary people, it is impossible unless one knows human feeling and historical change. In these circumstances, this novel also contains exhaustive accounts of human feelings in various contexts and good descriptions of the way in which times continue to change. For the poems and the prose, [Murasaki Shikibu] described the temperaments of the characters as though she were drawing their portraits. This again is the great marvel of this novel's grasp of human feelings.

[Kumazawa Banzan, *Zōtei Banzan zenshū*, vol. 2, pp. 420–21; IJM])

BUDDHISM

Banzan attributed to a number of causes the demise of the royal age, the transition to warrior rule, and the instability that he believed to have characterized Japanese history since that time. Most salient were the ascendancy of Buddhism and the related problem of extravagance. He passionately believed that Buddhism had an almost entirely destructive influence in Japan. Like other Confucians of the period, he directed a sustained and vehement polemic against this rival persuasion, of whose numerical superiority and deep roots he must have been acutely aware. Banzan's hostility was directed both against the fundamental metaphysical assumptions of Buddhism and its belief in transmigration and against what he perceived as the moral degeneracy of particular sects. He especially delighted in quoting Buddhists' own self-recrimination.

Some time ago, a friend of mine questioned a Zen believer, asking him his opinion of the present-day Pure Land, Nichiren, and Honganji sects.

The Zen believer replied: "They are the lees and chaff of Shakyamuni, shards and pebbles craving for Buddhahood."

"How about Shingon?"

"It incorporates Daoism and Shinto and possesses only the form of Buddhism. They are the stupid ones among the masters of yin and yang."

"How about Tendai?"

"It is as though they cling to the theories of the sutras and become fixated with the footprints of the hare in the snow. They also bear a resemblance to Shingon. The rest are not worth speaking of."

"What about Zen?"

"Our sect is referred to as the sect of the Buddha's heart and regards enlightenment as the ultimate."

My friend said, "You are clear about other [sects]. Why should you be in the dark about yourselves? Tendai, Shingon, and Zen all may have been good in the past, but now they are 'pillagers of the people.'[33] Although the [miscreant rulers] Jie and Zhou were the descendants of [the paragon emperors] Yu and Tang, their evil had to be smitten. Lees, chaff, shards, and pebbles do no harm. But the harms inflicted on the realm by the Buddhists of the present are very great. The attitude and conduct of the rice wholesalers are to crave for a typhoon when the rice is in bud and flowering. In summer, they rejoice in expectation of a drought. Their purposes are to inflict pain and suffering on the people of the realm, to cause them to starve to death and so to get the profit for themselves. People like these are the disciples of the Ikkō and Nichiren sects, and when they go to a temple, they are told, with no attempt made to enliven their evil hearts that through the efficacy of the *nenbutsu* [invocation of the Amida Buddha], still with their evil desires, they will attain Buddhahood. When they go to a Nichiren temple, [they are told that] 'even those who have slandered the Lotus [Sutra] will actually attain Buddhahood.' The reason is that even slandering [implies] having heard the name of the sutra. Still more, they are told that even if only with one voice, when they invoke *Namu myōhō rengekyō* [Hail to the Lotus Sutra of the Marvelous Law], even an evil man who has killed lord or parent will, without doubt, achieve Buddhahood. There can be no greater demons in the world than they. To call them lees and chaff is flattery.

---

33. *Mencius* 6B:9 (i).

"The Zen sect has an even worse aspect than this. One understands that in the Zen of former days, unless one had the incipient springs of enlightenment, [monks] would have nothing to do with one. But the Zen of the present deludes even those who were not deluded. Provided only that one has obtained enlightenment, they say, it does not matter what one does. When the minds of eminent men of great estate have thus become confused [by Zen], they become overwhelmed by debauchery, take extravagance to the limit, impoverish the peasantry, cause suffering to the samurai, forget their civil and military occupations, and possess none of the attitudes and actions [appropriate to] rulers of men. This is the symbol of the destruction of the state. But without this kind of teaching, there would not be this many followers of Zen, nor would they achieve ascendancy. Offer your defense."

When [my friend] spoke thus, the Zen believer blushed and was speechless.

[Kumazawa Banzan, *Zōtei Banzan zenshū*, vol. 2, p. 76; IJM]

DEFORESTATION

Another, related cause of instability was extravagance. For Banzan, this was both a moral vice, in the form of pride, and an economic failing, in the form of excessive consumption. The excessive consumption of timber, in particular, was dangerous, for it resulted in deforestation, the silting of rivers, and flooding. Banzan believed that the condition of a country's forests determined its political fortunes, and he went so far as to base a theory of history on this belief.

From the three generations of the houses of [Minamoto] to the beginning of the Hōjō house, the aftermath of an age of disorder persisted, and the commodities of the realm were in insufficient supply. Thus, spontaneously, there was frugality, and halls and temples were not erected at will. During this period, the mountains grew luxuriant and the rivers became deep. Hōjō no Yasutoki and Tokiyori liked frugality and exercised nonextravagant control, so that [the Hōjō house] continued for nine generations. But with the long period of civil order, the temple buildings became more numerous year by year, and the spirit vapors of mountains and rivers again became weak. Since the world could not persist on this basis, the Taiheiki disturbance resulted. For a long time, the world was disunited. During this period, the rivers, marshes, and mountain forests again became deep. The house of Ashikaga continued for several generations; the extravagance of the world grew; temple buildings were everywhere constructed; and the strength of the mountains and rivers was again exhausted. When you see the splendid fancier's implements that have survived until the present as "articles from the age of Lord Higashiyama" [Ashikaga Yoshimasa], the extravagance of that age is obvious. After that, a major disorder followed; there was competition for possession of the realm; the government became only a name; and the disorder of the realm lasted a long time, until [Oda] Nobunaga. During this time, the hills grew luxuriant, as they originally had been, and the rivers again grew deep. During the fourteen generations of the descendants of [Ashikaga] Takauji, for 240 years, Nobunaga's exercise [reign] was [mere] twelve or thirteen years. Since Nobunaga, the unification of the world proceeded rapidly, and the world has become tranquil. The campaigns of Sekigahara and Osaka were sedentary affairs and were concluded with just one battle each. Hence they did not constitute an age of disorder. In fact, from [the time of] Lord [Toyotomi] Hideyoshi continuing to the present, the extravagance of the realm has grown day by day and month by month.

[Kumazawa Banzan, *Zōtei Banzan zenshū*, vol. 2, p. 236; IJM]

THE RELEVANCE OF RITUAL TO MODERN TIMES

Extravagance or excessive consumption separated contemporary Japan from the ancient Chinese past and made the rituals of the Confucian canon impracticable. What was needed was moral suasion, example, and education rather than reliance on formal institutions.

The abundance of utensils and objects and the extravagance of men must now have surpassed the richness of the height of prosperity of the Zhou dynasty. But the unfamiliarity of the people's minds with rituals and ceremonies is like [that in] the time of Fu Xi. Although the people of Fu Xi were unfamiliar with rituals and ceremonies, they were frugal, pure, and bounteous; their emotions and desires were few; and they had no [sense of] profit and loss The strength of the emotions and desires of the people of today and the depth of their [concern with] profit and loss were not acquired in mere decades or centuries. Their roots are hard and their dyes are deep. If we were suddenly to suppress the human feelings of worldly custom and abruptly block [its concern with] profit and loss, the Way [still] would not be practiced.

Teaching the people of today is like leading an infant. With children, one nourishes them and awaits the onset of their spirit wisdom (*shinchi*). With the world, one should put education first and await the desire for rites and ceremonies. When [a sense of] righteousness begins to show in a child of three, four, or five, it has an attitude of bashfulness. When it first acquires knowledge, it has the ability to distinguish between the beautiful and the ugly. But it cannot yet distinguish between righteousness and unrighteousness, nor has it acquired knowledge of good and evil or right and wrong. When it [a child] reaches the age of six to eight years, his attitude of declining and yielding (*jijō*) is born. Therefore, the sage waited until they reached the age of eight and only then admitted children to school. Instead of coercion, there was compliance with their endowment and age.

For the last five hundred or six hundred years, worldly customs have been like the age of a child of five or six. Through school ordinances, one should first teach the knowledge that discriminates between right and wrong and good and evil and stimulate the righteousness that knows shame. After the passage of several decades and centuries, one should await the superior man of the future and have him inaugurate rites and ceremonies.

[Kumazawa Banzan, *Zōtei Banzan zenshū*, vol. 1, pp. 122–23; IJM]

THE ECONOMY

Banzan's interest in the contemporary world extended to economic problems. He provided one of the earliest analyses of the operations of the system of exchanging rice for money, showing how it worked to the disadvantage of the samurai estate. Indeed, the reactionary, antimercantilist tone of his writing in this area influenced the direction of samurai economic thought for much of the Tokugawa period.

QUESTION: In latter ages, when there is a good harvest and food is abundant, the gentlemen are in "distress and want";[34] [but] when the crops fail and food is scarce, the people starve, high and low by turns suffer, and the impasse results in civil disorder. Why is this?

ANSWER: There are many causes for this, but the major sources are three:

First, when large and great cities alike are located in places of easy access by river or sea, extravagance grows daily and is difficult to stem. Merchants grow rich and gentlemen poor.

Second, the use of unhulled grain as a medium of exchange has gradually declined. When gold, silver, and copper are predominantly used, commodities gradually become expensive, and the gold and silver of the realm gradually go into the hands of the merchants, and those of great and small estate alike do not have enough for their use.

Third, when the appropriate ceremonial forms (*shiki*) are not used, matters become complicated, and objects proliferate. Gentlemen exchange their stipend rice for gold, silver, and copper to purchase things. When the price of rice and unhulled grain is low and that of commodities is high, they do not have enough for their use. Furthermore, when business becomes complicated and things proliferate, they [gentlemen] become increasingly poor and in distress and want. When gentlemen are in "distress and want," they demand twice as much from the people. Therefore, in years of good harvest there is insufficiency, and in years of crop disaster, [the people] suffer from starvation

---

34. *Analects* 20:1.

and exposure. When gentlemen and people are in distress and want, the artisans and merchants lose the means to exchange for rice. Only the great merchants become wealthier and wealthier. This is because the power over resources is in the hands of the commoners. But the ruler of a state or lord of the world should not for a moment entrust the power over wealth and honor to others. When one entrusts power over wealth and honor to merchants, a struggle will ensue with the feudal princes over wealth. Later, the wealth of the domains will disappear; the state will perish; and the realm will be thrown into disorder.[35]

When the realm is in disorder, the wealth of merchants becomes their enemy. Because the tiger's fur has a distinctive pattern, it suffers the calamity of the hunt; because merchants have a lot of gold and silver, they become the slaves of bandits or lose their lives. Even insentient plants and trees, when their time comes, drop their leaves and wither. Their prosperity and decline are natural to them. Why should there be any reason for those who devote themselves to their own profit and cause suffering to the crowd to last long?

[Kumazawa Banzan, Zōtei Banzan zenshū, vol. 1, pp. 333–35; IJM]

QUESTIONS ON THE GREAT LEARNING
(DAIGAKU WAKUMON)

In the final years of his life, Banzan, fearing an invasion by the Manchus and a crisis in his country, was inspired to propose a program of reconstruction. His views are expressed in his Questions on the Great Learning, written around 1686. Since he held no official position entitling him to propose policies, when his opinions became known to the political authorities in Edo, they were interpreted as seditious, and Banzan was imprisoned in Koga Castle. In sum, he proposed the devolution of samurai society, de-urbanization, a degree of demilitarization, and the reversion to rice as a staple currency. These measures would be accompanied by a reduction in taxes and a program of reforestation. Banzan also proposed measures for cultural renaissance through the diffusion of court culture to the feudal provinces.

The following passage, urging the promotion of the Neo-Confucian Way (Dōgaku), echoes the ideal of universal schooling that Zhu Xi proposed in his preface to the Great Learning.[36] Banzan believed that instead of withdrawing from society into

---

35. Accepting the emendations to the second edition attributed to Banzan himself.
36. See de Bary and Bloom, eds., Sources of Chinese Tradition, 2nd ed., vol. 1, pp. 721–25.

Buddhist orders, the court nobility should take the lead in encouraging education as the best means of achieving a national reformation.[37]

The Court Nobility as Carriers of the Neo-Confucian Way to the Provinces

QUESTION: If only those who embraced Buddhism with their hearts and practiced the three disciplines of the precepts, meditation, and wisdom were permitted to take Buddhist orders, those among the imperial princes and sons of the court nobility who were sincerely motivated would be rare. How would [the others] do?

ANSWER: When the Way is practiced, there is a solution, without royal children and the sons and daughters of the nobility [needing to] take Buddhist orders. . . . At some time in the past, when because of civil disorder, there was no income from the estates of the palace and the court nobility, many people sought out relatives and stayed in the country. I heard that among those court nobles, there was someone who cherished [the following] hope:

"Would that the person who unified the realm and became shogun might be fond of the Neo-Confucian Way (Dōgaku)! If the ancient schools were revived in the capital and there were schools as of old in the provinces, there would not be enough qualified teachers. Even the school that survives in form only at Ashikaga has no teachers and so has been entrusted to monks. There is no justification for entrusting schools for human relationships to monks. In order to increase the numbers of teachers in the provinces, in the schools of the capital all the sons of those from the emperor down to the court nobility, with no grant of office or rank made from birth, would go to school as commoners do and be made to learn letters and music. The sons of [professional court] musicians and of Shinto priests would [also] be enrolled to wait on and serve the princes and court nobles, and the government would pay their expenses. During classes they would have the same seats and study together, so that [the princes and nobles] would learn music. A prince among them who has the virtue of humaneness would succeed to rank, and those among the court nobility who possessed talent and knowledge would be made to perpetuate their lineages, while those who have gained expertise in letters and music would be sent to the provinces.

"[In the provinces,] princes would be awarded a rank equivalent to [that of] the sons of regents or ministers; the sons of regent families,

---

37. For the plan for Banzan's Shizutani School in Okayama, see chap. 25.

a rank equivalent to [that of] councillors, [thus] lowering their ranks; and they would be made the guests of their respective provinces. They could have salaries of 2,000 *koku* for a large province, and those provinces of around 1,000 *koku* could combine [them] to hire a teacher. Some would be attached to those provincial schools assessed at more than 100,000 *koku*. Those among the sons of musicians and Shinto priests able in music and letters would become their assistants. Large provinces would take five to six [assistants]; medium-size provinces, four to five; small ones, three to four; and they should be granted income-support lands separately. The princesses and daughters of court nobles would go as brides for those provincial guests.

"These arrangements would be restricted to one generation. From their sons on, they would become commoners in their provinces. Some might become rural primary school teachers. Those with talent and aptitude would carry out the province's [administrative] business. But new appointees would be sent from the capital to the provincial schools. If this happened, the manners in the provinces would become civil and not rude. The lord of the province would, *a fortiori*, learn the correct rites and music and not learn from evil. Those even more talented would be appointed teachers to the government and summoned as guests. They would be called 'national teachers,' [for] to regard monks as national teachers here, too, like the teachers of the Ashikaga school, is a mistake.

"Since all warriors are vassals of the shogunate, the rituals are strict and the dialogue is difficult. But since the court nobility would be like guests of the shogunate, if the shogun were to make a man of learning and talent his teacher and a man expert in scores his musical companion, there would be many benefits. The feudal princes, also, are rulers of their provinces. so that the [samurai of the] entire province are their vassals. Here, too, if the sons of the court nobility were to come as guests [to serve as] teachers at schools, there would be friendship and [other] benefits."

So he spoke. This person's words were right.

The Institutional Reconstruction of Society

The institutional framework of society was to be reformed through "ceremonial forms" (*shiki*), codes of conduct whose sanction, in the high Confucian manner, would be social shame rather than laws and punishments.

QUESTION: How should the ceremonial forms be determined?
ANSWER: A person of warrior provenance who knows the Way and who is expert in human feelings and historical change would be made an

officer to determine the ceremonial forms. He would be aided by someone knowledgeable in matters Japanese and Chinese, and they would draw up several tens of articles. The ruler, his senior vassals, [and] the upper, middle, and lower samurai would be seated close together to discuss and classify them. They would express their opinions about [any] disadvantages, and the ruler and officer would decide on a [reasonable solution] and have a fair copy [of the articles] made. Again, orders would be issued to the domains and discrepancies with place and human feelings would be audited, the "admirable words"[38] of people of intelligence obtained, and adjustments made. Every fifty years the world undergoes small changes, and every five hundred years, a major change. Some of the ceremonial forms of old may be used now, and others may not be used.

Ceremonial forms are not legal regulations (*hatto*). With legal regulations, the fewer there are, the better it is. Gaozu of the Han [dynasty] shortened the law into three articles, and the realm was well governed. But when ceremonial forms are detailed, the world becomes calm, and honorable and base [people] are at peace. Those who violate law are punished, but those who violate ceremonial forms are not punished but merely face shame. When shame accumulates, it becomes impossible to appear in company. Therefore, although there are no punishments, offenses die out.

There follows a detailed discussion of the ritual forms and courtesies that should govern conduct of lords and samurai.

[Kumazawa Banzan, *Zōtei Banzan zenshū*, vol. 3, pp. 274–78; IJM]

NAKAE TŌJU'S SUCCESSORS IN THE ŌYŌMEI SCHOOL

After Nakae Tōju died, his disciples split into two streams, one emphasizing introspective self-cultivation and personal ethics and the other applying Tōju's teachings to the practical problems of government and public ethics. The latter direction, as we have seen, was typified by Kumazawa Banzan. Tōju's most prominent disciple of the introspective bent was Fuchi Kōzan (1617–1686), a samurai from Sendai who went to Edo to serve a *bakufu* vassal with a fief in Ōmi. When his lord sent him to Ōmi, Kōzan heard about Tōju and became his disciple in 1644. After Tōju's death some four years later, Kōzan opened a small academy in Kyoto and built a shrine in Tōju's memory. His reverence

---

38. Legge, trans., *Book of Documents*, "Counsels of the Great Yü," p. 125.

for Tōju and promotion of his teachings seem to have contributed significantly to Tōju's later reputation as a sage. Kōzan is said to have had disciples in twenty-four provinces, the most prominent being in Osaka, Mimasaka, Ise, Edo, Kumamoto, and Aizu.

Later, in the early eighteenth century, Miwa Shissai (1669–1744) revived the Wang Yangming school (J. Yōmeigaku), propagating it for three decades as a distinct teaching separate from other strands of Neo-Confucianism. By contrast, Satō Issai (1772–1859) (see chap. 32) was an outstanding example, at the very center of late-Edo-period *bakufu* education, of an influential teacher of Yangming's ideas who synthesized them with those of Zhu Xi.

Miwa Shissai's earlier efforts at propagation helped make Yangming learning widely known during the eighteenth century, to the point that it became one of the four schools of learning prohibited at the *bakufu* college in the Kansei Prohibition of Heterodoxy of 1790. It is not clear how much this prohibition reflected a perception of the subversive potential of Yōmeigaku; a long time had passed since Hayashi Razan had accused Banzan of involvement in subversive plots, and teachers like Shissai taught nothing that was politically questionable. After the prohibition, however, the number of Yōmeigaku followers paradoxically grew more rapidly than ever before, largely through the influence of Satō Issai and Ōshio Chūsai.

FUCHI KŌZAN

INNATE KNOWLEDGE (FILIALITY) AS THE ESSENTIAL LIFE FORCE

The emphasis in Tōju's teachings on family-centered ethics and the link between the natural/spiritual world and human society, in contrast to the Zhu Xi school's emphasis on scholarship and political ethics, helps account for their appeal to the peasantry, especially the rising class of independent cultivators in Aizu. Fuchi Kōzan seems to have stressed even more than Tōju did that innate knowledge (here equated with filial piety) is the fundamental life force generating, underlying, and pervading all things and affairs.

1. Human beings are originally born with innate knowledge (*ryōchi*).

2. There is nothing that innate knowledge does not penetrate and nothing of human concern that it does not touch. . . . The perfect sincerity (*shisei*) of innate knowledge does not cease to operate even in the most ordinary person. . . . All the idiosyncrasies of the mind come from believing in thoughts. . . . If you believe instead in innate knowledge, how will the various desires be able to move your mind?

3. The way of ordinary human relationships should not be seen as just a realm of moral effort unconnected with the original substance. If one seeks

innate knowledge in the realm of high abstractions, one will make it only into something far away. One's facial expression and manner of speaking are themselves the basis of virtue.

4. People tend to stiffen up when fearful or worried. But if your body has the slightest stiffness, everything you do will be difficult and you cannot feel free. Teaching people how not to stiffen up is the whole secret of Tōju's teaching.[39] . . . The original mind is the true master (*shusai*) of the self. When it is expanded, it reaches beyond Heaven and earth; when it is contracted, it hides in the mystery of the square inch [of the heart]. Accordingly, we should revere this master (*shujinkō*) as the highest thing in Heaven and earth and as the first principle of human life.

5. A person who wishes to realize the great Way for himself should first purify his body and mind and seek the assistance of the gods. No one has ever achieved something great without some reliance on divine assistance.

[Fuchi Kōzan, "Kōzan sensei jikyōroku," *kan* 5, 1, 3, 4; BS]

MIWA SHISSAI

Miwa Shissai was born in 1669, the son of a Kyoto physician whose ancestors had been officiants at the Miwa Shrine. He resolved early in life to become either a physician or a Confucian scholar. At the age of nineteen, he became a disciple of Satō Naokata of the Kimon school. But after five years of study under Naokata and three of service as a tutor to Naokata's lord, Shissai resigned his position because of growing doubts about Naokata's version of Confucianism. Between 1697 and 1699, Shissai openly rejected Naokata's teaching of seeking moral principles externally, with its emphasis on intellectual inquiry (*kyūri*) over everyday moral practice, turning instead to the philosophy of Wang Yangming. In general terms, Shissai's rejection of Naokata shares some similarities with Itō Jinsai's critique of Zhu Xi, and indeed Naokata lumped together both the Wang Yangming school (Yōmeigaku) and Jinsai's learning under what was for him a pejorative term, "practical learning" (*jitsugaku*)—that is, learning that gave too little attention to the correct understanding of objective moral principles. It was several years before he forgave Shissai's apostasy.[40] In 1712 Shissai published the first Japanese-annotated edition of Wang Yangming's *Chuanxi lü* (*Instructions for Practical Living*). In 1726 he founded his own

---

39. Literally, "the family recipe" of Tōju, a metaphor based on the tradition of keeping the knowledge of specific medicines secret within a family to ensure its future livelihood.

40. Perhaps with the Ako *rōnin* in mind, Naokata wrote *A Discussion on Wang* [*Yangming*] *Learning* (*Ōgaku rondan*): "If you just act with the belief that you have loyalty and filial piety within yourself, but without a knowledge of moral principles, then even if you have no selfishness in your heart, you may end up as a criminal in the eyes of your lord and father."

academy in Edo, the Meirindō (Hall for the Clarifying of Moral Relations), where he taught many disciples until his death at age seventy-six in 1744.

EVERYDAY METHOD OF THE MIND
(SHISSAI NICHIYŌ SHINPŌ)

The method of mind control central to Neo-Confucian moral cultivation and spiritual praxis is based on Zhu Xi's sixteen-word formula (set forth in his preface to the *Mean*) concerning the human mind and mind of the Way, and the need to direct human thought and feelings according to the dictates of moral principle in the mind of the Way. The following extracts are from an account of Miwa Shissai's views on the matter, referring to those of the Cheng brothers, Zhu Xi, Wang Yangming, and the Korean scholar Yi T'oegye. Shissai views the matter primarily in relation to a person's active engagement of the will—his personal resolve (*kokorozashi*) or fundamental commitment to the Way.

1. At fifteen, Confucius set his heart on learning. At thirty, he established himself; that is, he established his resolve (*kokorozashi*). At forty, he was no longer perplexed; that is, his resolve no longer vacillated. Passing through age fifty and sixty, [finally] at seventy he was able to follow whatever his heart desired without overstepping the bounds,[41] in other words, without overstepping the bounds of his resolve. Thus we know that resolve is the whole substance of learning from the stage of beginner right through to sagehood. . . . Establishing this resolve is the practice (*kufū*) of preserving the Heavenly principle of the original mind-and-heart. . . .

2. If the mind is truly set on sagehood, like a cat waiting to pounce on a mouse, there will be no leisure for the mind of [selfish] desire to arise. . . . A person's words and actions are the vestments of his resolve; if they are released for a moment, his resolve will freeze. Rightness and the Way are the nourishment of a person's resolve; once neglected, the resolve will starve. . . . [pp. 228–30]

4. According to Zhu Xi, that which feels hunger and thirst and perceives heat and cold is the human mind, while that from which the four beginnings of virtue arise is the mind of the Way. . . . But if the so-called mind of the Way exists outside physical nature, it is something other than the everyday practice of human ethics. That would make it something empty, mysterious, and silent like the deviant Buddhist teachings of directly perceiving one's nature and achieving Buddhahood. [pp. 260–61]

[*Shissai nichiyō shinpō; Nihon no yōmeigaku*, vol. 1, in *Yōmeigaku taikei* 8, pp. 228–30, 260–61; BS]

---

41. *Analects* 2:4.

[handwritten notes at top:]
- Threat of christianity
- Thought christians may have been trying to conquer them, which they were

Chapter 23

THE EVANGELIC FURNACE:
JAPAN'S FIRST ENCOUNTER WITH THE WEST

[handwritten notes:]
- San Filipe Incident
• Spanish Captain threatens Hideyoshi, tells him methods they use to conquer people, which is similar to the situations going on in Japan

The first Europeans known to have visited Japan were two or three Portuguese traders who arrived there in 1543 or possibly 1542 aboard a Chinese junk. The date varies according to the source, as do the names and number of the voyagers. Their landfall was Tanegashima, an island to the south of Kyushu. Within a few years, the Europeans were calling regularly at Kyushu ports, having identified Japan as an immensely profitable market for Chinese silk and other luxury goods from overseas. A "new and deranged greed" seized his compatriots and carried them there, according to the Portuguese adventurer and fabulist Fernão Mendes Pinto (ca. 1510–1583). Mercantile cupidity, however, was by no means the sole or the most significant factor in the history of the initial encounter between Europe and Japan. Indeed, that history has a far broader dimension. Some Europeans were drawn to Japan by a "fervent zeal for the glory of God," as Mendes Pinto also noted correctly. Luís de Camões (ca. 1524–1580) put it best of all in the Portuguese national epic, *The Lusiads,* by combining the two referents as he invoked Japan. Richard Fanshawe's translation of 1655 renders Camões's lines memorably: "*Japan* . . . yeelding the best *Silver-mine*: / Which th' *Evangellic Furnace* shall refine."[1]

---

1. Pinto, *Peregrinação*, chaps. 137, 203; Camões, *The Lusiads* 10:131.

The first evangelists to preach the Christian gospel in a country described by its inhabitants as the "Land of the Gods" were three Jesuit missionaries led by the Basque priest Francis Xavier (1506–1552), who landed at Kagoshima in southern Kyushu in 1549. Xavier, who had earned a master of arts degree and held a teaching position at the University of Paris before becoming one of the founding members of the Society of Jesus—a man whose indefatigable spirit led him through many travails to the glory of sainthood—was surely as splendid a representative of sixteenth-century Counter-Reformation Europe as could be imagined in Japan. Indeed, Catholic missionaries proved to be Europe's most important representatives in the first encounter between the two cultures.

The merchants remained peripheral. Their ships never ventured beyond Kyushu and mainly used harbors in that island's westernmost province, Hizen. From 1571, they largely confined themselves to one of those harbors, Nagasaki. The missionaries were more venturesome. From the start, they sought recognition from not only local but also national authorities and accordingly tried to establish themselves in Kyoto, the political and cultural center of the Japanese realm. By the 1640s, when persecution brought their activities in that realm to an end, the missionaries had penetrated almost all of its more than sixty provinces.

The missionaries came to Japan in order to convert it. Put another way, their mission was to transmit a central complex of Western culture—their religion— to that country. But they also acted as the disseminators in the West of knowledge about Japanese civilization. The many and effusive accounts of their trials and triumphs in Japan that were published throughout Catholic Europe proved to be best-sellers then and remain of interest to historians now. Even more significant were the Jesuits' Japanese publications. The movable-type printing apparatus they brought from Portugal in 1590 was the first of its sort in Japan. Their mission press, which remained active in that country until a nationwide persecution broke out in 1614, not only contributed some splendid adaptations of European masterpieces, including *Aesop's Fables* and *The Imitation of Christ* by Thomas à Kempis, to Japanese literature, but also published lexicographic and linguistic works that remain of great importance to an appreciation of contemporary Japanese language and culture. The mission's effect on Japanese intellectual history in the early modern era was not inconsiderable, as controversialist works of a high level were produced on both sides of the vast ideological divide separating apologists intent on establishing the paramountcy of Christian truth from defenders of the East Asian value system's Japanese variant. To be sure, it would be fruitless to look in Japan for an equivalent of the sophisticated intellectual interchange that Christian missionaries enjoyed with representatives of the elite in China from the 1590s onward. The scholarly traditions of China's governing class made its members more interested in dialogue with the European priests, some of whom were highly educated and cultured men, than was the case in Japan, a country dominated not by literati but by samurai. Indeed, the Japanese ruling class had a tradition forged in war, which was seemingly Japan's natural condition when the first Jesuits arrived. The violent temperament of the samurai had not yet been tamed by the climate of peace brought on by the very same rulers who forcibly terminated the mission. Japan was not as amenable as China to intellectual methods of penetration, and so the Jesuits, while pursuing their characteristic strategy of first persuading the elite and then capturing the populace, used different tactics in the two countries.

In the end, the missionaries' Japanese enterprise foundered on a fundamental antinomy. The First Commandment demands of all Christians absolute loyalty to God. That dependence on an extraterrestrial sphere of justification could not be reconciled with the system of secular loyalties imposed on Japan by the founders of its early modern state. To be sure, insofar as obstacles from political authority were concerned, the mission enjoyed relatively clear sailing for most of the first four decades of the "Christian century" of Japan, as the years 1549 to 1639 are sometimes rather fancifully called. But that was due to extraordinary historical conditions.

At the time of the first missionaries' arrival, Japan was in a state of great disorder. Conflicts among regional grandees, provincial barons, armed leagues of yeomen, and confederations of militant Buddhist sectarians had swept the country for the better part of a century, reduced the institutions of central authority—the imperial court and the Ashikaga shogunate in Kyoto—to ciphers, and turned Japan into a fragmented realm. The epoch from 1467 to 1568 is justly called the era of Sengoku, the "country at war." Where assorted petty powers, constantly on the lookout for the main chance, competed with one another, a niche existed for the foreigners whose commerce might put one of the ambitious contenders at an advantage over his adversaries. Hence the daimyo and the smaller barons of Kyushu eagerly courted the Portuguese traders, whose ships bore not only merchandise but also missionaries and munitions.

Paradoxically, their pursuit of temporal interests made some of these lords accessible to a spiritual message. Put more concretely, they welcomed the priests in order to attract the traders. So there existed a good environment for a symbiosis. In a few remarkable cases, Japanese lords not only converted to Christianity themselves in order to demonstrate their bona fides to the Europeans but even forced the populace of their domains to adopt the alien faith, persecuting the native religions in their eagerness to accommodate the foreigners.

For a time, Japan's fragmented state permitted the spread of Christianity on a domanial and even a regional scale. But from 1568 to 1615—the Azuchi–Momoyama era of Japanese history—the country was reunited under a single system of authority by the three hegemons Oda Nobunaga (1534–1582), Toyotomi Hideyoshi (1537–1598), and Tokugawa Ieyasu (1543–1616). In the realm built by these unifiers, there was no room for a competing structure of allegiances. For that reason, they were unyielding in their aim to eliminate the secular power of the Buddhist ecclesiastical institutions. Unfortunately for the Christian church of Japan, they looked at it in an analogous light and concluded that it, too, was a dangerous structure.

Anti-Christian decrees began to be issued by the regime of the unifiers in 1587, under Hideyoshi. At first, they were not rigorously or universally enforced. In 1614, however, the Tokugawa shogunate started a general persecution of Christianity. The missionaries were forced to leave the country or go underground. Those who stayed were hunted down. The members of their flock confronted a choice between apostasy and martyrdom. Most abjured Christianity, if only on the surface, but many defied their tormenters, refused to recant, and were put to death for their faith. More than two thousand cases of martyrdom, many of them involving multiple individuals, are recorded. Japanese Christianity was melted down in the crucible of the early modern regime.

For twenty-five years after the Bateren—as the padres, Christian priests, are called in contemporary Japanese sources—were banned by the shogunate in 1614, the Portuguese traders were permitted to conduct business in Nagasaki, although they were suspected, with good reason, of secretly sustaining whatever Japanese Christianity there was left. To be sure, after 1632 no missionary was smuggled into Japan without being immediately arrested.[2] Nevertheless, the authorities did not relax their vigilance. In 1639 Portuguese merchants, too, were expelled, as the shogunate sought to isolate the country from all possible contact with Catholic influences. For 215 years thereafter, the Dutch merchants of the United East India Company (VOC), which had maintained a trading factory in Japan since 1609, were the only Europeans permitted to reside there. Those years are often called the era of Sakoku, the "closed country," although in view of the continuous Dutch presence this formula is not entirely sound, as it would lose much of its meaning if the anti-Catholic elements were taken out of the equation. The Protestant Dutch could stay because the Tokugawa realized that they were not carriers of the Catholic contagion. Even so, they were quarantined on Deshima, an artificial island in Nagasaki harbor.

So the "Christian century" ended in 1639. But how did it run its course?

After some initial missteps, the mission's founding father, Francis Xavier, came to appreciate that his religious endeavor would not prosper in Japan unless it gained the favor of secular lords; that those lords' measure of involvement in this spiritual enterprise could increase only if associated with their pursuit of material self-interest; and that ceremony and a display of authority were necessary in dealing with the powerful in that country, for one gained nothing by

---

2. Mancio Konishi, S.J. (b. 1600), returned to his native country in 1632 after being ordained in Rome. He was the last priest to remain at large, but he appears to have been tracked down and put to death in 1644.

addressing them as a beggar. This realization became the cornerstone of the Jesuits' mission policy in Japan. Xavier's successors continued to court feudal lords who might shelter them and further their activities. Some of those lords they managed to convince and even to convert.

The first great (if, in the end, fatal) success of that policy and the illustrative specimen of that famous (if thoroughly unstable) category, the so-called Christian daimyo—Kirishitan daimyo, in the parlance of those days—was Ōmura Sumitada (1533–1587). The case of Dom Bartolomeu, as Sumitada was known after his baptism in the early summer of 1563, is the perfect example of the symbiosis among Japanese magnates, Jesuit missionaries, and Portuguese merchants. It is clear from the records of the Jesuits themselves that having identified Sumitada as one who was likely to cooperate, they targeted him for special attention, suggesting that he would derive not only spiritual but also temporal profits from converting to Christianity. The Jesuits not only persuaded him to embrace their religion but, in the end, also got him to cede a portion of his domain to their society. It is just as clear from the context of Japanese history that Sumitada cooperated with the foreigners because he thought he must in order to survive. His lordship was precarious. Far from being a great name, he was in fact one of the weaker of the barons fighting over his corner of western Kyushu. Among his few valuable assets, however, were harbors convenient to the Portuguese traders from Macao on the South China Sea. Desperate for the support that he was assured would come his way from the Portuguese, he became the Jesuits' client.

Sumitada's expectations were substantiated in the 1560s and 1570s, as were those of the missionaries and the merchants. Armed Portuguese trade ships were steered to Dom Bartolomeu's harbors. On more than one occasion, those ships were given the opportunity to demonstrate the superiority of Western weapons on behalf of this Kirishitan baron. Made fully aware that privileged access to the Portuguese vessels and their cargoes was vital to his interests, Sumitada went to extremes in order to secure that access. In 1574, he was persuaded by the Jesuits to extinguish "idol" worship in his lands—that is, to destroy the icons, the abodes, and the practice of the native religions and to require all his subjects, under pain of exile, to turn Christian. Some sixty thousand of the populace were baptized, and the Ōmura domain became a solidly Christian territory. In 1580, Dom Bartolomeu went even further. About to be reduced to fealty by Ryūzōji Takanobu (1529–1584), a far more powerful regional lord, Sumitada concluded that he could keep an interest in the most valuable part of his domain by giving it away to a third party, and so he donated the magnificent harbor of Nagasaki, the habitual anchorage of the Portuguese trading ships, to the Society of Jesus.

The man who formally accepted Dom Bartolomeu's preemptive cession of Nagasaki and was responsible for making elaborate plans to safeguard the new Jesuit colony with forts, munitions, and artillery was Padre Alexandro Valignano

(1539–1606). In 1573 the general superior of the Society of Jesus in Rome had appointed him visitor of its Indian Province, making Valignano the society's plenipotentiary in a vast mission area that extended across the regions penetrated by the Portuguese in South, Southeast, and East Asia. The general's confidence in him was not misplaced, as Valignano had truly exceptional creative powers, even if those powers were not so much intellectual or spiritual as organizational and political. He is known particularly for fostering methods of "accommodation" with the missionaries' host cultures. (As will be seen, he prescribed them for the Jesuits of Japan.) In the history of the Jesuits in Asia, Valignano's name deserves to be ranked right alongside Xavier's.

Valignano first set foot in Japan in July 1579 for a tour of inspection that lasted for two and a half years and was marked by his intense involvement in the politics of symbiosis. He persuaded the captain who brought him to Japan to steer for a harbor in the territory of the Kyushu lord Arima Harunobu (1567?– 1612), rather than sail to the Portuguese ships' habitual port of call in the Ōmura domain, because he wanted to attract Harunobu to Christianity. Valignano attained his purpose by supplying Harunobu's forts with food and munitions purchased with a considerable outlay of the Jesuits' meager funds. The foreign aid saved this beleaguered baron from disaster. Shortly before Easter 1580, Harunobu reciprocated by adopting the Christian religion, the baptismal name Protasio, and the characteristic policy of the "Kirishitan daimyo." Throughout his domain, the "idols" were destroyed, their shrines demolished, and their priests banished; by the beginning of 1582, some twenty thousand of the domain's population had been led to the baptismal font.

When Valignano left Japan in February 1582 at the end of his first visit, no fewer than 150,000 converts were under the Jesuits' spiritual care there. Over the previous decade, their number had quintupled. These were grounds for optimism.

When Valignano returned in July 1590 for his second visit, however, Japan was a different country. Oda Nobunaga, who had humored the missionaries, was dead. Nagasaki was no longer a Jesuit colony. Nobunaga's erstwhile vassal Toyotomi Hideyoshi had inherited the task of national unification and made spectacular progress toward completing it. On conquering Kyushu in 1587, he had confiscated the Europeans' port city and made it a part of his immediate domain. Since that conquest, the Jesuits had operated in Japan under a stay of execution. Having anathematized their actions as "unheard of" and "miscreant," Hideyoshi made it apparent that if he tolerated their presence in the country at all, it was only on account of his forbearance. The scale of the difficulties they faced had expanded. No longer could a niche for the Christian mission be defined in regional terms. Rather, the question of the mission's continued existence or extinction was subjected to the verdict of the head of a national regime. In other words, Hideyoshi made Christianity into a national problem.

What were the reasons for his harsh judgment? Their history of forced conversions harmed the missionaries. Their pretensions in regard to Nagasaki made them suspect in the eyes of the unifier. Moreover, Hideyoshi was not blind to the display of willful ecclesiastical politics put on by Vice Provincial Gaspar Coelho (d. 1590), whom Valignano had left in charge of the Jesuits' Japanese enterprise. This mission superior was a military adventurer intent on forming an axis of "Kirishitan daimyo" ready, if need be, to forswear their terrestrial allegiances and make war for their religion's sake. Because the Japanese lords were realists, Coelho could not make this mirage materialize, but he was inveterate in its pursuit. Worse, he made his willingness to act as a broker of military assistance known to Hideyoshi just as the hegemon (with an eye toward an invasion of Korea and China) was planning his descent on Kyushu.

Coelho failed to realize how deeply Hideyoshi distrusted priests of any kind who had political pretensions and meddled in military affairs. Hideyoshi dissimulated. Before Kyushu was conquered, he did not want to dismiss the possibility that Coelho might prove useful. In June 1586 he even issued the vice provincial a charter guaranteeing him and his padres the freedom to preach their gospel "in all the lands of Japan." Even after all of Kyushu had been subjugated by Hideyoshi's overwhelming military force and all the island's great and petty lords had submitted to him abjectly, Coelho continued to parade his magnificence before the hegemon. The would-be daimyo of a Kirishitan Nagasaki sailed on his own naval vessel, a European-rigged ship armed with artillery, to congratulate the conquering hero on his victory and entertained Hideyoshi on board this vessel. Less than a week later, on the morning of July 25, 1587, Hideyoshi presented Coelho with the notorious decree that ordered the Bateren out of the country.

Having issued his edict, the hegemon chose not to enforce it. Not wanting to jeopardize the smooth flow of the Portuguese trade, he, too, in his way, became part of the symbiosis. For the better part of a decade, he did not pursue the solution of the Christian problem any further. Indeed, in the early 1590s Christianity reemerged in public and in fashion at his court. Kirishitan lords were prominent among the generals who served Hideyoshi loyally in the war of aggression that he fought from 1592 to 1598 in Korea. Jesuit chaplains accompanied the Kirishitan soldiers who sailed to the peninsula in his invasion force.

A shipwreck brought this period of temporary grace to an end. In 1593 a group of Franciscan monks arrived in Japan as ambassadors from the Spanish colonial authorities in the Philippines. Not content with conducting diplomatic business with Hideyoshi, they stayed on to preach the Christian faith with what the Jesuits viewed as an excess of evangelic zeal. When caution was urged on the friars, because in fact they were flouting Hideyoshi's law, they responded by condemning their fellow missionaries for a lack of courage and reliance on subterfuge. By itself, this intramural wrangle might not have brought about a fatal outcome. When the Spanish galleon *San Felipe* ran aground off the coast of Shikoku in October 1596, however, the ship's pilot apparently tried bombast as a means of saving the rich cargo from confiscation. According to the Jesuits, he regaled Hideyoshi's agents with tales of the Spanish Empire's might and asserted that a missionary fifth column commonly paved the way for its conquests. Franciscan sources, on the contrary, maintain that it was not the ship's pilot but their Jesuit confreres who maligned them. Which side's account was more accurate cannot be ascertained, but whichever it was, the incident's consequences were tragic. The missionaries' mutual recriminations engendered suspicions of their European patrons' imperialist designs and incited Hideyoshi into ordering the first bloody persecution of Christianity in Japan. Six Franciscans, three Jesuits, and seventeen Japanese laymen were paraded in tumbrels from Kyoto to Nagasaki and crucified there on February 5, 1597. They are known as the Twenty-six Saints of Japan. Christianity was demonstratively proscribed once again.

The tyrannical Hideyoshi had only a year and a half left to live, but his demise merely opened the way for the rise of even grimmer anti-Christian despots. It is true that under Tokugawa Ieyasu, Hideyoshi's successor as national hegemon, Christianity enjoyed a kind of Indian summer that lasted for a dozen years. Indeed, in the first decade of the seventeenth century the mission, at least numerically, reached the height of its success in premodern Japan. No fewer than 300,000 of the country's population were Christian.

In 1612, however, a serious incident occurred when the "Kirishitan daimyo" Arima Harunobu sought to obtain favored treatment from the Tokugawa shogunate by bribing another Kirishitan, Okamoto Daihachi (d. 1612), the retainer of one of Ieyasu's closest advisers. (Both principals were sentenced to die.) The regime used this scandal, which touched, if only tangentially, its inner circle of power, as a pretext to prohibit Christianity in its immediate domains. The theoretical justification for the policy of persecution was proclaimed early in 1614 when the shogunate issued a statement, drafted on Ieyasu's orders, that branded the foreign religion a "pernicious doctrine" of social subversion. Written at the behest of its founding father, this document became part of the Tokugawa regime's ancestral law. What awaited Japanese Christians in the rest of the long Tokugawa era was the continuing prospect of persecution and—for those who defied the shogun and stayed loyal to the Lord—martyrdom.

Even after the "Kirishitan daimyo" turned against Christianity, the populace of their domains—the descendants of people coerced into the religion—clung to it. For example, Dom Protasio's apostate son sought to demonstrate his allegiance to the shogunate in 1612 by unleashing a fierce persecution on his completely Christian region, but that merely damped down the practice of the faith, leaving it to smolder. The embers of Christianity were not stamped out in the Arima domain until 1637/1638, when the Tokugawa regime intervened massively to crush a peasant uprising, known in history as the Shimabara Rebellion, that swept the area. The number of rebels slaughtered by the armies mobilized by the shogunate is usually given as 37,000. Extortionate taxation, not religious zealotry, had caused the rebellion's outbreak, but the authorities chose to interpret it as Christian inspired. This diagnosis was the proximate cause of the final "closed country" edict of 1639.

In the Ōmura domain, where Dom Bartolomeu's son and successor as daimyo turned against Christianity in 1606, as many as 665 persons suspected of practicing the religion were arrested, and 468 of them were executed as late as 1657 and 1658, more than a dozen years after the last missionary still active in Japan had been arrested. Indeed, Christianity persisted in Japan throughout the Tokugawa period, albeit in a form that cannot, strictly speaking, be called orthodox. A cruel and methodical inquisition drove most Japanese Christians to renounce their faith early on. Many, however, continued to practice it underground. Centuries of worship under hermetic conditions, in hiding from the agents of the persecution; the total lack of contacts with the European heartland of Catholicism; the absence of expert guidance from priests; the consequently irresistible drift toward syncretic accommodation with Buddhist and Shinto beliefs and practices—all these factors diluted the essence of their religion. Nevertheless, communities of people who considered themselves Christian and were willing to suffer for their beliefs remained in existence in Kyushu even as the Meiji Restoration overthrew the Tokugawa shogunate in 1868. The shogunate's anti-Christian smelter did not function perfectly after all.

EUROPEAN DOCUMENTS

ALEXANDRO VALIGNANO'S JAPANESE MISSION POLICY

While the political character of Alexandro Valignano's activities in Japan is obvious, they were not exclusively related to problems of power, status, and authority. Valignano also dealt with cultural questions, using his plenipotentiary office as Visitor of the Indian Province of the Society of Jesus to lay down rules of social behavior for the Jesuits of Japan. His major concerns and their proposed solutions are detailed in his *Sumario de las cosas de Japon* (*Summary of Japanese Matters*), a lengthy report to the Jesuit general superior in Rome that Valignano composed in India in 1583 after completing his first visit to Japan. The following selections from that work show Valignano's high estimate of the qualities of the Japanese, display his optimism regarding the prospects of disseminating Christianity among them, and illustrate one of the key aspects of his approach to his mission terrain: the accommodative method. The accommodation, to be sure, was to be limited to the sphere of manners. No compromise regarding morals, let alone concessions with respect to Catholic dogma, would be permitted for the sake of finding some sort of middle ground with Japanese religious beliefs and social practices. But the underlying principle of Valignano's method appears truly enlightened (if hard to follow) even today: Europeans who cross over to Japan must fit themselves to Japanese standards; that is, they must abandon their original habits and customs and learn Japanese modes of behavior; in short, they must eat, drink, dress, live, and act *à la japonaise*. Only by doing so, Valignano insisted, could the foreign missionaries hope to retain the support of their Japanese patrons and co-workers and, with their help, gain the affections of a wider public.

This principle was considered extravagant by some of the visitor's subordinates, including most notably the Mission Superior of Japan, the Portuguese padre Francisco Cabral (ca. 1533–1609), a former soldier who resisted acculturation, maintaining that no other nation he had seen was as conceited, covetous, inconstant, and insincere as the Japanese. Apparently, Cabral was so convinced that the Japanese culture was unpalatable that he even refused to drink tea. The barbed references to "ponderous men and men of the past" and to bigoted Portuguese that are found in the following text are part of an internal critique directed at the likes of Cabral. The far more urbane Valignano (not that he himself was free of prejudices, as the text makes apparent) realized how counterproductive was the barely disguised racism of such Eucharistic warriors, so he dismissed Cabral from his position of authority, replacing him with Padre Gaspar Coelho. (As seen in the introduction of this chapter, this was not one of the great administrator's most inspired personnel decisions.)

SUMMARY OF JAPANESE MATTERS

In Alexandro Valignano's *Summary of Japanese Matters*, the word *padres* refers to Jesuit priests. *Irmãos* (Portuguese for "brothers") are members of the Jesuit order who are not—or not yet—priests. *Dōjuku*, a term borrowed from Japanese Buddhist institutions and literally meaning "cohabitant," describes auxiliary personnel who are not members of the Jesuit order but are affiliated with it in such capacities as acolyte, verger, and catechist; "paramissionary" would be a fairly accurate rendition. "Secular priests" (*clérigos*) are priests who are not members of a religious order.

Chapter 6: Of the Importance of This Enterprise and of the Great Benefit Being Gained and Still to Be Gained in Japan

This enterprise of Japan is without a doubt the most important and beneficial of all being undertaken in these oriental parts and, indeed in all of discovery, for many reasons:

1. The first is that Japan is a very large territory which comprises . . . sixty-six kingdoms and is inhabited wholly by a white people distinguished by great politeness, prudence, and intelligence and completely subject to reason. On

account of all this, as experience has shown, a very great harvest may be expected here.

2. The second reason is that in our actual observation so far, among all these oriental peoples, only the Japanese are moved to become Christians out of their own free will, convinced by reason and desiring their salvation. What all the rest have in common is that human considerations and self-interest move them to accept our faith. From this it follows that the Japanese take in our doctrine much better, quickly becoming capable of apprehending it and receiving the sacraments; once they are converted, they completely unburden themselves of their idolatries. The contrary is the case among all the rest of the oriental peoples.

3. The third reason is that in Japan, unlike the rest of these oriental parts, it is not only the lowly and humble who become Christians. Gentlemen, great lords, and even kings likewise subject themselves willingly to our holy law. Accordingly, the harvest reaped in Japan is incomparably greater, less onerous, and more valuable.

4. The fourth reason is that the Japanese are naturally much inclined to religion and reverence and are very obedient to priests. This is evident from the grand status attained by the bonzes of all the sects of Japan. . . .

5. The fifth reason is that the door is open to the Holy Gospel and to conversion in all the kingdoms of Japan. Given the laborers and the funds necessary where the work of making Christians is begun, the padres can settle and preach the law of Our Lord wherever they wish. . . .

6. The sixth reason is that the Japanese are capable not only of receiving our holy law but also of absorbing our sciences with ease. What is most important, however, is that they are absolutely capable of being ordained secular priests or of living a holy life in a religious order. . . .

7. The seventh reason is that because this people is so much and so excellently inclined and subject to reason and because all have one language in common, they are easier to cultivate after being made Christian than any other nation. Members of our Society find incomparably greater satisfaction in living among them than among any others. . . .

8. The eighth reason is that this enterprise is one from which the Society can obtain much honor and benefit for the glory of Our Lord. Above and beyond what is accomplished in Japan, by its achievements there the Society gains a great name throughout Europe. Japan is in itself a country with superb human resources, which it will make available to the Society so we can avail ourselves of their help. . . .

9. The ninth reason is that the Society has already invested much capital in Japan and has gained much credit. We can say that the major difficulties have been conquered because by now [our padres there] know the customs of the Japanese and the mode of procedure to be observed with them. Moreover, they have many fellow workers who know the language, many native *irmãos*, much

authority among the Christians, and a good reputation among the heathen. Witness the great lords and gentlemen who every day turn Christian. Note that all the other sects of Japan are declining, whereas our religion continues to expand and advance. Observe the many houses and the beautiful, large churches that the Society has in this country. All this has shed much luster on our religion. In previous years the opposite was true. Ours were few and held in little account, and they lacked all these facilities of support and comfort. They therefore encountered many difficulties in carrying forward this enterprise.

10. The tenth and last reason is that Our Lord appears to have reserved such a great enterprise for the Society alone, because . . . members of other religious orders and foreign secular priests neither should nor, it would seem, can come here. As the Society has all this Christianity in its charge, without the interference of others who would use different methods of guidance, one purpose prevails and the flock can be guided in the manner considered appropriate. . . .

Chapter 16: Of the Great Care and Method to Be Observed in Maintaining Unity Among the Japanese *Irmãos* and *Dōjuku* and Our Europeans

Many difficulties are encountered . . . in carrying on with this enterprise of Japan, but among them all I consider none greater than maintaining unity of spirit among the Japanese *irmãos* and *dogicos* (*dōjuku*) and our Europeans. There is no doubt that without it, which is the foundation of this entire edifice, the Society of this province will before long cast itself into ruin. For that reason much solicitude and vigilance, and much dexterity and prudence, are required of the superiors if the ones and the others are to be governed in such a way that this unity is maintained. So that all this be understood better, we shall now deal with the particulars.

The difficulty of maintaining this unity will be clearly understood from the following reasons. The first is that the difference between the Japanese and the Europeans is so great that it appears to be not accidental but intrinsic and innate, as though founded in nature, inasmuch as the two groups generally disagree and diverge in their intellectual perceptions as in their corporal sensations to such a degree that what appears good to the ones fails to content the others. They do not accord with each other on practical matters, because the Japanese are guided by their precedents and customs, which are so contrary to ours that we can never hope to understand them. Likewise, the two groups fail to agree in matters having to do with the senses. In food as in song and instrumental music, in savor as in odor, the contrariety between them is so great that what delights the ones disgusts the others. In the presence of so much natural contrariety, unity is difficult.

The second reason is the great difference in modes of behavior. The Japanese are deliberate in their dealings, so they never show agitation or anger even when they are highly offended on the inside, and they neither complain readily nor grumble and speak ill of others. They are very covert in their hearts. They are much given to ceremony and external compliments, and they endure much, biding their time until they can get their own back. We, however, communally are the reverse of all this: We are hasty, choleric, and frank, quickly reveal what is in our hearts, and are no friends of all these ceremonies and external compliments. That a particular mode of behavior should be natural and habitual to each group makes it hard to relinquish; thus the ones are loath to compose their differences with the others. This is anything but conducive to achieving unity.

The third reason is the great contrariety that prevails in customs, in what is considered good breeding and polite behavior, and indeed in all norms of conduct between people. The ceremonies and courtesies current among the Japanese are so different from ours that we can never completely understand them, and many of the actions that we regard as courtesies are considered grave discourtesies by them. Some of their customs are so new and strange to us that for a long time we are bogged down like idiots because it costs us so much toil to learn them. As a result we neither know how to seat ourselves, nor how to eat or drink, behave or speak, after their fashion. The way we comport ourselves in all this is very ridiculous by Japanese standards. But because it would cost ponderous men and men of the past a good deal to accommodate themselves to those standards (so they do not), we are stuck with the reputation of savages and people of no breeding. Our Japanese members neither can nor want to accommodate themselves to us in these regards—and it would in any event be uncalled for, because outsiders would take it in extremely bad form. As long as habits that are intolerable by Japanese standards of good breeding and politeness persist, they will always occasion contrasting opinions and disputes on whose customs are better. Vexation is the result; unity suffers.

The fourth reason is the great difficulty of learning their language, which is so elegant and so rich that . . . one speaks in one manner, writes in another, and preaches in yet another, conversing in one vocabulary with nobles and in another with the humble. People's children and wives also have their own varied vocabularies. The writing system has an infinite number of characters, so none of our Europeans has yet succeeded in learning how to write, much less compose books that could be shown to people. To be sure, some have reached the point that they can preach to Christians, but it is so different from what any Japanese *irmão* can do, even if he knows nothing, that the padres have wisely embraced the resolution to keep their silence wherever Japanese *irmãos* are available. Never or rarely do the padres attain the ability to preach to the heathen—not, in any event, to bonzes or nobles and courtiers. From all this it follows that in time, once the Japanese have acquired knowledge and come to be ordained priests, they will be able to hear confessions and say mass and preach good doctrine at their own will and pleasure. Knowing the language and the customs, and being natives, they will always have greater talents in everything than our Europeans and will always be loved and esteemed more by the Japanese—and that is hard to bear, especially for the Portuguese who are accustomed to calling even the Chinese and the Japanese by the name of Negroes.

Inasmuch as the damage sure to follow unless unity is achieved is so evident and so palpable, there is no need to take much additional time in demonstrating it. First, where there is no unity, everything is destroyed. But there is so much occasion for disunity between the Japanese and us that if one begins to give ground before it, it will be impossible to keep that disunity from becoming immense; every step of the way, there will be material for it to feed on. The second is that we are unable, for the aforesaid reasons, to live or accomplish anything in Japan without them. But if a good many of them enter our houses only to live there in disunity, one can easily imagine to what sort of end the whole business will come. The third is that they are natives and we are foreigners. Once they have studied and become priests, and once there are many of those, there is no doubt that they will be able to do with us and with the Society what they wish. The fourth is that unless we achieve a more perfect unity with them and they with us, they will never enter into the spirit. Without it, they will not have the strength to defeat the dangers and occasions of vice that abound in Japan, and as a consequence the Society could easily be cast into perdition.

What is the way to ensure unity? Next to the grace and charity extended by Our Lord, it consists principally of keeping the following rules.

The first is that the Japanese members of the Society be in every respect treated equally to the European *irmãos*, the same applying in proportion to the *dōjuku*, because nothing destroys unity and brotherly love in congregations as much as the unequal treatment of *irmãos*.

The second is that the Japanese be treated and governed gently and lovingly, in accordance with the constitution of the Society. One should make the effort to instruct them in virtue and religious discipline in such a way that they have no reason to sense any asperity, anger, or choleric agitation in us, and no occasion to endure affronts and discourteous language, because all this is so incompatible with the Japanese mode of behavior. On the contrary, they should always be guided and persuaded by reasoning, in such a way that even when they are being penalized or chastised, they realize that they are being treated not in anger but with love, their own good and benefit being the objective in all respects.

The third is that our regulation enjoining the members of one nation not to think or speak ill about the customs and behavior of another be rigorously observed. Accordingly, notwithstanding how contrary the customs, ceremonies, and sensibilities of the Japanese may be to ours, no ill shall be said of them, and our Europeans shall not show that they find them strange, wishing to convince the Japanese that those of Europe are better; for that is the nursery of discord.

The fourth is that inasmuch as for the love of God we leave our countries and pass through so many hardships in order to come help the Japanese, we should not waste our labors and their fruit by not wanting to accommodate ourselves to them. Because for Japan its own customs, ceremonies, and modes of behavior are better; because from our observing them a more perfect unity follows, more abundant fruit is reaped among our neighbors, and the reputation of the Society and of our holy law increases; and because the contrary follows from our not observing Japanese mores, let us make every effort to learn them diligently and observe them enthusiastically. . . .

The fifth is that we mollify our taste buds and accommodate ourselves to their food, entirely forswearing our European foods. This is one of the principal things expected from us by the Japanese, who are amazed and disgusted at many of the things we eat. If, all at one stroke, we make up our minds and apply ourselves, we shall easily succeed in this. . . .

And so by these means and especially, as already stated, with the grace and help of Our Lord, it may without any doubt be expected that the due and desired unity will develop between the Japanese and us Europeans.

[Valignano, *Sumario de las cosas de Japon*, pp. 131–34, 198–202; JSAE]

A JESUIT PRIEST'S OBSERVATIONS OF WOMEN

Padre Luís Fróis, S.J. (1532?–1597), is best known as the author of the monumental *History of Japan* (*Historia de Japam*) and of voluminous other reports on the progress of the Christian enterprise in that country during his lifetime. A native of Lisbon, he entered the Society of Jesus in that city in 1548. The same year, he sailed to India, where he was active in various missions before he completed his studies of rhetoric, philosophy, and theology at the Jesuits' college in Goa and was ordained a priest in 1561. In 1563 Fróis arrived in Japan, where he spent thirty-one of the next thirty-four years and where he died. He personally knew and vividly portrayed many of the leading Japanese figures of his day, from Oda Nobunaga on down. Moreover, Fróis's lengthy experience in Japan gave him the opportunity to observe and the authority to dissect the peculiarities of that country's customs. This is the topic to which his *Treatise on Contradictions and Differences of Customs Between the People of Europe and of This Territory of Japan* is devoted.

The device that Fróis uses is to juxtapose European practices with Japanese, point by point, in the form of short, couplet-like statements. There emerges the image of total contrariety. Since Fróis goes into the most banal of details, the picture he paints—one that calls to mind the genre scenes depicted on contemporary Japanese folding screens—is more colorful, if less affecting, than the weighty treatment of the same topic found in Alexandro Valignano's *Summary of Japanese Matters*. In this treatise at least, Fróis is content with making observations without constantly being judgmental. It is left up to the reader to draw the conclusions.

TREATISE ON CONTRADICTIONS AND DIFFERENCES OF CUSTOMS
BETWEEN THE PEOPLE OF EUROPE AND OF THIS TERRITORY OF JAPAN

The selection presented here is from Luís Fróis's chapter "On Women." As a priest engaged in the cure of souls, he would certainly have been familiar with many of the problems of all classes of Japanese women. As one who was received in the high circles of the Japanese military aristocracy, he was no doubt knowledgeable about the fashions and conventions of "women of the Japanese nobility," as he calls them. More problematic is the extent of his knowledge of European actualities. It is clear that the "Europe" of his experience was limited to Portugal, a country that he left at about the age of sixteen, never to revisit. Moreover, when he departed, he was already a Jesuit. Before he became one, however, Fróis had held a post in the chancery of the king of Portugal. His career as a courtier, however brief, suggests that he knew more of the world than might ordinarily be expected of one so young.

Chapter the 2nd: On Women, Their Character, and Their Customs

1. In Europe, a young woman's sense of shame and the inviolate tabernacle of her purity are her highest honor and supreme treasure; Japanese women make nothing at all of virginal purity, and they lose neither honor nor nubility for lack of it.

2. European women are proud of their light hair and go to great efforts for it; Japanese women abhor it and do all they can to keep their hair black.

4. European women perfume their hair with fragrant essences; Japanese women always smell of the oil with which they grease their hair.

5. European women rarely use someone else's hair to tie into their own; Japanese women buy many wigs imported from China.

9. European women wash their head and their hair at home; Japanese women do so in public baths, where there are special washstands for hair.

11. European women take pride in well-formed and cultivated eyebrows; Japanese women pull them out with a pair of tweezers, leaving not a single hair.

14. European women pierce their ears and fill the apertures with ornaments; Japanese women neither pierce their ears nor wear earrings.

15. Among European women, conspicuous makeup is a defect; Japanese women consider the more face paint, the better.

16. European women value white teeth and expend much artifice and labor on keeping them so; Japanese women laboriously apply vinegar and iron to make their mouth and teeth black as [illegible].

19. European women's sleeves reach down to their wrists; Japanese women's sleeves go only halfway down the arm, and they do not consider it dishonorable to expose their arms and the breast.

20. Among us, a woman who went barefoot would be considered crazy or shameless; Japanese women, whether noble or base, for the greater part of the year always go barefoot.

21. European women gird themselves tightly with a belt; Japanese noblewomen so loosely that the belt keeps slipping down.

24. The dresses of European women are closed in front and cover the feet down to the ground; those of Japanese women are open in front and reach down to the ankles.

29. In Europe, men go first and women behind; in Japan, the men behind and the women first.

30. In Europe, property is held in common by the married couple; in Japan, each has his or her property separately, and sometimes the wife lends hers to the husband at interest.

31. In Europe, apart from its being a sin, it is considered the worst sort of infamy to divorce one's wife; in Japan, one can divorce as many wives as he pleases, and the women lose neither their honor nor their nubility on that account.

32. It is the men who divorce the wives, on account of the corruption of nature; in Japan, it is often the wife who divorces the husband.

34. In Europe, daughters and young ladies are kept strictly sequestered; in Japan, the daughters go wherever they please for a day or more without bothering to tell their parents.

35. European wives do not venture outside the house without their husband's permission; Japanese women are free to go wherever they wish without their husband's knowledge.

38. In Europe, although the practice does exist, the abortion of infants is infrequent; in Japan, it is so common that some women have aborted twenty times.

39. In Europe, infants are rarely or almost never killed after birth; Japanese women, by stepping on the infant's neck, kill all those whom they think they will not be able to bring up.

43. In Europe, the discipline of the cloister is strict, and nuns are kept under rigorous monastic seclusion; in Japan, the nunneries of the *biqunis* (*bikuni* [female religious]) serve, in effect, as prostitute quarters.

44. Among us, it is uncommon for nuns to set foot outside the cloister; the Japanese *bikuni* are always to be found at entertainments and sometimes go along on military expeditions.

45. Among us, it is not very common for women to know how to write; among women of the Japanese nobility, it is considered degrading not to know how.

49. European women ride on chair saddles or sidesaddle; Japanese women ride the same way as the men.

51. In Europe, the women ordinarily prepare meals; in Japan, the men do that, and even knights consider it an elegant accomplishment to know how to cook.

54. In Europe, it is considered disgraceful for a woman to drink wine; in Japan, it is very common, and at feasts they sometimes indulge to the point of drunkenness.

[Fróis, *Tratado*, . . . pp. 118–33; JSAE]

JAPANESE DOCUMENTS

ANTI-CHRISTIAN PRONOUNCEMENTS

In July 1587, after concluding his conquest of Kyushu, Toyotomi Hideyoshi made the decision to ban the Christian padres—Bateren—from Japan. His rationale is laid out in the first document translated here, the "Notice" dated on the day before the actual decree of expulsion and intended for an internal audience, the Japanese lords. Two major indictments are set down in detail. First, the hegemon considers the forced conversions of the populace of entire domains to Christianity to be "miscreant." Second, he accuses Christians of being "even more given to conjurations" than Buddhists of the Single-Minded sect (Ikkōshū), also known as the True Pure Land sect (Jōdo shinshū), which emphasized faith in Amida Buddha.

There is no doubt that Hideyoshi had ample evidence for the first indictment. Whether or not there was any substance to the second charge—that Christian "conjurations" represented a threat to the realm—is a moot question. Regardless of its accuracy, the comparison between Christianity and the Single-Minded sect of Buddhism was the most dangerous assessment that could have been made in the historical context of the struggle waged by the regime of the unifiers against the power of organized religion. It had taken Hideyoshi's predecessor Oda Nobunaga more than ten years to reduce the Ikkō sect's citadel, the temple-fortress Honganji, in Osaka; to conquer the provinces that owed allegiance to that sect's pontiff; and to destroy his medieval religious monarchy. The Single-Minded sectarians fought to the bitter end for the belief that faith alone brought salvation. That this was a "Lutheran" proposition was a theological point clearly perceived by the Catholic missionaries, who damned both the European Protestants and the Japanese Amidists as children of Satan. But Hideyoshi was incognizant of such distinctions. He was a man of power, not a theologian.

On the site of the Honganji, Hideyoshi built his own nonesuch, Osaka Castle, from which he presided over the creation of a new order in Japan. When it matured under the Tokugawa shogunate in the seventeenth century, that new, early modern order developed its own political ideology, in which there was little room for anything but secular loyalties.

Hideyoshi's "Decree" of July 24, 1587, was not yet the final verdict passed on Christianity and its servants in early modern Japan. The Portuguese merchants were specifically exempted from the edict of expulsion. The missionaries, too, were able to stay in Japan; that is, Hideyoshi closed his eyes to their presence. Knowing that they must behave discreetly or face dire consequences, the Jesuits trimmed their sails to the prevailing wind. Their partners in the policy of forced conversions had their wings clipped. With the striking exception of the daimyo of Akashi, Dom Justo Takayama Ukon (1552?–1615), who refused to compromise his faith and was disenfeoffed, the "Kirishitan daimyo" bent before their lord and master Hideyoshi and forswore their militant Christianity.

DECREE

1. Japan is the Land of the Gods. That a pernicious doctrine should be diffused here from the Kirishitan Country is most undesirable.

2. To approach the people of our provinces and districts, turn them into [Kirishitan] sectarians, and destroy the shrines of the gods and the temples of the Buddhas is something unheard of in previous generations. Whereas provinces, districts, localities, and fiefs are granted to their recipients temporarily, contingent on the incumbent's observance of the laws of the realm and attention to their intent in all matters, to embroil the common people is miscreant.

3. In the judgment of His Highness, it is because the Bateren amass parishioners as they please by means of their clever doctrine that the Law of the Buddhas is being destroyed like this in the Precincts of the Sun. That being miscreant, the Bateren can scarcely be permitted to remain on Japanese soil. Within twenty days from today they shall make their preparations and go back to their country. During this time, should anyone among the common people make unwarranted accusations against the Bateren, it shall be considered miscreant.

4. The purpose of the Black Ships is trade, and that is a different matter. As years and months pass, trade may be carried on in all sorts of articles.

5. From now on hereafter, all those who do not disturb the Law of the Buddhas (merchants, needless to say, and whoever) are free to come here from the Kirishitan Country and return. Be heedful of this.

That is all.

Tenshō 15.VI.19

[Kuwata, *Toyotomi Hideyoshi kenkyū*, pp. 347–49; JSAE]

LETTER TO THE VICEROY OF INDIA

On his second visit to Japan, Valignano traveled with an ambassador's credentials and presents from the Portuguese viceroy of India to Hideyoshi. After being made to cool his heels for half a year, Valignano was at length permitted to proceed to Kyoto, where Hideyoshi, by then the all-powerful ruler of Japan, received him in audience in March 1591. Valignano delivered a courtly letter from the viceroy, who professed admiration for Hideyoshi's unprecedented victories, avowed that he undoubtedly enjoyed the protection of Heaven, and recommended the padres to his continued, favorable attention. Hideyoshi's response was a typical example of the fustian that he considered the proper stuff for his foreign correspondence. Shocked at the letter's rude tone, its insults, and its threats, Valignano concluded that he could not possibly bear such an undiplomatic note to the viceroy, and the Jesuits requested that Hideyoshi change his wording. This boon was granted them, according to Luís Fróis's *Historia de Japam* (*History of Japan*), which includes an evidently doctored Portuguese version of the revised message.

Fatuous bombast is not all there is to Hideyoshi's original letter, which was drafted for him by the Buddhist priest Seishō Shōtai (1548–1607) of Shōkokuji, one of the Five Great Zen Temples (Gosan) of Kyoto. On the contrary, it has very serious contents. Japan is proclaimed the "Land of the Gods," but its divinity is multifaceted, resting on the concomitance of godlike functions and essences drawn from all the Three Countries: India, China, and "these Precincts of the Sun." In other words, as a basis for condemning Christianity, the universality of East Asian concepts of the divine is contrasted with the particularity of the current European concept of God. The critique begins by referring to *shin*—mind—as the base ground of all existence. *Shin* (Skt. *citta*) is a fundamental Buddhist term with a wide range of significations, "the Prime Meaning" and "the True Aspect of Transcendental Wisdom" among them; it is further described as an entity that "encompasses all space and generates the ethereal."[3] Mind is neither created nor is it a personal Creator, but it can signify something akin to the all-encompassing consciousness that is the seedbed of all elements. (The Stoic and Neo-Platonic analogues termed *nous*—mind—were surely familiar to the better-educated Jesuits of Japan, such as Valignano.) Having subordinated the universe to

---

3. See de Bary et al., eds., *Sources of Japanese Tradition*, 2nd ed., vol. 1, p. 312.

"the one mind," Hideyoshi goes on to plumb "the unfathomable functioning of yin and yang" and then enunciates the principle of the ultimate identity of the Three Teachings: Shinto, Confucianism, and Buddhism. He sets forth the Confucian formula for social ethics and concludes his argument by censuring the Christians for their narrow-minded and deluded insistence that they have a monopoly on the truth.

You have sent me a letter from afar. Opening it and reading it, I feel as though a vista of myriad miles of seas and mountains had opened before my eyes.

As your letter intimates, this empire, which comprises more than sixty regions, for many years knew more days of disorder than of peace. Hence evildoers fomented foul plots, provincial warriors banded together, and the imperial court's orders could not be enforced. In the prime of my life, I spent all my days and nights deploring and lamenting this state of affairs. I studied the art of self-cultivation and the essentials of governing the country, formulated deep designs, and made plans for the future. Founding myself in the three virtues of humanity, perspicacity, and martial valor, I nourished the warriors with affection and treated the farmers with compassion. I rectified rewards and punishments and set the state on a safe course free of perils. Consequently, before many years had passed, the realm was unified and now rests solid as a rock. There is no foreign land or territory however distant that fails to offer tribute. East and West, North and South: I order and they obey.

And now, disseminating His Sacred Majesty's decrees throughout his dominions and brandishing the authority proper to his worthy captain as far as the borderlands, I have opened all the barriers and bridges within the Four Seas, permitting free passage. I have struck down the bandits on land and the pirates on the sea, bringing peace to the state and the people. Our country is now secure. For all that, I have formed the ambition to rule over the country of Great Ming. Any time now, I will set sail for China aboard my palace-ship, and it will be as easy as pointing to the palm of my hand. Then I will have a convenient route for proceeding to your part of the world. Why should we let distance or differences come between us?

Now, then: Our empire is the Land of the Gods. God is mind. The universe and the myriad phenomena do not exist apart from the one mind (*shin*). Were it not for this god, no spirit would be generated; were it not for this god, no Way would be established. During all the kalpas of degeneration, this god does not diminish; during all the kalpas of regeneration, this god does not increase. The unfathomable functioning of yin and yang is called god.[4] That is why we say that god is the root and wellspring of all the myriad things. In India, this godlike functioning is called the Law of the Buddhas (Buppō); in China, the Way of the Sages (Judō); in these Precincts of the Sun, it is called the Way of

---

4. "Xizi shangjuan," in *Concordance to Yi Ching* [*Yijing*], p. 5.

the Gods (Shintō). To know the Way of the Gods is to know the Law of the Buddhas and to know the Way of the Sages as well.

As long as humans are active in society, humanity will be their basic principle. Were it not for humanity and rightness, a lord would not act as a lord or a subject as a subject.[5] It is by applying humanity and rightness that the essential ties between lord and subject, father and son, and husband and wife are perfected, that the Way of these relationships is established. Should you want to learn about the gods and the Buddhas in depth, kindly ask, and I will explain.

In lands like yours, one doctrine is taught to the exclusion of others, and you are unaware of the Way of humanity and rightness. You therefore fail to revere the gods and the Buddhas or to distinguish between the lord and the subject. Instead, you seek to destroy the True Law by means of a pernicious doctrine. Hereafter, stop fabricating wild, barbarous nonsense in ignorance of right and wrong!

Some years ago that notorious group, the Bateren, came to this country, seeking to bedevil and cast a spell on religious and lay folk, men and women alike. At that time I subjected them to only some slight punishment. Were they to return to these parts with the intention of proselytizing, however, I shall extirpate them without sparing any of their ilk, and it will then be too late for the gnashing of teeth. Should you have the desire of maintaining friendship with this land, however, the seas have been rid of the pirate menace, and merchants are free to come and go anywhere within these borders. Think this over. . . .

Tenshō 19.VII.25 [September 12, 1591] The Imperial Regent

[To] Injia Bisorei

[Kuwata, *Toyotomi Hideyoshi kenkyū*, pp. 253–55; JSAE]

STATEMENT ON THE EXPULSION OF THE BATEREN

The following is the fundamental anti-Christian statement of the Tokugawa shogunate. It was prepared at the behest of the retired shogun Tokugawa Ieyasu (r. 1603–1605) by the Zen monk Ishin Sūden (1569–1633), who was the abbot of Nanzenji, another of the Five Great Zen Temples of Kyoto, when he was called to Ieyasu's residence in Sunpu in 1608. One of the principal services that Sūden performed for Ieyasu was drafting foreign correspondence and other important documents, such as the Kinchū narabi ni kuge shohatto (Code for the Imperial Court and Court Nobility) of 1615. In 1612 Sūden was put in charge of Buddhist and Shinto institutional affairs,

---

5. Allusion to *Analects* 12:11.

a responsibility he shared with the shogunate's Kyoto deputy (*shoshidai*), Itakura Katsushige (1545–1624).

According to the *Diary of Foreign Affairs* (*Ikoku nikki*), a calendar of state papers kept by Sūden between 1608 and 1629, he was summoned into Ieyasu's presence at Edo Castle on Keichō 18/12/22 (January 31, 1614) and ordered to produce a statement on the expulsion of the Bateren. He worked through the night to write this document and presented it to Ieyasu the next day. The statement was issued over the vermilion seal of Shogun Hidetada (1579–1632; r. 1605–1623), and instructions were given to disseminate it throughout the country so that "everyone would be aware of its purport." It was then taken to Itakura's office in Kyoto, where it was reproduced in multiple copies. It is known that daimyo who received this notification interpreted it as an order to rid Japan not only of the padres but also of their adherents. In the Kyoto area, the order was put into effect on February 14. The missionaries were packed off to Nagasaki, and there was a mass roundup of Kirishitans, who were exposed to public humiliation in an effort to make them apostatize.

Sūden's basic argument resembles the one advanced by Seishō Shōtai, his fellow diplomatist of the Gosan school of Kyoto, on Hideyoshi's behalf. Sūden, too, exalts Japan as the "Land of the Gods," a realm triply blessed because the sublime traditions of all the Three Countries were amalgamated to form its unique national polity. Shinto, however, retains primacy in that fusion: it is through the assistance of the Shinto gods, Sūden asserts, that Buddhism and Confucianism were brought to Japan.

Heaven as father, Earth as mother, and Man born between them: here the Three Powers are determined.

Japan is by origin the Land of the Gods. The unfathomable functioning of yin and yang, given a name, is called god. Who would fail to hallow and revere the sacredness of the sacred, the spirituality of the spirit? All the more so because it is entirely as a result of the functioning of yin and yang that man gains life! None of the five bodily parts or the six senses, indeed no human action or undertaking, is for as much as an instant separate from god. God is not to be sought anywhere apart. What human beings are all endowed with, what each and every individual is invested with—that is the substance of god.

Japan is also called the Land of the Buddhas, and not without reason. It is written: "This is the land where the Buddhas manifest themselves as gods, the homeland of Dainichi."[6] And the Lotus says: "As saviors of the world, the Buddhas abide by their great godlike faculties; for the sake of bringing joy to sentient

---

6. Dainichi (Great Sun) is the Japanese name of Mahavairocana (Cosmic Buddha). Opportunely, if the characters for "the homeland of Dainichi" (Dainichi no honkoku) are written without being interrupted by a possessive case marker, the resulting compound may be read Dainihonkoku (Great Japan).

beings, they display boundless divine powers."[7] These are golden words, wonderful phrases. The names "gods" and "Buddhas" differ, but their purport is the same; they are just like the two halves of a tally joined.

In antiquity priests and laymen, each blessed with the gods' assistance, crossed the ocean and went to faraway China, exerting themselves in the endeavor to seek out the Law of the Buddhists and the teachings of the Way of humanity and to bring back the interior and the exterior scriptures. Their latter-day successors have passed on the learning of those scholars from one master to another, transmitting it generation by generation. The Law of the Buddhas flourishes here with greater vigor than in other lands. How could this be anything but the Eastward Progress of Buddhism!

And now the band of Kirishitans has unexpectedly come to Japan. They do not merely sail trading vessels here to traffic in commodities. Rather, they recklessly desire to spread a pernicious doctrine, confound true religion, change the governmental authority of this realm, and make it their own possession. These are the germs of disaster. This band must not be left unsuppressed.

Japan is the Land of the Gods and the Land of the Buddhas. The gods are hallowed here and the Buddhas revered; the Way of humanity and rightness is followed assiduously, and laws regarding good and evil are perfected. Any malefactor is subjected to the Five Penalties—tattooing the forehead, slicing off the nose, cutting off the legs, castration, and capital punishment—according to the severity of his offense. It says in the *Rites*: "There are many kinds of death, but only the Five Types of Mourning; there are many kinds of crime, but only the Five Penalties."[8] Should there be some doubt regarding culpability, then a divine proof is administered, the categories of crime and punishment determined, and innocence distinguished from guilt beyond a hairbreadth of uncertainty.

Criminals who commit the Five Violent Acts or the Ten Evil Deeds are execrated by the Buddhas and the gods, by the Three Treasures, and by the multitude of humans and of heavenly beings. To escape retribution for an overplus of evil is not easy. Either the sword or the stake—that is what the consequence of crime is like. This is the way of encouraging good and inhibiting evil. For all the desire to suppress evil, however, evil accumulates easily; for all the desire to promote good, good is difficult to preserve. How, then, could one not issue a clear warning: If this is what it is like in the present world, then what of the world to come? All the Buddhas of the Three Worlds will not save you from the torments meted out by Enma, the ruler of the Realm of Darkness,

---

7. Lotus Sutra 21, probably cited from the Kyoto Gosan monk Zuikei Shūhō's preface to the compendium of diplomatic correspondence, *Zenrin kokuhō ki* (1470), which also contains a statement similar to the previous quotation.

8. *Liji* (*Record of Rites*) 36:8.

and all the generations of your ancestors will not be able to do anything. Dreadful, dreadful!

All of that notorious band, the Bateren, contravene the aforesaid governmental regimen, traduce the Way of the Gods, calumniate the True Law, derange righteousness, and debase goodness. When they see that there are criminals to be executed, then they rejoice, then they rush to the scene, then they do reverence and pay obeisance in person. This [sort of death] they make out to be a consummation to be devoutly wished in their religion. If this is not a pernicious doctrine, then what is it? These are truly the enemies of the gods and the enemies of the Buddhas. If they are not banned immediately, the state will be sure to suffer grief in the future. Indeed, unless they are checked, those in charge of enforcing the ordinances shall themselves become the targets of the punishment of Heaven. So purge Japan of them! Expel them quickly without giving them an inch of land to grasp, a foot of ground to stand on! And if any dare resist these orders, they shall be executed.

Happily, these Precincts of the Sun have for some years now been ruled by a recipient of the Mandate of Heaven to hold sway over the state. Outwardly, he manifests our cardinal virtues, the Five Constants; inwardly, he turns to the great teachings of the Tripitaka. Therefore the country prospers and the people are at peace. The sutra says: "Peace and tranquillity in the present world, a good repose in the life to come."[9] And Confucius says: "Our bodies, down to the hair and the skin, are received by us from our fathers and mothers. Not to let them be injured or disfigured presumptuously: this is the beginning of filial piety."[10] To keep that body whole: this means to revere the gods. To repulse the pernicious doctrine of the foreigners without delay is to prosper our True Law all the more. Although the world may already have entered an age of decline, our government pursues an excellent course: It steadily increases the traditional patronage of the Way of the Gods and the Law of the Buddhas. Let all under Heaven and within the Four Seas take note! Let no one dare to err!

Keichō 18, the year of water junior and the ox, XII. VERMILION SEAL [Hidetada]

[Sūden, "Bateren tsuihō no fumi," pp. 33–34; JSAE]

FABIAN FUCAN PRO AND CONTRA

Fabian Fucan (1565?–1621?) has few, if any, competitors for the billing as the principal intellectual actor in the drama of the "Christian century" or the designation as the most notorious Japanese defector from the Society of Jesus.

---

9. Lotus Sutra 5.
10. *Xiaojing (Classic of Filiality)* 1.

A native of the Kyoto area who was raised in a Zen temple, where he evidently received an excellent education, he abandoned the Buddhist cloister for a Jesuit seminary in his late teens and in 1586 entered the society as an *irmão*. By 1592, Fabian was teaching Japanese literature to other *irmãos* at the Jesuit college of Amakusa, where his duties included making an adaptation of the great military romance *Tale of Heike* (*Heike monogatari*) in colloquial Japanese "for the sake of those desirous of learning the language and history of Japan." His version of the medieval classic was published by the Jesuit mission press in a romanized edition entitled *Feiqe no monogatari*. "Fucan Fabian" is how he signed the preface, dated 1592.

In the following years, Fabian built a formidable reputation as a rhetorician. In 1605 he wrote the elaborate Christian apologetic work *The Myōtei Dialogue* (*Myōtei mondō*), signing its epilogue, in Chinese characters, with the name Fukansai Habian. This work, which has been transmitted in manuscript, has the design of a popular treatise (*kana zōshi* [feuilleton in simple letters]), one with a fine fictional frame containing a colloquy between two women: Myōshū, a widow who seeks solace in religion, and Yūtei, a religious recluse who guides her "from the shallows to the depths" by exposing the emptiness of Buddhism, refuting Confucianism and Shinto, and exalting Christianity. The names of the participants in this three-part dialogue are contracted into "Myōtei" in the work's title. The epilogue identifies the target audience as "ladies of quality and widows" who "cannot easily find a proper way of conversing with men, even with monks, and even to inquire about true doctrine," but that is nothing more than a literary convention. It is known that such luminaries of the age as the Neo-Confucian scholar Hayashi Razan (1583–1657) and the shogunal adviser Honda Masazumi (1565–1637) were made familiar with Fabian's apologetic by the Jesuits. *The Myōtei Dialogue* puts on display not only Fabian's extraordinary range of knowledge of East Asian systems of thought but also his great skill with words. He presented his complex and challenging argument in plain Japanese (the Sinophile Razan called his language "plebeian"), reducing its alien character and making it accessible to the public. For that, if nothing else, Fabian deserves also to be considered one of the lead actors on the literary scene of the Azuchi-Momoyama era. Yet *The Myōtei Dialogue* is not a satisfactory performance from all points of view. For all the vigor of Fabian's defense of Christianity—or rather, paradoxically, because of the cerebral fervor with which he tries to demonstrate the rationality of his religion's underpinnings— he gives the impression of being a Christian out of persuasion rather than faith. His Jesuit superiors would surely have considered that a severe defect in his spiritual makeup.

Whatever the reason, despite his long and distinguished service as an *irmão*, Fabian was not promoted to the priesthood. Resentful, he avers, of what he viewed as the perfect example of a general pattern of discrimination within the society against its Japanese members, by 1608 Fabian had quit the Jesuits. There is evidence, however, that righteous indignation was not his sole reason for leaving their company; he apparently decamped together with a woman from a Christian religious community adjoining the society's rectory in Kyoto. In the event, Fabian was co-opted by the enemies of his former confreres. As the persecution gained force, he turned informant. In 1620 he published the corrosive anti-Christian tract *Deus Destroyed* (*Ha Daiusu*), a work organized in seven steps in emulation of the seven-step sequence of instruction undergone by Christian proselytes in Japan. In this recantation of Fabian's previous career, Christian claims are rebutted by his counterclaims just as vigorously as he upheld them in *The Myōtei Dialogue*. *Deus Destroyed* became the foundation of the subsequent anti-Christian polemic of the Tokugawa period.

THE MYŌTEI DIALOGUE
(MYŌTEI MONDŌ)

In the following texts, Fabian Fucan is presented as a debater against himself, *pro* and *contra* Christianity. The selections from *The Myōtei Dialogue* and *Deus Destroyed* deal with the same crucial question: Can the Christians be loyal to the Japanese state, in view of the exclusive loyalty to God demanded by the First Commandment? It is hard to say who wins the debate, Fabian or Fucan, because these two treatises are equally forceful.

Seeking to avoid unwelcome analogies with Japanese religious concepts, the Christian missionaries had since the early 1550s shied away from indigenous terminology and used the unmistakably orthodox Latin and Portuguese word *Deus* for God. To make assurance double sure, the Holy Name and a few other sacrosanct terms were usually tabooed in Christian texts composed in Japanese, being represented in them by monograms consisting of Roman or Greek letters. In Fabian's anti-Christian work, too, Deus—the un-Japanese notion of God—is written with the stylized letter 囚. The term translated as "adherents of Deus" is *Daiusu*, which occurs in *Ha Daiusu*, the original Japanese title of *Deus Destroyed* and recurs throughout that work. It is a different case, being a synonym for "followers of Christianity," the same general group that Hideyoshi called "sectarians of the Bateren." Not referring directly to God, Daiusu need not be singled out. Fabian writes this term with Chinese characters.

Points of Doubt Regarding the Kirishitan Teachings

MYŌSHŪ: There is something else I want to talk to you about, something about the Kirishitan teachings that may perhaps be considered dubious; in any event, the people of this realm think so. I mean simply this. Japan is a territory where the Law of the Buddhas has been widely propagated. Land of the Gods is the special name applied to our country by custom. It is by virtue of the Buddhas' and the gods' protection that the nation enjoys peace. Moreover, the Royal Sway could not possibly exist apart from the Law of the Buddhas and the Way of the Gods. Therefore, if all Japan were to become Kirishitan, the land would be in tumult and the Royal Sway would perish. "O what an insufferable religion!" is what everyone seems to be saying about the Kirishitan faith. How do you respond?

YŪTEI: "A woman or a preacher will talk on for seven days": that's it, more or less. Whatever people may say, let them say it. You, however, must have understood this much by now: All this talk that the Japanese nation enjoys peace because of the power of Buddhism and Shinto, and that the Royal Sway cannot exist without the Law of the Buddhas and the Way of the gods is laughable. Why do I say that? To start with, . . . Shinto may in the immediate sense be taken, in terms of the human body, to signify the Way of intercourse between man and wife. Its more distanced interpretation points to the functioning of the twin energies of Heaven and Earth, yin and yang. But yin and yang are what our religion calls creatures of 無; they are things that have no mind and no wisdom. Accordingly, they are incapable of bestowing rewards or inflicting punishments on human beings. So what will it profit one to pray to them? What miracles will result?

The claim that the nation enjoys peace by virtue of the gods' power is nonsense. Even more unreasonable is the claim that the majesty of Buddhism ensures good order. That is because the Law of the Buddhas, in the final analysis, is a doctrine posited on the absolute void. Accordingly, it considers good and evil undifferentiated, perniciousness and righteousness the same; its postulate is that our mind in itself is void and that there is no master over condemnation or bliss. How can such a doctrine be construed into a basis for peace? On the contrary! Here is the origin of revolts and disturbances. . . .

So that's the kind of benefit one gets from Buddhism! Is it really the way to bring about peace in the realm? Then what else shall we designate, what else abominate as the root of rebellion?

Shaka had not yet been born in the reigns of Yao, Shun, Yü, Tang, Wen, and Wu. Of the Law of the Buddhas no one had yet heard the words "Buddhas" or "Law." For all that, when you come right down to it, there is no report either in China or in our empire of a time when the Royal Sway was as blessed with felicity as it was then. The superior treated his inferiors with compassion; and since the sovereigns acted as sovereigns, the subjects also acted as subjects; inferiors honored their superiors. People's hearts were gentle, and that is because "the people of Yao and Shun patterned their hearts on the hearts of Yao and Shun."[11] They conceded the partitions of their rice fields to

---

11. *Shiba shi lüe* 1: Xia.

one another and did not stoop to quarrels. Thus the land was prosperous and the people wealthy, and there was no one to strike the
Drum of Plaints. Now this is what I call an example of the reign of
order! Japanese as well as Chinese may with right call this the propi-
tious mirror of the Royal Sway. To say that without the Law of the
Buddhas, the Royal Sway is forsaken, and that without reverence for
the Way of the Gods, the land cannot be safe is the verbiage of people
who know nothing. My advice to you is: Don't believe a word of it!

Let alone during the disturbances of the Shōhei and Tengyō eras,
at the time of the Hōgen and Heiji incidents not even the syllable
"Ki" of "Kirishitan" had been heard in our empire. Buddhism and
Shinto were in flower. And the realm was in uproar; the Royal Sway
was held for trifles; warrior subjects showed no sign of submission to
the imperial court. From that time on, beginning with the wars between the houses of Minamoto and Taira, steeped in pride, through
the Jōkyū disturbance, all the way down to our times, you will find in
the histories nothing but the assault on this place, the battle at another.[12] As for the recent past, our elders will tell you how this place
was burned, that one ruined in the rout of such-and-such a year, the
uprising of another. That's all you'll hear. Peace by benefit of the
Buddhas and the gods, indeed! What period in our empire's history
does that designate? Because of the worship of the pernicious Buddhas
and gods, Japan has been cursed with the punishment of Heaven, so
military conflicts have proliferated here more than in any other land—
that's the one thing I'm sure of.

In any event, unless all of Japan turns Kirishitan, the country cannot
be put to order perfectly. That is because Kirishitan doctrine teaches:
Worship the Lord 𝄖. Next, love and honor your master from the bottom of your heart; serve and obey him, from the emperor and shogun
on down to each and every lord below. This is the constant exhortation
of our faith. For that reason, I have heard it said, for more than one
thousand years there has been nothing describable as war, and not the
slightest trace of treason or rebellion in Kirishitan lands.

If all of Japan turned Kirishitan, the land would be in tumult and
the Royal Sway abandoned—on what kind of reasoning do these
assertions rest? In the Kirishitan countries there is no Law of the

---

12. The disturbances of the Shōhei (931–938) and Tengyō (938–947) eras were the rebellion
of Taira no Masakado in eastern Japan (935–940) and the massive disorder in western Japan (940–
942) caused by Fujiwara no Sumitomo and his pirate fleet. The Hōgen (1156) and Heiji (1160)
incidents were coups d'état fomented by courtiers with the connivance of military aristocrats in
Kyoto. The wars between the houses of Minamoto and Taira are usually called the Genpei War
(1180–1185). The Jōkyū disturbance (1221) was the failed attempt organized by the retired emperor
Go-Toba (r. 1184–1198) to overthrow the Kamakura shogunate by force of arms.

Buddhas, but the Royal Sway flourishes there, and its virtue abounds within the Four Seas.

[Fabian, *Myōtei mondō*, part 3, in *Kirishitan sho*, in *NST*, vol. 25, pp. 173–75; JSAE]

DEUS DESTROYED
(*HA DAIUSU*)

Seventh Step

The adherents of Deus claim: The First *Madamento* (*Mandamento* [Commandment]) is "You shall hold 𝕯 dear above all things and Him shall you worship." It means that one should esteem this 𝕯 above even one's master, above even one's father and mother. If complying with your master's or your parent's orders would mean acting contrary to 𝕯's will, then refuse to obey, not grudging your life! . . .

To counter, I reply: So you propound a statute in ten articles called *mandamentos*. But apart from the first of the ten articles, nothing here falls outside the scope of the Five Commandments [of Buddhism] that prohibit killing, theft, adultery, falsehood, and drunkenness. . . . The initial article states, in effect, "In case complying with your lord's or your father's orders would mean acting contrary to 𝕯's will, then disobey them, making light of your life!" In this article lurks the intention to subvert and usurp the country, to overthrow and destroy the Law of the Buddhas and the Royal Sway. Quick, quick! Put this gang in stocks and shackles.

"One does not usually expect to find precepts for attaining to ultimate good outside the realm of morals constantly preserved in the people's daily life."[13] There are many components in moral law, but in sum they amount to no more than the Five Human Relationships. Lord and subject, father and child, husband and wife, elder brother and younger brother, friend and friend—once they discharge their proper duties, what more can they do? And one who deranges these—to what iniquity, to what atrocity would such a one not stoop?

The duties proper to the lord and the subject are loyalty and its reward. The duties proper to the father and the child—filial piety and parental affection; the duties proper to the husband and the wife—the righteous observance of their separate functions; the duties proper to the elder brother and the younger brother—fraternal service and love; and the duties of friend and friend to each other are fidelity and sincerity. To bestow on humans a nature concordant with these Five Human Relationships is the proper part of Heaven's Will. And here is how you regard this, you adherents of Deus! To keep from acting contrary to

---

13. Zhu Xi, introduction to *Daxue zhangzhu*.

D's will, you say, cast aside the subject's loyalty to the lord, repudiate the bonds of filial piety and of fraternal service! What greater iniquity than this?. . .

. . . Because the Law of the Buddhas and the Way of the Gods exist here, the Royal Sway also flourishes; and since the Royal Sway exists, the majesty of the Buddhas and the gods increases. The adherents of Deus therefore have no recourse but to subvert the Royal Sway, overthrow the Buddhas and the gods, eliminate the customs of Japan, and import the customs of their own countries. Then only will their plan of usurpation advance.

They have sent troops and taken over such countries as Luzon and Nova Hispania, lands of barbarians close to animals in nature. But our empire surpasses other lands by far in its fierce bravery. For that reason the ambition to usurp this country by diffusing their doctrine, even if it takes a thousand years, has penetrated the very marrow of their bones. But what a gloomy prospect awaits them! For the sake of their doctrine they value their lives less than dust or ashes. *Maruchiru* (*mártir*), they call this. When a wise ruler governs the realm, good is promoted and evil chastised. Rewards promote good and punishments chastise evil. There is no greater punishment than to take away life, but the adherents of Deus have no fear of being killed and will not change their religion. How horrible it is! And where did this flagrant wickedness arise? Its origin, one look will show, is in the First *Mandamento* (Commandment): "You shall hold D dear above all things and him shall you worship." The spread of such a pernicious doctrine is completely the working of the devil. . . .

Who is there that would not hate them? . . .

[Fabian, *Ha Daiusu, Hai-Ya sho,* in NST, vol. 25, pp. 440–42; JSAE]

Chapter 24

CONFUCIAN REVISIONISTS

FUNDAMENTALISM AND REVISIONISM IN THE CRITIQUE OF NEO-CONFUCIANISM

Neo-Confucianism in seventeenth- and eighteenth-century Japan, as represented by the Cheng–Zhu learning of the Way, was only the culmination of a movement begun much earlier in the Song period to revive the original Confucian tradition and reassert its validity for later times. One feature of this movement had been a strong reaction against Buddhism as being antithetical to the Confucian belief in an enduring moral order, the moral self, and the value of social action. For the most part, Tokugawa scholars appreciated the role that Song thinkers had played in reasserting and revitalizing the basic teachings of the Confucian school. Some, however, came to recognize and deplore the extent to which these teachings had been amplified and, they thought, distorted by the Neo-Confucians in ways adapted to a Song spiritual climate much influenced by Buddhism and Daoism.

The thinkers represented in this chapter were not members of the same school or scholarly lineage, but together they represent a tendency—both revisionist and fundamentalist—to reexamine the Neo-Confucian synthesis and purge it of later interpretations (as, to some extent, the Song thinkers themselves had done in revising the Confucian scholarship of the Han and Tang periods).

As revisionists with regard to received tradition, they manifested a broader trend and stage in the evolution of East Asian Neo-Confucianism, continuing the critical reexamination of tradition. Often this critique combined an urge to simplify and reduce the teaching to its bare essentials (presumed to be based on the original Confucian classics), but that process itself reflected revisionist inclinations adapted to local culture and contemporary trends. Thus, in the case of Yamaga Sokō, the new formulation was adapted to the mentality and changing social role of the samurai class; in that of Itō Jinsai (an independent teacher, not a samurai), to the tastes and interests of the new bourgeois culture of the townspeople (*chōnin*); and in that of Ogyū Sorai, to the growing scholarly awareness of conceptual change and sophistication in regard to historical, linguistic, and contextual study. In each case also, these claims to rediscover and repossess the authentic classical Confucianism were adapted to major long-term trends in Japan: the military code ("feudal" values combined with "Confucian" ethics), which remained powerful into the twentieth century; the importance of middle-class culture in the later process of modernization; and the increasing diversity and sophistication of Japanese scholarship into the late nineteenth and early twentieth centuries.

YAMAGA SOKŌ AND THE CIVILIZING
OF THE SAMURAI

The first important thinker to challenge the Neo-Confucians was Yamaga Sokō (1622–1685), a figure known for his intellectual powers and independence of mind. A brilliant student of Hayashi Razan, he had established while still a young man a wide reputation for his mastery of Shinto, Buddhism, and Daoism as well as Neo-Confucianism. It was especially as a student of military science, however, and one with decided convictions about the role of the warrior class in peacetime, that Sokō attracted attention from numerous samurai eager to employ their leisure time in self-improvement.

Like Kumazawa Banzan, Sokō was concerned about the prolonged inactivity of the warrior class under peaceful Tokugawa rule. Even in these circumstances, he believed that samurai had an important function to perform that justified their special status, something more than simply keeping themselves fit for possible military service, important as that was. If samurai were given a stipend by their lord, it was not so they could enjoy a parasitic existence at the expense of the other social classes—eating the food of the peasant and using the goods of the artisan or merchant—but so they would be free to cultivate those arts and virtues that would enable them to serve as models and leaders for all others. Above all, samurai should set a high example of devotion to duty (*gi*, or rightness). If this sense of duty required the other classes to perform their respective functions conscientiously, it specifically required samurai to serve their lord with the utmost loyalty and in general to put devotion to moral principle (rightness) ahead of personal gain. The achievement of this high ideal involved a life of austerity, temperance, constant self-discipline, and readiness to meet death at any time, qualities long honored in the Japanese feudal tradition but now given systematic form by Sokō in terms of Confucian ethical philosophy. To set forth the lofty mission of the warrior class and its attendant obligations, he wrote a series of works dealing in detail with "the teaching for warriors" (bukyō) and "the Way of the samurai" (shidō). In the twentieth century, this series was taken to be the first systematic exposition of what came to be known as the Way of the warrior (bushidō).

It is good to remember, however, that for Sokō the Way of the warrior was not all moral indoctrination and martial discipline, and his contribution to it was more than simply codifying and providing a philosophical basis for Japanese feudal traditions. Sokō also stressed the so-called peaceful arts—letters and history—as essential to the intellectual discipline of the samurai. In this he reflects a characteristic feature of the age: the union of military power, as represented by the shogunate, with the civil arts, as the Tokugawa encouraged them through a Confucian type of humanistic studies. At the same time, Sokō exemplifies a historical trend of momentous significance: the conversion of the samurai class during the long Tokugawa peace from a military aristocracy to an increasingly political and intellectual leadership. This development helps explain why instead of becoming an idle and effete class relying on its hereditary privileges, the samurai could serve as the brains of the Restoration movement, take the initiative in dismantling feudalism itself, and play an important role in Japan's subsequent modernization.

Significantly, however, Sokō's intellectual interests did not conform exactly to the Confucian pattern of civil arts and peaceful pursuits. He was intensely concerned with military science, devoting himself to the study of strategy and tactics, weapons, and the acquisition of military intelligence, subjects for which the average Chinese Confucian would have expressed great disdain. But considering later Japanese thinkers' emphasis on moral indoctrination as the essence of bushidō, Sokō's affirmation that intelligence, too, was one of the martial virtues had important implications. He himself drew attention to the need for studying and adopting Western weapons and tactics as introduced by the Dutch, and it is striking that his claimed heirs in the nineteenth century, antiforeign though they were, quickly realized the necessity for "knowing the enemy" and thus for learning more about the West. Yoshida Shōin, the hero of the Restoration era who was arrested for stowing away on one of Commodore Matthew Perry's ships in order to visit the West, was from a family that ran a military school based on the teachings of Yamaga Sokō.

Considering the purpose to which he wished to put his Confucianism in a feudal age, it is not surprising that Sokō should have chosen as his teacher Confucius himself, who had lived in a period of feudal transition, rather than the Neo-Confucians, whose social concerns were those of a highly developed civil bureaucracy in a centralized state and whose philosophical outlook reflected the greater urbanity of the Song. In 1665, however, no such allowances could be made to mitigate Sokō's offense when he publicly avowed his antipathy for Neo-Confucianism in the *Essential Teachings of the Sages* and was sent into exile the following year at the instigation of Hoshina Masayuki, lord of Aizu, a prominent member of the Tokugawa house and a stout defender of Zhu Xi. In this work, Sokō proclaimed his belief that the unadulterated truth could be found only in the ethical teachings of Confucius and that subsequent developments in the Confucian tradition—especially the metaphysical theories of the Song Neo-Confucians—represented perversions of the original doctrine.

A main target of Sokō's attack was the notion that through quiet sitting, one might contemplate one's nature in its quiescent state. This he compared with the "direct apprehension of one's own nature" in Zen.[1] For Sokō, man's moral nature, as Mencius had defined it, consisted in the innate seeds or sprouts of goodness that, if cultivated and acted on, would become perfected in true humanity. Sokō's was a dynamic conception of human nature and principle, which could be fulfilled or realized only in action.[2] Because there was no such thing as a static, unitary principle or quiescent nature, whatever principle one attained in quiet sitting was, to him (using Zhu Xi's own language), like the "principle of dead and withered wood."[3]

It would be a mistake to conclude from Sokō's dynamic, functional view of the individual that he was a purely secular man without a religious dimension. For Sokō, Neo-Confucian "reverence" remained an essential value but directed outward in the form of respect for Heaven-and-earth and the objective standards exemplified in the ritual system of the sages. Moreover, for Sokō, the rituals also extended to the Shinto traditions of Japan. In this respect, his religiosity has a theistic quality that contrasts with the undifferentiated, rationalized "reverence" of the Cheng–Zhu school, which recognized no external object of devotion but was largely internalized.[4]

After Sokō was sent into exile, in the custody of the lord of Akō, his studies and writing turned more toward the Japanese tradition than to the Chinese. He became convinced that the civilization of Japan was even more glorious than that of its neighbor and wrote *True Facts Concerning the Central Kingdom* (*Chūchō jijitsu*) to show that his own country, not China, was the center and zenith of all culture. This claim Sokō based on the fact that Japan was divinely created and ruled by an imperial line coeval with heaven and earth. The truths

---

1. Yamaga, *Seikyō yōroku*, in *NST*, vol. 32, pp. 21, 24–25; *Haisho zanpitsu*, in *NST*, vol. 32, p. 334; and *Yamaga gorui* 33:233.

2. Yamaga, *Seikyō yōroku*, in *NST*, vol. 32, pp. 24–26, and *Yamaga gorui* 33:185–200.

3. Yamaga, *Yamaga gorui* 41:265–72, 296–97.

4. Yamaga, *Seikyō yōroku*, in *NST*, vol. 32, pp. 21–22.

that Confucius taught had already been revealed by the divine ancestors of the imperial house and, of course, were no less true on that account. But the Japanese alone had been true to the highest concept of duty as set forth by Emperor Jinmu and Confucius; they alone had set an example of unswerving loyalty to the dynasty. Conversely, in China, dynasties had come and gone, and Confucian teaching itself had been corrupted almost beyond recognition.

By pointing to the emperor as the focus of all loyalties, Sokō had no intention of undermining the shogunate's authority. Indeed, he contended that the recognition by Japan's successive military rulers of the imperial sovereignty was proof of both the continuity of imperial rule and the legitimate exercise of power by the shoguns as deputies of the emperors. Loyal service to the shogunate was therefore one more manifestation of that hierarchy of loyalties uniquely upheld by the Japanese. After being pardoned in 1675, Sokō was allowed to return to Edo and continue his teachings, albeit in a very circumscribed way. During his final decade, his thinking moved away from the relatively nativistic themes extolling Japan espoused in the *Chūchō jijitsu* and toward an exploration of the numerical foundations of change permeating the cosmos. Sokō's *Exploring the Origins of Things and Our Springs to Action (Gengen hakki)*, vaguely modeled on the Chinese *Classic of Changes (Yijing)*, a work crucially important to Neo-Confucians, signaled in part Sokō's coming full circle, returning to the kind of philosophical abstractions that he had earlier criticized Neo-Confucians like Zhu Xi for expounding.

PREFACE TO THE *ELEMENTARY LEARNING FOR SAMURAI* (*BUKYŌ SHŌGAKU*)

This preface, written by two of Yamaga Sokō's students, illustrates the transition from Neo-Confucian studies to the Way of the warrior, showing how Zhu Xi's primer, the *Elementary Learning*, was adapted to instruction for the samurai, taking into account the very different tradition and lifestyle of the Japanese military elite from the more civil-minded literati whom Zhu addressed. Although ostensibly intended for young people eight to thirteen years of age, Zhu's "primer" actually presupposed much familiarity with Chinese classical culture and history. Sokō (and his students) simplified this greatly, but in presenting the very different and more rigorous standards to which samurai must adhere, they invoke the prestige of the prevailing culture by citing Confucian texts (e.g., the *Record of Rites, Classic of Filiality, Great Learning*, and even the Song thinkers referred to in the text) to support the idea that Japanese traditions are native forms embodying universal truths.

In the Song dynasty [960–1279], the Chinese philosopher Zhu Xi wrote a book entitled *Elementary Learning* [J. *Shōgaku*, Ch. *Xiao-xue*]. It is a textbook for children between eight and fourteen (*sai*), teaching everything from sweeping up, responding to others, when to advance or retire, love for parents, respect for elders, and kindness for friends. Zhu's *Elementary Learning* is tied together by its emphasis on felicitous speech and goodness in action. Its contributions to elementary education have been notable.

Nevertheless, Japanese customs and traditions differ from those of China. Times and circumstances change. The conduct of common samurai in this country has become thoroughly corrupt. Even while living in this country, they are attracted to Chinese customs or study rites and ceremonies in a foreign way or perform Shinto rituals in a strange manner. This is all the fault of not investigating principles. Learning consists in investigating things and extending knowledge, not imitating Chinese customs. How could the Way of the samurai (*shi taru no michi*) be fulfilled by practicing common Chinese customs? Truly the pursuit of the Way of the Sage [Confucius] lies in studying it from childhood, being transformed by the wisdom gained from its practice, and having it become thoroughly integrated into one's own mind-and-heart. Our teacher Sokō's military instruction is quite lucid. Those who wish to become his disciples and study the Way of the samurai (*shidō* or *samurai no michi*) must accept his instructions as if they were commands! They must never allow their commitment [resolve (*shi*)] to lapse into self-indulgence or selfishness. . . .

The eighth lunar month of Meireki 2 [1656]

Respectfully recorded by Teacher Yamaga's disciples

Sokō's Elementary Learning deals with many of the same matters of daily life, training, and comportment as Zhu Xi's text does, but it speaks to the samurai as mature men (not to the early training of children, as in Zhu Xi's case) and as a class (with little of Zhu Xi's emphasis on the cultivation and formation of the individual self). The following excerpts from the first and last chapters include a notable section about the education and treatment of women in samurai families.

Early to Bed, Early to Rise

The samurai code requires that samurai rise at dawn, wash their face and hands, groom themselves, dress properly, and prepare their weapons. Then samurai should harmonize themselves with the soothing, calm ethers (*ki*) of the early morning air. With due appreciation for the graciousness of their lord and their father, samurai should deliberate on their daily responsibilities to them, remembering the adage of the *Classic of Filiality*:

> I received my body, its skin and hair, from my father and mother. Keeping myself from harm is the first duty of filial piety. Establishing myself, practicing the Confucian way, leaving an honorable name to posterity, and thus conferring distinction on my parents, that is the consummation of filial piety.

Then samurai should attend to their family affairs and receive guests. [When] serving their lord, samurai must be prompt. [When] attending their parents, samurai should call on them, personally looking after their comfort. When executing tasks, samurai must not exceed their station or their lord's directives. When serving their superiors, samurai need to treat them with respect as they would their own parents, being deferential and not quarrelsome. "They should make friends through culture and learning and, through friendship, cultivate humaneness."[5] When among comrades, samurai should exchange many questions.[6] Samurai must be honest, never deceitful. Avoiding laziness, they should remember their proper duties. Such is the Way of intercourse with friends.

For samurai the path of official service finds them first out in the morning and ahead of others in dispatching business; in the evening they are the last to go home. [When] returning to their families, samurai should greet their parents first, then relax. [When] seated, they should ask what happened in their absence. They must deal with urgent matters promptly. In their free moments samurai should reflect on the events of the day; read philosophy, history, and biographies; and reflect on the true Way of the samurai (shi no seidō) so that they will understand the nature of righteous and unrighteous conduct. At dusk samurai must prepare for the evening hours, taking the necessary precautions to guard against accidents from fires and darkness. Having secured the safety of their household, samurai should retire to their bedroom to rest. Thus they give ease to the body and rest to those who serve them.

Precepts for Posterity

[When] instructing their daughters, samurai must use exceptional care. Often femininity and softness are deemed—albeit quite mistakenly—to be the norm in teaching them. Because samurai are invariably preoccupied with official matters, they are not fully aware of the problems of the inner household. In their stead, their wives must administer family matters. Given these responsibilities, how can they be soft and effeminate? Men should not override their wives in domestic matters; women should not have the final say in official matters. In order to differentiate their concerns, official life and that of the home, husband and wife should not presume to judge each other's domains.[7] Nor should men and women share a clothing rack, as their apparel should not be mixed together, and women should never dare to hang their robes on a man's clothing rack. In addition, the wife of a samurai should treat her parents-in-law properly.

---

5. *Analects* 12:24.
6. *Analects* 16:4.
7. *Record of Rites [Liji]*, "Family Regulations" (chap. 10).

In the Han and the Tang dynasties, many Chinese women chose death for the sake of rightness in defending their duties. Likewise in Japan the wives and daughters of samurai have not let considerations of success or failure alter their sense of rightness, nor have they allowed matters of life and death to change their minds about what is right. Thus some sacrificed themselves [while] fighting rebels, and others died [while] combating enemy warriors. What can femininity and softness have to do with defending propriety or standing for what is right? In women the yin forces predominate; their bodies are naturally weaker and they are more submissive in mind and heart. Therefore yielding and compliance characterize their activities, but these are to be governed by resoluteness. Lewdness should never, not even at play or in jokes, be part of one's relations with women. Taught by the moral Way of rightness and duty, shown in what is essential to the Way of the samurai, the Way of husband and wife will then be correct, and the great Confucian Way of human moral relations will be illumined [made manifest in action].

[Adapted from *Yamaga Sokō zenshū: Shisōhen*, vol. 1, pp. 481–82, 485–86, 495–97; JAT]

THE WAY OF THE SAMURAI
(SHIDŌ)

The opening passage of *The Way of the Samurai*, which follows, lays the groundwork for Sokō's exhaustive discussion of this subject as recorded by his disciples. Reflecting the general Neo-Confucian approach to ethics (compare, for example, Yamazaki Ansai's discussion of the guiding principles of Zhu Xi's school), it is entitled "Establishing One's Fundamental Aim: Knowledge of One's Own Function." Here Sokō stresses the correct understanding of one's place and function in a feudal society and its application to Confucian ethics based on personal relationships.

The master once said: The generation of all men and of all things in the universe is accomplished by means of the marvelous interaction of the two forces [yin and yang]. Man is the most highly endowed of all creatures, and all things culminate in man. For generation after generation, men have taken their livelihood from tilling the soil, or devised and manufactured tools, or produced profit from mutual trade, so that peoples' needs were satisfied. Thus the occupations of farmer, artisan, and merchant necessarily grew up as complementary to one another. But the samurai eats food without growing it, uses utensils without manufacturing them, and profits without buying or selling. What is the justification for this? When I reflect today on my pursuit in life, [I realize that] I was born into a family whose ancestors for generations have been warriors and whose pursuit is service at court. The samurai is one who does not cultivate, does not manufacture, and does not engage in trade, but it cannot be that he

has no function at all as a samurai. He who satisfies his needs without performing any function at all would more properly be called an idler. Therefore one
must devote all one's mind to the detailed examination of one's calling.

Human beings aside, does any creature in the land—bird or animal, lowly
fish or insect, or inanimate plant or tree—fulfill its nature by being idle? Birds
and beasts fly and run to find their own food; fish and insects seek their food
as they go about with one another; plants and trees put their roots ever deeper
into the earth. None of them has any respite from seeking food, and none
neglects for a day or an instant in a year its flying, running, or going about [for
food]. All things are thus. Among men, the farmers, artisans, and merchants
also do the same. He who lives his whole life without working should be called
a rebel against Heaven. Hence we ask ourselves how it can be that the samurai
should have no occupation, and it is only then when we ask about the function
of the samurai that [the nature of] his calling becomes apparent. If one does
not apprehend this by oneself, one will depend on what others say or [will
understand] only what is shown in books. Since one will not then truly comprehend it with one's heart, one's purpose will not be firmly grounded. When
one's purpose is not firmly grounded, owing to one's long ingrained bad habits
of lethargy and vacillation, one will be inconstant and shallow. [In this condi-
tion] can the samurai's purpose by any means mature? For this reason, one must
first establish the basic principle of the samurai. If one follows the suggestion
of someone else or leaves matters to the shifting dictates of one's own heart,
even though one may, for example, achieve what one wants in a given instance,
it will be difficult for one to fulfill one's purpose in any true sense.

If he deeply fixes his attention on what I have said and examines closely his
own function, it will become clear what the business of the samurai is. The
business of the samurai is to reflect on his own station in life, to give loyal
service to his master if he has one, to strengthen his fidelity in associations with
friends, and, with due consideration of his own position, to devote himself to
duty above all. However, in his own life, he will unavoidably become involved
in obligations between father and child, older and younger brother, and husband and wife. Although these are also the fundamental moral obligations of
everyone in the land, the farmers, artisans, and merchants have no leisure from
their occupations, and so they cannot constantly act in accordance with them
and fully exemplify the Way. Because the samurai has dispensed with the business of the farmer, artisan, and merchant and confined himself to practicing
this Way, if there is someone in the three classes of the common people who
violates these moral principles, the samurai should punish him summarily and
thus uphold the proper moral principles in the land. It would not do for the
samurai to know martial and civil virtues without manifesting them. Since this
is the case, outwardly he stands in physical readiness for any call to service, and
inwardly he strives to fulfill the Way of the lord and subject, friend and friend,
parent and child, older and younger brother, and husband and wife. Within

his heart he keeps to the ways of peace, but without, he keeps his weapons ready for use. The three classes of the common people make him their teacher and respect him. By following his teachings, they are able to understand what is fundamental and what is secondary.

Herein lies the Way of the samurai, the means by which he earns his clothing, food, and shelter and by which his heart is put at ease; and he is able to pay back at length his obligation to his lord and the kindness of his parents. If he did not have this duty, it would be as though he were to steal the kindness of his parents, greedily devour the income of his master, and make his whole life a career of robbery and banditry. This would be very unfortunate. Thus I say that he first must study carefully the duties of his own station in life. Those who have no such understanding should immediately join one of the three classes of the common people. Some should make their living by cultivating the fields; some should pass their lives as artisans; and some should devote themselves to buying and selling. Then the retribution of Heaven will be light. But if by chance he wished to perform public service and to remain a samurai, he should commit himself to performing even menial functions; he should accept a small income; he should reduce his indebtedness to his master; and he should be ready to do simple tasks [such as] gatekeeping and nightwatch duty. This then is [the samurai's] calling. The man who takes or seeks the pay of a samurai and wants a stipend without understanding his function at all must feel shame in his heart. Therefore I say that what the samurai should take as his fundamental aim is to know his own function.

[*Yamaga Sokō bunshū*, pp. 45–48; RT, WTdB]

SHORT PREFACE TO THE *ESSENTIAL TEACHINGS OF THE SAGES* (*SEIKYŌ YŌROKU*)

In this preface to the *Essential Teachings of the Sages* (1665), Sokō's pupils explain the risks of publishing this work and the reasons why Sokō nevertheless insisted on going ahead with it. Indeed, the year after its publication, Sokō was sent into exile.

The sages lived long ago in the past, and their precise teachings have gradually been lost. The scholars of the Han, Tang, Song, and Ming dynasties have misled the world, piling confusion upon confusion. And if this has been true in China, how much the more has it been true in Japan.

Our teacher appeared in this country two thousand years after the time of the sages. He has held to the Way of the Duke of Zhou and Confucius and was the first to address their essential teachings. Whatever the problem—of the individual, of the family, the state, or the world—and whether it has concerned the arts of peace or the arts of war, his teaching has never failed to solve it and deal with it effectively. Truly the presence of such a teacher among us is a sign of the beneficial influences emanating from our good government.

In order to preserve his teachings for posterity but not knowing whether the general public should be allowed to share in its benefits, we, his disciples, collected his sayings and then made this request of our master: "These writings should be kept secret and sacred to us; they should not be spread abroad among men. Your criticisms of Confucian scholarship in the Han, Tang, Song, and Ming dynasties contradict the prevailing view among scholars. Some readers might complain to the authorities about it."

The master answered, "Ah, you young men should know better. The Way is the Way of all-under-Heaven; it cannot be kept to oneself. Instead, it should be made to permeate all-under-Heaven and be practiced in all ages. If this book can help even a single man stand on his own convictions, that will be a contribution to the moral uplift of our times. The noble man must sometimes give his life in the fulfillment of his humanity. Why should my writings be kept secret?

"Moreover, to talk about the Way and mislead people concerning it is the greatest crime in the world. The textual exegesis of the Han and the Tang, the Song and Ming school of principle, so clever in speech and full of talk, wanted to clear up the confusion but ended up only making it worse. The sages were left sitting in filth and mud—a dreadful spectacle!

"The sages' scriptures are self-evident to all-under-Heaven; there is no need for lengthy comment. And I, deficient in scholarship and no master of letters—how could I aspire to write a new commentary on these sacred texts or engage in controversy with other scholars about them? And yet unless this is done, the filth and defilement of these other scholars cannot be cleansed away and the texts restored to their original purity.

"I am 'mindful of future generations' and aware of my own shortcomings. Once my sayings are out in public, all the world will publicize them, condemn them, and criticize them. Should these reports, accusations, and criticisms help correct my mistakes, it will be a great blessing to the Way. They say, 'A pig of a barbarian invites ridicule; the boastful ass is apt to fall on his own knee.' The weakness of us all lies in seeing only our own side and not seeing that of others, in the lack of open-mindedness.

"I look up to the Duke of Zhou and Confucius for guidance, but not to the Confucians of the Han, Tang, Song, or Ming. What I aim to master is the teaching of the sages, not the aberrant views of deviationists; in my work I occupy myself with everyday affairs, not with a transcendental feeling of being 'unconstrained.'[8] . . . The Way of the sages is not one person's private possession.

---

8. Reference to the serenity of mind that Zhu Xi attributed to his teacher Li Tong, attained through quiet sitting.

That which can be practiced by one individual, but not by all the world, is not the Way. My sole aim is to reveal it to the world and await the judgment of noble men in the future."

[*Yamaga Sokō shū*, vol. 6, pp. 167–68; NST, vol. 32, pp. 8–9; RT, WTdB]

ESSENTIAL TEACHINGS OF THE SAGES
(*SEIKYŌ YŌROKU*)

The following are excerpts from the distillation by Sokō's students of his *Essential Teachings of the Sages*. They show that despite Sokō's break with the Song Neo-Confucians, the topics he addressed largely follow the Neo-Confucian agenda and conceptual vocabulary. By contesting the latter, he showed why it was difficult to escape from its orbit completely. The classified titles themselves come from Zhu Xi's writings or reflect the ordering of topics in Chen Beixi's *Neo-Confucian Terms Explained* (*Xingli ziyi*).

Establishing Teachings

Unless taught, people do not understand the Confucian Way. When they misunderstand the Way, humans can wreak more havoc than birds and beasts. If not ethically transformed through instruction, people fall prey to heterodoxies, believe perverse theories, worship phantoms, and ultimately even "murder their rulers and parents."[9] In founding states and establishing themselves as rulers, ancient kings thus instituted school systems as one of their first tasks. If rulers govern by morally educating their people, then both their ministers and people will be truly transformed. With sustained instruction, people will see moral teachings as their customs, and then all will live in natural peace and security. Families, states, and the world have teachings specific to them. Nevertheless, when morality is unified, the customs of mankind become the same for everyone.

Reading Books

Books convey the surviving wisdom of ancient and modern times. We thus should read them with all our strength. Indeed, we must read energetically as each day we pursue practical affairs, because Confucian education depends largely on book learning. Education will conflict with daily practical matters if we obsessively read books, neglecting to practice the moral Confucian way as well. If we read books after having made moral learning our purpose in life, we will benefit immensely. But if we read books thinking that learning consists of

---

9. *Mencius* 3B:9.

nothing else, we will end up like a commoner who, amusing himself with useless playthings, loses his purpose in life.

The books we should read describe the sages' moral teachings. Confucian teachings are very plain and simple. . . .

The Succession to the Way

Sokō's fundamentalism is based on Confucius as the sole authentic source of the Way and regards all his successors as falling short of the Master. But the very term and concept of "Succession to the Way" (J. *dōtō*, Ch. *daotong*) was Zhu Xi's, so Sokō is only perpetuating and redefining Zhu's account of the attenuation of the Way while insisting that the original "pure" Way, shorn of all later, synthetic efforts to embrace new ideas, represents the true universal Way of all humanity.

The ten ancient sages—Fu Xi; Shen Nong; the Yellow Emperor; Yao; Shun; Yu; Kings Tang, Wen, and Wu; and the Duke of Zhou [ca. 1045 B.C.E.]— extended their virtue and knowledge to the world, supplying myriad generations with their blessings. As the Zhou dynasty [1045–249 B.C.E.] declined, Heaven blessed humanity with the birth of Confucius. As Mencius remarked, "Since the creation of humanity, there has never been another as great as Confucius."[10] With his demise, however, the transmission of the sagely teachings nearly ceased. Although they tried, Zengzi, Zisi, and Mencius could not peer beyond the vision that Confucius offered. Some Han and Tang scholars sought to revive the transmission of the Confucian Way, but they could not even match Mencius, Zengzi, and Zisi. Following the rise of Song thinkers like Zhou Dunyi [1017–1073]; the two Cheng brothers, Cheng Mingdao [1032–1085] and Cheng Yichuan [1033–1107]; Zhang Zai [1020–1077]; and Shao Yong [1011–1077], Confucian teachings underwent egregious transformations. Those Song academics believed that Confucianism was yang and heterodoxies were yin, as though the two were complementary halves of some greater whole. In the Song, the transmission of the moral Confucian way was thus obliterated! The situation became even worse with the rise of Lu Xiangshan [1139–1193] and Wang Yangming's [1472–1529] many disciples. Only Zhu Xi made major contributions to studies of the Confucian classics, but even he could not transcend his predecessors' excesses. . . .

From Mencius's demise to the Song [dynasty], Confucianism underwent three degenerations. The first, during the Warring States period [403–222 B.C.E.], was the rise of the amoral schools of the Legalists and the theorists of the horizontal and vertical alliances. The second, evident in Han and Tang literature, was the

---

10. *Mencius* 2A:2.

sterile work of commentators, specialists, and logicians. The third transformation was the abstractions of the Song schools of principle and the mind. From Confucius's death to the present, more than two thousand years have passed. With these degenerations, the Way of the Duke of Zhou and Confucius lapsed into mere subjective ruminations, deceiving and confusing people.

The Way

The Way is practical. Unless it can be followed everyday, it is not the Way. The sagely Way is the Way of humanity; thus it consists of what everyone should follow in their daily activity, regardless of time and place. If it were artificial or contrived so that only one person could follow it but others could not, or so that the ancients could follow it but moderns could not, then it would not be the Way of humanity, nor would the *Mean* have said that it "follows human nature."[11]

As a concept, the notion of "the Way" arose from the word for a road that people follow. When traveling, people must follow roads. For example, wagons and carriages traverse the great highways linking the imperial capital with every direction. Because these highways facilitate the flow of people and commodities, everyone wants to use them.[12] Back alleys, while convenient for locals, are narrow, cramped, and difficult to navigate; nevertheless, they are occasionally attractive. Confucius's Way is a great thoroughfare, while heterodox ways are mere alleys.

Principle

Principle refers to rational order (*jōri*).[13] Everything has a rational order. If that order is thrown into confusion, then matters of precedence and hierarchy will never be right. A person errs greatly if he views human nature and heaven as principle. A natural and rational order (*shizen no jōri*) pervades Heaven, earth, people, and physical things. Ritual propriety (*rei*) embodies that order.

Rites

Rites are the patterns of behavior that people should follow in their lives. People follow them so that they can regulate their actions to the Mean and bring order

---

11. *Mean* 1.

12. *Mencius* 1A:7: "Travelers all would wish to get onto the king's roads (if he ruled humanely)"; *Mencius* 6B:2: "The way is like a large road."

13. *Mencius* 5B:1: "Proceeding along with . . . the rational order of things is the work of wisdom."

to their daily tasks.[14] A person who can both understand and practice rites is a sage. Without rites, people would not know what to do with their hands and feet or what they should look at or listen to! Without rites, people would not know when to advance and when to retreat or when to press on and when to yield.[15] With rites, peace prevails in the home, the community, and the imperial house, as well as in the civilian and military arenas. Rites do not distort feeling, nor do they simply embellish appearances: instead, they provide natural regulation (*shizen no setsu*). Rites are thus the Way from which we cannot depart. The sagely Confucian teachings consist simply of rituals and music.

Reverent Seriousness and Respectfulness

Whereas Zhou Dunyi emphasized "quiescence" (*jing*) as a contemplative ideal, the Cheng brothers and Zhu Xi preferred another *jing*, which combined the classic Confucian virtue of religious reverence with a seriousness focused on moral principle, as preferable to anything redolent of Daoist or Buddhist quietism. For Sokō, even this amendment was unsatisfactory, since it still was associated with the Neo-Confucian practice of "quiet sitting" and a focus on the unity of principle, which Sokō rejected as too metaphysical.

Reverent seriousness refers to being earnest and respectful in conduct and refraining from doing things in a wild and unregulated way. If a person perfectly manifests seriousness in every aspect of the rites, he is behaving with proper vigilance. When discussed apart from the rites, reverent seriousness sounds oppressive, cramped, and uncomfortable.

Confucius's sagely teachings focused on ritual decorum. When practicing the rites, a person becomes reverent and serious. Yet dwelling in seriousness is not the way to master ritual decorum. Song Confucians nevertheless declared that reverent seriousness was the foundation of learning; they also claimed that it was the means by which a person could perfectly embody the sagely Confucian learning from beginning to end.[16] However by following the Song Confucian

---

14. *Record of Rites*, "Evolution of Rites": "Confucius said, ' . . . to neglect (the rites) is to die, while to follow them enables one to live a proper life'" (Legge, trans., *Li Chi*, vol. 1, p. 367); *Record of Rites*, "Confucius at Ease in His Home": "Confucius said, ' . . . with rituals one adjusts one's behavior to the mean'" (Legge, trans., *Li Chi*, vol. 2, p. 271).

15. *Record of Rites*, "Confucius at Ease in His Home": "Without the rites, one would not know how to dispose of his hands and feet, or how to apply his ears and eyes; and his advancing and retiring, his bowing and giving place would be without any definite rules" (Legge, trans., *Li Chi*, vol. 2, p. 273).

16. Zhu Xi, *Zhuzi quanshu* 2:21b: "Reverent seriousness is the first principle of the Confucian school. From beginning to end, it must not be interrupted for an instant" (Chan, *Source Book in Chinese Philosophy*, p. 606).

methods of "concentrating on unity" (*shuitsu*) and "quiet sitting" (*seiza*), people become overly scrupulous, submerged in silence, and oppressively narrow. Confucius explained seriousness as being cautious and apprehensive.[17] Accordingly, the caution and apprehension produced by reverent seriousness in ritual decorum engenders a natural calmness and serenity. Dwelling exclusively on seriousness imprisons the human mind so that it [can] penetrate nothing.

Respectfulness (*kyō*) refers to reverent seriousness displayed externally.

[Yamaga Sokō, *Seikyō yōroku*, in NST, vol. 32, pp. 14–21; JAT]

AN AUTOBIOGRAPHY IN EXILE
(*HAISHO ZANPITSU*)

In *An Autobiography in Exile*, written during Sokō's years in exile, he traces his own intellectual development from Neo-Confucianism through Daoism and Buddhism to his "rediscovery" of the authentic traditions of Confucianism and Shinto.

In the autobiography, Sokō describes his spiritual odyssey and the doubts he experienced, like many Neo-Confucians before him, until he found the teaching that could become his way of life. His early education was in the Cheng–Zhu school, which was, as he came to realize later, very "Chinese." It was also a very "catholic" training, including both orthodox book learning and spiritual discipline. The latter he identified with the practice of "sustained reverence" (J. *jikei*, Ch. *chijing*) manifested mainly in the form of quiet sitting. But apparently, he found it too constraining and wondered whether it was making him too grave, overserious, and withdrawn. Turning to Daoism and Buddhism, especially as synthesized by Zen, Sokō found that their mystical insights provided greater access to spiritual freedom and spontaneity.[18] These were the values that the Neo-Confucians themselves had recognized, and at this stage of his development Sokō found them immensely liberating.

In pursuing an "inexpressible state of selfless purity and mystical freedom," however, Sokō became aware that it took him away from society, not into it. His continued search for a practicable, livable "way" for the Japanese of his time led him back to both the original teachings of the Confucian classics and the original Japanese way of life in Shinto, from which he derived a simplified system of basic ethics that would serve as a kind of common denominator adaptable to any social situation in life, whether that of the samurai, townsman, or peasant.

Sokō's autobiography, written while he was living in exile in Akō following the publication of his *Essential Teachings of the Sages* (*Seikyō yōroku*), reflects the nativistic developments in his thinking as expressed in the *True Facts Concerning the Central*

---

17. *Mean* 1.
18. Yamaga, *Haisho zanpitsu*, in NST, vol. 32, pp. 33–34.

Kingdom (Chūchō jijitsu). It does not, however, refer to the final stage of Sokō's intellectual development during his last decade in Edo following his pardon: his numerical analyses of change as explained in *Exploring the Origins of Things and Our Springs to Action (Gengen hakki).*

I am taking this occasion to write down some of my views about learning. For a long time I have been fond of studying foreign books. Although I am not acquainted with those writings that have reached this country only in recent years, I nonetheless have gone through all the books received from China a decade or more ago. I feel, therefore, that at least I am well acquainted with things Chinese.

I once thought that Japan was small and thus inferior in every way to China, that "only in China could a sage arise." This was not my idea alone; scholars of every age have thought so and devoted themselves to studying Chinese. Only recently I have become aware of the serious errors in this view. We have "believed too much in what we heard and not enough in what our own eyes could see; we have ignored what is near at hand in our search for the distant." Truly this is, without doubt, the chronic weakness of our scholars. This point I tried to make clear in my *True Facts Concerning the Central Kingdom (Chūchō jijitsu).* The following is a short summary of what I said there:

In Japan the one true imperial line, legitimate descendants of the Sun Goddess, has ruled from the divine ages to the present time without the interruption of a single generation. The Fujiwara, too, loyal vassals and supporters of the throne, have survived, with men of every generation serving as premier or minister. Such unbroken succession has no doubt been due to the inability of rebels and traitors to succeed in treachery and intrigue, but has this not in turn been due to the wide prevalence in Japan of the cardinal virtues of humanity and rightness? . . .

No less deserving of mention is Japan's pursuit of the Way of martial valor. The three kingdoms of Han[19] were conquered and made to bring tribute to the court. Korea was subjugated and its royal castle made to surrender.[20] Japanese military headquarters were established on foreign soil, and Japanese military prestige was supreme over the Four Seas from the earliest times to the present day. Our valor in war inspired fear in foreigners. As for invasion from abroad, foreigners never conquered us or even occupied or forced cession of our land. In fact, in the manufacture of armor for man and horse, the manufacture and use of sword and spear, and, again in military science, strategy and tactics, no

---

19. Three kingdoms of Han refers to Korea. The name derives from three early kingdoms in southern Korea known to Japanese as Bakan (Na-han), Shinkan (Mu-han), and Benkan (Hinhan). The conquest of Korea referred to here is that of the Empress Jingō (r. ca. 362–380). At the time of this invasion, the three kingdoms of Korea were Silla, Koguryo, and Paekche.

20. Reference to the invasion of Korea by Hideyoshi in 1592.

other country can equal us. Within the Four Seas, then, are we not supreme in military valor? . . .

Many paths to learning have existed in the past and present. Confucianism, Buddhism, and Daoism each has its own basic principle. In my own case, from boyhood to manhood I devoted myself to studying the Cheng–Zhu system, and consequently my writings in those days were generally in accord with this system. Then in middle age I became interested in Laozi and Zhuangzi and accepted as basic such mystical concepts as emptiness and nothingness. At the same time I also developed a particular admiration for Buddhism and visited the eminent masters of the five Zen monasteries, including even Abbot Ingen, because of my eagerness to pursue the path to enlightenment.

While I was studying the Cheng–Zhu system, I was too much given— perhaps owing to my own ineptitude—to the practice of sustained reverence and silent sitting and found myself becoming too taciturn and grave. Compared with the Cheng–Zhu system, however, the approach of Laozi, Zhuangzi, and Zen proved far more full of life and freedom. The identification of human mental activity with the mystic activity of nature led to a deep insight. From that point on I followed the impulse of my own nature; all was spontaneous. Heaven and earth might fail, but there would be no doubt that the eternal and unchanging principle would remain active and untrammeled.

Nevertheless, there was still much that I did not understand about everyday matters. Thinking that this might again be due to my own ineptitude, I pursued this method all the more diligently in the hope that I might improve. It might be, I thought, that daily affairs are of such little importance that it is better to let them take their own course. Still, we find ourselves bound by the five obligations of human relationship and are so much involved in everyday affairs that we cannot go on in that way; we are held in their grip. If we should make our abode under the trees or on some rock in lonely solitude, scorning worldly honor and fame, we might be able to attain an inexpressible state of unselfish purity and mystical freedom. But when it comes to the affairs of the world or the state, and of the four classes of the people, needless to say we would not be able to accomplish anything in that manner. We would have less understanding of even minor things than does the uneducated man in the street.

Some say that if the perfection of humanity (*jin*) could be fully realized in the mind, all the things of this world and all the affairs of men would be taken care of; others say that if the compassion of Buddha were made the basic principle, all would work out for good in the three existences: past, present, and future. But all these ideas serve only to keep learning apart from the real world. Whatever others may think, I myself cannot believe otherwise or accept that kind of learning as satisfactory. . . .

Then, early in the Kanbun era [1661–1672], it occurred to me that my failure to comprehend might be because I had been reading the scholars of the Han, Tang, Song, and Ming. By going directly to the writings of the Duke of Zhou and Confucius and using them as my model, I could correctly ascertain the guiding lines of thought and study. After that I stopped using later writings but day and night applied myself to the works of the sages. Then for the first time I understood clearly the guiding teachings of the sages, and their underlying principle became firmly fixed in my mind. . . .

Now to learn the guiding principles of the sages, neither language nor scholarship is needed, because [the principles are so simple that] if I am told about them today, I can understand what I am to do today. Neither the "moral training" nor the "sustained reverence" nor the "silent sitting" [of the Neo-Confucians] is required. . . .

Among the paths to learning is one that emphasizes personal virtue and cultivates benevolence through the intensive practice of moral training and silent sitting. Another involves personal cultivation, the guidance of others, the maintenance of peace and order in the world, and the winning of honor and fame. There also is one arising from a love of books and stressing the writing of poetry or prose. Scholars may be divided into these three classes, each with his own attitude or approach.

As far as I can observe, however, it is difficult in our times for men to reach the degree of rightness that prevailed in the days of the Yellow Emperor and the sage-kings Yao and Shun, so that rule by virtue alone is sufficient through its beneficent influence to keep the country under control without a word of command being given, or to make peace reign supreme within the Four Seas so as to win without coercion the willing submission of an enemy. Even though we should take the sage-kings as our model, no good result would come of it. Scholars who advocate such a course have lofty aims, but in the end they turn their backs on the world and return in solitude to commune only with the birds and the beasts. But the love of books and literary pursuits are merely scholarly diversions, not matters of everyday concern. Writing is a corollary of learning, and I do not cast any aspersions on it. Writing poetry and prose is something that should not be neglected "if one has spare time for them."[21]

To me, therefore, the guiding path to the sages' teaching involves personal cultivation, the guidance of others, the maintenance of peace and order in the world, and the winning of honor and fame. I come from a samurai family, and my person and station are ruled by the five obligations of human relationship. My own thought and conduct, as well as my five obligations in relations with others, are what I as a samurai must first attend to. In addition are the major and minor matters to which the samurai must attend. In minor matters such as dress, food, dwelling, and all implements and their uses, he must live up to the best samurai traditions of good form. This is particularly true in connection with training in the arts of war and with the manufacture and use of armor and

---

21. Paraphrase of *Analects* 1:6.

horse trappings. Among major matters are the maintenance of peace and order in the world; rites and festivals; the control of feudal states and districts; mountains and forests; seas and rivers; farms and rice fields; temples and shrines; and the disposition of suits and appeals among the four classes of people. In addition, there is military command and organization, strategy in war and tactics in battle, the quartering and provisioning of the troops, and the building of fortifications—all those preparations for war that are the daily concern of generals and officers.

No matter how much training a samurai undergoes, if the studies he pursues do not enable him to get results in all these fields, then they serve no useful purpose and do not follow the guiding principle of the sages' teaching. . . . [But] if a man follows this approach to learning, his intelligence will be renewed; virtue itself will be heightened; humanity will be deepened; and courage will be strengthened. Finally, he will reach a state of mind in which success and fame are of no account, in which unselfishness and self-forgetfulness will be the rule. Thus he starts out with the idea of success and honor but arrives at a stage in which success and honor have no meaning, and he simply goes on fulfilling the Way by which man becomes truly human. The *Classic of Filiality* says: "Cultivate yourself and follow the Way; fame will be the natural outcome of filial piety."

[*Yamaga Sokō bunshū*, pp. 481–88; RT, WTdB]

ITŌ JINSAI'S SCHOOL OF ANCIENT MEANINGS

The tendency to break with Neo-Confucianism and return to the classical sources of Confucianism was given added impetus by a very different type of scholar from Yamaga Sokō, the gentle but persuasive Itō Jinsai (1627–1705). Whereas Sokō stood for the basic Confucian virtues as exemplified in the samurai, Jinsai, the son of a Kyoto townsman (*chōnin*), represented dedication to humanistic ideals, regardless of class. What they had in common was an independence of mind, which Jinsai demonstrated in his thinking and by making study and teaching a profession in itself and refusing all offers of lucrative employment from powerful feudal lords. In this respect, he followed the example of Confucius himself, who was probably the first to establish teaching in ancient China as an independent profession rather than as an official function.

Jinsai himself enjoyed great success as a teacher, attracting students in even larger numbers than Sokō did. The private school that he opened with the able assistance of his son Tōgai was devoted to the study of the original classics and was known as the Kogi-dō, or, roughly, Hall for Study of Ancient Meanings. Here the *Analects* of Confucius and the *Mencius* were the basic texts. Besides reducing Zhu Xi's Neo-Confucian canon, the Four Books, to these two texts,

Jinsai even went so far as to impugn the authenticity of the *Great Learning*, which Zhu had elevated to the rank of first importance as a Confucian classic.

In so doing, Jinsai broke with his earlier intellectual and spiritual formation from the standard works of the Neo-Confucian curriculum: in Zhu's lucid commentaries on the Four Books; in his anthology of the major Song philosophers, *Reflections on Things at Hand* (Ch. *Jinsilu*); and in the official Ming compilation of Neo-Confucian thought, the *Great Compendium of Human Nature and Principle* (Ch. *Xingli daquan*). Of special significance in this process was Jinsai's earlier fascination with Zhu's dialogues with his teacher, Li Tong, in the *Dialogues with Master Yanping* (*Yanping dawen*), offering a method of self-cultivation that held out the prospect of attaining the same lofty serenity of mind that Zhu so admired in Li.

This strong spiritual attraction of Neo-Confucianism was indicated by Jinsai's adoption of the pen name Keisai, expressing his dedication to a life of reverent seriousness (*kei*). (It previously was the pen name of Hu Juren [1434–1484], probably the most religiously inclined of Ming Cheng–Zhu schoolmen.) By the age of twenty-nine or thirty, however, Itō had changed his pen name to Jinsai, indicating a new commitment to humaneness (*jin*) as his highest ideal. From this we learn something about the intensity with which Jinsai devoted himself to studying Zhu Xi. We learn, too, how disenchanted he eventually became with his former spiritual ideal. As in the case of Sokō, what had first recommended itself as a demanding discipline and austere dedication to lofty goals eventually generated a reaction against its very rigorism and scrupulousness. From this experience of disenchantment with the Song model, style, and practice of sagely serenity, when Jinsai tried to articulate the intellectual and philosophical implications of his new stance, he could draw on the earlier work of the Ming Neo-Confucian Lo Qinshun, representing a brand of Neo-Confucian teaching that stressed material force, or ether, as the prime reality.[22]

Here Jinsai took issue with the Neo-Confucians on metaphysical grounds, rejecting Zhu Xi's dualism of principle (*ri*) and material force (*ki*) in favor of a monism that denied any standing to *ri* as a first principle. It was *ki*, conceived as the vital force, that underlay all three realms of existence: heaven, earth, and humankind. By conserving and developing the life force within, a person could achieve self-fulfillment in the virtue of humanity (*jin*), which for Jinsai meant "love."

From this vantage point, Jinsai saw the "reverence" or "seriousness" of the Song school as a deadening, life-denying attitude in much the same way as Sokō had spoken of the Song masters as searching out the "principle of dead and withered wood." . . .

---

22. See de Bary and Bloom, eds., *Sources of Chinese Tradition*, 2nd ed., vol. 1, chap. 24.

According to Jinsai, it was the subtle and pervasive influence of Buddhism that had led to the belief in sudden enlightenment as the culminating experience of sagehood. The Song was a time, he observed, when all educated persons of all classes, ages, and sexes were immersed in Zen, and they read into the Confucian classics Buddhist meanings that were not really there. Jinsai's principal written work, *The Meaning of Terms in the Analects and Mencius (Gomō jigi)*, is a critical analysis of key terms in the Neo-Confucian lexicon intended to show that their original meanings had been corrupted by Daoism and Buddhism. This corruption arose from the identification of man's essential nature with "principle." To Jinsai, principle was a "dead term," meaning that it applied to fixed norms or to the structure of inanimate objects. Principle was static and morally inert, whereas human nature and the Way were a living, dynamic reality. . . .

To Jinsai, the significance of humaneness could not be understood apart from the complementary virtues of reciprocity (mutuality) and rightness. Humaneness was given a practical definition only through a loving sense of identification with others and through actions responding appropriately to their needs. In other words, humaneness was expressed in the total context of a Way extending beyond the individual and his self-centered experience. . . .

As a Confucian fundamentalist, Jinsai wanted to return to the original "pure" teaching in the *Analects* and *Mencius*. As a Neo-Confucian revisionist, however, his return to the literal meaning of these ancient texts required that he critique the subsequent use of the same terms, as well as sort out the new terms, concepts, and practices that had intruded on the Song revivalist interpretation of Confucianism. In other words, Jinsai's literal reading of supposedly pure scripture had to have been affected by his reactions to the subsequent received tradition as he attempted to purge the latter of unwanted accretions. Finally, both the fundamentalist and revisionist views, albeit projected from a historical high ground, could not be unaffected by strong currents in the contemporary culture of Jinsai's own day. Thus what he saw as fundamental in the *Analects*— humaneness understood primarily as love—came close to the same theme in the Genroku literature of Jinsai's own townspeople, among whom love and human feeling (*ninjō*) reigned as the supreme values.

THE MEANING OF TERMS IN THE ANALECTS AND MENCIUS (*GOMŌ JIGI*)

From its title, we might assume that this major work of Itō Jinsai is a gloss on the *Analects* and the *Mencius*. Actually it is more a philosophical lexicon of terms prominent in Neo-Confucian discourse, whose prototype is Chen Beixi's *Neo-Confucian Terms Explained* (Ch. *Xingli ziyi*). Reflecting an awareness of the different uses of these terms in successive ages, Jinsai typically gives a historical account of these uses (abbreviated here), critically comparing them with the original meanings as he interpreted them in his two prime sources of authority: the *Analects* and *Mencius*. Jinsai's general approach is to view these key terms as having been distorted by Neo-Confucians in a misguided attempt to theoretically refute, or adapt to, Buddhism and Daoism.

The Way of Heaven

The word *michi* denotes a road or pathway: something that people follow in coming and going. Our conception of "the Way" thus refers to that through which everything comes and goes. The Way of Heaven refers to yin alternating with yang, ceaselessly coming and going. The *Classic of Changes* states, "Yin alternating with yang is called the Way."[23] The word "alternating" describes the ceaseless and successive motion by which yang follows yin and yin follows yang. It also conveys their coming and going, their growth and decline.

A unitary generative force (*ichigenki*) pervades all Heaven and earth. Sometimes it exists as yin, sometimes as yang. These two aspects of the generative force fill things and empty them, promoting both growth and decay. They actively come and go and respond ceaselessly to everything. As the whole substance of Heaven's way and the activating force of nature, yin and yang produce myriad transformations and manifold beings. . . .

The myriad things are rooted in the five elements, which in turn are grounded in yin and yang. If we further seek the origins of yin and yang, we cannot help but return to the notion of principle. That is the conclusion at which common sense inevitably arrives. However, in addition, Song Neo-Confucians devised their theory of the non-finite yet Supreme Ultimate. The analogy of square pegs being jammed into round holes aptly conveys the very mistaken nature of their reasoning. The claims of the Song Neo-Confucians, such as that "principle exists and then generative force exists" and "before the existence of heaven and earth, there was principle," are nothing more than subjective opinions. Like legs added to a picture of a snake or a head growing atop another head, they will never really be confirmed by experience!

The *Classic of Changes* states, "The great virtue of Heaven-and-earth is life-giving productivity."[24] Thus, ceaseless reproduction is the Way of Heaven-and-earth. . . . Because the Way of Heaven-and-earth is manifested only in life-giving creation, even though one's ancestors might have passed away, their spiritual essence has still been transmitted to their descendants. In turn the descendants transmit some of the same to their progeny. Spiritual essence is produced and reproduced ceaselessly. It is never exhausted and therefore attains immortality. The same is true with numerous living things. . . . [pp. 14–19]

---

23. *Concordance to Yi ching* [Yijing], p. 40; Legge, trans., *I ching*, p. 355.
24. *Concordance to Yi ching* [Yijing], p. 45; Legge, trans., *I ching*, p. 381.

The Decree of Heaven

We must discuss moral issues, but sometimes we must also discuss fate. Why? Going forward or standing still and advancing or retreating are indeed matters over which we have some control. We correctly understand them as moral issues. But matters like the preservation or destruction of a state and the prevalence or neglect of the Way depend ultimately on Heaven. Even the sage Confucius was not able to control them entirely as he wished! Therefore the *Analects* observed that "when the Way prevails, it is due to fate. When the Way is abandoned, that is also due to fate."[25] Mencius furthermore related that "Confucius said that success and failure are matters of fate."[26] The sage Confucius thus deemed fate to be worth discussing. While people must discuss morality, in some cases we can attribute circumstances only to fate. We are mistaken, however, in concluding that fate is not worthy of discussion.

When we lack the nobility that Heaven confers, it is morally wrong to claim the noble titles that humans invent.[27] We should simply not accept them. But if we have received the nobility that Heaven confers, then we may rightfully accept those titles bestowed by humanity. Indeed, we should accept them. Yet when we have the nobility that Heaven bestows, but not what man bestows, it is due to fate. [pp. 23–25]

Note in the foregoing Jinsai's assertion of a meritocratic basis for holding rank and office. A person should not accept an office if he is not morally and intellectually qualified to fill the position. According to that standard, townspeople, no less than samurai, could qualify, although fate (circumstances) might not allow for it.

The Way

Michi, meaning "the Way," denotes a road (*michi*), that is, something that all people follow in coming and going. Ancient Confucian writings explained that yin alternating with yang indicates the Way of Heaven. Firmness interacting with resilience embodies the Way of earth. Humaneness practiced along with rightness constitutes the Way of humanity. In each characterization, "the Way" signifies complementary activities.

Another ancient Confucian saying observes, "The Way is like a road."[28] By following it, you make progress. If you do not, you will never make any [progress] at all. Other statements like "Why does nobody follow the Way?"[29] and

---

25. *Analects* 14:36.
26. *Mencius* 5A:8.
27. That is, moral qualities (*Mencius* 6A:16).
28. Yang Xiong (53 B.C.E.–18 C.E.), "Questions About the Way," in *Fayan*, "Wendao" sec.
29. *Analects* 6:17.

"We cannot depart from the Way for even an instant"[30] illustrate the same point. They suggest that only by choosing a route and following it can we make real progress. They also indicate that the Way must be followed because it alone allows for complementary activities. While embracing these various nuances, the Way truly exemplifies a single unified principle. . . .

The Way is the path that people should follow in their daily ethical conduct. It does not exist simply because it was taught. Nor does it exist simply because it corrects human tendencies. Rather, it naturally exists. Throughout the four directions and eight corners of the world, everyone understands the moral relationships naturally existing between ruler and minister, parent and child, husband and wife, elder and younger brother, and friends. Everyone also understands the ways of parental affection, rightness, differentiation, precedence, and trustworthiness.[31] For many generations, this has been and will be true. Therefore these are called the Way. The statement in the *Mean*, "People cannot deviate from the Way for an instant,"[32] refers to this very universality of the Way.

The same is not true of the so-called teachings of Buddhism and Daoism. . . . Buddhists, Daoists, and recently "Zen-Confucians"[33] all have advocated principles that are quite empty and abstruse. They apparently enjoy formulating lofty, unattainable notions. They are not pleased with anything that is not mysterious; nor are they fascinated with a doctrine that is not abstract. But how can their supposedly lofty teachings adequately convey the all-penetrating Way that extends throughout time and space, that is, the Way that can never be discarded for an instant? Lengthy arguments are not necessary to distinguish our Confucian teachings from heterodox ones. . . .

Buddha believed that emptiness (*kū*) is the Way. Laozi saw it as vacuity (*kyo*). Buddha thought that mountains, rivers, and continents were all illusions (*genmō*). Laozi claimed that everything was born from nothingness (*mu*).[34] Now for many ages, Heaven and earth have sustained life; the sun and moon have illuminated the world; the seasons have followed one another; mountains have stood and rivers flowed; [and] birds, beasts, fish, insects, trees, and grasses have lived as they do even now. For myriad generations, creatures that metamorphose have been metamorphosing; life-forms that transform have been doing so. Transmitting and mutating, life has been produced and reproduced without limit! How could Buddhists and Daoists claim that everything is emptiness and vacuity? Their views crystallized after they stopped studying and indulged in speculative wisdom! Buddhists and Daoists retired to mountain forests, sat silently (*mokuza*), cleansed their minds (*chōshin*), and indeed achieved a certain

---

30. *Mean* 1.
31. The values that attach to the preceding Five Human Relationships (*Mencius* 3A:4).
32. *Mean* 1.
33. "Zen-Confucians" refers to Neo-Confucians and their followers.
34. *Daodejing*, chap. 40.

perspective on things. But their so-called principles exist neither inside this world nor outside it!

Fathers and sons love each other; husbands and wives love each other; [and] among friends, there is camaraderie. Not only is this true of humanity, the same applies to many animals. These relationships exist even among bamboo plants, trees, and other forms of inanimate life! Among them are distinctions between male and female, parent and child. How much more so must these distinctions be present in the minds of people endowed with the four beginnings,[35] moral intuition (*ryōchi*), and moral capacities (*ryōnō*).[36] Not only do noble persons (*kunshi*) behave in accordance with such moral relationships, even roadside beggars do! . . . [pp. 26–29]

Principle

The word "principle" (*ri*) is similar in meaning to the notion of "the Way." The Way refers to paths by which we go and come, whereas principle refers to the rational order of physical things. . . .

Someone asked, "Why did Confucius discuss Heaven and humanity in terms of the Way, and physical things in terms of principle?"

I replied, "The Way is a dynamic, living concept (*katsuji*), one capable of describing the reproductive and transformative mysteries of living things." "Principle" is a dead word. Dictionaries classify it under the jade radical, and its pronunciation derives from the word "mile" (*ri*).[37] Principle originally referred to the veins in a piece of jade. By extension, it came to refer to the rational order of inanimate things. Thus, principle can neither convey nor capture the mysteries that Heaven and earth spawn through productive transformative life. . . .

As a dynamic concept (*katsuji*), the Way signifies organisms alive with activity (*kō*). Principle, an inanimate, dead term (*shiji*), denotes things that exist (*son*) but are not alive. Because the sage Confucius saw the Way (*michi*) as real and substantial (*jitsu*), his accounts of its principles were dynamic (*katsu*). Laozi envisioned the Way as emptiness (*kyo*), and so his interpretations of its principles were morbid (*shi*). Confucius regularly discussed Heaven's Way and Heaven's decree, but never Heaven's principles (*tenri*). He explained the Way of humanity

---

35. *Mencius* 2A:6. These are (1) the mind of compassion (*sokuin no kokoro*), which is the beginning of humaneness (*jin no tan*); (2) the mind of shame (*shūo no kokoro*), the beginning of rightness (*gi no tan*); (3) the mind of deference (*jijō no kokoro*), the beginning of ritual decorum (*rei no tan*); and (4) the mind of right and wrong (*zehi no kokoro*), the beginning of wisdom (*chi no tan*).

36. *Mencius* 7A:15.

37. The *Shuowen*, a Han etymological dictionary, explains the meanings of words in terms of their written forms. Jinsai suggests that "principle" derived its meaning from inanimate things, such as jade, and abstract quantities, such as the measurement for a mile.

and human nature, but never the principle of humanity (*jinri*). Zhuangzi discussed principle more than any ancient thinker. He did so because he believed that the Way was emptiness and nothingness. In describing his vision of the Way, Zhuangzi inevitably turned to principle. We must conclude, therefore, that Neo-Confucians followed Laozi in making principle their main concern. . . .

Emptiness (*kyo*) and quietude (*jaku*) were originally coins of Buddhist and Daoist discourse. They never appeared in our sagely Confucian literature. . . . Zen learning spread across the world during the Song dynasty. Everyone who could read—scholars and soldiers, officials at all levels of government, men and women, young and old—studied Zen. Even Confucian scholars studied Zen! Unconsciously they began interpreting sagely Confucian literature in terms of it! Later, students believed that Confucianism consisted of the Zen notions that the Song Neo-Confucians had attributed to it. In particular, they never realized that the Neo-Confucians had so badly distorted Confucianism. [pp. 30–34]

Virtue

Virtue (*toku*) is a comprehensive notion that refers to virtues like humaneness (*jin*), rightness (*gi*), ritual decorum (*rei*), and wisdom (*chi*). . . .

Confucius discussed virtue but not the mind! Neo-Confucians philosophized about the mind, but gave virtue short shrift. Virtue, however, constitutes the world's highest good. It embraces several moral qualities. The sage Confucius thus instructed his students to pursue and practice virtue. . . .

Neo-Confucians emphasized the mind but neglected virtue. Stressing the mind's importance, they devoted all their talents to it. Each of their teachings concluded with a discourse on the mind. Their learning therefore seems withered and dry, lacking the calm composure and energetic magnanimity characterizing the teachings of the sage Confucius. This disparity flows from the very different focus that is at the basis of their learning. [pp. 35–37]

Humaneness and Rightness

Humaneness and rightness are the two great beginnings of the Way and virtue. They also stand as the comprehensive mind that wills all goodness. Ritual decorum (*rei*) and wisdom (*chi*) thus emerge from them. Heaven's Way encompasses yin and yang; earth's Way embraces the firm and resilient. Similarly, humaneness and rightness assist and complement each other, enabling our full realization of the Way of humanity. . . . [p. 38]

Reverence

In the Cheng–Zhu school, *jing* (J. *kei*), which combined religious reverence and moral seriousness, was a generalized attitude toward all life and creation, fundamental to both action and contemplation. Cheng Yi and Zhu Xi preferred it to the quiescence (*jing*) emphasized by Zhou Dunyi. Jinsai, however, rejected all such conceptions as too quietistic.

The word "reverence" (*kei*) signifies respect and veneration. Thus the ancient *Classics* discuss "reverencing Heaven,"[38] "reverencing ghosts and spirits,"[39] "revering a ruler," "reverencing parents," "reverencing older brothers,"[40] and "reverencing duties."[41] In those contexts, the *Classics* use the word "reverence" to signify veneration and worship. But never do they mention "reverence" apart from an object of reverence! . . .

Master Zhu Xi's *Questions and Answers on the Great Learning* claims, "Reverence completes the teachings of the sage from start to finish." Master Zhu also stated, "Reverence is the mind's ruling master and the foundation of the myriad things."[42] I cannot agree with such claims. The sagely learning of Confucius reveres humaneness and rightness while making loyalty and trustworthiness its masters in practice. . . .

Reverence is indeed essential to students. Yet loyalty, trustworthiness, reverence, and diligence all must be observed; none can be discarded! We greatly violate the Sage's teachings by insisting that reverence alone should be preserved. . . .

Humaneness and wisdom are ultimate virtues. Yet if our fondness for them is not enlightened by learning, we will end up being confused. How much more so might this be true of focusing solely on reverence? . . . [pp. 71–72]

The *Great Learning* Was Not by Confucius

Following a growing trend in the Song period, Zhu Xi singled out the *Great Learning* (a chapter in the *Record of Rites*) as a prime text of Neo-Confucian cultivation and first among the Four Books. Jinsai puts the *Analects* and *Mencius* first.

The words of the *Analects* are plain and honest, but its principles are deep and profound. Adding even one word would be excessive. Taking away one word would leave it imperfect. The *Analects* is the most perfect work of literature in the entire world. It exhaustively explains the principles of the world. It is truly the greatest book in the universe!

---

38. Legge, trans., *The Shoo king*, p. 437.
39. *Analects* 6:22.
40. *Concordance to the Hsiao ching* [*Xiaojing*], p. 2.
41. *Analects* 1:5.
42. This remark from Zhu Xi's *Daxue huowen* is quoted in Chen Beixi, "Seriousness," p. 48b; Chen Beixi, *Neo-Confucian Terms Explained*, trans. and ed. Chan, p. 102.

The *Mencius* explains the *Analects*. The words of the *Mencius* are very clear, and its principles [are] quite pure. The *Mencius* is not like the *Record of Rites*, which was reconstructed by Han Confucians after the first emperor of the Qin dynasty tried to burn all Confucian literature and execute all Confucian scholars. Other than the *Analects*, the only Confucian work that is free of textual corruption is the *Mencius*.

Students should immerse themselves in these books, savor their meanings, never depart from them in speech, nor refrain from following them as guides in action. . . .

The *Great Learning* was originally part of Elder Dai's *Records of the Rites*. No one knows who edited it. . . . My view is that while Confucius and Mencius often discussed the outline of learning, they never articulated a sequential learning formula as that in the opening paragraphs of the *Great Learning*.

The *Analects* states that the sage Confucius "taught four subjects: culture (*bun*), moral conduct (*kō*), loyalty (*chū*), and trustworthiness (*shin*)."[43] Clearly these were Confucius's teachings. The *Analects* also says, "A person of wisdom has no doubts; a humane person, no worries; a courageous person, no fears."[44] These three—wisdom, humaneness, and courage—refer to the ultimate virtues of the world.[45] Progress in learning involves nothing more than progress in these. . . .

But the *Great Learning* suggests that progress along the moral way is as difficult as climbing a nine-story pagoda.[46] We climb up story after story, until finally reaching the top. Yet the Confucian way is nothing other than the moral way of humanity. Because it was meant to be cultivated, how could it be so remote? . . .

The *Great Learning* also claims, "A state should not deem petty profit to be real profit; real profit comes from rightness."[47] But even this statement endorses a kind of profit-seeking mentality. Mencius remarked, "Must the king mention profit? Humaneness and rightness are my only concerns!"[48] In practicing the Confucian way, the noble person respects rightness but never acknowledges the profitability of any kind of profit.[49] . . . [pp. 160–64]

---

43. *Analects* 7:25.

44. *Analects* 9:29.

45. *Mean* 20.

46. *Daodejing*, chap. 64.

47. *Great Learning*, in Legge, trans., *Confucian Analects, the Great Learning, and the Doctrine of the Mean*, p. 380.

48. *Mencius* 1A:1.

49. *Analects* 4:16: "The Master said, 'The common person only recognizes profit while the Noble Person, only rightness'" (J. *gi*, Ch. *yi*); *Analects* 14:12: "The master said, ' . . . A person who sees profit, but thinks of rightness . . . should be called a complete person'" (J. *seijin*, Ch. *chengren*).

The Revival of Heterodoxies

Many people think that heterodoxies and heinous deeds arose only in the Warring States period [403–221 B.C.E.] but did not exist before. That is not so.
Propagators of heterodox ideas and doers of riotous deeds existed even before
Yao and Shun. Yet when Yao and Shun appeared, they fled, "afraid and
unwilling even to listen"[50] to the sages. . . . Thus, later generations never realized that heterodoxies and violence had actually existed before Confucius.
Even after Confucius, however, the dregs of the teachings of the Yellow Emperor and Laozi remained for some time. During the Han dynasty, they re-
surfaced.

Siddhartha Gautama's Buddhism entered China from abroad and soon
spread across the realm. It flourished during the Sui [581–618] and Tang [618–
907] dynasties and was still causing an uproar in the Song. The next wave of
Confucians angrily rejected Buddhism, sharply distinguishing Buddha's doctrines from their own. They struggled against Buddhism until their energies
were spent. But the more they attacked it, the greater it became. The more they
rejected its tenets, the more popular it became. Confucians could not extinguish its flames because in combating them, they stooped to use, as the Buddhists use, empty words rather than the moral virtues taught by Yao, Shun, and
Confucius.

When the Way and virtue flourish, debate subsides. When the Way and
virtue decline, debate and argument abound. When they flourish, the Way and
virtue grow more distant. The rise of debate, argument, and rhetoric thus marks
the pinnacle of a degenerate age. At the heights of such empty polemics, we
arrive at the very extremes of Zen Buddhism! Nothing is further from morality,
more distant from daily life, and more lacking in benefits to society and the
state than Zen. . . .

The *Spring and Autumn Annals* shows that the best way to halt heterodoxies is to personally cultivate the Confucian Way and its virtues. Opposing heterodoxies with ethical theories is the next best approach. The least effective
strategy is debating whether or not principle exists or whether we should remain still or respond ethically. Han Yu and Ouyang Xiu chose the second
method, and the Cheng brothers and Zhu Xi followed the last strategy. Sadly
enough, since Confucius and Mencius, no one has used the best approach.
[pp. 165–67]

[Itō Jinsai, *Gomō jigi*, in NST, vol. 33, pp. 14–38, 71–72, 160–67; JAT]

---

50. *Concordance to Yi ching* [*Yijing*], p. 32; Legge, trans., *I ching*, p. 33.

OGYŪ SORAI AND THE RETURN TO THE CLASSICS

Umegaka ya   The scent of plum blossoms!
Tonari wa   And close to it—
Ogyū Soemon   Ogyū Soemon.

Thus wrote the poet Bashō, who at one time was Sorai's neighbor, associating this great Confucian of the Tokugawa period with the plum flower, which thrives despite the vicissitudes of winter and early spring. Having spent more than a decade in the land of his father's exile, during which he kept working away at his studies, Ogyū Sorai (1666–1728) returned at the age of twenty-five to the metropolis of Edo, where he started a free, open-air lecture course beside the front entrance of the famous temple Zōjōji. There he eventually attracted the attention not only of the prelate of that Buddhist center but also of the shogun himself. With the shogun's special permission, equivalent to a recommendation, Sorai was made private secretary to Premier Yanagisawa and thereafter rose rapidly to earn an unusually large stipend.

At his school, which he later set up in the very stronghold of the officially favored Zhu Xi teaching, Sorai offered a radically new approach to Confucian studies. For a time, he had followed both the official school and Itō Jinsai but concluded that they both had failed to fulfill the basic aim of scholarship: to provide for the needs of the people and the general social welfare. The Neo-Confucians were too preoccupied with metaphysics, philosophical idealism, and personal cultivation. Although Jinsai was correct in trying to rediscover the original basis of Confucian teaching, he had likewise concerned himself with personal ethics, to the neglect of political issues and social questions. By insisting on the authority of the *Analects* alone, Jinsai had failed to recognize that this work could be properly understood only in relation to its historical context. Taking a broader view of things, Sorai could see that the Six Classics (including the *Classics of Documents, Odes, Rites,* etc.) were the basic depository of China's classical heritage and that the Four Books (including the *Analects* and the *Mencius*) merely represented personal interpretations. In fact, from Sorai's point of view, the classical philosopher Xunzi was a much better guide in such matters. Sorai upheld Xunzi's realism in regard to the evil nature of man and the necessity for correcting it through social institutions, against Mencius's more subjective, idealistic, and optimistic view that social betterment had to be achieved through self-cultivation in order to fulfill the original goodness of human nature. Sorai therefore stressed the importance of rites (understood broadly to include virtually all social institutions) and political administration, as opposed to the virtues of humaneness and rightness emphasized by Mencius and Jinsai. Indeed, Sorai is utilitarian in asserting that morality, as embodied in the traditional Confucian "Way," has no other basis than the social function of bringing peace and security to the people, which is what the ancient sage-kings intended. In this respect, Sorai did not hesitate to give primacy to law, its strict enforcement through a system of punishments and rewards, and the need to reform institutions as well as men.

Sorai's key manifesto, *Distinguishing the Way* (*Bendō*, 1717), presents his view of the Confucian Way in the broadest terms. It opens with a sweeping critique of previous Confucian thought but leaves no doubt about his basic intellectual orientation toward the Confucian tradition or the unprecedented role he says that Heaven entrusted to him as the rediscoverer of its true significance after the Way had been obscured for more than a thousand years. Implicitly working within Zhu Xi's concept of the "succession to the Way" (*daotong*) but adapting it to his own purposes, Sorai clearly presents himself as fulfilling the Confucian teaching, not breaking with it.

The issues that Sorai takes up in the *Bendō* are those shaped by the Neo-Confucians and later redefined by Jinsai. He joins Jinsai in challenging the Cheng–Zhu theory of human nature, sharing with both Yamaga Sokō and Jinsai the view that in seeming to deprecate the physical nature, the Song school had allowed Buddhist and Daoist influences to distort the original Confucian teaching. Like Sokō and Jinsai, too, Sorai went over the heads of the Song masters and invoked the original teaching of the Confucian classics as the test of orthodoxy. It was for this that the three have been classed together as advocates of the "Ancient Learning," even though this did not represent a single school.

The crux of the issue between Sorai and his Neo-Confucian predecessors was their central doctrine of sagehood as the ultimate goal of self-cultivation. Earlier, in accordance with the universality of the moral nature in all human beings, Neo-Confucians had asserted that sagehood could be acquired through individual study and self-discipline. In the *Bendō*, however, Sorai attacks the "fatuous idea that sagehood could be attained through study or that one could become a sage all by oneself."[51] Here he directly repudiated the words of Zhu Xi in his commentaries on the Four Books, as well as Zhu's essential message in *Reflections on Things at Hand*. Sorai further analyzed this prevalent fallacy in terms of the Daoist notion of "sageliness within and kingliness without." For Sorai, true sageliness and kingliness were inseparable. The true sages were not those who claimed to have subjectively realized their ideal human nature within, but the early kings who displayed their virtue outwardly through the construction of an all-encompassing social and political order.

In part, Sorai's rejection of the Song model for sagehood can be seen as a defense of man's physical nature against the excessive demands of a moral ideal

---

51. Ogyū, *Bendō* 2, in *NST*, vol. 36, p. 12 (200).

that spoke of achieving "complete unity with Heavenly principle without a trace of selfish desire."[52] Against this, Sorai quoted both Confucius and Zisi to the effect that even the early sages had their human limitations and Confucius himself was not without human desires. Moreover, in his commentary on the *Great Learning*, when Zhu Xi spoke of the sage as "plumbing the ultimate of Heavenly principle and being without so much as one iota of selfish human desire,"[53] it meant for Sorai a lack of realism in three respects.

First, individual natures differ and cannot be made to conform to a single ideal. To set up such a goal for human cultivation is to do violence to individual natures. The more a man becomes aware of the discrepancy between himself and the norm, and the more conscious he becomes of his own shortcomings, the more dissatisfied he will be with himself and the further he will be from achieving a sense of fulfillment. "To force on the common man a standard that he is not capable of achieving is to make him lose all hope in goodness."[54]

Second, Sorai insisted that man's psychophysical nature could not be changed and that attempting to curb fundamental human desires would lead only to frustration and resentment:

The physical nature is the Heavenly nature. To try to use the force of man to overcome Heaven and thwart nature is not possible.[55]

The scholars of later times, ignorant of the Way of the early kings, have presented their own superior wisdom, thinking to promote the performance of good and the avoidance of evil and to enlarge [the effective domain of] Heavenly principle while restricting human desires. Once such a view is adopted, however, it will become evident to all that their rulers are not Yaos or Shuns, that men are not sages, and that evil inevitably abounds while good is scarcely to be seen. Accordingly, a deadly spirit of faultfinding will spread throughout the world. Thus when [Zhu Xi's version of] the *General Mirror* is followed in government and the [*Great Compendium on*] *Human Nature and Principle* is the guide to moral discipline, no one will be able to endure their rigors, and everyone will end up thinking that the Confucians take delight in oppressing people.[56]

Third, given the differences in men's natures, as well as the extent of their common needs, it is apparent that only an all-encompassing approach to the human economy will allow for individual differentiation while providing for

---

52. Ogyū, *Bendō* 11, in *NST*, vol. 36, p. 22 (204).
53. Zhu Xi, *Daxue zhangju*, commentary on chap. 1.
54. Ogyū, *Bendō* 6, in *NST*, vol. 36, p. 17 (202).
55. Ogyū, *Bendō* 14, in *NST*, vol. 36, p. 24 (204).
56. Ogyū, *Bendō* 9, in *NST*, vol. 36, p. 21 (203).

the needs of all. To try to deal with the governance of men through self-cultivation and the practice of reverence — that is, through self-examination and mind control to root out unworthy desires — is fatally to misconceive the nature of the problem: to meet the needs of human society as a whole, not just to achieve individual serenity of mind. The early sage-kings had dealt with the larger needs of the state and society, leaving the finer points of individual cultivation to be taken care of in the natural course of events. Action to meet the needs of mankind could not await the ruler's attainment of a lofty frame of mind. Similarly, for men in later ages, their task was to study and follow the pattern established by the early kings, not to engage in quiet sitting, "sustained reverence," or the other disciplines of Neo-Confucian mind-control.[57]

Here Sorai betrays a basic ambiguity concerning the autonomy of the individual and his independent role in society. On the one hand, he takes a radical stand on the fundamental individuality of each man's nature:

> The inborn nature differs with each individual, and for him, virtue varies according to his nature. There is no single way for men to achieve fulfillment or for their talents to be perfected.[58]
>
> Heaven's decree is not the same for all . . . the gentleman understands this and does not try to force it [i.e., conformity to a specific norm or model]. In regard to perfecting their own talents, even the sages did not achieve complete success, and therefore they did not try to force it on others. Consequently, the idea that all men can achieve sagehood is false, and so is the idea that men's natures can be changed.[59]

Sorai resisted any solution to the problem that would further enhance the status of the subjective self or assert a single principle on the basis of which anyone could achieve sagehood. In his view, if it was not possible by studying the principles of things one by one eventually to achieve a personal integration of them (in the way that Zhu Xi did), neither was it possible to assert an a priori principle as the ground on which one could experience unity with Heaven-and-earth and all things.[60]

A man of broad learning himself, Sorai nevertheless believed that neither comprehensive knowledge nor an exhaustive objective investigation of things could be made a condition for one's self-fulfillment. At the same time, he resented what seemed to him the crude and boorish dogmatism of those like Yamazaki Ansai, whose intensely subjective method of self-cultivation enabled

---

57. Ogyū, *Bendō* 10–12, in *NST*, vol. 36, pp. 21–23 (203–4).
58. Ogyū, *Gakusoku* 7, in *NST*, vol. 36, p. 196 (258).
59. Ogyū, *Gakusoku* 7, in *NST*, vol. 36, p. 196 (258).
60. Yoshikawa, "Sorai gakuan," in *NST*, vol. 36, pp. 730ff.

them to acquire strong convictions about moral principles, to the extent that their religious "seriousness" and zealotry became quite overbearing.[61] According to Sorai,

> principle is formless; therefore it provides no definite standard. To think that the Mean can serve as the principle of proper conduct is to leave it to each man's view of it, and each man's view of it is different. Then everyone takes his own mind as the judge of what the Mean is and what proper conduct is. . . . It is like the people of two villages disputing the boundary between them, without any magistrate to hear and judge the merits of the case.[62]

Here Sorai's concern is with the question of objective public authority. For him, there could be only one ultimate standard, and it was not the Supreme Ultimate or norm in the mind that the Song school had spoken of as unlimited or open-ended (*wuji*); it had to be something more objectively defined. For him this was the rites of the early kings:

> The norm established by the early kings was the rites. . . . Such concepts as the Supreme Ultimate of the normative principles of things, the transforming of the physical nature, or studying to be a sage have no basis in the original teaching of the early kings and Confucius.[63]

There was indeed such a thing as the kind of sagely wisdom needed to lead the people, but it existed only in the past: "Sages existed in the past, but not in the present. Therefore study today must be addressed to the past."[64] Toward the sages of the past Sorai held a most worshipful attitude compared with that of the would-be sages of the present:

> The sages' extraordinary intelligence and wisdom were powers received from Heaven; how could one expect to acquire them now through study? The spiritual luminosity of their virtue was beyond all calculation; how could it be sought out and fathomed? Thus even in ancient times, only King Tang, King Wu, and Confucius tried to learn what it was to be a sage.[65]

---

61. Imanaka, *Sorai gaku no kisoteki kenkyū*, p. 485; *Ogyū Sorai shū*, in *Nihon no shisō*, vol. 12, p. 14.

62. Ogyū, *Bendō* 19, in *NST*, vol. 36, p. 28 (205–6).

63. Ogyū, *Bendō* 6, in *NST*, vol. 36, pp. 16–17 (201).

64. Ogyū, *Gakusoku* 4, in *Ogyū Sorai zenshū*, vol. 1, pp. 10, 76.

65. Ogyū, *Benmei, sei* 4, in *NST*, vol. 36, p. 68 (218).

The early sages were kings whose achievement lay in unifying the world and constructing a whole social order. This would be an unusual ambition in the present and would have to be matched by a natural endowment of extraordinary proportions. Certainly it could not be achieved by intuiting and following a natural principle within the mind, as the Cheng–Zhu school would have it:[66]

> The mind is formless, and there is no way of controlling it. Therefore the Way of the early kings used rites to control the mind. For anyone to speak of governing the mind except through rites is to imagine things. Why? If it is the mind that is to govern and the mind that is to be governed, this means that my mind is trying to govern itself—like a madman governing his own madness. How can there be any governing that way?[67]

Here the real significance of Sorai's views cannot be understood simply in terms of the individual or "individualism." We must distinguish between individuality and individualism: the recognition of individual differences and a realistic acceptance of them, on the one hand, and the active advocacy of an enlarged role for the individual, a wider scope for his autonomous choices, and a generally greater measure of what we call individual freedom, on the other.

There can be no doubt that Sorai was highly conscious of human individuality in the psychophysical sense; he clearly believed in the need to give the individual scope for satisfying his own needs and talents. By stressing man's physical nature *as* his Heavenly nature, Sorai affirmed the inherent value of individual qualities:

> For the scholar/samurai who wishes to study the Way of the early kings in order to fulfill virtue in himself, he must recognize this Way as manifold and multiform and men's natures also as diverse. If he can recognize that the Way of the early kings consists in providing peace and security for the world, and on this basis, if he can exert himself for the sake of humanity, then each man should follow what is closest to his own nature in order to achieve his potentiality of the Way.[68]

Sorai realized that in arguing for personal fulfillment on the basis of individual talents, he was exposing himself to criticism for sacrificing a man's essential humanity to his functional utility, that is, for treating him as a mere "utensil" (*ki*). Thus he tried to explain:

---

66. Ogyū, *Bendō* 4, in *NST*, vol. 36, p. 1415 (201–2).
67. Ogyū, *Bendō* 8, in *NST*, vol. 36, pp. 27–28 (205).
68. Ogyū, *Bendō* 7, in *NST*, vol. 36, p. 18 (202).

Confucius's teaching of his disciples can be seen as adapted in each case to their individual talents so as to perfect them. His saying that "the noble man is not a utensil"[69] refers to the humane man and to the instruments used by the ruler and his ministers, just like the [tools of the] craftsman and [the medicine of] the physician. Those who say that Confucius refers to [and rules out functional specification like that of] the ship sailing on the sea and the cart traveling by land [but not vice versa] have no reason whatever for this view.[70]

Here Sorai contended that Confucius's pronouncement about "not being a utensil" did not rule out functional specialization, but he asserted that such functionality not only served humane ends but was a moral value itself. What clearly emerges, then, is that his affirmation of the value of the individual in no way enhanced the status of the autonomous self. Man's "humanity" exists only as a part of the collectivity and is fulfilled only in a total polity or cooperative community. Sorai stated that

the Way of the early kings is the way of bringing peace and contentment to the world. Although it takes manifold forms, they all must conform to this end of bringing peace and contentment to the world. . . . Thus the Way cannot be spoken of in terms of one man but only in terms of millions of men collectively. . . .

In general, according to the Way of the early kings and Confucius, everyone had his own function to perform and his own purpose to serve, and the essential thing was to nurture and fulfill that capability. However, later men with a more dogmatic view insisted on "humaneness" as a comprehensive virtue, and they could not help but leap on it as a single all-encompassing principle. In the end, however, it comes down to no more than the Buddhist doctrine of the law-body (*dharmakaya*) as the ultimate principle embracing all things.[71]

Sorai set two significant limits on the early kings' effective authority: first, their Way could be followed only in general terms, rather than as a precise model for later times; and second, this Way could be known only through the most exacting contextual study and was not immediately knowable for direct application. Thus Sorai was skeptical of present-day pundits and would-be sages because they failed to meet the demanding requirements of his critical scholarship and objective, evidential inquiry. But belief in the early kings did not

---

69. *Analects* 2:12.
70. Ogyū, *Bendō* 14, in *NST*, vol. 36, p. 24 (204).
71. Ogyū, *Bendō* 7, in *NST*, vol. 36, pp. 17–20 (203).

have to meet the same test. On the contrary, it was the inherent limits of human knowledge that made the sages' achievements not credible in rational terms but compelling in their extraordinariness. To believe in the sage, man must make a leap of faith, and to do so is reasonable enough when he recognizes that his own rational powers fail to produce certain knowledge. Thus Sorai was skeptical of man, not the divine, and his faith in the sages sustained him while he engaged in the scholar's critical tasks:

> The sages' extraordinary intelligence and wisdom were powers received from Heaven. How could one expect to acquire them through study? The spiritual luminosity of their virtue was beyond all calculation. How could it be sought out and fathomed?[72]

While thus redefining sagehood and eliminating it as a model of personal self-cultivation, Sorai made it into a remote, though nonetheless commanding, symbol of external authority. Here there can be no mistaking his deep distrust of the Neo-Confucian idealism and individualism that drew so powerfully on the moral egalitarianism and ethical mysticism of Mencius, or his fearful reaction to the liberal humanism of the Song and the Ming, which proclaimed that every man had within him the making of a sage.

The fact that Sorai was permitted to propagate these ideas openly in competition with the Hayashi family school suggests that the enforcement of Zhu Xi orthodoxy was much less strict than is commonly supposed. From a political point of view, however, Sorai's nonconformism held no great risks for the shogunate. His respect for the rule of law backed by superior force accorded well with the realities of this period, seeming to justify the maintenance of a military government rather than reliance on the virtue of the imperial house and its subjects to keep order. Moreover, Sorai's dim view of individual autonomy, his deep respect for higher authority, and his insistence on the recognition of superior expertise rather than trust in the judgments of the common man were easily adapted to the authoritarianism of the *bakufu* regime.

It is understandable, then, why Sorai's ideas were positively received by the eighth shogun, Yoshimune, who was greatly impressed by the breadth of his scholarship and his practical approach to political problems. Sorai's *Discourses on Government* (*Seidan*), written expressly for Yoshimune, offers detailed suggestions about a wide variety of such problems, pointing to the need for stricter controls and more uniform policies to achieve a stable social order. Yoshimune, it is said, was about to give him a high post in the government when Sorai, who had been in poor health much of his life, suddenly died at the age of sixty-three.

---

72. Ogyū, *Benmei, sei* 3, in *NST*, vol. 36, p. 68 (218).

Although Sorai was much concerned with political and social institutions in contemporary Japan, it was with the study of ancient China that his school became most closely identified. Sorai's strong point was scholarship, and from the start he put a premium on a thorough knowledge of the Chinese language. Thus, as the leading Sinologist of his time, he communicated to his disciples a love of all things Chinese and perhaps also a touch of intellectual snobbery, which made the most of his own Sinological mastery while deprecating the competence of other Japanese scholars in Chinese studies. It was this attitude that carried over to his leading disciple, Dazai Shundai (1680–1747), a committed Sinophile. Thereafter, the tide ran strongly in a nationalistic direction, as if in reaction to the excessive adulation of Sino-Confucian culture. But it is significant that here, too, Sorai's teaching was felt. One of his own students was the first to show that the study of antiquity and classical learning could be applied to Japan as well as to China, which led to the National Learning school.

THE CONFUCIAN WAY AS A WAY OF GOVERNMENT

In the following passage from Ogyū Sorai's *Distinguishing the Way* (*Bendō*), which is aimed at both Itō Jinsai and the Neo-Confucians, he tells how the Way arose from cumulative human efforts to meet social needs and not from Confucius's unique discovery of a constant moral order or natural process, or something within the power of a single sage-king to produce.

The Way of Confucius is the Way of the early kings. The Way of the early kings was the way by which all under Heaven were brought peace and contentment. Confucius always wished to serve the Eastern Zhou dynasty by training his disciples and perfecting their talents so that they could be employed in the government. In the end, however, failing to achieve a position of authority, he devoted himself to editing the Six Classics so that they might be handed down to posterity. Thus the Six Classics[73] embodies the Way of the early kings, and they are quite wrong who say today that the Way of Confucius is not the same as the Way of the early kings.

The basis for bringing peace and contentment to all-under-Heaven was personal cultivation, but always with a mind to achieving peace in the world. This was what one called humaneness. After the appearance of Zisi and Mencius, when the Confucians became a separate school, they devoted themselves to the reverent following of their master's way and foolishly thought that through study alone they could achieve sagehood. Having once achieved sagehood, they could then set an example for all-under-Heaven, and the world would govern itself.

---

73. The Six Classics are the *Classics of Documents, Odes, Changes, Rites,* and *Music* (later lost) and the *Spring and Autumn Annals.*

This was like the theory of Laozi and Zhuangzi concerning "sageliness within and kingliness without." But to deprecate the importance of what lies outside [politics] and to attach all importance to what lies inside [personal virtue] is quite contrary to the old Way of Confucius and the early kings. Therefore, inside their schools the Confucians have been unable to train students to develop their capacities, and outside their schools they have been unable to mold the character of the nation by perfecting its customs. This is why the Confucians could not escape the charge that their learning was useless.

The Way is an all-embracing term. It brings together rites, music, law enforcement, and political administration—everything the early kings established—under one designation. There is no such thing as the Way apart from rites, music, law enforcement, and political administration. . . . The Way of the early kings was something the early kings themselves created; it was not the natural Way of Heaven and earth. Through their high intelligence and perspicacity, the early kings received the mandate of Heaven and ruled over the world. . . .

[Inoue, *Nihon rinri ihen,* vol. 6, pp. 12–13; RT, WTdB]

DISTORTION OF THE WAY THROUGH IGNORANCE OF THE PAST

Sorai's critique of the later Confucian tradition, which appears as a kind of prolegomenon to his *Distinguishing the Way*, points to the need for broader and more intensive study of the classical age and ancient Chinese writing in order to rescue Confucianism from the effects of historical change and subjective partisanship.

The Way is difficult to know and difficult to express because of its magnitude. What the Confucians of later times saw of the Way was only one aspect of it. The true Way is the Way of the early kings of China, but after the appearance of Zisi and Mencius it degenerated into the Confucian school, which began to contend for supremacy among the "hundred philosophers" of the late Zhou, and, by so doing, itself demeaned the Way. . . .

. . . The sense of sympathy and shame point to the fact that humaneness and rightness have their origin in nature, but the sense of sympathy is not all there is to humaneness, and the sense of shame and aversion may not necessarily constitute rightness. This is a slight misstatement that has led to a tremendous error. The latter-day Learning of the Mind had its inception in this. Xunzi's criticism of it was correct. So I say that Zisi and Mencius were defenders of the Confucian school while Xunzi was a loyal minister to Zisi and Mencius.[74]

---

74. In Confucian parlance, "loyal minister" is most often used to signify a forthright critic devoted to his master's best interests.

Nevertheless, this was not long after Mencius's time, and things had not changed greatly, so their world of discourse was essentially the same. But by the time Han Yu appeared in the Tang [dynasty], writing had undergone a great change. Thereafter came the two Chengs and Zhu Xi, admittedly scholars of great stature yet nonetheless unacquainted with the ancient language. Unable to read and understand the Six Classics properly, they showed a preference for the *Mean* and the *Mencius* because these texts were so easy to read. Thus, the writings of philosophers contending with other philosophers came to be regarded as the true expression of the Way of the sages in its original form. In addition to that, they read the ancient style of writing as if it were the modern style, and since they were ignorant of what was actually referred to, a discrepancy arose between reality and discourse, in which sense and reasoning took separate paths. Consequently, the teaching of the early kings and Confucius disappeared.

In recent years Itō Jinsai, also a scholar of great stature, has become aware of this general state of things. Nevertheless, in his interpretation of the *Analects* he depended on *Mencius* and read the ancient style of writing as if it were the modern one, just as the people in the Cheng and Zhu school did. Moreover, he [Jinsai] openly divided the Way of the early kings and Confucius into two ways and put aside the Six Classics in favor of the *Analects* alone. He also did not succeed in avoiding the errors of those who read Chinese in Japanese fashion. So when I read what Jinsai presented as the ancient meaning, I wonder indeed how it could ever be called "ancient"! . . .

Thanks to Heaven's special favor, this writer obtained access to the works of two eminent scholars, Wang and Li,[75] and for the first time became acquainted with the ancient style of Chinese writing. Thus equipped, I painstakingly went through the Six Classics for many years. Gradually I began to understand the terms and their corresponding realities, and after that the interpretation of the texts became clear. Only then did I feel able to discuss the Six Classics properly. The Six Classics contain facts, whereas the *Record of Rites*[76] and *Analects* offer interpretations. Interpretations must be supported by facts, however, before they can be accepted as definitive explanations of the Way. If we disregard the facts and accept interpretations at face value, it will scarcely be possible to avoid generalizations, exaggeration, and arbitrary judgment. These are the faults found among scholars following Han Yu and Liu Zongyuan, the Chengs, and Zhu Xi.

I am already past fifty. If I do not exert myself before I die, what will be Heaven's judgment? Mindful of this, whenever I have had time to spare, I have

---

75. Wang Shizhen and Li Panlong were sixteenth-century Chinese scholars who advocated a return to the language and prose style of ancient times.

76. The compilation containing the *Great Learning* and the *Mean*.

begun writing in appreciation of Heaven's favor. The contents of this work include many tens of items, all intended for students who may come under my guidance.

[Inoue, *Nihon rinri ihen*, vol. 6, pp. 11–12; RT, WTdB]

DISTINGUISHING TERMS
(*BENMEI*)

Sorai's major work, *Distinguishing Terms*—which is in the same Neo-Confucian genre as Yamaga Sokō's *Essential Teachings of the Sages*, Itō Jinsai's *Meaning of Terms in the Analects and Mencius*, and Chen Beixi's prototypical *Neo-Confucian Terms Explained*—is a philosophical lexicon explaining how key concepts have changed from ancient times to the present. The change, usually seen as a distortion from the true meaning to be found in the correct contextual interpretation of the Confucian classics, reflects Sorai's fundamentalist faith in the possibility of arriving at a literal reading of the scriptures. Using this golden age of revelation as the basis for a critique of his own predecessors, Sorai liberates himself from received tradition and gains the freedom to adapt the Way to his own contemporary situation.

Preface

. . . Because terms convey teachings, rulers (*kunshi*) must use them cautiously. Confucius thus observed, "If terms are used incorrectly, then language will not accord with the truth."[77] Even if a single word is misused, people may be unable to secure their livelihoods. Can we afford not to be cautious?

After Confucius's death, the hundred schools of philosophy proliferated. These philosophers first misrepresented things by using words according to their own various perspectives. . . . Thereafter, words and the meanings assigned to them changed over time. In the Tang dynasty with Han Yu, literary studies were divided into the "ancient" and "modern" schools. During the Song dynasty, philosophical scholarship also was divided into the "ancient" and "modern" schools.[78] Possessing preeminent natural genius, those gentlemen heroically scrutinized their age, indignant over its degeneracy. Accordingly, they decided that manifesting the Way of the sages would be their own personal mission.

---

77. *Analects* 13:3: "The Master said, 'If terms are used incorrectly, then language will not be in accord with the truth. If language is not in accord with the truth, then things cannot be accomplished. If things cannot be accomplished, then ceremonies and music will not flourish. If ceremonies and music do not flourish, then punishment will not be just. If punishments are not just, then the people will not know how to move hand or foot.'"

78. Reference to the "new" commentaries that Zhu Xi and other Song scholars produced.

But in doing so, the Song scholars indulged their subjective views without ever recognizing how words and their meanings had changed over the generations. Instead, they selected some of their personal ideas, calling them "principles." Moreover, they claimed that the Way of the sages existed in them. Most egregiously, however, the Song scholars failed to understand that contemporary language was not identical with that of the ancient sages. . . .

No one has ever comprehended the Way of the sages while misunderstanding the right relationship between language and reality. The concepts defined by the Cheng brothers and Zhu Xi were indeed little more than their own subjective ideas. . . .

Those who wish to seek the Way of the sages must do so through the Six Classics. Then those things that the sages created will be correctly understood. Students of the Way of the sages must also seek it in the various texts written before the Qin and Han dynasties. When we completely understand language and reality, we will understand the Way of the sages. To make this easier, I have written *Distinguishing Terms*.

The Way

1. The Way is a comprehensive term, signifying something that is followed. In antiquity, the early sage-kings defined this concept so that later generations would follow it in their conduct. . . . The early kings were sages. Some passages thus refer to "the Way" as "the Way of the early kings," and others call it "the Way of the sages." Since rulers regard following the Way as their duty, some passages call it "the Way of rulers." Confucius transmitted it, and the Confucian scholars (*ju*) preserved it. The Way is therefore known as "Confucius's Way" or as "the Way of the Confucian scholars." Nevertheless, it is only one single reality, the Way. . . .

Because of the ineffability of the Way, the early kings formulated both philosophical concepts and practical tasks to enable people to adhere to it. And they had the *Classics of Documents, Odes, Rites,* and *Music* compiled to teach people the Way. . . .

Commenting on the *Analects*, Kong Anguo observed that "the Way refers to rites and music." How could subsequent scholars have hoped to surpass that statement? . . .

In formulating the Way, the early kings focused on the problem of bringing peace and security to all-under-Heaven and posterity. . . . Therefore, the early kings followed the mind of all people to love, nourish, support, and perfect one another. And the early kings appropriated the people's ability to work together and undertake tasks cooperatively. . . . The Way of the early kings is best displayed in external things. The six arts, for example, are parts of the Way of the early kings. Thus, in antiquity, "the Way" and "the six arts" were spoken of in tandem. . . .

The expression "the universal Way" refers to the accessibility of the Way of the early kings: all people, the elite and the despised, the wise and the foolish, the worthy and the unworthy—everyone can follow it. Other ways, like "the Way of the Son of Heaven" and "the Way of the feudal lords," cannot be practiced by everyone. Similarly, "the Way of the ruler" cannot be practiced by everybody. "The universal Way" thus differs from these more restricted ways. . . .

Later Confucians misconstrued the meaning of "universal" and mistakenly explained that it meant "the universally acknowledged filial piety of King Wu and the Duke of Zhou." Alas! If all the world acknowledged filial piety, why would they restrict their praise to only King Wu and the Duke of Zhou? [pp. 41–48]

The Sage

Fuxi, Shennong, and the Yellow Emperor all were sages. But during their time, the Way of correct virtue had not been fully founded. Rites and music were not propagated until later ages. Yao and Shun systematized the rites and music, first completing the Way of correct virtue. Then rulers were able to complete their virtues, and the common people, to perfect their vulgar customs. Corporal punishments were unnecessary. The world was so well ordered that from it emerged the Way of the true king. This age thus manifested the perfection of morality. . . .

The sages were merely men, and the virtues of men differ with their natures. Even among the virtues of the sages, why would we expect them all to be the same? They are called sages because they systematized the civilized order. Traces of their systematization can still be seen. We call them sages because of what we can see. But we dare not discuss their virtues! This approach conveys our utmost respect for the sages. And such indeed was the Way of the sages. . . .

The sages received from Heaven their virtues of quick apprehension, intelligence, perception, and wisdom! How could these virtues possibly be acquired through study? How could anyone ever fathom such unfathomable mysteries? . . . Although Mencius did not emphasize following the rites and music of the sages, that was precisely what he meant when he stated that people could become Yao or Shun by wearing the clothes, using the words, and practicing the actions of Yao and Shun. He never meant to suggest that people should try to become sages!

Instead of considering the contexts of Mencius's and Zisi's writings, later Neo-Confucians embraced the absurd notion that they might try to become sages. In the process they advanced theories minutely detailing the virtues of the sages. Their accounts were meant to serve as models for students hoping to become sages. In them the Neo-Confucians described the mind of the sage as completely embodying the principles of Heaven, with its yin and yang harmonizing the virtues of their human nature without partiality or prejudice.

With their supposedly sharp methods of mind control, Neo-Confucians tried to control themselves with sagely wisdom, naively hoping to fathom the unfathomable. . . . [pp. 62–68]

Reverence

Reverence means never being irreverent when there is something that one should worship and revere. . . . The Way of the early kings referred to Heaven as its basis; therefore, the early kings devised many words meaning reverence so as to encourage people to practice their Way and thereby serve the Way of Heaven. . . .

The ruler (*kun*) is the heir of the early kings and the very representative of Heaven. The ruler, therefore, must be reverenced! But Heaven itself decreed that the people be the subject of government. Therefore, they too should be reverenced! . . .

Neo-Confucians who value rational principle and esteem knowledge neither believe in ghosts and spirits nor revere Heaven. Rather, they view Heaven as principle and ghosts and spirits as the spiritual forces of yin and yang. They claim that principle exists within us and that if we can exhaust principle, then Heaven will dwell within us as well! Thus, their minds are rather presumptuous and disrespectful. . . . Stressing the maintenance of stern dignity, the Neo-Confucians, to some extent, distance their outlook from human emotions. They have failed to realize that this reverence is rooted in the reverence for Heaven. Because of their ignorance of the latter, they vainly insist on "holding onto reverence" instead. . . .

. . . Because they tried to relate everything to the mind, the Neo-Confucians understood "about oneself" as a state of solitude in which other people were ignorant of a person's actions, even though he remained aware of them. Thus the Neo-Confucians advocated focusing a person's mental energies on even their most minute and trifling thoughts. That is a fabricated and absurd notion. It has never been part of the Way of the early kings and Confucius! [pp. 96–97]

[Ogyū Sorai, *Benmei*, in NST, vol. 36, pp. 41–48, 62–68, 96–97; trans. adapted from Tucker, *Benmei*, pp. 1–21, 58–67, 122–29]

CONCLUSION TO *DISCOURSES ON GOVERNMENT* (*SEIDAN*)

Sorai's *Discourses on Government* take up at great length and in great detail a variety of problems affecting Japanese society. In this conclusion, Sorai sums up his general approach and principal recommendations. Note his emphasis on strong legal controls and his comparative deprecation of the ruler's personal example (such as leading a life of austerity) as an influence on the people.

The Way of government is not a series of disconnected affairs; [rather,] a knowledge of the whole world and what goes on in it is essential to the ruler. The important thing to understand today is that all the present conditions are based on two facts: first, that people are living like transients in a hotel and, second, that everything is out of legal control. Therefore, family registration should be instituted so that people would settle down in a fixed residence. Controls should be adopted to maintain the distinction among military households, merchants, and farmers. Controls over the daimyo should also be established. Finally, the government should stop buying in the rice market.[79]

For the most part, these measures will help the nation recover and become prosperous. Other measures will follow in natural sequence as things improve. The ruler himself may adopt economic and austerity measures to put his household on a sound basis, but they will do no good if the people continue to suffer from poverty. My fervent desire is to see that both ruler and ruled grow rich and prosperous together, so that Your Highness's [Yoshimune's] reign will last forever.

[*Ogyū Sorai shū*, pp. 214–15; RT, WTdB]

FOR A MERIT SYSTEM IN GOVERNMENT

As we have seen, Sorai not only favored the hereditary class system but also advocated strict controls to preserve it. For government, however, he believed that the hereditary succession to high office inevitably resulted in power falling into the hands of incompetents. Although he did not recommend a general replacement of the hereditary system with a civil service, like many Confucians before him Sorai had to plead for a man of ability if he was to have an opportunity to put his own ideas into effect. No doubt Sorai's criticisms were directed in part at the Hayashi family, whose hereditary position in state education he attacked elsewhere in the *Discourses*.

It is a general law of nature that old things gradually disappear and new things appear. All things in heaven and earth are like this. We might like to keep old things forever, but that is beyond our power. Timber rots; grain varies in yield from year to year. So too with men: the old die, and the young come of age. In this they follow the law of nature, by which things from below rise gradually

---

79. This was an attempt to control the price of rice by buying when the price was low and selling when the price was high. It also aimed at storing surpluses that could be used for relief in times of famine.

to the top and, upon reaching the top, decline and disappear. This is an invariable rule, with which even the law of [the *Classic of*] *Changes* accords. It is in keeping with the principles of good government that a family that has rendered distinguished service be well treated so as to preserve it as long as possible. In a family with old people, prayers are said for great-grandparents, grandparents, and parents in hopes of their living until the end of time. It is only human not to be concerned that they die easily, but the law of the universe is one thing and human sentiment is another; the things of old, which you want to preserve so much, are destined to disappear. To say that things of the past might just as well disappear immediately is to go too far in the other direction and is not in accord with the Way of the sages. Nonetheless, trying to preserve the things of the past forever is sheer stupidity and also not in accord with the Way of the sages. The Way of the sages gives due place to human sentiments so that human feelings will not be outraged, but at the same time the everlasting law is abundantly clear and there is no way of ignoring it. Consequently, not dwelling foolishly on human sentiment is the key to fairly treating all mankind.

Because of this law, the descendants of Kings Yao and Shun, Yu and Tang, Wen and Wu, have vanished without a trace in China. In Japan there is no longer any trace of the once great shoguns Yoritomo and Takauji. It is the same with all famous families. But the powerful families we call daimyo today were of little account in earlier days. Because of their achievements in war they have risen to the top. Even so, today few powerful families have maintained a direct, legitimate succession. To try foolishly to preserve hereditary status by forever keeping those on top at the top and those below at the bottom violates the law of the universe, for it helps preserve from oblivion those at the top who have reached the point that they should give way. When men of talent and wisdom are no longer at the top, it signifies the end of a regime; confusion and disorder will open the way for men of talent and wisdom to rise up and overthrow the dynasty. Being aware of this truth and careful to preserve the dynasty, the sages instituted the system of punishments and rewards in order to raise up men of talent from below and at the same time leave to Heaven's will the elimination of those who have no legitimate heir to succeed them or whose wickedness has doomed them to destruction.

If this [advice] were followed, the wise would always be on top, and the stupid would always stay at the bottom, in perfect accord with the universal law; and thus the reign would go on forever. To be unaware of this natural balance is to be ignorant of the law that prevails over heaven, earth, and humankind. In turn this means to be out of accord with Heaven's will, which again is not the true way of government. . . .

Why is it that during a period of prolonged peace, men of ability are found only in the lower classes, while men of the upper class grow increasingly stupid? As far as I can see, men's abilities are developed only through hardship and tribulation. In the case of our bodies, use makes the members strong. Use your hands and your arms will grow strong; use your legs and your feet will become hardened. If you practice aiming, as in archery or gunnery, your eyesight will improve. Likewise, when you use your mind, your intelligence will develop. If you encounter hardship and tribulation in different forms, these experiences will bring out your abilities; that is the natural law. So the *Mencius* notes that when Heaven has a great mission for a man to perform, it first puts him to an acid test. When he develops his ability through such an acid test, he is especially fit for the task of government because he is familiar with conditions among the people. Therefore, in the Way of the sages, too, it is recommended that able men be advanced by bringing them up from below. . . .

Even when men of the hereditary nobility have come to that high estate, it is because their forebears risked their lives during the Warring States period, developed their abilities the hard way through bitter experience, and rendered distinguished service in order to attain high office and large feudal stipends. Their descendants, however, having held high office and large feudal stipends for generations, find themselves on top from birth and suffer no hardship at all. How, then, can they develop their abilities? . . . Although they may be intelligent and clever enough, they live so far apart from the people that they are simply unaware of how the people feel. . . . For this reason, the Way of the sages placed the prime importance on raising up wise and talented men of low station and strongly disapproved of hereditary succession in high office from generation to generation.

[*Ogyū Sorai shū*, pp. 124–28; RT, WTdB]

SETTLEMENT ON THE LAND

In general, Sorai believed that owing to adverse circumstances, Japan had not had proper laws and institutions for several shogunates. Although it would not be possible, he thought, to reverse this situation all at once, a proper government could not be established except with a sound agrarian economy, for which it would be necessary to settle people—and especially the military class—on the land.

The main point of Sorai's policy was that the system of alternate residence of military households in Edo should be modified to allow the members of the military class to return to the country and make their permanent homes on their land and to establish institutions that would enable the military government (*bakufu*) to maintain control over the country and ensure future stability. Through these measures, the military class would be freed from its dependence on the merchants, and in the future the *bakufu* would be able to prevent the changes in status and occupation that had taken place throughout the preceding century. The benefits that Sorai expected from the return of the military class to its land were, first, that the "extravagance" of town life, with its debilitating effects, would cease; second, that relations between the military class and the peasantry would be improved; and, third, that the military class would be able to overcome the power of the merchants by no longer being dependent on them to supply its needs.

If the members of the military class lived in the country, they would not incur any expenses in providing themselves with food, clothing, and shelter, and for this reason their financial condition would be much improved. Now it is generally true that extravagance originates among the female members of the family, and since the wives and daughters of the military class have lived in Edo, increasing extravagance has weakened their health and made them a prey to disease, with the result that the children whom they bear are weak and unfit for the service of the *bakufu*. But if these women were also[80] made to live in the country, they would exercise their bodies by working at the loom and, having few luxuries, would become strong and healthy, as befits the wives and daughters of warriors. The men, too, would have strong limbs from walking and riding all over the countryside. . . .

The members of the military class would be at leisure most of the time, which would be of more benefit to them than is the case in Edo, for they have no other forms of recreation than the practice of the military arts and the pursuit of learning. If their retainers were given plots of land assessed as yielding five or ten *koku*[81] and they were allowed to keep the produce of that land, its yield would soon increase from five *koku* to ten *koku* and from ten *koku* to twenty *koku*. And since they would be living in a country style, five *koku* would be equivalent to twenty, and ten *koku* to forty, and hence it would be possible to keep many retainers amply supplied, and any military duties that might be required would be easily discharged. . . .

If the members of the military class settled on the land, the peasants, from their earliest childhood, would look up to their steward (*jitō sama*) with feelings of respect that would become deeply impressed on their minds, and good order would be preserved in the district. . . . Again, if the military class lived in the country, they would become familiar with the land, with the construction of river dikes and with other such matters. . . .

Once the military class had settled on the land, their period of attendance at Edo would be fixed at one month or one hundred days. . . . By going through the country on foot and horseback, by fishing and hunting, they would become more familiar with the topography of their districts, used to moving over rough country, and expert in all the matters making up the warrior's art. At present they live in Edo and have neither familiarity with nor feelings of obligation

---

80. That is, as well as their husbands.

81. One *koku* is approximately five bushels. *Koku* was the unit used to measure rice as well as the productivity and value of land, reflected in the stipends for the military class.

toward the people of their distant fiefs. The peasants think of them merely as the men who take the rice tax from them, while warriors regard the peasants simply as the source from which they collect the rice tax. The only feeling that exists between them is, on the one side, a desire to exploit and, on the other, a determination not to be exploited, and some members of the military class inflict great cruelties on their peasants. If they lived on their lands and grew used to seeing and speaking with their peasants, they would naturally acquire feelings of sympathy for them, and naturally, too, would not treat them with excessive severity. . . .

A major consequence of the existing system was the impoverishment of the samurai because of their dependence on the merchant class. Sorai wished to "restore" a proper four-class system by reversing the relations between samurai and merchants.

At least one-quarter of the harvest must be stored, and when possible, no rice in excess of this proportion should be sold. For if rice is kept in the hands of the military class, the merchants, who will be forced to buy the rice in exchange for money, will be utterly confounded, and it will be possible to lower prices to any level desired. The question is who will be in the dominant position and who will be in the subordinate position. At present, the merchants are in the dominant position, and the military class is in the subordinate position because the military class lives as though they were at an inn where they cannot do without money and must sell their rice in exchange for money with which to buy their daily necessities from the merchants. It is for this reason that the military class has no control over prices. If the military class lived on their land, they would have no need to sell their rice, while the merchants would wish to buy it, and thus the military class would be in the dominant position and the merchants in the subordinate one. In that case, the military class would be able to determine prices at their pleasure. . . .

If these proposals were carried out, the price of rice could be set very high and the townspeople of Edo would be obliged to eat coarse grains. In this way a distinction would arise between the food of the rulers (*kunshi*) and the ruled (*shōjin*), which also is in accordance with the ancient Way. . . . [pp. 59–63]

Economic Policy

The most important recommendations in Sorai's economic policy were a part of his measures for ending the state of "living in an inn" at Edo. The military government would no longer make purchases from the townspeople but would accept payment directly from the daimyo and the producers of the goods that the state required. Natural resources such as forests and mines would be brought under the *bakufu*'s direct control. At the same time, the practice of contracting work by townspeople would be discontinued, and artisans would work directly under the *bakufu*'s officers. Unskilled laborers would be selected from the servants of the middle-ranking samurai and from the townspeople.

Ending the situation of "living in an inn" requires ending money purchases by the *bakufu*. Now, as to how this is to be accomplished: during the Three Dynasties the feudal lords presented tribute (*gong*) [to the emperor], and it is clearly recorded in the histories that since that time, under the rule of successive emperors in China and in ancient Japan during the period of the centralized (*gunken*) administration, local products were always presented to the court from the provinces. But if you ask why the lords should present tribute when they have been given complete control of their lands, observe that because they have received these lands, the lords have the duty of supplying rice and labor to their sovereign from the grain that their lands produce and from the people who live there. In the case of other products, certain localities produce goods of particularly high quality; in this respect not all the fiefs are alike. Thus presenting local products to the overlord is not at all unreasonable but is quite logical and indeed has been the established practice in both ancient and modern times. That the daimyo of the present day, who correspond to the feudal lords of ancient times, do not make presentations of local products despite the requirements of both logic and precedent, is because at the end of the rule by the Muromachi, when the country was in a state of civil war, the military lords (*buke*) seized the provinces and prefectures and stopped paying even the three taxes *so*, *chō*, and *yō*[82] long established under the centralized system of government, quite apart from any presentation of local products. Later, Toyotomi Hideyoshi unified the country, but because he was illiterate, he was ignorant of these matters, and when the succession passed to the Tokugawa, Ieyasu died in the year after the siege of Osaka without establishing this institution. It is entirely wrong for the daimyo to accept this as a precedent for believing that they need not make presentations of local products. . . . [pp. 95–96]

Law

Sorai did not propose compiling an all-embracing code of law, believing, as a Confucian, that the fewer laws (as opposed to moral sanctions) a state had, the better its government would be. His proposals were limited to systemizing and simplifying the existing legislation.

The *bakufu* has issued scores or hundreds of edicts (*ofure*) since the Tokugawa took power, and there now are so many that it is impossible for the middle-ranking samurai or the people in the city and in the provinces to remember all of them. Some edicts reverse those previously issued, and the people are often

---

82. Taxes in grain, cloth, and labor.

confused when they do, not knowing which edict is in force. I have also heard that the *bakufu* authorities have been prosecuting people not under recent edicts but under edicts issued as much as forty or fifty years ago. The issuing of a large number of legal enactments (*hatto*) confuses people and has the opposite effect of that intended. I would advise that the provisions of all the legal enactments issued up until the present should be reviewed, selecting those to be observed and revoking those not to be observed. One of the principles in antiquity was to have as few legal enactments as possible. If there are [too] many, the common people will not be able to remember them and [so] will not observe them. . . . [p. 122]

Education

In his discussion of education, Sorai was concerned with only higher education, "learning" (*gakumon*)—that is, studies in the Chinese language conducted from a Confucian standpoint. Such studies, Sorai believed, should be pursued only by members of the upper classes, for they could be of no use to the lower orders and, indeed, might encourage rebellion:

It is not necessary that the common people be taught anything apart from the virtues of filial piety, brotherly submission, loyalty, and trustworthiness. . . . The study of other works will merely increase their cunning and will lead to disruption. For when the people are filled with cunning, they are difficult to rule. The techniques of government should be employed for their instruction.

Sorai held that the function of Confucian studies was to train members of the military class in matters that would prepare them to govern. Instruction was to begin with thorough training in the Chinese language, and later this linguistic knowledge was to be used to study subjects of practical utility in government, of which history was the most important.

Sorai particularly objected to lectures by Confucian scholars at the shogunate. Known as *kōshaku*, these lectures were an adaptation of a Neo-Confucian practice in the Song, Yuan, and Ming, and, in Korea, were known as the "lectures from the Classics Mat."[83] They were so identified with the whole system of Zhu Xi learning that Sorai dismissed them as unsuitable for Japan.

Lectures on the texts of the classics (*kōshaku*) are one of the greatest evils of the day. People of all classes believe that undertaking scholarly studies (*gakumon*) necessarily means attending *kōshaku* lectures. These lectures follow a particular pattern, which consists of reading through from beginning to end the texts of the Four Books, the *Jin si lu* (*Reflection on Things at Hand*), and other

---

83. See de Bary and Bloom, eds., *Sources of Chinese Tradition*, 2nd ed., vol. 1, pp. 628–38.

books of that sort. In the Song Confucians' system of study, this reading of the Four Books and the *Jin si lu* is a form of religious exercise meant to teach a person to become a sage. Since, of course, no one ever "became a sage," this means that the Song Confucians have a mistaken view of the nature of the classics. There can be no more roundabout method of doing things than to insist that we must set aside all consideration of government matters until we have become sages. . . .

Zhu Xi's commentaries, however, are generally regarded as the correct interpretation, and the idea that *kōshaku* lectures are an indispensable part of scholarly studies has also come to be accepted as a general rule, so that now no other form of scholarly study is recognized. The attitude of those who attend the lectures is reverence for the books, rather than confidence in the lecturers, and the aim is to have the lecturer explain the meaning of the text so that his audience may apply it at their own discretion. But if someone tries to discern the meaning of what is written in these books with a mind completely immersed in the customs of the time, the result will merely be a statement of his prejudices. . . .

Shogun Tsunayoshi had some fondness for learning, but even though this made learning fashionable, the *kōshaku* lectures were emphasized, and composition in prose and verse was neglected. Because people had no experience using the Chinese written language, these lectures were of no use. Since that time, scholars in the *bakufu*'s service have neglected their studies. Chinese poetry competitions would be of much greater benefit than the *kōshaku* lectures of the time of Shogun Tsunayoshi. If learning were encouraged to the same degree in the households of all the daimyu in Japan, scholars would be encouraged, many fine scholars would appear as a result, and the scholars in the *bakufu*'s service would be forced to attend to their studies. . . .

Furthermore, if the Hayashi family is favored by being the only school of Confucian scholars (*jusha*) employed by the *bakufu*, those scholars not employed by the *bakufu* will probably neglect their studies. The Way of the sages is essentially the Way of ruling the state, and in ancient and modern times its first concern has always been with matters of government. . . .

I would propose that the *bakufu* have the scholars in its service select one of the eight subjects—Chinese poetry, [Chinese] prose, history, law, Japanese studies, military science, mathematics, and calligraphy—and that they instruct their pupils in their subject with the object of preparing them for the *bakufu*'s service. . . . If this became an established procedure, all scholars would be of service to the *bakufu*, and nonprofessional scholars would be directed to study matters that also would be of use to the *bakufu*. All the futile discussions of the method of the mind-and-heart (*xinfa*) and arguments about metaphysical points may properly be described as useless learning.

[Adapted from McEwan, *Political Writings*, pp. 59–63, 95–96, 122, 133–34, 140–44]

MURO KYŪSŌ'S DEFENSE OF
NEO-CONFUCIANISM

Muro Kyūsō (1658–1734), the son of a physician (as were many other thinkers of his time), defended Zhu Xi's philosophy at a time when it was being criticized by such able men as Yamaga Sokō, Itō Jinsai, and Ogyū Sorai. Having acquired his belief in the rightness of Zhu Xi only after a long intellectual struggle, it was a matter of intense personal conviction for Kyūsō and not just a passive acceptance of the established teaching. Therefore, he did not try to formulate any new philosophy of his own but was far more effective in revitalizing the Neo-Confucian teaching than was the official Hayashi school. In this role, he strongly reinforced the ethical attitudes that the Tokugawa shoguns had endorsed as a means of stabilizing their own rule. Among these was the sense of duty (*gi*, or rightness), as manifested in personal relationships, especially in service to one's lord or ruler, which in Japan was regarded by many as the highest duty. Related to this was a deep sense of one's indebtedness or obligation (*on*) to one's parents for the original gift of life and to one's ruler for sustaining and protecting it.

In contrast to Sokō, however, whose sense of loyalty was increasingly directed to the imperial house, Kyūsō remained a staunch supporter of the shogunate, for which he found a justification in Mencius's theory of the Mandate of Heaven being conferred on those who best served the interests of the people. On this basis, for instance, he regarded Ieyasu as virtually heaven-sent to bring order out of chaos and establish a benevolent regime after centuries of bloodshed and disorganization. Indeed, Kyūsō contributed in no small measure to the hero-worshiping cult of Ieyasu, which persisted until the end of the Tokugawa period, and to the general buttressing of the shogunate's position and authority. By thus identifying himself so wholeheartedly with the existing regime and Zhu Xi's teaching, however, Kyūsō stood squarely in the face of two powerful currents of thought that eventually swept all before them: incipient nationalism (particularly as embodied in the revival of Shinto, which he considered unworthy of association with Neo-Confucianism) and the growing sense of loyalty to the imperial house.

IN DEFENSE OF ZHU XI'S NEO-CONFUCIANISM

In his prefatory remarks to the *Conversations of Suruga-dai* (*Shundai zatsuwa*), Muro Kyūsō, identified as the "Old Man," describes how he became a convinced Neo-Confucian only after many years of study. Now, with the Cheng–Zhu school under attack from many quarters, he feels that he has a mission to defend it similar to that of the great Han Yu in Tang-dynasty China, who turned the tide against Buddhism and Daoism and led the way to the later revival of Confucianism. Kyūsō sees himself not only as a follower of Zhu Xi but also as another in the line of Zhu's successors upholding the True Way during the Yuan and Ming periods.

One day as the Old Man was talking with his students, the discussion turned to developments in Confucian thought since the Song school, and one of those present expressed doubts about the Cheng–Zhu philosophy. The Old Man said to him:

"When I was young I pursued conventional Chinese studies, memorizing and reciting the classics and studying composition. I had devoted many years and months to this when suddenly I realized the folly of it and thought of devoting myself to that teaching of the ancients that was concerned with one's true self. Unhappily, however, I had neither able teachers nor worthy friends to guide me and was simply bewildered by the many theories of the different philosophers. I half believed in the Cheng–Zhu system and half doubted it. Unable to arrive at any settled view of things, I saw the years and months pass by without gaining anything. Then at about the age of forty I arrived at the realization that nothing could take the place of the Cheng–Zhu teaching. For thirty years I have studied the writings of the Cheng–Zhu school, considering them in my heart and reflecting on them in my mind. Neither too abstruse nor too superficial, these teachings would undoubtedly obtain the full assent of even a sage, should one rise again. For the Way of Heaven-and-earth is the Way of Yao and Shun; the Way of Confucius and Mencius is the Way of Cheng and Zhu. If we refuse to follow the Way of Cheng and Zhu, we cannot attain the Way of Confucius and Mencius; if we refuse to follow the Way of Confucius and Mencius, we cannot attain the Way of Yao and Shun; and if we refuse to follow the Way of Yao and Shun, we cannot attain the Way of Heaven-and-earth." . . .

At this everyone seemed to listen all the more intently, and the Old Man went on:

"What I say has already been confirmed by five centuries of scholarly opinion and consequently does not need an oath from me to affirm it today. After the time of Zhu Xi, beginning with such eminent scholars as Zhen Xishan (Dexiu) and Wei Haoshan (Liaoweng) in the Song dynasty, Xu Luzhai (Heng) and Wu Caolu (Cheng) in the Yuan dynasty, and Xue Jingxuan (Xuan) and Hu Juren (Zhuren) in the Ming dynasty, many others were devoted to studying the True Way, and all of them believed in Cheng and Zhu. . . . Thus until the middle of the Ming period, scholarship was conducted along correct lines, and the true teaching suffered no decline. But when Wang Yangming appeared, he proclaimed the doctrine of innate ["good"] knowledge and attacked Zhu Xi. Thus the temper of thought in the Ming changed, and after Yangming's death, such followers of his as Wang Longqi turned toward Zen Buddhism. Thereafter scholars became intoxicated with intuitive knowledge and grew tired of pursuing first principles. By the end of the Ming the deleterious effects of this were such that scholars throughout the land became Confucians by day and Buddhists by night. . . .

"In our state, peace has endured for a hundred years and learning has flourished, so that scholars have appeared in great numbers. Their scholarship may not always have been the best, but at least they held firmly to the Cheng–Zhu philosophy and preserved what was worthy of imitation from the past—which must be counted a blessing. More recently, however, some of them have misled men into new and dangerous paths, trying to set up their own schools of thought and gathering followers around them, so that they might enjoy some kind of ascendancy in the company of scholars long used to prostituting themselves and making much of their own wild ideas, without the least sense of shame. All the dogs join in when one starts barking, and that is the reason why vile teachings and outrageous doctrines abound in the world today. Truly the Way is in a critical phase. Therefore, just as Han Yu rose up when Buddhism and Daoism were flourishing and attacked them single-handedly, likening himself to Mencius and swearing an oath by the gods of Heaven-and-earth, so this man swears too, that although his merits may not equal those of Mencius, still he dares not fail to answer the call of Han Yu. And you, too, see that my words are not listened to in vain!"

[Inoue, Nihon rinri ihen, vol. 7, pp. 82–84; trans. adapted from Knox,
"Japanese Philosopher," pp. 28–31]

ECONOMICS AND TRADITIONAL VALUES

The next two selections from Kyūsō's *Conversations* are typical of the official attitude toward the rising merchant class and the spreading influence of bourgeois life and values. It springs from concern about the deterioration of samurai standards and from a feeling that the merchants' prosperity was gained at the peasants' expense and tended to discourage agriculture. Kyūsō obviously was guided by the traditional Chinese policy, which became established as early as the Han dynasty (second century B.C.E.), of discrimination against the merchant class and at least nominal support for agriculture. His reflections on the contemporary scene are a striking commentary on the rapid social and economic changes Japan was undergoing, despite the shogunate's attempt to preserve the status quo.

Nothing is more important to the samurai than duty [rightness]. Second in importance comes life, and then money. Since both life and money are also of value, when confronted by a life-or-death situation or when faced with money matters, a man is likely to depreciate the precious thing called duty. Hence, only if the samurai is careful not to think or speak of greed for life or greed for money can he remove himself entirely from avaricious desires. What I call avaricious desires is not limited to love of money, for the concern with one's life also is avarice. Is one's life not more precious than money? When faced with an unpleasant duty, the Way of the samurai is to regard his own wishes — even his life itself—as having less value than rubbish. How much less should he value money? Since [life and money] are of intrinsic value, it is good to take care of one's health and avoid spending money heedlessly. Even so, to cherish one's heart or even to speak of overfondness for one's life or the worship of money may be all right for merchants, but it is hardly so for a samurai. . . .

In ancient Japan, in keeping with its name of "the country of the sages," manners were pure and simple and not perverted by [consideration for] prices and profits. Even when duty was not rigorously defended, the inbred sense of honor had not entirely disappeared. Although manners changed greatly with the coming of military government, the samurai still knew nothing at all about money matters, and they were frugal and direct and not the slightest bit given to extravagance. This was true until recent times. . . .

As I remember in my youth, young men of that time never mentioned prices, and some blushed when they heard erotic stories. Most of them delighted in listening to stories about old battles and loved to discuss duty to their lord or father and the samurai's resolute will. I hear that nowadays when young men get together, they often amuse one another by telling stories of profit and loss or talking about sexual pleasures. Thus the social standards have changed from fifty or sixty years ago. . . .

Some years ago, when Arai Chikugo-no-kami [i.e., Arai Hakuseki] was attendant lecturer in the Confucian temple, I heard him say: "Never say, in reporting about another man, that he is greedy, for if he is greedy about money, then you can be sure that he will be greedy about life. In that case, you should use the blunter word and say that he is cowardly." This is quite true.

[Inoue, *Nihon rinri ihen*, vol. 7, pp. 82–84; trans. adapted from Knox,
"Japanese Philosopher," pp. 81–84]

THE PEOPLE SHOULD BE AS HEAVEN TO THE KING

Once, at the end of his exposition of the tenth book of the *Analects*,[84] concerning the passage "He bowed to those who bore the tables of the census," the Old Man asked his guests: "What is the meaning of the phrase 'The king takes the people to be Heaven, while the people take food to be Heaven'?"

"The people," replied one, "are the foundation of the state; when they are obedient the state remains, but when they rebel it is destroyed. Because the state's preservation or destruction is up to the people, the king must always

---

84. *Analects* 10:16.

honor them as Heaven. Food is the people's life. With it they live, but without it they die. . . . Therefore, the people honor food as Heaven."

"You have explained both of them correctly," continued the Old Man. "Both phrases refer to the idea that agriculture should be highly valued. When Heaven begets humankind it brings forth grain for their food. If there are humans there is grain, and if there is grain there are humans; if there is no grain there are no humans. Nothing on earth is more important than food. The farmers produce it and are entrusted by Heaven to the king, who must honor them as he honors Heaven itself. He should not despise even one of them. This is why the census in ancient times was received with honor by the king, and Confucius bowed when he met those who were carrying it. The people too should remember that they are entrusted with producing the most essential thing in the land, given by Heaven for the continuance of human life, and should honor it as Heaven itself. They must not be idle, for their industry is the basis of social standards and customs and has a bearing on the tranquillity of the state. . . .

"From what I have heard about the recent state of the capital, the provinces are full of avaricious officials, and the towns are full of money grubbers. While they seem outwardly to obey the law and be above bribery, many of them work privately for profit and love luxury. Furthermore, they flaunt their cunning and hide their faults; they deceive the government, slander others, and plot shrewdly. From what I hear of their intercourse with one another, they strive for sumptuousness in their banquets; they vie with one another in the elegance of songs and dances and spend immense sums in a day. They take all this to be in refined taste. . . . Gold and silver are scarce. But food is produced every year, so money grows dear while grain grows cheap. The samurai who are paid in rice must exchange cheap grain for expensive cash and do not have enough, whereas the money grubbers buy cheap grain with scarce coins and increase their goods. But with few coins their extravagance is unlimited, and useful money goes for useless things. . . .

"This has not come about in a day. Until sixty or seventy years ago there was greater prosperity than there is today. Some vulgar people liked luxury, but the majority were frugal, for many old men of the former age still remained, men who . . . had endured hardship as soldiers and had known no luxury even in their dreams. They trained their sons and grandsons too in the family traditions. Even though we would speak of them today as having rustic ways, they were naturally without ostentation and were rich in character. They were lacking in falseness and full of genuineness. They were earnest, dependable, hardworking, and kind. Later, such men disappeared. Samurai and officials now wallow in their hereditary pensions. In times of peace, they know nothing of hardships. All they want is comfort. . . . In the country there still remains some of the old spirit that has already disappeared from the capital. Of course, country folk are often foolish and profligate, and some commit great crimes; moreover, usually having little discretion, they become angry when faced with hard times and sometimes rise against the government. Still, they are not devious like the townspeople. They are naturally honest, simple, easily moved by blessings, quick to follow reason, and satisfied with their daily food.

"When the officials of a province remember the spirit that takes the people to be as Heaven, modify the taxes according to circumstances, and so treat the people that they may nourish parents and children without fear of death from cold and hunger, then the people will be content and will not abandon their land to escape suffering. When the laws are made known, showing the punishments that will be meted out to criminals, forbidding extravagance, and reproving the idle and dissolute, then the people of that province will respectfully obey, and their customs will be improved. As customs improve in one province after another, their influence will naturally be felt in the capital. The townspeople are not one-tenth so numerous as the country folk; yet whatever is in fashion at the capital soon spreads to the provinces. Were the farmers content and prosperous, then still more readily would their fashions go throughout the empire conquering extravagance and evil. Without doubt, extravagance would give way gradually to frugality."

[Inoue, *Nihon rinri ihen*, vol. 7, pp. 155–59; trans. adapted from Knox, "Japanese Philosopher," pp. 81–84]

Chapter 25

VARIETIES OF NEO-CONFUCIAN EDUCATION

Whatever the different views espoused by individual thinkers of the Tokugawa period, as shown earlier, Neo-Confucian education had a significant life of its own. As in China and Korea during the same period, the spread of education was a major factor in the development of these maturing civilizations, and in the case of Japan especially, it had much to do with the readiness of the Japanese to receive and adapt to new civilizational influences in modern times.

This educational development drew on three key features of the Confucian revival in the Song, features that distinguish the new stages of growth from the earlier received tradition. First, while drawing on classical ideals, Neo-Confucianism reformulated them in ways roughly comparable to the neoclassicism of the Western Renaissance and Enlightenment. Hence the prefix "Neo-." Second, it strongly asserted the need for universal schooling. This was a major aim of the Song reformers and particularly emphasized by Zhu Xi, the dominant figure in the cultural and educational movement identified with him as "the learning of Master Zhu" (in Japan, Shushigaku). But—and this is the third feature—Zhu Xi not only advanced schooling (i.e., formalized, institutionalized, "public" learning open to all) but also provided the texts, sequential curriculum, and even an appropriate reading method for general use. Again, these were not wholly new, but they were neoclassical and Neo-Confucian in that Zhu Xi gave them a specific definition, articulation, and codification that proved widely serviceable in the new age. And because of their widespread adoption as a new educational program in all East Asian countries—spreading as the core texts of the new movement in much the same way as the Lotus, Vimalakirti, Golden Light, Flower Garland, and Pure Land Sutras had done in the earlier Buddhist age—they became the basis of educated discourse in the shared culture of the new East Asia.

Thus schools as physical institutions, texts that had been newly interpreted and codified, and a new core curriculum gave a definite shape and concrete content to education, making it to some extent independent of the interpretations of individual thinkers. Scholars might dispute philosophical issues among themselves and promote distinct schools of thought in that sense. But the shared discourse among educated persons, and the terms and concepts that largely emerged from Zhu Xi's commentaries on the Four Books and ancillary texts that he edited, provided the common ground on which individual scholars erected their own diverse theories.

What contributed to the intellectual diversity was the relative autonomy of the schools that grew so rapidly in the seventeenth and eighteenth centuries. Before this, most education had taken place in the home or had been part of religious training centered in monasteries. It had been "private" or privileged in the sense that the transmission of learning—whether in the dominant Buddhist forms or in the more attenuated Confucian learning—was in the hands of teaching lineages that tended to regard themselves as special custodians of their own brand of learning, often as conveyors of exclusive or even secret transmissions. But in contrast to the state-sponsored education of China and Korea, which was closely tied to the civil service examination system, the growth of schools in the Tokugawa period was more like the spread of local semiprivate academies in China (shu-yuan) and Korea (sŏwon). In other words, Neo-Confucian education spread on its own intellectual and cultural merits and had begun to dominate the cultural scene even before it was officially recognized or to any degree an "enforced" ideology.

To say this is not to ignore the powerful effect on others of the shogun's own patronage of Neo-Confucianism. The prestige of the Tokugawa house was such that many followed the leader and emulated his example in sponsoring such schools in their own domains (han), whether in the influential branches of the Tokugawa house itself or in the outlying domains. But the Tokugawa feudal system had enough local autonomy so that independent teachers could operate in their own fashion with the benign support—and usually loose supervision—of the local lord. In addition, there were private schools (shijuku) with their own teachers and their own teaching style. What was so striking amid this diversity and autonomy was the extent to which Zhu Xi's basic texts and curriculum were voluntarily adopted as the standard for the basic level of instruction, despite so much independent initiative and diversity on the upper levels and in the higher reaches of Japanese scholarship.

The following selections illustrate both the standard content and the pedagogical diversity of Neo-Confucian education, including the ways in which those who took issue with Zhu Xi nevertheless used his system as their point of departure and argued their case largely in the terms of the Neo-Confucian discourse.

PRINCIPLES OF EDUCATION

YAMAZAKI ANSAI

Yamazaki Ansai was a powerful teacher who, as we saw earlier, established a major school of Tokugawa Confucianism and had a strong sense of Zhu Xi's importance as an educator. An independent scholar himself, Ansai had come to appreciate the contribution of the scholarly academies that had survived official repression in the Song and carried on this tradition of learning independently of the state in Yuan and Ming China, as well as in Korea under the Chosŏn dynasty. Many of these academies had adopted Zhu's *Articles of the White Deer Grotto Academy* as their basic charter, and Neo-Confucian scholars had often commented on their significance, among them the outstanding Korean philosopher Yi T'oegye, whom Ansai greatly admired. Although Ansai refers to these as "regulations"—the common appellation in schools transmitting the Zhu Xi tradition—Zhu himself identified them as "articles," and in an epilogue he specifically disavowed the idea of disciplinary rules, preferring to think of them as values voluntarily subscribed to. They were to be a set of stated precepts, posted for all to see as the basis for the conduct of instruction in the academy when it was reopened in 1180.

PREFACE TO THE *COLLECTED COMMENTARIES ON ZHU XI'S REGULATIONS OF THE WHITE DEER GROTTO ACADEMY*

Yamazaki Ansai's preface emphasizes the systematic character of Zhu Xi's educational philosophy and the comprehensive, sequential, and cumulative order of Zhu's curriculum, in which the cultivation of personhood was correlated with social relations and intellectual development went hand in hand with moral refinement.

The philosopher Zhu, styled Huian, was conspicuously endowed with intellectual leadership. Following in the line of [the Song philosophers] Zhou Dunyi and the Cheng brothers, he advanced the cause of Confucianism in both elementary education and higher education. For the guidance of his students he established these regulations, but they could not gain wide acceptance in his own time because of opposition from vile quarters. . . .

It would seem to me that the aim of education, elementary and advanced, is to clarify human moral relationships. In the elementary program of education the various human relationships are made clear, the essence of this education in human relationships being reverence for the person (oneself and others). The "investigation of things" in advanced studies [as set forth in the *Great Learning*] simply carries to its ultimate conclusion what has already been learned from elementary instruction. . . .

Zhu Xi's school regulations list the Five Human Relationships as the curriculum, following an order of presentation that complements the curriculum of advanced education [as found in the *Great Learning*]. Studying, questioning, deliberating, and discriminating: these four correspond to the "investigation of things" and "extension of knowledge" in advanced education. The regulation dealing with conscientious action goes with the "cultivation of one's person." From the emperor to the common people, the cultivation of one's person is essential, including both "making the intentions sincere" and "rectifying the mind." The "managing of affairs" and "social intercourse" [in Zhu's *Regulations*] refer to "regulating the family," "governing the state," and "establishing peace" [in the *Great Learning*]. These regulations thus contain everything, and they should be used for instruction together with the book of *Elementary Learning* and the book of the *Great Learning*. But so far they have gone almost unnoticed among the items of Zhu's collected works, scarcely attracting any attention from scholars in Japan. I have taken the liberty, however, of bringing them out into the light of day by mounting and hanging them in my studio for constant reference and reflection. More recently I have found a detailed discussion of these regulations in *Some Reflections of Mine* by the Korean scholar Yi T'oegye. It convinced me more than anything else that these regulations are the true guide [to education].

[Signed] Yamazaki Ansai
Keian 3 [1650]: 12th month, 9th day

REGULATIONS OF THE WHITE DEER GROTTO ACADEMY

As the prefect of Nangang, Jiangxi, Zhu Xi led an effort to revive the White Deer Grotto Academy, located at the foot of Mount Lu by the great bend of the Yangtze River, a scenic spot famous as the site of Buddhist temples and Daoist sanctuaries. It is significant that Zhu took a strong interest in both public schools and the "private" (i.e., quasi-independent) academies that were centers of scholarship and ritual for the educated elite in local settings. The latter became important media for the propagation of his teachings.

As was typical of Zhu's work, the articles (or precepts) consist mostly of quotations from the classics or other early writings (not attributed, since he assumed that his readers would recognize the source from memory). Zhu Xi's contribution was putting them together in a definite order and sequence. Particularly to be noted are the balance he strikes between personal cultivation and social relations, as well as between moral and intellectual development.

Between parent and child, affection.
Between ruler and subject, rightness.
Between husband and wife, differentiation.
Between elder and younger, precedence.
Between friends, trust.[1]

These are the items of the Five Teachings, that is, the very teachings that Yao and Shun reverently commanded Xie, as minister of education, to propagate. For those who engage in learning, these are all they need to learn. As for the proper procedure for study, there also are five items, as follows:

Study extensively, inquire carefully, ponder thoroughly, discriminate clearly, and practice earnestly.[2]

This is the proper sequence for the pursuit of learning. Study, inquiry, pondering, and sifting are for fathoming principle to the utmost. As for earnest practice, there also are essential elements at each stage from personal cultivation to the handling of affairs and dealing with others, as separately listed next:

Be faithful and true to your words and firm and sincere in conduct.[3]
Curb your anger and restrain your lust; turn to the good and correct your errors.[4]

The foregoing are the essentials of personal cultivation.

Be true to moral principles and do not scheme for profit; illuminate [exemplify] the Way and do not calculate the advantages [for oneself].[5]

The foregoing are the essentials for handling affairs.

Do not do to others what you would not want them to do to you.[6] In your conduct, when you are unable to succeed, reflect and look [for the cause] within yourself.[7]

The foregoing are the essentials for dealing with others.

To these precepts, Zhu Xi added a postscript of his own, emphasizing important points that were not explicit in the quoted precepts:that learning should be both individual and

---

1. *Mencius* 3A:4.
2. *Mean* 20.
3. *Analects* 15:5.
4. *Yijing*, hexagrams 41 and 42.
5. Dong Zhongshu, in *Han shu* 56:12b.
6. *Analects* 12:2; 15:24.
7. *Mencius* 4A:4.

social, with appropriation by oneself and discussion with others essential to both self-integration and the conduct of affairs. The same approach had been recommended in Zhu's memorials and lectures to the emperor: that he should first form his own opinion of things and then discuss his opinions with others before making up his mind.

I, [Zhu] have observed that the sages and worthies of antiquity taught people to pursue learning with one intention only, to make students understand the meaning of moral principle through discussion so that they can cultivate their own persons and then extend it [moral principle] to others. The sages and worthies did not wish them merely to memorize texts or compose poetry and essays as a means of gaining fame or seeking office. Students today obviously do the contrary [to what the sages and worthies intended]. All the methods that the sages and worthies used in teaching people are found in the classics. Dedicated scholars should by all means read them frequently, ponder them deeply, and then inquire into them and sift them.

[*Zoku Yamazaki Ansai zenshū*, vol. 3, pp. 1–5 (commentary deleted);
Zhu Xi, *Wenji* 74:18a; WTdB]

KAIBARA EKKEN

Like Zhu Xi and Yamazaki Ansai, Kaibara Ekken qualifies not only as a major Neo-Confucian thinker but also as a leading educator. In addition to writing for many different audiences, he summed up the basic principles of Neo-Confucian learning that underlay all forms of education in his *Precepts for Daily Life in Japan (Yamato zokkun)*, written in 1708 in vernacular Japanese, a medium that served popular education and not just the cultivation of an elite trained in classical Chinese (as was the case for most schooling in China and Korea).

Although "popular" can mean many things, in Ekken's case one ingredient of this effort to write for a larger vernacular audience was his effort to summarize and explain in simple language the basics of Zhu Xi's learning method. There is perhaps no comparable work in Neo-Confucian East Asia that digests in such concise, plain, and straightforward language the essentials of Zhu Xi's approach, including the basic steps of the learning process, the Neo-Confucian core curriculum, the central aim of Confucian "learning for one's own sake," and the methodical, cumulative course of personal growth from elementary to higher learning. Other remarkable features of this piece are Ekken's emphasis on the proper and efficient use of time—not just a bourgeois virtue but a Confucian one applicable to all classes and ages—and on the importance of education for all people, regardless of rank or class.

The Pursuit of Learning, Part 1

There are many paths of learning. There is the scholarly interpretation of old texts, namely, philology and exegesis; there is memorization; there is the study of poetry and prose; and there is the learning of the Confucians.[8] Exegesis means trying to learn in detail the meanings of the sentences and phrases in the books of the sages. Memorization is reading widely the books of past and present and remembering the historical facts and evidence. The study of poetry and prose is learning to compose poems and essays. The learning of the Confucians is understanding the Ways of Heaven, earth, and humankind and learning the way of self-discipline for the governance of humankind. If it involves scholarly pursuits, it must be a subject of Confucian learning. Although exegesis is a mode of comprehending the meaning of sentences in the Four Books and the Five Classics, if we do not understand moral principles, it will be of little use. Memorization and the study of poetry and prose are still further from the Way and do not constitute Confucian learning. But if one is single-minded in the pursuit of Confucian learning. it is all right for one to combine with it the practice of exegesis and memorization. . . .

With regard to Confucian learning, someone might ask: isn't it all right just to learn the Human Way? Why is there a need to learn the Way of Heaven-and-earth? In reply I would say: the Way of Heaven-and-earth is the root and the source of the Human Way, and unless we know the Way of Heaven-and-earth we will not understand the root from which truth emerges. If we do not know the root, the Human Way will not be clear because we will not recognize the natural principles inherent in human beings, and we will not understand the unity between Heaven and humankind that we receive from nature. Therefore, after first learning the Way of daily human relations, we should learn the Way of Heaven-and-earth. . . .

In the pursuit of learning, both knowledge and action are essential. We call being diligent in these two essentials "extending knowledge" and being "vigorous in practice." Extending knowledge is penetrating to the limits of learning. Vigorous practice is making an effort in action. When knowledge of the Way is not clear, we cannot act. . . . If we are not conscientious in our practice, even though we know something, it is useless. . . . When we cannot see, we are unable to discern the way in which we ought to proceed. When we are not equipped with both sight and movement, it is difficult to progress along the path.

---

8. Learning for moral improvement, as distinct from purely literary or technical studies.

First comes knowledge, then comes action. In all things if we do not know what comes first, it is difficult to act. In order of precedence, knowledge comes first. Knowledge is for the sake of action. . . .

If we differentiate the two methods of knowledge and action into greater detail, there are five steps. They are stated in the *Mean* as study widely, question thoroughly, ponder carefully, discriminate clearly, and practice earnestly.[9] This is the method for the pursuit of learning by knowing the Way and practicing it.

The method of "studying widely" implies diligence with respect to seeing and hearing. It is seeking truth by reading the books of the sages, hearing the Way from others, and reflecting on the past and present. The Way of human moral relations is recorded in the writings of the sages and worthies. . . . There is no limit to the Way and its principles in this world. If we do not learn the Way and its principles and do not know the method by which we should act, our mistakes will be numerous. The Way and its principles are established in our hearts, and they function in all things and affairs. Thus, by first delving into the Way and its principles in our own hearts and then widely searching out the principles in-all things, we will "get it for ourselves" in our own mind and heart. This is learning widely. . . . However, simply loving words without seeking moral principles is not wide learning.

In "questioning thoroughly," we should resolve our doubts by clarifying these principles through association with enlightened teachers and good friends. We may question them in greater detail concerning things that we have already learned but about which we may still have doubts.

As for "pondering carefully," we should try to understand doubtful things in what we have already investigated by calming our mind-and-heart and reflecting seriously on them until we understand. Even if we investigate something, if we do not completely understand it, it will not become our own. . . . The pursuit of learning values "getting it oneself." "Getting it oneself" means acquiring knowledge by careful and thorough consideration and, by realizing the Way and principles within our hearts, making them our own.

When we "discriminate clearly," if we still are confused about good and evil after we have already considered something carefully, then by clearly investigating the rightness or wrongness of the situation, we can distinguish good and evil. These four [steps] all are techniques of knowing in order to discriminate the Way clearly.

As for "practicing earnestly," if we learn a truth through studying, questioning, and discriminating, we must deliberately practice the truth that we know. When we do not, the Way will not be established. The way of practicing

---

9. *Mean* 20:19.

earnestly is being true to our words, being without deception, being prudent in action, and having few faults. . . .

Confucius said, "In ancient times one studied for one's own sake; nowadays one studies for the sake of others' [approbation]."[10] "For one's own sake" means real [practical] learning to cultivate oneself. "For others" means learning for fame and profit, which is learning to be known by others. The original meaning of learning is cultivating ourselves without concern for whether or not we are known by others. . . . This is real [or practical] learning. However, the Confucianism of the petty person is learning in order to be known by others. This is simply intending to seek fame and profit without the aim of disciplining oneself. It is false learning. . . . If we read books, it should be our single-minded aim to assimilate them for ourselves. . . .

Although we read many books, if we do not assimilate them, it is only what is called "learning of the mouth and ear,"[11] for it is only what comes in the ear and immediately goes out the mouth, without being kept in the heart or personally practiced. This is useless learning.

When people begin their studies, they should first earnestly read the Four Books and then carefully read the Five Classics.[12] The Five Classics are the teachings of the sages of early antiquity; they represent the fountainhead of letters and the ancestral source of moral principles. The Four Books are the teachings of the Confucian school. Reading them is like listening directly to the teachings of the sages. We ought to respect them. If we wish to understand the meaning of these writings, we should first look at his [Zhu Xi's] commentaries on the Four Books, then at *Questions Concerning the Great Learning* and *Questions Concerning the Mean*, and then at the commentaries on the Five Classics. Next we should look at the books of the [Song masters]: Zhou Dunyi, the Cheng brothers, Zhang Zai, and Zhu Xi. Among these we should carefully read the books of the Cheng brothers and Zhu Xi. The *Elementary Learning*[13] is concerned with an especially important method for self-discipline. The Way of human moral relationships is almost completely supplied there. By reading this at an early age, we should learn its meaning. Furthermore, it is good to look at the histories of past ages, namely, the *Zuo Commentary on the Spring and Autumn Annals*, [Sima Qian's] *Records of the Historian*, and Zhu Xi's *Outline and Details of the Comprehensive Mirror*. This is the method of learning

---

10. *Analects* 14:25.

11. Watson, trans., "Encouraging Learning," in *Basic Writings: Hsün Tzu*, p. 20.

12. The Four Books were designated by Zhu Xi as central to the process of self-education. These, along with Zhu's commentaries, became the basis of all schooling and of the civil service examinations in China.

13. The *Elementary Learning* (J. *Shōgaku*, Ch. *Xiao xue*) was compiled by Zhu Xi as the basis for primary education, preceding higher education through the *Great Learning.*

by which we understand the Way and penetrate past and present. If we understand the classics, the commentaries, and the histories, we will not fail to grasp the principles of events, past and present.

The books of the sages are called *classics*. Classics are constants. The words of the sages reveal the constant Way throughout the centuries. The writings of the worthies are called *commentaries*. These commentaries explain the Way of the sages and transmit them to later generations. The Four Books and the Five Classics are constants. The annotations [on the classics] and the writings of the Song Confucians are commentaries on these. The books that record past ages are called *histories*. These are records of past events. The philosophical texts include those of Xunzi,[14] Yangzi,[15] Huainanzi,[16] Wenzhongzi,[17] and the Shuo yuan.[18] These books are not as clear or detailed as the books of the Cheng brothers and Zhu Xi in clarifying the Way and its principles, but they are useful as an aid to [understanding] the moral principles expressed in the classics, and we should read them.

The "collected works" (*shū*) are books containing essays and the like by various authors. These also reveal moral principles. These four types of books, namely, classics, histories, philosophical treatises, and collected works, are of varying importance, but they all are useful in the pursuit of learning. If we wish to learn the Way, we should devote ourselves mainly to diligent study of the classics for our whole lifetime. Next come the histories, which also are of great benefit. Then we should look at the philosophers and collected works. The *Outline and Details of the Comprehensive Mirror* by Zhu Xi is an especially good book. It is not simply for learning about the remaining records of past ages, their periods of order and disorder, rise and decline, but it is also a great help for the study of moral principles. It is an especially clear mirror for those who rule the country. Also, since it shows the way to victory or defeat in war, it is definitely helpful for people studying military arts. This book describes numerous important events of the past and present, many things of great benefit, and we should apply ourselves to reading them over and over. Truly it is one of the great classics for the governance of the world.

In addition, we should look as much as possible at the records of China and Japan. If we still have time left, it is good to look at the writings of the hundred philosophers in order to clarify the meaning of the classics and broaden our grasp of moral principles. . . .

To be diligent in study from our youth, we must use time wisely. . . .

---

14. The *Xunzi* is attributed to Xunzi (298–238 B.C.E.).

15. The *Yangzi* is attributed to Yang Xiong (53 B.C.E.–18 C.E.).

16. The *Huainanzi* is a Daoist text of the former Han, written by a number of authors under the patronage of Liu An, king of Huainan (d. 122 B.C.E.).

17. The *Wenzhongzi* is a Sui-period text representing the views of Wang Tong (583–616?).

18. The *Shuo yuan* is attributed to Liu Xiang (b. 77 B.C.E.).

. . . If the superior person does not use time prudently, he will not be able to discipline himself or regulate his family. The farmer, artisan, and merchant will lose the work of their family and will not be able to escape poverty, starvation, and cold. Scholars will assuredly lack refinement in learning and have no capabilities. Doctors will inevitably become like lowly craftsmen. Various skills will be lost if we do not use time wisely. Therefore, time is a treasure for people, and we should use it well. . . .

Wisdom is understanding the Way of the Five Human Relationships; humaneness is preserving and exercising them; and courage is practicing them diligently. Knowing and practicing is having courage and making an effort. These three virtues are the method of the mind-and-heart, which is the learning of the noble person (*kunshi*). The Way that we ought to practice is that of the Five Human Relationships. . . .

The Pursuit of Learning, Part 2

The teachings of the *Elementary Learning*, as something studied by children, are a form of learning for the young. In the past, all children at the age of eight, regardless of rank, became students and learned by receiving the instruction of a teacher. This was elementary learning. What they were taught was to have filial piety for their parents, respect their seniors, and serve their master, [also] the way to receive guests, sweep the room, prepare food and drink, advance and withdraw in the presence of notable people, and respond to questions and requests;[19] [further,] they were taught the skills of the six arts for daily use, namely, ritual, music, archery, driving [a horse or chariot], reading, and arithmetic. From their youth they nurtured their mind-and-heart by these means, and as they became older they made them the basis for studying the greater [higher] learning. In general, the *Elementary Learning* teaches such matters.

The *Great Learning* is the learning for adults from the age of fifteen, and it is concerned with the important principle of governing people through self-discipline. The earth is extensive, but it consists [essentially] of nothing but the self and others. The study of the Way of governing people through self-discipline is the greatest and most important of studies. Therefore, it is called the "Great Learning." "Making clear one's luminous virtue" [i.e., manifesting the moral nature] is to discipline oneself. "To renew the people"[20] is [the means of] governing people. "Resting in the utmost good" means that by manifesting illustrious virtue and by renewing the people, we attain the utmost goodness and should abide there. . . .

---

19. Described as the branches of learning in *Analects* 19:12.

20. According to Cheng Yi and Zhu Xi, this is the second "mainstay" or "guiding principle" of the *Great Learning*.

In the *Great Learning*, clarifying principles by investigating things and extending knowledge is the beginning of "governing people through self-discipline." "Investigating things" is thoroughly exploring and understanding the principles of all things and affairs; "extending knowledge" is fathoming what is known in our own mind-and-heart and clarifying it. . . .

Next is making our intentions sincere. Intentions are like seedlings; they indicate when the mind-and-heart is first aroused. The substance of the mind-and-heart is quiescent before good and evil appear. When it is first moved, both good and evil arise and so do likes and dislikes. To dislike means to hate. At this point, making our intentions sincere means loving the good, disliking evil, being honest and not deceitful. For example, loving the good is like loving beautiful colors; disliking evil is like shunning bad smells. We should be honest in such things, for it is the beginning of effort and practice. . . .

Thus the Way of the Great Learning is expanding our knowledge by fathoming the principles of everything through the investigation of things and the extension of knowledge. Then, making our heart sincere by loving the good and shunning evil, we practice what we know. This is making our intentions sincere. If our knowledge is insufficient, we cannot distinguish between good and evil in everything. If we do not make our intentions sincere by loving good and shunning evil, we will lack genuineness and cannot carry out the Way. These two are the essence of the Way of the Great Learning, and they represent the method of [both] knowing and acting. . . .

In the morning we learn from a teacher; in the afternoon we review what we learned in the morning; and in the evening we study it again. At night we reflect on our mistakes during the day, and if there are no failings we can sleep peacefully. If there are failings we should be repentant and ashamed and take this as the lesson for the following day. . . .

The Way to pursue learning is to respect the teacher. In respecting the teacher, we naturally honor the Way; in honoring the Way, we revere the Way of the people. Therefore, even though a person might have a high rank as a lord, he should not look down on the teacher as a retainer. In ancient times, in the Royal College, the teacher did not face north when teaching the emperor. This was because the teacher was venerated.[21] . . .

Nevertheless, it is difficult for ordinary people to know and practice the Way well. Therefore, the ancient sages appeared in the world, established their teachings, made clear the Way and principles, and described them in books. There is nothing that is not clearly presented in the writings of the sages concerning the principles of all things under heaven, whether great or small, fine or coarse. . . .

---

21. Customarily, the emperor sat facing south, while his ministers stood below him facing north. However, because a teacher was to be held in high esteem as a mentor (according to the Confucians), he should sit beside the emperor.

If we pursue learning by reading books, [our] knowledge of seeing and hearing will increase daily. However, if we do not practice what we know, virtuous deeds will daily decline and will not increase. If we do not act, what we learn is not true learning. Today's scholars greatly distort what is learning and what is practice because they do not "learn for their own sake."[22] . . .

Even if poor people have only the resolve to do good, they will encounter many instances when they can help people. How much more, then, do the rich and noble have the power to do good on a wide scale? Thus the learning of people of wealth and rank should not be simply concerned with their self-cultivation but should, by taking a heart of humaneness and love as the basis, concentrate their efforts on helping others. All this is useful learning.

[Kaibara Ekken, *Yamato zokkun*, pp. 55a–71b; MET]

"THE GREAT LEARNING FOR WOMEN"
(ONNA DAIGAKU)

From its first publication in 1733,[23] "The Great Learning for Women" was attributed to Kaibara Ekken, and therefore it has had the status of a classic work on women's education. Some scholars have questioned this attribution, but whatever the ultimate verdict may be, the reader should note that the treatment of women in this essay is completely different from that in the preceding excerpts from the *Yamato zokkun*, with its concept of self-cultivation and self-development. Indeed, we cannot call it "education" at all in the sense—whether Western or Confucian—that it is meant: to bring out the potentialities and capabilities of the human being. Here women are seen as having no life of their own, no individual character or personhood. Womanhood is total self-subordination to the needs of her husband and his family, in keeping with the identification of her nature with the yin principle, characterized here as "dark," inferior to men, and essentially passive.

Basil Hall Chamberlain, an early translator of this essay and a leading nineteenth-century British contributor to Japanese studies, appended a note to his translation, commenting that "anyone having the least acquaintance with the doctrines of the Chinese philosophers will see how directly the moral and social ideas current in Japan flow from those in vogue in the Middle Kingdom." This may be true of those having some "acquaintance with things Chinese," but it ignores other possibilities latent in the Neo-Confucian conception of the shared human moral nature, as shown in the different treatment of the subject in "Instructions for the Inner Quarters,"[24] possibilities that are, indeed, implicit in the other writings by Ekken himself.

---

22. *Analects* 14:25.
23. An earlier version was reported for 1729, but is no longer extant.
24. This is part of the Four Books for Women by the Ming empress Xu. See de Bary and

Seeing that it is a girl's destiny, on reaching womanhood, to go to a new home and live in submission to her parents-in-law, it is even more incumbent on her than it is on a boy to receive with all reverence her parents' instructions. Should her parents, through excess of tenderness, allow her to grow up self-willed, she is bound to show herself capricious in her husband's house and thus alienate his affection; while if her father-in-law is a man of correct principles, the girl will find the yoke of these principles intolerable. She will hate and decry her father-in-law, and the end of these domestic dissensions will be her dismissal from her husband's house and the covering of herself with ignominy. Her parents, forgetting the faulty education they gave her, may, indeed, lay all the blame on the father-in-law. But they will be in error, for the whole disaster should rightly be attributed to the faulty education the girl received from her parents.

More precious in a woman than a beautiful face is a virtuous heart. The vicious woman's heart is always excited; she glares wildly around her; she vents her anger on others; her words are harsh; and her accent [is] vulgar. When she speaks, it is to set herself above others, to upbraid others, to envy others, to be puffed up with individual pride, to jeer at others, to outdo others—all things at variance with the way in which a woman should talk. The only qualities that befit a woman are gentle obedience, chastity, tenderness, and placidity.

From her earliest youth a girl should observe the line of demarcation separating women from men, and never, even for an instant, should she be allowed to see or hear the least impropriety. The customs of antiquity did not allow men and women to sit in the same apartment, to keep their wearing apparel in the same place, to bathe in the same place, or to transmit anything directly from hand to hand. A woman going abroad at night must in all cases carry a lighted lantern, and (not to speak of strangers) she must observe a certain distance in her relations even with her husband and with her brothers. In our days the women of the lower classes, ignoring all rules of this nature, behave in a disorderly manner; they contaminate their reputations, bring down reproach on the head of their parents and brothers, and spend their whole lives in a vain manner. Isn't this truly lamentable? Likewise it is written in the *Elementary Learning* that a woman must form no friendship and no intimacy except when ordered to do so by her parents or middlemen.[25]

In China, marriage is called "returning," for the reason that a woman must consider her husband's home as her own, and that, when she marries, she is

---

Bloom, eds., *Sources of Chinese Tradition*, 2nd ed., vol. 1, chap. 23, and, for a work of the same title by Queen Sohye of Korea, Ch'oe et al., eds., *Sources of Korean Tradition*, vol. 2, pp. 49–52.

25. The middleman is the go-between. It was the parents' duty to secure a suitable partner for their child, and, in turn, the conduct of the affair was customarily entrusted to a third person (generally a married friend of theirs). The middleman thus negotiated the marriage and often remained through life a godfather to the young couple.

therefore returning to her own home. However low and needy her husband's position may be, she must find no fault with him but consider the poverty of the household that it has pleased Heaven to give her as the ordering of an unpropitious fate. The sage of old taught that once married, she must never leave her husband's house. If she should forsake the Way of womanhood and be divorced, shame shall cover her until her last hour. With regard to this point, there are seven faults termed the "Seven Reasons for Divorce": (1) A woman shall be divorced for disobedience to her father-in-law or mother-in law. (2) A woman shall be divorced if she fails to bear children, the reason for this rule being that women are sought in marriage for the purpose of giving men posterity. A barren woman should, however, be retained if her heart is virtuous and her conduct is correct and free from jealousy, in which case a child of the same blood must be adopted; neither is there any cause for a man to divorce a barren wife if he has children by a concubine. (3) Lewdness is a reason for divorce. (4) Jealousy is a reason for divorce. (5) Leprosy or any like foul disease is a reason for divorce. (6) A woman shall be divorced who, by talking too much and prattling disrespectfully, disturbs the harmony of kinsmen and brings trouble to her household. (7) A woman shall be divorced who is addicted to stealing. All the "Seven Reasons for Divorce" were taught by the sages.[26] A woman once married and then divorced has wandered from the "Way" and is covered with great shame, even if she enters into a second union with a man of wealth and position.

It is the duty of a girl living in her parents' house to practice filial piety toward her father and mother. But after marriage, her duty is to honor her father-in-law and mother-in-law, to honor them beyond her father and mother, to love and reverence them with all ardor, and to tend them with a practice of filial piety. While thou honorest thine own parents, think not lightly of thy father-in-law! Never should a woman fail, night and morning, to pay her respects to her father-in-law and mother-in-law. Never should she be remiss in performing any tasks they may require of her. With all reverence she must carry out, and never rebel against, her father-in-law's commands. On every point must she inquire of her father-in-law and mother-in-law and accommodate herself to their direction. Even if thy father-in-law and mother-in-law are disposed to hate and vilify thee, do not be angry with them, and murmur not. If thou carry piety toward them to its utmost limits and minister to them in all sincerity, it cannot be but that they will end by becoming friendly to thee.

A woman has no other lord; she must look to her husband as her lord and must serve him with all worship and reverence, not despising or thinking lightly of him. The Way of the woman is to obey her man. In her dealings with her husband, both the expression of her countenance and the style of her address

---

26. That is, based on precedents in the canonical books of rites.

should be courteous, humble, and conciliatory, never peevish and intractable, never rude and arrogant—that should be a woman's first and principal care. When the husband issues his instructions, the wife must never disobey them. In doubtful cases she should inquire of her husband and obediently follow his commands. If her husband ever asks her a question, she should answer to the point; to answer carelessly would be a mark of rudeness. If her husband becomes angry at any time, she must obey him with fear and trembling and not oppose him in anger and forwardness. A woman should look on her husband as if he were Heaven itself and never weary of thinking how she may yield to him and thus escape celestial castigation.

Because brothers-in-law and sisters-in-law are the brothers and sisters of a woman's husband, they deserve all respect. If she lays herself open to ridicule and shows dislike for her husband's kindred, she will offend her parents-in-law and do harm even to herself; whereas if she lives on good terms with them, she will likewise make happy the hearts of her parents-in-law. Again, she should cherish, and be intimate with, her brother-in-law and his wife, esteeming them as she does her own elder brother and sister.

Let her never even dream of being jealous. If her husband is dissolute, she must expostulate with him but never either nurse or vent her anger. If her jealousy is extreme, it will render her countenance frightful and her speech repulsive and can only result in completely alienating her husband from her and making her intolerable in his eyes. If her husband acts ill and unreasonably, she must compose her countenance and soften her voice to remonstrate with him; and if he is angry and does not listen to the remonstrance, she must wait over a season and then expostulate with him again when his heart is softened. Never set thyself up against thy husband with harsh features and a rancorous tone.

A woman should be circumspect and sparing in her use of words and never, even for a passing moment, slander others or be guilty of untruthfulness. If she ever hears of calumny, she should keep it to herself and repeat it to no one, for it is the retelling of calumny that disturbs the harmony of kinsmen and ruins the peace of families.

A woman must always be on the alert and keep a strict watch over her own conduct. In the morning she must rise early and at night go late to rest. Instead of sleeping in the middle of the day, she must be intent on the duties of her household; she must not grow tired of weaving, sewing, and spinning. She must not drink too much tea and wine, nor must she feed her eyes and ears on theatrical performances (kabuki, jōruri), ditties, and ballads. Until she has reached the age of forty, she should go only seldom to Shinto shrines or Buddhist temples and other such places where many people come together.[27]

---

27. Buddhist temples and Shinto shrines were favorite sites for festivals and fairs, where crowds went for pleasure rather than for religious devotions.

She must not let herself be led astray by mediums and shamanesses or enter into the degenerate rituals of gods and buddhas or indecent religious practices. If she satisfactorily performs her duties as a human being, she may ignore prayer without ceasing to enjoy divine protection.

In her capacity as a wife, she must keep her husband's household in proper order. If the wife is evil and profligate, the house will be ruined. In everything she must avoid extravagance, and in regard to both food and clothes, she must act according to her station in life and never give in to luxury and pride.

When she is [still] young, she must avoid the intimacy and familiarity of her husband's kinsmen, comrades, and retainers, always strictly adhering to the rule of separation between the sexes; and on no account whatsoever should she correspond with a young man. Her personal adornments and the color and pattern of her garments should be unobtrusive. It is enough for her to be neat and clean in her person and in her wearing apparel. It is wrong for her, by an excess of care, to try to attract attention to herself. She should practice only what is suitable.

She must not selfishly think first of her own parents and only second of her husband's relations. At New Year's, on the seasonal festivals,[28] and on other similar occasions, she should pay her first respect to those of her husband's house and then to her own parents. Without her husband's permission, she must go nowhere, and she should not offer a gift on her own.

Because a woman brings up her children not for her own parents but for her father-in-law and mother-in-law, she must value the latter even more than the former and tend them with filial piety. In addition, after marrying, her visits to her parents should be few. Much more than with regard to other friends, it should generally be enough for her to send a message inquiring after their health. Again she must not be filled with pride at the recollection of the splendor of her parental house or talk boastfully about it.

However many servants she may have in her employ, it is a woman's duty not to shirk attending to everything herself. She must sew her father-in-law's and mother-in-law's garments and prepare their food. Ever attentive to the requirements of her husband, she must fold his clothes and dust his rug, raise his children, wash what is dirty, be constantly in the midst of her household, and never abroad except when necessary.

Her treatment of her servant girls will require circumspection. Those low-born girls have had no proper education; they are stupid, obstinate, and vulgar in their speech. When anything in the conduct of their mistress's husband or parents-in-law bothers them, they will fill her ears with their invectives, thinking thereby to render her a service. But any woman who listens to this gossip must beware of the resentment it is sure to breed. Easy it is by reproaches

---

28. Certain festivals, like the seventh day of the first month, the third of the third month, the fifth of the fifth month, the seventh of the seventh month, and the ninth of the ninth month.

and disobedience to lose the love of those who, like a woman's marriage connections, were all originally strangers; and it is surely folly, by believing the
prattle of a servant girl, to diminish the affection of a precious father-in-law and
mother-in-law. If a servant girl is too loquacious and bad, she should be dismissed right away, for it is the gossip of such persons that upsets the harmony
of kinsmen and disorders a household. Again, in her dealings with these low
people, a woman will find many things to disapprove of. But if she is always
reproving and scolding and spends her time in a rush and angry, her household
will be in a continual state of disturbance. When there is real wrongdoing, she
should occasionally notice it and, without anger, point out the path of correction. While in her heart she sympathizes with her subordinates' weakness, she
must outwardly admonish them strictly to walk in the path of propriety and
never allow them to fall into idleness. If she wants to comfort someone, she
should be generous with her money, but she must not foolishly shower her gifts
on servants who serve no useful purpose just to please her individual caprice.

The five worst infirmities that afflict women are indocility, discontent, slander, jealousy, and silliness. Without any doubt, these five infirmities are found
in seven or eight of every ten women, and it is they that cause women to be
inferior to men. A woman should counteract them with self-inspection and self-
reproach. The worst of them all and the parent of the other four is silliness. A
woman's nature is passive (yin). The yin nature comes from the darkness of
night. Hence, as viewed from the standard of a man's nature, a woman's foolishness [means that she] fails to understand the duties that lie before her very
eyes, does not recognize the actions that will bring blame on her own head,
and does not comprehend even those things that will bring calamity to her
husband and children. Nor when she blames and accuses and curses innocent
persons or when, in her jealousy of others, she thinks only of herself, does she
see that she is her own enemy, alienating others and incurring their hatred.
Lamentable errors. Again, in the education of her children, her blind affection
induces an erroneous system. Such is the stupidity of her character that it is
incumbent on her, in every detail, to distrust herself and obey her husband.

It is said that after the birth of a baby girl, the custom of the ancients was to
let her lie on the floor for the space of three days.[29] Even in this may be seen
the likening of the man to Heaven and the woman to earth; and the custom
should teach a woman how necessary it is for her in everything to yield to her
husband the first [place] and to be herself content with the second place. She
should avoid pride even if her actions deserve praise. Conversely, if she makes
blameworthy mistakes, she should find her way through the difficulty and cor-

---

29. *Book of Odes*, no. 189: "And so he bears sons; they lay them on a bed, . . . [they will be]
rulers of hereditary houses. And so he bears daughters; they lay them on the ground, . . . they
shall have nothing but simplicity" (Karlgren, *The Book of Odes*, p. 131).

rect her faults, and conduct herself so as not again to lay herself open to censure. She should endure without anger and indignation the jeers of others, suffering such things with patience and humility. If a woman conducts herself in this way, her relationship with her husband will be harmonious and enduring, and her household will be a scene of peace and concord.

Parents! Teach the foregoing maxims to your daughters from their earliest years! Copy them out from time to time so that they may read and never forget them! Better than the garments and diverse vessels that the fathers of the present day so lavishly bestow on their daughters when giving them away in marriage, they should carefully teach them these precepts, which they should guard as a precious jewel throughout their lives. How true is the ancient saying: "A man knoweth how to spend a million pieces of money in marrying off his daughter but knoweth not how to spend a hundred thousand in bringing up his child!" Those men who have daughters must take this to heart.

The translator, Basil Hall Chamberlain, adds a revealing postscript: "Thus far our old Japanese moralist. For the sake of fairness and completeness, it should be added that the subjection of women has never been carried out in the lower classes of Japanese society to the same extent as in the middle and upper. Poverty makes for equality all the world over. Just as among ourselves woman-worship flourishes among the well-to-do, but is almost, if not entirely, absent among the peasantry, so in Japan the contrary or rather complementary state of things may be observed. The peasant women, the wives of artisans and small traders, have more liberty and a relatively higher position than the great ladies of the land. In these lower classes the wife shares not only her husband's toil, but his counsels; and if she happens to have the better head of the two, she it is who will keep the purse and govern the family."[30]

["Onna daigaku," in NST, vol. 34, pp. 202–5; trans. adapted and revised from Chamberlain, "Educational Literature of Japanese Women," pp. 325–43; WTdB]

THE SHIZUTANI SCHOOL

The Shizutani School was established by the lord (*daimyō*) of the Okayama domain, Ikeda Mitsumasa (1609–1682), who became inspired by the Neo-Confucian ideal of universal schooling, which was based on the idea that sound government depended on the educational level of the people and, rather than being exclusively for the elite, should be extended as widely as possible.

---

30. Fifty years later, Mao Zedong made similar observations concerning the differing conditions of Chinese women in elite and peasant households. See de Bary and Lufrano, eds., *Sources of Chinese Tradition*, 2nd ed., vol. 2, p. 410.

Therefore in addition to maintaining a domain school for samurai, modeled on the shogunal school in Edo, Mitsumasa established the Shizutani School at a rural location outside Okayama, intending it to be part of a system of local schools. In the latter sense it was a kind of public school, open to all classes, but because it was independently endowed with its own lands, it managed as a semiprivate institution to survive the vicissitudes of political change, economic crisis, and fiscal stringency that handicapped many of the other local schools.

An avid student of Neo-Confucian learning, Mitsumasa at one point supported the ideas and programs of Kumazawa Banzan, but from early on the school's program followed the standard curriculum of the Zhu Xi school, including the sequential reading of texts—especially the *Elementary Learning*, the *Classic of Filiality*, *Articles of the White Deer Grotto Academy*, the Four Books, and the Five Classics—that had become common to virtually all education in East Asia. These were supplemented by special lectures presented by local and visiting scholars, as well as Confucian rituals such as the annual sacrifices to Confucius. This student population included commoners as well as samurai, full-time residents, and part-time commuters (both local and regional), with a fair number of them from farming families whose seasonal labors allowed for only limited schooling and literacy.

The physical layout of the school, which still stands, is typical of that of other such schools and academies, with instructional halls, a library, and a refectory surrounding a shrine to Confucius and, to one side, dormitories and a memorial hall to the founder (in this case, Ikeda Mitsumasa).

REGULATIONS OF THE SHIZUTANI SCHOOL

Early versions of the school regulations were short and pertained mostly to admission to and management of the school. The following, more detailed regulations of 1814 represent the cumulative experience of the school in the seventeenth and eighteenth centuries.

1. Those [students] wishing to apply for admission to the Shizutani School should submit to the professors of the school an application form, a consent form of the head of their house, and a recommendation from landowners of their village to the professors of the school. After the *han* education official certifies admission, they will be allowed to live in a dormitory and be served meals.

2. Those [students] who can commute from neighboring villages should also submit application forms. When permission has been granted, they can attend calligraphy lessons and lectures.

3. Those [students] who apply from another region need to submit a recommendation from a relative in the region or someone else of good lineage in

the region. They also need the permission of their domain official permitting them a home stay in the region for one year. It is the home stay family that should present [the student's] application form to the *han* educational official.

4. Each young student is given a desk, a wooden ink slab, a stone tablet and five pieces of thick paper, a brush, and a water container. When the stone tablet and small or large brushes become worn out, new ones will be issued. A calligraphy form is given out on those days [numbered] with twos and sevens.

5. Instruction in the Shizutani School, as in the domain school, is based on Zhu Xi's teachings.

6. In class, the students do "plain reading" [recitation] from the *Classic of Filial Piety*, the *Elementary Learning*, the Four Books, and the Five Classics. They learn to paraphrase the *Elementary Learning* and then the Four Books as preparation for studying the Five Classics, the *Chronicles of Mr. Zuo* (*Zuo Zhuan*), standard histories, and various masters [of ancient China] and worthies [of the Song]. Most sons of commoners leave school after they learn plain reading [recitation], in order to take up farming. Thus we teach them the way of filial piety and trustworthiness and encourage them to practice it. Those able to do more are encouraged to broaden their learning and to practice standard poetry and prose.

On the days with ones and sixes

At 10:00: All should be present in the lecture hall.
After the lecture until 1:00: calligraphy and reading in the practice hall.

On the days with twos and sevens

10:00–1:00: Calligraphy and reading new materials in the practice hall.
2:00: Attendance in the Hall for Study of the Arts (Shūgeisai)

On the days with fours and nines

10:00–1:00: Calligraphy and reading new materials in the practice hall.

On the days with fives and tens

No school; time for taking a bath.

This is the students' routine. After school, students visit professors' and teachers' houses and study. Except on the days with fives and tens, they study from 7:00 A.M. to 10:00 P.M., with an interval between 4:00 and 6:00 in the afternoon. . . .

1. The lectures on the days with ones and sixes are on the Four Books and are given by different professors in turn.

2. On the morning of the first of every month, a reading teacher gives a lecture in the Hall for Study of the Arts (Shūgeisai) on the *Articles of the White Deer Grotto Academy*. This is to encourage students to study hard.

3. On the first of every month in the practice hall, the students' memorization is checked using wooden cards on which four or five characters are written, taken from the *Elementary Learning*, the Four Books, and the Five Classics. In a group of four to seven students, each chooses several wooden cards and writes down the characters in his notebook and learns them by heart.

4. In the Hall for Study of the Arts (Shūgeisai) on the days with threes and eights, reading teachers give lectures on the Five Classics and Song commentaries in turns. Then a group of older students leads a discussion, and the younger students read aloud.

5. Every day, professors, overseers, and teachers of reading and calligraphy are present in the practice hall. Younger students practice writing and reading while the older ones read. Reading teachers share bamboo sticks, on each of which a student's name is written. In a small group a teacher calls on two students near him to listen to their reading.

6. Four or five students of different ages live together in a dormitory. The room master is an older student who manages all the matters of the dormitory and sometimes teaches reading to the younger students.

7. Twelve times a month, the students visit the houses of professors or reading teachers for intensive study with one another. . . .

On the evenings of the days with ones, students gather at teachers' houses for two hours from 6:00 P.M. First they read by themselves the *Elementary Learning*, the Four Books, and Five Classics. Then in groups of three or four, they read these texts by checking forgotten characters and correcting one another's misreadings and write them down in their notebooks. Students sit in order of merit.

On the days with twos, poetry gatherings are held. Before each gathering, students are assigned to compose a poem. The person who composes a superior poem is given a book for a prize.

On the fifteenth of every month, a gathering for essays is held.

At the end of the year, professors and overseers recommend excellent students to the domain education official. They are rewarded with money, notebooks, texts, or the like.

Students can borrow books from the library.

[Taniguchi, *Zōtei Shizutani gakkō shi*, pp. 392–94; MET]

THE MERCHANT ACADEMY OF KAITOKUDŌ

The Kaitokudō, a school to reflect on human "virtue," was a merchant academy established in 1727 in Osaka through the initiatives of Osaka merchants and formally chartered by the Tokugawa *bakufu*. It developed into a renowned academy until its demise with the Meiji Restoration of 1868, which ushered in the modern era.

After Miyake Sekian (1665–1730), Goi Ranshū (1697–1762), and the Nakai brothers, Chikuzan (1730–1804) and Riken (1732–1817), the influential teachers at the Kaitokudō took the teachings at the academy far beyond certain basics offered at the beginning. Graduates of the academy included Tominaga Nakamoto (1715–1746), Kusama Naokata (1753–1831), and Yamagata Bantō (1748–1821). The Kaitokudō was frequented by various scholars, including the famous historian of the Bakumatsu era (the end of Tokugawa period), Rai Sanyō (1780–1832). Among the supporters of the academy were the merchant houses of Kōnoike, Hiranoya, Sumitomo, Masuya, and Dōmyōjiya.

The following translations are of the inaugural lecture delivered in 1727 by Sekian, the first headmaster of the academy, before seventy-nine leading Osaka merchants; and two "items of understanding" (*jō*), posted in the academy, one at the time of its founding and the other, drafted by Nakai Chikuzan, some thirty years later.

LECTURE ON THE EARLY CHAPTERS OF THE *ANALECTS* AND *MENCIUS* AT THE OFFICIALLY CHARTERED ACADEMY OF OSAKA: KAITOKUDŌ, FIFTH DAY, TENTH MONTH, WINTER, ELEVENTH YEAR OF KYŌHO

Prepared with great care for a merchant audience, Miyake Sekian's lecture on a few early passages from the *Analects* and *Mencius* speaks metaphorically about universal ethical principles as being pertinent to commerce. The work of market people was not to be condemned but must be infused with basic ethical values. At the same time, Sekian's manner of presentation reflects the heightened awareness in his time of how the circumstances, context, language, and genre in which a classic text was composed affected one's understanding of it.

The *Analects*

The *Analects* is made up of the teachings of Confucius that were transcribed and transmitted by his disciples to their students. They eventually took the form that we call the *Analects*.

CHAPTER I: LEARNING

"Learning" is the term taken from the opening lines of the *Analects* and used as the title of the first chapter. In antiquity, words were written or carved on bamboo slips which were preserved by being bound with tanned leather. They thus have survived in exceptionally good condition. The *Analects* comprises ten volumes and twenty chapters.

When we speak of "learning," we also are referring to its purpose. This purpose is to learn the Way. What, then, is the Way? It is the way of being human. For those who are not human, this may not be of any consequence, yet those who are born human must learn the way of being human. The birds and beasts remain as they are, whereas humans must learn to become human. The Way, therefore, is the way of being human, and learning means to study it. In the Way, the relationships between ruler and subject, father and son, husband and wife, older and younger brothers, and friends are divided. You should know that all things fall within each of these five relationships, as they are in accordance with the Way. Thus the ruler must be a ruler, the subject a subject, the father a father, the son a son, the husband a husband, the wife a wife, and brothers and friends accordingly. This is the way of being human and the reason why we are called that. Because of our prejudicial temperament and sensual desires, however, we quickly lose what is within us at birth. The sages did not lose this and remained true to their original inner selves. Learning is about this, that is, studying those who have retained their innate qualities. Such is the meaning of learning or teaching it. The sages did not establish their teachings with willful intellectual contrivance. Their aim was to teach people to be true to their original selves. Thus humans must pursue this aim simply because they are human. Still, because people also are born with varying habits, some believe that it is completely beyond them to attain this aim, no matter how hard they try. Others assume that since it [being human] is already known within, not much effort is required. While it may already have been known once, it should be considered neither trivial nor utterly beyond recovery. The sages were human. We here now also are human. If humans pursue the way of being human, they will realize it. However, since we are swayed by our prejudicial temperament and sensual desires, it may seem difficult to realize [this]. We tend to feel that it is beyond our reach. Also, because we are not aware of the profound and exquisite nature of what we already know, we regard this as insignificant. Both these views are distorted and biased, and we should open our hearts and receive with reverence the teachings of the sages.

Confucius is the greatest of all the sages. Indeed, since the beginning of heaven and earth, he has been alone among the sages. As Mi Yuan Zhang said in his eulogy: "Before Confucius there was no Confucius; and there will be no Confucius after him." And in the Song era, the following line was anonymously inscribed on a pillar: "If Heaven had not given birth to Confucius, ten thousand generations would have lived as though in eternal darkness." He understood very well the significance of Confucius.

Everyone of us receives the grace and benefits of Confucius, yet these are of such magnitude that we are unable to fully realize their importance. Isn't this like being grateful for the kind light received for one's lantern on a dark night while not giving thought to the sun and the moon? In the *Mean* (*Chūyō*), descriptions of the sages are followed by the passage: "As far as ships and carriages travel, human endeavors reach, heaven and earth nourish, the light of the sun and moon spread, and the frost and dew fall, all who possess the breath and blood of life honor and revere him." The reference is to Confucius, as written by Zisi in stating his vision of the future. Everywhere, even among the barbarian tribes living in various directions, the *Analects* that carried the teachings of Confucius came to be honored and revered. We are extremely fortunate, therefore, to receive Confucius's teachings. Still, if you simply read and hear the words without going beyond them, what benefit would there be for you? You must reach into your own hearts and reflect on them to grasp their meanings. Likewise, mere speculation is of no use. The teachings must lead to action on your own part. When things do not work out even after careful thought and action, seek the help of a teacher or friends. There is in our world a saying that one can "read the *Analects* but not know them" and also that one can "read the *Analects* and thus not know them." Each is understandable. The former [first saying] is a warning to scholars to take heed. When people speak knowingly even when they have not engaged in scholarly study, the Way does not seem to exist at all. The latter [second saying], "read the *Analects* and thus not know them," is a sound warning for those without much learning to reflect on themselves. When scholars say it, the Way may not seem to exist at all. It states, however, why there is no other way but to reflect on how one may not be correct. It is extremely dishonest to see oneself as always being right and others wrong. It is a weakness common to everyone.

"Isn't it truly joyful to have studied something and to learn from it regularly?"[31]

"To study" means following examples or receiving knowledge from without. "To learn" means doing things on one's own and becoming familiar with them. The word "regularly" means doing things steadily and not abandoning them. By "joyful" is meant the deep feeling of happiness that one feels in one's heart. The expression "Isn't it truly joyful?" is stated rhetorically to make people fully aware of how deeply enjoyable it is. The essential nature of all humans is the Way itself, or humaneness. . . . With ceaseless effort, ordinary humans can rise to become sages. Of course you will not at once become as awakened as those predecessors were. Only after acquiring general knowledge and learning about things close at hand and becoming familiar with them, reflecting on them, and practicing them regularly and steadily, then what might have seemed perplexing and murky will suddenly, in due time, become clear. What seemed troubling

---

31. *Analects* 1.

and difficult to realize will then unfold with ease. Your heart will then be joyful and your efforts ceaseless. As you proceed fully in this manner, you will gradually realize your virtue.

"Isn't it deeply satisfying to be visited by friends from afar?"

"Friends" refer to those who belong to the same order of things. If they come to visit even from a great distance, it means that those living nearby will surely come as a matter of course. If you are known for a special scholarly virtue, those who share this will be moved. If they visit you from near or afar, your feelings of delight will grow stronger, and you will be truly joyful. The phrase "deeply satisfying" means not being able to contain the feelings of happiness in your heart.

"Isn't it being a gentleman to take no offense against others who fail to appreciate your abilities?"

The phrase "fail to appreciate" means that despite your learning and virtue, others do not recognize them, and despite your humaneness, you are seen, on the contrary, to be a wicked person. The wording "take offense" points to a feeling at the bottom of your heart that somehow things are not being accurately stated about you in one way or another. The "gentleman" is one who, through studying and learning the Way, has realized his virtue.

When you are thought to be wrong, even though you know you are correct and even though you are good, others see you as wicked, you might seek by whatever means to convince them that this or that is not so, and you might eagerly assert that there is nothing at fault on your part. Such an attitude might surface from within. If even the slightest feeling of this sort becomes manifest, it is no longer an expression of true learning. Although one might be aware that learning is not meant to be put on display, when one is trapped by worldly sentiments one will take offense when criticized, as in the previous example, and feel within one's heart that the situation should not be the way it is. The gentleman of complete virtue, by comparison, is always critical of himself and is not mindful at all of what others say but simply sets his sights on the proper course that he must take.

. . . The words "to study" and "to learn steadily" apply to each person. The phrase regarding "friends visiting from afar" refers to humans interacting with one other in shared activities. The understanding of one's self as well as one's relationship with others is entirely clarified by these, even for those whose abilities are not appreciated or are objects of criticism and face uncertainty and adversity. For when "friends come from afar," one gains a sense of constancy and steadiness. Human beings have in common the sincere intent of being fond of goodness and hateful of evil. Thus a person who is joyful in his heart as he studies and learns should be respected and revered by everyone. It also follows that although one may feel confident of having realized a favorable goal, if one fails to influence others, one's virtue will still be incomplete. Also, as in the previous case, even if one is joyful with constancy and steadiness inside but takes offense when faced with unsteadiness and adversity, then one is still lacking [something]. . . .

Mencius

CHAPTER 1, PART 1, "KING HUI OF LIANG"

As with the *Analects* of Confucius, the title of this chapter in *Mencius* is taken from the first words used, King Hui of Liang. "Chapter" refers to the way in which words are ordered. Words are put together in passages, and passages add up to a chapter. Ordered in this manner, the meanings of the writing can be presented and comprehended from beginning to end. A certain scholar named Zhao of the late Han dynasty rendered this part of *Mencius* as a "chapter," and this designation has been adopted since.

"MENCIUS VISITS KING HUI OF LIANG"

In Mencius's time, a hundred years or so had already passed since the death of Confucius. Although Confucius lived around the end of the Zhou dynasty, the people of his day had not yet completely abandoned the practices of humaneness, rightness, ritual decorum, and music. By Mencius's time, however, the pursuit of success and self-interest had come to occupy the minds of the people, and humaneness, rightness, ritual decorum, and music were completely eradicated and no longer existed in the lives of the people. There thus were great differences between the times of Confucius and Mencius. Because of these differences, Confucius taught humaneness, while Mencius advocated rightness in addition to humaneness.

Although both Confucius and Mencius discussed the importance of virtue, Mencius often placed more emphasis on human beings' inner spirit. There was a reason for this. Because the people in his day devoted themselves solely to advancing their own interests, Mencius emphasized rightness to correct such selfishness. Selfishness could be corrected only with the rightness of inner spirit. If the realization of virtue and inner spirit were in accord, inner spirit could have been called virtue. But a distinction was necessary because the world had fallen into disarray and the realization of virtue alone no longer was enough to bring goodness to the minds of the people. Only by placing a special emphasis on the inner spirit could people be made aware of self-centeredness and be reminded of goodness. By teaching in this way, each person could be made aware of this. It was, therefore, the decline of the world that led Mencius to stress the inner spirit along with humaneness and rightness. This should be kept in mind when reading the chapter. It was during the Warring States period that Mencius was active. As each kingdom sought the advice of scholars in order to gain prominence, Mencius visited the kingdom of Liang at the courteous invitation of King Hui.

"The king said: 'Venerable sir, having come this long distance without even thinking of traveling a thousand *ri*, you must surely have an idea about how to bring profit to my kingdom?'"

"Venerable sir" refers to an old man, a term used to address an aged person. "Thousand *ri*" does not literally mean that exact distance. It simply means a great distance. "Profit" refers to greed, selfish desire. The ideograph for profit originally meant something positive. Once it came to be associated with "profit," it came to assume the meanings of greed and selfish desire. At that time King Hui was planning to engage in warfare with other states, and thus he sought, as a matter of the highest importance, to strengthen the army by enriching the kingdom. The words "bring profit to my kingdom" point to a particular concern of his. The king is intentionally using the idea of profit here to mean a selfish purpose. The king believed that Mencius had come from a thousand *ri* away without heeding the distance because he, Mencius, wanted to help the king realize his kingdom's interests. During this period, scholars served lords by promoting the skills needed to create a wealthy and militarily strong kingdom (*fukoku kyōhei*). The king assumed that Mencius's visit was to serve such a purpose.

"Your Majesty," Mencius replied. "Why mention the word 'profit'? All that matters is that there be humaneness and rightness."

In King Hui of Liang's time, humaneness and rightness had disappeared, and the people concerned themselves only with their own interests. The king's query reflects his age. Only after the selfish mind is abandoned can the Way be properly promoted. The renunciation of the selfish mind therefore comes first. Mencius's question asks why a person of King Liang's stature would focus on self-interest only. Such a concern was totally unnecessary, as only humaneness and rightness are required.

We should read the character for humaneness (*jin*) as *megumi*, meaning "empathy," and rightness (*gi*) as *kotowari*, meaning "reason." Humaneness means compassion for the emotional truthfulness in things, or *mono no aware* as we say, and rightness means accuracy in the assessment of things. Both are essential to the inner human spirit. Humaneness and rightness are sometimes said to emanate from natural energy or from knowledge gained through the senses, but these are not true to their ideas of humaneness and rightness. True humaneness and rightness spring from the basic inner self. And because they are from within the self, humans can reflect on them. Sometimes certain views seem to resemble humaneness and rightness but are actually far from them. Thus the phrase "there should be only humaneness and rightness." The idea here applies to kings and [also] to officials and commoners. It is especially important to persons in high places, and certainly so for those who lived during the Warring States period.

"If the king asks, 'What must I do to bring profit to my kingdom?' then councillors will ask, 'What should be done to do so for my families?' and lower officials and commoners will say, 'What must I do to benefit myself?' Those on high and those below will then seek profit at the expense of one another, and so the kingdom will be endangered. . . ."

Because the king is the head of the kingdom, he speaks for the interest of the entire country. Similarly, great officials represent the interests of their families, and lower officers and commoners represent themselves. These are the ways in which the term for profit was used. . . .

. . . When the king assumes such a selfish attitude, selfishness will prevail throughout the land, since the low always emulates the high. People of all statuses will act irresponsibly in all directions. As they do so, they will lose [their] humaneness and love of others. The harm done to the country will be extreme. . . .

Those who govern the kingdom must let humaneness and rightness prevail throughout the land and prevent the spread of selfishness. If humaneness and rightness and desire for profit compete with one another in one's mind, one must have a special plan to deal with it. Sages like Zi Xia foresaw a difficulty here. One truly must have a good plan. The word "profit" refers to doing something according to one's wishes and about which there is nothing that may be deemed wrong. The term "profit," however, always contains the meaning of partiality to the self. It is thus regarded as immoral. Profit is thus about the mind's desiring self-satisfaction. While one may not lose one's life for this, one will lose the essential inner spirit endowed by Heaven. The spirit of humaneness and rightness must be made to prevail over the desire of selfishness. This desire is pervasive in the social world. It is manifested even in small acts at the individual level. Although the acts appear the same as when emanating from one's rightness, subtle shifts in attitude take place in which those acts are pursuits of one's willfulness. Deep reflection is required here. The mind of the gentleman is bright and perceptive of the future. His mind is not blinded by selfishness. Lesser people are blinded by these desires and are preoccupied with only the immediate gain before their very eyes and are unable to see into the distant future. This is not any different from being birds and beasts. We should make every effort to understand this point.

[Signed by seventy-nine merchant leaders in attendance]

ITEMS OF UNDERSTANDING (JŌ), 1727

In the "items of understanding" posted in the academy, the allowance for samurai privilege included in 1727 is conspicuously absent in the version of 1758, whose emphasis is on collegial learning. Equally noticeable is the point that education is not free.

Scholarly study is based on the purpose of realizing loyalty and filiality and fulfilling one's occupational calling. Since this is the sole purpose of the lectures, even those who do not have books may listen to them without feeling ill at ease. Should an unexpected emergency arise, however, one may leave even while the lecture is in session.

Those of the samurai class shall be given priority seating at the front. But if they enter after the lecture has already begun, no special consideration will be given.

Those attending the lectures for the first time must seek permission from Nakai Chūzō/Shūan. If Chūzō is absent, permission should be sought from the managing officer Dōmyōjiya Shinsuke.

ITEMS OF UNDERSTANDING (*JŌ*), 1758

Students will interact with one another as colleagues without regard to high and low or rich and poor.

Distinctions should certainly be made between adults and children, and seating should be offered in accordance with academic seniority and levels of achievement.

Boarding students must not leave by themselves on their own accord [i.e., without permission]. However, if something unexpected comes up or the family requests permission, such departures will be permitted.

Students fifteen years and older will be expected to make a contribution in money or kind for attending the lectures. Younger children may, of course, attend the lectures as well.

Eighth month of the year of the tiger [August 1758]

[Nishimura et al., eds., *Kaitokudō isho*, unpaged facsimile; TN]

OGYŪ SORAI'S APPROACH TO LEARNING

When he was twenty-five, Ogyū Sorai (1666–1728) started a free, open-air lecture course beside the front entrance of the famous temple Zōjōji. At his school, which he later established in the very stronghold of the officially favored Zhu Xi teaching, Sorai offered a radically new approach to Confucian studies. The title of the following work, which in Japanese is *Gakusoku*, is a standard term in Neo-Confucian discourse for "school regulations," but it could cover anything in school routines from curriculum to daily conduct and discipline. Sorai uses the term *gakusoku* in the same broad sense as Zhu Xi does, as a basic approach to learning and not as either a course of study or a set of rules. Nevertheless, he is clearly challenging the presumptions of Neo-Confucian education as formulated by Zhu Xi and summed up earlier in this chapter by

Kaibara Ekken. Reflecting a growing consciousness of linguistic and conceptual change in his time, Sorai questions the possibility of any direct personal appropriation of the Four Books, even with the aid of commentarial literature (usually misleading). Each age has its own manner of speaking, which can be understood only in relation to the concrete realities of life in that age, not through the subjective interpretations of later writers in different times and places. Scholarly exactitude and linguistic precision are necessary. The essential teachings of the ancient sages may not be understood, and their significance for one's own time and place may not be appreciated except by those with the necessary linguistic, historical, and sociological competence. Not everyone could just read the Four Books hoping to cultivate himself on the model of the sages. There is no such thing as a common human nature, only different individual endowments and learning capabilities; thus the study of the classics requires the special competence of the Sinologue.

Ironically, the erudition that Sorai brought to his subject, and its obvious display in his writing, may have dazzled his readers, but it obscured his meaning. Thus it was left to a later commentator to summarize each of Sorai's points in simpler and more understandable terms, as we do here.

LEARNING PRINCIPLES
(GAKUSOKU)

One

In which it is stated that the Way of the sages exists in the *Odes*, the *Records*, and the other books of the Six Classics; that all these six classics are in the Chinese language; that if a Japanese person wishes to understand the Chinese language, the main thing is not to use Japanese readings; that instead he must labor with eye and heart; that if he does this, then for the first time there will be no difference between Chinese and Japanese; and that if there is no difference between Chinese and Japanese, then afterward he can study the Six Classics.[32]

Two

In which it is stated that just as the world's languages differ, so ancient and contemporary literature are not alike; that the study of commentaries is not necessary; and that if one is able to study and compare the old books and thus to read the old books correctly, this is to deal night and

---

32. The précis reprinted here is not by Sorai but by the commentator Itō Randen.

day with the thousand ages and to receive instruction in the same room
with the disciples of Confucius.

Three

In which it is stated that the sages did not teach by means of theoretical
terms and discussion; that they established forms and conditions of action
and taught by means of these; and that students must follow these forms
and conditions of action and thereby learn.

Four

In which it is stated that one who would master the classics must study
the annals of the various dynasties and use them to see the differences
between antiquity and today; and that thereafter he will be able to understand the Six Classics clearly and rule the realm.

In ancient days there were sages. Now there are no sages. Hence, to study
necessarily means to study the past. . . . A man is conversant with the past and
thereby sets himself facing the proper standard. He knows the present and
thereby makes this standard his own. He distinguishes among the ages and
thereby observes their histories. If he does all these things, their customs and
human feelings will become as clear to him as if he were seeing them in the
palm of his hand.

To be sure, past and present are different. Where can we see their differences? Only in concrete things (*mono*). Concrete things change with the age;
ages change with concrete things. . . .

Five

In which it is stated that the latter-day distinctions between right and
wrong and virtue and evil arose when the way of Shen Buhai and Han
Fei was practiced in the realm; and that these distinctions are not a part
of the governance of the rites and music of the former kings.

Six

In which it is stated that the way of scholarship prizes breadth and does
not disdain diversity; that a man must first "establish his greater part" and
nourish and protect it; and that even the hundred schools are all part of
our Way.

Seven

In which it is stated that all men have what is ordained for them by Heaven; that even each of Confucius's disciples took what was closest to his nature, being unable to combine all virtues; that for this reason it is the Way of the sages and the former kings that each person follow his nature, develop his talents, and perfect his virtues, and thereby conform with what Heaven has ordained[33] for him.

"What Heaven bestows on men we call human nature."[34] People differ in their natures. Natures differ in their virtues. "Furthering talent"[35] and "developing capacity"[36] cannot be done in a uniform manner. The fact that each of the various disciples of Confucius took what was closest to his own nature: how can this be taken to mean that there were inadequacies in Confucius's teaching? Confucius's teaching is "like the seasonal rain that transforms things";[37] there is nothing that it does not cause to grow. The large grow large; the small grow small. We cannot help wishing that the small grew large. But "what Heaven has ordained for men is in fact not equal."[38] The *junzi* knows what Heaven has ordained; therefore, he does not force things. In developing capacity there are things even a sage cannot do. For this reason a sage does not force things. Hence it is not true that "all men can become sages."[39] It is not true that "human nature can change."[40] It is not true that [Confucius's saying] "the *junzi* is not an implement"[41] means that in the water he cannot be a boat or on land, a cart.

What the world esteems is worldly success, not success in Heaven's terms. Therefore, he who attends to what the world esteems in order to seek recognition from others does not know what Heaven has ordained for him.

Now the Six Classics are fragmentary and incomplete. Born into today's world, who can see them in their completeness? This is as Heaven ordains it. The rural areas offer no teachers, no friends. That is as Heaven ordains it. "One's family is poor and has no books."[42] That is as Heaven ordains it. Still, "if the heart sincerely seeks,"[43] "Heaven will come to its aid."[44] A man serves in the

---

33. What is ordained for one in terms of both one's individual nature and the circumstances in which one must act.

34. *Mean* 1.

35. *Mencius* 7A:40.

36. *Yijing*, "Xici, shang"; *Concordance to Yi ching* [*Yijing*], sec. 11, p. 44.

37. *Mencius* 7A: 40.

38. *Book of Odes*, no. 21.

39. *Mencius* 6B:2.

40. Zhu Xi, *Zhuzi yulei*, chap. 4.

41. *Analects* 2:12.

42. *Hou Han shu* 49, *lie juan* 39, p. 1629.

43. *Great Learning* 9:2.

44. *Book of Odes*, no. 272.

government and has no energy left over, no free time to study. That is as Heaven ordains it. This being so, those who themselves are unable to study take delight in others' study. Those who have means sufficient to enable other people to study enable them to study. Why must there be rejoicing only when ability and wisdom and virtue and moral action [are seen to] come from within a man's own self? Truly, what Heaven ordains is something about which nothing can be done. Hence, studying to gain what is closest to a man's nature is also like this. To "further one's talent," "develop one's capacity," and thereby serve in one of Heaven's offices—this is the way of antiquity.

Study to become masters of one of the orthodox philosophical schools, or masters of the minor arts if you will, but do not try to become a teacher of the [Neo-Confucian] Learning of the Way.

> [*Gakusoku*, in NST, vol. 36, pp. 29–46; trans. adapted from Minear, "Ogyū Sorai's 'Instructions for Students,'" pp. 10–32; WTdB]

HIROSE TANSŌ'S SCHOOL SYSTEM

Hirose Tansō (1782–1806) was a Confucian scholar born into a wealthy merchant family in the small domain of Hita in Kyushu, a remote appendage to the larger Tokugawa house. At his private academy, the Kangien, Tansō became known as an outstanding teacher, attracting thousands of students from all over Japan, some of them influential in the later Restoration and Renovation movements. Tansō's learning reflected a wider eclectic trend among his contemporaries to accommodate different strands of Neo-Confucianism. Although he drew on the scholarship of Itō Jinsai and Ogyū Sorai, as an educator he adhered closely to a standard Neo-Confucian curriculum.

ROUNDABOUT WORDS
(UGEN)

The following excerpts are from a larger work, entitled *Roundabout Words*, giving Hirose Tansō's general views on political, social, and cultural matters. Thus his educational views expressed here go beyond what Tansō could teach in his own private academy and offered instead what he would recommend for official domain scholars and the country as a whole.

The main features of Tansō's plan are his attempt (1) to integrate aristocrats and commoners in a single universal school system, in order to overcome the debilitating effect of hereditary aristocracy, and (2) to provide a common classical education for everyone, after which students would go on to specialize in different fields, without trying to encompass them all. These ideas were not new,[45] but Tansō's curriculum

---

45. Song Neo-Confucians had already advocated universal schooling and some degree of

recognized the weakness of the feudal system and the increasing cultural and technological complexity of nineteenth-century Japan, which created a need for common humanistic core values in general education and for individual specialization on a more advanced level. In this he anticipated and prepared the way for some of the reforms of the Meiji period.

Promoting the wise and worthy and eliminating the unqualified is the basis for governing the country. When the wise and worthy are employed, the country flourishes, and when the unqualified are employed, the country perishes. . . . However, under the present feudal system, members of the ruling class have become accustomed to receiving hereditary stipends generation after generation, and it is difficult to dismiss members of such stipended families, even though they may not be qualified. . . . Consequently, since it is not possible to eliminate the old families, there is no alternative but to educate the children of these families, enhance their good points, and try to eliminate their shortcomings. However, as stated before, the present school system is unsuitable, and the methods of education do not measure up, so the ancient's original intentions in establishing schools has been lost. Therefore, with the ancient rites in mind, I now propose to reform the school system. . . .

In broad terms, one should send the children of the nobility to school along with those of ordinary people of the country, without distinguishing between the noble and the lowborn, so that the children of the whole body of officials and commoners would mix together, and seniority in age would be the only determinant of who sits higher than the other. In this way the heirs [of the hereditary aristocracy] will naturally come to respect the worthy and learn to defer to their elders, so that when they grow up and assume noble rank, they will not be arrogant and will listen to the words of the wise and worthy. . . .

We do not hear much about heirs and young noblemen attending today's schools in the domains; their families usually invite teachers to instruct them at home. When the children of retainers attend school, their seating priority is based on family rank rather than age. This is fundamentally incorrect. Even in their study of the classics, 70 to 80 percent of it is merely simple repetitive reading of texts (*sodoku*). Furthermore, although some study for a longer time, they only work at interpreting texts philosophically or write poems and prose; they do not apply themselves to useful study. Consequently, instruction in schools is merely formalistic; it never nurtures human talent. But if we eliminate what is not useful and maintain what is useful in the course of training and then add rewards and punishments, promotions and demotions, we can realize great reform in our customs. . . .

technical specialization. See de Bary and Bloom, eds., *Sources of Chinese Tradition*, 2nd ed., vol. 1, chap. 21.

The school system should be established with a division between the civil and military arts. Civil arts should include the subjects of Confucian classics, history, the [non-Confucian] philosophers, composition, military science, medicine, astronomy, Japanese studies, administration, government service, Dutch studies, calligraphy, mathematics, and the various [books of] rites. All these subjects involve speech and language and are of use to the nation. They should be classified as curricular subjects and an instructor appointed for each. Military arts will be discussed later, not here.

As for the students to be sent to school, they should, starting with the sons of the nobility, from the sons of the lord's principal retainer down to the sons of foot soldiers, all those ten to twenty-two years of age, not excepting even the heir apparent, should be made to attend. A magistrate should be installed to oversee the instructors, jointly administering the schools of civil and military arts. . . .

Because of the gravity of the responsibility, the appointee should be chosen from among the lord's principal retainers. . . .

Next is a detailed procedure by which the supervisor should direct and monitor the studies of all students, including their personal conduct; keep records for each; and eventually certify them for whatever their duties in life may be.

Upon entering school, a student's training begins with simple repetitive reading (*sodoku*). At the same time he studies penmanship, various rites, and stratagems. Simple repetitive reading is divided into three levels, top, middle, and bottom. After works such as the Four Books, Five Classics, *Elementary Learning*, and *Reflections on Things at Hand* are completed, and recitation has advanced nicely, the student reaches the upper level. On the upper level, the students read and explain by turns (*rindoku*) and also listen to lectures (*kōshaku*). Students read works such as the *Spring and Autumn Annals* and *Classic of History*, which they have not yet been taught, as materials to read and explain one by one. As they read in succession, students who have clear, pleasant voices and make no mistakes in punctuation (*kutō*) reach the top level of reading and explaining by turns. Thereafter, the students read and lecture by turns (*rinkō*). They sit in line and lecture one by one on the classics and histories. Those with clear language and a mastery of moral principles reach the top level of reading and lecturing. . . .

The method of study is for the teaching official to raise questions before the assembly. He asks questions that gradually test the complex significance of litigation judgments, negotiations with neighboring domains, petitions made to the government, or official notices directed to people of lower status. He has the students write reports based on what they know about these issues. Students whose compositions are thoroughly moral, whose phraseology is accomplished, and who gain the admiration of all are at the top level of the civil arts. If students begin the above-described training from simple reading to composition at eleven or twelve years of age, they can complete it in as few as five or six years, or in as many as eight or nine years. Generally by twenty years of age they should have completed this training. General education ends with this. . . . This is necessary for people above warrior rank, but if a person does not want to make a profession out of learning [teaching], it is not necessary for him to study more than this. . . .

Those who assume the responsibility of becoming Confucian teachers should divide up courses of instruction and keep to one of these divisions. They should devote themselves according to their particular strengths to one, or a combination of any two, of the subjects listed above after Confucianism. It is impossible for a person to be well versed in all subjects. . . .

If there are people qualified to teach simple repetitive reading to the family servants, let the sons of nobles and principal retainers of the feudal lords first be taught by them . . . . When it is time for the student to go to school, even if he is of noble rank, he must not wear fine clothes, and he must not have more than two men servants at most. When he is walking to school, he must not have other people move out of his way on the road. . . .

The course of classical study in school begins with simple repetitive reading and ends with composition. After that each person may follow his own bent. Some may study how to interpret the classics, and some read extensively in the many schools of philosophers; some study poetry and Chinese-style prose, and some study Japanese literature or barbarian [i.e., Western] learning, and so forth, each according to his desire. If there is nothing that appeals to a person in the above, he may stop studying. However, those above warrior status [those who take teaching as a profession] must not stop reading books in their leisure time for the rest of their lives. As I have stated before, unless he reads books, even a correct person or a person of talent and wisdom will not be knowledgeable and will be susceptible to vulgar opinions. Unless a person reads many books, is well versed in the thinking of the sages and worthies, and knows about the great men of the past, he cannot avoid being a common, witless man. . . .

The students who read and lecture, or the students who read and explain, should direct the students of simple repetitive reading. The composition students or students who read and lecture should supervise students who read and explain. The education official himself should supervise students who read and lecture and students who work at compositions. . . .

Virtuous conduct, speech, political affairs, and literary studies are the four branches of Confucian scholarship. These are the marks of a man of perfect virtue, and they cannot be expected of children. Nevertheless, children should be aware of their general meaning. The conduct of the students in schools must conform with decorum and propriety. Students must not try to stand on their own social rank but should defer to older students of ability. This constitutes virtuous conduct. If a student's lectures are refreshing to hear and rouse the listeners, he has mastered speech. If a student can elucidate moral principles in his compositions and manages well all aspects of affairs, he has the talent for combining political affairs with literary studies. In assessing human conduct, the men of old esteemed the ability to understand the significant aspects of a person's character by observing his small points. This does not merely consist of considering the quality of his achievements in the arts.

The hall for military arts should be built more than one *chō*[46] away from the civil arts area. The curriculum should be divided into fencing, lancing, archery, horsemanship, gunnery, *jujitsu*, and so forth, all the things that accompany military training, with an instructor for each, just as is to be done for the civil arts. The students should be divided into A and B groups according to their ability, as is also done for the civil arts. This will provide a unified course of acceptable instruction in the knowledge and skills that a warrior must acquire. Mastering the secrets of civil and military arts is not something to be done only by those who aspire to be teachers. . . .

Mixing the sons of lords with sons of those of lower rank not only nourishes men of talent and reforms current evils but also brings many other benefits. As I have previously described, there is to be no gap between noble and base or high and low among the students. They all will have cordial relations and feel very much at ease. Consequently, when the young nobles become rulers in later years, they will understand the feelings of those [former fellow students] below them in rank. They will remember their general impression of a person's character, even down to the infantry officers. This will be advantageous when they employ men in government service. . . . Furthermore, because these lower-ranking [former fellow students] can know the characters of those higher-ranking [former fellow students], they need not be unnecessarily suspicious or apprehensive and will think fondly of those of higher rank. As a rule, for those of lower rank to be familiar with those of higher rank is the most desirable way to rule a country, but it is also the most difficult. . . .

[Hirose Tansō, *Ugen*, in *NST*, vol. 38, pp. 316–26; trans. adapted from Kassel, *Tokugawa Confucian Education*, pp. 157–69; WTdB]

---

46. One *chō* equals 2.541 acres.

Chapter 26

POPULAR INSTRUCTION

Although Neo-Confucian instruction was generally carried on by an educated elite, whose leadership role varied in the different societies of East Asia, the basic texts of the Neo-Confucian core curriculum, and especially Zhu Xi's prominent preface to the *Great Learning*, stressed the importance of education for all. The actual results may have varied from place to place, but in Tokugawa Japan significant efforts were made to extend education beyond the samurai elite to the townspeople (*chōnin*) and farming (*nōmin*) classes. While based on essentially the same texts as those featured in the preceding chapter, to some extent the contents and teaching methods were adapted to different audiences. If Japan in the nineteenth century showed a relatively wide literacy and shared attitudes toward the importance of learning on all levels of society, it may be credited to the kind of popular education illustrated in the following excerpts.

ISHIDA BAIGAN'S LEARNING OF THE MIND AND THE WAY OF THE MERCHANT

It was among the townsfolk of Kyoto, a busy center of textile and handicraft production, that a Confucian-inspired religious movement first made its influence felt beyond the samurai-oriented academies and domain schools of Tokugawa Japan. The founder of this movement, Ishida Baigan (1685–1744), was of peasant origin but moved to Kyoto in his youth and worked there for many years as a clerk in a dry-goods store. While a young man, he became interested in various forms of learning, beginning with traditions centered on the worship of native Japanese deities but soon ranging over the Confucian classics, Neo-Confucian commentaries, and various popular Buddhist texts. His commitment to his studies is legendary: he is said to have read books early in the morning, late at night, and during every spare moment, without ever neglecting his shop duties. In 1729, when Baigan was in his mid-forties, he left his employment and began to lecture on his version of the "Way" to anyone who cared to listen. At first his audiences were small, but he gradually developed his speaking skills and in time attracted a number of serious students, some of whom later spread his ideas throughout Japan. By the end of the Tokugawa period, about 180 study centers associated with Baigan's movement had been established at one time or another in most parts of Japan, and public presentations of the founder's ideas by traveling lecturers had become commonplace, not only in the major urban centers of Kyoto, Osaka, and Edo, but also in the rural towns and villages.

Ishida Baigan's religious and moral life was the main source of the teaching, which he referred to as "Shingaku," using the expression for the learning of the mind-and-heart well established in Cheng–Zhu learning of the Way. He engaged in prolonged periods of meditation, after which he had two enlightenment-like experiences in which he reportedly gained profound insights into his own nature and its relation to moral truth and the universe. He formulated and expressed these insights for his followers by drawing freely on a wide range of Japanese and Chinese philosophical traditions. The dominant influence in his thought was Mencius's rendition of Confucian thought, particularly as elaborated by the Song Neo-Confucian masters. In his writings, Baigan reiterates in various ways that all human beings are naturally endowed with moral goodness and that our task in life is to identify our innate moral sense and allow it to guide our behavior. He justifies this idea by referring, for example, to Mencius's assertion that we can know the order of the universe ("Heaven") by thoroughly examining the truth in our own heart and thus coming to an understanding of our nature,[1] or to chapter 1 of the *Doctrine of the Mean*, which identifies the Way as "following one's own nature." The ultimate aim of Baigan's system was in fact the enactment of the "Way of the sages," which he defined in accordance with Confucian tradition as harmony between ruler and minister, parent and child, husband and wife, older and younger siblings, and friends (the so-called Five Human Relationships). The direct, personal insight into one's own nature that Baigan advocated thus had eminently practical implications: it entailed observing in everyday life such

---

1. *Mencius* 7A:1.

time-honored values as loyalty and filial piety, along with the related ideals of frugality, honesty, and diligence.

In order to prepare his students to experience the moral quality of their own natures, Ishida Baigan encouraged them to engage in meditation, which he called "contemplative practice" (*kūfū*) or, following the Song Neo-Confucian masters, "quiet sitting" (*seiza*). The purpose of the meditation was to restore their minds to a state of serenity and selfless openness, in which all objects of experience, including other people and one's own body, would be experienced as directly constituting one's own mind. Baigan referred to this rather mystical perspective as "the mind that depends on form." His successor, Teshima Toan (1718–1786), who along with the famous preacher Nakazawa Dōni (1725–1803) was largely responsible for disseminating Baigan's teaching after the founder's death, further emphasized the notion of a selfless, nondualistic mind and systematized the training process through which practitioners came to experience this mind directly. It was because of this continuing insistence on the importance of knowing one's own true mind or nature that Baigan's teaching came to be called Sekimon Shingaku (the Learning of the Mind-and-Heart according to Ishida Baigan's school).

Baigan first addressed his teaching to members of the Kyoto merchant milieu and thus often found himself answering questions about the relevance of his ideas to people who spent most of their time selling, buying, and distributing goods. At that time, many members of the educated class of the day regarded commerce in a negative light. Some Tokugawa writers even argued that merchants were worthless because they did not generate goods themselves but merely lived off profits made from others' productions. Merchants were in fact ranked lowest among the four classes of the Tokugawa order (after samurai, peasants, and artisans). Baigan accordingly took pains in his writings to assure his critics of the value of learning for merchants (as, of course, the merchant academy Kaitokudō had done). Thus he was not alone in defending the moral capacity of merchants in the face of high-minded Confucian polemics against the immorality of profit making, but his arguments were certainly vigorous for his time and have struck even some modern observers as being politically charged. We should note, however, that Baigan typically cited the samurai as the model of integrity that merchants should emulate. He fully accepted the Tokugawa social hierarchy and its associated value system, according to which samurai occupied the top levels of society and, in effect, controlled the content and channels of formal education. It was within these parameters that Baigan and his successors pursued the implications of the Mencian theory of the original goodness in human nature for all social classes.

The Shingaku teachers in fact developed a powerful educational movement that took for granted the natural capacity of commoners to create and disseminate their own forms of knowledge. The impressive spread of this movement during the late Tokugawa period seems to have been part of a larger trend in which greater numbers of ordinary people were creating religious systems suited to their own needs. The popularity during the early nineteenth century of traveling Shingaku teachers who used humor and storytelling to engage the interest of large audiences may well have reflected the preoccupation of privileged townsfolk and rural gentry with maintaining moral consensus in their communities at a time when the fabric of Tokugawa society appeared to be deteriorating.

CITY AND COUNTRY DIALOGUES
(TOHI MONDŌ)

Ishida Baigan's best-known work, City and Country Dialogues, is based on records of his conversations with students and critics of his teaching. The following excerpt typifies the Shingaku founder's response to debates among Confucian scholars of the time about the nature of the Way that is delineated in the classical texts. One cannot understand these texts, says Baigan, unless one has a direct, personal insight into one's own nature.

A student asked: "The great sage Confucius explained the path of the Three Bonds [Mainstays] and the Five Constant Virtues,[2] but he did not address the issue of human nature and principle. Mencius for his part stated that 'the nature of human beings is good.'[3] He also spoke about 'nourishing my all-encompassing vital energy.'[4] Gaozi said that 'the inborn is what is meant by "nature"' and that 'there is neither good nor bad in human nature.'[5] He also said that 'human nature is like the qi willow' and that it is 'like whirling water.'[6] Moreover, Han Yu asserted that 'there are three kinds of human nature,'[7] and Xunzi said that 'the nature of human beings is evil; goodness is the result of conscious activity.'[8] Yangzi claimed that 'good and evil are mixed together [in

---

2. The Three Bonds (Mainstays) are the moral standards for relations between ruler and minister (lord and retainer), parent and child, and husband and wife. The Five Constant Virtues are humaneness, rightness, ritual decorum, wisdom, and trustworthiness.

3. For statements in this vein, see, for example, Mencius 6A:2, 6.

4. Mencius 2A:2.

5. Mencius 6A:3, 6.

6. Mencius 6A:1, 2.

7. Han Yu, Yuan xing, Kanbun taikei 3, Tōsō hakka bun 1:8 (Tokyo: Fuzanbō, 1972). Baigan may be following Zhu Xi's commentary on Mencius 6A:6, in which he cites Han Yu. See Shisho shūchū 2:337, 527b, in Shushigaku taikei, vol. 8.

8. Xunzi, Xing'e, sec. 23; Watson, trans., Basic Writings: Hsün Tzu, p. 157.

human nature]."⁹ In addition, the theories of Lao, Zhuang, and the Buddha regarding human nature are innumerable. Which of these views should be considered right and which wrong? . . ."

Master Baigan answered, " . . . Whether Mencius's view about its goodness is right and consistent with your nature is an issue that you can resolve for yourself later. For now, let us leave aside the matter of the goodness of human nature. How do you understand Confucius's 'single thread'?"

The student said, "Zengzi said it consists of 'loyalty and reciprocity,' being true to oneself and considerate of others, that is all.¹⁰ How can we doubt this?"

Master Baigan replied, "Zengzi's 'loyalty and reciprocity' is excellent. It is natural for those of later generations who are ignorant of the principle of human nature to claim in their turn that the single thread is loyalty and reciprocity. In fact, however, it is absolutely wrong for them to say that the single thread means loyalty and reciprocity. . . . The 'single thread' is the utterly marvelous principle of the goodness of human nature. It represents the understanding of the sages, so it is beyond words and phrases—something you must apprehend on your own.

" . . . Zengzi had learned the transmission of the Way, so he explained the single thread of utmost sincerity as 'loyalty and reciprocity.' Persons who have attained the Way freely explain the single thread as loyalty and reciprocity, and [in their case] this view is right. Whether it is right or not depends on whether you have attained the Way. . . .

" . . . Everything written in the *Analects* represents the mind of the Sage [Confucius], and if you do not know that mind, what doctrine will you use to cultivate your person and teach others?"

The student noted, "The Way of Confucius is nothing other than the Five Human Relationships and the Five Constant Virtues. How can we possibly doubt this?"

Master Baigan replied: "If you do not know the meaning of 'one' in Mencius's 'there is only one [Way],' then you do not know the Way. Confucius said, 'People can enlarge the Way; the Way cannot enlarge people.'¹¹ 'To say that the mind can bring human nature to complete realization means that people can enlarge the Way.' 'There is no Way outside people, and there are no people outside the Way. Insight into the Way takes place inside people's minds.'¹² By

---

9. Yang Xiong, *Fayan*, "Xiu shen" sec. Baigan is probably following Zhu Xi's commentary on *Mencius* 6A:2, in which he refers to Yangzi (Yang Xiong). See *Shisho shūchū* 2:331, 526a, in *Shushigaku taikei*, vol. 8.

10. *Analects* 4:15.

11. *Analects* 15:29.

12. Both quotations are from Zhang Zai, cited in Zhu Xi's commentary on *Analects* 15:28. See *Shisho shūchū* 1:287; 432a, in *Shushigaku taikei*, vol. 7.

means of this insight one enlarges the Way. The mind that gains insight is the substance. The great human relationships among people are its functions. When the substance is established, its functions are carried out. Those functions are the interactions between lord and retainer, parent and child, husband and wife, elder and younger siblings, and friends. The innately good mind of humaneness, rightness, ritual decorum, and wisdom is the mind that causes these Five Human Relationships to be enacted. You do not realize that this mind is one and only one." [pp. 435–38]

Baigan developed his own theory of the state of mind that results from knowing one's own nature. In the following excerpt, he describes this "wisdom of the sages" as a frame of consciousness in which self-centered, subjective impulses give way to a perfectly other-centered outlook. In this state, the exigencies of the external forms that one encounters in any given moment determine the content of one's mind-and-heart at that particular time. In short, one's mind, emptied of selfish considerations and projections, is simply made up of what it apprehends. This state of selfless openness results in a spontaneous naturalism, akin to the simple attitude of animals, which fulfill their physical needs without becoming involved in subjective speculations. Baigan identifies the Japanese gods as well as the ancient Chinese sages as the ultimate paragons of this other-centered consciousness. His formulation of this theory, which may have been inspired by Zen Buddhist and Daoist as well as Neo-Confucian sources, is not always clear or internally consistent. Nevertheless, his theory of the "mind that depends on form" had important implications for Shingaku ethical teaching: when one knows one's true nature, one identifies completely with other people and thus places priority on their needs rather than on one's own.

A student noted, "The sage is born with knowledge.[13] It is not the sort of knowledge that someone like you could have. How is it that you nevertheless discriminate easily between the wisdom of a sage and self-centered, individual knowledge?"

Master Baigan replied, "Even you can easily distinguish between black and white. Distinguishing between the wisdom of the sages and self-centered knowledge is similar. When Yu regulated the waters, it was simply a matter of his knowing that one place was high and another was low; there was nothing unusual about it.[14] Because self-centered knowledge combines with all kinds of willful notions, it is not natural knowledge; it differs from the wisdom of the sages. To render the wisdom of the sages in familiar terms, Master Cheng said, 'The people of today use a bridle to control a horse. But they do not use it to restrain an ox. All people know that bridles were created by human beings, but

---

13. Allusion to *Analects* 16:9: "Those who are born with knowledge are the highest."
14. Allusion to *Mencius* 4B:26.

they do not know that bridles came into being because of horses. The sage's moral instruction is also like this.'[15] It was only after the sage observed horses that he created bridles and used them on horses. He did not know about horses from birth, from when he was in his mother's womb. He took exactly what he saw in front of him as his mind. This is the superior quality of a sage's wisdom. In his ability to reflect the things he encounters without any distortion he resembles a bright mirror or still water.

"In the beginning, the minds of human beings were no different from those of the sages; but people's minds became obscured by the Seven Emotions,[16] and they began to believe that the wisdom of the sages was something unusual, outside themselves. Hence they grew ignorant and began to have various sorts of doubts. Originally, one could directly apprehend the forms of things as one's mind. For example, if one scratches oneself while asleep, one is unconsciously assisting one's body: one's body directly becomes one's mind. Also, when mosquito larvae are in water, they do not bite people; but once they change into mosquitoes, they suddenly bite people. This is due to the mind that depends on form. . . .

" . . . Mencius said, 'Our body and our complexion are given to us by Heaven. Only a sage can bring his body to complete fulfillment.'[17] To bring one's body to complete fulfillment means to carry out exactly the Way of the Five Human Relationships. Those who cannot carry out the Way, thereby bringing their bodies to complete fulfillment, are small persons.

"Animals and birds do not have self-centered minds. Rather, they bring their bodies to complete fulfillment. These all are natural principles, and the sage understands them. The *Chronicles of Japan* [*Nihongi*] states: 'The god O-Onamuchi and the god Sukuna-bikona combined their powers, came to an agreement, and created the world under heaven. For the sake of the lovely people and the animals, they also established the methods for curing diseases. Moreover, in order to drive away the calamities of birds, animals, and insects, they established rules for preventive incantations. Through these methods and rules, the entire populace has enjoyed the gods' protection until today.'[18] The Way is the same, no matter where. In China the *Classic of Documents* says that Fu Xi raised sacrificial animals and kept them in his storehouse. In fact, because human beings and animals belong to different categories, both birds and animals fear human beings and will not approach them. The sages and gods do not have self-centered minds, so they observed the birds' and animals' fear and regarded it as constituting their own minds. . . . They made into their own minds what

---

15. Cheng Hao and/or Cheng Yi, cited in Zhu Xi's commentary on *Analects* 5:25. See *Shisho shūchū* 1:109–10, 406b, in *Shushigaku taikei*, vol. 7.

16. The Seven Emotions are joy, anger, sorrow, fear, love, hatred, and desire.

17. *Mencius* 7A:38.

18. *Nihon shoki*, "Kami no yo," in *NKBT*, vol. 67, p. 128.

they encountered and became familiar with the inborn characters of all animals. They accustomed the animals to human beings and thus domesticated many of them." [pp. 451–52]

In the next exchange, Baigan's efforts to spread the Way among his fellow merchants are harshly criticized. His famous response, equating the merchant's profit with the samurai's stipend, gave Baigan a place in history as a champion of the moral capacity of business people.

A student stated, "Merchants make their living by gaining profit through deceit. Under the circumstances, learning is definitely not something they can engage in. I understand, however, that it is mostly tradespeople who come to you to study. You teach case by case, modifying your teaching to suit each person's needs; you are what Confucius meant when he said, 'The village paragon is the ruin of virtue.'[19] Not being a scholar, you pander to the trend of the times: you follow the immoral spirit of the age and curry favor with the world. You are a petty man who leads people astray and deceives his own heart. Your disciples do not know this. Aren't you ashamed to consider yourself a scholar?"

Master Baigan replied, "Confucius said, 'When a gentleman is ignorant, one would expect him not to offer any opinion.'[20] You should always leave aside matters you do not know about. Don't you think it is base to circulate rumors without understanding this principle? Now then, the matter you have mentioned is something people in the world have doubts about, too. First of all, there is only one Way. However, warriors, farmers, artisans, and merchants each have a path to fulfill; even beggars—not to mention merchants—who are outside the four classes of people, have a Way."

The student asked, "You mean to say that even beggars have a Way?"

Master Baigan replied: ". . . The Way of beggars is not to steal, even if one is starving to death. Confucius said, 'It comes as no surprise to the gentleman to find himself in extreme straits. The small man finding himself in extreme straits would abandon all restraint.'[21] One who upholds what is right even when in distress is a gentleman. One who becomes wayward and confused when in distress is a petty man. Isn't it deplorable to be a petty man, inferior, or beggar?"

The student remarked, "But merchants are extremely greedy and make their living by constantly coveting things. To teach them not to have desires is the same as making a cat guard the bonito fish. To encourage them to engage in learning is mixed up and illogical. Isn't it a fraud to be teaching merchants, even though you are aware that it will not work?"

19. *Analects* 17:13.
20. *Analects* 13:3.
21. *Analects* 15:1.

Master Baigan replied: "Those who do not know the Way of the merchant invest in greed and bring ruin to their households. When one knows the Way of the merchant, one abandons desires, strives to maintain a humane attitude, and regards prosperity that accords with the Way as the virtue of learning."

The student asked, "In that case, do you teach students to forgo sales profits and to sell at cost? If those who practice under you learn not to take a profit openly but to take it behind their back, this is not a true teaching; on the contrary, you are teaching a lie. Your teaching is incoherent in this way because you insist on what is inherently impossible. That a merchant can get along without loving profit is absolutely unheard of."

Master Baigan replied: "My teaching is not a lie, and I can tell you the reason why it is not. One of you here is probably in the service of a lord. Is it possible that a retainer could serve his lord without receiving any remuneration?"

The student said, "That is unlikely. Even Confucius and Mencius stated that 'not to receive a stipend is against the rites.'[22] Why should it be a problem to receive a stipend? This is in accordance with the Way of receiving. To receive a stipend in accordance with the Way is not avarice."

Master Baigan answered: "To gain a profit from a sale is the Way of the merchant. I have never heard that selling at cost is the Way. If making a profit from sales is greed and thus not the Way, then why did Confucius accept Zigong [a successful merchant] as his disciple? Zigong applied Confucius's Way to his buying and selling activities. Without any profit from his transactions, Zigong would not have been able to grow rich. The merchant's profit is the same as the samurai's stipend. For a merchant not to take a profit is like a samurai serving his lord without receiving a stipend." [pp. 420–25]

The following excerpt typifies the practical advice that Baigan offered merchants on how to prosper financially without losing their moral integrity. Partly in reaction to the extravagances of the Genroku period (1688–1704) and the shogunate's subsequent pressure on the city classes to economize, many merchants of the time were concerned with maintaining a reputation for frugality and integrity.

The student asked, "How, then, should I put into practice the rules for the conduct of a merchant?"

Master Baigan replied, "As I said earlier, place priority on 'knowing everything by means of one thing.'[23] For example, a warrior who begrudges his life for the sake of his lord cannot be called a samurai. If the merchant understands this, his own path is clear. As long as you do not neglect the customers who

---

22. Baigan is alluding to *Analects* 6:3 and *Mencius* 2B:14.

23. Baigan is referring to a proverb that says, "By means of one thing, one knows everything and anything."

support you and you serve them wholeheartedly, you will meet their desires in eight cases out of ten. If you invest your energy in your business in such a way as to meet the wishes of your customers, surely you will not need to worry about making a living. Also, to begin with, you should be frugal; you should manage expenses that until now have cost you one *kanme* with seven hundred *monme*, and reduce your profit from one *kanme* to nine hundred *monme*. Thus, from sales proceeds of ten *kanme*, reduce the profit by one hundred *monme*.[24] If you take only nine hundred *monme*, you don't need to worry that you will be accused of selling goods at a high price. Because you won't have any worries, you will feel easy in your heart. Furthermore, do not take double profits based on inconsistent measurements, as I mentioned earlier; do not be unreasonable with the dyer about dyeing mistakes; do not make advance agreements to receive fees from people who are bankrupt, thereby stealing the money that is owed to their creditors;[25] and do not unfairly violate agreements about account balances. Abandon luxuries; do not indulge in costly tea ceremony accessories; give up pleasure sprees; and do not cultivate a taste for building lavish houses.

"When you restrain yourself and give up all sorts of practices, even if you take a profit of only nine hundred *monme* instead of one *kanme*, you should easily be able to support your household. . . . One hundred *monme* of immoral money makes all the remaining nine hundred *monme* immoral. Many do not know that accumulating one hundred *monme* of immoral money, and thus turning nine hundred *monme* into immoral money, leads to the destruction of their descendants in the same way that one *shō* of water is thrown away because of one drop of oil. Even if you combined all your double profits, fees from bankrupt people, and illicit money gained through sleight of hand at payment times, you would not be able to make a living from it.

"This principle may be applied to everything. Wouldn't it be sad if, because your greed won out and you found it difficult to part with the one hundred *monme*, you made immoral money without realizing that your beloved descendants would thereby die out? As I said earlier, today one should regard the Way of the samurai as a model of the integrity of all things. Mencius said, 'Only a gentleman can have a constant heart without having a constant means of support.'[26] . . .

---

24. One *kanme* was equal to 1,000 *monme* (of silver, in this context). Baigan is thus advising his listener to reduce his profits from 10 percent to 9 percent (from 1 *kanme* to 0.9 *kanme*) per 10 *kanme* of gross proceeds.

25. Baigan is referring to the practices of making a "double" profit by buying at a reduced price a piece of cloth that measures a bit short and then selling the same piece at the price of a standard measure without informing the customer; of paying cloth dyers less for pieces that have small dyeing defects but selling them at full price to customers; and of accepting secret payments from people who are facing bankruptcy in return for holding off their creditors.

26. *Mencius* 1A:7.

". . . From this perspective, a samurai is one who can be a model for the people of the world. Confucius said, 'There must be such cases, but I have not come across them.'[27] The world is large, so there must be samurai who hush up things and condone injustice. If such persons exist, they may carry swords in imitation of the samurai, but they are thieves. . . . Today, in this age of peace and order, how can there possibly be a samurai who is not loyal? You should realize that for a merchant to take double profits or accept money on the sly betrays a lack of filial piety and loyalty to his ancestors—and you should bear in mind that the merchant's heart should not be inferior to that of the samurai. Why should the Way of the merchant be any different from the Way of the samurai, the farmer, or the artisan? Even Mencius said, 'There is only one Way.'[28] Samurai, farmers, artisans, and merchants all are creatures of Heaven. Is there more than one Way in Heaven?" [pp. 432–34]

[Ishida Baigan, *Tohi mondō*, in NKBT, vol. 97, pp. 435–38, 451–52, 420–25, 432–34; JS]

THE HOUSE CODES OF TOKUGAWA MERCHANT FAMILIES

The Hakata merchant Shimai Sōshitsu left his descendants a set of instructions that he claimed should be "as important to you as the Great Constitution of [Shōtoku] Taishi." He wrote those instructions in 1610, about the same time as the trader Suminokura Soan established a series of rules for the sailors whom he employed for voyages overseas (see chap. 20). These codes are among the very earliest house laws written by merchants. Military houses, of course, had possessed written codes far earlier.[29] Merchant house codes did not begin to appear in large numbers until the eighteenth century and, even then, only in wealthier and older merchant houses.

Despite the wide variations among these houses, certain generalizations about the codes are possible. When the patriarchs of the large Tokugawa merchant houses wrote codes to leave to their descendants or to use in instructing their workers, they devoted considerable attention to economic matters. In fact, they seem to have written the codes primarily to ensure the continued economic stability of their houses. Despite this concern, however, these men did not preach an entrepreneurial ethic but instead approached their businesses with a financially conservative attitude, suggesting that these merchants shared many of the samurai's philosophical assumptions. One thing they did not share, however, was a low opinion of mercantile activity, for they were, above all, self-confident men.

---

27. *Analects* 4:6.
28. *Mencius* 3A:1.
29. See de Bary et al., eds., *Sources of Japanese Tradition*, 2nd ed., vol. 1, chap. 18.

Many writers of merchant codes showed their concern for the future prosperity of their houses by exhorting their successors or workers (1) to work diligently, (2) to be frugal, (3) to obey the government, and (4) to protect the reputation of their houses. In these instructions, too, they reflected a Confucian ethic widely shared among most classes.

Frugality, however, is even more strongly stressed in these codes than diligence. Many worried that their heirs, who inherited their fortunes instead of earning them, would squander that wealth. Money was hard earned but easily spent, and a spendthrift could quickly waste an enormous amount of money wooing a distinguished courtesan. The instructions vary from generalized comments about the wisdom of frugality to specific rules forbidding merchants to wear fancy clothes, visit the pleasure quarters, gamble, or drink excessively.

The Shimai code illustrates how parsimonious some merchants could become. Not only does Shimai Sōshitsu prohibit his heirs from going on moon-viewing and flower-viewing excursions, playing games of go and chess, and becoming devotees of the tea ceremony, but he also advises them to pick up bits of trash and use the pieces to make rope, plaster, or paper. He tells them never to trust their servants, and he even suggests ways of spending less money on the servants' food.

The path to luxury lay on a slippery slope, according to the writers of the codes, and it was a path that all merchants should avoid. "No one actually decides that from now on he will live extravagantly," the merchant Itō Chōjirō explains in his code. "Rather, he tells himself, 'Such-and-such would be too much, but this much is fine,' and before he knows it, he has slipped into extravagant habits."[30] And once a merchant adopts such habits, he has endangered the entire fortune of the house. In his book *Chōnin kōken roku*, Mitsui Takafusa cites the example of the Ginza merchants as a warning to his descendants:

> When they played music for nō plays or went sightseeing or on pilgrimages to temples, they wore elegant clothes. . . . Their wives and daughters rode around in palanquins, and even their ladies' maids and menservants were the height of fashion, making a splendid show. Before they knew where they were, their houses and storehouses were broken up and sold off; the lords and masters were without servants; their ladies went on foot; and the utensils were put out as pledges or auctioned off.[31]

Although the writers of the codes seem preoccupied with economic matters, they do not preach an entrepreneurial ethic. They clearly teach not boldness but caution: urging the reader not to expand the family fortune, but to guard

---

30. Yoshida, ed., *Shōka no kakun*, p. 252.
31. Crawcour, trans., "Some Observations on Merchants," p. 107.

and maintain it, and often forbidding him to change business practices or engage in risky business ventures.

Many codes specifically prohibit risky ventures or changes in business practices. The merchant houses old and rich enough to write codes seem to have considered it best to play it safe, to avoid risking their wealth for the sake of new possible profits. The testament of the founder of the Mitsui house states: "Be always careful and cautious in your work or your business will fail."[32]

Moreover, they were conservative in other ways as well, preaching a moral philosophy that in many ways resembles the professed values of the ruling elite. They insisted on the duty they had to provide for their descendants and the debt that they owed their ancestors. "Our parents are the 'cause' of our existence," states the code of the Okaya, a Nagoya hardware-store family, and the family must "remember the debt of gratitude we owe our parents."[33]

A merchant owed service not only to his descendants and ancestors but also to his superiors within the house hierarchy. These superiors, of course, were supposed to return the service with benevolent care. A Mitsui code, for example, instructs family members in a typical Confucian manner: "Those who stand above should be kind and charitable to those below, and those who are low should be respectful to those on high."[34] According to the codes, the relationship between a clerk and his employer is a reciprocal one that echoes the way a merchant must not only repay his ancestors but also provide for his descendants.

Wealth is a result of hard work and frugal habits, many code writers imply, and any merchant who is frugal and diligent is almost certain to become rich. As Mitsui Takafusa puts it, "One who keeps working will never be poor." "Your work determines your 'luck,'" states the code of the Itō. "If you are frugal and work hard, 'luck' will reward you." And a Mitsui code assures the reader: "If you work diligently and scrupulously avoid luxury, you will ensure the prosperity of your family and descendants."[35]

[Adapted from Ramseyer, "Thrift and Diligence," pp. 209–20]

THE TESTAMENT OF SHIMAI SŌSHITSU

During the Warring States (Sengoku) period, the Shimai house of Hakata in northern Kyushu traded in saké and lent money. Then, under the leadership of Shimai Sōshitsu (1539–1615), it expanded the scope of its activities, lending even to important lords and trading with merchants in Korea. When Hideyoshi decided to invade Korea, Sōshitsu

---

32. Mitsui, "Chōnin kōken roku," p. 82.
33. Mitsui, "Chōnin's Life Under Feudalism," p. 72.
34. Yoshida, ed., *Shōka no kakun*, p. 252.
35. Yoshida, ed., *Shōka no kakun*, pp. 250, 83.

apparently tried to dissuade him, reasoning that war would disrupt his trade with the peninsula. But Hideyoshi persisted, and Sōshitsu made a handsome profit supplying his armies. Although the Shimai house safely weathered the national transition to Tokugawa rule, by then it had abandoned its own international ventures and turned to financing other traders. This code, written in 1610, is addressed to Shimai's adopted son and heir. It is in seventeen articles, and its conclusion invokes the model of Prince Shōtoku's Seventeen-Article Constitution.[36]

1. Live an honest and sincere life. Respect your parents, Sōi and his wife, your brothers, and your relatives, and try to live harmoniously with them all. Honor and treat with respect everyone you meet, even those you see only occasionally. Never behave discourteously or selfishly. Never lie. In fact, never say anything that even resembles a lie, even something you heard from someone else. Loud and garrulous people are not liked, and such behavior is not profitable, anyway. Say nothing that might later be considered official evidence, even if you are asked about an incident that you have seen or of which you have heard. Above all, ignore anyone who criticizes or slanders someone else. Indeed, try to avoid hearing such comments at all.

2. Although those who are elderly may reasonably pray about the life to come, you should ignore all such issues until you are fifty. You may follow only the Pure Land or Zen Buddhist faiths, and you must have absolutely nothing to do with the Christian religion. . . . Such a faith is an intolerable obstacle to anyone devoted to his house. Not one person in ten understands the things of this life or of the next. Birds and beasts worry only about what is immediately before them, and humans are no different. In this life they first should make certain that they do not sully their reputations. If even Buddha himself is said to have known nothing of the world to come, how can any ordinary mortal know such things? Until you reach fifty, therefore, do not worry about the future life. . . .

3. Dice, backgammon, and all other forms of gambling are strictly forbidden in this life. Even *go*, chess, the martial arts, the nō chants, and the nō dances are forbidden for people under forty. Although those over the age of fifty may enjoy any of those entertainments, those who are younger must avoid even such amusements as trips to pine groves or rivers, or excursions for moon viewing, flower viewing, or any other form of sightseeing. If a master of the nō dance or drama holds a series of performances, you may attend perhaps two in a series of seven. If you wish to make a pilgrimage to a temple or shrine, take along a servant, but remember that the gods and Buddhas do not recognize pilgrimages undertaken even partly as recreation.

---

36. Prince Shōtoku lived from 573 to 621. See de Bary et al., eds., *Sources of Japanese Tradition*, 2nd ed., vol. 1, chap. 3.

4. Until you are forty, avoid every luxury, and never act or think like one above your station in life. In matters of business and moneymaking, however, work harder than anyone else. But do not invest heavily in trading or outfit ships to send to the Chinese or to the Southern Barbarians, even though you may envy the profits that others have made trading with those people. Always behave as one whose station in life is half that of yours. Although some people may suggest that you [should] be more visible and assertive, ignore all such advice and maintain a low profile. Until you turn fifty, be temperate in all things, and avoid all ostentation and finery, anything, in fact, that might call attention to yourself. Do not cultivate expensive tastes, for you should ignore such things as the tea ceremony, swords, daggers, and fine clothes. Above all, do not carry weapons. If you own a sword or some armor that someone gave you, sell it and carry the money instead.

Until you are forty years old, wear only material like cotton, loosely woven cloth, or knotted silk, materials that will not attract attention. As for your house, worry only about keeping it repaired, and do only such work as that of replacing rotten ropes holding together a fence or a wall. Do not build a new house unless you are over fifty. Those who are that old may build what they like and can afford. Yet most people are poor by the time they die, for fewer than one in ten or twenty who build a fortune by their own talent carry it to their graves, and those who inherit their wealth are even more likely to lose it and die impoverished. Remember this.

5. Until you are forty, do not invite out others or let others invite you out. Once or twice a year you may invite out your parents, brothers, or relatives, or go out at their invitation, but—do not forget—even this you may do only occasionally. Never, however, attend a party in the evening, even one to which your brothers invite you.

6. Do not covet other people's tools or display your own tools. You may accept a tool as a gift only if it is from a relative. Take good care of your valuables and never show them to anyone.

7. You may befriend those who enjoy mercantile work, who take good care of their family businesses, who are unobtrusive, and who are trustworthy. With such unobtrusive and fine people, you may become close friends. Conversely, you should not befriend those who are quarrelsome, who criticize others, who are ill natured and detestable, who slander government officials, who like crowds, who have a passion for shamisen music and ballads, or who talk too much. You should not even sit beside such people.

Addendum. Include masters of the martial arts in the last group of people.

8. Never wander outside the shop or visit places where you have no business being. . . . Since you will generally be in the house, you yourself should tend the morning and evening cooking fires and handle the firewood and embers. You should pick up all trash inside and behind the house, chop up the pieces of rope and short bits of trash to use in plaster, and use the long pieces to make rope.

Collect and clean pieces of wood and bamboo longer than five *bu* and use them as firewood. Save all paper scraps, even pieces only three or five *bu* long, to use in making fresh paper. Do as I have done, and waste absolutely nothing.

9. When you need something, go and buy it yourself, regardless of whether it is firewood, two or three *bu* of small fish or sardines, other purchases from the seaside or the town, or even timber. Bargain for the items and pay as little as you can, but remember the range of possible prices for each item. . . . Firewood, coal, and oil are said to be essential provisions, but of these three, firewood is the most important. Since the amount of firewood used depends considerably on how it is burned, you should try doing the cooking yourself so that you will know how much firewood a person needs for such regular tasks as cooking a day's worth of rice or soup. You can then give the maid only the precise amount she will need. . . .

10. In general, use few servants, especially few female ones. When wives go out, they must not take along more than one male and two female servants. If they have children, they may not dress the children in fine clothes or take along for each child more than one nurse and one maid. Nor should they take along servants carrying umbrellas or swords. They should wear small braided hats instead.

11. Keep a steady supply of coarse *miso* on hand for your servants, and when you make the *miso* soup in the mornings and evenings, carefully filter the *miso*. You should add to the residue salt and cucumbers, eggplants, gourd melons, and onions, and serve this as a side dish to the servants. You can give them the stalks as well, and when rice is expensive, you may feed them some sort of hodgepodge. But if you do give your servants such a dish, you and your wife should eat it as well. Even if you intend to eat rice, first sip at least a bit of the hodgepodge, for your servants will resent it if you do not. In fact, in everything you do, you must consider how your servants will react. People always used to do so. Even my mother did, and thus when I was young, I always ate what my servants ate. . . .

13. Those with even a small fortune must remember that their duty in life is to devote themselves to their house and its business. They must not become careless, for if they buy what they want, do as they please, and, in general, live sumptuously, they will soon spend that fortune. They may be shocked at their loss, and they may regret that they were not more careful, but they will no longer have the funds to run a business. The fortune they should have guarded carefully will be gone, and they will have little choice but to beg. . . .

Although a samurai can draw on the produce of his tenured lands to earn his livelihood, a merchant must rely on the profit from his business, for without that profit, the money in his bags would soon disappear. No matter how much profit he makes and packs into his bags, however, if he continually wastes that money, he may as well pack it into bags full of holes. Remember this.

14. Rise early in the morning, and go to bed as soon as the sun sets, for you will waste oil if you burn lamps during evenings when you have nothing im-

portant to do. Never wander about at night if you have nothing to do. And never stay long when you visit people, whether during the day or during the evening. Deal with pressing business at once, and never think, "I'll do it later," or "I'll do it tomorrow." Never procrastinate.

15. As much as possible, do things yourself. Rather than send someone else after an item, for example, get it yourself. And when you travel, carry things such as your bags and inkstone box yourself. If you need to travel only three or five *ri*, walk instead of riding a horse, for merchants should travel by foot as much as possible. When I was young, I never rode a horse. During your trips, record such information as the distance traveled and the amounts paid for horses, board, meals, and ferries, for then you can anticipate the expenses involved when you send someone else. In fact, you should remember even the names of the innkeepers. Although you may buy things for your friends and relatives during these trips if you absolutely must, you may transact no other unofficial business. Never violate this rule.

16. No matter what meeting you are attending, if a fierce argument breaks out, leave at once. It is, of course, a different matter if your brothers or relatives are involved, but otherwise go home immediately. Avoid all possible quarrels, and even if someone treats you rudely or otherwise insults you, ignore him. If people call you a coward for avoiding a fight, tell them that to violate Sōshitsu's Seventeen-Point Testament would be tantamount to breaking an oath.

17. Live in harmony with your wife, for the two of you must work together diligently. Both of you should live modestly and carefully and consider always the good of the house and its business. A contentious, unhappy marriage destroys a house, for it distracts the husband and wife from their work. . . .

Addendum. Since you will accomplish nothing if your health is poor, you should take medicine and have moxa applied five or six times a year.

These seventeen articles were written not for Sōshitsu's sake but for yours. They are his testament, and you should follow them closely. They should be as important to you as the Great Constitution of Prince Shōtoku. Read them every day, or even twice a day, and be careful to forget nothing. Write a vow on the back of a votive tablet promising never to violate any of the articles and put it in my coffin when I die.

> *Keichō 15 [1610], 1st month, 15th day*
> *Kyohaku [Shimai] Sōshitsu [seal]*
> To: *Kamiya Tokuzaemon [adopted son of Sōshitsu]*
> [Yoshida, ed., *Shōka no kakun*, pp. 35–62; trans. adapted from Ramseyer,
> "Thrift and Diligence," pp. 210–26]

THE CODE OF THE OKAYA HOUSE

A samurai named Sōshichi founded the Okaya house when he moved to Nagoya and started a hardware store. The business grew gradually until it flourished eight generations later under the leadership of the author of this code, Okaya Sanezumi, who wrote it in 1836.

1. Remember your duties to your parents.

We cannot distinguish between cause and effect unless we remember that our parents are the "cause" of our existence. Neither can we make filial piety the "cause" of our actions unless we remember the debt of gratitude we owe our parents.

2. Honor your superiors.

Everyone, young or old, should consider the distinctions between master and servant and between superior and inferior to be basic, and so honor those above him.

3. Maintain peace within the neighborhood.

Peace in a neighborhood depends on peace in each house, but peace in a house depends on the attitudes of its members. If each person in your house maintains a healthy attitude and works faithfully, everyone will be on good terms with his colleagues, and your house will win the respect of the neighborhood.

4. Instruct your descendants.

Teach your children when they are young to lead pure lives. Teach them to obey their parents, to respect their elders, never to tell even a small lie, to move about quietly, never to neglect their work, to be always alert, never to walk about aimlessly, and never to dress or eat extravagantly.

5. Be content with your Way.

Samurai study the martial arts and work in the government. Farmers till their lands and pay their taxes. Artisans work at their family industries and pass on to their children the family traditions. Merchants have trading as their duty and must trade diligently and honestly. Each of the four classes has its own Way, and that Way is the true Way.

6. Avoid bad behavior.

Although the world is limitless, everything in it is either good or bad. That which follows the Way is good, while that which goes against it is bad.

> Revised: Tenpō 7 [1836], 7th month, auspicious day.
> Okaya Sanezumi

[Yoshida, ed., Shōka no kakun, pp. 114–24; trans. adapted from Ramseyer, "Thrift and Diligence," pp. 227–30]

IHARA SAIKAKU

Ihara Saikaku (1642–1693), a poet and novelist, wrote voluminously for a popular audience about the life of the townspeople, dominated by sex and money, often referred to as the "floating world," celebrated also at this time in the drama of

Chikamatsu Monzaemon and in the arts by the famous *ukiyo-e* (woodblock prints). Saikaku's works reflect the ethos and lifestyle of the merchant class and the ebullient sensuous culture produced by the new affluence of thriving commercial centers like Osaka, Kyoto, and Edo.

Much of Saikaku's writing shows a fascination with the complexity, perversity, and foibles of human nature, about which he often makes wry and sardonic comments. Relatively uninfluenced by Confucianism, and by no means an unqualified exponent even of the merchant ethic, Saikaku is skeptical, too, about people's religious motivations as identified with Buddhism and Shinto. These reservations indeed provide a perspective for his own ironic observations on the life of the merchant: driven by the pursuit of profit but eventually succumbing to the self-indulgence and luxuriance that success and affluence afford. If hard work and single-minded concentration on acquiring wealth produce worldly success, this merchant ethic nevertheless leads to its own undoing. Only the wisest of men can escape these inevitable consequences of such passionate involvements with a life so seductive.

THE JAPANESE FAMILY STOREHOUSE
(*NIHON EITAIGURA*)

The following are excerpted from a collection of tales about the lives of Japanese merchants.

Riding to Success on a Lucky Horse

Heaven says nothing, and the whole earth grows rich beneath its silent rule.[37] Men, too, are touched by Heaven's virtue; yet in their greater part, they are creatures of deceit. They are born, it seems, with an emptiness of soul and must take their qualities wholly from things without. To be born thus empty into this modern age, this mixture of good and ill, and yet to steer through life on an honest course to the splendor of success—this is a feat reserved for paragons of our kind, a task beyond the nature of the normal man.

But the first consideration for all throughout life is earning a living. And in this matter, each one of us must bow before the shrine of the Heavenly Goddess of Thrift (not Shinto priests alone, but samurai, farmers, traders, artisans, and even Buddhist bonzes), and we must husband gold and silver as the deity enjoins. Although mothers and fathers give us life, it is money alone that preserves it.

But in the longest estimate, the life of man is a day that knows no tomorrow. To some it seems a day cut short at eventide. Heaven and earth, the poets say,

---

37. Echo of a passage from the Chinese classic *Lun-yü*, *Yang Ho P'ien*: "Does heaven speak? The four seasons come and go, and the earth yields its fruits. Does heaven speak?"

are but a wayside inn for Time, a traveler, on journey through the ages, and our fleeting lives are phantoms in Time's dreams.[38] People will tell us that when we die and vanish in a moment's wisp of smoke, all our gold is less than dross and buys us nothing in the world beyond. It is true enough, and yet—is not what we leave behind of service to our sons and our posterity? And while we live (to take a shorter view) how many of life's desirable things is it not within the power of gold to grant us? In all the world there are five[39] perhaps, no more than that. Has any treasure that we see on prints of treasure ships more power? Those invisible-making hats and capes, for instance, worn by devils on an island no one has ever seen—they would leak as much as any in a cloudburst. So lay aside your dreams of things beyond man's reach, turn your minds to what lies close at hand, and work with a will at the trade you have chosen. Since luck and profit come only to those who persevere, let none of you squander a moment in sloth between dawn and dusk.

Above all you must make humanity and rightness the basis of your conduct, and worship the gods and the Buddhas. This is the custom of Japan.

It was the day of the horse, the first in the second moon. Through the spring haze shrouding the hills men and women, rich and poor, were making their way on pilgrimage to the shrine of Kannon at Mizuma Temple in Izumi Province. None went in search of enlightenment. The road they trod together was the road of greed. Passing along endless mossy byways and over weary new-swaled wastes of reed and mugwort and coming in time to this desolate village, still bare of any form of blossom, they made their vows to the temple's Buddha—but their prayers were mere requests for wealth, varying only in the quantity that each considered his due. Even for Kannon the thought of replying to them all, one by one, was too much. Instead, a general pronouncement was made, in a miraculous voice issuing from behind the sacred alcove's curtain.

"Nowadays, in this vale of sorrow," it said, "there is no such thing as easy money, and it is obvious enough, without your asking me, what each must do. You country people have your allotted means and skills. The men must dig the fields; the women must weave at the loom; and each must work at his task from dawn to dusk. To every one of you I say the same."

But (such is human stupidity) even this inspired advice failed to sink into the pilgrims' ears. . . .

All human beings have eyes and noses, and all alike are born with hands and feet. But in one respect the ordinary townsman is different from the nobility, the great military families, and the practitioners of the various arts: his hopes

---

38. Translation of a poem by the Chinese poet Li Bo, included in the *Kobun shinpō*, Xulei.

39. Elements of life borrowed from various Buddhas at birth and returned at death. According to one source they are bones, flesh, blood, sinews, and breath; according to another, they are heart, liver, spleen, lungs, and kidney.

of worldly fame rest solely on the acquisition of money. It is a pitiful thing for him if he works from early youth and dies without the reputation of a man of wealth. Birth and lineage mean nothing: money is the only tree for a townsman. A man may be descended from the noblest of the Fujiwara, but if he dwells among shopkeepers and lives in poverty, he is lower than a vagabond monkey trainer. There is no alternative for a townsman: he must pray for wealth and aim to be a millionaire. To be a millionaire he must have the will of a hero, the heart to climb a great mountain. He must also, even to rise to middling wealth, employ good clerks. . . .

But an ordinary man who enjoys good health and makes a living sufficient for his needs and station can be yet more fortunate than the greatest of millionaires. A household may be rich and prosperous, but if it lacks a son to succeed or if death has separated master and mistress, its happiness will not be complete. Disappointments of this and many other kinds are common enough in our world.

In a village at the foot of the hills to the north of Kyoto lived a celebrated family, the envy of all, known as "The Three Couples." First there were the grandfather and grandmother, still safely together after all the years; then there was their son, with the new wife he had taken; and last the grandson, and he too had grown up and was married. The three husbands and three wives lived together in the same house, and in each case the man and his wife had been childhood friends before their marriage. Few parallels could be found for such good fortune. When the grandfather reached the [auspicious] age of eighty-eight, his wife was eighty-one; the second couple were fifty-seven and forty-nine; the third were twenty-six and eighteen. Not once in their lives had any of them suffered the slightest illness, and what is more, they had always lived together in perfect harmony. They were farmers, and their paddy fields, tilled land, cattle, horses, and rows of adjoining houses for men and women helpers were such as farmers dream of; and since they had been granted tax exemption, every harvest they reaped was for themselves alone. Living thus in perfect contentment, worshiping the gods and holding the Buddhas in deep reverence, their hearts came naturally to be endowed with every virtue. . . .

Money is still to be found in certain places, and where it lies, it lies in abundance. Whenever I heard stories about it, I noted them in my great national stock-book, and in order that future generations might study them and profit thereby, I placed them in a storehouse to serve each family's posterity. Here they now rest, as securely guarded as the peace of Japan.

[Adapted from Sargent, trans., *The Japanese Family Storehouse*, pp. 13–14, 144–46]

MITSUI TAKAFUSA

The following excerpt is from a work compiled in 1727/1728 by a scion of the famous Mitsui merchant house, Mitsui Takafusa (1684–1748), and his father,

Takahira (1653–1737). It contains accounts of about fifty once-wealthy merchant families of Kyoto now impoverished by their gradual neglect of business, extravagance, injudicious lending and borrowing, and speculation.

The context of these cautionary tales is of a feudal society composed of hereditary classes expected to perform their customary roles, but it assumes that the rise and fall of families is a universal phenomenon. The preface excerpted here cites the experience of Chinese dynasties and of Japanese military shogunates as equally relevant to Kyoto merchants. Advice to the merchants, however, is quite specific with regard to their conduct of business and is not clearly based on any Confucian or Buddhist ethic.

SOME OBSERVATIONS ABOUT MERCHANTS
(CHŌNIN KŌKEN ROKU)

The world is divided into four classes—samurai,[40] farmers, artisans, and merchants. Each man works at his calling, and his descendants carry on the business and establish the family. Merchants in particular, although divided into various lines of business, are all concerned primarily with the profit to be earned on money. In rural areas, merchants pay deference to their provincial lords and squires. When they look at their superiors, they see no great splendor and so do not get carried away. Thus most of them work at their business generation after generation. As for the merchants of Kyoto, Edo, and Osaka, the founder of the firm, starting either in a country area or as someone's clerk, gradually works his way up, expands his business, and, with the idea of leaving a fortune to his descendants, lives frugally all his life, paying no heed to anything but his family business. After he has built up a record of difficulties and sufferings, his son inherits the family business. Having learned from observing his father's frugality and having passed his formative years while the house was still not so prosperous, he just manages to keep things intact during his lifetime. When it comes to the grandchildren's time, however, having been brought up after the family already had become rich and knowing nothing of physical hardships or of the value of money, they unconsciously pick up the ways of the world, get big ideas, leave their family business to others, and pass their time in idleness. With their personal expenses mounting, they gradually grow older. Even if they pay attention to their business affairs, they do not know how to run them. While letting their expenses rise, they borrow ready money from other people. The usual thing is for them to gradually become saddled with interest payments and to end by ruining their houses. We know from our own observation that notable merchant houses of Kyoto generally

---

40. The identification of the leadership class as samurai (shi) follows the typical Japanese understanding and ignores the considerable difference from Chinese literati (shi) at this time.

are ruined in the second or third generation and disappear from the scene. The old sayings "Some begin well, but few end well" and "When you are in safety, do not forget dangers" are applicable to one who in his own generation starts up a family business and becomes rich. How much more do they apply to one who receives his father's savings by inheritance and has had wealth from his upbringing? . . .

In his august testament, the divine Lord Tōshō[41] graciously expressed his feelings thus: "When the country is in a state of war, one behaves prudently and does not relax one's vigilance. As one works at governing the country, both one's own retainers and the people at large are kept well under control. In times of peace, however, both ruler and people grow lax and forget their tribulations, and it therefore is hard to maintain good government." Such famous sayings are numerous in both ancient and present times.

Moreover, Lord Yoritomo[42] may have created a model for military leaders, but his son Lord Yoriie[43] was fond of football,[44] and Lord Sanetomo[45] devoted himself to Japanese poetry. Neglecting its government, the family finally lost the country in their third reign. The Ashikaga shogun[46] quelled the great disturbance that had continued for more than forty years and gained control of the country. Although his family passed on the shogunate for more than ten reigns,[47] the fifth shogun, Lord Yoshimasa,[48] neglected his duties and was fond of the tea ceremony and entertainments, with the result that the Ōnin rebellion[49] broke out. Finally, the Ashikaga became shoguns in name only and might as well not have existed. The declines and falls of various other houses were exactly the same. By neglecting their duties, they brought to naught the great works of their founders. How much truer is this of merchants! Farmers and artisans keep their families going for several generations because they would lose their livelihood immediately if they relaxed for even a day. Naturally, therefore, they work hard. Merchants are the only ones who after a time leave things to clerks and, neglecting the family business as generation succeeds generation, eventually lose their estates. Just as "the tipping over of the leading cart is a

---

41. Tokugawa Ieyasu (1542–1616) was the founder of the Tokugawa shogunate. The work referred to is the *Tōshōgū goyuikun*, compiled about 1614, an unauthorized collection of a series of political instructions dictated by Ieyasu for the benefit of his successor, Hidetada. The passage is not a direct quotation but the gist of Ieyasu's opinion.

42. Minamoto Yoritomo (1542–1616) was the founder of the Kamakura shogunate.

43. Yoriie was the second Minamoto shogun.

44. *Kemari*, of Chinese origin, was a game in which the players tried to keep in motion a ball made of deerskin on a bamboo frame.

45. Sanetomo was the third Minamoto shogun, brother of Yoriie.

46. Ashikaga Takauji (1305–1358) was the founder of the Muromachi shogunate.

47. There were sixteen Ashikaga shoguns over 235 years.

48. Ashikaga Yoshimasa (1436–1490) was actually the eighth Ashikaga shogun.

49. The Ōnin War broke out in 1467.

warning to the following cart,"[50] in this spirit I record here briefly what I have seen and heard of the rise and fall of merchants of Kyoto.

[Adapted from Crawcour, trans., "Some Observations on Merchants," pp. 31–34]

MURO KYŪSŌ

The so-called Six Instructions or Precepts (drawn originally from the works of Zhu Xi for popular instruction) were first promulgated officially by the founder of the Ming dynasty in the fourteenth century, at which time they became best known in the Ming as an imperial instruction subsequently renewed as the so-called Sacred Edict of the Kangxi emperor in the early Qing period.[51] Intended for popular instruction—part of what came to be known as "Village Lectures" in the Ming and Qing periods—these instructions underwent successive adaptations and expositions in the vernacular, one of which, the *Extended Meaning of the Six Precepts* (*Liuyu yanyi*), by the late Ming scholar Fan Hong, reached Japan by way of the Ryūkyūs in the time of the Tokugawa shogun Yoshimune. Yoshimune had Ogyū Sorai punctuate Fan's text in Japanese style and had Muro Kyūsō (1658–1734) translate it into the Japanese vernacular, which he did with the assistance of a professional translator from Nagasaki who was more expert in the Ming vernacular.

Kyūsō's *The General Sense of the Extended Meaning of the Six Precepts* (*Liuyu yanyi dayi*) was not, however, simply a translation of Fan Hong's work but a digest in the same genre as Xu Heng's digest of Zhu Xi's *Elementary Learning* (*Xiao xue dayi*) and other works by Zhu Xi summarized by Xu in vernacular form for the Mongol emperor Khubilai. Fan's *Extended Meaning*, by contrast, expanded on the Six Precepts in the same way as Zhen Dexiu had done in his *Extended Meaning of the Great Learning* (*Daxue yanyi*). Thus popularization underwent successive phases of expansion and contraction.

Kyūsō was both a strong adherent of Zhu Xi and a notable advocate of Zhu's ideal of universal schooling—for women as well as men. In this light, Kyūsō's *General Sense* may be seen as a fair and sympathetic representation of Zhu's overall intent. Sorai, conversely, was critical of Zhu Xi, had doubts about the wisdom of raising people's political consciousness through popular education, and opposed the dissemination of the *Extended Meaning of the Six Precepts*.

Subsequently, the shogun Yoshimune authorized the promulgation of Kyūsō's *General Sense of the Extended Meaning of the Six Precepts* not only to

---

50. One should learn, that is, from the mistakes of predecessors. The quotation is from the *Han shu, jiayi chuan*.

51. See de Bary and Bloom, eds., *Sources of Chinese Tradition*, 2nd ed., vol. 1, chap. 21; and de Bary and Lufrano, eds., *Sources of Chinese Tradition*, 2nd ed., vol. 2, chap. 25.

his own domains but to outer ones as well. More than forty versions were in print and still extant in the Meiji period. Indeed, the code of the Okaya merchant house, presented earlier, is based on the same Six Precepts. They also became a prime source for the celebrated Imperial Rescript on Education of the Emperor Meiji, even though few scholars today are aware of its origin or the successive adaptations of the *Six Precepts*.

The Meiji version stresses loyalty to the emperor, which is lacking in Zhu Xi's original, which emphasizes filial piety as the common human ground of public morality and says nothing about loyalty to the ruler. Kyūsō's version is faithful to that of Zhu Xi. If he had wished to promote loyalty to the ruler, he might have done so in his vernacular exposition of the second precept, excerpted here. Instead, he kept to Zhu Xi's original concept of family and communitarian roles, not loyalty to the state or emperor. In a postface to his *General Sense*, Kyūsō states:

> The *Rites of Zhou* speaks of people meeting for the reading of the laws, and later worthies [especially Zhu Xi] spoke of community compact meetings. These were to supplement education in the schools so as to support and sustain public morality. . . . But after the school system ceased to be maintained [as provided in the *Rites* and advocated by Zhu Xi], the people received instruction only by government edict, so the ruler had to worry about how effectively his efforts at edification reached down into the villages. Laws proliferated, punishments increased, regulations multiplied, and enforcement became more strictly detailed [to no avail]. . . . Then in the Ming there was a plethora of imperial admonitions and edicts, of laws and regulations promulgated throughout the land, which were followed by the Six Precepts of the Qing emperor [Kang Xi] for the regulation of his conquered empire and for emulation by his subjects. But how could this be done with barbarians imposing on the civilized Chinese? As it happened, however, Fan Hong of Huiji had [already] written his *Extended Meaning of the Six Precepts* in vernacular Chinese, which served the educational purpose well.

Kyūsō then explains that his work in Japanese may serve the same purpose for Japan, which claims to be a "land of Confucian noble men."

THE GENERAL SENSE OF THE EXTENDED MEANING OF THE SIX PRECEPTS
(RIKUYU ENGI TAII)

Muro Kyūsō's vernacular Japanese commentary stays close to Fan Hong's version, which itself keeps to the original Six Precepts without the more legalistic and bureaucratic additions of the Qing. As such, Kyūsō's interpretation reflects Zhu Xi's original emphasis on filiality as the basis of public morality. Had he been inclined to substitute loyalty to the ruler for filiality, the natural place to have done so would have been in his interpretation of the second maxim, respect for seniors and superiors, extending it upward to include those on high. In the following discussion of "respect your seniors and superiors," Kyūsō did not do this but kept to Zhu Xi's basic family and communitarian model and did not go along with the Qing adaptation of the Precepts to serve the purposes of the ruler and his state—or, it may be added, with the inclination of other Tokugawa-period thinkers who, writing for samurai and not commoners, put the virtue of loyalty to one's lord ahead of filial piety.

The Six Precepts are

1. Be filial and obedient to your parents.
2. Respect your seniors and superiors.
3. Harmonize and cooperate with your community.
4. Instruct your children and grandchildren.
5. Be content with your own livelihood.
6. Do nothing you shouldn't do.

Following the rendering of filial service to one's parents, respect for one's seniors and superiors comes next as the second precept. "Seniors and superiors" means people older in age and higher in standing, that is, people "above us." First of all, in the family, come those kinfolk senior in age, regardless of whether they are male or female. However, the Way of respecting seniors begins with one's older brothers and sisters. Here "those above us" means those born ahead of us. In the case of someone who takes the place of one's father, the one to be respected next to one's parents may not be one's older brother. For instance, on the death of one's father, usually it is the senior member of the extended family (*honke*), perhaps in another household, who disposes of the family finances and property. Nevertheless, one must still accept the judgments of one's elder brother. In that disposition of things, there must be no less intimate affection between brothers. Even if the older brother is no good and does one wrong, the Way of the Younger Brother must be fulfilled; one must never show disrespect to one's older brother. Besides that, with those who serve as foster parents (father or mother), older members of the same extended family, one should fulfill the forms of ritual respect due each of them and never subject them to any indignity. . . .

Moreover, in other cases those of the same generation and age as one's father are to be respected on the same level as one's father, and those of the same age as one's older brother are likewise to be respected the same as he. . . . Furthermore, among those to be considered "senior and superior," it is hardly necessary to say, there are persons whose conduct is correct and who are worthy to serve as a mirror for others, as well as those with exceptional knowledge and abilities, worthy to serve as a teacher to others—these are especially to be respected. Also, those who may stand higher than oneself include the aged and infirm, even if they are not of great virtue or ability; if they have established themselves in a status superior to one's own, they are to be regarded as "senior and superior" and entitled to all forms of ritual respect. . . . . From of old, men of high station, men of worth and wisdom, men of great age—they have been regarded as among the three [types] Meriting Full Respect, persons to be respected anywhere in the world.

> [Muro Kyūsō, *Rikuyu engi taii*, in *Nihon kyōiku bunko*, pp. 548–84; WTdB]

HOSOI HEISHŪ

Hosoi Heishū (1728–1801) was the younger son of a wealthy peasant in the rural village of Hirashima in Owari. He spent the first nine years of his life in his native village, where he so distinguished himself as a student at the local temple school that on the recommendation of the priest, his father sent him to Nagoya and then to Kyoto for further study with private tutors. There Heishū received his formal education in the Confucian classics and the Song commentaries. As a young man, he gave formal lectures to the sons of daimyo and high-ranking samurai on the Way of the sages. When he spoke to commoners, however, Heishū used colloquial language and illustrated his message with examples that would be readily understood and enjoyed. Wherever he went, his lectures appear to have been received with great enthusiasm by audiences numbering in the thousands.

Central to Heishū's teaching is the concept of *makoto*, an important value in the Shinto religion and one that would have been familiar to Heishū's listeners. *Makoto* expressed the idea that there is an innate purity in nature and, in man, is the foundation of the ethical nature of Heaven-and-earth. All creatures are born with *makoto*, so a newborn baby is pure. Only in his life on earth is a person polluted by evil. People who retain *makoto* are in sympathy with one another and with nature, and this sympathy gives rise to peace and harmony in human society and in the natural world as well.

Heishū directs many of his remarks to women. His message closely resembles that of the *Great Learning for Women* attributed to Kaibara Ekken, which was a blueprint for the upbringing of women in the samurai class. In colloquial language directed at commoners, Heishū emphasizes that parents should not spoil their daughters in childhood, for otherwise girls will develop into self-willed, luxury-loving women who cannot adjust to the demands of society when they grow up and marry. Indeed, he is quite outspoken about his low regard for women in general. A woman can redeem herself only by becoming a good wife.

SERMON, DECEMBER 14, 1783

From the seventeenth century, the central Tokugawa government (*bakufu*) and the domain governments employed Confucian scholars to address samurai formally assembled in lecture halls built for the purpose, but when those lectures were opened to commoners in the early eighteenth century, very few people could understand them. Therefore, to attract a wide audience of commoners, the authorities also supported popular preachers who could translate the message of the Confucian lecturers into terms that would be understandable to ordinary people. Some of these preachers drew large audiences who listened intently to their sermons. Under the aegis of the Owari domain government, Hosoi Heishū delivered a popular sermon in the city of Nagoya on December 14, 1783, excerpts from which are translated here.

I would like to talk to you today about the meaning of learning. Please listen carefully to what I have to say. Learning is the perception of reason; it is through reason that we know the difference between good and evil. We can achieve reason by studying the classics. I myself have come to understand reason from books, and I give talks to lords about its meanings.

The number of books in the world is staggering. All of you here, men and women alike, whether you are warriors, artisans, or merchants, are far too busy to study the classics on your own. You couldn't possibly read them all, and it would take me a long time, months in fact, just to summarize them for you. I certainly couldn't do it in a day or two.

I can make you understand far more easily by telling you a few stories. Learning is not something that can be found only in books; you can find it in your daily lives as well. Everything around you contains great teachings if you only look for them.

Of all creatures in the universe, man is the most blessed. He alone is good at heart, and his goodness comes from *makoto*. Because of *makoto* man is born free from evil. An example of *makoto* is the relationship between mother and child. A mother cherishes her child. If she leaves the child with another woman while she goes to the toilet, the child will cry for her, and no amount of comforting will console him. The child will stop crying only when the mother returns. He will be happy then, even if she scolds him for crying. The child is innocent; his only desire is to be close to his mother. Likewise, the mother loves her child and is happy. Their feelings for each other are an expression of *makoto*. Human beings must never lose such innocence and purity, for without it they will become evil.

The lessons of nature are all around us and teach us about *makoto*. In every year there are four seasons. Spring is warm; summer is hot; autumn is cool; winter is cold. It has been that way for millions of years. While there is some variation—such as an occasional cold day in spring or summer—the general pattern remains the same. Spring weather makes the seeds sprout. Summer brings thunderstorms and, along with them, cicadas and mosquitoes. The sun rises in the east; the moon waxes and wanes. Everything follows the laws of nature that emanate from *makoto*. . . .

The foundation of all human relationships was laid down by our ancestral gods, Izanagi and Izanami. Those two gods gave birth to many deities, and from their descendants human beings were born. We can see from this creation story that marriage between a husband and wife is the most fundamental of all human relationships.[52] . . . Because their relationship is the basis of all other relationships, it is vitally important that a husband and wife be guided by *makoto*. A husband loves his wife, and she in turn respects him. The husband goes out to work, and the wife stays home to take care of the house. . . .

Now it is one thing if the wife's attitude stems from frugality, but that is seldom the case. In general, because relations with the outside world are a man's responsibility, men try to live up to their duties and obligations, while women do not understand them at all. If the wife's real concern is for the family budget, she can economize on her own clothing and cosmetics, rather than on social obligations. Women seldom do that. . . .

The husband earns money by the sweat of his brow, and he has to work very hard just to support his family. Only an ignorant and selfish wife could fail to appreciate his efforts. Such a woman is blind to her husband's anguish. She indulges herself with expensive clothes instead of helping her husband meet his social obligations.

There is no need for women to be extravagant in their dress. By nature, males are better looking than females, anyway. Take birds, for example. A cock has far prettier feathers than a hen. Male birds, in general, are more beautiful than female birds, and the same is true of humans. Men are simply better looking than women. They are born that way, and women should accept it. Consider how ugly a woman would look if she did not use cosmetics and shaved her head or dressed up in men's clothing. She would certainly not look as nice as a man does. . . .

There is a saying that it is the lot of girls to be obedient. When she is young, a girl must obey her parents. When she is married, she must obey her husband. When she grows old, she must obey her sons. These are the three obligations of a woman, and like it or not, it is a fact of life. You must be careful to prepare your daughters to fulfill their obligations. . . .

All human relations must be based on harmony. This applies not only to the members of a family but to all of society. Each member of a family—father,

---

52. Among the Five Human Relationships, the parent–child relationship, seen as the starting point at birth of any given life, usually has first priority (*Mencius* and *Mean*). But some texts (*Classic of Filiality*) and scholars in both China and Japan emphasize the primacy of the conjugal relations as essential to conception and procreation, even before birth takes place.

son, son-in-law, daughter-in-law—has individual needs and desires. But nothing can be gained if each one insists on having his own way without compromise. I'm not saying that such individual wishes are necessarily bad, only that every person has a place in society and that if we are to fulfill our roles we must try to achieve harmony. . . .

A poem by the cloistered emperor Go-Mizunoo[53] goes as follows:

> Having *makoto*,
> An old man collects
> The last grains of rice
> From the bottom of the bowl
> And gives them to his wife.

To share one's food with others is true *makoto*. This poem shows that even very poor people have *makoto*. A poor old couple share their meager rations with each other. When the old man in the poem can get only a spoonful of rice from the pan, he gives it to his old wife rather than eating it himself. This is an expression of *makoto*. That is what the poem means.

In general, people who make a great display of their sincerity are not really sincere. They do not have *makoto*; they only pretend to have it. If a person truly has *makoto*, it will be seen in all aspects of his life, in his business dealings and in his work. That is the basis of human ethics. . . .

As I have emphasized many times in this talk, *makoto* is a gift of heaven. You must make a sincere effort to preserve it. If we all abide by this rule, we can avoid bad deeds. I have a lot more to tell you, but it's getting late, and so I will end on this point.

[Hosoi Heishū, *Heishū zenshū*, pp. 915–49; trans. adapted from Aoki and Dardess, "The Popularization of Samurai Values," pp. 393–413]

HOW TO BEHAVE AT TEMPLE SCHOOLS

Much of elementary learning and literacy in the Tokugawa period was provided at so-called temple schools (*terakoya*), but usually not by Buddhist clergy. It consisted of conventional guidance and proverbial wisdom couched in maxims such as are recorded here, a few of them surviving from earlier texts like Annen's *Precepts for the Young* (*Dōjikyō*) that show a certain continuity of traditional lore. Noticeably missing, however, is anything like the priority Annen attached to Buddhist religious goals and their transcendence over human concerns in the Heian period. Instead, these maxims emphasize "the Human Way," and

---

53. Emperor Go-Mizunoo (1596–1680).

the basic texts of the temple schools almost universally accepted in the Tokugawa period are the Confucian *Classic of Filial Piety*, Zhu Xi's *Elementary Learning*, and the Four Books of Neo-Confucianism. The precepts themselves, though nondenominational, amply attest to what was known in the twentieth century as the "Confucian ethic" common to East Asian peoples, which stresses strict morality, frugality, hard work, and the importance of education.

Several of the following maxims appeal to the sense of shame, a fact that may help explain why some Western writers have characterized Confucianism as a "shame ethic." It is true that such references go as far back as Confucius and Mencius, but other considerations weigh no less heavily on the Confucian conscience, including the senses of commiseration, deference and respect, and right and wrong (as in Mencius's sprouts of virtue, 6A:6).

PRECEPTS FOR THE YOUNG
(DŌJIKYŌ)

To be born human and not be able to write is to be less than human. Illiteracy is a form of blindness. It brings shame on your teacher, shame on your parents, and shame on yourself. The heart of a child of three stays with him until he is a hundred, as the proverb says. Determine to succeed, study with all your might, never forgetting the shame of failure.

Goodness and badness depend on the company you keep. Cooperate with one another to behave yourselves as you should; check in yourselves any tendencies to be attracted to evil ways; and put all your heart into your brushwork.

At your desks, let there be no useless idle talk, or yawning or stretching, or dozing or picking your nose, or chewing paper, or biting the end of your brush. To imitate the idle is the road to evil habits. Just concentrate wholeheartedly on your writing, giving each character the care it deserves.

Never write too fast. There never yet was a hothead who earned fame and success. Write your characters firmly, deliberately, and quietly.

Don't lean on your desk, or rest your elbow, or write just with the tips of your fingers, or easily and automatically without concentration. You will never develop a good hand if you do. Put all your effort into every character, making sure you hold your brush properly and giving proper attention to each stroke.

One who treats his brushes or his paper without due respect will never progress. The boy who uses carefully even the oldest, most worn-out brush is the one who will succeed. Treat your brushes carefully.

Don't litter the floor around you with scraps of paper. Keep your desks and your drawer neat and tidy and don't spill ink.

Torn and dirty clothes look bad. Even more they are a sign of a torn and dirty spirit. Always behave with proper decorum so that your clothes do not get torn.

Mischievous pranks benefit no one. One thing leads to another and fighting results. You should always be ready to admit your own faults and learn to control yourself. Sumo wrestling, arm wrestling, leg wrestling, tugs of war, and such games of strength are unbecoming to young children and are forbidden.

Don't run about on the banks of ditches or rivers, near walls, or verandas, stone steps, or platforms. To do so is unfilial conduct, for it is the beginning of filial piety to take care and preserve yourself from injury. Behave with proper gravity and avoid roughness.

Ill-natured pupils can never learn to write a good hand. Honor your parents, revere your teacher, respect your elders, and be kind to your juniors, for this is the heart and origin of the Human Way. Follow the rules of correct etiquette, and use polite language even among friends.

Purity of heart is of the first importance. Those who come to school to learn the Human Way with mud on their boots and ink on their hands and faces smudged like used practice paper show great disrespect. Grubbiness in others should be a warning to yourself and an incentive to take proper care.

A pupil who keeps his hair properly in place, his kimono properly folded across the front, his belt properly tied, and his teeth properly white is a model for all and a testimony to the training of his teacher and his parents. You should always remember this and avoid untidiness of dress.

A friend is to a friend as a brother to brother, as a fish is to water. Be nice to your friends and always put their interests first at the expense of your own.

A child who is overclever and tells untruths will end up as a criminal. Never tell untruths and never hide the truth, even in fun.

Luxurious habits begin with the palate. Eat what you are given without fads and complaints. Any child who buys food in secret is guilty of unworthy conduct and can expect to be expelled.

You will never write a good hand unless you learn to practice and go on practicing even when you are cold and hungry. Don't overeat. Meanness of spirit starts with the indulgence of appetite. Eat only what you are given.

The lazy are always eager to eat, like a starved monkey gobbling nuts, as the old proverb says. It is the mark of the idle child to be always wanting to go for tea and water even when he is neither hungry nor thirsty, to be always going to the lavatory even when he has no need to go, but only as a pretext for play. This is mean and unworthy conduct of which you should be thoroughly ashamed.

Nobody likes a child who smokes or drinks saké or is always sipping tea. And those who are disliked by their fellowmen in the end incur the wrath of Heaven. To those who are liked by their fellows the gods also afford protection. This is clear as day. In this as in all other things, carefully avoid making yourself disliked.

When you need something say so clearly and precisely. Never under any circumstances take things from other people without telling them, even a single sheet of paper. It is also strictly forbidden for pupils to buy and sell things from one another, and you should refrain from taking things from younger pupils.

A three-inch axle pin takes a cart a thousand miles. A three-inch tongue can be the ruin of a body five feet tall. No one hates the crow because he is black, only because he is obstreperous. Take heed from this. Useless gossip, rude language, [and] shouting are the marks of beggars and outcasts. There must be no uncalled-for remarks, telling tales, butting in, provocative questioning, nasty innuendo, talking behind people's backs. Accusations and whispering that embarrass others are signs of a wicked nature.

It is an idle child who speaks ill of his home at school and, when he goes home, talks disparagingly of his school—all to cover his own wrongdoing. Be on your guard against this.

Be careful where you tread and what you touch. When walking about the room, opening doors or lining up desks, move quietly and carefully.

Be careful not to put on other people's sandals and clogs. It is the height of rudeness. If you should happen to do so by mistake, always apologize properly.

Avoid rough or quarrelsome companions. In your dealings with them, speak politely and without provocation. Fences and fights never have just one side, as the saying goes. If there are bickerings and altercations leading to quarrels, both parties shall be held to blame.

There shall be no scrawlings on the walls of temples or public buildings or in school. Likewise, breaking the paper or partitions, carving on pillars or dirtying the *tatami* shall be considered grave offenses.

All games of chance, lotteries, penny in the pool, and so on are strictly forbidden, for they lead to meanness of spirit. Within limits, however, a certain amount may be permitted at New Year's up to January 15.

Children who waste their time on their way to and from school, watching sideshows and peddlers and street hucksters, bring their parents and their teacher into disrespect and are guilty of great thoughtlessness.

Those who, thinking no one will hear them, sing songs or hymns, or snatches of *jōruri* in a loud voice at night, in open spaces or in the streets, show a lack of respect for their neighbors and betray a vulgar nature. It is a disgusting habit. In places where you cannot be seen or heard, you should be all the more careful of how you behave.

Boys who speak roughly to, or pick quarrels with, girls or younger children do not deserve to be considered pupils of this school. They are merely lower animals disguised in human form.

Whatever happens, however unusual, there is no need to clamor and shout. And when going to the privy, go one at a time.

Make appropriate greetings to your parents when you leave home and when you return. At school, enter and leave according to your teacher's instructions. Truancy is a very grave offense.

Men deserve the name of men only when they behave like men. Show due respect for your fellows, and in particular be kind to your juniors and do all you can to help them along.

Take off your hat to walk under a young tree. Training is more important than lineage. So the sayings go. You should not hate or despise your friends even if they are naughty. It only makes matters worse. "When I am good, how can others be bad?" runs the poem. Reprove your bad companions and shame them into goodness, for even the mugwort will grow straight among reeds.

However much better than others your handwriting may be, never lose a proper modesty, never be proud or boastful. The small seeds of pride in a young heart will grow later into a great obstacle to success in life.

Keep seven feet behind your teacher and never tread on his shadow, as the saying goes. Every letter you know you owe to him. Never answer back to your parents or your teacher, observe carefully their admonitions, and seek their instruction that you may walk ever more firmly in the Human Way.

Those who do good shall gain happiness. Those who do ill shall be visited by misfortune. He who is born a man but lacks a spirit of filial piety is no more than a beast. He who does not believe in the Way is little better than a stick or stone. He who thinks these precepts foolish and fails to obey them shall bring shame on himself, lose his good name, and soon live to repent his ruination. This is what is meant by the Punishment of Heaven.

> [Sasayama, *Terako seikai shikimoku*, pp. 145–52; trans. adapted from Dore,
> *Education in Tokugawa Japan*, pp. 323–26]

Chapter 27

"DUTCH LEARNING"

In the seventeenth, the eighteenth, and into the nineteenth century, while the Netherlands lived on its flourishing international trade and commerce, especially through the remarkable East India Company (Vereenigde Ostindische Compagnie [VOC]), Japan adopted a so-called closed-country (*sakoku*) policy, to keep external contacts to an absolute minimum and to allow only a smidgeon of foreign trade under the closest government control. Nonetheless, through the tiny "window on the West," which first Hirado and then, after 1640, Deshima became, bilateral trade with the Dutch continued, even though its monetary significance to the Netherlands steadily declined. And through that same "window" into Japan by way of the very few Dutchmen who arrived each year or of Chinese reports about the West entered most of what the Japanese in their self-imposed isolation were able to learn about European culture, society, and politics.

The initial contact between the Dutch and the Japanese came in the year 1600 the same year in which the battle of Sekigahara brought an end to a bloody civil war and confirmed the supreme power of the Tokugawa house while the daimyo remained in local control of their own domains, a relationship that in theory was not to be disturbed as long as the Tokugawa regime held secure.

The study of the West, however, began some fifty years before this. Three Portuguese castaways reached the shores of the southern coastal island of

Tanegashima in 1543, and in a very few years, Lusitanian ships were trading at several ports in Kyushu. In 1549, Francis Xavier and two other Spanish Jesuits arrived in Japan in order to spread the doctrines of the Catholic faith (see chap. 23). This began what became known to some Western historians as the "Christian century," an era marked by considerable tension and conflict that terminated in the *bakufu*'s firm resolve to eradicate forever the despised religion from the island empire. Despite the potential political advantages of trading with foreigners, the government's fear that native converts might harbor divided political loyalties and might even facilitate an invasion by a European power was conviction enough to ban from Japan both Christianity and its Iberian propagators.

At the beginning of the *sakoku* (closed-country) era, which lasted from 1640 to 1853, only the Dutch remained among the Westerners who had had contact with Japan before that time. Consequently, knowledge of the West that Japan absorbed during the *sakoku* period eventually came to be known as *rangaku*, or Dutch learning. The actual word *rangaku* seems to have originally been used by the Japanese in the 1770s to differentiate from the Nagasaki interpreters those Japanese scholars with a particular interest in the West. At first the *rangaku* scholars narrowly defined Dutch studies as the scholarship of Holland ([O]Ran). However, since commerce during the *sakoku* era was permitted only with Holland, all the knowledge and techniques from the West were transmitted through the medium of the Dutch language, and so it is not surprising that *rangaku* became the prevalent appellation for all Western learning.

Rangaku had two main strands: medicine and astronomy. The first included botany, pharmacopeia, mineralogy, chemistry, physics, and zoology, all deriving in some way from Western-influenced medical science. The second strand concentrated on calendrical science but eventually included surveying, cartography, and geography. The practical considerations attracting "Dutch" scholars to medicine and astronomy were the desire to prolong and save lives in the former instance and to correct the calendar to better manage the agricultural cycle in the latter.

Rangaku scholars initially concentrated on those Western technological skills that had the most obvious immediate application in Japan. Although the Tokugawa authorities recognized the potential value of practical scientific knowledge from Europe, at the same time they curbed inquiries into European history, philosophy, law, literature, and religion. Fearing any repetition of what was seen as the disruptive effect of introducing Christianity into Japan, the *bakufu* set specific limits on the scope of Western knowledge in Japan. But since most of the *rangaku* scholars were themselves either government employees or scholars well versed in Neo-Confucian instruction, they had little inclination to regard such study as outside the limits of the Neo-Confucian "investigation of things and extension of knowledge."

Dutch studies in Japan had certain distinct characteristics. The mainstreams of medicine and astronomy are indicative of the *bakufu*'s and daimyos' support of the investigation of Dutch techniques by official physicians and astronomers in their respective fields. As the ruling authorities came to recognize the practical value of skills learned from the Hollanders, the *bakufu* engaged the services of scholars, knowledgeable in certain aspects of Western astronomy, who could serve a number of official purposes. First, since the traditional function of making the calendar in China and Japan had always been assigned to court astronomers, the establishment in Edo of an astronomical bureau, with greater competence in calendrical science than the traditional imperial astronomical bureau in Kyoto had, gave the shogunate an important reinforcement of its claim to political and cultural predominance. Second, as Tokugawa officials who supposedly understood Dutch, these astronomers were useful to have on hand in Edo, where in times of emergency their language skills could be pressed into service. Third, under government supervision certain of the astronomers were encouraged to study Russian and even Manchu in order to give the *bakufu* expertise in the problems emerging on Japan's northern frontiers. Fourth, by using the astronomical bureau as an official translation center, the government could supervise and control the *rangaku* scholars brought into government service.

In Edo, the astronomers focused on making calendars, which continued to be based on the traditional Chinese model, to which they simply added a few elements of Western astronomy. Such European concepts as Copernicanism and Newtonianism were introduced into Japan by the work of either the Nagasaki interpreters or private amateur astronomers. However, even these men often had difficulty understanding the theories with which they were working, especially in view of the prevailing acceptance of the Chinese dualist yin-yang cosmology. According to this, since heaven was positive and earth negative, heaven was seen as round and moving, and earth as square and motionless (quiescent), in diametric opposition to the Copernican theory. Conversely and by contrast, heliocentrism did not conflict with the centrality of the Sun Goddess in Shinto and of Dainichi (Great Sun) in Esoteric Buddhism. Yet given the particular intellectual environment into which Western astronomy was introduced, it is not surprising that the immediate Japanese comprehension of its theoretical basis was minimal, as was its general influence during the Tokugawa period.

The principal obstacle to the maturation of Dutch studies was that many of its practitioners, like the *bakufu* itself, saw it as a utilitarian technological supplement to a well-ordered, harmonious, intellectually "satisfying" ethical system derived from Zhu Xi Neo-Confucianism. Like Ancient Learning (Kogaku) or even National Learning (Kokugaku), Dutch studies was not a complete system of knowledge constructed on the basis of a single worldview. Rather, it was a random accumulation of certain quasi-scientific and technological information acquired from western Europe through restricted contact with the Dutch or indirectly through the Chinese trade in Nagasaki. It was only exceptional scholars like Miura Baien and Honda Toshiaki who saw in it a greater challenge than this.

ENGELBERT KAEMPFER

The carefully recorded experiences of Engelbert Kaempfer (1651–1716), a German physician in the employ of the Dutch East India Company, on two trips to Edo in 1691 and 1692 are unique. Both these trips were in accordance with the requirement that the Dutch make annual pilgrimages to the capital to pay their respects and give appropriate presents to the shogun. Not only were these annual visits mandated by the original charter granted to the Dutch by the first Tokugawa shogun, Ieyasu (1542–1616), but they were understood as giving the Dutch *opperhoofd* (chief of the Dutch factory at Deshima) a status equivalent to that of a daimyo. These journeys, known in Dutch as *De Hofreis naar Edo* and in Japanese as *Edo sanpu* or *Edo sanrei*, were the only opportunity for the Dutch to know something about Japan outside Nagasaki. Likewise, the trips afforded a significant segment of the Japanese populace an opportunity to find out about the existence of the Dutch and, accordingly, the West.

It became customary for the *opperhoofd* to be almost always accompanied by the physician and the company secretary. Appropriate gifts in both number and value had to be selected and prepared. Accompanying Japanese personnel — that is, officials, interpreters, servants, and porters — also had to be hired. Since the trip from Nagasaki to Edo usually took around ninety days, an immense amount of baggage — including tables, chairs, wines, European foodstuffs, and the like — had to be packed.

The Dutch usually spent two to three weeks in Edo. They were housed at and, of course, confined to the Nagasakiya, the official inn for visitors from Nagasaki. Obviously the high point of their trip was their actual audience with the shogun. In Kaempfer's account of his experience in 1691, he refers to the shogun as emperor, as his understanding was that the emperor in Kyoto was the spiritual ruler of Japan and that the shogun was the temporal ruler.

ACCOUNT OF VISITS TO EDO

On the 29th of March, therefore, being Thursday, and the day appointed for our audience, the presents design'd for his Imperial Majesty were sent to court, attended by the deputies of Sino Cami[1] and of the commissioners for inspecting foreign affairs, to be there laid in due order, on wooden tables, in the hall of the hundred mats, as they call it, where the emperor[2] was to view them. . . .

Having waited there upward of an hour, and the emperor having in the meanwhile seated himself in the hall of audience, Sino Cami and the two commissioners came in and conducted our resident into the emperor's presence, leaving us behind. As soon as he came thither, they cry'd out aloud Hollanda Captain, which was the signal for him to draw near and make his obeisances. Accordingly he crawl'd on his hands and knees, to a place shew'd him, between the presents rang'd in due order on one side, and the place, where the emperor sat, on the other, and then kneeling, he bow'd his forehead quite down to the ground, and so crawl'd backward like a crab, without uttering a single word. So mean and short a thing is the audience we have of this mighty monarch. Nor are there any more ceremonies observ'd in the audience he gives, even to the most powerful princes of the empire. For having been call'd into the hall, their names are cried out aloud, then they move on their hands and feet humbly and silently toward the emperor's seat, and having shew'd their submission, by bowing their forehead down to the ground, they creep back again in the same submissive posture.

Formerly all we had to do at the emperor's court was compleated by the captain's paying him the usual homage, after the manner above related. A few days after, some laws concerning our trade and behavior were read to him, which, in the name of the Dutch, he promis'd to keep, and so was dispatch'd back to Nagasaki. But for about these twenty years, last past, he and the rest of the Dutchmen that came up with the embassy to Jedo were conducted deeper into the palace, to give the empress and the ladies of her court, and the princesses of the blood the diversion of seeing us. In his second audience, the emperor and the ladies invited to it attend behind screens and lattices, but the counsellors of state and other officers of the court sit in the open rooms, in their usual and elegant order. . . .

The emperor and his imperial consort sat behind the lattices on our right. As I was dancing, at the emperor's command, I had an opportunity twice of seeing the empress thro' the slits of the lattices and took notice that she was of a brown and beautiful complexion, with black European eyes, full of fire, and from the proportion of her head, which was pretty large, I judg'd her to be a tall woman, and about thirty-six years of age. By lattices, I mean hangings made of reed, split exceeding thin and fine and cover'd on the back with a fine transparent silk, with openings about a span broad, for the persons to look

---

1. Kawaguchi Munetsune, the bugyō (magistrate) of Nagasaki.
2. Actually not the emperor, but the shogun Tokugawa Tsunayoshi.

through. . . . The emperor himself was in such an obscure place that we should scarce have known him to be present had not his voice discovr'd him, which yet was so low, as if he purposely intended to be there incognito. . . . On our left, in another room, were the counsellors of state of the first and second rank, sitting in a double row in good and becoming order. The gallery behind us was fill'd with the chief officers of the emperor's court and the gentlemen of his bedchamber. The gallery which led into the room where the emperor was, was fill'd with the sons of some princes of the empire then at court, the emperor's pages and some priests lurking. After this manner it was, that they order'd the stage on which we were now to act. . . . After the usual obeisance made, Bengo[3] bid us welcome in the emperor's name. The chief interpreter receiv'd the compliment from Bengo's mouth and repeated it to us. Upon this the ambassador [*opperhoofd*] made his compliment in the name of his masters, withal returning their most humble thanks to the emperor for having graciously granted the Dutch liberty of commerce. . . .

The mutual compliments being over, the succeeding part of this solemnity turn'd to a perfect farce. We were ask'd a thousand ridiculous and impertinent questions. Thus, for instance, they desir'd to know, in the first place, how old each of us was, and what was his name, which we were commanded to write upon a bit of paper, having for these purposes took an European inkhorn along with us. This paper, together with the inkhorn itself, we were commanded to give to Bengo, who deliver'd them both into the emperor's hands, reaching them under the lattice. The captain, or ambassador, was ask'd concerning the distance of Holland from Batavia and of Batavia from Nagasaki. Which of the two was the most powerful, the director general of the Dutch East-India Company at Batavia, or the prince of Holland? As for my own particular, the following questions were put to me: What external and internal distempers I thought the most dangerous and most difficult to cure? How I proceeded in the cure of cancerous humors and imposthumations of the inner parts? Whether our European physicians did not search after some medicine to render people immortal, as the Chinese physicians had done for many hundred years? Whether we had made any considerable progress in this search, and which was the last remedy conducive to long life, that had been found in Europe? To which I return'd in answer, that very many European physicians had long labor'd to find out some medicine, which should have the virtue of prolonging human life and preserving people in health to a great age; and having thereupon been ask'd, which I thought the best? I answer'd that I always took that to be the best which was found out last, till experience taught us a better; and being further ask'd, which was the last, I answer'd, a certain spirituous liquor, which could keep the humors of the body fluid and comfort the spirits. This general answer

---

3. Makino Narisada, the grand chamberlain at the shogunal court.

prov'd not altogether satisfactory, but I was quickly desir'd to let them know the name of this excellent medicine, upon which, knowing that whatever was esteem'd by the Japanese, had long and high-sounded names, I return'd in answer, it was the Sal volatile Oleosum Sylvii. This name was minuted down behind the lattices, for which purpose I was commanded to repeat it several times. The next question was, who it was that found it out, and where it was found out? I answer'd Professor Sylvius in Holland. Then they ask'd me, whether I could make it up? Upon this our resident whisper'd me to say no, but I answer'd yes, I could make it up, but not here. Then twas ask'd, whether it could be had at Batavia? and having return'd in answer, that t'was to be had there, the emperor desir'd that it should be sent over by the next ships. The emperor, who hitherto sat among ladies, almost opposite to us, at a considerable distance, did now draw nearer and sat himself down on our right behind the lattices, as near us as possibly he could. Then he order'd us to take off our cappa, or cloak, being our garment of ceremony, then to stand upright, that he might have a full view of us; again to walk, to stand still, to compliment each other, to dance, to jump, to play the drunkard, to speak broken Japanese, to read Dutch, to paint, to sing, to put our cloaks on and off. Meanwhile, we obey'd the emperor's commands in the best manner we could, I join'd to my dance a love song in High German. In this manner and with innumerable such other apish tricks, we must suffer ourselves to contribute to the emperor's and the court's diversion. The ambassador, however, is free from these and the like commands, for as he represents the authority of his masters, some care is taken that nothing should be done to injure or prejudice the same. Besides that he shew'd so much gravity in his countenance and whole behavior as was sufficient to convince the Japanese that he was not at all a fit person to have such ridiculous and comical commands laid upon him. Having been thus exercis'd for a matter of two hours, though with great apparent civility, some servants shav'd came in and put before each of us a small table with Japanese victuals and a couple of ivory sticks, instead of knives and forks. We took and eat some little things and our chief interpreter, tho' scarce able to walk, was commanded to carry away the remainder for himself. We were then ordered to put on our cloaks again and to take our leave, which we gladly and without delay complied with, putting thereby an end to this second audience. We were then conducted back by the two commissioners to the waiting room, where we took our leave of them also.

[Kaempfer, *The History of Japan*, vol. 3, pp. 85–94]

SUGITA GENPAKU

Sugita Genpaku (1733–1817), descended from a family of physicians, was trained in traditional Chinese-style medicine, studied with one of the Nagasaki Dutch interpreters, and closely questioned the Hollanders on their annual visits to

Edo. Perhaps Genpaku's outstanding achievement was the famous autopsy that he, Maeno Ryōtaku (1723–1803), and Nakagawa Jun'an (1739–1786) performed. On the night of March 3, 1771, a letter from a man called Tokunō Manbei, a retainer of one of the Edo magistrates (*machi bugyō*), reported that the corpse of a convicted criminal would be in Senju Kotsugahara at the execution grounds the following day. The corpse that the three *rangaku* scholars were permitted to view was that of Aochababa (Green Tea Hag), a woman of about fifty from Kyoto. Both Ryōtaku and Genpaku had with them copies that each had purchased of the Dutch translation (*Ontleedkundige tafelen*, 1734) by Gerard Dicten, a practitioner in Leiden, of the *Anatomische tabellen* (*Tabulae anatomicae in quibus corporis humani*, 1722) by Johan Adam Kulmus (1689–1745) of Breslau, who had studied medicine in Halle, Leipzig, Strasbourg, and Basel and with Hermann Boerhaave in Leiden and who was a teacher of medicine and pathology in Danzig. In accord with the experimental spirit of the times, Genpaku and Ryōtaku compared the anatomy of the woman's body with Kulmus's charts, and they were amazed and impressed with the accuracy of the Western, in contrast to traditional Chinese, descriptions. Realizing the importance of their discovery, Genpaku, Ryōtaku, and Jun'an agreed to translate Kulmus's book. With the help of other scholars of Dutch learning, after working for three years and five months they published the fruit of their labors as A New Book of Anatomy (*Kaitai shinsho*).

Despite the breakthrough that it definitely represented, A New Book of Anatomy had a number of weaknesses. Ryōtaku was the only one of the translators who knew a fair amount of Dutch, and no dictionaries were available. Kulmus's original work was a brief text with extensive footnotes, but the Japanese version omitted the footnotes. Since the Japanese physicians who worked on the translation had not learned Western medicine systematically and since they were still viewing the Kulmus volume as supplementary to their basic grounding in Chinese-style medicine, the translation's inaccuracies were due to the translators' not understanding several of the basic concepts familiar to Western medical practitioners. In addition, the illustrations were reproduced as woodcuts, thus diminishing their clarity and precision when compared with the engravings of the original.

Nevertheless, these negative observations pale into insignificance when compared with the remarkable impact of A New Book of Anatomy on the Japanese scholarly world. This undertaking, as a cooperative scholarly venture among already recognized physicians, had a particular distinction that, in turn, meant that other similarly qualified physicians became interested in medical knowledge from the West. Clearly, too, the translators' reliance on demonstrable proof of the correctness of Kulmus's anatomical charts laid the groundwork for scientific medicine and subsequently a more scientific attitude among a significant segment of the growing Japanese intelligentsia. Accordingly, the appearance of A New Book of Anatomy marked the opening of a new era in the history of *rangaku* in which the physical center of Dutch studies moved from Nagasaki to Edo and the intellectual mainstream broadened from the frequently part-time and often dilettantish scholarship of the official interpreters to the national scholarly community, with Edo's prestigious physicians in the vanguard.

Perhaps the greatest importance for the future of Dutch studies was the translators' foresight in securing the *bakufu*'s sanction to publish their work. They did this by presenting *A New Book of Anatomy* to the authorities for their approval before its actual public release. While this act obviously reinforced the shogun's control of *rangaku*, it also was an implicit signal that the government was ready to permit further scholarly activity, at least in order to enhance medical knowledge.

For all its "newness," however, and the opening it gave to Western science and technology, Dutch studies did not stand entirely apart from the Neo-Confucian learning that held sway in the Tokugawa period. Although he was impressed by the new learning, Genpaku gave credit to the Neo-Confucian promotion of rational inquiry, critical inquiry, and "practical learning" that helped prepare the Japanese for their encounter with the West.

THE BEGINNINGS OF DUTCH LEARNING
(*RANGAKU KOTOHAJIME*)

At the outset of *The Beginnings of Dutch Learning*, Sugita Genpaku compares the new European learning with the Confucian learning of China.

Dutch Learning Compared with Chinese Learning

It is really surprising that "Dutch learning" has gained such great popularity lately. Farsighted intellectuals study it with enthusiasm, while the ignorant praise it in grandly glowing terms.

This pursuit of Dutch learning was casually started by us—very few of us—about fifty years ago. We never expected that it would come into such a great vogue.

The way Chinese learning was begun and promoted was quite different. In old Japan, envoys were sent to Tang China (618–906), and some great Buddhist monks were sent there to pursue their studies under the direct tutelage of Chinese scholars. On coming back, these men were commissioned to educate the Japanese, high and low, in Chinese learning. It was natural, therefore, for Chinese learning to become gradually diffused among the people.

Nothing like this happened with Dutch learning. Yet it has come into such popularity that it makes me wonder what made it so. Was it because in medicine, teaching was first of all practical and it could be followed easily? Or was it because some old foxes, seeking after fame or gain, took advantage of the curiosity of the masses who considered Dutch medicine as a new, exotic, and mysterious cure?

National Isolation; Surgery in South Outlanders' Style; Surgery in Dutch Style

Let us consider here how the Japanese contact with outsiders has changed since early times. Western ships began to visit the extreme western part of Japan about the Tenshō (1573–1592) and the Keichō eras (1595–1615). Their avowed purpose was trading with Japan, but in fact they had an ulterior object, and this caused all sorts of trouble.

After the establishment of theTokugawa government (1603), all trade with Westerners came to be forbidden. This is a historical fact we all know about. The direct cause for this drastic measure, that is, the strict ban on heretical Christianity, is alien to me, and I have nothing to say about it. But I am quite positive in stating that some of the surgical knowledge, which the Japanese acquired from the doctors aboard the foreign ships coming to Japan in those days, is still with us as useful techniques in healing. These are designated as surgery in "south outlanders' style (nanban-ryū)."

In spite of the general ban on Western ships visiting Japan, the Dutch were allowed to keep on coming to Hirado, Hizen Province, as they were not considered "conspirators." Thirty-three years later, that is, in 1641 (the eighteenth year of Kan-ei era), all the other "south outlanders" who had been in Dejima of Nagasaki were expelled to allow the Dutch alone to reside there. Ever since, Dutch ships have made it a rule to drop anchor at Nagasaki every year. It is reported that on board the ships which visited there, there was not a small number of doctors who were instrumental in initiating the Japanese into the knowledge of surgical operations. The medical art thus transmitted was called the "surgery in Dutch style." Needless to say, the Japanese doctors did not acquire it by reading Dutch books but by watching what the Dutch performed and taking notes on their prescriptions. Since many of the drugs they applied were not available in Japan, some substitutes were used. . . . [pp. 1–3]

Dutch Learning Prospers

In the beginning, I did not think the Dutch learning would flourish and advance as we see today. This was due to my poor intellect and lack of foresight. Looking back now, I see that the Chinese learning took long to develop in this country, perhaps because it was primarily a rhetorical language while Dutch developed fast, because it expressed facts as they were and it was easier to learn. Or perhaps it was that Chinese had trained the Japanese mind and had made a foundation whereupon Dutch was able to make a rapid stride. I cannot tell.

Or it may be that the time was just ripe for this type of learning. Takebe, whom I came to know by correspondence, as I mentioned before, wrote in his letter that he was beside himself with joy to receive my answer, proving our intellectual coincidence. This gentleman was twenty years my senior. Claiming that he was too old to study himself, he sent his son Ryōtaku and one of his pupils, Ōtsuki Gentaku, to Edo to be tutored by me.

I watched this man, Gentaku, and found him very positive in learning. He would not say or write anything unless he was convinced of it himself. He was not necessarily of vigorous mind, but he disliked frivolousness. He was exactly the man for the study of Dutch science. I loved his talent and personality and made a conscious effort to teach him. Afterward, I entrusted him to Ryōtaku's guidance. As was expected, he proved a diligent scholar, and Ryōtaku instructed him in the fundamentals of Dutch language. Thus in a short while Gentaku became thoroughly versed in the essentials of Dutch learning.

During this time, he made the acquaintance of such "Dutch" scholars as Nakagawa Jun'an, Katsuragawa Hoshū, and Lord Fukuchiyama, resulting in a rapid advance in his studies. Ever enthusiastic in its pursuit, he expressed his desire to receive lessons directly from interpreters in Nagasaki. Ryōtaku and I happily supported him in this idea. "Go, young man—and study!" we said. "You will achieve greatness in your cherished desire."

Gentaku decided to go to Nagasaki, but the trouble was the question of expense. Impressed by his fervor, I wanted to do something for him. But I myself was pressed financially then. Still, I did everything possible within my capacity. Our companion, Lord Fukuchiyama, himself a student of Dutch, kindly rendered him generous help. Thus he had the good fortune of going to Nagasaki. Having carefully disciplined himself for some time under the guidance of Motoki Einoshin,[4] an interpreter, and having sought every possible acquaintance with many experts in the line, he came back to Edo and became a permanent resident there.

After he returned to Edo, Gentaku put out the book *A Guide to Dutch Learning* (*Rangaku kaitei*) which he had compiled but had laid aside unpublished. Many of the scholars who read the book were deeply moved and were stirred to fresh exertions. I am thankful to the providence which obliged us with the appearance of such a man and such a book in support of my cherished dream. [pp. 51–53]

Report on an Autopsy

In his autobiographical account of the development of Dutch learning in Japan, *The Beginnings of Dutch Learning*, Genpaku vividly recounts the famous autopsy and the

---

4. Motoki Einoshin (1735–1794) was a scholar knowledgeable about astronomy, humanities, and natural history.

subsequent labors involved in the publication of A *New Book of Anatomy* (*Kaitai shinsho*).

All of us together arrived in the designated place in Kotsugahara. The executed body to be dissected was of a female criminal about fifty years old, who, born in Kyoto, had earned for herself the nickname of "Aochababa" (Green Tea Hag). She had committed a heinous crime, we were told.

Toramatsu, an *eta* and a skillful dissector, was expected to perform the task, but he failed to appear on account of a sudden illness. His ninety-year-old grandfather, a sturdy-looking man, took his place. He said that he had performed a number of dissections ever since his youth. In dissecting the human body, the custom till then was to leave everything to such outcast people [like the *eta*]. They would cut open the body and point out such organs as the lungs, liver, and the kidneys while the observing doctors simply watched them and came away. All they could say then was: "We actually viewed the innards of a human body." With no labels attached to each organ, all they could do was listen to the dissector's words and nod.

On this occasion, too, the old man went on explaining the various organs such as the heart, the liver, the gallbladder, and the stomach. Further, he pointed to some other things and said: "I don't know what they are, but they have always been there in all the bodies that I have so far dissected." Checking them later with the Dutch charts, we were able to identify them to be the main arteries and veins and suprarenal glands. The old man also said: "In my past experience of dissection, the doctors present never seemed puzzled, or asked questions specifically about one thing or another."

Comparing the things we saw with the pictures in the Dutch book Ryōtaku and I had with us, we were amazed at their perfect agreement. There were no such divisions as the six lobes and two auricles of the lungs or the three left lobes and four right lobes of the liver mentioned in old medical books. Also, the positions and forms of the intestines and the stomach were very different from the traditional descriptions.

The shogun's official doctors—Okada Yōsen and Fujimoto Rissen—had beheld dissections seven or eight times before, but always what they saw was different from what had been taught in the past thousand years. They said they had been making sketches every time they saw something that struck them as strange. On this basis, I suppose, they had written that perhaps the Chinese and Japanese were different in their internal structures. This I had read.

After the dissection was over, we were tempted to examine the forms of the bones, too, and picked up some of the sun-bleached bones scattered around the ground. We found that they were nothing like those described in the old books but were exactly as represented in the Dutch book. We were completely amazed.

On our way home, three of us—Ryōtaku, Jun'an, and I—talked of what a startling revelation we had seen that day. We felt ashamed of ourselves for having come this far in our lives without being aware of our own ignorance. How presumptuous on our part to have served our lordships and pretended to carry out our duties as official doctors when we were totally without knowledge of the true makeup of our bodies, which should be the foundation of the art of healing! Based upon today's experience, suppose we should, by some means, learn even the bare outline of the truth about the body and practice our medicine according to that knowledge, we should be able to justify our claim as medical professionals.

Thus we talked and sighed. Ryōtaku, too, said all of this was very true, and he was in complete agreement. I broke the spell by saying, "Even this one volume of *Ontleedkundige Tafeln*—suppose we translate it—many facts about the body will be clarified and the art of healing will be greatly benefited. I would like, in some way or another, to read this book without the aid of a Nagasaki interpreter."

Ryōtaku replied: "I have had the cherished idea of reading a Dutch book, but I have not found a friend to share that purpose, and I have been passing the days in regret. However, if you are all for it—I have been to Nagasaki and learned something of the language—shall we, then, make mine the seed of our knowledge and start work on the book?"

"That makes me glad!" I said, "If you would join forces as comrades, I too will show you I can rouse myself to action."

Ryōtaku, very much elated, said, "'For good purpose, do not dally,' the proverb says. Let us meet in my home tomorrow. We will find some way to go at the work."

I promised earnestly to follow his words, and we parted.

Next day, we gathered at Ryōtaku's house. We talked over the experience of the day before. Then we faced the book.

But it was as though we were on a boat with no oar or rudder adrift on the great ocean—a vast expanse and nothing to indicate our course. We just gazed at each other in blank dismay.

Ryōtaku, however, had studied the Dutch language for some years. He had been to Nagasaki and had learned something of the Dutch words and syntax. He was also an old man ten years my senior. So we decided to make him our leader and respect him as our teacher.

As far as I was concerned, I knew nothing of the Dutch language, not even the twenty-five letters of the alphabet. As the project was such a sudden event, I had to begin by learning the letters and gradually familiarize myself with the language.

We conferred and discussed together how to approach the translation and put it into proper and intelligible Japanese.

We thought it too difficult to attack the internal structure of the body at the incipient stage of our work. At the beginning of the book, there were illustrations of the full view of the human body, front and back. As we were familiar with all parts of the body's outside, we thought it would be easy to pair off the signs on the illustrations and on the explanatory notes, thus to learn the names of the parts of the body; at any rate, these were the first of the illustrations—we decided to begin with them. The result of this work was the compilation of the volume called *Atlas and Nomenclature of the Human Body* (*Keitai-meimoku-hen*) in *A New Book of Anatomy* (*Kaitai shinsho*). . . .

Needless to say, we did take questions to the interpreters who came to Edo annually. Also, between times we attended the dissections of human bodies, and more often we opened animal bodies to confirm what we read.

When I first obtained that book of anatomy and ascertained its accuracy by actual observation, I was struck with admiration by the great difference between the knowledge of the West and that of the East. And I was inspired to come to the determination that I must learn and clarify the new revelation for applying it to actual healing and also for making it the seed of further discoveries among the general physicians of Japan. I was anxious to bring the work to completion as fast as possible. I had no other thought in those days than to write down in the evening what we had deciphered in the day's meeting. I considered the forms of expression in many ways, trying and retrying, and in the four years, I rewrote the manuscript eleven times over before feeling ready to hand it to the printers. Thus the work *A New Book of Anatomy* (*Kaitai shinsho*) was completed. [pp. 29–37]

[Sugita, *Dawn of Western Science in Japan*, pp. 1–3, 51–53, 29–37]

ŌTSUKI GENTAKU

One of the most noted and most learned of the scholars of things Dutch was Ōtsuki Gentaku (1757–1827), whom Sugita Genpaku referred to in the preceding excerpt. Gentaku began his study of medicine at age thirteen, and eager to acquire both language competence and Dutch medical skills, he studied with the official interpreters in Nagasaki and the Dutch-style physicians in Edo. Revered by both Tokugawa officialdom and Dutch studies specialists, by the time of his death Gentaku had reached the pinnacle of scholarly esteem for his all-encompassing knowledge. His *A Clarification of Misunderstandings in Theories [About] the Dutch* (*Ransetsu benwaku*, 1797), which was supposedly written down verbatim by one of his disciples, shows evidence of both the kinds of inquiry that were commonly addressed to *rangaku* scholars and the level of their "scholarly" achievement.

MISUNDERSTANDINGS ABOUT THE DUTCH
(*RANSETSU BENWAKU*)

Short Life

Q: It is rumored among the public that all Hollanders are short-lived. Is there really any basis for this in fact?

A: Where this story sprang up or the reason for it, I do not know. Human life, both long and short, is exacted in heaven, and there is no difference throughout the whole world in all countries and in all places. This fact is well known in both China and in Japan. However, among those peoples [of the earth] who continuously sail over great expanses of rough waters, it is said that there are many who are short-lived and who generally die around forty. . . . On looking at the people who come to this country, [we see that] those who say they are twenty-two, twenty-three, twenty-four, or twenty-five all appear to be around forty. People who remain in that country [Holland] are no different from those in this country, and their spans of life are not all the same. There are those who live on to a hundred years and those who die after ten or twenty fleeting years. [*jō*, pp. 2–3]

Without Heels

Q: It is said that it is a natural characteristic of the Hollanders not to have heels or that they have eyes like animals or that these people are tall. What is really the truth?

A: Where did these false stories develop? Since the eyes of the people of this country are very different from [the eyes of] those people [Hollanders], are they scorned as though they were animals, or is this because they are from a different continent? There is some degree of difference in the coloring of Europeans and Asians. However, there is none at all in the physical composition [of their bodies], nor is there the slightest difference in how they use [their bodies]. When I was at Nagasaki and saw people who were Indians and blacks, they differed slightly in their eye structure. There is a small difference among the Chinese, Koreans, and Ryukyuans, and even in people of our same country I think I can discern some variations in the appearance of the eyes among the people of Tōō , Hokuetsu, Shikoku, and Tsukushi. There is a little difference in color and appearance, but as far as practical application is concerned, we are all the same. It goes without saying that citizens of a continent over ten thousand *ri* away will be different. Even though there are the same conditions of creation, there must be slight variations conditioned by the location of their homeland. Moreover, since the heel is the base of one's body—and without heels how could one move about?—this [question] is not even worthy of comment. [*jō*, pp. 4–5]

Wine

Q: I hear that as intoxicants they have various things such as grape wine, *araki* [Du. *arak* (Arab spice wine)], *chinda* [Port. *vinho tinto* (red wine)], etc. How do they manufacture them?

A: As for the Dutch wines in general, there are many purchased abroad or imported from various countries. They are all fermented from grapes. They have various names depending on the method of manufacture. Saké is called "uein." This is taken from [the word for] grapes "ueingaarudo" with the last part omitted. Therefore they are all grape wines and only have different names according to their manufacture.

That country [Holland] has a great many kinds of wine. Grape wine, *araki*, and *chinda* are not different things. They have names which differ according to the method of manufacture. And the thing specifically called "biiro" [Du. *bier*] is an alcoholic drink manufactured from grain. This is used after eating and is said to aid in the digestion of food and drink. [*jō*, pp. 9–10]

Various Glass Utensils

Q: The kinds of Dutch-made glass wine cups in this area are all called "koppu"; the wine containers are called "flasks" (*furasuko*); and the glass is called "biidoro" [Port. *vidro*]. Are there any distinctions among each of these?

A: From ancient times, glass has been called "biidoro," and this is not a Dutch word. It is a Latin and Portuguese word. Years ago when Portuguese ships came to our country, this word was transmitted and became a common term. In Holland they say "garasu." Originally the thing known as "koppu" referred to an object like a *chawan* [teacup]. Now what is called "koppu" by the public is generally the "kerukii" [Du. *kelk*]. There are various names depending on the shape. As for "furasuko" [Port. *frasco*], the original name is "furesuku" . . . the glass container in which is put medicinal oils, saké, etc. Here I have selected and included suitable pictures. They should be looked at together. [*jō*, pp. 12–18]

Food

Q: What sorts of things do the Hollanders have for food? People say that they are like the Chinese in eating inferior food and that like the Chinese also, they smoke tobacco a great deal.

A: This [story] must arise because it is said that foreigners have varieties of beef and pork as staple foods. This [diet] is not limited to Holland and China. All foreign countries have such foodstuffs. Since Japan is a country surrounded on four sides by water, and since ample food is derived from things produced in the sea, it seems that from days of old we have not made use of mountain products. Since foreign countries for the most part are states that continue far inland, distances from the seashore may extend from one hundred to three hundred *ri*. Therefore it is difficult to have a sufficiency [of food] by using sea products, and naturally people eat things that live on land. It is thought that pigs and the like were created and put on earth by heaven for food. Since even in our country there are places such as the northern provinces that are deep in the mountains and are far from the sea, it is said that there are many places where, besides salted fish, wild boar and deer are always eaten. This practice is probably the same [as in Holland and China]. The cuisine of both Holland and China, according to what I hear of the appearance of their food, might not be what common people rumor it to be; they have from the beginning used as staple foods varieties of fowl, cow, and pig which are raised by people. Of course, as far as their method of cookery is concerned, everything they eat is very well cooked, and they never eat things that are boiled alive or things like raw fish which, after entering the intestines, are difficult to digest. It is said that Hollanders and others, though they be lowly persons, have no wish to eat animals and fish of unusual shapes which from ancient times they have been unaccustomed to eat. They do not eat things like the sea-devil [devil fish], squid, and octopus. It is said that they eat such varieties of fish as the sea bream, halibut, salmon, trout, and carp. In reference to birds it is said that they do not make much use of birds like the pheasant and duck that are fat and deleterious. From the first they say that species such as the dog and the horse have not been [considered] edible. Of course, they have regular times for eating and drinking, but it is said that beyond these they never drink or eat to excess. When they [Hollanders] hear it said that all the people here ordinarily eat fish and that our town bullies can down two bonitos or . . . a great amount of saké in one gulp, the [Hollanders] must be horrified and must deplore it.

As for the saying that they smoke tobacco a great deal, this must be because they are seen using a long-stemmed pipe with a large pipe bowl. The whole pipe is made of porcelain. Since it has a long stem, it does not fill up with exudations over a long period of time, and from the way it is made one would think it would easily break in a short time. Its length is more than a *shaku* [0.994 foot], probably with the idea that the fragrance of the tobacco on the throat should be slight.

Although the pipe's bowl is relatively large, the hole that transmits [the smoke] is extremely narrow. And the thing they call tobacco is first boiled in hot water and then dried after thus being separated from its violent poisons. Of course, as far as their smoking tobacco is concerned, they don't swallow [the smoke] but blow it all out. Always filling their cheeks up to the point of exhaling, they stop at two or three puffs. They are more moderate than our people who used short pipes that can be used coming or going and sitting and lying down. [ge, pp. 1–3]

Black-boys

Q: It is said that "black-boys" who come over on Dutch ships submerge in water easily and grow up practicing swimming or that they are a kind of monkey.

A: "Black-boys" are poor people from India. The Dutch have engaged them as servants at "Jagatara" [Jakarta]. In that area are people from various places, and all of them have homelands which have their origins in the deep south and therefore have very hot climates. Hence their bodies are bathed in the sunlight, and their coloring becomes extremely black. And since they are menial people, it is said that they do not clothe their bodies and only cover their private parts. Often they are said to have frizzled hair like Shaka who was born on a tropical island called "Seiran" [Ceylon] in India and whose swirled hair was curled by the extreme heat. Furthermore, it must have been owing to the heat of the land that the five hundred disciples of Buddha were either stripped to the waist or entirely nude. Among "black-boys" there is certainly a distinction between the noble and the lowly and the wise and foolish, and those people are no different from the rest of mankind. From the beginning I have not paid any attention to the story that they grow up practicing swimming. People are not what others say they are. Each Hollander has his own servant, and each is useful in different circumstances. Without distinction the various waiters and chambermaids and seamstresses assist in washing, drawing water, rice-hulling, and cooking. The Dutch call them "suwaruto yongo" [Du. *zwarte jongen* (young black)]. "Suwaruto" is black , and "yongo" is a servant, a young person. This must mean a servant-slave. [ge, pp. 3–5]

Electricity

Q: "Erekiteru" [electrostatic generator] is said to be an instrument for taking fire from the bodies of human beings. What sort of thing is this?

A: A diagram of this [instrument] has already been detailed in Morishima's book *Kōmō zatsuwa* (*Miscellany of Dutch Studies*). ["Erekiteru"] is a version of the original word "erekiseriteito" [Du. *electriciteit* (electricity)]. The Dutch use the words "hiyufuru sutein karakuto" [Du. *vuur steen kracht* (fire-stone power)]. There is no justification of taking fire from human bodies. Fire emerges by contact with something. Rocks and minerals are rubbed against each other causing fire. Since this action is like steel striking flintstone to produce fire, we use the name "fire-stone power." And it is this device which, by causing friction among the forces of heaven and earth, proves the principle which is manifested in a flash of lightning. Fire does not emerge from the tip of the thing which is struck but erupts from the place which has been rubbed with this instrument and brings forth fire. In this light, it is not at all a mysterious thing. It is an implement which has been devised according to this principle and creates fire. It should be known that this fundamental principle is the same as that of the igniting stone which is used every morning and evening in every home. [*ge*, pp. 6–7]

First Entry into the Harbor and Accommodations at Nagasaki

Q: When were the Dutch first in this country, and have they come to Nagasaki since ancient times? Further, what sort of accommodations do they have in that place [Nagasaki]?

A: As I have already explained in my *Rangaku kaitei*, they began [coming here] about the time of Toyotomi [Hideyoshi (1536–1548)] in the Keichō period [1596–1615] and reached Hirado in Hizen. After that, during the Kan'ei period [1624–1644], they entered the harbor of Nagasaki in the same province. Not yet two hundred years have gone by. Ignorant and stupid women think that Nagasaki is a place in China, and there are those that think that the people of this country [Japan] are mixed with the people of that country [Holland]. These are gross errors. Both the Chinese and Dutch have places of residence. The Dutch live on a small island constructed on the shore of the place called Edo machi in the same city [Nagasaki]. It has been given the name Dejima. Facing northward from this place there is a gate by which various officials, interpreters, etc. may come and go. Nishikawa [Joken (1647–1724)] of this place has detailed this in a book called *Nagasaki yawagusa* (*Evening Thoughts of Nagasaki*). The abode of the Chinese is a place called Jūzenji-mura. At the east of the harbor on the outskirts of the city there is a place called Umegasaki. Here the Chinese ships anchor. Facing this is a temple called Daitokuji. Below is a common. At the right on a high place there is a village called Kojima. In the area between this village and the temple is the [Chinese compound]. From Dejima the terrain can be viewed very widely. In years gone by, when I went there to study, they were making prints at that place, and I bought some pictures of Nagasaki that were for sale. Pictures that showed the general outline of the quarters of both the Chinese and Dutch could be obtained, and I keep them at home. [*ge*, pp. 11–13]

The Origins of the Visits to Edo and Commerce

Q: Why do the Dutch come to Edo every year in the spring? Their ordinarily being called merchant foreigners is very strange. What is the origin of this?

A: This [visit] is to obtain permission to cross the sea [to Japan]. I hear that they are permitted to come every spring bringing products of their country in order to pay homage in an audience with the shogun. As is the established custom, they leave Nagasaki on the fifteenth of January, and at the beginning of March various officials of the Nagasaki garrison, three Hollanders, the senior and junior interpreters, etc., leading several tens of men, go up to the castle for an audience and offer products of their country. When they take their leave, they are granted gifts from the shogun. I understand that they divide up these gifts into seven portions, send them to the seven provinces of their homeland, and distribute them respectively. As far as the conduct of their trade is concerned, after entering the harbor in early autumn, during the three months of July, August, and September, they exchange various goods at Dejima, Nagasaki. Those who come into port in early fall of the current year alternate with those who have remained on Deshima since the previous year. At the audience in the following spring the captain will take the secretary and the physician, and it is said that these are as a general rule the three who make the visit to [Edo]. [*ge*, pp. 13–14]

Surgery

Q: You speak as though all the Dutch doctors are ordinarily only surgeons. Is this really true?

A: As far as this [question] is concerned, when the first ships came into port skilled surgeons were on board, and the interpreters of that time [who were] learning the various unusual skills that they [the surgeons] had to offer were the founders of surgery and, before one knew it, formed a school. Following those people [these ideas] were handed down by hearsay and gradually became widespread, and it seems like Nagasaki was the source of surgery. At that time, since the books of that country could not be read directly, those studying these marvelous arts could only learn by memory, and it seems that these [students] did not extend their questioning into matters of internal medical treatment. Even when one speaks of Holland, how can external treatment alone be used to treat external injuries resulting from wind, cold, heat, and dampness, the various ailments brought on by internal injuries, conditions of women before and after childbirth, children's smallpox and boils, and varieties of measles? This is utterly unthinkable. Even aboard ship the same situation exists. Are there only external ailments and not internal ailments? On board ship, although [their doctors] do not distinguish between internal and external treatment, [they] combine both internal and external medical science. In their books, internal medical treatments and methods are very minute and detailed, and that country [Holland] has a great many books which can be selected from among the work of its wise men. Generally those persons who are doctors consider that it is of first importance to know the whole human body under ordinary conditions. The four extremities and the whole external human body from the skin, flesh, body hair, and hair on the head to the viscera, veins, and membranes on the inside are all vivisected and investigated, and on the basis of these [studies] the [doctors] consider the source of the illness and give treatments. Learning these facts in detail by research in these techniques, they know their procedure. Among medical skills, internal medicine is especially difficult to master easily. . . . As for the whole field of medicine, even among the medical profession, it is said that there are men of [especially] good repute. They are called "heneisuheiru" [Du. *geneesheer* (physician)]. This is a title of respect. Another name is "dokutōru" [Du. *doktor* (doctor)]. Men such as these do not come over on ships, and it is understood that they recklessly [go] to other countries. They also are skillful surgeons. As far as [the doctors] who come over on the ships are concerned, many of them are persons who in a general way know the techniques. It is said that they come for the sake of pursuing their studies and that they endeavor to succeed in both medicine and surgery. From time to time there are people whose main endeavor is medicine, and for study and research they also come over to try to get better acquainted [with such work]. In their language a surgeon is called "heiru meisuteru" [Du. *heelmeester* (surgeon)] or "hando uerukerusu" [craftsman; i.e., surgeon] but since on the ships he combines medicine [with surgery] he is called "dokutōru." Two men come over on each ship. One is called "oppuru meisuteru," and the other is called "onderu meisuteru." Our comparable terms for these are senior surgeon and junior surgeon. "Oppuru" is senior. "Onderu" is junior. The one who pays his respects at Edo is the "oppuru meisuteru." However, as noted above, they are called "dokutōru." [*ge*, pp. 15–18]

[Ōtsuki, *Ransetsu benwaku*; Goodman, trans., "Translation of Ōtsuki
Gentaku's *Ransetsu benwaku*," pp. 71–99]

SHIBA KŌKAN

Shiba Kōkan (1747–1818), an Edo man, was a painter of traditional Chinese and Japanese styles (especially *ukiyo-e* [woodblock prints]) before he developed an interest in Western art and, in association with the leading scholars of Dutch studies, became an enthusiastic advocate of Western art and civilization, manifested in his work as a painter, etcher, and engraver.

DISCUSSING WESTERN PAINTING
(*SEIYŌGA DAN*)

The distinguished historian Sir George Sansom saw Shiba Kōkan as representing a significant restlessness among educated Japanese of his day: "[He] felt that his native culture was exhausted and stale . . . a man in revolt against contemporary Japanese life, . . . [and] impressed by the material and scientific aspects of Western culture."[5] The following comments by Kōkan, from *Discussing Western Painting* (1799), reflect his sense of impatience with his own countrymen for failing to appreciate things Western.

1. The diameter of the world is more than seven thousand miles, and the sea route circumnavigating it is over twenty-four thousand miles. The land known as the West is in the region lying to west of China and Japan. The most distant region of the West is called Europe. It is one of the great continents and contains several thousand countries the size of Japan. One of them, the Netherlands, is divided into seven districts, one of which is Holland.

The various countries of the West all have the same style of painting. Since this style was introduced to Japan by the Dutch, and since today there are numerous examples of Dutch art in Japan, we call all Western paintings "Dutch paintings." The technique employed in this art produces a true representation of reality, greatly different from the style that is used in Japan. Many persons in Japan—among them those who paint in the traditional Chinese or Japanese technique—consider Western-style painting absurd and have no desire to learn the Western method. Not only do they think it unworthy of study, but they feel that it has no artistic value and cannot be called painting at all! They seem to think that the artistic creations of the West are mere artisan's work. This is indeed an extremely foolish notion.

The Japanese and Chinese painting that we refer to as *saiga*, or minutely painted pictures, actually come under the category of *saiku*, or artisan's work. Take, for example, the manner in which the Japanese draw hair and beards: every single strand of hair is drawn individually. The Western technique of

---

5. Sansom, *The Western World and Japan*, pp. 232–33.

drawing hair, however, is to suggest the hair in a few brush strokes, so that the resulting appearance is one of real hair, not a mere mass of lines. In ancient times people were not concerned with the stress and character of the brush stroke. Fundamentally, a brush is a tool for drawing pictures. If one attempts to draw an ox without expressing the actual appearance of the ox, if one is concerned mainly with the impression given by the brush technique, then a mere spot of ink could just as well be called a picture of an ox.

For example, medical science cures illness with medicine. Relating this metaphorically to painting, let us call medical science the brush, illness the picture, and medicines the colors. The attempt of medical science to cure a specific illness with general medicine, or the attempt of the brush to correct a picture with color, is like not knowing exactly where the illness originates or just what is at fault in a painting. The primary aim of Western art is to create a spirit of reality, but Japanese and Chinese paintings, in failing to do this, become mere toys serving no use whatever.

By employing shading, Western artists can represent convex and concave surfaces, sun and shade, distance, depth, and shallowness. Their pictures are models of reality and thus can serve the same function as the written word, often more effectively. The syllables used in writing can only describe, but one realistically drawn picture is worth ten thousand words. For this reason Western books frequently use pictures to supplement written texts, a striking contrast to the inutility of the Japanese and Chinese pictures, which serve no better function than that of a hobby to be performed at drinking parties. . . .

2. Instead of using glue as we do to mix our pigments, Western artists use oil. This means that even if their paintings get wet, they are not damaged. These pictures are commonly called oil paintings. Although many artists in Japan have copied this technique, few have ever attained a genuine knowledge. When I visited Nagasaki some years ago, a Hollander named Issac Titsingh gave me a book on art entitled *Konst Schilderboek*. Perusing this work carried me into an intoxicating world. After a careful study of it, I finally attained a perfect command of its principles and can now draw whatever I wish with complete ease—landscapes, birds, flowers, men, or beasts.

Pictures that are intended to give information, because of the vast amount of accurate detail that they contain, are far more effective than simple words of description. All things depicted in paintings—from the great wild goose down to the tiny sparrow, and even further to the components of eyes and beaks and legs—differ in shape and feeling. Even the color in plumage varies exceedingly. The written word in black and white cannot possibly recreate an accurate image of the true form. For this reason, the pictures drawn in Western countries are regarded even more highly than writing. Painting and writing both serve the nation; they are not devised merely for amusement.

3. Many Easterners consider Western art to be no more than "perspective pictures," but this belief is utterly fallacious for the reason I have stated previously: a picture that does not represent reality faithfully is not well executed.

There is far more to realistic painting than the mere drawing of perspective. Eastern pictures have no accuracy of detail, and without such accuracy, a picture is not really a picture at all. To paint reality is to paint all objects — landscapes, birds, flowers, cows, sheep, trees, rocks, or insects — exactly as the original objects appear, thereby actually animating the drawing. No technique other than that of the West can achieve this feeling of reality. When a Western painter looks at the work of an Eastern artist, he surely must see it as the mere playing of a child, hardly worthy of the name "painting." But when an Oriental artist, who is used to living with his wretched paintings, has an opportunity to compare his work with the distinctly superior Western art, he stupidly considers the latter merely another school of art, calling it "perspective painting." Obviously, such categorizing represents an extreme misunderstanding of Western painting.

4. Western books contain pictures made by the copper-engraving process. They have, for example, botany books (something like our medicinal herb books) in which illustrations and words are equally important for description. Without illustrations it would be impossible to obtain a clear understanding of the plant's appearance. Similarly, in order to construct an unfamiliar article, one must know its shape. What better way could there be to describe this than by means of a picture? Being realistic representations, the drawings of Western countries are executed according to the "three-face method" of shading. . . .

The three-face method of shading in Western art must be studied carefully and understood thoroughly: (1) Keep pure white that part of the painting which is to depict objects in direct sunlight. (2) Paint in pale tones those objects on which the sun shines obliquely. (3) Paint in deep tones those objects that are shaded from the sun and are therefore dark. The effect of light and dark shadows is achieved in engraving by the use of parallel lines: when single parallel lines are used in close proximity, the tonality is light; when two sets of parallel lines are used crossing each other, the tone becomes dark. . . .

No one in Japan knew the proper method of making a copperplate. I therefore turned to the formula given in a book by a Hollander named Boisu. I consulted with Ōtsuki Gentaku, who assisted me in translating the text so that I could manufacture copperplate pictures in Japan. In 1783, I produced the first engraving. Unfortunately, Asians are different in nature from Europeans, who have achieved such great skill in this art, and I could hardly hope to attain an equal perfection.

At the time of this writing I am more than fifty years old, and gradually my energy wanes. Though I have still much to learn, I should like to offer what slight knowledge I possess on the art of copperplate engraving to those whom it might interest. I therefore intend to publish another book, called *Oranda kikō*, which will explain the engraving technique.

5. Western artists apply their theories to a technique of precise representation, and their works cannot be viewed in a frivolous manner. There is, in fact, a

specific way to look at them. Perhaps to facilitate this, the pictures are usually framed and hung on a wall. Even when a painting is to be looked at casually, it should be hung directly in front of the observer. In the picture there is always a horizon line between sky and land. The viewer should move back five or six feet to a position where the horizon in the picture is level with his eyes. In this manner perspective is expressed in its truest form, clearly delineating the foreground from the background and setting off objects in space. Often a mirror is used in looking at small pictures, giving them an even greater appearance of depth and reality.

6. Portraiture is an important art form in the West, where the faces of sages and political figures are recorded in copperplate engravings for the benefit of future generations. The portrayal of these men gives one as clear an understanding of their physiognomies as seeing the men themselves. Again, the contrast to Japanese and Chinese paintings is striking, for without the technique of copying reality, the Eastern artist can paint only a subjective impression of an object or a face. The same man, if painted by two different Japanese artists, will appear to be two different men. Consequently, since the true form is not described, only a vague image appears. An image of grass and flowers that does not resemble the actual plants can hardly be called a picture of them.

7. The indigenous art technique of Japan and China cannot possibly reproduce reality. In drawing a spherical object, a Japanese artist will simply draw a circle and call it a sphere because he has no method for representing roundness. Being unable to deal with convexity, should he draw the front view of a man's face, there is no way of expressing the height of the nose! This difficulty is not due to the way in which the lines are drawn, but to the total disregard of shading in Japanese art. I shall discuss the drawing of Western pictures in greater detail in a later book, called *Seiyōga den.*

[French, *Shiba Kōkan*, pp. 171–74]

Chapter 28

EIGHTEENTH-CENTURY RATIONALISM

As Japan moved into the eighteenth century, the Tokugawa shogunate was already a century old, with its power and prestige firmly established and its policy of peace enforcement a proven success. The country was entering a stage of economic and cultural prosperity that was accompanied by an outburst of intellectual activity and originality unprecedented in Japan's long history. Despite the shogunate's adherence to a seclusion policy, the events of the late sixteenth century leading up to its adoption also had left indelibly printed on many Japanese minds the vision of a new and larger world in which the West played a dynamic part. At the same time, the program of instruction based on Zhu Xi's texts, which for almost a century had been spreading its influence throughout the land, greatly stimulated scholarly study in general, sometimes along lines not anticipated by its Tokugawa sponsors. Furthermore, in the port cities and towns around the feudal castles, members of the growing merchant class, restricted by the lack of opportunities for overseas trade, developed new outlets for their energies and talents at home. As patrons of men like the novelist Ihara Saikaku, the poet Bashō, and the playwright Chikamatsu, they helped create a variety of popular arts that displayed the people's increasing wealth and culture. In some instances, these merchants and their fast-growing towns also contributed materially to the development of independent thinkers and scholars.

One epoch-making development in peaceful eighteenth-century Japan was the construction of a new calendar by an official commission of scholars, working with new methods similar to those then used in the West. It had been the fond dream of Yoshimune (1684–1751) to issue a calendar using the services of his newly built observatory, and there was great satisfaction with the proclamation of a new era name, Precious Calendar (Hōreki), in 1751. The satisfaction was doubly felt because it meant that the Japanese no longer had to rely on the Chinese for what was considered to be the almost sacred duty of calendar making.

The newly awakened sense of cultural independence was far reaching in its effect. As the eighteenth century brought to full flower the needs of the independent and, particularly, scientific thought sown in the preceding period, there was a steady rise in both rationalist and nationalist thinking. The latter trend is dealt with in other chapters. Here we offer a few examples of the growing rationalism in this period. One proponent was Tominaga Nakamoto (1715–1746), the son of an Osaka merchant, whose name is associated with an original method of historical criticism. Another is Miura Baien (1723–1789), a rural physician in Kyushu, under no feudal bond, who carried on in the tradition of Kaibara Ekken, another Kyushu man, who had brought Zhu Xi's spirit of objective investigation into the open field of nature, regarding the study of man and nature as one. Baien went further to insist that man cannot be understood except in terms of nature and that nature can be understood only if man divests himself of his anthropocentric point of view. The third representative is Kaiho Seiryō (1755–1817), who was born by the shores of the Japan Sea into a warrior family of good standing. He renounced his hereditary status, however, to become a teacher among merchants and farmers. Seiryō argued in favor of the realistic study of the laws governing social and economic behavior, as compared with the moralistic approach of the traditional Confucians.

None of these figures had a wide influence in his own time, and none can be considered representative of the eighteenth century as a whole. They are, rather, symptomatic of an intellectual ferment that threatened to eventually break through the narrow limits of humanistic scholarship. It is true that this trend toward greater independence in thought, which had expanded steadily throughout the eighteenth century, was partly checked by a shogunal decree in 1790 known as the Prohibition of Heterodox Studies. Nevertheless, the fact that such a prohibition was felt to be an urgent necessity indicates in itself the extent to which independent minds were active and articulate by the end of the century.

Before turning to these more striking cases of independent thought, however, we shall see how, in the person of a far more widely recognized scholar and statesman, Arai Hakuseki, this rationalist tendency was supported by the ranks of orthodox Confucianism. He also serves as a reminder of the fact, sometimes lost to modern sight, that this rationalist temper of mind owes more to the Neo-Confucianism that it sought to displace than to any other single influence in Japanese thought. Neo-Confucianism itself provided the means of its own self-criticism.

ARAI HAKUSEKI'S CONFUCIAN PERSPECTIVE
ON GOVERNMENT AND SOCIETY

Arai Hakuseki (1657–1725) was notable among Tokugawa Confucian scholars for his great influence on government policy. Although he did not hold an official post in the *bakufu*, as the personal adviser to the sixth Tokugawa shogun, Ienobu, and Ienobu's attendant, Manabe Akifusa, Hakuseki succeeded in promoting a number of changes in *bakufu* policy. After Ienobu died in 1712, having served for only four years as shogun, Akifusa continued to consult with Hakuseki during the following four-year reign of Ienobu's young son Ietsugu. But with Ietsugu's premature death in 1716, both Akifusa and Hakuseki fell from favor. The following shogun, Yoshimune, promptly discontinued most of the projects that Hakuseki had promoted, many of which had already encountered fierce opposition from ranking members of the *bakufu* bureaucracy.

Hakuseki's key aim as shogunal adviser was to transform the shogun from a feudal hegemon, one of the 260-odd daimyo writ large, into a national monarch, a "true" king in the Confucian sense. He was inspired in this effort by two key premises of Chinese Confucian political thought. One was a belief that the preservation of political and social stability depended on the establishment of a clearly defined hierarchy. The other was the assumption that the figure standing at the pinnacle of such a hierarchy, the king, not only had to possess actual power but also had to be endowed with various symbols of legitimate authority. In Confucian terms, he should combine in his person both the "substance" (J. *jitsu*, Ch. *shi*) of power and the "names" (J. *mei*, Ch. *ming*) that appropriately manifested his authority to others. This combination would signal that the shogun was the recognized holder of the Mandate of Heaven.

Considered from this perspective, the Japanese polity was anomalous in several regards. Rather than presenting a single, clear hierarchy, it rested on a system of bifurcated sovereignty. Two figures, the emperor in Kyoto and the shogun in Edo, might plausibly claim to head the polity, but neither, in Confucian terms, combined the "substance" and "names" of authentic rulership. By the Tokugawa period, the imperial court had long lost effective power. First, within the framework of Heian court politics from the ninth to the twelfth century, the Fujiwara regents had encroached on the function of the emperor in whose name they acted. Then, at the end of the twelfth century, with the establishment of the Kamakura *bakufu*, the governmental powers had become divided, with the Kamakura shogun assuming authority over military and peace-keeping matters. From that point on, successive military leaders steadily absorbed the court's remaining responsibility for civil administration. The Tokugawa shogun had signaled his de facto authority over all aspects of government by issuing a code that defined the parameters of imperial court activities in the same manner as the Code for the Warrior Households (Buke shohatto) set out the responsibilities and obligations of the daimyo. The shogun also demonstrated his superior power by awarding the emperor and nobility their source of livelihood in the form of landholdings, in effect enfeoffing them as he did the daimyo. Simultaneously, however, the Tokugawa continued to treat the court as the repository of ultimate symbolic authority. The shogun formally received his appointment from the emperor, and within Tokugawa warrior society, the long-standing system of noble ranks and offices awarded by the court in Kyoto continued to be an important demarcation of status (see chap. 20).

Regarding such anomalies as a potential source of instability, Hakuseki set out to correct them. In China, on occasion, "name" had been separated from "substance" at the time of transition from one dynasty to another. The noted Northern Song statesman and historian Sima Guang had held that in such cases, the possessor of the substance of power had the greater claim to legitimacy. Following this argument, Hakuseki took for granted that it was the shogun—by the Tokugawa period universally acknowledged as the holder of the substance of power—who should properly assume the role of an autonomous national monarch recognized by Heaven and endowed with the authentic symbols of rulership. He recommended a range of measures to enhance the status of the shogun as the national ruler. These included adoption at the shogunal court of more kingly forms of dress and furnishings modeled after those of the imperial court and revision of the Code for the Warrior Households to emphasize that the daimyo had civil as well as military responsibilities in a comprehensive national government headed by the shogun. Hakuseki failed to win acceptance of a proposal to adopt a new system of honorary ranks centered on the shogun instead of the emperor. But in a dramatic step toward showing the shogun to be an autonomous national monarch, he convinced Ienobu to adopt the title of king of Japan (Nihon kokuō) in relations with other countries (primarily Korea).

Through these measures, Hakuseki in effect presented the Tokugawa house as the ruling dynasty, the successor to the Mandate of Heaven held originally by the imperial line. In so doing, he adhered to the premises of Chinese Confucian political thought, which accepted dynastic change as a norm of human society. To justify his position in the face of criticism from inside and outside the *bakufu*, Hakuseki turned to the classic form of political analysis used by Chinese Confucians like Sima Guang: the writing of history. Hakuseki wrote several major works dealing with Japanese history from this perspective. Among those that survive, of particular importance are *Views on the Course of History* (*Tokushi yoron*), an account of the evolution of the Japanese polity from the early Heian period to the eve of the establishment of the Tokugawa *bakufu*, and *An Interpretation of Ancient History* (*Koshitsū*), in which he interpreted as an epoch of human history the so-called Age of the Gods depicted in the *Kojiki* and *Nihon shoki*. Both *Views on the Course of History* and *An Interpretation of Ancient History* emphasize that dynastic change in accordance with the will of Heaven had characterized the history of Japan no less than that of China. In this way, Hakuseki's analysis of history supported his argument that the shogun should adopt the symbols of kingship appropriate to a national monarch recognized by Heaven. He did not intend, however, that the shogun should oust the emperor. On the contrary, he also used Chinese political ideals to argue that as a sign of his virtue, the shogun should make various efforts to show respect for the emperor in Kyoto as the representative of the former dynasty.

THE FUNCTION OF RITES

The Confucian political tradition stressed the importance of ritual forms as a means of establishing correct hierarchical relations throughout human society. As part of his effort to transform the shogun into a more complete monarch, Arai Hakuseki thus placed great emphasis on the adoption of appropriate forms of dress and titles. In a memorial calling for the revision of various current *bakufu* practices in this area, he explained both the power of ritual and the reasons why his own time (rather than one hundred years earlier, when the Tokugawa *bakufu* had been founded) was the right moment to establish proper ritual forms.

When the founder of this house [Tokugawa Ieyasu] came to rule the realm, he wished to revive the ancient ways of the shogunal houses; however, of the elders among the military class, only Hosokawa Fujitaka was still alive. The founder seems to have consulted with him about various matters . . . but although Hosokawa far surpassed others of the day in his accomplishments in civil and military affairs, he had been born at a time when the realm had been in total disorder for two hundred years and when the ancient ways of the military houses had all been lost. . . . Had the founder lived longer, doubtlessly he would have had the ritual forms appropriate for this house discussed and settled upon. However, in the fourth month [of 1616] he passed away. . . . During the reign of Lord Hidetada [the second shogun], there was at length a declaration that the ancient ways of the military houses should be revived. I wonder if the founder did not leave posthumous instructions to this effect. Among the elders entrusted with the handling of government affairs at that time, however, there was one who objected, and so in the end this matter was not carried out. The objections to establishing ritual forms at that point in time were not totally unfounded.

In antiquity, at the beginning of his reign, Han Gaozu,[1] observing the effects of the excessively harsh laws of the Qin, sought to make everything uncomplicated and direct. The people who held office during his reign were all fierce and experienced warriors, fresh from having fought in a hundred battles. They had no idea of such a thing as the ritual of court; they became drunk and

---

1. Han Gaozu (247–195 B.C.E.) was the founder of the Han dynasty.

quarreled over whose martial exploits were greater, going so far as to draw swords and strike a pillar. Gaozu was greatly troubled by this, and following the advice of a scholar named Shusun Tong, he commanded that scholars of ritual from the state of Lu be summoned and put in charge of the matters of court. The scholars were summoned, and taking some one hundred senior officers and disciples, they made a practice stage in the field in the shape of a palace, like our cordoned-off arenas today, and there they studied ritual. In the seventh year of Han, the Changle Palace was built, and there Gaozu held audience and received tribute. From the rulers of principalities to the most lowly officials, all presented tribute in order, and there was none who did not tremble in awe and reverently correct his posture. After the ritual wine was distributed, and from the reception of tribute to the completion of the drinking of the wine, there was not a single person who failed to observe the proper ritual forms. "Today I know what the dignity of the Son of Heaven is," declared Gaozu, greatly delighted. This was the start of the majesty of Han officialdom.

Now, when Shusun Tong summoned the scholars of ritual, there were two Confucians from Lu who did not respond. "Peace has just been established in the realm," they said. "The dead have not yet been buried; the wounded are not yet healed. And yet you wish to establish the rites. To establish the rites requires the accumulation of a hundred years of virtuous rule. What your lord seeks to do does not accord with ancient practice. We will not go." Thus, the attempt during Lord Hidetada's reign to revive the ancient ceremonial of the military houses was the same in spirit as the wish of Gaozu to establish the rites of the Han dynasty, and the objection of the elder was the same as those of the two scholars from Lu. Now, in those remarks of the two scholars, it says that the rites are to be established after the accumulation of a hundred years of virtuous rule. Thus the time for the present house, taking account of the ancient ceremonial of the military houses, to settle the ritual forms appropriate for ten thousand generations to come is precisely today, a hundred years since the founding of this house!

[*Arai Hakuseki zenshū*, vol. 6, pp. 477–78; Nakai, *Shogunal Politics*, pp. 188, 293–94]

THE EVOLUTION OF JAPANESE HISTORY

In *Views on the Course of History*, Hakuseki adopted an innovative approach to show how the pattern of bifurcated sovereignty, so irregular from a Confucian perspective, had emerged over the course of Japanese history from the Heian to the Tokugawa period. In the prologue he noted, "In our country, after nine epochal changes, the government of the realm was assumed by members of the warrior class; in the age of warrior rule, there were five further epochal changes leading to the rule of the present house." These two eras did not constitute two chronologically distinct blocks of time. Rather, the final three epochs of court rule and the first two of warrior rule overlapped. In line with this conceptualization of the stages of the Japanese polity's evolution, Hakuseki traced in the first part of *Views on the Course of History* the nine stages in the history of imperial rule from the early Heian period to the reign of Go-Daigo in the early fourteenth century. Applying the traditional criteria of Confucian historiography, he showed how the imperial line had progressively disqualified itself as rulers of Japan. The lack of virtue requisite in a ruler was evident in contests over the succession and in the failure of emperors to give due care to the critical matter of designating an heir. It was laxity in this latter matter that had opened the way to the Fujiwara family's usurping imperial authority as regents, a development that over time weakened the position of the court as a whole. The decline in court rule culminated in the division between two rival courts at the time of Go-Daigo. As Hakuseki interpreted it, Go-Daigo's reign marked the irrevocable loss by the imperial line of Heaven's mandate.

In the second part of *Views on the Course of History*, Hakuseki turned to the way in which warrior rule had evolved within the framework of the decline in imperial competence. He noted that just as the emperors had not paid proper attention to the choice of an heir, they also had neglected military affairs. They had delegated campaigns of pacification to others, and instead of reintegrating meritorious generals into the civil officialdom upon completion of the campaigns, the emperors had treated them as specialized military officials and distinguished them from civil officeholders. This development had led to the rise of the warrior class and, with it, the movement toward the division of civil and military authority that contradicted the way of the true king:

> As kingly virtue slackened and favorite ministers came to monopolize power, little importance was placed on the appointment of generals. No military figures obtained high civil office, and both civil and military posts became hereditary in nature. As a consequence, the court's authority declined daily; meritorious vassals [i.e., warriors] came to oversee military prerogatives; the tide of the times underwent a fundamental change; and things became such as to make impossible a return to the ways of antiquity.

The court's formal recognition of the prerogatives of the Kamakura *bakufu*, which marked the first epoch of warrior rule, was a fateful step. During the Kamakura period, the court's authority continued to diminish, and the actual power of the military class continued to grow. Following the debacle of Go-Daigo's reign, there was no way for the court to recover the authority it had lost. From that point on, "the court existed only as a facade propped up by others, and the realm was completely under the rule of the military class."

Unlike in China, however, the collapse of court rule did not result in the rapid establishment of a legitimate new dynasty. Rather, until the founding of the Tokugawa *bakufu*, a succession of warrior leaders continued to help prop up the facade of court rule. In analyzing this phenomenon, a key theme of the third part of *Views on the Course of History* (which covers the three epochs of warrior rule after Go-Daigo's downfall), Hakuseki employed another key notion of Chinese Confucian political thought: the *ba*, or hegemon. The term *ba* referred historically to the succession of feudal lords of the late Zhou who sought to establish themselves as supreme over their peers by championing the cause of the increasingly powerless Zhou king and by carrying out, with the king's nominal sanction, certain of his functions as ruler. As Hakuseki put it, "Since *ba* means 'chief,' it refers to one who, becoming chief of the feudal lords, raises up the Son of Heaven and issues orders [in his name]." The *ba* did not try to replace the ruler, but by effectively absorbing what remained of the substance of the ruler's authority, they both contributed to the further decline of kingly government and made themselves liable to the charge of usurpation. In Hakuseki's view, this was exactly what had happened under warrior leaders from Yoritomo down through Hideyoshi. Depicting them as a series of variations of *ba*, he in effect rejected previous warrior regimes as a viable model for the Tokugawa house and implicitly tried to justify his alternative vision of the shogun as a true Confucian king.

Following an established tradition of Confucian historiography, in *Views on the Course of History* Hakuseki presents many of the main points of his argument in the form of short appraisals of major political figures. The following selections illustrate his use of this technique.

VIEWS ON THE COURSE OF HISTORY
(*TOKUSHI YORON*)

Tenmu as Usurper

Hakuseki held that the first contest over the imperial succession took place in 672, when the future emperor Tenmu raised an army against his deceased brother Tenji's legitimate heir, Prince Ōtomo. As Hakuseki described the situation, despite Tenmu's apparent triumph, the fate of his descendants clearly reflected Heaven's disapproval of his usurpation.

While Tenmu succeeded for the moment in defeating the imperial forces and claiming the realm, only seven reigns and a hundredsome years later, his line terminated with his great-great-grandchild, the female ruler Shōtoku [r. 749–758, 764–770]. The grandchild of Tenji, Kōnin [r. 770–781], succeeded to the throne, and his line has continued to the present. One must say that it is clear that Heaven joins with those who uphold the Way. This was the beginning of the rivalry for the throne between two rulers that marked later ages; clearly, kingly virtue had already slackened, and social customs had begun their decline.

Go-Daigo as Loser of Heaven's Mandate

In his summation of Go-Daigo's reign, Hakuseki painted the emperor in the classic colors of the last ruler of a dynasty, fated as a result of his own lack of virtue to lose Heaven's trust.

Even in the best of times, is not restoration a more difficult enterprise than founding? Founding is like building a house anew. Even if the construction is not that great, once accomplished, the house will stand for hundreds of years. But to try to restore to its former state a great mansion that has started to collapse is a major task. . . . That, after the Fujiwara regents began to use their power as they pleased and the rites of the court declined, Emperor Go-Sanjō [r. 1068–1072] was able readily to restore things to what they had been in the past, was because the degree of decline was not yet that great. It was like a house repaired when the damage to it is yet small.

After Yoritomo had divided the powers of the realm and Hōjō rule had continued for nine generations, the warriors of the sixtysome provinces had grown used to exerting power and having their way. How could they be expected now to bow and plead before those without any merit? To attempt to restore things to what they had been in the days before the court's decline, as if such a task required no particular effort, was like propping up the walls and adding embellishments to a building whose foundation is crumbling. Certain collapse was only a matter of days. And when the people had not yet been relieved of the burden on their shoulders, to seek to build a palace and to award grants of land first to palace attendants, female servants, actors, and priests, allotting nothing to those with military merit, or else soon retracting what rewards were given—this was to invite revolt.

Again, at a time like this, it is essential to handle rewards and punishments equitably. Unless one deals properly with such matters, one can evoke neither feelings of gratitude nor awe. But in dealing with those of great merit, let alone those whose accomplishments were slight, the emperor failed completely to make rewards appropriate to the accomplishments of those concerned.

Minamoto no Yoritomo and the Tradition of the *ba*

In Hakuseki's eyes, Yoritomo was one of the main figures responsible for setting the evolution of military rule in Japan along the path of the *ba*. He began his appraisal of Yoritomo by comparing Kitabatake Chikafusa's praise of Yoritomo for having maintained order and stability in an age of chaos[2] with Confucius's admission that Guan Zhong, a key adviser to the *ba* of ancient China, "might be termed benevolent."

---

2. See de Bary et al., eds., *Sources of Japanese Tradition*, 2nd ed., vol. 1, chap. 11.

Like Guan Zhong, Yoritomo had demonstrated a political competence that temporarily improved the unstable conditions of his day. But seen in its entire context, his
actions were far from praiseworthy.

When Yoritomo first raised an army, he did not do so out of a desire to uphold
the ruler and succor the people. Coming at a time when the evils brought
about by the Taira were rampant and when the powerful houses of the realm
were quarreling among themselves, one talented and fleet got his deer. In the
years from the time Yoritomo first raised his forces until the campaign against
Yoshinaka,[3] there is no evidence of his having taken a single warrior west to
chastise evildoers and uphold the ruler. Moreover, under broad Heaven to the
far reaches of the nation, who is not the subject of the ruler? Where is the land
that is not the ruler's? The people whom Yoritomo destroyed, the land that he
claimed for his own, whose subjects were these? Whose land? . . . His army
may have appeared righteous, and it may have seemed that it was for that reason
that he readily accomplished his task. But had the Taira succeeded, as they
plotted, in taking Retired Emperor Go-Shirakawa with them when they fled
the capital, or had Yoshinaka succeeded, as he plotted, in taking the retired
emperor with him to the western regions when fighting broke out between him
and Yoritomo, then under what name would Yoritomo's army have attacked
Yoshinaka; under what pretext would he have put down the Taira? That Go-
Shirakawa managed to stay in the capital and that the Taira left the fourth prince
[the later Go-Toba] in the capital was none other than the doing of Heaven, an
indication that the imperial lineage was not to be extinguished. Claiming [the
destruction of Yoshinaka and the Taira] as his own merit, however, Yoritomo used
these acts as an excuse for pressuring and controlling the court. Should it not be
said that in truth he was stealing the accomplishments of Heaven? . . .

Having succeeded in rallying a band of defeated fighters, Yoritomo gained
the trust of the warriors and people of the eastern provinces. With his military
triumphs, the realm ultimately submitted to his martial accomplishments. This
was not owing solely to the legacy of the merit of his ancestors. He himself had
heroic qualities, and he was able to get capable people to assist him. . . . But
as a person, he was extremely cruel and suspicious. Intending to secure the
benefit of his own house and descendants, he destroyed his brothers and their
families. Instead he allied himself with his wife's family [the Hōjō] and left his
young sons in their charge, only to have their actions result in the termination
of his line. It is said that Heaven never errs in its retribution, but this is something that Yoritomo brought about himself.

---

3. A cousin of Yoritomo, Yoshinaka took part in the campaign against the Taira and drove
them out of Kyoto. Displeased with Yoshinaka's acting too independently, in 1184 Yoritomo dispatched his younger brother Yoshitsune to drive Yoshinaka in turn from the capital.

Ashikaga Takauji: Military Rule After the Collapse of the Court

Hakuseki portrayed Ashikaga Takauji, the founder of the second *bakufu*, as an opportunistic figure whose lack of personal virtue made it impossible for him to establish his government on a stable footing. The degree of success he did enjoy, however, was further evidence of the bankruptcy of court rule.

Takauji established his house by casting aside the ties of his family [to the Kamakura *bakufu*] of many generations' standing and going over to the side of the emperor. Shortly thereafter he turned against the emperor and brought the realm to turmoil. The emperor had rewarded his small merit far beyond its due. However, having raised his army with his own interests rather than those of the emperor in mind, Takauji no doubt always had planned to turn against the emperor in the end. . . . From the time he first raised his forces in battle, for twenty-six years there was not a day without fighting. In the end, he was unable to pacify the realm, and the fighting between lord and vassal, father and son, brother and brother, was without parallel, past and present. It all resulted from the fact that lacking rectitude himself, he was unable to rectify others. That nevertheless Takauji was able to become leader of the military houses was because both warriors and the populace knew that government under the court was far inferior to what had existed during the period of warrior rule [under the Kamakura *bakufu*]. Thus everyone, no matter who, throughout the realm longed to take as ruler whoever could revive the age of warrior rule. Takauji opportunely having become an enemy of the court, [they followed him], for although they disliked the name [of traitor], they longed for the substance of what Takauji represented.

Ashikaga Yoshimitsu

Among previous warrior rulers, the third Ashikaga shogun, Yoshimitsu, presented a special challenge to Hakuseki's skills in historical analysis, for he had come the closest to trying to make the shogun into a more monarchal figure. In trying to justify his own recommendations, Hakuseki sometimes alluded to the third shogun as a positive precedent, but in *Views on the Course of History* he criticized the ambiguities of Yoshimitsu's position relative to the court. In particular, he condemned Yoshimitsu for having tried to stay within the shell of the authority of the court even while he in fact, in the manner of a *ba*, dominated it.

In antiquity, Confucius said, "If names be not correct, language is not in accordance with the truth of things. If language be not in accordance with the truth of things, affairs cannot be carried on to success. . . ." Now, the term "minister" refers to a subject who serves the ruler in an official capacity. When one holds an office, there necessarily are functions specific to it. . . . Since the court had already fallen into decline, and the military houses, governing the realm, had set up the emperor as the ruler, although [Yoshimitsu] called himself by the name of subject, what he was in substance differed from that name. If, receiving the office of minister to the king, one does not undertake to carry out the affairs of the king, how can he expect true submission from those whom he in turn commands to carry out his affairs?

Further, the office [Yoshimitsu] held was that of minister to the king; the offices his vassals held were also those of minister to the king. When both lord and vassal hold the post of minister to the king, in substance they may be lord and vassal, but in name they are both ministers of the king. In such a situation, how can the vassal in fact revere his lord? The unending succession of rebellious vassals during Yoshimitsu's reign may be attributed to his lack of virtue, but it also had its source in the lack of true reverence for the lord. Moreover, while assuming the status of a subject, Yoshimitsu summoned ministers of the court to serve him, calling them attendants or retainers of his house; how could he escape the condemnation of the ages for such an act of overt usurpation? Since the age had already changed, he should have established the rites for his reign in accordance with those changes. This is the principle of according with change. Had he not been unlearned and unlettered, at that time he could have investigated the practices of the Minamoto house and of our country, old and new, and established his title, making it one rank below the emperor and clarifying that apart from the ministers of various ranks serving the court, the entire populace of the sixtysome provinces were his subjects. Had he done so, his efforts would be of use even in this age today.

Toyotomi Hideyoshi

In his critique of Hideyoshi, Hakuseki noted that Hideyoshi had sought the old court office of regent to the emperor and had issued orders to various daimyo as if commanded by the emperor.

As for one who had the intention to become a true *ba* and who succeeded in the work of a *ba*—may Hideyoshi be counted as such? This person followed the policies of Nobunaga in everything he did, but perhaps because he was impatient to achieve his aim, unlike Nobunaga he did not bother to exterminate the established daimyo and lesser lords. Instead he awarded their existing lands to those who submitted to his military power. The only house he destroyed was the Hōjō of Sagami. Thus he soon was able to show evidence of the achievement of his aim. The missives he sent to the Shimazu and the Hōjō all purported to express the will of the emperor. This was indeed an instance of raising up the Son of Heaven and issuing edicts in his name. However, at that time who knew anything of respect for an edict from the Son of Heaven? Thus neither the Shimazu nor the Hōjō responded to those purported commands. It was like putting on the mask of a demon to frighten a child. When one thinks about it today, it was most ridiculous.

[Nakai, *Shogunal Politics*, pp. 255–57, 262–64, 279–81, 283–86, 302]

HAKUSEKI'S VIEW OF CHRISTIANITY AND THE WEST

Among the most dramatic events of Hakuseki's career was his meeting with the Italian priest Giovanni Battista Sidotti, who in 1708 tried to enter Japan to reinaugurate the proselytizing of Christianity. Sidotti was quickly discovered and eventually taken to Edo, where Hakuseki interviewed him on several occasions. Hakuseki subsequently also met a number of times with representatives of the Dutch East Asia Company when they visited Edo. Through his interviews with Sidotti and the Dutch and his readings of a range of works in Chinese about the West and Christianity, Hakuseki acquired a degree of knowledge about these things unmatched by anyone of his time. He recorded his findings and described his meeting with Sidotti in *Tidings of the West* (*Seiyō kibun*), written between 1715 and 1725. Because it deals with matters concerning the proscribed religion of Christianity, *Seiyō kibun* was not published until the 1880s. It seems to have circulated to some extent in manuscript form, however, and after the reopening of Japan to the West in the 1850s, it was one of the first works translated from Japanese into English.

In *Tidings of the West*, Hakuseki reported on various aspects of what he had learned about the customs and political systems of Europe (he discussed at some length the events of the War of the Spanish Succession and noted the existence of parliamentary forms of government as well as monarchies). He also provided a summation of Christian doctrine. Hakuseki's evaluation of Christianity had two distinct sides. On the one hand, he argued that those who, like Sidotti, sought to spread Christian teachings to other countries did not have aggressive designs on those countries. He further expressed admiration for Sidotti's knowledge of science and mathematics. These aspects of Hakuseki's analysis of the West are held to have paved the way for the more open attitude toward the study of Western scientific learning that began under the next shogun, Yoshimune. But, on the other hand, Hakuseki's appreciation of Western science did not extend to religion. Appraising Sidotti's knowledge from the perspective of Confucian rationalism, he noted that when the Italian priest began to speak of religion, "it was as if stupidity had taken the place of intelligence, and as if I were listening to the words of a completely different person. I thereupon realized that while the learning [of the West] may be advanced in regard to forms and objects, it pertains only to the so-called physical realm and has nothing to do with the higher realm of principle and moral knowledge." And while he did not see any immediate danger of an invasion by Christian countries, Hakuseki remained convinced that to allow Christian missionaries to resume their activities would have socially and politically subversive consequences. Reflecting his emphasis on the importance of establishing a clear overarching hierarchy, he particularly stressed the dangers that Christian doctrine posed to such a goal.

TIDINGS OF THE WEST
(SEIYŌ KIBUN)

As I see it, when [Sidotti] says that discussions of a country must not be based upon that land's small or great size, near or far distance, he has a good argument. And when he says that what corrupts a country is not its religion but its people, his words also have the ring of truth. But [the Christians] teach that Deus produced heaven and produced earth and make him out to be the Great Lord and Great Father who generated the myriad things. In other words: I have a father, but I do not love him; I have a lord, but I do not revere him. Now this is what we call impious and disloyal. Nor is that all! This Great Lord and Great Father cannot be served without exhausting all one's love and all one's reverence—is what they say. But the Book of Rites reserves the rites of serving Shangdi, the Lord on High, to the emperor, the Son of Heaven; no such prerogative of worshiping Heaven is given the various princes or those ranking below. And that is in order to prevent the disturbance of the distinction between the exalted and the base. Rather, the sovereign is Heaven to the subject; the father is Heaven to the child; the husband is Heaven to the wife. And therefore, he who serves his sovereign with loyalty thereby serves Heaven. He who serves his father with filial piety thereby serves Heaven. She who serves her husband with propriety thereby serves Heaven. Outside the constancy of these Three Bonds, there is no way of serving Heaven. If I have a Great Lord to serve beyond my lord and a Great Father to serve beyond my father, and if this [Great Lord and Father] is sacred beyond my lord and my father, then not only are there two sacred personages in the house and two lords in the land, but the highest duty must be to set at naught the lord and set at naught the father. Even if they do not go as far as teaching to set the father and the lord at naught, still the atrocious nature ingrained in their doctrine is of such enormity that even at the point of regicide or parricide they must not look back and, in the end, think nothing of it.

[Arai Hakuseki, *Seiyō kibun*, pp. 16, 79; Elison, *Deus Destroyed*, p. 241]

HAKUSEKI'S APPROACH
TO FISCAL POLICY AND TRADE

As an adviser to Ienobu and Manabe Akifusa, Hakuseki also gave extensive attention to *bakufu* fiscal policy. By the late seventeenth century, the *bakufu* faced a financial crisis. The combination of general economic growth and a marked decline in the yield of domestic gold and silver mines had led to a shortage of currency. The *bakufu*'s expenditures were also outpacing income. To solve these problems, *bakufu* officials resorted to successive debasements of the currency, but they led to rampant inflation. Hakuseki was highly critical of the debasements and argued vigorously for restoring the original metallic value of the currency (among other things, in an early recognition of Gresham's law that bad currency will drive good from the market, he pointed out that the lack of popular confidence in the debased coins had resulted in people's hoarding the older, more metallically pure coins). In line with standard Confucian economic thought, Hakuseki also called for reducing expenditures rather than increasing income.

Hakuseki took a similarly conservative position regarding the foreign trade conducted in Nagasaki by Chinese and Dutch merchants. Because this trade largely involved the importation of foreign goods (particularly Chinese silk, books, and medicine) in exchange for Japanese precious metals, it had a direct bearing on the currency problem. From the 1680s on, *bakufu* officials tried to limit the outflow of precious metals by limiting the amount of foreign goods that could be imported each year, but various loopholes in the regulation of trade had allowed extensive smuggling outside the officially set quotas. Hakuseki was highly critical of this situation. Among the types of wealth that could be extracted from the soil, he noted, the five grains and the raw materials used for cloth were like the blood, flesh, and hair of the human body. Even if used excessively, they could be replenished. But gold and silver were the "bones of the earth," and "once removed, they will not grow again." To stop the loss of the "bones" of the country, Hakuseki argued for more comprehensive regulatory measures, including the adoption of a tally system like that employed by the Chinese Ming dynasty to control more effectively the number of foreign ships allowed to enter *bakufu* ports. He also advocated trying to reduce the country's dependence on imports of foreign goods and instead to increase the domestic production of items like silk. In the following passage from his autobiography, *Musings by a Brushwood Fire* (*Oritaku shiba no ki*), Hakuseki reviews developments in trade policy up to his time.

MUSINGS BY A BRUSHWOOD FIRE
(ORITAKU SHIBA NO KI)

During the spring of this year, in the second month, the opinions of the port commissioner and other local officials of Nagasaki were sought regarding the shortage of copper coins for foreign trade. As there was nothing worthy of official adoption in the written reports they submitted, I was assigned to write out and submit a set of revised regulations along the lines suggested during the rule of the former shogun [Ienobu (d. 1712)]. These regulations that I drafted contained 211 articles in some eight fascicles. . . .

I will not go into events that occurred before the present dynasty of shoguns. For some time after 1601, foreign ships coming here to trade were not regulated.

This was at a time when Ming China maintained strict prohibitions against overseas trade, especially during the Wan-li era [1573–1620]. Thus, Chinese ships were not seen here, as they are now. Only Western ships cast their anchor at Nagasaki. . . . During these days the number of foreign ships coming here or the volume of trade permitted was not restricted.

In 1685 the first regulation was enacted, limiting trade with the Chinese to six thousand *kan*[4] in silver and with the Dutch to fifty thousand *ryō*[5] in gold. Then in 1688 the number of Chinese ships permitted to trade was set at seventy. This was because the number of Chinese ships arriving annually in Japan had reached two hundred, following the lifting of trade restrictions in China during the reign of the Kangxi emperor. After 1695 a system was established of using copper, in addition to silver, as a medium of exchange. As a consequence, from 1698 onward ten more Chinese ships were allowed to come to Japan each year, increasing the number of Chinese ships to eighty and the volume of Chinese trade by two thousand *kan* in copper in addition to the amount permitted in silver. Because the number of Chinese ships permitted to trade was fixed, all ships over the fixed number were called "cargoes to be sent home" and were not allowed to trade. Moreover, in accordance with the regulations limiting trade, even ships within the specified number were permitted to trade only to the extent of 160 *kan* per ship, and any cargo beyond that amount was termed "leftover goods." Since those who had come, traveling a great distance and braving many dangers, had no desire to return empty-handed, without selling the large quantity of goods they had brought, they tried to dispose of their merchandise in any manner they could, even at the risk of violating the law. Our merchants, too, tried to buy in any manner possible the "cargoes to be sent home," for buying legal cargo entailed paying high commissions and incurring heavy expenses and consequently low profits. Thus, the volume of illicit trade rose each year.[6]

During the rule of the previous shogun, the Port Commissioner's Office in Nagasaki was ordered to find out the volume of gold, silver, and copper that flowed out from Nagasaki in exchange for foreign goods. It reported that the records for the forty-six years from 1601 to 1647 are not clear. In the sixty years that followed—from 1648 to 1708—2,397,600 *ryō* of gold and 374,229 *kan* of silver left the country. For copper the figures are not clear for the sixty-one years before 1662, but in the forty-four years from 1663 to 1707, the total reached 1,114,498,700 catties (*kin*). These figures, which come from the records of the Nagasaki port commissioner, represent only the trade of Nagasaki and only the outflow from 1648 on. But trade was not limited to Nagasaki. As I wrote above, in earlier years foreign ships came to trade at various ports in our country, and

---

4. One *kan* of silver was about 8.25 pounds.

5. At this time, the *ryō* was roughly equal to a half-ounce.

6. This trade and illegal cargo were known variously as "outside trade," "trading through brokers," "chance goods," and "chance trading."

ships from here went overseas to trade at various places. Apart from that, there is Tsushima's trade with Korea and Satsuma's with the Ryūkyū Islands. It thus is impossible to make a comprehensive estimate of the total amount of the gold, silver, and copper that has left the country.

On the basis of reports submitted by the Nagasaki commissioner, if a rough estimate of the volume of gold and silver lost to foreign countries for the 107 years since the Keichō era [1596–1615] is compared with the amount of gold and silver coined in our country for the same period, we must conclude that one-fourth of the gold and three-fourths of the silver have been lost.[7] At this rate, half the gold remaining will be lost in another hundred years, and the silver left for use in our country will be completely lost before another century has passed. As for copper, there is a shortage not only in meeting the present needs of foreign trade but also in meeting our country's annual expenditures. The treasures of permanent value produced in our country are being diverted to pay for curios of momentary value that come from afar. Indeed, such transactions for commercial profit work against our national interest and prestige. If payment abroad is necessary for the purchase of medicines and books, we should estimate the current need for them in our country and the annual amount of domestic production in the various provinces. On that basis, we can fix a limit on the annual payment for such products [coming] through Nagasaki, Tsushima, and Satsuma. Merely limiting the annual volume of gold, silver, and copper to be used for foreign trade at Nagasaki without taking further measures is meaningless. Even if limits are set, private illicit trade will continue unchecked unless the number of ships and the cargo of each ship also are regulated. Therefore, I suggest estimating the annual production of gold, silver, and copper in our country relative to the volume of their flow into foreign countries [and] fixing the annual limit on their use for foreign trade accordingly. Similarly, we should estimate the amount of cargo carried here by foreign ships and fix a limit for both the numbers of ships allowed to come and the amount of cargo they may carry. If the permitted volume of cargo is purchased [through regulated channels] in its entirety, we shall no longer lose our national treasures in illicit trade, nor will foreigners continue to defy our country's laws. Our national prestige will prevail far and wide, and our national wealth will prove adequate for all time.

[Arai Hakuseki, *Oritaku shiba no ki*, in *NKBT*, vol. 95, pp. 391–93; KN]

TOMINAGA NAKAMOTO'S HISTORICAL RELATIVISM

Osaka, where Tominaga Nakamoto (1715–1746) was born, had something of a reputation for independence and individual initiative. It was there, at the end

---

7. Although often cited, Hakuseki's estimates of the total outflow of precious metals have been strongly questioned.

of the Middle Ages, that a militant Buddhist organization had asserted its independence by resisting the attacks of Nobunaga for nearly a decade. Subsequently, Osaka had been proud to serve as headquarters for the ambitious Hideyoshi in his heyday of power; and even after Ieyasu's triumph, it was the first city to recoup its economic fortunes, win a measure of self-rule from its Tokugawa masters, and lead in the development of a new bourgeois culture. Here Saikaku's novels were written, with sex and money as their leading themes, and here Chikamatsu's dramas, with their love triangles and suicides, filled theaters to capacity (see chap. 26). In Osaka, too, in 1726, the shogun Yoshimune saw an opportunity to start a Confucian educational center, with financial support from the town's merchants. It was from this new center that the son of one such enterprising merchant struck out on his own, against formidable opposition from many quarters, to explore the past.

Tominaga, who died at the age of thirty-one after a protracted illness aggravated by persecution and penury, did not live to write the complete history of Japan that he had in mind. Apparently much of his writing was lost as a result of the Prohibition Act of 1790, according to which it would have been classed as nonconforming and dangerous. But fortunately two of his important works, *Discourses After Emerging from Meditation* (*Shutsujō kōgo*) and *Testament of an Old Man* (*Okina no fumi*), preserve for us something of his critical historical method. Another work, now lost, *Failings of the Classical Philosophers* (*Seppei*), seems to have been a critical examination of Chinese thought in the pre-Qin period. That it was an outspoken and provocative piece is certain, for it started the stone of persecution rolling over him before he was twenty. Not only did it lead to his expulsion from the Confucian school that his father had helped establish (the Kaitokudō), but it also forced the young man out of his father's home. Thereafter, he is said to have earned a meager living at a Zen monastery in Uji, working as a proofreader of the newly edited *Tripitaka*. This gave him an opportunity to test his historical method and textual criticism in the field of Buddhism. *Emerging from Meditation* was a result.

At that time, thirteen Buddhist sects with sixty-three subdivisions were established throughout the nation, and Tominaga's historical analysis left none of them unscathed, causing a great furor. "The rise of the sects and denominations is due to everybody's striving for 'advancement,'" he wrote in the second chapter of *Emerging from Meditation*.

> It is an effort to promote a certain teaching by making an additional contribution of one's own, without which religion would never spread. In the past as in the present, it is the nature of religion to develop in this way. Students of later times, however, consider that all religions were the same originally as they are found to be in later transmission, unaware that a great many innovations and reforms have taken place.

Elsewhere (in paragraph 9 of the *Testament*), Tominaga says that in all historical religions, the followers appeal to the founder's authority by seeking to rise above or push beyond those who preceded them. That is the rule and not the exception, and it is the reason why, in the study of religion, historical criticism is indispensable. It is not difficult to see in this the logical extension to other schools of thought of the critical method that Ogyū Sorai had advocated for the study of Confucianism.

As criteria for textual criticism, Tominaga specified three "things" and five "categories." "My method of study emphasizes three things by which all human discourse can be properly understood," he wrote. "As long as one's approach is made through these three things, there is no discourse that defies clear understanding." First, discourse has man behind it, and just as one man or one group of men differs from another, so does discourse. Tominaga illustrates this by showing how the terminology used in the various Buddhist scriptures reflects the difference in various authors' language and outlook and shows that they do not derive from one original source. Second, discourse is related to time, and just as each age has its own characteristics, so does human discourse. Third, discourse falls into different "categories." Although Tominaga did not fully explain these types or categories, they seem to have referred to the ways in which different teachings or truths were further developed or modified by others. First, there was assertion or expansion; second, generalization; third, collision or contradiction; fourth, revision or inversion; and fifth, transformation or modification.

The terms that Tominaga used to represent these terms or categories are metaphorical and suggest the movement of water at the seashore as a wave swells up and rolls forward, spreads out, breaks against the shore, washes back, and then turns away. The examples he gives, however, are drawn from Buddhist teaching, and their exact significance is not always clear. First, when a Buddhist says that the historical personage Shakyamuni achieved Buddhahood, it is a case of assertion or expansion. Second, to say that all creatures are potential Buddhas is a case of generalization. (The original meaning of Tathagata as applied to the Buddha was "He who comes thus." As the storehouse of the mind, however, it is described in the Lankavatara Sutra as the source of good and evil, and in the Prajnaparamita Sutra, all creatures from heaven to hell are seen as embraced in the storehouse of the Tathagata.) Third, to say that the Truth-body (Dharmakaya) does not exist apart from the world of passion or, in other words, that in the storehouse of the Tathagata, the Tathagata is found amid all the passions of the sentient world, is a case of collision or, in this instance perhaps, paradox. (That is, as absolute Truth, the Tathagata transcends good and evil, but as the perfection of virtue Tathagatahood proceeds from the stilling of the passions.) Fourth, the use of the expression "to follow one's own bent" as a translation from the Sanskrit *pravarana* is a case of inversion. ("To follow one's own bent" originally had the bad connotation of lacking restraint; here it takes on the good connotation of acting spontaneously in accord with one's true nature.) Fifth, that a member of the shudra caste, originally considered to be lacking a Buddha nature, should—as a sentient creature capable of spiritual conversion—possess the seeds of Buddhahood is an example of modification or transformation (i.e., a modification or transformation of the idea of potentiality for Buddhahood as deriving from the possession of spiritual selfhood rather than from one's status among men).[8] Thus Tominaga goes on to show in detail how Buddhism evolved over time into so many different schools, sects, and denominations through individual contributions following the different possible lines of development.

In his *Testament*, Tominaga tried to synthesize his historical interpretations of the three existing religions—Shinto, Buddhism, and Confucianism—into a kind of ethical culture that he called Makoto no oshie, or "the Teaching of Genuineness." It was long preserved in a manuscript from which only a few copies were made and did not attract the attention it deserved until 1923 when Professor Naitō Konan of Kyoto Imperial University had reproductions made of it for distribution among his friends. To Dr. Anesaki Masaharu, a modern authority on the history of Japanese religion and the author of *Historical Criticism of the Buddhist Scriptures* (*Bukkyō seiten shiron*), Tominaga Nakamoto seemed like a lotus in the muck because of the critical powers and broad knowledge of cultural history that he displayed at a time when the historical sense was almost wholly lacking in the study of Buddhism.

TESTAMENT OF AN OLD MAN
(*OKINA NO FUMI*)

Having provoked great hostility from the established religions because of his unorthodox views, Tominaga Nakamoto found it prudent to represent this short work as expressing the opinions of an anonymous old man rather than himself. It nevertheless provides a convenient summary of his own philosophy and his critique of established teachings.

This writing is the work of a certain Old Man and was lent to me by a friend. Even though this is a degenerate age, the author appears to be a wise old man. Departing from the Three Teachings of Buddhism, Confucianism, and Shinto, he advocates what he calls the Way of genuineness (*makoto*). Truly, it seemed to me that if one conducted oneself in accordance with what the Old Man said, one would make no mistakes in life. And having thus subscribed to his teaching, I asked my friend what the Old Man's name was, only to be told that he did not know and there was no way of finding out. The Old Man must have been like those personages in ancient times who chose to live in obscurity so that they might be free to say what they thought. Wishing to preserve this as my

---

8. As reconstructed from *Shutsujō kōgo*, sec. 11, in NST, vol. 43; Ishihama, *Tominaga Nakamoto*, pp. 96–107.

own family teaching and also to pass it on to others, I have copied it all down from beginning to end.

Genbun 3 [1738]: 11th month, Ban no Nakamoto

I. In the world today there are three religions: Buddhism, Confucianism, and Shinto. Some think they represent the three different countries—India, China, and Japan—while others consider them essentially one or else dispute with one another over the truth or falsity of each. However, the way that may be called the Way of all ways is different from these, and what each of these Three Teachings calls the Way is not in accord with the Way of genuineness. The reason is that Buddhism is the Way of India, and Confucianism is the Way of China. Because they are peculiar to these countries, they are not the Way of Japan. Shinto is the Way of Japan, but because of the difference in time, it is not the Way for the present generation. Some may think that the Way is always the Way despite differences in nationality and differences in time; but the Way is called the Way because of its practicality, and a Way that is not practical is not the Way of genuineness. Thus, the Way as taught by these three teachings is not a Way practicable in present-day Japan.

Deleted here are four sections dealing with the Indian character of Buddhist practices and their unsuitability to Japan; similarly with regard to the Chinese practices prescribed for Confucians; and ancient practices associated with Shinto, which are impractical in the present day—as are all the traditional practices of the Three Teachings.

VI. What is the Way of genuineness, then, that will be practicable in present-day Japan? It is simply this: Be reasonable in everything you do. Consider today's work of primary importance. Keep your mind upright. Comport yourself properly. Be careful in speech. Be respectful in manner and bearing. Care for and honor your parents.

(A note by the Old Man refers to the [Buddhist sutra] Rokkōhai-kyō, in which the Five Human Relationships are specially dealt with. Confucians also consider these relationships important, and the Shinto regulations likewise mention these five things. Therefore just as these three are indispensable to the Three Teachings, so are they to the Way of genuineness.)

If you have a master, serve him well. If you have children, educate them well. If you have an elder brother, show him every respect; if you have a younger brother, show him every sympathy. Toward old people, be thoughtful; toward young people, be loving. Do not forget your ancestors. Be mindful of preserving harmony in your household. When associating with others, be completely sincere. Do not indulge in evil pleasures. Revere those who are superior while not despising the dim-witted. What you would not have done to yourself, do not do to others. Do not be harsh; do not be rash. Do not be obstinate or stubborn. Do not be demanding or impatient. Even when you are angry, do not go too far. When you are happy, be so within bounds. You may take pleasure in life, but do not indulge in sensuality. Do not lose yourself in sorrow; whether or not you have enough, accept your lot as good fortune and be content with it. Things that you should not take, even if they seem insignificant, do not take; when you should give, do not hesitate to do so, even if it means giving up everything, even [rulership of] the state and empire. As for the quality of your food and clothing, let it conform to your station in life, and avoid extravagance. Do not be stingy; do not steal; do not lie. Do not lose yourself in lust; be temperate in drinking. Do not kill anything that does not harm mankind. Be careful in the nourishment of your body; do not eat bad things; do not eat too much.

(A note by the Old man says: in the [Buddhist] Yoga Shastra, cases of untimely death are listed under nine types as [1] too much eating, [2] untimely eating, [3] eating again before food has digested, and so forth. The *Analects*, too, say that one should not eat in the wrong proportions or at the wrong time or in excessive amounts. They all have insight into the Way of genuineness.)

In your free time, study the arts of self-improvement; try to be better informed.

(A note by the Old man says: The *Analects* has it that when one has energy to spare, one should study the polite arts. The [Buddhist] Discipline [Vinaya] also says that to understand order and gradation, you should study history. Also, the young *bhikshus* [acolytes] are permitted to study arithmetic. These, too, are in accord with the Way of genuineness.)

To write with present-day script, to use present-day vernacular, to eat present-day food, to dress in present-day clothes, to use present-day utensils, to live in present-day houses, to follow present-day regulations, to mix with present-day people, to do nothing bad, to do all good things—that is the Way of genuineness. That is the Way that is practicable in present-day Japan.

(All these things are mentioned in Confucian and Buddhist writings and do not need to be made a special point of. But the Old Man is presenting these ideas as if they were something new of his own, so as to persuade people to discard all that is useless and go straight to the Way of genuineness. His aim is truly praiseworthy.) . . .

VIII. That it is difficult to invent any system of teaching that can do without the Way of genuineness can be surmised from the fact that Buddha preached the Five Commandments and Ten Virtues; called greed, anger, and folly the Three Poisons; and declared filial piety to parents and loyal service to teachers to be one of the Three Blessings. "Not to do anything bad but to do everything good and keep one's motive pure is the essence of all the Buddha's teaching," it is said.

Confucius also talked about filial piety, brotherliness, loyalty, and tolerance. He taught fidelity and reverent devotion. Wisdom, Humaneness, and Valor he called the Three Cardinal Virtues. Restraint of anger, stifling of passion, correction of mistakes, and conversion to goodness also were emphasized. "The

superior man is always poised for action, while the inferior man is ill at ease,"
he said.[9]

Shinto people also taught purity, simplicity, and honesty.

These all are in accord with the Way of genuineness, well expressed and to
the point, each resembling the other. As long as the followers of the Three
Teachings abide by their respective beliefs, without bias or prejudice, not giving
themselves over to the strange and exotic, but living in the society of men to
the end of their lives—then they also are following the Way of genuineness.

(In the foregoing the Old Man has expressed his main ideas. He does not
mean to discard the Three Teachings in their entirety. He simply wants everyone to act on the Way of genuineness.)

At this point, however, the Old Man has his own theory. Generally speaking,
it has been the rule that all those who have started teaching what they call the
Way as handed down from ancient times have inevitably appealed to the authority of a founder while at the same time trying to go further than any predecessor has gone. Posterity, however, has been ignorant of this fact, and it has
resulted in great confusion.

*Tominaga proceeds to explain how the teaching of the Buddha and the various schools
of Buddhism successively appealed to some earlier authority while at the same time either
reacting against or attempting to surpass their immediate predecessors. Instead of representing a pure and untouched revelation from the past, these teachings were actually
the product of a considerable development in human hands. The same pattern of evolution is indicated for the Confucian tradition. Finally he takes up Shinto.*

XII. As for Shinto, it is what certain medieval Japanese dressed up as ancient
traditions of the Divine Ages and called the Way of Japan in an attempt to outdo
Confucianism and Buddhism. In the time of Abhasvara in India, for instance,
or of Ban Gu in China,[10] there were no definite teachings like Buddhism and
Confucianism. What later came to be known as Buddhism and Confucianism
were wholly purposeful and conscious creations of men in later times. In exactly
the same way, there could be no such thing as Shinto in the Divine Ages. The
first Shinto taught was the syncretism known as Dual Shinto, which was a
combination of Confucianism and Buddhism arbitrarily put together to suit the
occasion. Then followed the Shinto called Honjaku engi, which regarded
Shinto deities as Japanese manifestations of Indian gods and buddhas. This was
an attempt by Buddhists envious of the rise in popularity of Shinto, who taught
Shinto outwardly but inwardly wanted to capture it for Buddhism. Then came
another form of Shinto known as Yui-itsu sōgen [the One and Only Original

---

9. *Analects* 7:36.
10. The first beings to appear in these countries.

Source]. It was an attempt to separate from Confucianism and Buddhism and to claim Shinto as pure and unique. All three of these appeared in medieval times.[11] A new type of Shinto that has recently appeared is known as Ōdō Shinto, the Shinto of the sovereign way. It teaches that Shinto has no particular way of its own and that the Way of the sovereign is the Way of the Gods. There is also a form of Shinto that professes Shinto outwardly but inwardly identifies it with Confucianism.[12] None of these things existed in divine antiquity; they have simply arisen from the struggle of each one to get ahead of the other. But not realizing this, ignorant people of the world believe one of these to be the true Way, identify themselves as partisans of this teaching or that, and start violent controversies. It is at once pitiful and ridiculous to this Old Man's way of thinking.

XIV. The distinguishing feature of Buddhism is magic, which today [in Japan] is known as *izuna*. India has a love of magic, and when those who wish to propagate a teaching mix it with magic, people there accept it without question. . . . Many of the sutras speak of supernatural transformations, supernatural breakthroughs, supernatural powers, and the like. . . . This is the way people are led on in India, but it is not anything needed in Japan.

XV. The distinguishing feature of Confucianism is rhetoric [literate discourse]. Rhetoric is what we call eloquence. China is a country that greatly delights in this. In the teaching of the Way and in the education of men, if a man lacks proficiency in speech, he will find no one to believe in or follow him. For example, take the word "rites" (*ri*). It simply signified the ceremonies on the four great occasions in life: coming of age, marriage, mourning, and religious festivals. But as you know, they talk now about what the rite of a man as the son to his father is, what the rite of a man as the subject to his sovereign is; they speak of it in connection with human relationships, they speak of it in regard to seeing, hearing, speaking, and acting. They also assert that rites owe their inception to the division of heaven and earth and embrace the whole universe. Take again the character for "sage," which originally signified a man of wisdom. They have gradually stretched it to the point that a sage is the highest type of humanity, even capable of working miracles. Thus we know when Confucius talked about humaneness, Zengzi about humaneness and rightness, Zisi about sincerity, Mencius about the Four Beginnings and the goodness of human nature, Xunzi about the badness of human nature, the *Book of Filial Piety* of filial piety, and the Great Learning about [what the superior man] loves and hates, the *Book of Changes* about Heaven and earth—that all of these were just ways of presenting the plainest and simplest things in life with a

---

11. Concerning the foregoing types of Shinto, see de Bary et al., eds., *Sources of Japanese Tradition*, 2nd ed., vol. 1, chap. 15.

12. Reference to Yamazaki Ansai, *Suika Shintō*.

rhetorical flourish in order to arouse interest and make people follow them. Chinese rhetoric is like Indian magic, and neither of them is particularly needed in Japan.

XVI. The distinguishing feature of Shinto is secrecy (mystery), divine secrets, secret and private transmission, such that everything is kept under the veil of secrecy. Hiding things leads to lying and theft. Magic and oratory are interesting to see or to listen to—they thus have some merit. But this vice of Shinto is of the lowest sort. In olden times people were simple, and so secrecy may have served certain educational purposes, but the world today is a corrupt world in which many people are addicted to lying and stealing, and it is a deplorable thing for Shinto teachers to act in such a way to protect and preserve these evils. Even in such lowly things as farcical performances (*sarugaku*) and the tea ceremony, we find them all imitating Shinto, devising methods of secret transmission and authentication, and attaching a fixed price to the transmission of these "secrets" for selfish gain and benefit. It is truly lamentable. If you ask the reason why they devise such practices, their answer is that their students are immature and untried and must not be granted too ready an access to their teachings. It sounds plausible, but any teaching that is kept secret and difficult of access and then is imparted for a price cannot be considered in accord with the Way of genuineness.

[Tominaga Nakamoto, *Okina no fumi*, in *Nihon jurin sōsho*, vol. 6, pp. 1–14; WTdB]

DISCOURSES AFTER EMERGING FROM MEDITATION (*SHUTSUJŌ KŌGO*)

The title of this work recalls the traditional account of the Buddha's original experience of enlightenment: that it was inexpressible in words, and it was only as a concession to ordinary beings that he attempted to explain the truth in conventional language. Tominaga's title also conveys the sense that he himself left the monastic life to engage in scholarly inquiry and intellectual discourse.

Preface

When I was young and had time for it, I was able to read the texts of Confucianism, and later on, when I had time, I also read those of Buddhism. Thus I can now say that the ways of Confucianism and Buddhism are alike in that they aim to do good. But when we try to trace the meaning of the Way in detail, we find that we do not get a satisfactory explanation because there are gaps and inconsistencies in the textual record. This state of affairs gave me the idea of "Emerging from Meditation." I have had this idea in my mind for ten years, but when I have spoken to people about it, they all have been uncomprehending. As the years accrued to my age, my hair has begun to whiten. [Meanwhile] everyone has accepted the Confucian and Buddhist Ways just as they appear to be, Confucian and Buddhist, and there has seemed to be no point trying to persuade them otherwise.

Alas, I am now in a deplorable condition and painfully sick, of no use to anybody. Yet, as I am nearing my end, how can I not pass my thoughts on to someone? I am already more than thirty years old and can no longer hold back. I hope that those who take it up will tell it to many, passing it on to Korea and China, from Korea and China to the peoples west of China, and on to the land of Shakyamuni's divine descent. If it helps the people to be illumined by the Way, then my death will not be a mere putrefaction. Nevertheless, some may charge that this is a kind of "bad wisdom"—which is difficult [for me to deal with]. In regard to this, I must await [judgment by] the combined efforts and supplementary work of later scholars.

> *First year of Enkyō [1744], autumn, 8th month,*
> *Tominaga Nakamoto*

Part 1: Sequence

In this section, Tominaga cites the conflicting testimony of several canonical Buddhist works with regard to the sequential order of the Buddha's teaching.

Divisions appeared among the various teachings because they all first arose by superseding others. If it had not been for this relationship of superseding, how would the path of Dharma have been extended? This is the natural path for Dharma, whether old or new. However, scholars of later generations vainly say that all these teachings came directly from the golden mouth [of the Buddha] and were personally transmitted by those who heard him frequently. They do not realize that on the contrary, there are many gaps as well as connections. Is this not sad? . . .

From the six statements [cited], we can conclude the following: We can tell that for long after the Buddha's death there was no definitive exposition among his followers and there were no writings on which a person could depend. Everyone revised the teaching according to his own opinion and passed it on orally. Thus it is that there are endless differences in the exegesis of the scriptures, and this again is why no one can trust them. When the Zen school says, "Do not rely on the written word," perhaps this is what they mean!

The bulk of Emerging from Meditation *is an analysis of the conflicting textual evidence with regard to doctrinal issues, orthopraxis, and contingent factors in the development of Buddhism. Finally, in the conclusion of the work, Tominaga affirms that despite their contradictory sectarian claims, Buddhism and Confucianism can be seen as serving an underlying common purpose.*

Teachings may be diverse, but their main point comes back to doing good. If these teachings are sincerely and well kept and each is fervent in doing good, what need is there to choose some and criticize others ? Buddhism is all right. Confucianism is all right. If they sincerely try to do good, then they are of one school. How much more so with those who claim the religion of the Buddha as their own while differentiating it into sects! I know of none who, though vainly quarreling over differences among the sects, is not trying to do good. Letters are all right. Magic is all right. If the intention sincerely lies in doing good, then why should they not be all right? I know of none who, though they may vainly indulge in magic or letters, is not concerned with doing good.

[Tominaga Nakamoto, *Shutsujō kōgo*, in NST, vol. 43, pp. 12 [106], 19–21 [109], 105 [128]; trans. adapted from Pye, *Emerging from Meditation*, pp. 71, 81–83, 183]

MIURA BAIEN'S SEARCH FOR A NEW LOGIC

Miura Baien (1723–1789) was a philosopher before there was a word for the discipline in his language. The pen name Baien means "plum garden," from his plum orchard above the village of Nakamoto in the Kunisaki peninsula, in northeastern Kyushu. In contrast to his more itinerant scholarly contemporaries and predecessors, Baien kept to this garden as the single center of his sixty years of scholarship. No other Japanese thinker of his era could match his elaborate philosophical system, yet behind even his most abstract thoughts we find, in some guise, sunlight and shade, cold and heat, wet and dry, which govern the life of a valley where summers are hot and the sun sets early in winter.

Baien studied first at a temple school and then at the private school in Kitsuki taught by Ayabe Keisai, but learned mostly through his own reading. Like many scholars of his day, he wrote about a wide variety of topics. The school in Kitsuki fostered an interest in astronomy. Ayabe's fourth son became Edo Japan's foremost astronomer, Asada Gōryū (1734–1799), who was Baien's close friend and correspondent. Quiet Kitsuki was not isolated in those days, for foreign books from the port of Nagasaki came in overland to Kitsuki's harbor and were loaded into boats for Osaka. At sixteen, Baien had already constructed a celestial globe, and at twenty-three he made the first of two journeys to Nagasaki, to hear for himself about the latest foreign learning.

By tradition, the heads of the Miura family were landlords and physicians. Baien studied anatomy and wrote about it at great length, eventually incorporating some of that knowledge into his own philosophical system. He conscientiously applied his analytic skills to meet the needs of a village at the mercy of the floods and droughts. In 1756, a time of hardship, he wrote

Mutual Charity (*Jihi mujin*), describing a cooperative scheme that he organized among his villagers to set aside reserves for lean times. More than once he refused to take office in the Kitsuki fief, choosing to remain at home as head of his small household, landlord of the village, and, most important, teacher of a small school at his home. In a letter to Asada Gōryū, he describes waking his pupils early and climbing with them to a vantage point to watch an eclipse of the sun.

Western materials reached Baien through several removes of translation and editing, but a great deal else came through China and Korea. His scientific mind was encouraged by seventeenth-century critiques of earlier doctrines, such as the theory that the world was composed of five phases (or elements): fire, water, wood, metal, and earth; or the idea that the stuff of the universe (J. *ki*, Ch. *qi*) was simple and homogenous. Among all his scholarly interests his overriding mission was to discover and set out in writing what the universe really was. This was the motive for his *Deep Words* (*Gengo*). Such a realist attitude was common among Edo scholars. In 1730 Nishikawa Seikyū stated, "Even the words of the ancient sages are useless when they do not fit the phenomena of the earth and sky." Baien himself maintained. "Although we may come to truly understand fire, fire will continue to burn as it did before, and water will continue to flow as it did before we came to understand it. Names are indeed made by people and thus the reed of Naniwa has come to be called the reed of Ise. But we ourselves cannot alter reality."[13]

The works often referred to as "The Three Go"—*Gengo*, *Kango* (*Daring Words*), and *Zeigo* (*Superfluous Words*)—are quite dissimilar in structure and content. *Kango* was completed well before the others. *Zeigo* was a late work, more an anthology of essays and letters on such subjects as cosmology, astronomy, ancient theories, zoological classification, and anatomy. Baien revised *Gengo* at least twenty-three times in as many years, but his final draft went far beyond his earlier ones in originality and importance.

Baien was familiar with the protoscience of the old cosmologies and with the much more substantial advances made by astronomers such as Nishikawa Joken and in botany by Kaibara Ekken in *Plants of Japan* (*Yamato honzō*). In his later years, Japanese progress in science accelerated, and Baien was in touch with several scientists. Two brilliant models in particular inspired him, the astronomy of his friend Asada Gōryū and the courageous undertaking of Sugita Genpaku (1733–1787) and his friends, who, noticing that drawings in a Dutch anatomy text were at odds with the familiar Chinese ones, first established the correctness of the Dutch anatomical drawings by observing a dissection, and then translated the Dutch text against almost insuperable odds. It is as though Baien had thought that if Asada Gōryū and others could devise theories for

---

13. *Baien zenshū*, vol. 2, p. 100.

special fields of study, it might be possible to devise a theory that would reveal the order of the whole universe. *Gengo* is his attempt to do just that. From the practicing scientists, he recognized the importance of observation and objectivity, but *Gengo*'s outstanding features are its technical language and orderly system. In short, Baien set out alone to write an objective account of the universe in which each thing and phenomenon had a place. Although the Chinese classic *Yijing* was an ordered system, it was useless for organizing new scientific knowledge and empirical observation.

Baien's bold endeavor brought new problems. How could such diversity and complexity fit into a single order? How could it be expressed in a single language? *Jōri* (logic) was Baien's answer to both those questions. What Baien calls *jōri* has to do with opposition, which gives him a superficial resemblance to numerous philosophers, ancient Greeks, Chinese, European dialecticians, and others. Nevertheless, his *jōri* is unique. Baien's objectivity required that it be discovered in the universe and confirmed or corrected by observation. He began with a relatively simple principle and eventually modified it beyond recognition. He came to see that setting out a system for the whole universe was more than one man could do, but he was convinced that it was theoretically possible. He never abandoned *jōri* and persisted in fitting it to his observations and theories, in the course of which he invented an ingenious machine for generating terminology. Words from ordinary language, while always related to their meanings, are precisely defined as members of pairs of opposites.

The name of Miura Baien does not occur often in the works of his contemporaries and immediate successors, but his contribution to Tokugawa thought is beyond doubt. He corresponded and sometimes talked with several prominent scientists, especially those of the Kaitokudō, the famous academy in Ōsaka, to which he sent some of his pupils. (One of them was the grandfather of Fukuzawa Yukichi.) He learned much from these colleagues, and they received ideas and encouragement from him. For him, it was not enough just to ask questions; the more elusive the answers were, the harder one should work to find them. A Baien revival began early in the twentieth century with the publication of his complete works, and in Japan since the 1970s there has been a vigorous study of many aspects of his work.

The near oblivion into which *Gengo* fell and remained for one hundred years or so after Baien's death is attributable in part to its difficult and unconventional style. Miura Baien appreciated something about science proper, in contrast to the old protoscientific five phases (or elements) and yin-yang theories that were relatively accessible to any reader. That is, he realized that significant science was for the specialist, for much of it was not widely accessible even to the educated, and he saw his own theory as the same. He wrote to Asada Gōryū, "The more advanced my investigations [are], the less they will be accepted. But that does not matter."

"THE ORIGIN OF PRICE"
(KAGEN)

Miura Baien was not one of those scholars who despised merchants; on the contrary, he believed that each of the four classes—samurai, farmers, artisans, and merchants—should be respected for its necessary role in a balanced community. The Kaitokudō in Osaka, where some of his friends and pupils studied, was a merchant academy. In 1773, when asked his view of local problems, Baien wrote "The Origin of Price." One of its themes is managing the currency in a closed economy, discussed already by his predecessors, Ogyū Sorai and Arai Hakuseki. Other parts of the essay have the ring of a Confucian teacher. The following passage is more topical.

As the quantity of gold and silver increases, the rich accumulate greater wealth, and the poor collect greater debts. As bad money is circulated, good money disappears. . . . Thickets and deep pools do not draw fish and sparrows; hawks and otters drive them there. Likewise, the wealthy themselves do not draw in gold and silver; it is the borrowers who pay interest that drive gold and silver to the wealthy families, where it might increase five times, ten times, then a hundredfold, while the debtors have insufficient income for years to follow. Nowadays, perhaps nine out of ten wealthy people are merchants. The 10 percent who are not merchants perform no service; they are carefree itinerants who follow the merchants around. Samurai, farmers, and artisans are the poor. . . . Two or three out of every ten samurai and farmers reject their proper work for trade and commerce, and three or four out of every ten become itinerants. There is a constant drift away from farming; when farming declines, assets decline, and the foundations of the nation are weakened. . . . For example, until quite recently, many people from my own village would return from Tokyo or Osaka with their children to make their home here, where some now have grandchildren. But nowadays many who go to Tokyo or Osaka do not return.

When the supply and distribution of goods are controlled by merchants and tradesmen, common necessities such as rice, millet, silk, cotton, fish, and salt all are sent to the towns. Poor families begin the year short of food and clothing; in some years the wealthy may sell some food and cloth, but the farmers have no reserves. When commodities from all over the country converge in the cities, the surplus is stored there. If trading ceases, people in the provinces are deprived of food, and when the day comes that they can no longer sell rice, they receive no gold or silver. Surplus from the provinces goes to the big merchants in the cities. If the country people can no longer make money, they will abandon their proper business to work for gold and silver. Although the price of grain rises, the same sum buys less than before. Add to this the cost of transport, and where does that find them?

The city is the place of abundance. There the itinerant merchants gather day and night, captivating eyes and minds with patterns and colors, carvings and inlays, sounds and songs, gadgets and gimmicks. They fish the purses of good people for gold and silver, the fruits of honest labor. Thus the fishers are fished, and people have spent sweat and blood in vain. We small people, who cling to our money because we need it, might ignore all this, but it is not a reason for the nation to rejoice. When the circulation of money is looked at from the point of view of heaven and earth, it is nothing but the shifting of things from left to right, right to left. How can this be compared with the art of producing today rice, cloth, and implements that yesterday did not even exist, thus protecting us from cold, heat, and starvation?

[Miura Baien, *Baien zenshū*, vol. 1, pp. 917–20; RM]

DEEP WORDS
(GENGO)

Preface

The volumes of *Deep Words* give an account of just what I see. I have added the several hundred thousand words of *Superfluous Words* (*Zeigo*), assembling various doctrines and criticizing them according to *jōri*. *Zeigo* is superfluous in contrast to *Gengo*. Those who read *Gengo* well do not need to read *Zeigo*. Heaven and earth are there already. Because it is nothing but written words, *Gengo* itself is superfluous. Anyone skilled in observation would not need to read *Gengo*. . . . How miserable it would be always to have one's eyes fixed beyond moral principles and neglect mankind. Therefore I have added the one volume of *Daring Words* (*Kango*) to clarify moral principles and complete the task. In *Gengo* I have borrowed no words from the ancients. But in *Zeigo* and *Kango* I deal with current matters in the usual way. . . . Nevertheless, quoting ancient writings, or examining their many doctrines, is like looking cross-eyed or walking with a limp and should invite ridicule from the learned.

[*Gengo*, in *Miura Baien*, in *NST*, vol. 41, p. 383; RM]

BAIEN'S SYSTEM OF "LOGIC" (JŌRI)

From any approach, *Gengo* is a difficult work. Traditional terminology was inadequate for Baien's detailed analysis. His "logic" (*jōri*) system enabled him to create a vast lexicon of old words with new meanings. Pairs of terms are defined precisely by their opposition. By using the same word as a member of several different pairs, he could give it several definitions without confusion. The following gives a clue to what he meant by *jōri*.

If we want the word to identify the subject correctly, we must infer the meaning from the pair. That is the method of seeking *jōri*. . . . When I use "spirit," there are the kinds: heaven and spirit, essence and spirit, spirit and object, spirit and soul, phantom and spirit, spirit and man, sagacity and spirit, and so on. When I use "heaven," there are the kinds: heaven and earth, heaven and spirit, heaven and object, heaven and man, heaven and destiny, and so on. . . . If we did not rely on pairs, we might mistake the subjects. [p. 381]

On the first pages of Gengo, *the dense text suddenly breaks out into the metaphor of a brocade robe, which illuminates many distinctive features of Baien's work. The* jōri *pairs in the first lines of the following passage are "object and nature," "nature and body," "object and ki," "merging and distinctness," "whole and side," and so on. Already the words "object" and "nature" have occurred in two different pairs. By such a shift in meaning, Baien was able to make fine, precise distinctions where natural language makes none. The pair "whole and side" exemplifies Baien's theory. The two sides of the brocade are not two parts that can be separated and be put together. What we call the right side, with dragons and phoenixes, is intrinsically different from the wrong side, intertwined scarlet and green threads. Although each of these is the whole brocade, the functions of the warp and woof are not at all the functions of the dragons and phoenixes. A twentieth-century expression of this would be to say that the functions of atomic particles are not at all the functions of trees and rivers. Unifying theories are constantly sought in various fields of science, and some, like Baien, seek a unifying theory for everything that exists.*

Object has nature, and nature is endowed with object. Nature and object merge seamlessly. They are thus one whole. Nature pairs with body; object pairs with *ki*. Nature and object stand distinct; this is *jōri*. Thus they are two sides. Nature is nature alongside object; object is object alongside nature. Therefore, one is one and one; and one and one is one. *Ki* is heaven; object is earth. Nature is endowed by one, and bodies are divested from one. This endowment by one and divestment as two corresponds to the warp from the aspect of division and to the woof from the aspect of the contrast of one *ki* and one object.

As an illustration, take a piece of brocade. The raw side consists of warp threads and woof threads, scarlet threads and green threads, but on the finished side are flowers, grass, and fabulous birds. The spirit of these comes from the imagination of a clever woman. . . . One piece of brocade has a nature that is endowed with two bodies, the raw side and the finished side; the weaver's skill brings spirit to it; objects are fixed to it by silk threads; and an incomprehensible human art attains the mystery of heaven's creation.

Now, the great object becomes *ki* and object. Warp threads pass through it, and woof threads fill it up; the fine is concealed; the coarse is manifest. The passage of the warp threads makes the hours in which spirit produces events.

The filling up of the woof threads makes the places in which objects have the bodies of objects.

Thus, in a single piece of brocade, warp and woof comprise an object; their weaving is an event. Dragons leap and phoenixes dance. They give brilliance to the finished side, but if one looks into the obscurity of the raw side, one will see the opposition of warp thread to woof thread, and the alignment of like thread with like. So we discover the way of contrast. The whole is a single piece of brocade, but it has two sides, front and back. So we discover what division is. Thus, the piece of brocade is originally one and therefore a whole, but the front and back as two, are two sides. Being a whole requires that front and back merge, and the seams between them are concealed. Being two sides means that front and back stand distinct and reveal *jōri*. The brocade is ordered by *jōri*. Without overlooking a single scale or feather, the clever seamstress weaves dragons and phoenixes. When leaping dragons and dancing phoenixes are traced out with warp and woof, how lifelike they are! [p. 389]

[*Gengo, Honsō*, in *Miura Baien*, in *NST*, vol. 41, pp. 381, 389; RM]

HEAVEN-AND-EARTH IS THE TEACHER

If we were to rely entirely on books for knowledge, believing this knowledge to be thorough—as though the lords of creation themselves had spoken to us and things could not possibly be otherwise—we would still be relying on human habits of thought; there would be no escape.

Thus I may visit schools and speak to the masters; I call them educated and well informed because when I question them, I find that they share my own ideas and attitudes. I ponder the relics of the past and study the geography of distant lands, how far away they are to east or west, and a hundred other such things. For noting things beyond what I see and hear directly and confirming other people's discoveries, books are indeed important.

Nevertheless, heaven and earth are not old or new, ancient or modern; they are always constant and unchanging. The fire in my fireplace is the same fire that is ten thousand miles away; the water in my bowl was the same water a thousand years ago. Since this is so, if we try to understand heaven and earth and to understand this fire and this water, we must first apply ourselves to the unchanging. When we consult the books beside us, we should reject anything contrary to our findings and accept only what does agree.

When it comes to seeing Heaven-and-earth with insight, some people have been called "sages" or "buddhas," but because they were nothing other than human beings, their place is in the long line of companions in our continuing discussion. Heaven-and-earth is the teacher.

[Miura Baien, Reply to Taga Bokkei (1777), in *Baien zenshū*, vol. 2, p. 88; RM]

JŌRI AND SCIENCE

I am nearsighted; my measurements are clumsy. I observed celestial phenomena when I was young and have not abandoned the old teachings. Every book I read reveals my ignorance. At the beginning of this spring, I reread several of the passages you recommended. I spent several days unrolling volumes. At last I understood your meaning and was overjoyed. I applauded you and sighed, "Oh my dear friend, your understanding is almost godlike. What things you have understood! . . . Although I cannot understand all your methods, you have given me a great notebook for the study of *jōri*." [p. 753]

Jōri pairs are seen as genuine features of the universe, hence sun and moon, or circle and square, are false oppositions. Astronomy gives no foundation for the former, and in the latter case, circles are natural phenomena, but squares are artificial, constructed from natural straight lines.

In the method of inquiry according to *jōri*, if I have one trace and cannot find a pair for it, I postulate some other object and try to pair it. If this does not give me the truth, I pair it with another object; if that fails, with another; and so on, stopping when I reach a pair that matches. Before hitting on the straight line as the pair for the circle, one might first try the square; before pairing the sun with shade, one might first try the moon and finally arrive at the straight line and shade in this way. Since the time of the ancients, no one has put forward the theory of *jōri*. I myself do not expect to have found all the true pairs, although I have devoted my efforts to this for fifty years. Therefore in my book you will find the false intermingled with the true. [p. 754]

[Miura Baien, Letter to Asada Gōryū (1785), in *Baien zenshū*, vol. 2, pp. 753, 754; RM]

KAIHO SEIRYŌ AND THE LAWS OF ECONOMICS

Kaiho Seiryō (1755–1817) was born into a warrior-class family of some standing, the eldest son who gave his inheritance to a younger brother. When called to serve as secretary and lecturer to one of the three Tokugawa families, he resigned this, too, citing poor health. He was thus free of any allegiance or responsibilities and spent most of his life as a wayfarer, covering the length and breadth of the country. That he never married was due not to any ascetic convictions on his part but simply to his love of independence. Although Seiryō's early education reflected the influence of Ogyū Sorai's school—its critical scholarship and its revisionist views of Neo-Confucianism—much of his own learning was based on his direct observations of Japanese life. In an autobiographical sketch at the end of his *Lessons of the Past (Keikodan)*, he wrote:

After I resigned from service, I visited Echigo for a year. The following year I made my way to Kaga, spending more than a year there and climbing Mount Tate for the sake of my health. After that I visited Kyoto twice and traveled to the eastern circuit (from Edo to Kyoto) back and forth, ten times. Twice I journeyed to remote Kiso; the northwestern coast, by the Japan Sea, I also visited. All together, the places I visited for longer or shorter stays numbered nearly forty, and the mountains I climbed numbered a few hundred. I never had a wife, never spent money on concubines, and have no children. . . . Being fifty-nine years old, I have so far been fortunate enough not to have starved and free enough to keep on writing whatever I wanted to write. Without a guilty conscience, without obligation to any offspring, I have felt that my way of life was quite enjoyable.[14]

As he traveled through Japan, Seiryō talked with farmers, shopkeepers, and tradesmen, emphasizing that human society rests on two pillars: labor and the exchange of merchandise. Society is basically economic in character, and the first principle of government is the law of economic balance: unless both ends meet, distress and disaster are inevitable. In order to achieve this balance of goods and needs, the size of unproductive classes such as Buddhist priests, Confucian scholars, and hereditary warriors should be strictly regulated. The first two should never be allowed to increase in number; in fact, their total elimination is desirable. Handicrafts and home industries should be encouraged in the warrior class, for it is the law of Heaven that everybody should work. It is preposterous to assume that the ruling warrior class is exempt from this fundamental law of economics, for according to this economic rationalist, warriors themselves are only so much human merchandise sold into the hands of a feudal lord. Feudal service is basically a business transaction. The exchange of commodities is the primary mechanism for sustaining society. But, unfortunately, the ruling class is unwilling to recognize this basic mechanism of society, so its members are condemned to a life of poverty or utter destitution.

This rationalist and mercantilist also believed in the rule of law instead of the arbitrary rule of man, but it was human law grounded in natural law (Heaven's principles as the inherent infrastructure of the universe). "To act in strict accordance with Heaven's principles, completely restricting one's own arbitrary desires, is the secret for bringing happiness and forestalling evil," Seiryō wrote.[15] In respect to legal codes, however, he advocated a minimum of laws with a maximum of enforcement. An extensive and detailed code with vague means of enforcement more often than not defeats its own purpose. In this way,

---

14. *Keikodan*, in *Kaiho Seiryō shū*, pp. 19–92.
15. *Yorozu-ya dan*, in *Kaiho Seiryō shū*, p. 294.

Seiryō mediated between the traditionally opposed Confucian and Legalist positions: he agreed with the former that too much legal regulation is self-defeating and with the latter that ultimate authority must rest in the law rather than in the individual ruler. His view of law as universal and transcending all personal considerations thus reflected his general belief in a system of natural law prevailing throughout the universe—in the political and economic sphere as well as in the physical or moral sphere.

Despite the universalizing trend of Seiryō's economic thought, as a practical matter he had to accept that Japan was divided into feudal domains that were more or less autonomous in regard to matters of local governance not specifically related to Tokugawa military control. Thus he could only hope to prescribe more realistic household management for feudal domains (akin to the provisions of household law [*kahō*]), but not policy or organization on the scale of a unified national regime, as Honda Toshiaki and Sato Nobuhiro did later (see chap. 33).

The fact that Seiryō conceived of the natural order in characteristically Neo-Confucian terms as the "principles of Heaven (or Heaven-and-earth)" suggests again how much even the most independent Japanese rationalists owed to the conception of a rationally ordered universe that was part of their Neo-Confucian heritage. In Seiryō's case, however, as in that of Miura Baien, the moral aspect of things (or the moral order as understood in human terms) assumed much less importance than their factual or empirical base and intelligibility in scientific terms. For Seiryō, "a sage is one who understands the law of nature, who keeps the ways of Heaven-and-earth and all creatures in mind. Since he knows the quality of the soil and the nature of the tree, the trees planted by him have a better chance of taking root."[16] Thus it is his intelligence, not his virtue, that really makes a man a sage or saint. For Seiryō, the great founders of Buddhist sects in Japan like Kūkai, Shinran, and Nichiren were to be appreciated simply because their intelligence, not their moral character, was far above that of contemporary Confucians.

THE LAW OF THE UNIVERSE: COMMODITIES TRANSACTIONS

The following selections are from *Lessons of the Past (Keikodan)*, a summation of Kaiho Seiryō's economic thought written in 1813. The title, as he explains in the opening lines of the work, means "comparing the past with the present, considering the outstanding excellencies of the past and making use of them." "Study should not be for the acquisition of detailed information concerning the past," he writes elsewhere. "It should seek detailed accounts of affairs today." Seiryō's use of his own classical learning

---

16. *Yorozu-ya dan,* in *Kaiho Seiryō shū,* p. 299.

is well illustrated in the references to Mencius in the following passage. Even his style demonstrates his freedom from conventional practices and his independence of mind. Not content to quote verbatim the words of the sage, he paraphrases them expansively, almost in the language of the marketplace.

Seiryō's frequent references to the *Rites of Zhou* also indicate his esteem for this classic as providing a more realistic model for the organization of the political economy than do the texts featured in Zhu Xi's Four Books. Despite its attribution to the "feudal Zhou," the *Rites of Zhou* (often referred to as the *Offices* or *Institutes of Zhou* [*Zhouguan*]) embodied an ideal of unified, centralized administration.

It is ridiculous that the aristocracy and military class in Japan should disdain profit or that they should say that they disdain profit. When a man does not disdain profit, he is called a bad person. Such is the perverse practice of the times. In China it is the same. A man who is clever at making profits is called a sharp enterpriser or some such bad name. But if collecting taxes from those beneath you is to be a sharp enterpriser, then the *Rites of Zhou* is a book for sharp enterprisers; and if lending rice and money to the people and extracting interest from them is to be a sharp enterpriser, then the duke of Zhou himself was a sharp enterpriser. Let us first make a general case of this, go to the root of it, and examine it close at hand.

What sort of thing was it when rice fields were originally handed over to the people and rice was collected from them in return? By what logic was rice taken from the people? If we recognize only the natural principle by which this was done, we shall understand it completely. Rice fields, mountains, the sea, gold, rice, and everything between Heaven-and-earth are commodities. The gathering of rice from rice fields is no different from the gathering of profit from gold. The gathering of timber from mountain land, the gathering of fish and salt from the sea, and the gathering of profit from gold and rice are the natural principle of Heaven-and-earth. If one lets a field go uncultivated, nothing will be grown on it; if one lets gold go unused, nothing will be produced from it. But if one lends a rice field to the people and exacts an annual tribute [tax] of one-tenth on it, then one will make a profit of 10 percent. . . . Of course, the realization of profit is fast or slow depending on the case, so the rate of interest should vary accordingly. Taxes on the rice fields and taxes on mountain land are similar forms of interest, levied on commodities that have been lent. Such commodities are things on which interest must be levied. This is not sharp enterprise or anything of the sort; it is the natural principle of Heaven-and-earth.

Bo Gui was an economist in ancient times. He said to Mencius: "I think I shall take a twentieth of the produce as a land tax." He boasted that since the state had become wealthy, even a tax that small would be enough for its needs. Then Mencius said: "You had better exact a tax of one-tenth. A tax of one-twentieth would be the way of the barbarians, but the barbarians have no fortifications, no palaces, and no rites or music, so even that little is sufficient for the needs of the state. However, China has a splendid way of life, so a tax of one-tenth must be levied."[17] . . . From ancient times it has been said that the relationship between lord and subject is according to the way of the market-place.[18] A stipend is offered for the service of a retainer, and the retainer is a seller. It is simply a business transaction, but business transactions are good, not bad. When it is said that business transactions are not things for a superior man to worry about, this is a misunderstanding that comes from everyone's having swallowed whole the idea that Confucius despised profit. Much parasitism and wasted labor have resulted from the notion that the relationship between lord and subject is not a trade relationship. . . .

Heaven-and-earth consist of principle; buying, selling, and paying interest are inherent principles. If one wishes to enrich the country, one should return to principle. The ruler is the landlord who owns the land as a commodity. The feudal houses also are landlords who own the commodities known as feudal domains. They lend these commodities to the people and live on the interest from them; ministers and high officials sell their knowledge and abilities to the ruler and live off the daily wages he pays. Porters carry a sedan chair, and for each *ri* they carry it, they get paid so much money, with which [in their own turn] they can buy some rice cakes or wine. . . .

In Seiryō's Lessons of the Past, *it is often the Chinese past rather than the Japanese past from which he draws his lessons. From his detailed knowledge of Chinese thought and history, he generally expresses a low opinion of the Confucians' performance as practitioners of the art of rulership, while giving far more credit to the Legalists. The Confucians tended toward a humanitarian benevolence that was liberal and lax; the Legalists served a higher humaneness in insisting on the exactness characteristic of monetary exchange. Seiryō's constant theme is strictness in enforcing punishments and in monetary exactions lest people become lazy, frivolous, and wasteful. The following passage makes clear his agreement with basic Legalist assumptions.*

The unity of law and punishment is also a law of the universe. . . . In Chinese antiquity when a death sentence was passed, the sentence was reported to the sovereign; then the sovereign would request a reprieve three times, but the penal officer would not listen to the request and proceeded to execute the death sentence. To repay a capital crime offender with capital punishment is a matter of simple business arithmetic. That the death sentence had to be executed, despite the sovereign's request for a reprieve, is proof that Heaven's principle

---

17. *Mencius* 6B:10.

18. Reference to *Shiji*, chap. 81: "Relationships in the nation are according to the way of the marketplace. If the lord is powerful, I shall follow him. If he is without power, I shall leave him."

weighed more heavily than the will of the ruler and that business arithmetic was more important than the will of the sovereign. [pp. 11–14]

Nowadays what is thought of as "loving the people" means only letting the people do as they please, but this is only "lesser humaneness." To condone crime is a form of "lesser humaneness" and greatly damages "greater humaneness"; when 10 percent interest is appropriate, to charge only 5 percent is "lesser humaneness" and again does damage to "greater humaneness." It is good for people to work. If one lets up on one's demand for taxes, even though it might be regarded as a way of encouraging savings on the people's part, since the people are generally foolish, they will only squander the balance on frivolous enjoyments. [p. 16]

The warrior laughs when told that the king of Holland engages in commerce. But he himself buys and sells commodities; it is a law of the universe that one must sell in order to buy and hardly a thing to be laughed at. [p. 37]

[*Keikodan*, in *Kaiho Seiryō shū*, pp. 11–37; RT, WTdB]

Chapter 29

THE WAY OF THE WARRIOR II

The Way or ethos of the warrior (*bushidō*), which achieved its first notable articulation in medieval times,[1] continued to assert itself under the Tokugawa shogunate, a basically military regime. As we have seen, the Way of the warrior strongly influenced the Japanese understanding of the Five Human Relationships, a core Neo-Confucian teaching, by transforming the second of these relationships—for the Chinese, a predominantly civil conception of ruler/minister—to one between lord and samurai, giving the highest priority to personal loyalty to one's lord, over the mutual dedication to principle stressed by Chinese Neo-Confucians.

As the shoguns tried to give their military supremacy an aura of civil legitimacy, they and their scholarly adherents found themselves in conflict with old samurai loyalties entrenched in feudal relations. This conflict underlay the debate over the Akō vendetta, the subject of the excerpts immediately following, inviting a diversity of opinion among many schools of Tokugawa-period thought and even dividing scholars within the same school.

The spread of Neo-Confucianism in vernacular forms also brought it into contact with popular culture, especially the drama and fiction of the so-called floating world. One of the most famous works of the puppet theater, and later

---

1. See de Bary et al., eds., *Sources of Japanese Tradition*, 2nd ed., vol. 1, chap. 12.

the kabuki, dramatized the same issue of samurai loyalty versus the claim to "public" authority questionably asserted by the shogunate. Both the scholarly debate and the popular dramatization reflect the uneasy coexistence of Neo-Confucian civil culture with many feudal values persisting not only in the samurai class but in the popular mind as well.

As the Way of the warrior became increasingly codified in literary form, other long-standing religious influences showed themselves. One of the most famous of these is found in *In the Shadow of Leaves* (*Hagakure*), which reflects the persistent influence of Zen in the Tokugawa period (see chap. 31), especially Zen in the cult of swordsmanship—the cult that Ruth Benedict referred to in her classic characterization of Japanese culture, *The Chrysanthemum and the Sword.*

THE DEBATE OVER THE AKŌ VENDETTA

Few events both fascinated and frightened the peaceful world of eighteenth-century Tokugawa Japan as much as the Akō vendetta of 1703. The vendetta had its beginnings in the spring of 1701, when a *tozama daimyō*, Asano Naganori (1667–1701), lord of the Akō domain, attacked and wounded Lord Kira Yoshinaka, a high-ranking master of shogunate court ritual. The reason for the attack remains unclear, but the usual explanation is that Lord Asano lost his temper because Lord Kira continually humiliated him. The attack occurred on the final day of an important state ceremony in which the shogunate hosted imperial emissaries sent from Kyoto to convey the emperor's New Year greetings to the shogun. Lord Asano, who had been serving as one of the shogunate's representatives during the ceremony, was detained, interrogated, and sentenced to die by committing *seppuku* on the very same day.

After learning of their master's death, the now masterless samurai (*rōnin*) of Akō disagreed about the appropriate response. Some advocated the peaceful surrender of Akō Castle. Others recommended defending the castle to the death. Still others called for immediate revenge on Lord Kira. The matter was resolved when most of them agreed to surrender Akō Castle in the hope that the Asano family would be allowed to continue as daimyo of Akō. After the shogunate decreed that Naganori's branch of the Asano family would be discontinued and the domain confiscated, the castle at Akō was surrendered and Asano's retainers became *rōnin*. A number of them had vowed in Akō to protest what was regarded as an unjust punishment by the *bakufu*, and after many months of debate on how to accomplish their goals, in the late summer of 1702 they resolved on revenge. A contingent of forty-seven of the Akō *rōnin*, led by Ōishi Yoshio (Kuranosuke), took their revenge on Lord Kira one year and ten months after their master's suicide. The *rōnin* next marched to Sengaku Temple and presented Kira's severed head to the grave of their deceased master. They then reported their deed to the shogunate and awaited its verdict. After long deliberations, the shogunate decided that the *rōnin* had broken the law and would have to be punished: each was sentenced to die by *seppuku*.

A lengthy debate over the revenge vendetta soon followed, centering on issues of the samurai code, duty, and ethics but also, implicitly, issues related to religious practice, such as the possibility of venerating figures otherwise sentenced to death as felons.

Much of the debate hinged on the interpretation and importance of Japanese concepts of loyalty (J. *chū*, Ch. *zhong*) and duty or righteousness (J. *gi*, Ch. *yi*). To Chinese Confucians, *zhong* had strong connotations of personal fidelity, or being true to oneself, and not necessarily blind loyalty to a ruler. To the Japanese, in keeping with earlier feudal traditions of the samurai class, *chū* had more emphasis on self-sacrificing loyalty to one's lord. Here the Chinese Confucian term *yi* is rendered as "rightness" because it has a contingent, contextual character (what is right or proper in a given situation), whereas Japanese writers tend to assign to *gi* an absolute value and religious intensity, translated here as "righteousness." Much of the Akō debate was spent assessing priorities among the universalistic values and particularistic duties affirmed in each case. We should also note the difference in the meaning of the term *chen* (J. *shin*), which Chinese Confucians generally understand as "minister" (usually civil) and Japanese regard as "retainer," harking back to the medieval, feudal traditions of the samurai. A certain asymmetry and incongruity was inevitable in the adaptation of Confucian concepts to the different Japanese scene.

Along with the debate, the Akō vendetta inspired numerous dramatic productions, including one of the most famous of the Japanese stage, *The Treasury of Loyal Retainers* (*Kanadehon chūshingura*), excerpts from which follow the passages presented here from some of the most important early statements in or related to the debate.

OKADO DENPACHIRŌ

Okado Denpachirō (1659–1723), a deputy inspector (*ometsuke*) serving the shogunate, was on duty overseeing the ceremony when Lord Asano attacked Lord Kira. Immediately after the attack, Denpachirō interrogated both men and reported his findings to the junior councillors (*wakadoshiyori*) serving the shogun. After interrogating the two men, Denpachirō and the other inspectors submitted their reports to their superiors. These ultimately reached Lord Matsudaira, the governor of Mino, who was also known as Yanagisawa Yoshiyasu and was the shogun's favorite and arguably one of the most powerful men in the shogunate. Later the same day, the shogunate's verdict was read by Nagakura Chin'ami, the chief of servants at Chiyoda Castle.

MEMORANDUM

In the following document, Okado Denpachirō presents himself as an eyewitness who twice protested the shogunate's decision to punish only Lord Asano. Some modern scholars argue that this document, which gives readers the impression that it was composed shortly after Asano's suicide in 1701, was probably written well after the 1703 revenge vendetta and is questionable on a number of counts.

Lord Asano, the chief of the Imperial Bureau of Carpentry, earlier today failed to respect the fact that he was in the shogun's castle. He succumbed to his own resentments and attacked Lord Kira, the lieutenant governor of Kōzuke. Such behavior is insufferable. It is decreed that Lord Asano be put in the custody of Tamura Tateaki, high steward of the Right Division, and that he commit *seppuku*. Lord Kira was mindful of [being in] the shogun's castle. He did not even lift a hand during the altercation. This is extremely admirable. A physician serving the shogunate, Yoshida Ian, will prescribe medicine, and a surgeon, Kurisaki Dōyū, will tend his wounds. This should greatly facilitate his recovery. Lord Kira and his entourage are free to go as they please.

Disturbed by the verdict, Denpachirō requested a meeting with the junior councillors. During the meeting, he emphasized Lord Asano's high standing and his status as a tozama daimyō. In particular, Denpachirō asked for further investigations of the cause of the attack, suggesting that Kira was more to blame than had been established. Apparently Denpachirō believed that the shogunate should resolve the conflict according to the legal principle of kenka ryōseibai, *or punishment for both parties in any altercation.*

As I reported earlier, during the interrogation Lord Asano stated that he bore no personal grudge against the shogunate. However, he did admit that he harbored a deep grudge against Lord Kira, which caused him to forget the occasion and behave disrespectfully in the shogun's castle, wounding Lord Kira with his sword. He agrees that this was an outrageous act and regrets it. He admits that whatever the verdict, he will abide by it, without complaint against the shogunate.

Still, Lord Asano is the lord of a castle and the recipient of a stipend of fifty thousand *koku*. Moreover, the main branch of the Asano clan, to which he is related, is one of the most powerful daimyo families in the realm. Might we be proceeding without sufficient concern for the gravity of the situation in sentencing him to commit *seppuku* on this very day? My standing is low, but still as an inspector serving the shogunate, it would be disloyal for me not to speak up now.

True, Lord Kira behaved admirably. Nevertheless, it seems that even if Lord Asano, a daimyo with a stipend of fifty thousand *koku*, was deranged, if he bore a grudge that prompted him to discard his family, forget his presence in the shogun's castle, and wound Lord Kira with his sword, then is it so difficult to conclude that Lord Kira must have pushed him over the limit?

To base the verdict on an investigation conducted by only two inspectors, and doing so hastily, might later prompt the main branch of the Asano family, who are *tozama daimyō*, to decide for some reason or another that the verdict was reached without concern for the gravity of the case. Therefore we suggest that the inspectors reinvestigate matters related to the verdict that Lord Asano commit *seppuku*. Then, after several days of investigation, whatever verdict is arrived at will be handed down. Until that time, Lord Kira should be advised to proceed cautiously. He, too, should be reinvestigated. If he proves to have behaved admirably and done nothing to provoke a grudge, and the attack is found to have resulted from the deranged mind of Lord Asano, then Lord Kira should be treated favorably. According him such treatment today, however, might make the verdict seem ill considered. This we humbly suggest.

The junior councillors to whom Denpachirō made his plea relayed it to the senior councillors, but they did not accept it. Instead, the junior councillors were informed that Lord Matsudaira had already decided the matter and refused to reconsider it. The following is Denpachirō's response.

If Lord Matsudaira arrived at the verdict by himself, then I humbly suggest that my recommendations be forwarded to the shogun. The verdict is much too one-sided. Any *tozama daimyō* would be shamed by it. Please make my suggestions known to the shogun immediately. If the shogun has deliberated the matter, then we will abide by the verdict. [But] if Lord Matsudaira alone decided it, I request that my suggestions be forwarded to the shogun.

Denpachirō's objection was taken to Lord Matsudaira, who responded by having him placed under house arrest. Shortly thereafter, he was pardoned and then appointed to serve as a witness during Lord Asano's seppuku, which occurred around 6:00 P.M. the same day.

[Okado Denpachirō, *Kinsei buke shisō*, in NST, vol. 27, pp. 167–74; trans. adapted from Satō, *Legends of the Samurai*, pp. 307–20; JAT]

RELIGIOUS NUANCES OF THE AKŌ CASE

HAYASHI RAZAN

After the revenge attack by the forty-seven Akō *rōnin* against Lord Kira, the debate centered on the question of whether the *rōnin* were "loyal retainers and righteous samurai" (*chūshin gishi*). In China, this term was understood in a more civil context as "loyal ministers and dutiful officers" (Ch. *zhongchen yishi*) and was defined in *Neo-Confucian Terms Explained* (*Xingli ziyi*) by Chen Beixi (1159–1223), a disciple of Zhu Xi. Beixi suggested that "loyal ministers and dutiful officers" were men who had sacrificed themselves, or had met some violent death, in fidelity to a dynasty. Beixi added that "loyal ministers and dutiful officers" could be legitimately venerated at shrines built to honor their spirits. Hayashi Razan (1583–1657) wrote a colloquial version of Beixi's work, which became a text widely read in Tokugawa Japan. Indeed, many scholars participating in the debate were familiar with it. Whether the common Japanese understanding of *chūshin gishi* as "loyal retainers and righteous warriors" (*samurai*) included this nuance is open to question, but if it did, the shogunate might face the prospect that men it had sentenced to die as criminals could later be apotheosized at shrines dedicated to them.

Razan quoted the *History of the Tang Dynasty*, which says that Xu Yuan and Zhang Xun defended the city of Suiyang during the final year of the An Lushan (d. 757) rebellion. After they were killed by rebel troops, Xu and Zhang were enshrined as *zhongchen yishi* because of their heroic defense of the dynasty. Razan next presented an account from the *History of the Song Dynasty*, that Su Jian was enshrined after he burned himself to death following defeat by an invading barbarian force from areas south of China. Razan turned to the *History of the Tang Dynasty* and the *History of Fukien* for information about Chen Yuanguang, enshrined for his successful defense of the Tang dynasty against invaders from the north. None of these Chinese cases, however, involved revenge or a vendetta, and Razan's account of them was written well before the Akō incident. Japanese Confucians familiar with Razan's explications of Beixi's accounts interpreted the notion of *chūshin gishi* as signifying a loyalist martyr who could be legitimately venerated. In 1912 the Ōishi Shrine was built for Ōishi Kuranosuke and the other Akō *rōnin*. At the time of the Akō incident, the religious aspects of the case as it appears in the eighteenth-century version of the popular play *Chūshingura* were connected to a Buddhist temple celebrating the feudal values of revenge and honor redeemed.

In the following extract, because Razan is translating from Beixi's Chinese, the English rendering of the key terms first gives the Chinese meaning and then the way they might be understood in the Japanese samurai context.

"LOYAL RETAINERS AND RIGHTEOUS WARRIORS"

In later ages, loyal ministers [retainers (*chūshin*)] and dutiful officers [righteous warriors (*gishi*)] threw themselves against unsheathed blades to avert disaster. For example, both Zhang Xun (709–751) and Xu Yuan died in defending Suiyang. Twin temples were erected for them there. Su Jian (d. 1076) died in Yongzhou, and so a temple was founded for him there. The King of the Manifest

Spirit of Zhangzhou sacrificed his life to defend his people. Therefore the people of Zhangzhou built a temple so that they could offer sacrifices. These temples for loyal ministers (retainers) and dutiful officers (righteous warriors) were, in each case, legitimate ones. These temples must be closely supervised so that they open and close at certain times. Vandals must not be allowed to desecrate them. To show their respect for the loyal ministers (retainers) and dutiful officers (righteous warriors) enshrined at these temples, commoners should be allowed only to burn incense at them. . . .

[Hayashi Razan, *Seiri jigi genkai*, vol. 7, pp. 27a–29a; JAT]

HAYASHI HŌKŌ

In 1691, the shogun Tsunayoshi appointed Hayashi Hōkō (Nobuatsu, 1644–1732), the son of Gahō (1618–1680) and the grandson of Razan, to a newly created post, *daigaku no kami*, head of the Confucian academy. The same year, the academy, known as the Hall of Sages (Seidō), was moved from Shinobu-gaoka to the top of Shōhei Hill, named after Confucius's birthplace and located in the Yushima district of Edo. The new site served primarily as the venue of semiannual *sekiten* ceremonies held in the spring and autumn to honor Confucian masters and their teachings. "On Revenge" (Fukushū ron) reveals Hōkō's admiration of the "forty-six men," as well as his ultimate respect for the integrity of the law.

"ON REVENGE"
(FUKUSHŪ RON)

Forty-six men, including Ōishi Yoshio's[2] samurai retainers of a certain Kansai daimyo, united their hearts in forming a league to avenge the death of their deceased lord. On the fourteenth day of the twelfth lunar month in the winter of Genroku 15 [1703], they took revenge on his enemy and were arrested. The shogunate commissioned a thorough and official investigation of the crime and

---

2. Although forty-seven *rōnin* took part in the revenge attack, one of the group, Terasaka Kichiemon, apparently was ordered to leave before the *rōnin* reached the Sengaku Temple and thus neither surrendered himself to the *bakufu* nor was forced to commit suicide with the others, living instead for another forty-five years to the ripe old age of seventy-eight. Essayists have thus variously referred to the participants as being either forty-six or forty-seven in number, with those seeking to justify the *bakufu* verdict citing the number of those sentenced to die, forty-six, and more sympathetic writers referring to forty-seven. Also, the participants in the vendetta were variously described as "men," "*rōnin*," or "samurai," depending on the extent to which praise or condemnation was intended.

then handed down its verdict: the members of the league were asked to commit suicide.

Someone asked the following question:

The Three Bonds and the Five Constant Virtues[3] are the great substance of ritual propriety and the foundations of our moral transformation by means of education and learning. Throughout history and the entire world, there has never been any deviation from these. Based on them, the early kings of antiquity established laws and formulated detailed regulations, promulgating them throughout the realm and transmitting them to posterity. Now the relationships between a ruler and his ministers and between a father and his sons are most essential and basic to the Three Bonds and the Five Constant Virtues. Those relationships represent the pinnacle of heaven's principles and human ethics. Nowhere between heaven and earth can one escape them. Therefore the *Book of Rites* states, "One should never live under the same sky with the enemy of one's ruler or one's father."[4] This injunction issued from a natural and irresistible human feeling; in no respect is it the product of selfishness. Forbidding revenge contradicts the regulations established by the early kings and wounds the hearts and souls of loyal retainers and filial children (*chūshin kōshi*). Executing those who take revenge is an extreme example of destroying the ethical models of the early kings and violating the laws they formulated. Thus, how can forbidding revenge possibly help rectify human ethics or conform to the law?

I replied that the rightness [or duty (*gi*)] of revenge is evident in the *Record of Rites*, the *Institutes of the Zhou Dynasty*, and the *Spring and Autumn Annals*. Moreover, many Tang- and Song-dynasty Confucian scholars who discussed revenge came to the same conclusion. A Ming-dynasty scholar, Qiu Jun [1420–1495], also discussed revenge in considerable detail in his "Supplement" to the *Extended Meaning of the Great Learning* (J. *Daigaku engi*, Ch. *Daxue yanyi*).

I, too, would like to analyze the matter, noting relevant insights from the ancient Confucian classics and commentaries on them. First, I will view their vendetta from the perspective of the hearts of the forty-six men. It was imperative that they "not share the same sky with their master's enemy" and that they "sleep on reeds, using their sword as a pillow" [*Record of Rites*]. To hang onto

---

3. The Three Bonds refer to the proper relations between ruler and minister, parent and child, and husband and wife. The Five Constant Virtues are humaneness, rightness, ritual decorum, wisdom, and trustworthiness.

4. The *Record of Rites* makes this remark only in reference to one's father. The *Rites of Zhou*, however, suggests that the same ethic can be legitimately applied to one's ruler.

life by enduring shame and humiliation is not the way of the samurai. We must also consider the vendetta from the perspective of the law. Anyone who sees the law as his enemy must be put to death. Although the forty-six men were carrying out the last wishes of their deceased lord, they could not do so without committing a capital crime in the process. Stubbornly rebellious, they blatantly defied the authorities. They were arrested and punished in order to clarify the laws of the nation for the realm and for posterity.

These two perspectives are hardly identical, but they might complement each other in operation, without contradiction. Above, there must be humane rulers and wise ministers who govern by clarifying law and promulgating decrees. Below, there must be loyal retainers and righteous samurai (*chūshin gishi*) who readily vent their anger in the determined pursuit of their cause. In doing so, if the forty-six men had to sacrifice their lives because they broke the law, what could they possibly regret? The vendetta let the world know that a lord can indeed trust his retainers and that retainers are loyal to their lord. . . .

[Hayashi Hōkō, *Kinsei buke shisō*, in NST, vol. 27, pp. 372–75; BS, JAT]

MURO KYŪSŌ

Muro Kyūsō (1658–1734) was born in Bitchū Province, the son of a *rōnin*. At fifteen, he entered the service of Maeda Tsunanori (1643–1724), daimyo of Kanazawa domain. Soon thereafter, Kyūsō was sent to study in Kyoto under the Neo-Confucian scholar Kinoshita Jun'an (1621–1698). In 1711, with the recommendation of Arai Hakuseki, Kyūsō became a scholar serving the eighth shogun, Yoshitsune. Kyūsō's *Records of the Righteous Men of Akō Domain* (*Akō gijin roku*), one of his longer works, was written in 1703, shortly after the suicide of the *rōnin*. It offers a detailed narrative of the incident from beginning to end and was one of the earliest writings to proclaim the righteousness (*gi*) of the *rōnin* vendetta. In the form of a dialogue with three of Kyūsō's students, the preface suggests that the vendetta of the Akō samurai was grounded in a Confucian tradition, dating back in ancient China to Bo Yi and Shu Qi, when ministers remonstrated against unwise policies adopted by their rulers.

PREFACE TO *RECORDS OF THE RIGHTEOUS MEN OF AKŌ DOMAIN* (*AKŌ GIJIN ROKU*)

Now that autumn is here, the rain has at last given way to clear skies. Outside my door I hear footsteps approaching. Looking out to welcome my visitors, I see that they are several of my students. I take out my *Records of Righteous Men* (*Gijin roku*), and we read it together. Once we stop reading, with tears we lament that loyalty and goodness are not rewarded and that no one seems to understand the Way of Heaven. Alas! We sigh over these things because Mencius did not deceive us when he said that "ethical principles and righteousness (*rigi*) delight the human heart."[5]

One of my students, Ishi Shinmi, remarked, "The authorities have settled the matter involving the samurai of Akō domain according to the law. However, you, Master Muro, have written boldly on this subject, extolling their actions and praising them as righteous men. Your intentions in this are admirable, but does this not amount to offering a private opinion that contradicts a matter of public law?"

Another disciple, Tani Kyōzen, observed, "No, that is not the case! In ancient times Bo Yi and Shu Qi strongly opposed King Wu's plan to overthrow King Zhou and the Shang dynasty. Thus they stood in front of the horses of King Wu's army, hoping to prevent the overthrow with their own bodies. Now the samurai of Akō domain strongly opposed the pardon of Lord Kira Yoshinaka, and so they banded together to take revenge on him in Edo. Bo Yi and Shu Qi sought to fulfill their humanity and succeeded.[6] The Akō samurai chose to give up their lives for the sake of righteousness.[7] While these examples differ in scale, they are the same in that both were based on giving primary importance to the righteousness that binds lord and retainer. For that reason, King Wu's political adviser, Lü Shang, did not shrink from praising Bo Yi and Shu Qi as righteous men, and this did not reflect unfavorably on King Wu's wisdom. How will the fact that Master Muro today does not shrink from praising the samurai of Akō domain as righteous men undermine the prosperity of our state? Considering Bo Yi and Shu Qi as righteous did not imply condemnation of King Wu. Why, therefore, should praising the Akō samurai as righteous suggest that one is casting aspersions on the shogunate?"

The third disciple, Oku Shifuku, added, "While I agree with what you have said, King Wu's political adviser was able to bypass Bo Yi and Shu Qi with just one order to his troops, sending them to the right and left of the two protesters. [But] Master Muro's discussions are conducted in isolation from the shogunate, here in his school. It was impossible for him to spare the Akō samurai the verdict of the shogunate's legal representatives. Was that not a matter of accepting fate?"[8]

After a long sigh, my three students departed. I immediately recorded what they had said for the benefit of prospective readers of these *Records*.

[Muro Kyūsō, *Kinsei buke shisō*, in NST, vol. 27, pp. 272–73; BS, JAT]

---

5. *Mencius* 6A:7.
6. *Analects* 7:15.
7. *Mencius* 6A:10.
8. That is, accepting the limiting circumstance in which one must act.

OGYŪ SORAI

Ogyū Sorai (1666–1728) was the second son of a physician serving Tsunayoshi, the Tokugawa heir who later became the fifth shogun. Sorai later entered the service of Yanagisawa Yoshiyasu, grand chamberlain to Tsunayoshi. Sorai's "Essay on the Forty-seven Samurai" (Shijūshichi shi ron) endorses the shogunate's verdict on the *rōnin* but extols a superior path for those intent on civil disobedience, that of peaceful remonstration. Another essay, "Giritsusho," allegedly written by Sorai, suggests that his thinking about the incident was similar to Hōkō's and far less critical of the *rōnin*. "Giritsusho" is often cited as Sorai's representative statement on the incident, but some scholars believe that it is a forgery. In any case, Sorai's essay on the Akō vendetta reflects his early thinking as a Neo-Confucian scholar rather than his later thought.

"ESSAY ON THE FORTY-SEVEN SAMURAI"
(SHIJŪSIIICHI SHI RON)

An unofficial historian related,

On the fourteenth day of the third month of Genroku 14 [1701], imperial emissaries visited Edo. That day, the lord of Akō domain, Asano Naganori, because of a personal grudge, unsheathed his sword and attacked, inside the shogun's palace, the major general of the Right Division,[9] Kira Yoshinaka. Lord Kira was wounded in the attack but not killed. That very evening, Lord Asano was sentenced to death, and his domain was confiscated. Lord Kira was not punished. Then, in December of Genroku 15 [1703], a band of Lord Asano's retainers led by Ōishi Yoshio, totaling some forty-seven men, broke into Lord Kira's residence and beheaded him. Subsequently they were arrested and confined. In the second month of the following year, they were sentenced to death. Everyone concluded that the forty-seven men had decided to sacrifice their lives following their lord's death so that they could act loyally, without desire for reward. People thus praised them as righteous samurai (*gishi*).

In my view, however, their behavior was as senseless as that of the five hundred men who followed Tian Heng in death by committing suicide on a desolate island. After all, it was Lord Asano who wanted to kill Lord Kira. Lord

---

9. "Major general of the Right Division" (*ushōshō*) was an honorary imperial government title that had been conferred on Lord Kira, largely as a reflection of his high status.

Kira had no desire to kill Lord Asano! Therefore, we cannot say that the forty-seven men took revenge on their lord's enemy. Furthermore, it was because the lord of Akō had tried to kill Lord Kira that the Asano family lost their domain. Lord Kira did not destroy their domain. Therefore, again, the forty-seven men cannot be said to have exacted revenge for their lord's death.

Forgetting his ancestors and acting no more courageously than a common fellow, Lord Asano yielded to a moment of anger that morning and thus failed in his attempt to kill Lord Kira. Lord Asano's behavior must be deemed unrighteous (*fugi*). At best, the forty-seven men can be said to have deftly carried out their master's evil intentions. How can that be called right (*gi*)?

Lord Asano's samurai, unable to save their lord from his unrighteousness in life, chose to die in the process of completing his unrighteous intention. Circumstances led them to their fate. Even if we try to empathize with them, how can the whole matter not be deemed an enormous tragedy? Thus I judge the forty-seven men much as I do the five hundred followers of Tian Heng who killed themselves on an island in the sea.

Let us consider the loyal servant Ichibei,[10] who was by far superior to Lord Asano's retainers. Diligently and intelligently, Ichibei applied his strength to the way of loyally serving his master, persistently doing what he should have done. Ichibei's sincere intentions eventually persuaded the shogunate to restore his master's family to their former position among the good people of the realm. How could such behavior not be deemed superior to the deeds of Lord Asano's retainers? Alas! Although Ichibei's circumstances were not the same as those of the forty-seven men, his intentions must be praised as righteous (*gi*).

[Ogyū Sorai, *Kinsei buke shisō*, in NST, vol. 27, pp. 400–401; BS, JAT]

SATŌ NAOKATA

Unlike Hayashi Hōkō and Ogyū Sorai, who were born in Edo, Satō Naokata (1650–1719) came from the castle town of Fukuyama, in southwestern Japan, between Okayama and Hiroshima. After studying Zhu Xi Neo-Confucianism under Yamazaki Ansai, he served as a Neo-Confucian scholar to daimyo in

---

10. In "On the Loyal Servant Ichibei," Sorai recounts that the peasant Ichibei, a native of the village of Anesaki in Kazusa, assumed responsibility for the family of his village headman, Jirōbei, after the latter was exiled to Ōshima because of his supposed complicity in a murder. Convinced of his master's innocence, Ichibei petitioned the shogunate for the return of his master's estate. In Hōei 2 (1705), Ichibei's petition was granted. Sorai notes that Ichibei abstained from sexual relations with his wife during the eleven years of petitioning for fear that her pregnancy might curtail his efforts on behalf of his lord. Noting that conjugal relations were among the few pleasures that Ichibei might otherwise have enjoyed, Sorai praises the loyalist for his sacrifice for his master.

Fukuyama, Maebashi, and Hikone domains. Unlike Ansai, who advocated a blend of Neo-Confucianism and Shinto religiosity, Naokata strongly rejected mixing Shinto with Neo-Confucianism, instead defending the Zhu Xi orthodoxy against all other versions of the Confucian Way. Although Naokata and Asami Keisai were Ansai's most prominent disciples, they eventually formed opposite views of the vendetta. Naokata, one of their most severe critics, denounced the *rōnin* as utterly lacking righteousness.

NOTES ON THE FORTY-SIX MEN (SHIJŪROKU NIN NO HIKKI)

At two o'clock in the morning on the fifteenth day of the twelfth month of Genroku 15 [1703], the chief retainer of Lord Asano, Ōishi Kuranosuke, and his band of forty-six men entered the main residence of Lord Kira. The men wore helmets and armor and carried bows, arrows, and spears. They decapitated Lord Kira, wounded his son Sabei, and killed or wounded many of Lord Kira's retainers. Later that morning, the men retreated to Sengaku Temple in Shiba. Before the grave of their deceased lord, they offered up Lord Kira's severed head. There they remained.

On the way back from Lord Kira's residence, the men sent two members of their band, Yoshida Chūzaemon and Tomimori Suke'emon, to the residence of an inspector general, Sengoku Hisanao, the governor of Hōki Province. Chūzaemon and Suke'emon were supposed to report the incident to the inspector, deliver a letter to him, and await the shogunate's verdict regarding their fate. The shogunate decreed that the forty-six men be placed in the custody of four daimyo: (1) Hosokawa Tsunatoshi, governor of Etchū; (2) Matsudaira Sadanao, governor of Oki; (3) Mizuno Tadamoto of Yamagata (Dewa); and (4) Mōri Tsunamoto, governor of Kai. On the fourth day of the second month of Genroku 16 [1703], the shogunate handed down its death sentence, which was promptly carried out. The verdict read as follows:

The shogunate asked Lord Asano to assist in entertaining imperial emissaries from Kyoto visiting Edo. Lord Asano, showing no regard for the occasion or the fact that he was inside the palace, acted in an outrageous (*futodoki*) manner, for which the appropriate punishment was ordered. Lord Kira committed no crime and so was not punished. Because of this, the forty-six men banded together to take revenge against their master's enemy; forced their way into Lord Kira's mansion armed with bows, arrows, and spears; and killed him. The shogunate deems this whole matter, from beginning to end, to be disrespectful to the authorities and most outrageous. Thus, it decrees that they commit *seppuku*.

The ethical principles of honorable behavior (*giri*) informing the shogunate's verdict are clear. The forty-six men were allowed to disembowel themselves rather than be put to death by decapitation. The forty-six men should consider themselves fortunate that the shogunate decided to give them a compassionate sentence. Despite this, the common people chime in, praising the forty-six men as "loyal retainers and righteous samurai" (*chūshin gishi*).

It is understandable if uneducated people not familiar with the ethical principles of honorable behavior (*giri*) make mistakes like these. But even Master Hayashi Hōkō eulogized their passing, comparing them with Yu Rang and Tian Heng and praising them as "loyal and righteous retainers" (*chūgi no shin*). Hōkō further stated that the forty-six men "took revenge on their lord's enemy and thus promoted righteousness."[11] Many scholars have joined the refrain, similarly regretting the deaths of the forty-six men. Some, like Hōkō, even claim that the verdict was in accordance with ethical principles (*ri*) and that the intentions of the forty-six men were righteous (*gi*). But if the shogunate's verdict was in accordance with ethical principles, how could the forty-six men not have been unrighteous (*fugi*)? Such claims are groundless errors resulting from ignorance of righteous principles [of honorable behavior] (*giri*).

The common people regard as a teacher anyone who reads Confucian literature and then has something to say about ethical principles. But it is truly sad when mistakes are made and the minds of the people are misled. The forty-six men indeed made an egregious error when they deemed Lord Kira to be their deceased lord's enemy and invoked the *Record of Rites'* statement that "one should not coexist under the same sky with the murderer of one's lord or father." Lord Kira was not their enemy, although he might have been if he had actually attacked Lord Asano. Lord Asano was sentenced to death because he was a criminal who violated the great law of the land and defied the authorities.

Moreover, if we consider the matter in terms of the dedicated spirit (*kokorozashi*) appropriate to a samurai, then if Lord Asano's rancor against Lord Kira was irrepressible, he should have waited until his ceremonial duties were completed and then found a more appropriate place to attack Lord Kira. To attack Lord Kira during the great ceremony hosting the imperial emissaries was a reckless, unmanly, and cowardly way of acting. Lord Kira was standing and chatting with Kajikawa Yosobe when Asano approached him from behind, suddenly drew his short sword, and slashed him even as he attempted to flee. Lord Kira was not fatally wounded, and Kajikawa apprehended Lord Asano before he could finish his task. Lord Asano's lack of courage and skill

---

11. This remark is in the preface to another version of the poem that Hōkō composed to conclude his essay "On Revenge." Both the preface and the other version of the poem are in *Hōkō Hayashi gakushi shū*. See NST, vol. 27, p. 375.

were laughable in the extreme! That he was sentenced to death and his domain confiscated was indeed in accordance with the ethical principles proper to such matters.

Lord Kira never even drew his short sword. He collapsed in surprise, and his face turned pale, making him the laughingstock of samurai throughout the realm. He behaved so shamefully that even death would have been a better fate. What could the shogunate have done to punish him any further? Clearly Lord Kira was not the mortal enemy of [the forty-six men's] master, Lord Asano.

Rather than regretting their master's crime, the forty-six men defied the shogunate's verdict, armed themselves, and used passwords, secret signals, and military strategy to murder Lord Kira. Thus they too committed a capital crime. Nevertheless, obsessed with their master's anger toward Lord Kira, their muddled minds became totally intent on taking revenge. If later they had reflected on the nature of their crime, a violation of the shogun's law, and committed suicide at Sengaku Temple, their intentions would have merited sympathy despite the wrongness of their deed.

Instead they reported their deed to the inspector general and waited for a verdict from the shogunate. In both the letter they presented explaining their deed and in their first remarks to the inspector general, the men declared that they respected the authorities. But was not such behavior part of a scheme meant to win them praise, help them escape the death penalty, and perhaps even be given a stipend? Having committed a capital crime and blatantly disobeyed the authorities, there was no need for them to report anything, nor was there any need to wait for a verdict. These were not the acts of men who had readied themselves for death.

The Asano family had long revered Yamaga Sokō's teachings on military science. Ōishi had thus studied these teachings from the start. [The forty-six men's] plot arose out of their virulent reaction to the prospect of being reduced to the status of masterless samurai. Their attack was the product of calculation and conspiracy; it did not arise from any real sense of loyalty (*chūgi*) to their lord or from any feelings of commiseration with their lord in his misfortune. Someone who presumes to be a samurai should instead analyze things in detail and make clear distinctions so that he can resolve the confusion clouding the common people.

Examining the matter further, there is a reason why people join in praising the forty-six men as loyal and righteous retainers (*chūgi no shin*): Lord Kira was by nature a very greedy man. The world hated his arrogance, deceitfulness, and perverseness. Thus people overlooked Lord Asano's crime and felt sad over his death and disgust that Lord Kira still lived. Upon hearing that the forty-six men had taken revenge, killing Lord Kira, they were overjoyed, praising the forty-six as loyal and righteous retainers. Alas! Because of the perverseness of this one person, so many others ended up being killed, all of Edo was put in an uproar, and people's minds were thrown into confusion. Lord Kira is indeed the one whom we all should despise.

[Satō Naokata, *Kinsei buke shisō*, in *NST*, vol. 27, pp. 378–80; BS, JAT]

ASAMI KEISAI

Asami Keisai (1652–1711) was born near Kyoto, in the castle town of Takashima, in Ōmi Province. In 1677 he became a disciple of Yamazaki Ansai. Unlike Satō Naokata, Keisai avoided serving daimyo, preferring instead to remain a private teacher of Neo-Confucianism in Kyoto. Naokata and Keisai were two of Ansai's most brilliant students, but they strongly disagreed on a number of important issues. In this case, whereas Naokata judged the forty-six "men" to have been unrighteous (*fugi*), Keisai praised them as loyal servants and righteous samurai. Keisai's argument is couched in terms of the "supreme duty (or righteousness)" (*taigi*), for which he became well known. In "Essay on the Forty-six Samurai" (Shijūroku shi ron), written around 1706, Keisai refers indirectly to Naokata's views and attempts to refute them.

"ESSAY ON THE FORTY-SIX SAMURAI" (SHIJŪROKU SHI RON)

Everyone knows the story of the Akō vendetta carried out by men from Banshū [Harima Province]. While it is hardly open to question whether the forty-six men acted for the sake of their master, some who have misgivings about them claim that their behavior was unrighteousness (*fugi*) toward the government of the realm (*tenka*) because they took revenge on someone whom the government had deemed innocent.

Such reasoning has generated a great variety of rather tenuous arguments. Many people have written me from near and far asking about the truth or falsity, rightness or wrongness of such arguments. A cursory look at these arguments reveals that they all fail to make clear the fundamental issues involved. . . . Here I will try to clarify the main outlines of the matter to supplement what they have to say.

Kōzuke-no-suke (Lord Kira) was in charge of the shogun's representatives during the great ceremonies welcoming imperial emissaries from Kyoto. Because of his selfish desires, Lord Kira did not care whether Takumi-no-kami (Lord Asano) blundered through the great ceremony. Nor was Lord Kira concerned whether Lord Asano was disgraced and humiliated before the illustrious representatives of the imperial court. Such behavior greatly infuriated Lord Asano. In not devoting himself first and foremost to the ritual ceremonies of his lord, the shogun, and instead indulging his selfish desires, Lord Kira committed crimes of an extremely serious nature. Even if Lord Asano had not first attacked him, Lord Kira should not have escaped punishment for his offenses.

Even if he had been spared the death penalty, he should at least have been forced to relinquish his titles and resign his office. At the very least, he should have been stripped of his rice stipend.

On Lord Asano's part, his inability to control his private anger on the occasion of a major court ceremony and his rash behavior in attacking Lord Kira at such a time also were very serious errors. Nevertheless, these acts were not in the slightest degree directed against the shogunate. More than that, [Lord Asano] did not even intend to act without deference to the occasion. Whether it was because of repeated disgrace or the insult he endured on that day, his heart so burned with indignation that without taking time to consider the consequences, he struck out at Lord Kira. Lord Kira fled, and a person on the scene subdued Lord Asano, so before he knew it, Asano found himself unable to finish his attack. If he had been able to attack and kill Lord Kira as he wanted to, he should then have committed suicide immediately. Or if he had been subdued before he managed to commit suicide, he should of course have been prepared to receive the death sentence.

In that case, if we ask what established legal principle would have been applicable here, it would have been the law stipulating that both parties in an altercation are to be punished equally (*kenka ryōseibai*). If we grant that Lord Asano's offense was the disturbance he created during the great ceremony, it was not unprovoked. Rather, it resulted entirely from Lord Kira's selfish intent. If Lord Asano was held responsible as one party in the altercation, then Lord Kira should have been held responsible as the other party. But Lord Asano alone was sentenced to die for disrupting a state ceremony, while the other party, Lord Kira, was not punished at all. Thus there is no question that in the last analysis, Lord Asano died on account of Lord Kira. Accordingly, had Lord Asano's retainers not killed Lord Kira, completing the work begun by their master's sword, their supreme duty (*taigi*) would never have been fulfilled. This was simply a matter of a lord's retainers killing his adversary in fulfillment of their lord's intention to kill him himself, and it is clear that the forty-six men showed not an iota of enmity toward, nor any thought of rebellion against, the shogunate. All they did was to carry out revenge against a person who had been pardoned by the shogunate. There is no concept of supreme duty (*taigi*) that justifies refraining from taking revenge against the murderer of one's lord or father simply because the government has pardoned the murderer. . . .

The adage "merit and demerit do not cancel out each other" means that a person's earlier good deeds are not undone by later mistakes that he might commit. From beginning to end, Ōishi's actions showed not the slightest intention of rebelling against the shogunate. On the contrary, one should say that the righteousness displayed by the forty-six in not committing suicide but instead holding their necks out and entrusting their fates to the shogunate was something that they had learned from their lord's lifelong loyal service to the shogunate.

Gradually the whole story of what had transpired came to light. Lord Kira's heir was later punished for his disloyalty in not defending his father to the death, while the heirs of the forty-six men were treated leniently and their relatives were spared from punishment.[12] Moreover, the forty-six were allowed to choose their grave sites, next to their master's at Sengaku Temple. From these facts it appears that the loyalty and righteousness of the forty-six men have been recognized by the shogunate and that the shogunate's councillors have come to recognize them as well. But even if this were not the case, and the bones of the forty-six men's sons and grandsons had been crushed to dust, it would not have prompted hatred in their loyal and righteous hearts. It is just like the case of Fang Xiaoru.[13] There is nothing particularly ambiguous or open to doubt in such things: it is simply a matter of the principles of honorable behavior (*giri*) that are clear to everyone in the realm, whether educated or not. Some scholars who like to espouse exceptional and high-sounding views have offered all sorts of half-baked ideas, and it is not surprising that heterodox theories also emerge from their midst. Such views are not worth taking seriously.

A certain person has argued that if Ōishi and the others had immediately committed suicide at Sengaku Temple, their deed would have been comparable to those included in the "Exemplary Behavior" chapter of the *Elementary Learning*, but because they did not kill themselves right then and there, they were unrighteous. This is also a case of reasoning that confuses what came after with what came before. Even if we allow that their failure to commit suicide at Sengaku Temple contradicted the principles of honorable behavior (*giri*), in taking revenge on their lord's adversary, they were surely loyal and righteous (*chūgi*). . . . How much truer this is of the forty-six men who, instead of committing suicide, discarded their swords, reported their deed to the inspector general, and left their fate to the authorities, doing all this gallantly and with perfect composure. This act of self-surrender was admirably and skillfully performed, and it is not the sort of thing for which one seeks posthumous fame and honor. Even an ignorant person would have known that they could not

---

12. Satō notes that East Asian law provided for the punishment of not only the criminal but family members as well. Collectively, the forty-six men had nineteen sons. Four of them, all fifteen years of age or older, were exiled but pardoned three years later. The remaining fifteen sons were to be exiled when they turned fifteen, but they all became Buddhist monks, which excused them from punishment. The rice income of Lord Kira's adopted son, Yoshichika (1686–1706), was confiscated because he had not fought to the death to protect his father. He also was placed under house arrest, in the custody of a daimyo, before his death four years later (*Legends of the Samurai*, p. 333).

13. Fang Xiaoru (1357–1402) was a Confucian tutor to the second Ming emperor. After the prince of Yan, the emperor's uncle, seized the throne, Fang was asked to compose the accession edict. For writing "The rebel Yan usurped the throne," he and his clan to ten degrees of relatedness were sentenced to death, resulting in the execution of several hundred relatives and disciples. Fang's case, however, in no way involved revenge or a vendetta.

expect to be pardoned simply because they did not commit suicide. If they were so attached to life, how could they have set their minds so firmly on the supreme duty, which by its very nature entails giving up one's life? . . .

Some foolish people are confused by the allegation that the vendetta was carried out in defiance of the shogun's pardon of Lord Kira. However, as I said before, there is no principle (*kotowari*) stating that a son should not take revenge on his father's murderer just because the murderer has been pardoned by the authorities. Such revenge does not amount to defying the authorities. Because the vengeance seeker thinks of nothing but the enemy of his father, it does seem in retrospect that he has acted in defiance of the authorities. But it is really the same as Mencius's statement that if Shun's blind father Gu Sou had killed a man, Shun would have fled the empire carrying his father on his back.[14] He would not have done this with any intention of defying the authorities. Nor would a son be defying his father if he refused to participate in a rebellion that he started, trying unto death to dissuade him. For rulers and parents, the same principles apply. It is here that we find the pinnacle of loyalty and filial piety.

Another theory that this person has offered is particularly despicable. According to this argument, the forty-six men, having nowhere to turn and no master to serve, staged the vendetta as a subterfuge to obtain a stipend from some admiring lord. This must be the most slanderous allegation of all. From beginning to end, the forty-six men, without exception and without regrets, chose to discard their lives, having already written their last testaments. . . . How could even one of them have hoped to return alive? To allege that they did this in the hope of obtaining a stipend makes no sense whatsoever. . . .

A certain person asked, "How would it have been if Lord Asano's private grudge against Lord Kira had not reached the breaking point at this important ceremony, but in some other circumstances? Would that not have been more acceptable?" In the last analysis, I answer, it would still be the same thing. When one disregards one's public responsibilities because of a private grudge, one cannot escape punishment for the crime. But as long as the act is committed with no trace of disrespect toward the authorities, then it is the same, no matter what the occasion. Even the letters and last testaments of the forty-six men had no hint of ill will toward the shogunate. On the contrary, their attitude was moderate and reasonable in the extreme, demonstrating an acute awareness of the rules of ritual decorum. . . . Samurai in the service of a lord generally do not feel a deep sense of personal commitment to their master's feuds, because once the occasion has passed, the matter of revenge becomes a collective responsibility. After all, the house retainers are not usually related by blood to their lord, and the custom is for retainers to change

---

14. *Mencius* 7A:35.

masters quite readily. This is all because in the normal course of their lives, no one pays enough attention to the principle of righteousness between lord and retainer. Ever since the *Chronicle of Great Peace* (*Taiheiki*), in all quarters of our land, in times of disorder, there have been many heroic deeds and many courageous men. Yet if we examine how many of them truly merited the name "loyal retainer and righteous samurai" (*chūshin gishi*), we will find few indeed. . . .

Someone asked, "The forty-six men formed themselves into a vigilante band, armed to the hilt [and] using passwords, secret signals, and techniques of military strategy to carry out their deed. That itself is a capital offense. What do you think about this?" As you have described their actions, I answer it appears as if they were indeed an armed band acting in defiance of the shogunate. But they were only a small band formed with the intent of entering the mansion of an important person in order to take revenge on their lord's adversary in some way or other, without fail. Thus they had no choice but to make such preparations. They never tried to defy the shogunate or to create a civil disturbance. . . . What is more, the forty-six planned their vendetta in such a way that the neighboring residences were not disturbed in the slightest, and even inside Lord Kira's residence, they avoided killing those who remained out of the fray. After accomplishing their task, they even took care not to start any accidental fires as they left Kira's mansion.

In consideration of all this, to say that what they did amounts to surreptitiously raising an army [and] deceiving the authorities is to fail to recognize their fundamental objective. Generally speaking, when analyzing a major incident like this one, it is best to deemphasize the minor infractions while trying to comprehend sympathetically the basic intention underlying them, in order to avoid impugning the loyalty and righteousness of the parties involved. . . .

A certain person has contended, "The forty-six men revered the military strategies taught by Yamaga Sokō's school. Their conspiracy to take revenge thus arose not from sentiments of loyalty, righteousness, and compassion but, rather, from exasperation over becoming vagrant *rōnin*." This is a most laughable theory! The military strategies of Kusunoki Masashige, the Han-dynasty scholar Zhang Liang, and Zhu Geliang often involved stratagems and deception. Yet the deeds of these men shine brilliantly even today, and no one questions the fact that they possessed a Confucian nobility of character and were true exemplars of loyalty and righteousness. This is because their lives clearly manifested the original mind-and-heart and sense of supreme duty. Even apart from the original mind, if only the supreme duty is established, there inevitably will be loyal armies and righteous wars fought in its name. This fact is shown in the way Zhu Xi wrote the *Digest of the Comprehensive Mirror* (*Tongjian gangmu*), as well as, in our own country, in the accounts of the loyalists of the Southern Court recorded in the *Chronicle of Great Peace*. In the writings left behind by the forty-six men, their unswerving dedication to the memory of their lord is clear beyond a shadow of doubt, and no amount of effort to find fault with their motivation can stand up to scrutiny. This is what people in ancient times meant by the saying "If you are determined to accuse a person of a crime, you can always drum up a charge."[15]

A certain person has also remarked, "If one person says that the forty-six men were loyal and righteous, then all the other scholars will chime in" (*raidō*). The expression "chime in" refers to a situation in which, regardless of the number of people, people fawn on and conform to the words and ideas of those in a position of authority or those with power and influence. In that case, if a person's words arise from a mind that is given to flattery, even one person can be said to "chime in." When it comes to things like praising the filial piety of Shun or revering the loyalty of King Wen, even if the whole realm has agreed on the same thing for ten thousand generations, it cannot be said to be "chiming in." It is necessary only to understand the true principles of honorable behavior; whether or not one speaks the same way as others do is not something about which one should be concerned.

Ultimately, my thesis is neither circuitous nor ambiguous: if one's ruler or father attacks someone but fails to kill him and, for that reason, loses his life while his adversary continues to live as if nothing had happened, what purpose would be served if his retainers or sons simply looked on from the side, just because of some blunder made by their lord or father? And what purpose would be served if such retainers or sons were regarded as loyal vassals and righteous samurai (*chūshin gishi*) and, on that basis, were given stipends and employment by the lords of the land? These are questions that do not arise in ordinary examinations of the master-retainer relationship. Other matters are relevant here as well, but it is not possible to mention them all. Actually, their essential outlines can be inferred from what I have already said.

[Asami Keisai, *Kinsei buke shisō*, in NST, vol. 27, pp. 390–96; BS, JAT]

DAZAI SHUNDAI

Dazai Shundai (1680–1747) was born in the castle town of Iida, in Shinano Province (modern Nagano Prefecture). After briefly serving as a samurai retainer to Matsudaira Tadanori, Shundai moved to Edo and began studying under Ogyū Sorai in 1711, two years after the death of the fifth shogun, Tsunayoshi. While Shundai's views are consistent with Sorai's insofar as they condemn the *rōnin*, they also resemble Satō Naokata's conclusions. Especially significant is that Shundai, like Naokata, blamed Yamaga Sokō's teachings for the

---

15. *Zuo zhuan*, "Duke Xi, 10th Year," in Legge, trans., *The Ch'un ts'ew, with the Tso chuen*, p. 157.

vendetta. Shundai's bold "Essay on the Forty-six Samurai of Akō Domain" (Akō shijūroku shi ron, ca. 1731–1733), condemning the *rōnin* and their vendetta, sparked a second round of debate over the incident. A number of essays that ensued refuted Shundai's views, much as Asami Keisai and others had written to rebut Naokata's earlier claims. From the mid-eighteenth century, the debate over the Akō vendetta continued through the remainder of the Tokugawa period.

Given Shundai's Sinological orientation, it is significant that after citing Chinese precedents, he acknowledged a different Japanese Way: "For samurai of this Eastern country there is an indigenous Way: if a samurai sees his lord murdered, he will immediately lose all self-control and become crazed for revenge. Without thought about what is right or wrong, he will leap into the fray believing that it is only through death that he can demonstrate his righteousness."

"ESSAY ON THE FORTY-SIX SAMURAI OF AKŌ DOMAIN"
(AKŌ SHIJŪROKU SHI RON)

A visitor asked Master Dazai, "The whole world praises the righteousness of the forty-six men, but you alone condemn them. Can you explain your views?"

I replied, "I can indeed.

"From the time that Lord Asano attacked and wounded Lord Kira inside the shogun's castle to the time that the Akō samurai murdered Lord Kira and were sentenced to death, I was in Edo, and on the basis of what I saw and heard, I have been able to ascertain all the facts of the matter. When it occurred, I was in my twenties and had some understanding of the principles of honorable behavior (*giri*). At first, I simply followed public opinion, thinking that what Yoshio and the others had done was righteous and mourning their deaths. But soon I began to have second thoughts about the matter. There is a saying that in human life, 'it is not easy in the morning to plan for the evening.'[16] After all, who would have known that they could wait until the winter of the following year without Lord Kira's dying in the meantime? And if Lord Kira had died before that winter, how would the Akō samurai have been able to accomplish their mission? In such a situation, what could they have done? Taken the tonsure, shaved their heads, and become Buddhist monks? Fled to some remote island, as Tian Heng and his men did? Exhumed Lord Kira's corpse and flogged it as Wu Zixu in ancient China did to the man who killed his father? None of these would have been proper courses of action.

---

16. *Zuo zhuan*, "Duke Shao, 1st Year," in Legge, trans., *The Tso chuen*, in *The Ch'un ts'ew, with the Tso chuen*, p. 578.

Had the forty-six men chosen one of these alternatives, would they not have become the laughingstock of the world? As it turned out, Lord Kira did not die of illness before the vendetta, so he ended up dying at the hands of the men of Akō. Although this has been called 'the punishment of Heaven' (*ten-chū*), it was really due to nothing more than the good fortune of the men of Akō. It is on account of this that I have doubts about the actions of Yoshio and his band.

"Moreover, for several years I have read and studied the Six Classics so that I have a rough understanding of what the supreme duty (*taigi*) is all about. Accordingly, I feel that I can make a retrospective judgment regarding the men of Akō on the basis of the laws of the *Spring and Autumn Annals*. The *Record of Rites* states, 'One should not remain alive under the same sky as the murderer of one's father.' Although there is no clear statement regarding the murderer of one's lord, the *Classic of Filial Piety* states that one's lord should be respected the same as one's father. Accordingly, the murderer of one's lord is analogous to the murderer of one's father. This is a principle that has remained unchanged since ancient times and that all people understand. It is only for this reason that praise has been heaped on Yoshio and his band.

"However, because Lord Asano's death did not result from Lord Kira's murdering him, Lord Kira cannot be deemed his enemy. Why, then, did Yoshio and his band kill him? They did so because they did not understand where their resentment should be directed. For this reason, I judge the actions of Yoshio and his band to have been wrong. Ultimately, I came to hold this view and have debated with many people about it. But my view has displeased many. Therefore, for years I kept my thoughts to myself, considering them idiosyncratic, personal views.

"When I began studying under Master Sorai, I asked him about his views, and it seemed that they tallied perfectly with my own conclusions. Master Sorai said, 'The Akō samurai did not understand righteousness. Their killing of Lord Kira represented nothing but their study of Yamaga Sokō's military strategies.' I have heard that according to the laws established by our divine founder, Ieyasu, anyone who commits murder in the shogun's palace must die. But Lord Asano only wounded Lord Kira. That is not a crime punishable by death. Nevertheless, the government (*kokka*) sentenced him to die. Thus, the punishment exceeded what was proper. The retainers of Lord Asano should have felt resentment about *that*. However, Yoshio and his band did not resent what they should have resented but instead resented Lord Kira. What an insignificant target for their resentment! When the shogunate treats the lord of a domain with respect, the retainers serving that lord should obey him and stand in awe of the shogunate. If the shogunate does not treat their lord with respect, however, his retainers should feel resentment against the shogunate. Retainers of the lords of the various domains are aware only of their particular lords. What do they know about the shogunate?

"Moreover, for samurai of this Eastern country there is an indigenous Way: if a samurai sees his lord murdered, he will immediately lose all self-control and become crazed for revenge. Without thought about what is right or wrong, he will leap into the fray believing that it is only through death that he can demonstrate his righteousness. Humane men inevitably see such self-sacrifice as a vain waste of life, but they also realize that the state depends on this Way, and thus they strive to preserve it. They also know that this Way is effective in maintaining morale among the samurai. Therefore, it cannot be abandoned. Now Yoshio and his band did not resent what they should have resented but instead resented Lord Kira. Because they stood in awe of the shogunate, they refused to act against it. Not only did they not realize the righteousness expected of retainers; they also abandoned what the samurai of this Eastern country consider as their Way. Is that not pathetic?"

The visitor then asked, "Well then, what should the Akō samurai have done for their lord?"

I replied, "Nothing would have been better than for them to have died at Akō Castle. I have heard that Akō is a wealthy domain and that for generations the people there have been happy with their lord. If Yoshio and his band had put their lord first on the basis of righteousness, who would have dared to oppose them? Would he have had only forty-six soldiers? With such support to rely on, Yoshio and his band could have stood before Akō Castle and put up a good fight against the shogun's troops. Then they could have climbed inside the castle, set it afire, and committed suicide one by one, letting their corpses go up in flames with the castle. Then the men of Akō would have done all that could be done. But Yoshio and his band did not know how to make such an honorable showing of themselves. Instead, they just folded their arms and turned over the castle to emissaries of the shogun. They surely lost their great opportunity!

"But even if they were unable to die at Akō Castle, they still could have gone right away to Edo and attacked Lord Kira. If they had succeeded in killing him, they should have immediately killed themselves. If they did not succeed, they should have died in the effort. Whatever the outcome of the attack, they would have had no choice but to die. With death, their duties to their lord would have been fulfilled completely.

"Yet Yoshio and his band were not capable of such behavior. They bided their time leisurely, waiting for the right moment, vainly plotting and conspiring how they might best murder Lord Kira. Their goal was to succeed in their plot and, by doing so, to achieve fame and profit (myōri). How despicable! The fact that Lord Kira did not die before they attacked him was due only to the good fortune of the Akō samurai. Once Yoshio and his band had killed Lord Kira and offered up their victory before their master's grave, they had completed their task and fulfilled their duty. For commoners it is a capital crime to murder a retainer of the shogun. Thus the forty-six samurai should have committed suicide. What need was there to wait for an official verdict from the shogunate?

"The fact that they were unable to bring themselves to commit suicide [and so] turned themselves over to the authorities could only be because they thought that having completed a task of the greatest difficulty, they would win the highest merit. If they were fortunate enough to avoid death, they thought, then to obtain a position would be as easy as bending down to pick up dust from the ground. If they were unfortunate and did die, then they would be dying according to the law, and they would not be criticized for not dying earlier. So why, they thought, should it be necessary to commit suicide?

"Is this not what I have called seeking fame and profit (*myōri*)? How ignominious! Are people like Yoshio who feign devotion to their supreme righteous duty (*taigi*) when in fact they are driven by a desire for profit in any way worthy of being deemed righteous? If the shogunate had mistakenly pardoned Yoshio and his band and allowed them to be offered an official position, they would have ended up eating the shogun's grain. This was all because they did not know the proper object for their resentment. It all began with Master Yamaga Sokō serving the lord of Akō domain as an instructor in military strategy. Yoshio studied under Master Yamaga. He and his band used Yamaga's teachings on strategy in every detail of their plot to murder Lord Kira. For this reason they made no tactical errors and were able to accomplish their mission. But because they did not understand the proper object for their resentment, they fell short of fulfilling the supreme duty they owed their master. Master Yamaga's teachings are indeed like that. . . ."

[Dazai Shundai, *Kinsei buke shisō*, in NST, vol. 27, pp. 404–11; BS, JAT]

GOI RANSHŪ

A native of Osaka, Goi Ranshū (1695–1762) was educated from youth as a Neo-Confucian scholar and eventually became a lecturer at the Kaitokudō merchant academy in Osaka. Later he traveled to Edo and briefly served the daimyo of Tsugaru domain. In 1739 he returned to the Kaitokudō and remained an influential force there, especially in regard to the academy's philosophical curriculum, until his death in 1762. Ranshū is often credited with leading the Kaitokudō toward a more orthodox, Zhu Xi–based version of Neo-Confucian teachings than had been evident in its earlier eclecticism. His rebuttal (ca. 1731–1733) of Dazai Shundai's view of the Akō incident was among the more important and influential pieces to emerge in the "second round" of the debate. It is especially significant insofar as it represents one expression of *chōnin* (townsfolk) thought regarding an incident involving samurai, *rōnin*, and the shogunate. Ranshū concludes by opining that the samurai's death-defying commitment is "something that Confucian scholars and men of letters can never really understand," in other words, that a great gulf remains between the code of the Japanese samurai and that of the Confucian scholar.

REFUTATION OF DAZAI SHUNDAI'S "ESSAY ON THE FORTY-SIX SAMURAI OF AKŌ DOMAIN" (HAKU DAZAI JUN AKŌ SHIJŪROKU SHI RON)

Even from a cursory examination of vendettas launched by loyal retainers and men of high principle (*chūshin sesshi*) since antiquity, we see that success can never be hurried. Rather, those who carried out vendettas had to keep their blades hidden from view, patiently gauging their strength before moving, and waiting for the right moment before striking. The essential thing was always that their mission be accomplished. This was true in every case, not just the case of the Akō men. If they had acted rashly because they could not be sure how long their adversary would live, without regard for their chances of success or failure, they would have truly been acting like petty-minded, fretful men. Moreover, one can never be sure how long one's own life will last, let alone the life of one's adversary. It is just a matter of fate, not something that one can debate. How can we treat it lightly? All we can do is live out to the best of our ability our destined span of life. How can the matter of length of life be taken as the basis for judging the righteousness of Yoshio and his band? If, unfortunately, Lord Kira had died in his sleep, Yoshio and his band would have had to report that fact to the spirit of their late master and then commit suicide, bewailing their misfortune. In this way they would have cleared themselves of blame. Why would they consider becoming monks and abandoning the world or exhuming Lord Kira's corpse and flogging it? . . .

Lord Asano committed a crime legally punishable by death. Can the law be considered his enemy? Lord Kira, of course, did not kill Lord Asano; therefore he cannot be called his enemy, either. Yoshio and his band did not claim that they were avenging their lord's death; they simply said that they were fulfilling the last wishes of their lord. When their late master faced death, how would he have dared to hold a grudge against the shogunate? It was just that Lord Kira escaped from his sword, leaving Lord Asano unable to kill him. Nothing, they thought, could be a greater cause of regret for a samurai at the moment of death! Therefore his retainers killed him on behalf of their lord only in order to console their late master's anger in the underworld. This is not what we call revenge. But if we trace the crime to its origin, it is true that it all began with Lord Kira. For this reason, the fact that people regard it as a case of revenge can also not be said to be mistaken.

Yoshio led a band of former retainers of the confiscated domain of Akō in an armed attack in the shogun's capital and there killed a high-placed person as if he were an orphan swine. This was a major crime. If they were judged according to the laws of the *Spring and Autumn Annals*, Yoshio and his band would certainly be guilty of a capital crime, murder of a government official. This crime merited severe punishment, such as the public exposure of their severed heads or their banishment from society along with common criminals. The shogunate did not place them in the custody of penal officials, however, but entrusted them to the care of daimyo. These daimyo did not begrudge the trouble; instead, they treated the men with utmost hospitality. After some time had passed, the shogunate granted them the honor of dying by their own hands and allowing them a proper burial.

Despite losing their domain and the possibility of continuing their lord's house, Yoshio and his band roused themselves to action without looking back and endured countless difficulties in order to fulfill their single-minded loyalty to their master. Accordingly, the shogunate must have considered their deed to have been righteous and empathized with their feelings, and so granted them lenient treatment. This is also the reason that scholars writing about the matter have taken their side. Then there also are scholars like Satō Naokata who like strange ideas and take pleasure in disagreeing with others and who have offered arguments condemning Yoshio and his band. Others agreed with them and stole their ideas. Now this Mr. Dazai has picked up their argument, declaring that if he does not write an essay on the matter, this principle of righteousness will never be clarified. This is laughable in the extreme.

Lord Asano intended to kill a man. By chance, the person he attacked did not die. The attack, moreover, occurred inside the shogun's castle during a major state ceremony, and Lord Asano was in the position of receiving instruction from Lord Kira. Suddenly, Lord Asano tried to slay Lord Kira on account of a personal grudge. This was extremely disrespectful, and the crime committed was serious. Even so, whether the punishment was right or wrong is not something that subjects like us should dare to judge! It is best to let it be without discussing it.

The death of Lord Asano was a result of his crime. How would he have dared to hold a grudge against the shogunate? If that was true of the lord, it was true of his retainers as well. If they held a grudge against the shogunate, that would have betrayed a selfish mind. "When one loses one's temper at home but vents this anger in the marketplace,"[17] one's crime will be punished by death. That is, it was because of Lord Kira's perverseness that Lord Asano viewed him as his enemy, and so it was proper for Yoshio and his band to bear a grudge against Lord Kira. What should they have done about that grudge? They would have no peace until they killed Lord Kira and offered up his head at their late

---

17. *Zuo zhuan*, "Duke Shao, 19th Year," in Legge, trans., *The Tso chuen*, in *The Ch'un ts'ew, with the Tso chuen*, p. 675.

master's grave. I have no idea why Yoshio and his band should have held a grudge against anything greater. Suggesting so is preposterous!

When enemy domains are at war, it is appropriate for each person to be devoted only to his own master. But when the realm is well governed, one deems unity to be the highest value. In such times, is there anyone who eats the produce of the land who is not also a subject of the realm?[18] Can anyone be ignorant of the shogunate's existence? If retainers who serve various domains were to band together in resentment against the shogunate whenever the shogunate happened to treat their lord with a little disrespect, great calamities would follow. . . .

Righteousness is the same thing anywhere in the world. If people's actions accord with righteousness, how can one claim they follow a way unique to our country alone? If people's deeds do not accord with righteousness, how are they worthy of being regarded as according with the Way? This all is the talk of military men and common officials and far from the words of a scholar of noble principle.

Regarding the shogun with respect is the basis of regarding one's lord with respect. If one does not regard the shogun with respect, calamities will befall one's lord. This is what is called not regarding one's lord with respect. In arguing that Yoshio and his band should have shown disrespect for their lord by practicing a righteousness that is not righteousness, Mr. Dazai is inciting people to evil. Is that not wrong?

If a lord commits a crime and his domain is confiscated and then his chief retainer rounds up all his lord's subjects to defend his castle to the death, refusing the orders of the authorities and murdering its officials, they are committing an extreme act of insurrection. Even if they all gave their bodies to the flames and perished with the castle, their grudge would not be dissolved, and they would only have added in vain to the mistake of their late master. In the end, misfortune would visit their entire lineage. Is this not also an evil course? Certainly *this* is a righteousness that is not righteousness, yet it is what Mr. Dazai takes as righteousness! . . .

Yoshio was determined to kill Lord Kira, and he believed that his duty to his master would be fulfilled by doing so. He believed that he could not fulfill his duty by dying in vain. Therefore, in order to ensure victory, it was absolutely necessary for him to plan meticulously and consider every possible contingency. . . .

When warriors go into battle, their hearts must be ready for death, free of any attachment to life. Otherwise, how could they charge into the unknown and submit their bodies to the blades of the enemy's swords? This is something

18. *Zuo zhuan*, "Duke Shao, 7th Year," in Legge, trans., *The Tso chuen*, in *The Ch'un ts'ew, with the Tso chuen*, p. 616.

that Confucian scholars and men of letters can never really understand. Throughout the attack, Yoshio's only concern was to take revenge against the enemy; he gave no thought to his possible death. How could he have had any room in his mind for thoughts of fame and profit? Allegations like these are what we call "a petty man using his belly to gauge a great man's mind."[19] Such allegations also exemplify how small-minded men love to argue but do not enjoy "helping others complete what is good in them."[20]

My late father also commented on the next argument of Shundai's essay, and I follow his views on the matter.[21] Although Yoshio's plan began in his own heart, it ultimately gained the support of all the other members of his band; thereafter it was executed. There has to have been a reason for this, so we cannot condemn him out of hand. It is probably that retainers should never dare to murder a high-ranking official. That notwithstanding, Yoshio's single-minded loyalty to his master was not compromised just because of his adversary's high status, and he carried out his mission. The only thing then was to turn himself over to the authorities to await the death sentence. Is this not an illustration of Mencius's saying that "when it is permissible both to die and not to die, it is an abuse of valor to die."[22] In the unlikely event that the shogunate had commended his resolve, bent the law, and pardoned him from death, he would have prostrated himself repeatedly in gratitude and respect and promptly committed suicide, entering the underworld with a smile on his face. He would not have tried to hang on to life at the cost of his honor. "It is easy to rend one's breast with emotion and then commit suicide, but it is difficult to retain calm and composure and follow righteousness."[23] Such was Ōishi Yoshio.

The final several hundred words of Mr. Dazai's essay are baseless and slanderous claims intent on bolstering his thesis that Yoshio sought fame and profit. They are not worth discussing.

[Goi Ranshū, *Kinsei buke shisō*, in NST, vol. 27, pp. 418–24; BS, JAT]

FUKUZAWA YUKICHI

Fukuzawa Yukichi (1830–1901) was born in Nakatsu domain in Kyushu, the second son of a lower-level samurai. A good student, Fukuzawa took up Dutch learning and later the study of English during the final decades of the Tokugawa period. Before the collapse of the shogunate, Fukuzawa was known as a

---

19. *Zuo zhuan*, "Duke Shao, 29th Year," in Legge, trans., *The Ch'un ts'ew, with the Tso chuen*, p. 675.

20. *Analects* 12:16.

21. Ranshū's father, Goi Jiken (1641–1721), was one of the early Kaitokudō scholars.

22. *Mencius* 4B:23; Lau, trans., *Mencius*, p. 132.

23. *Jinsu lu*, chap. 10, "Zhengshi"; Chan, *Reflections on Things at Hand*, p. 251.

promoter of Western learning. After the Meiji Restoration, he continued with that work even more energetically. One of his most popular writings, *An Encouragement of Learning* (*Gakumon no susume*), addressed the Akō *rōnin* incident in an effort to explain the sociopolitical ideas found in Francis Wayland's *Elements of Moral Science*. Wayland emphasized the importance of following national laws, as opposed to engaging in vigilante justice. To make the same point, Fukuzawa cited the example of the Akō *rōnin*, using it to promote a new concept of citizenship in a nation-state.

Fukuzawa's critique of the *rōnin*, much like Satō Naokata's and Dazai Shundai's earlier ones, elicited a barrage of criticism directed at Fukuzawa's writings as well as his person. It is noteworthy that Fukuzawa's attack occurred during an age when the Akō *rōnin* were becoming increasingly popular heroes of a new emperor-centered nationalism. One indication of this trend is the fact that after moving his capital to Tokyo (formerly Edo) in 1868, the new Meiji emperor early on paid homage to the grave of Ōishi Yoshio and the other Akō *rōnin*, praising the example they had set for other samurai.

AN ENCOURAGEMENT OF LEARNING
(*GAKUMON NO SUSUME*)

Private vengeance is evil. . . . In no instance can even the son of the murdered parent take it upon himself to kill this criminal in place of the government. This would be to mistake his duty as a subject of the nation and to violate his contract with the government. If the government disposes of the case with undue favoritism to the accused, the son should complain of this injustice to the government. Whatever one's reasons, one is not entitled on any account to initiate the process of punishment. Even if the murderer of one's parents is lingering before one's own eyes, one has no right to retaliate privately.

In the Tokugawa period, the retainers of the Asano family killed the major general Lord Kira Yoshinaka to avenge the death of their master, Lord Asano Naganori. Society called them righteous samurai (*gishi*). But was this not a great mistake? The Tokugawa shogunate constituted the government of Japan at that time. Lord Asano, Lord Kira, and the retainers of the Asano family all were citizens of Japan. They had contracted to obey the government and its laws, and in return they received the protection of the government provided under the rule of law.

Because of a mistake made one morning, Lord Kira was rude to Lord Asano. Lord Asano did not realize that he should have reported the offense to the government. Instead, he succumbed to his anger and personally tried to cut down Lord Kira. This was considered a vengeful attack. It was resolved legally when the chief of the Imperial Bureau of Carpentry [Asano] was sentenced to death by *seppuku*, while Lord Kira was not punished at all. This verdict should be deemed unjust.

If the samurai retainers of the Asano family thought that the verdict was unjust, why did they not petition the government? If each of the forty-seven samurai had planned to petition against the verdict, according to the law they might have obtained a more just verdict. A tyrannical government would not have accepted the appeal at first and might even have executed the person making the appeal. But if the remainder of the samurai were not frightened by that execution and instead proceeded, one by one, to petition the government for a just verdict, meeting each execution with another petition, then no matter how despotic the regime was, it would have eventually submitted to rational principles and provided for a more just verdict by punishing Lord Kira.

Using such a strategy, [the samurai] would have truly proved themselves to be righteous. But they did not understand the ethical principle behind such a strategy. While they were citizens of the state, they chose to ignore the importance of the laws of the land. Instead, they madly murdered Lord Kira. In doing so, they misunderstood their responsibilities as citizens, violated the rights of the government, and privately tried to pass judgment on people's crimes. Fortunately, the Tokugawa government sentenced these rebellious men to death, thus settling the matter. If the government had forgiven the Akō samurai, however, then the retainers of the Kira family would have taken revenge. One vendetta would have followed another until all family and friends on both sides had been annihilated. Such a process would have reduced society to a state of lawless anarchy. Such is the harm of private vigilante justice to the state. Such lack of respect must not be allowed.

> [*Fukuzawa Yukichi zenshū*, vol. 3, pp. 65–66; trans. adapted from Dilworth and Hirano, trans., *Encouragement of Learning*, pp. 37–38]

THE AKŌ VENDETTA DRAMATIZED

In the background of the debate about the Akō vendetta is what might be called a strong popular undertow of sympathy for the *rōnin*, as dramatized in the theater: the legend of *The Treasury of Loyal Retainers* (*Chūshingura*), the title of which evokes the feudal traditions of medieval samurai rather than the ethics of a Zhu Xi or even the popular Japanese Neo-Confucianism observed in chapters 25 and 26. At issue in the more formal debate is the question of legitimate authority, in which feudal traditions of individual honor and duty are at odds with the civil values and public order upheld by Neo-Confucianism.

Although the "loyal" samurai who appear in the following excerpts are commonly referred to as exemplars of Confucian values, the concepts of honor, duty, revenge, vendetta, and ritual suicide (*seppuku*) derive from medieval Japanese traditions, with Buddhism as their religious accompaniment, whereas references to proper decorum are merely a bow to the Tokugawa's fictive claim to ritual legitimacy or a mere cosmetic conformity to Confucian "propriety."

In this puppet play, attributed to Takeda Izumo (1691–1756) as the principal author, Lord Kira is identified as Kō no Moronao; Lord Asano is represented as Enya Hangan; and the senior retainer Ōishi Kuranosuke is thinly disguised as Ōboshi Yuranosuke. Enya Hangan's climactic ritual suicide is introduced here by reading the sentence from the shogunate.

THE TREASURY OF LOYAL RETAINERS
(*CHŪSHINGURA*)

LORD ISHIDŌ, REPRESENTING THE SHOGUNATE (*reads*): Whereas Lord Hangan Takasada, for reasons of long-standing private quarrel, did attack and wound the chief councillor Kō no Moronao and disturb the peace in the palace, his lands are confiscated and he is ordered to commit *seppuku*. . . .

HANGAN: I submit myself in all particulars to His Excellency's command. But now please relax and take a cup of wine, to refresh yourselves after your arduous duties.

YAKUSHIJI: Hold your tongue, Hangan. You should by all rights be strangled and then beheaded for the crime you've committed. You should be grateful that, thanks to His Excellency's clemency, you'll be allowed to commit *seppuku*. I should think you'd start making preparations at once, particularly since there are fixed precedents to be observed when committing *seppuku*. What do you mean by dressing yourself up in a long *haori*,[24] the latest in fashion? Are you drunk? Or are you out of your mind? This is a breach of courtesy toward Lord Ishidō and myself, who've come here by order of the shogun. . . .

HANGAN: I deeply appreciate your kindness. Ever since I wounded him, I have been prepared for this. My only regret is that Kakogawa Honzō held me back and kept me from killing Moronao. It rankles in my bones, and I can never forget it. Like Kusunoki Masashige,[25] who declared at Minatogawa that he would prolong his life by the strength

---

24. The *haori* is a kind of cloak worn with a kimono. The length of the *haori* was subject to shifts in fashion.

25. The great hero of the forces loyal to Emperor Go-Daigo, Kusunoki Masashige died in 1336. The passage in *Taiheiki* alluded to here is in the chapter "The Deaths of Masashige and His Brother."

of his resolve in his final hours, I vow that I shall be born and die, again and again, until at last I am avenged.

NARRATOR: His voice vibrates with wrath. . . . Rikiya, acting on his master's orders, takes the dagger which has been readied for this purpose and places it before him. Hangan calmly slips his hempen jacket from his shoulders and sits more at ease.

HANGAN: The official witnesses are to observe that the sentence has been carried out. . . .

NARRATOR: He takes up the dagger with the point toward him. Plunging it into his left side, he starts to pull it across his abdomen. His wife, too horrified to look, murmurs the invocation to the Buddha, tears in her eyes. . . . With both hands on the dagger, he pulls it across, piercing deep. He gasps with pain.

HANGAN: Yuranosuke, I leave you this dagger as a memento of me. Avenge me!

NARRATOR: He thrusts the point into his windpipe; then, throwing down the bloodstained weapon, he falls forward and breathes his last. His wife and the assembled retainers stand for a moment, transfixed, their eyes shut, their breaths bated, their teeth clenched; but Yuranosuke crawls up to his lord and, taking up the dagger, lifts it reverently to his forehead. . . . At this moment there takes root within Ōboshi that noble purpose which will give him a name for loyalty and rectitude to resound through all the ages. . . . [pp. 68–72]

After long preparation by Yuranosuke, he carries out the revenge vendetta at the mansion of Kō no Moronao.

YURANOSUKE: When I blow the signal whistle, it will mean the time has come to scale the walls. Remember, we need take only one head.

NARRATOR: In response to these commands from Yuranosuke, as one man they direct looks of fierce hatred at the distant mansion, then separate into parties bound for the front and back gates. . . .

(Though few in number, these are courageous men, deadly determined to succeed this night and employing every secret tactic.)

YURANOSUKE: Kill Moronao! Pay no attention to anyone else. . . . I am Ōboshi Yuranosuke, and this is Hara Gōemon. We have no quarrel with Takauji or his brother. Nor do we bear any grudge against either Lord Nikki or Lord Ishidō, so we promise to do nothing irresponsible. I have ordered our men to take the strictest precautions against fire, so you need have no worries on that account. We ask only that you peaceably refrain from interfering. . . .

NARRATOR: The samurai next door, hearing this bold proclamation, shout back.

SAMURAI: What superb courage! Every man who serves a master should behave as you are doing. Call if you have any need of us. . . .

NARRATOR: All at once the neighborhood becomes still. During the fighting, which has lasted about two hours, barely two or three of the attackers have been slightly wounded, but the enemy casualties are beyond numbering. Nevertheless, the enemy general Moronao eludes detection. The foot soldier Teraoka Heiemon runs around the mansion, searching the rooms . . . but no one can tell where Moronao has gone. . . . He rushes outside, afraid Moronao has somehow escaped the house, when a voice calls.

JŪTARŌ: Heiemon, wait!

NARRATOR: Yazama Jūtarō Shigeyuki drags out Moronao, all but carrying him in his arms.

JŪTARŌ: Hear me everyone. I found him hiding in the woodshed and took him alive.

NARRATOR: The others all rush up, bolstered in spirits like a flower touched with dew.

YURANOSUKE: Nobly done, a tremendous feat. But we mustn't kill him hastily. After all, he served for a time as a high officer of the government. The proper decorum must be observed even when killing him.

NARRATOR: Taking him from Jūtarō, he makes Moronao sit in the place of honor.

YURANOSUKE: We, who are merely retainers of a retainer, have broken into your mansion and performed acts of violence because we wished to avenge our master's death. I beg you to forgive this gross discourtesy and to give us your head without offering resistance.

NARRATOR: Moronao, master of deceit that he is, betrays no fear.

MORONAO: I understand. I have long been expecting this. Take my head.

NARRATOR: He puts Yuranosuke off guard with these words, only suddenly to draw his sword and strike at him. Yuranosuke wards off the blow and twists Moronao's arm.

YURANOSUKE: Ha—what a touching display of resistance! All of you, now is the moment to satisfy our long-accumulated hatred!

NARRATOR: Yuranosuke strikes the first blow, and the forty and more men raise shouts of joy and celebrate. . . . They jump and leap in exuberance, and using the dagger their lord left behind as a remembrance of him, they cut off Moronao's head. In their high spirits they even dance. . . . Yuranosuke takes from his breast the memorial tablet of his late master and places it on a table in the alcove. He cleanses Moronao's head of the bloodstains and offers it before the tablet, then burns the incense he has carried inside his helmet. He steps back respectfully and bows three times, then nine times, before the table.

YURANOSUKE: I humbly report to the sacred spirit of my late master, Renshōin Kenri Daikoji.[26] I have, using the dagger you bestowed on me after you committed *seppuku* and obeying your command to appease your spirit, cut off Moronao's head and offered it before your memorial tablet. Please accept it from your resting place under the sod.

NARRATOR: In tears he offers his prayers. . . . [pp. 173–78]

[*Chūshingura*, trans. Keene, pp. 68–72, 173–78]

HAGAKURE AND THE WAY OF THE SAMURAI

Hagakure (*In the Shadow of Leaves*), also known as *Hagakure kikigaki*, the *Hagakure Analects*, and the *Analects of Nabeshima*, became one of the most famous works of *bushidō* thought in the 1930s, although in the Tokugawa period it did not circulate beyond the remote southern province in northwestern Kyushu where it was written. The core parts of the narratives and reflections that compose the work were dictated by a retired samurai of Saga domain in Hizen Province, Yamamoto Tsunetomo (1659–1719), to a fellow samurai, Tashiro Matazaemon Tsuramoto (1678–1748), between 1709 and 1716. Tsunetomo, the scion of a family that had long served the Nabeshima house, had, from the age of nine, been a close attendant and confidant of his lord, Nabeshima Mitsushige, serving him in the capacity of secretary and document writer. When his master died, Tsunetomo wanted to follow him in death to fulfill his loyalty, but this custom of *junshi* had been forbidden by Mitsushige in 1661, four years after he became daimyo. Consequently, Tsunetomo chose to shave his head and take up the secluded life of a Buddhist teacher (thus he is referred to in contemporary documents as Zen master Yamamoto Tsunetomo). *Hagakure* was a testament of spirit to the samurai of his domain that grew out of his "determined mindset of *seppuku*," a cry of protest against the bureaucratization of Saga samurai life that was proceeding rapidly under the leadership of Mitsushige and his successor. Yamamoto's critique of the Akō vendetta for its delayed response, instead of taking immediate, direct action, echoed the thought of Dazai Shundai.

The teachings of the *Hagakure* have long been epitomized by the following passage: "I have found that the Way of the samurai is death. This means that when you have to choose between life and death, you must quickly choose death." In fact, this passage was used as a slogan in the militarist period during the twentieth century in order to encourage soldiers to throw themselves fear-

---

26. Enya Hangan's posthumous Buddhist name.

lessly and resolutely into battle, and the book as a whole was understandably revered by right-wing ultranationalists. Nonetheless, the original "logic" of always being prepared to die in a fight with another should be understood in the context of the samurai code of honor. Tokugawa law decreed that both parties to a fight would be punished equally (*kenka ryōseibai*), usually with death, without any investigation of either party's claims of who was right and who was wrong.

Becoming one with death in one's thoughts even in life, moreover, was regarded as the highest demonstration of a person's subjective purity and singleness of heart (*makoto, magokoro*). In one's readiness to die honorably for one's lord, "loyalty and filial piety are naturally present in their fullness," requiring no reflection on abstract moral principles. In Tsunetomo's view, seeking excuses to stay alive when one is faced with death arises from the mind of discrimination (*funbetsu*) and discretion or caution (*shiryo*), which leads to hesitation and second thoughts and only obstructs the enactment of true loyalty. The Way of the *bushi* is to throw oneself into loyal action without reserve, oblivious of personal danger, like a person fought into a corner by his enemy who, with no way out but death, fights with total self-abandonment (*shinigurui*). The connections with Zen teachings here are quite clear: both "discrimination" and "discretion" are Zen terms for the irresolute, attached state of mind that is to be overcome by Zen practice, a practice that needs to be fueled by contemplation of the reality of death and the transitoriness of life. For death is an absolute reality, whereas concepts of right and wrong, as objects of discriminating consciousness, are only relative.

Such a focus on death may seem morbid or negative to those used to the modern conception of death as the fearsome enemy of life, as indeed it did to Tokugawa-period spokesmen for Confucian ethical norms like Yamaga Sokō. However, Tsunetomo does not mean that men are to throw themselves away carelessly to a meaningless death just for the glory of dying. For one thing, the glorification of the resolution is rooted in the knowledge that a person who has resolved to die and has lost all fear of death is very difficult to defeat in battle. In all the martial arts, the highest level of mastery demands a complete abandonment of attachment to life and the desire to be a winner, not to mention a leap beyond the principles of logic and the dichotomy between means and ends. Thus the resolution to die may give rise to a higher state of life, a life infused with beauty and grace that is beyond the reach of the man concerned with self-preservation. For this reason, Mishima Yukio (1925–1970) held great reverence for this book, finding it an inexhaustible inspiration for the creative life. It is also this conception of the Way of the samurai that gave rise to Tsunetomo's views on the crucial matter of revenge.

In addition, Tsunetomo taught that the fundamental concern of the dedicated samurai is to strengthen the spiritual foundations of the realm—that is, of his domain—for which reason he must diligently study the history of the daimyo house that he serves. His fierce, almost fanatical (*kurui*) dedication to excellence in the pursuit of this goal merely reflects the fact that one cannot accomplish feats of greatness in an unaroused state of mind. Such a philosophy of action is naturally impatient with the conventional, rational norms of conduct by which a man restrains his impulses to act. Tsunetomo would agree with Laozi that the highest form of art seems like artlessness, the highest form of virtue knows nothing of goodness, and the highest form of wisdom resembles foolishness.

IN THE SHADOW OF LEAVES
(*HAGAKURE*)

Prologue: "Carefree Talks in the Shadows of the Night"

I suppose it does not become me now that I have shaved my head and taken up a reclusive life, but I have never thought of attaining enlightenment or achieving buddhahood and all that stuff. The resolution to devote myself to this domain has penetrated so deeply into my viscera that even if I were to die and be reborn seven times, I still would want nothing other than to be born as a samurai of Nabeshima and to be of service in the government of my domain (*kuni*). This does not require some special sort of strength or talent. To put it simply, it is just a matter of becoming resolved to take upon one's shoulders the entire destiny of one's domain. I have been born as a human being just like anyone else. Why should I be inferior to anyone? If I do not practice with the attitude that there is no one better than myself, then all my practice will come to naught. Yet while the kettle of determination can get very hot, it also tends to cool down very quickly. There is a way to keep it from cooling down. Let me tell you my own version of the Four Vows:

1. Do not fall behind in *bushidō*!
2. Be of use to my lord!
3. Be filial toward my parents!
4. Arouse great compassion, and be of use to other people!

If you recite these four vows every morning to the buddhas and the gods, you will obtain the strength of two people, and you will not backslide. Like an inchworm, you will move forward bit by bit. Even the buddhas and the gods became what they are through the power of vows. [part 1, pp. 218–19]

I have found that the Way of the samurai is death. This means that when you are compelled to choose between life and death, you must quickly choose death. There is nothing more to it than that. You just make up your mind and go forward. The idea that to die without accomplishing your purpose is undignified and meaningless, just dying like a dog, is the pretentious *bushidō* of the city slickers of Kyoto and Osaka. In a situation when you have to choose between life and death, there is no way to make sure that your purpose will be accomplished. All of us prefer life over death, and you can always find more reasons for choosing what you like over what you dislike. If you fail and you survive, you are a coward. This is a perilous situation to be in. If you fail and you die, people may say your death was meaningless or that you were crazy, but there will be no shame. Such is the power of the martial way. When every morning and every evening you die anew, constantly making yourself one with death, you will obtain freedom in the martial way, and you will be able to fulfill your calling throughout your life without falling into error.

A man of service (*hōkōnin*) is a person who thinks fervently and intently of his lord from the bottom of his heart and regards his lord as more important than anything else. This is to be a retainer of the highest type. You should be grateful to be born in a clan that has established a glorious name for many generations and for the boundless favor received from the ancestors of the clan, [and you should] just throw away your body and mind in a single-minded devotion to the service of your lord. On top of this, if you also have wisdom, arts, and skills and make yourself useful in such ways as these permit, that is even better. However, even if a humble bloke who cannot make himself useful at all, who is clumsy and unskilled at everything, is determined to cherish his lord fervently and exclusively, he can be a reliable retainer. The retainer who tries to make himself useful only in accordance with his wisdom and skills is of a lower order. [part 1, nos. 2–3]

A certain man was regarded as shameful because he did not take revenge after being involved in a fight (*kenka*). In taking revenge, you should just jump in and charge full speed ahead until you are cut down. If you do so, you will not incur any shame. . . . The reason we listen to people's stories and read books is to be constantly prepared. Especially in the case of *bushidō*, remember that one never knows what might happen even today, so it is imperative to consider things carefully and systematically day and night. Victory or defeat is decided by the momentum of events and is different from the actions by which we avoid incurring shame. It is enough just to resolve to die. If one is not successful on the spot, then one quickly takes revenge. In this there is no need for some special wisdom or technique. The real master never considers victory or defeat but just charges forward intently unto death (*shinigurui suru bakari*) without a second thought. [part 1, no. 55]

Until fifty or sixty years ago, samurai would take a bath every morning, put scent onto the shaven part of their head and into their hair, cut their nails, file them with a pumice stone and polish them with oxalis, and pay very careful attention to their personal appearance. They would be especially careful to see that all their weapons and armor were free of rust, wiping away all dust and dirt and polishing them so they always were ready for use. To take great pains with their appearance may seem to be merely decoration, but it is not just some kind of affectation of elegance. It was because they were always in a state of preparedness, thinking, "Today I might die in battle. If I were to be killed in battle with a sloppy appearance, my lack of preparedness in ordinary times would be revealed, and I would be regarded contemptuously by the enemy as a slovenly fellow." Thus, whether a samurai was young or old, he would always give careful attention to his physical appearance. Certainly it is troublesome and takes time, but this is what the work of the samurai is. Other than this, there is nothing that one needs to be particularly busy about or that needs to take a lot of time. If one's mind is always totally prepared to die in battle, already having become one with death, and one devotes oneself to one's work of service and to the martial arts, then a situation in which one incurs shame is not likely. Yet today people give not the slightest thought to this sort of thing, passing their days pursuing self-gratification, so that when the time arrives, they bring shame on themselves without even realizing that it is shame. They think only that if they themselves are feeling good, nothing else matters, so they end up performing all sorts of audacious and improper things. What an incredible shame! . . . [part 1, no. 63]

It is difficult to dislike unrighteousness (*fugi*) and hold steadily to what is right (*gi*). However, if you believe that holding to rightness is the highest thing and try to hold just to that exclusively, you will only end up making a lot of mistakes. There is a Way that is higher than rightness. It is very difficult to find, but he who does so possesses an unsurpassed wisdom. From its vantage point, rightness itself is something small and narrow. You can know it only when you have become aware of it in yourself. But even if you cannot find it on your own, there is still a way to reach it: "The onlooker gets the best view of the game." People also say, "Remain aware of your wrongs at every moment," and the best way of doing so is by talking with people. The reason that we remember the old stories we hear and what we read in books is so that we may discard our own personal discriminations and align ourselves with the discriminations of the ancients. [part 1, no. 44]

Bushidō is nothing but charging forward, without hesitation, unto death (*shinigurui*). A *bushi* in this state of mind is difficult to kill even if he is attacked by twenty or thirty people. This is what Lord Naoshige[27] used to say, too. In a normal state of mind, you cannot accomplish a great task. You must become like a person crazed (*kichigai*) and throw yourself into it as if there were no turning back (*shinigurui*). Moreover, in the Way of the martial arts, as soon as discriminating thoughts (*funbetsu*) arise, you will already have fallen behind. There is no need to think of loyalty and filial piety. In *bushidō* there is nothing but *shinigurui*. Loyalty and filial piety are already fully present on their own accord in the state of *shinigurui*. [part 1, no. 113]

---

27. Nabeshima Naoshige (1538–1618), Mitsushige's grandfather, was a famous general and the founder of the daimyo house of Saga domain. He won great merit in Hideyoshi's Korean campaigns in the 1590s and was enfeoffed by Ieyasu with the domain of Saga in 1601.

When Ōki Tetsuzan[28] was in his old age, he had the following to say: "I used to think that *jūjutsu* was different from *sumō* in that in a match, even if you found yourself on the bottom, it would not be a problem as long as you won in the end. But in recent years it has occurred to me that if someone came along to arbitrate while you were on the bottom, you would be judged to have lost. To win in the beginning is to win all the way through." [part 1, no. 84]

There is really nothing other than the thought that is right before you at this very moment. Life is just a concatenation of one thought-moment after another. If one truly realizes this, then there is nothing else to be in a hurry about, nothing else that one must seek. Living is just a matter of holding on to this thought-moment right here and now and getting on with it. But everyone seems to forget this, seeking and grasping for this and that as if there were something somewhere else but missing what is right there in front of their eyes. Actually, it takes many years of practice and experience before one becomes able to stay with this present moment without drifting away. However, if you attain that state of mind just once, even if you cannot hold onto it for very long, you will find that you have a different attitude toward life. For once you really understand that everything comes down to this one thought-moment right here and now, you will know that there are not many things you need to be concerned about. All that we know of as loyalty and integrity are present completely in this one thought-moment. [part 2, no. 17]

There is nothing that is impossible. If one thought is aroused, Heaven and earth will move in response. It is not that something is impossible but that people are too timid to make up their minds to do it. "To move Heaven and earth without expending any energy" is also just a matter of the One Mind.[29] [part 1, no. 143]

Yamazaki Kurando's admonition that "it is not a good thing for a man of service to be too discriminating" is truly a wise saying. It is awful if a samurai's mind gets stuck on judgments of right and wrong (*rihi jasei*), whether something is "loyal" or "disloyal," "righteous" or "unrighteous," "proper" or "improper," and so on. If one just devotes oneself totally and single-mindedly to the service of one's lord, forgetting all other considerations, and cherishes one's lord without second or third thoughts, that is enough. This is what it is to be a good retainer. If you devote yourself totally to your service and worry only about your lord, even though you may sometimes make mistakes, that is all part of fulfilling your original aspiration. It is said that in all things it is not good to go to excess but that only in the way of service is it actually better if you make mistakes

---

28. Ōki Tetsuzan (d. 1665) was a *bushi* who distinguished himself in the Shimabara revolt of 1637/1638.

29. The quotation, which in its original context refers metaphorically to the power of poetry to move the heart, is from the *kana* preface to the *Kokin wakashū* (ca. 913 C.E.).

owing to an excess of devotion. A person who is always looking for reasons and principles often just gets hung up on the small things and spends his whole life in vain. What a shame! Truly, you have just this one short life. There is nothing better than to just give yourself to only one thing, without any seconds and thirds. It is no good to split yourself into two. Drop all other things and just throw yourself into the *samadhi* of service—there is nothing higher. All those pretentious arguments about "loyalty" and "righteousness" and so on are really nauseating. [part 1, no. 195]

The highest form of self-absorption in love is secret love (*shinobukoi*). There is a song that says it well: "Only in the smoke that lingers after love-death can one really know that's what it was, that agony of longing that was never revealed to anyone." If one confesses one's love while one is alive, that is not deep love. A love that pines and burns within the heart until one dies with longing—only that is the supreme form of love. Even if you are asked by the object of your affections, "Are you not by chance in love with me?" you answer, "I never dreamed of such a thing." For there is nothing higher than going to one's grave with one's love still held inside as a secret. Love has to take the long way around; it is not something that you just come out and say. Some time back, when I spoke about this, a few [people] agreed with me, and I called them "my comrades of the smoke." I guess this is something that only people who have gone through quite a lot of things in this world come to understand. In things like the lord–vassal relationship as well, one should serve with this attitude of mind. By the same token, to keep watch over yourself when no one is watching you is the same as doing so in a public place. If you do not try to avoid unseemly actions when you are all alone and keep unseemly thoughts out of your mind even when no one is watching you, then you will not be able to present a pretty sight in public. As they say, a sudden attempt to fix yourself up will not get rid of the dirt. [part 2, no. 34]

[*Hagakure*, in NST, vol. 26, part 1, pp. 218–19, nos. 2, 3, 44, 55, 63, 84, 113, 143, 195; part 2, nos. 17, 34; BS]

Tokugawa = Neo-Confucian academics sort of going against it

Chapter 30

THE NATIONAL LEARNING SCHOOLS

Kokugaku = nationalist

— Japanese people already aware, didn't need Confucian morals

The earliest extant writings in Japan are about Japan, so it is no exaggeration to say that the Japanese interest in Japan—its mythology, heritage, culture, and traditions—is as old as Japanese history itself. During the seventeenth century, however, there was an eruption of interest in things Japanese to a degree not previously witnessed in that country, and during the eighteenth century this interest developed into a preoccupation with concepts of identity and character.

We have already seen how the domestication of the Neo-Confucian interest in history resulted in an unprecedented outburst of historical writing throughout Japan, especially in the Mito domain, and how leading seventeenth-century scholars like Hayashi Razan and Yamazaki Ansai sought to reconcile the "truths" of Confucian teaching with the traditional native belief in *kami*, or Shinto deities. In literary studies, too, there was a newly invigorated interest in the composition of verse and the study of Japan's prose and poetic classics as the spread of printing liberated them from the limitations of traditional modes of dissemination and opened them up to an enthusiastic audience of "towns-people" (*chōnin*) in Japan's burgeoning metropolises.

In this scholarly and intellectual activity in the seventeenth century, as in that in most earlier periods in Japanese history, the study of things Japanese went hand in hand with the study of things Chinese. Indeed, the two seemed to be seamless components of a singular "learning" whose fundamental purpose was enriching the human person through the pursuit of knowledge. In the eighteenth century, however, this changed with the rise of the nativist movement of "National Learning" (Kokugaku).

There are several reasons for this change. It was at least in part related to the comparative cultural isolation of the Japanese after their contact with Europeans (other than the Dutch) was curtailed after the 1630s and when Christianity was proscribed and driven underground, thereby heightening Japan's consciousness that its culture was distinct from that of Asia's other countries. Another factor may have been the growth of the popular academy as one part of a burgeoning popular culture that redefined the relationship between the producers and the consumers of culture. In this process, some scholars in Japan awakened to the fact that offering instruction in the Japanese heritage was one way to make a potentially lucrative livelihood, just as samurai understood the possibility for their own career development through Japanese studies and as merchants and other townspeople sought instruction in fields and traditional arts that had earlier been accessible to only a privileged few. Also a factor was the increasingly commodified nature of cultural and other transactions in the society.

Whatever the reasons, the initial fissure between Chinese and Japanese studies is apparent in the writings of Keichū (1640–1701), who since the eighteenth century had been regarded as a forerunner or pioneer of National Learning. Keichū was a Shingon Buddhist priest who, building on the work of such figures as Shimokōbe Chōryū (1624–1686), wrote an important commentary on Japan's oldest extant poetry anthology, the eighth-century *Anthology of Ten Thousand Leaves* (*Man'yōshū*), commissioned by Tokugawa Mitsukuni (1628–1701), the daimyo of Mito. In it, Keichū wrote:

> Japan is the land of the *kami*. Therefore in both our historical writing and our public matters, we have given priority to the *kami* and always place humans second. In early antiquity, our rulers governed this land exclusively by means of Shinto. Since it was not only a naive and simple age but an unlettered age as well, there were only the oral traditions called "Shinto," and there were no teachings like those in Confucian classics and Buddhist writings.[1]

Besides its resonant restatement of the opening words of Kitabatake Chikafusa's (1293–1353) *Record of the Direct Succession of Divine Sovereigns* (*Jinnō shōtōki*), identifying Japan as the land of the *kami*, the significance of Keichū's statement is that in the context of a commentary on the *Man'yōshū*, he wrote about the ancient past in terms that described the native tradition as sufficient, without Buddhism or Confucianism, for the task of ordering society and affairs of state.

---

1. *Keichū zenshū*, vol. 1, p. 292.

It was for this reason that other eighteenth-century "National Learning scholars" (Kokugakusha) saw in Keichū's writings a kind of genesis for their own endeavors.

A more publicly prominent authority on Japanese studies and the first major figure of this eighteenth-century movement was the Shinto priest Kada no Azumamaro (1669–1736), whose forebears had served for centuries as hereditary wardens of the Fushimi Inari Shrine in the suburbs of Kyoto. Azumamaro shared an interest in the ancient classics with his Confucian contemporary Ogyū Sorai, but whereas Sorai had argued that the ancient Way was to be found through the philological analysis of Chinese classics in historical context, Azumamaro believed that Japan likewise possessed a Way that could be found by studying the classics of Japan's own past. Apparently seeking to establish Japanese studies as an academic field equal to Chinese studies, Azumamaro petitioned the incumbent shogun to found "a school for studies of the imperial land," at which the "old learning might be taught." Although there does not appear to have been an official response to Azumamaro's petition, it did express the adversarial relationship between Chinese studies and Japanese studies that characterizes most of the leading nativist scholarship of the eighteenth century.

Among Azumamaro's identifiable students was Kamo no Mabuchi (1697–1769), who emerged as the foremost authority on the Man'yōshū. Born and raised in Hamamatsu, Mabuchi was taught to read by Azumamaro's niece. In 1728 he registered in Azumamaro's school and in 1733 moved for full-time study to Fushimi, where he quickly established himself as one of Azumamaro's most promising students. After Azumamaro's death in 1736, Mabuchi went east to Edo, a move representative of a broader cultural shift at this time. In Edo, Mabuchi again quickly established a reputation as an authority on the ancient Japanese classics, but it was his affiliation with the second son of Tokugawa Yoshimune, Tayasu Munetake, whom Mabuchi served from 1746 to 1760 as tutor in Japanese studies (wagaku goyō), that gave him the opportunity to concentrate on his nativist scholarship while gaining a window on affairs at the very heart of the bakufu. Toward the end of his life and after his retirement from service to Tayasu Munetake, Mabuchi adopted the sobriquet "old man of the fields" (agata no nushi), an ironic self-appellation for someone on the fringes of Edo, at that time the world's most populous city.

Almost all of Mabuchi's thought can be traced to his conviction that verse was superior to prose for communicating heartfelt sentiment. Suspecting that later poetry had a disproportionate concern with artistry rather than emotive truth, Mabuchi believed that of all Japanese poetry, the verses of the Man'yōshū were the most deserving of esteem. The value of these poems, he argued, was twofold. First, Mabuchi believed that when imitating ancient modes, the very act of versification—the composition of poetry—produced a socially beneficial transformation of one's spirit. Just as those in ancient times were able to ventilate powerful emotions and thereby become better citizens, people are comparably enabled in the here-and-now. Second, he believed that the value of the *Man'yō* verses came from their having been composed before the introduction of Buddhism and Confucianism, which rendered them useful for gleaning the virtues and sentiments of the "true heart" (*magokoro*) of the Japanese, a heart unsullied by exposure to Chinese morality and rationalism. By composing poetry in imitation of ancient modes, one might be able, Mabuchi argued, to disengage from the fallen present and reenter an idealized and beatific ancient past. As he wrote in *Inquiry into the Idea of Poetry* (*Kai kō*, 1764), by studying *Man'yō* verses and composing in imitation of the ancient styles, one could be transported away from the present, "an age that has descended like a river down from the mountains," and into the past, thereby resurrecting all those virtues—principally directness, manliness, and sincerity—that contributed to the beatific innocence of the ancient age.

Mabuchi was unrestrained in his criticism of China, which he viewed as addicted to rationalism and dependent on moral and ethical teachings needed to offset a Chinese propensity for unruliness. Evidence for Japan's superiority, he argued, lay in the fact that in ancient times Japan found such moral instruction unnecessary, since the people naturally and instinctively leaned toward behaviors that contributed to the harmonious operation of society. By turning to such sources as the *Man'yōshū* and reanimating their dormant "true hearts," the Japanese might reclaim the same ancient natural Way of Heaven-and-earth that was their birthright.

The mantle of Mabuchi's nativist scholarship was assumed by Motoori Norinaga (1730–1801), regarded as not just the greatest of the eighteenth-century National Learning scholars but also, as Donald Keene described him, "certainly one of the greatest Japanese scholars, perhaps the greatest."[2] Except for the years from 1752 to 1757, when he was a student in Kyoto, Norinaga lived his entire life in Matsusaka, near the celebrated Ise Shrines, where he founded his school, the Suzunoya, or House of Bells, in which more than five hundred students had registered by the time of his death. Although Norinaga inherited much of Mabuchi's perspectives on the past and on Japan's privileged position, there also were some differences. For example, whereas Mabuchi's thought emphasized a return to the natural Way and spontaneous spirit of the past, Norinaga regarded the Way as having been fashioned by the native *kami* of Japan and bequeathed by them to their terrestrial delegates, the succession of divine emperors who had continued to rule in an unbroken chain since time immemorial. Whereas Mabuchi had sought his ancient Way of Heaven-and-earth in the verses of the *Man'yōshū*, Norinaga turned to the slightly more ancient *Record of Ancient Matters* (*Kojiki*, 712), Japan's most ancient extant mythohistory, which he raised to the status of scripture. And whereas Mabuchi had asserted the

---

2. Keene, *World Within Walls*, p. 320.

superiority of Japan and Japanese culture vis-à-vis other countries of Asia, Norinaga argued for Japan's unique superiority on global terms, owing to the world's having been created by—and hence owing a debt of gratitude to— Japanese *kami*, especially the solar deity Amaterasu, whose radiant sunshine continued to succor and sustain the world.

Furthermore, Norinaga was the preeminent literary critic of his age, and in this regard he is best known for his theory of *mono no aware* (the pathos of things). Norinaga contended that in the classics of Japanese prose and poetry— above all, Murasaki Shikibu's *Tale of Genji* (*Genji monogatari*)—the discerning reader would find the depiction of emotional truth and, in this way, would acquire an empathetic understanding of the melancholic pathos—the touching sadness—of human experience. *The Tale of Genji*, Norinaga wrote, is

> simply a tale of human life that leaves aside and does not profess to take up at all the question of good and bad and that dwells only on the good-ness of those who are aware of the sorrow of human existence (*mono no aware*). . . . [The] illicit love affairs described in the tale [are] there not for the purpose of being admired but for the purpose of nurturing the flower of the awareness of the sorrow of human existence (*mono no aware*).[3]

Earlier interpretations of *The Tale of Genji* and other classics were based on a combination of Buddhist and Confucian understandings of morality, according to which promiscuity and adultery bring their own punishment—if not in this lifetime, then surely in the next. Indeed, even Kada no Azumamaro and Kamo no Mabuchi found the engagement of literature and verse to be fundamentally edifying. In contrast, by emphasizing the validity of the affective spheres of human experience, Norinaga's literary theory was closely attuned to the emo-tional vitality and exuberance of much mid-Tokugawa culture, and his literary criticism also represented an important break with the earlier didacticism. In-deed, Norinaga's interpretations proved to be so influential that they have con-tinued to dominate literary criticism of Japan's classics, and even his sense of which works were deserving of critical attention has shaped the modern un-derstanding of Japan's literary and poetic canon.

KADA NO AZUMAMARO

Kada no Azumamaro's petition—or memorial—submitted to the shogun, Yoshimune, in 1728, without contesting the position of the dominant

---

3. See Tsunoda et al., eds., *Sources of Japanese Tradition*, 1st ed., vol. 2, pp. 27–28.

Neo-Confucian school, appeals for the creation of a school that would rescue traditional Japanese literature from oblivion. The unquestioned heritage of Chinese learning at this time is apparent in the very form of the memorial itself: it is in an extremely ornate style of classical Chinese, full of obscure allusions to the Chinese classics, the furthest thing from the native language and literature that Azumamaro wished to revive. Even more significant is his adaptation of Neo-Confucian principles to his own purpose. Thus he uses the slogan of the Confucian revival in the Song dynasty, "Restore the Ancient Order (or Way)" (J. *fukko*, Ch. *fugu*), to justify a kind of Japanese neoclassicism. In Azumamaro's mind, however, it is clear that these classical studies must be literary and philological in nature, for the Ancient Way can be rediscovered only through textual research.

It is important to note, incidentally, how this text reflects the prevailing view that loyalty to the shogun and to the emperor go hand in hand. There is no suggestion of a conflict of interests or authority such as arose in the nineteenth century.

PETITION FOR THE ESTABLISHMENT OF A SCHOOL OF NATIONAL LEARNING

Respectfully submitted, craving your bountiful favor in promoting the creation of a school of National Learning. I bow my head in awe and trepidation; vile and base as I am, I abjectly offer my words.

Tokugawa Ieyasu rose in Mikawa Province and soon succeeded in assuming command of the various daimyo to bring peace to the nation. All were as grass before the wind; who could surpass him? Changes brought about by his renewal of the country first led to the establishment of the Kōbunkan,[4] which has grown and prospered. What could be added to it?

Enlightened rulers have successively ascended to power, and literary pursuits have grown increasingly splendid; their refulgence shines ever more. The military arts are more perfected than ever; how noble and accomplished they are! Could the respect of the Muromachi family for literature be mentioned on the same day? In keeping with this age of great peace, Heaven has sent us a generous and benevolent ruler.[5] The country has witnessed the mild rule vouchsafed by his innate gifts. No talented men are without employ; the court is thronged with upright men. Above, he respects the emperor and devotes himself to effecting a government without deceit. Below, he cherishes the daimyo, who offer him tribute. Because his policies are perfected and he has leisure for other

---

4. The Kōbunkan was the official Hayashi school of Neo-Confucianism, founded in 1630 by a grant of land in Edo from the shogun Iemitsu.

5. The shogun Tokugawa Yoshimune (1684–1751).

pursuits, he has turned his mind to ancient studies; when the teachings in them are not complete, he spends much time in studying the rule of the men of old. He buys rare books for a thousand pieces of gold. Following his example, the celebrated scholars of the nation search for rare and forgotten books. Visitors of unusual talent from all over the world flock to his court. . . .

Everywhere now, Confucian studies are followed, and every day the Buddhist teachings flourish more. "Humaneness" and "rightness" have become household words; even common soldiers and menials know what is meant by the *Classic of Odes*. In every family they read the sutras; porters and scullery maids can discuss Emptiness (*shunyata*). The people's manner of living has benefited by great advances, but our National Learning is gradually falling into desuetude. Cultivated fields are continuously being abandoned, and possessions are being exhausted by contributions to Buddhism. Most lamentably, however, the teachings of our divine emperors are steadily melting away, each year more conspicuously than the last. Japanese learning is falling into ruin and is a bare tenth of what it once was. The books of law are disappearing: who is there to ask about studies of the old learning? The way of the *waka* [poetry] is falling into oblivion; what can revive the great refinement of the old styles?

Those who now treat Shinto all follow the theories of yin-yang and the Five Phases.[6] Those who consider the *waka* tend to adopt the explanations of Tendai doctrines or of the Four Disciplines of Chinese poetry. If these scholars are not the dregs of Tang and Song Confucians, they are exudations from the Womb and Diamond Mandalas. If their writings are not fabrications composed of vain theories and idle hairsplittings, they are eccentricities without foundation or thought. They speak of "secrets" and "traditions," but of the true traditions of the wise men of old, what knowledge do they have? They speak of "depths" and "recondite meanings," but how many are the forgeries of recent men!

From the time when I was young, I went without sleep or food in order to combat such heterodox ideas. When I grew to maturity, I tried ceaselessly, with learning and with thought, to revive the Ancient Way. If now I do not rouse myself and try to explain the rights and wrongs, people later will certainly confuse the true and the false, for their ears will be stopped and their hearts shut. If I try to keep aloof, the old writings will become vague and obscure. If I try to pursue the matter, I will find how old and weary I am. In this state of doubt, I cannot make a decision. Uncertain, I fail to do what I should.

Prostrate, I here make my humble request: that I be given a quiet tract of land in Kyoto where I can open a school for studies of the imperial land. I have collected since my youth many secret and obscure writings and, since growing old, have corrected numerous old records and accounts. I propose to store them at this school to provide for researches of future days. There must be persons

---

6. For example, the school of Yamazaki Ansai.

living in remote villages who experience great difficulty in getting hold of such
books. There must also be many scholars in forsaken hamlets who cannot realize their ambitions to study the Japanese classics. We should lend the necessary texts throughout the country and enable scholars to read them. A familiarity with only a single volume would permit a scholar to find out about the
downfall of many kings; a careful study of antiquity could save the people
from countless suffering. If by great good fortune some extraordinary man
of talent arises, the way of Prince Toneri will not perish.[7] If there are men
who polish the gems of poetry, the teachings of Kakinomoto Hitomaro[8] will
again flourish. If the National Histories are clear, it will be no small aid to the
officials in improving the people. If the laws of the three reigns[9] are given new
life, this will also prove of great benefit to the prestige and permanence of the
nation. The *Man'yōshū* is [the *Shijing* of the East and][10] the pure essence of
our national temperament. He who studies it will not be slandered as an ig-
noramus. He who is unfamiliar with it will be admonished as being unfit to
converse with.

The first school established in our country was at the Ōmi[11] court. The first
teaching of the Way of letters originated at the time of the Emperor Saga. The
Sugawara and Ōe families[12] had academies of learning. The Minamoto,
Fujiwara, Tachibana, and Wake families followed them. At the Dazaifu in Kyushu, there was a school; in Ashikaga and Kanazawa, education was advanced.
However, they taught Chinese history and the Chinese classics in these schools,
even in those for the imperial family. Offerings were made to the spirit of
Confucius. Alas, how ignorant the Confucian scholars were of the past, not
knowing a single thing about the imperial Japanese learning. How painful, the
stupidity of later scholars—who cannot bewail the destruction of the ancient
learning? This is why foreign teachings have prevailed, and we encounter them
in street conversations and corner gossip. This is why, too, our teachings have
so deteriorated. False doctrines are rampant, taking advantage of our
weakness. . . .

I am an exceedingly ignorant man. What can I claim to know? If, indeed,
there is one thing I dare claim for myself some familiarity, it is the explanation

---

7. Prince Toneri (d. 735) was the compiler of the *Chronicles of Japan* (*Nihon shoki*).

8. Kakinomoto Hitomaro was the greatest of the *Man'yōshū* poets.

9. The codes of the Kōnin, Jōgan, and Engi eras. They are used here, however, to balance
the "National Histories" in the preceding sentence and mean, more generally, the laws of Heian
times.

10. The phrase in brackets is found in the rough draft of this petition, but it was deleted by
Kada in the final version. It is restored here because of its interest.

11. Ōmi was the site of the court, near the modern city of Ōtsu, during the reign of Emperor
Tenchi.

12. All the following are important families with literary traditions.

of words. There are many misconceptions about our national writings. The fact that some people seem to be aware of them today is probably because the books survive. There are few explanations for the old Japanese words. The fact that one does not hear of anyone who is thoroughly conversant in them must be because the documents and men are insufficient. It has indeed been several hundred years since the old learning was taught. Only three or four books explain the words, and these books vie with one another in claiming to be the authority, advancing new and outlandish theories to support their claims. Such books are exceedingly superficial; how can they hope to attain the true meanings? If the old words are not understood, the old meanings will not be clear. If the old meanings are not clear, the old learning will not be revived. The way of the former kings is disappearing; the ideas of the wise men of antiquity have almost been abandoned. The loss will not be small if we fail now to teach philology. We must devote ourselves to this project. I have given my life's energies to studying the old words. I humbly believe that the rise or fall of Japanese learning depends on whether or not my plan is accepted. I pray Your Excellency will grant it your attention and consider it favorably.

Your servant Kada submits the above in awe and trepidation.

[Kada no Azumamaro, *Kada zenshū*, vol. 1, pp. 1–6; RT]

KAMO NO MABUCHI

Kamo no Mabuchi regarded poetry as the medium best suited for expressing heartfelt emotion. He thus concluded that Japan's most ancient verses might offer insight into, and even evidence of, an archaic, purely Japanese "heart" (*kokoro*) untainted by exposure to continental moral and ethical teachings. He also believed that history—especially Japan's unbroken chain of imperial rule—demonstrated the inherent superiority of the Japanese polity.

INQUIRY INTO THE IDEA OF POETRY

Indeed, in early antiquity [before the Nara period (710–794)], people's hearts (*kokoro*) were straightforward and correct. Since their hearts were straightforward, there was little scheming, and since affairs were few, words were likewise unadorned. Accordingly, when matters arose in the heart, persons voiced these matters in song. These "songs" were called *uta* [which also means "poetry"]. Thus, since their verses were straightforward and heartfelt and since their words were correct using unadorned language, their composition was spontaneous and naturally poetic. Accordingly, as these verses were utterly heartfelt expressions, in ancient times there was no distinction between poets and nonpoets.

In the limitless fifteen-hundred-reign rule of far-off, majestic divine emperors, Chinese and Indian words and concepts (*kokoro*) entered our country and mixed with our native words and concepts, creating confusion. As a result, there are countless examples of how our people's correct hearts have been overwhelmed by these disorienting gusts and how even the spoken language has been corrupted by the [imported] garbage. Thus, in the most recent times, poetic words and spirit (*kokoro*) have come to differ from everyday words and spirit, and what we call poems have come to depend on classical models that distort the instinctively good heart and are overly concerned with verbal artifice.

Just as a dusty mirror can reflect only a clouded image and just as clean blossoms will inevitably become soiled when mixed with trash, these fallen [poetic] modes were perpetuated by the selection [of verses for anthologies] by later individuals whose hearts were completely defiled. However, it is not as if no one appears to lament this. . . . Truly, if, among things that remain unchanged from ancient times, one considers that birds, beasts, trees, and vegetation are all totally unchanged from ancient times, are we to believe that human beings alone have somehow changed from ancient times until now? Human beings naturally (*onozukara*) learn wickedness as they contend with one another's schemes, and society moves along similarly. How can we imagine that a person who has once turned to wrongdoing will somehow long to turn toward goodness? Rather, when the impulse to return to the past arises, it is from the wish to have one's prose and poetry more closely resemble the words and verses of the ancient past.

Since people today remain fundamentally the same as the people of the past, as one learns the [verses of the past], one's heart again becomes like the divine mirror, and one's words become as fresh as crossing a plain or [seeing] a mountain wildflower. If even the Chinese who change their masters in all things long for a return to the past, then should we, born into this country ruled by the heavenly succession, not long for a return to the lofty ages pacified prosperously by the imperial ancestor, and shall we cling to the present, an age that has descended like a river down from the mountains? . . .

Such decline notwithstanding, there is a legacy of that divine distant rule, and there are more than a few people who long for the past. When one looks at the writings of that vast and lofty age, the wise ways of those peaks seem to have ceased; one scarcely knows where to look to plumb the wisdom of the plains, and it all seems as ephemeral as a leaf blowing in the autumn wind. People in later ages were misled by the mists and lost their way—some have been duped by foreign ways of doing things and have forgotten their cultural roots. Just as the sun and moon remain unchanged, so too do the spirit (*kokoro*) and words of the ancient poems composed more than a thousand years ago by our forebears, and like the colors of spring and autumn, they remain the same from ancient times until now.

If you just give over your heart (*kokoro*) to the illustrious ancient courts at Fujiwara and Nara, if you put out of your mind thoughts of the colorless later ages, and if for months and even years you dedicate yourself to your versification, your heart will naturally (*onozukara*) return to the correct fold. Give over your thoughts to that time in particular, when people's hearts were correct and words were elegant and when there was not a trace of foulness or staleness in the practices of their lofty and manly hearts.

In this way, when you look on the manifold writings of the past, like a traveler who finally arrives home after having crossed the mountain depths or like a ship that reaches its destination after having crossed distant seas, you will, in this very world, attain the heart that is undisturbed by things and affairs and understands what is fruitless, a heart that, without help, with neither design nor force, and without [moral] teachings of any kind, conforms to Heaven-and-earth. It is the poems of the ancients that make it possible to know clearly the divine ages of the great Way of early antiquity that pacified the realm in ancient times. Study those ancient verses and make them your own.

[*Karonshū*, pp. 569–73; PN]

INQUIRY INTO THE IDEA OF THE NATION
(*KOKUI KŌ*)

Unlike Kada no Azumamaro, who presented in ornamental Chinese his petition for the establishment of a school of National Learning, Kamo no Mabuchi wrote *Inquiry into the Idea of the Nation* (*Kokui kō*) in almost pure Japanese. It was composed in 1765. Although it attacks Chinese, particularly Confucian, thought, it is conceived largely in Daoist terms, with numerous direct or indirect references to Laozi. The antiintellectual, intuitive teachings of Daoism proved congenial to later Shinto scholars as well, and in many instances we find in this work of Kamo no Mabuchi the arguments that Hirata Atsutane and other men presented less temperately.

Someone remarked to me, "I pay no heed to such petty trifles as Japanese poetry; what interests me is the Chinese Way of governing the nation."

I smiled at this and did not answer. Later, when I met the same man he asked, "You seem to have an opinion on every subject—why did you merely keep smiling when I spoke to you?"

I answered, "You mean when you were talking about the Chinese Confucian teachings or whatever you call them? They are no more than a human invention that reduces the heart of Heaven-and-earth to something trivial."

At these words he became enraged. "How dare you call our Great Way trivial?"

I answered, "I would be interested in hearing whether or not the Chinese Confucian learning has actually helped govern a country successfully." He immediately cited the instances of Yao, Shun, Xia, Yin, Zhou, and so on. I asked if there were no later examples, but he informed me that there were not.

I pursued the matter, asking this time how far back Chinese traditions went. He answered that thousands of years had passed from Yao's day to the present. I then asked, "Why then did the Way of Yao continue only until the Zhou and afterward cease? I am sure that it is because you restrict yourself to citing events that took place thousands of years ago that the Way seems so good. But those are merely ancient legends. It takes more than such specious ideas to run a country!"

When I said this, he grew all the more furious and ranted on about ancient matters. I said,

> You are utterly prejudiced. You say that Yao yielded the throne to that rascal Shun? That sounds as if it must have been a good thing for the country, but that is the sort of thing we avoid in Japan as being "too good."[13] In China there also were ruffians who, far from yielding the throne, sprang up from nowhere to kill their sovereigns and seize control of the country. That is what we find "too bad" and equally avoid. An excess of good can thus lead to excess of evil.

Mabuchi goes on to cite many other similar instances in Chinese history.

"Things in China grew more and more chaotic, although in the time of Emperor Wen of the Han dynasty, there seems to have been an interval of good government because the emperor took to heart what Laozi had said. As you can see, whenever some baseborn individual appeared to slay his lord and proclaim himself emperor, everyone bowed his head and served this upstart obediently. That is not the worst of it. Although the Chinese despise all foreign countries as 'barbarian,' when someone from one of the 'barbarian' countries became emperor, they all prostrated themselves before him. Wouldn't you say, then, that to despise others as 'barbarian' was irresponsible? It is not a word to be applied indiscriminately.

"Thus, even though their country has been torn for centuries by disturbances and has never really been well administered, they think that they can explain with their Way of Confucius the principles governing the whole world. Indeed, when one has heard them through, there is nothing to be said: anyone can quickly grasp their doctrines because they consist of mere quibbling. What they

---

13. That is, something that, although good in itself, can lead to unfortunate consequences.

value the most and insist on is the establishment and maintenance of good government. Everybody in China would seem to agree on this point, but belief in it did not in fact lie very deep. It is obvious that many gave superficial assent in their hearts. Yet when these principles were introduced to this country, it was stated that China had obtained good government by adopting them. This was a complete fabrication. I wish it were possible to send to China anyone who clung to such a belief! He would discover, as did Urashima Tarō[14] when he returned to his home, what an illusion he had been suffering from!

"In ancient days Japan was governed in accordance with the natural laws of Heaven-and-earth. There was never any indulgence in such petty rationalizing as marked China, but when suddenly these teachings were transmitted here from abroad, they quickly spread, for in their simplicity the men of old took them for the truth. In Japan, generation after generation, extending back to the remote past, had known prosperity, but no sooner were these Confucian teachings propagated here than in the time of Tenmu[15] a great rebellion occurred. Later, at Nara, the palace, dress, and ceremonies were Chinesified, and everything acquired a superficial elegance; under the surface, however, contentiousness and dishonesty became more prevalent.

"Confucianism made men more crafty and led them to worship the ruler to such an excessive degree that the whole country acquired a servant's mentality. Later it even happened that an emperor was sacrilegeously driven to an island exile. This occurred because the country had become infected with Chinese ideas. Some people speak ill of Buddhism, but since it is a teaching that makes men stupid, it does not represent a grave evil; after all, rulers do not prosper unless the people are stupid.[16]

"Just as roads are naturally created when people live in uncultivated woodlands or fields, so the Way of the Age of the Gods spontaneously took hold in Japan. Because it was a Way indigenous to the country, it caused our emperors to become increasingly prosperous. However, not only had the Confucian teachings thrown China into disorder, but they now also had the same effect on Japan. Yet those not knowing these facts revere Confucianism and think that it is the Way to govern the country! This is a deplorable attitude.

"Japanese poetry has as its subject the human heart. It may seem to be of no practical use and just as well left uncomposed, but when one knows poetry

---

14. Urashima Tarō is the hero of a Japanese fairy tale who returns to his village after extraordinary adventures in a dragon's palace to discover, like Rip Van Winkle, that many years have elapsed and he is an old man.

15. Emperor Tenmu (631–686) ascended the throne only after a struggle with Prince Ōtomo, the appointed successor to Tenchi.

16. On the ground that knowledge leads to greed and ambition, craftiness and contentiousness.

well, one understands also without explanation the reasons governing order and disorder in the world. They say that Confucius himself did not reject poetry but placed the *Classic of Odes* at the head of the classics. Things that are explained in terms of theories are as though dead. Those that spontaneously operate together with Heaven-and-earth are alive and active. I do not mean to say that it is a bad idea to have a general knowledge of all things, but it is a common human failing to tend to lean excessively in that direction. It is advisable not to cling too tenaciously to things once one has learned them. Even though some Japanese poems have evil desires as their themes, the poems do not corrupt the reader's heart but instead make it more gentle and more understanding of all things.

"When ruling the country, a knowledge of Chinese things is of no help in the face of an emergency. In such a situation some man will spontaneously come forth to propose things that are wise and true. In the same way, doctors often study and master Chinese texts, but very seldom do they cure any sickness. In contrast, medicines that have been transmitted naturally in this country, with no reasons or theoretical knowledge behind them, infallibly cure all maladies. It is good when a man spontaneously devotes himself to these things. It is unwise to become obsessed with them. I would like to show people even once what is good in our Way. The fact that the Confucian scholars know very little about government is obvious from the frequent disorders that arise in China whenever the government is left to them. . . .

"It is another bad habit of the Chinese to distinguish men from beasts, by way of self-praise for being man and dispraise for the rest. It is like their custom of despising all other countries as 'barbarian,' a meaningless expression. Are not all creatures that live between Heaven-and-earth so many insects? Why should only man be considered precious? What is so exceptional about man? In China they venerate man as 'the soul of all things' or some such, but I wonder whether man would not rather be called 'the most evil of all things.' By this I mean that just as the sun and moon have not changed, birds, beasts, fish, and plants all are exactly as they were in ancient days, but ever since man impetuously decided that knowledge would be of use to him, evil motives of every kind have sprung up among people and have finally thrown the world into turmoil. Even when they enjoy peaceful rule, men deceive one another. It might be desirable if just one or two men in the world had knowledge, but when everyone possesses it, a dreadful chaos ensues, and in the end knowledge is useless. If one looked through the eyes of a bird or a beast, one would say, 'Man is evil. His ways should not be followed.'" . . .

People also tell me, "We had no writing in this country and therefore had to use Chinese characters." From this one fact you know everything about the relative importance of our countries. I answer, "I need not recite again how troublesome, evil, [and] turbulent a country China is. To mention just one instance—there is the matter of their picture writing. There are about 38,000 characters in common use,[17] as someone has determined. . . . The name of every place and plant has a separate character for it that has no other use but to designate that particular place or plant. Can any man, even one who devotes himself to the task earnestly, learn all these many characters? Sometimes people miswrite characters, [and] sometimes the characters themselves change from one generation to the next. What a nuisance, a waste of effort, and a bother! In India, in contrast, fifty letters suffice for the more than five thousand volumes of the Buddhist scriptures. The knowledge of a mere fifty letters permits one to know and transmit innumerable words of past and present alike. . . . In Holland, I understand, they use twenty-five letters. In this country there should be fifty. The appearance of letters used in all countries is generally the same, except in China where they invented their bothersome system. . . . The opinion that the characters are precious is not worth discussing further.". . .

. . . When we look at things recorded in China by the learned men, we see that the country never profited by any Way unless it was in accord with Heaven-and-earth. Therefore the sayings of Laozi derived from the will of Heaven-and-earth were in consonance with the proper Way of the country. In ancient days China was also a decent country. . . . In ancient times words and things were few. When things are few, the heart is sincere; there is no need for difficult teachings. All will go satisfactorily even without teachings because men are honest. It is true that since men's hearts have many facets, there is always some evil in them, but evil itself cannot remain hidden in an honest heart. If it is not hidden, it will not develop into anything serious but will remain no more than a moment's aberration. Thus, in ancient days although the land was not absolutely devoid of the teachings of good men, a few easy ones sufficed. But since China is a country of wicked heartedness, no amount of profound instruction could keep the innate evil from overwhelming the country, despite the surface appearance. Japan has always been a country whose people are honest. . . . Nevertheless, Chinese doctrines were introduced and corrupted men's hearts. Even though these teachings resembled those of China itself, they were of the kind that, heard in the morning, are forgotten by evening. Our country in ancient times was not like that. It obeyed the laws of Heaven-and-earth. The emperor was the sun and moon, and the subjects, the stars. If the subjects as stars protect the sun and moon, they will not hide it, as is now the case. Just as the sun, moon, and stars have always been in Heaven, so our imperial sun and moon—and the stars his vassals—have existed without change from ancient days and have ruled the world fairly. However, some knaves appeared, and as a result the emperor is diminished in power, and his subjects, too, have fallen

---

17. This is an extraordinary exaggeration, since even in Mabuchi's day, not more than 2,500 characters could have been in common use.

off. The Age of the Gods is where we may gain a knowledge of this. To discover it, we should carefully examine the words and thoughts in the ancient poetry and thereby see clearly into the oldest writings.

[*Sekai daishisō zenshū*, vol. 54, pp. 2–10; Dumoulin, "Kamo Mabuchi"]

MOTOORI NORINAGA

PRECIOUS COMB-BOX
(*TAMAKUSHIGE*)

The following excerpt is from Motoori Norinaga's *Precious Comb-box* of 1786, whose contents are meant to "comb" out the snarls of intellectual confusion. In it, Norinaga upholds the traditional account of the divine creation in all its unembellished simplicity while rejecting the rationalistic cosmogony of the Chinese. The Sun Goddess Amaterasu is represented as a universal as well as a national deity, one who has shown special favor to the Japanese and is guiding them to a special destiny.

The True Way is one and the same, in every country and throughout Heaven-and-earth. This way, however, has been correctly transmitted only in our imperial land. Its transmission in all foreign countries was lost long ago in early antiquity, and many and varied Ways have been expounded, each country representing its own way as the Right Way. But the Ways of foreign countries are no more the original Right Way than the end branches of a tree are the same as its root. They may have resemblances here and there to the Right Way, but because the original truth has been corrupted with the passage of time, they can scarcely be likened to the original Right Way. Let me state briefly what that original Way is. One must understand, first of all, the universal principle of the world. The principle is that Heaven-and-earth, all the gods and all phenomena, were brought into existence by the creative spirits of two deities—Takami-musubi and Kami-musubi. The birth of all humankind in all ages and the existence of all things and all matter have been the result of that creative spirit. It was the original creativity of these two august deities that caused the deities Izanagi and Izanami to create the land, all kinds of phenomena, and numerous gods and goddesses at the beginning of the Divine Age. This spirit of creativity [*musubi*, literally "union"] is a miraculously divine act, the reason for which is beyond the comprehension of the human intellect.

But in the foreign countries to which the Right Way has not been transmitted, this act of divine creativity is not known. Men there have tried to explain the principle of Heaven-and-earth and all phenomena by such theories as the yin and yang, the hexagrams of the *Classic of Changes*, and the Five Phases. But all of these fallacious theories stem from assumptions of the human intellect, and they in no wise represent the true principle.

In deep sorrow at the passing of his goddess, Izanagi journeyed after her to the land of death. Upon his return to the upper world, he bathed himself at Awagihara in Tachibana Bay in Tsukushi in order to purify himself of the pollution of the land of death, and while thus washing himself, he gave birth to the Heaven-Shining Goddess who, by the explicit command of her father-god, came to rule the Heavenly Plain for all time to come. This Heaven-Shining Goddess is none other than the sun in heaven that today casts its gracious light over the world. Then, an imperial prince of the Heaven-Shining Goddess was sent down from heaven to the middle kingdom of Ashihara. The goddess's mandate to the prince at that time stated that his dynasty should be coeval with Heaven-and-earth. It is this mandate that is the very origin and basis of the Way. Thus, all the principles and the Way of humankind are represented in the different stages of the Divine Age. Those who seek to know the Right Way must therefore pay careful attention to the stages of the Divine Age and learn the truths of existence. These aspects of the various stages are embodied in the ancient traditions of the Divine Age. No one knows with whom these ancient traditions began, but they were handed down orally from the very earliest times, and they refer to the accounts that have since been recorded in the *Kojiki* and the *Nihon shoki*. The accounts recorded in these two scriptures are clear and explicit and present no cause for doubt. Those who have interpreted these scriptures in a later age have contrived oracular formulas and have expounded theories that have no real basis. Some have become addicts of foreign doctrines and have no faith in the wonders of the Divine Age. Unable to understand that the truths of the world are contained in the evolution of the Divine Age, they fail to ascertain the true meaning of our ancient tradition. Because they base their judgment on the strength of foreign beliefs, they always interpret at their own discretion and twist to their own liking anything they encounter that may not be in accord with their alien teachings. Thus, they say that the High Heavenly Plain refers to the imperial capital and not to Heaven and that the Sun Goddess herself was not a goddess or the sun shining in the heavens but an earthly person and the forebear of the nation. These are arbitrary interpretations purposely contrived to flatter foreign ideologies. In this way, the ancient tradition is made to appear narrow and petty by depriving it of its comprehensive and primal character. This is counter to the meaning of the scriptures.

Heaven and earth are one; there is no barrier between them. The High Heavenly Plain is the high heavenly plain that covers all the countries of the world, and the Sun Goddess is the goddess who reigns in that heaven. Thus, she is without a peer in the whole universe, casting her light to the very ends of Heaven-and-earth and for all time. There is not a single country in the whole world that does not receive her beneficent illuminations, and no country can exist for even a day or an hour without her grace. This goddess is the splendor of all splendors. Foreign countries, however, having lost the ancient tradition of the Divine Age, do not know the meaning of revering this goddess. Only through the speculations of the human intelligence have they come to call the sun and the moon the spirit of yang and yin. In China and other countries, the "Heavenly Emperor" is worshiped as the supreme divinity. Other countries have objects of reverence, each according to its own way, but some of their teachings are based on the logic of inference and some on arbitrary personal opinions. At any rate, they are merely manmade designations, and the "Heavenly Ruler" or the "Heavenly Way" has no real existence at all. That foreign countries revere such nonexistent beings and remain unaware of the grace of the Sun Goddess is a matter of profound regret. But because of the special dispensation of our imperial land, the ancient tradition of the Divine Age has been correctly and clearly transmitted in our country, telling us about the genesis of the great goddess and the reason for her adoration. The "special dispensation of our imperial land" means that ours is the native land of the Heaven-Shining God-dess who casts her light over all countries in the four seas. Thus our country is the source and fountainhead of all other countries, and in all matters it excels all the others. It would be impossible to list all the products in which our country excels, but foremost among them is rice, which sustains the life of man, to whom there is no product more important. Our country's rice has no peer in foreign countries, which is why our other products are also superior. Those who were born in this country have long been accustomed to our rice and take it for granted, unaware of its excellence. They can enjoy such excellent rice morning and night to their heart's content because they have been fortunate enough to be born in this country.

Our country's imperial line, which casts its light over this world, represents the descendants of the Heaven-Shining Goddess. And in accordance with that goddess's mandate of reigning "forever and ever, coeval with Heaven-and-earth," the imperial line is destined to rule the nation for eons until the end of time and as long as the universe exists. That is the very basis of our Way. That our history has not deviated from the instructions of the divine mandate testifies to the infallibility of our ancient tradition. It also is why foreign countries cannot match ours and what is meant by the special dispensation of our country. For-eign countries expound their own Ways, each as if its Way alone were true. But their dynastic lines, basic to their existence, do not continue; they change fre-quently and are quite corrupt. Thus one can surmise that in everything they say there are falsehoods and that there is no basis in fact for them.

[*Motoori Norinaga zenshū*, vol. 6, pp. 3–6; PN]

"FIRST STEPS INTO THE MOUNTAINS"
(UIYAMABUMI)

"First Steps into the Mountains," an essay written in 1798, represents the fullest state-ment of Norinaga's taxonomy of learning. Ever the precisian, he distinguishes among different academic traditions and expounds the advantages of Japanese studies. His disclaimer that "any methodology is acceptable" notwithstanding, Norinaga explains how one might resurrect the true Way of the Gods (*kami*).

In life, there are many routes to pursue learning, not just one. Among these routes is, first, the diligent study of the Way, based on the book on the Age of the Gods in the *Nihon shoki*. This is called the Learning of the Gods, and a student of this is called a scholar of the Way of the Gods. Then there is learning whose object of study is government offices, ceremonies, and legal codes. Yet another area of learning deals with ancient customs, costumes, and accoutrements. These last two are called the Study of Classical Procedures.

There is also an approach that is not based on any particular set path; it studies the records starting with the Six National Histories and other ancient writings, including the later records. There are further divisions in this approach.

Another is the study of poetry, which has two methods. Some people compose only poems, while others study the ancient poetry collections and tales.

These are the kinds of learning, and each student learns according to his preferred way. The method of learning also varies according to the intentions of the teacher and his students.

A person who is determined to learn and begins to study has a preferred route from the beginning. Some choose the methodology by themselves, while others have no preconceived way of learning or understanding in this matter. They approach a learned teacher and ask, "Which Way should I take?" or "Which book should a novice read first?" This is common and understandable.

You should begin studying your discipline in an orthodox manner, adopting a correct attitude; in this way you will not later deviate into erratic and improper directions. In addition, your learning will bear fruit sooner if the most effective methods are clearly outlined from the beginning. This is the most desirable way to approach scholarship.

Even when the energy expended is constant, there are advantages and disadvantages depending on the path and the methodology followed. But as for the choice of learning, a teacher should not force something onto a student; the choice should be left to the student's interests. No matter how much a novice he may be, a person who is determined to pursue scholarship is not entirely like an infant in regard to his intellect. There is invariably a route in which he is interested and which accords with his ability. He likes some directions and is uninterested in others. Furthermore, people are gifted by birth in some things and not in others. Success is seldom achieved in something that you do not like or are not gifted in, no matter how much effort you may put into it.

In any kind of study, it is easy enough to teach a method based on a set of superficial reasons, with the teacher instructing the pupil to follow this path or that. There is no way of knowing, however, whether the adopted method is indeed good or whether against all expectations it may turn out to be unhelpful. So the method should not be forced onto a student; the choice should be left entirely to his preference. In essence, the most important and fundamental requirement is that learning be pursued for many years, sparing no effort, without ever becoming boring or fatiguing.

In this respect, any methodology is acceptable, and it should not be a matter of great concern. Yet, however excellent your method of study, you will not be successful if you are lazy and make no effort. . . .

There are many types of foreign studies, starting with Confucianism, Buddhism, and so on, but since they are foreign to us, they need not be discussed here. I prefer to expend my efforts on studies of my country, rather than waste it on matters pertaining to foreign countries. Leaving aside for the moment the question of which is superior, is it not regrettable that some people study foreign things and remain ignorant of the matters of their own country?

What is the main principle of study that one should rely on? It is the study of the Way. This Way is the Way of the Sun Goddess. It is the Way in which the emperor governs his realm. It is the true Way that permeates all nations within the four seas and is transmitted exclusively in our imperial land.

The True Way of the Gods is totally different, dissociated from the teachings of Confucianism, Buddhism, or any other doctrine, having nothing whatsoever in common with them.

Since in recent years all the scholars studying the Way of the Gods are as I have described, they resemble the scholars of the Song school of Chinese studies. Displaying not the least discernment, they seek the Way with single-minded commitment. But fettered by their exclusive reliance on Chinese-style logic, they do not realize that they search for the spirit of ancient times. Their viewpoint is completely Confucian, so the more they progress in their studies, the further they depart from the meaning of the Way.

As a rule, the ceremonies of the Way of the Gods as performed by those who advocate relying on Buddhism are imitations of Buddhist ritual; the ceremonies are just inventions and are by no means the genuine ancient practices of our imperial land.

Confucian scholars of the Way of the Gods in recent years perform ceremonies such as funerals, memorial services, festivities, and other unorthodox rites. They claim that these, different from ordinary secular ceremonies, are the ceremonies of the Way of the Gods. In truth, they are not the ancient ceremonies, for they are mixed with Confucian ideas, and many features have been invented. . . .

The Way is enacted by the ruler. It is bestowed on subjects from above, so subjects should not privately interpret and carry it out. . . .

This is the just and public Way with which the emperor governs the world. It is therefore repulsive and sad when people turn it into their private, individual possession, changing it into something narrow and small. . . .

[Adapted from Nishimura, "First Steps into the Mountains," pp. 449–55]

LOVE AND POETRY

PERSONAL VIEWS OF POETRY
(ISONOKAMI SASAMEGOTO)

In this piece, *Personal Views of Poetry* of 1763, Norinaga acclaims Japanese poetry for its spontaneous expression of the deepest human emotions and justifies its defiance of Confucian canons of emotional restraint. Characteristically, Norinaga recognizes the worth of all Japanese poetry in this regard, whereas his teacher Kamo no Mabuchi singled out the *Man'yōshū*.

QUESTION: Why are there so many love poems in the world?

ANSWER: The oldest love poems are found in the *Kojiki* and the *Nihon shoki*, but the dynastic anthologies are particularly conspicuous for the great number of love poems that they contain. The *Man'yōshū* has sections . . . devoted entirely to love poems. . . . Even in the Chinese *Classic of Odes*, love songs are prominent. Why is this so? It is because love, more than any other emotion, stirs the human heart deeply and demands an outlet in poetry. It is to love poems that we must look for lines that profoundly express human emotions.

QUESTION: Generally speaking, man seems to be constantly concerned not so much with love but, rather, with personal success and the acquisition of wealth, in which he appears to be completely and unreasonably absorbed. Why is it that there are no poems expressing these sentiments?

ANSWER: There is a distinction between emotion and passion. All the varied feelings of the human heart are emotions, but those among them seeking something in one way or another are passions. These two are inseparable, for passions are generally a kind of emotion. Only such feelings as sympathy for others, sadness, sorrow, and regret are specifically called emotions. But poetry comes only from emotion. This is because emotion is more sensitive to things and more deeply compassionate. Passion is absorbed only in the acquisition of things; it does not move someone deeply or intimately. Thus, it has no capacity for tears at the sight of flowers or the song of birds. The desire to acquire wealth is an example of passion. It is so alien to the awareness of the sorrow of existence that there can be no outpouring of poetry from it. Although love has its origin in passion, it is a deep emotion that no living thing can avoid. And because man is most highly capable of understanding the meaning of the sorrow of existence, it is he who is most deeply moved—sometimes unbearably—by the sentiment of love. Outside love in which there is awareness of the sorrow of existence, there is poetry. And whereas it became the practice in later times to suppress emotion—for emotion was regarded as less profound than passion, a sign of a faint heart, and therefore a shameful thing—poetry alone retained the spirit of antiquity and continued to express truthfully and without adornment the real sentiments of the human heart. Nor has poetry felt constrained to apologize for femininity or faintheartedness. In later times, in order to enhance the charm of poetry, poets have emphasized awareness of the sorrow of existence and have turned against themes of passion. Passion is not a fit subject for poetry. Thus, poems like those in praise of wine found in the third volume of the *Man'yōshū* and so common in Chinese poetry are unappealing, if not odious. They evoke no affection and hold no attraction, because passion is regarded as tainted and not conducive to fine sentiment. Why is it that in other countries [meaning China] the feeling of emotion is regarded as something shameful, and base passion is regarded as something admirable?

QUESTION: The Chinese work, the *Record of Rites*, states that love is the cardinal passion of man. Conjugal sentiment is deep, for it is the feeling of husband for wife and wife for husband, and this is as it should be. But love in poetry is not always confined to love between man and wife. A man in the privacy of his own room yearns for the woman who is not acceptable to his parents; another, in the intimacy of the bedchamber, gives his love to a woman betrothed to another. Such conduct is licentious and wicked; yet it is regarded as an exquisite example of love.

ANSWER: It was stated above that the human is susceptible to love—no one can avoid it. Once involved in and disturbed by it, the wise and foolish alike frequently behave illogically in spite of themselves, and they end by losing control of the country[18] and ruining their bodies and their reputations. That has been the case in countless instances in the past, and it is so in the present. And this happens even though everyone fully realizes that such behavior is evil and that one must guard against becoming wildly infatuated. But not all men are sages. Not only in love but also in their daily thought and conduct, the good

---

18. It is characteristic of Confucian teaching, which is addressed initially to the ruling class, that it is most concerned with the political consequences of moral failings.

does not always prevail; in fact, the bad often does. Of all the things in life, love is most difficult to suppress, despite every effort to control it. And even realizing that conduct contrary to the dictates of his own mind is evil, man is helpless to control it; of this there are numerous instances. Inside the heart, unnoticed by others, there may be a fancy for someone else, even though outwardly one appears quite sober and admonishes others to beware of love. If one searches the bottom of one's heart, it is impossible not to find love there, especially the type of love forbidden by man. And try as one might to suppress it, there will be only melancholy and bewilderment in one's heart. Because love is thus unreasonable, the love poems issued on such occasions are especially touching. It is also natural that many love poems suggest impropriety and licentiousness. Be that as it may, poetry follows the principle of the sorrow of existence and attempts to express without adornment the bad as well as the good. Its aim is not to select and arrange for the heart what is good or bad. To advise against and check evil is the duty of those who govern the country and teach the people. While unruly love should be strongly cautioned against, it is not the responsibility of poetry to teach such discipline. The aim of poetry is different: it aims to express an awareness of the poignancy of human life and should not be judged on any other basis. This is not to say that poetry applauds evil conduct or implies that it is good. It means only that poems, as a medium for expressing emotion, are admirable. All forms of literature, including the novel, should be seen and appreciated in this light and an attempt made to grasp the spirit of their purpose. For further reference I have dwelled on this point separately and at greater length in my study of *The Tale of Genji*, which includes quotations from every chapter and explanatory notes. From this tale one can understand the spirit of poetry.

QUESTION: Chinese poetry and other forms of Chinese literature are rarely devoted to accounts of love, but our literature abounds in them, including many instances of licentious behavior involving high and low alike. Yet no one condemns this as evil. Is it because there is a taste for the frivolous and the voluptuous in our national character?

ANSWER: Man's predilection for love is the same now as it has been in the past, and it is the same here as it is elsewhere. An examination of Chinese historical accounts indicates that country has had more than its share of licentiousness affairs. The Chinese, however, customarily subject all things to long, tedious moralistic judgments. In particular, love affairs have been judged by would-be scholars as contemptible and despicable. Chinese poetry, likewise, has been subjected to this same national tendency; it has a taste for only the heroic, manly spirit and speaks not of the effeminate sentiments and sinful aspects of love, which it regards as shameful. This aspect of Chinese poetry is only its edited, ornamented, and outward appearance and not the true revelation of the human heart. But in a later age the readers of such poetry have accepted it without serious study as expressive of the true situation. It is ridiculous to believe on this basis that the people of that country are less susceptible to the temptations of love than are the people of other countries.

In general our countrymen are generous and not particularly discerning or critical. They have not engaged in painstaking and persistent disputations on the good or the bad in men. Instead they have transmitted in speech and in writing things as they were without adornment. This is particularly true of our poetry and our novels, which have as their aim the expression of a sensitivity to human existence; they are calm, straightforward revelations of the varied feelings of men in love.

Again, our national histories written according to Chinese models show no special distinction from their Chinese prototypes. It is a mistake to ignore these national histories and to fail to discern what is so clearly written in them, just as in their Chinese prototypes or to judge the Japanese solely on the basis of their poetry and novels as being especially susceptible to the temptations. Even the *History of the Wei* (*Wei zhi*), a Chinese history that may not be wholly reliable on all matters, says that the Japanese are not sexually licentious. Not only in love but in all other things as well, there have been many scoundrels in China. The Chinese persistently warn against evil; yet there are many evil men there because the country is bad. In our country, conversely, man's conduct has neither been excessively praised nor excessively decried; it has been dealt with calmly and straightforwardly. Thus, we do not make much of evil men in our country. And this is because our country is the land of the gods.

[*Motoori Norinaga zenshū*, vol. 6, pp. 524–29; PN]

POETRY AND MONO NO AWARE

A LITTLE BOAT BREAKING A PATH THROUGH THE REEDS (ASHIWAKE OBUNE)

Motoori's first published work, *A Little Boat Breaking a Path Through the Reeds*, is an honest attempt to confront the problems of composing poetry and not, like so many similar books, a mere restatement of platitudes. An encounter with Keichū's writings inspired Motoori to search for the truth about poetry and to make himself into "a little boat breaking a path through the reeds"—that is, resolved to brush aside the encumbrances hindering his boat and sail directly to the heart of poetry.

A *Little Boat* is written in a question-and-answer form and covers a wide range of topics. Most of its basic ideas remained characteristic of Motoori's later writings on literature. It opens with a statement and question.

The *uta* is a Way for assisting the government of the country. It must not be thought of as a plaything to be toyed with idly. That is why one finds statements to this effect in the preface to the *Anthology of Old and New Japanese Poems* (*Kokinshū*). What do you think of this opinion?

This question reveals a Confucian attitude toward literature and brings to mind the controversy over the eight essays and the statement that uta *(waka poems) are of no help in promoting good government. Although Motoori's answer to the question reveals his familiarity with Arimaro's arguments, he also introduces a distinctive note.*

ANSWER: This is incorrect. The basic function of the *uta* is not to assist in government, nor is it intended to improve the person. It is the outward expression of thoughts in the mind and nothing else. Undoubtedly some poems do help in government, and others serve as a lesson to the people. Some poems also are harmful to the country and do damage to the person. These effects surely depend on the particular poem produced by the mind of a particular person. A poem can be used for evil or for good; it can be used to express excitement, depression, grief, joy, or any other mood. . . . And moreover, if you wonder why there are so few poems with a didactic message and so many about love, it is because that is the area in which the true nature of poetry is naturally expressed. No emotion is as powerful as love, and it is precisely because every single person wants to be successful in love that there are so many poems on the subject. Few sages in the world are so given to improving themselves and obtaining the good that they think exclusively about didactic matters; that is why there are so few didactic poems.

The key expression in Motoori's aesthetic judgments is mono no aware. *The word* aware *was found in the* Man'yōshū *as an expression of wonder or awe. Motoori defined the word in terms of its original meaning.*

When we speak of knowing *mono no aware*, we refer to the cry of wonder that comes to our lips when our mind is moved by the realization that something we have seen, heard, or touched is *aware*. Even in our common speech today, people say *aa* or *hare*. When they have been impressed by the sight of the moon or the cherry blossoms, they say, "*Aa*, what splendid blossoms!" or "*Hare*, what a lovely moon." *Aware* is the combination of the two cries of *aa* and *hare*.

One is moved because one has recognized *mono no aware*. This means, for example, if something joyous makes us feel happy, it is because we have recognized the joyful nature of the thing. . . .

The true feelings of people are awkward and untidy. Suppose a beloved child dies—surely there would be no difference in the depth of grief of the father and mother. But the father would pretend this was not so, even as the mother, overcome by lamentations, is blinded by her tears. Why should this be the case? The mother, unable to conceal her true feelings, expresses them exactly as they are. The father unavoidably must worry about how he appears in others' eyes, and he will control or suppress his emotions for fear that people will think him softhearted. He will not shed a single tear, nor will he reveal on his face the terrible grief he feels in his heart but will present a picture of noble resignation. The mother's appearance will be unseemly, distraught, and disheveled. But this is what is meant by showing feelings as they actually are. The father's appearance is indeed masculine and severe, and it is admirable that he manages somehow not to appear distraught, but these are not his true feelings. . . . One may see, then, that the real appearance of human emotions is frail, untidy, and foolish. And since poetry is something that describes feelings, it is fitting that it should accord with one's feelings and also be untidy, clumsy, and frail. . . .

When a man who knows *mono no aware* encounters something that is *aware*, he may try not to think about it, but he cannot prevent himself from feeling the *aware*. It is like a man with good hearing who, though he tries not to hear the thunder, hears it and is afraid. . . . The words that naturally burst forth when the poet is unable to resist *aware* inevitably multiply and become decorated and eventually form themselves into a poem. . . .

A poem is not merely something composed to describe one's feelings when one can no longer bear the *mono no aware*. When one's feelings are extremely deep, one's heart still feels dissatisfied and unresigned, even after having composed a poem. In order to feel comfort, one must read the poem to someone else. If the other person hearing the poem finds it has *aware*, this will greatly comfort the poet. . . . Even though reading one's poem to someone else brings no material advantage to either the listener or the poet, it is quite natural that the poet feels compelled to read it aloud to another person. And since this is the intent of poetry, it is a basic principle and not an accident that poems must be heard by others. Someone who does not understand this might say that a true poem describes one's emotions exactly as they are, whether bad or good, and it has nothing to do with whether or not people hear it. Such an argument sounds plausible, but it betrays ignorance of the true meaning of poetry.

[Adapted from Keene, *Dawn to the West*, pp. 322–26]

GOOD AND EVIL IN THE TALE OF GENJI

THE EXQUISITE COMB
(TAMA NO OGUSHI)

Before Norinaga became involved in the National Learning movement, he devoted himself to studying Japanese literature, and his interpretation provided the basis for much of his later thought. The following selections from *The Exquisite Comb*, a study of Lady Murasaki's *Tale of Genji*, reveal his view of the novel as a record of human experience as we find it, not necessarily as we wish it to be. It is just such a realistic appreciation of the emotional life of man that confirms *The Tale of Genji* as one of the greatest expressions of the Japanese spirit and provides a key to all that is true and best in the Japanese national life.

There have been many interpretations over the years of the purpose of this tale. But all these interpretations have been based not on a consideration of the nature of the novel itself but, rather, on the novel as seen from the point of view of Confucian and Buddhist works, and thus they do not represent the author's true purpose. To seize on an occasional similarity in sentiment or a chance correspondence in ideas with Confucian and Buddhist works, and to generalize about the nature of the tale as a whole, is unwarranted. The general appeal of this tale is very different from that of such didactic works. [p. 472]

Good and evil as found in this tale do not correspond to good and evil as found in Confucian and Buddhist writings. . . . Good and evil extend to all realms. Even for human beings, good and evil are not necessarily limited to their thinking and conduct. Rank and position imply good and evil; thus, the noble person is regarded as good, the lowly as bad. In *The Tale of Genji*, persons of high rank are spoken of as good, while in common parlance there are such expressions as "of good family" and "of good or bad standing." Likewise, we speak of good or bad features of one's face. Again, longevity, wealth, and prosperity all are good things, and short life, poverty, failure, loss of material things, illness, and disaster all are bad things. In addition to these strictly human aspects of good and evil, there is good and evil in such things as dress, furniture, housing, and, in fact, all things. Thus, it is not only in the psychological and ethical realms of life that we find good and evil. Again, good and evil are not constant—they change according to time and circumstance. For example, an arrow is good if it penetrates its object, while armor is good if it is impenetrable. In the heat of a summer day, coolness is good, while in the cold of winter, heat is good. For the man walking on the road at night, darkness is bad, but for the one trying to conceal himself, moonlight is bad. In such a way all things may be good or bad. Thus too the good and bad in man's mind and in his acts may not be as opposed to each other as they seem: they differ according to the doctrines that one follows. What Confucianism deems good, Buddhism may not; and what Buddhism considers good, Confucianism may regard as evil. Likewise, references to good and evil in *The Tale of Genji* may not correspond to Confucian or Buddhist concepts of good and evil. Then, what is good or evil in the realm of human psychology and ethics according to *The Tale of Genji?* Generally speaking, those who know the meaning of the sorrow of human existence, that is, those who are in sympathy and harmony with human sentiments, are regarded as good; and those who are not aware of the poignancy of human existence, that is, those who are not in sympathy and harmony with human sentiments, are regarded as bad. Regarded in this light, good and evil in *The Tale of Genji* may not appear to be especially different from that in Confucianism or Buddhism. However, if you examine it closely, you will see that there are many points of difference, as, for example, in the statement about being or not being in harmony with human sentiment. *The Tale of Genji* presents even good and evil in gentle and calm terms, unlike the intense, compelling, dialectical manner of Confucian writings.

Since the object of novels is teaching the meaning of the nature of human existence, their plots contain many points contrary to Confucian and Buddhist teaching. This is because among the varied feelings of man's reaction to things—whether good, bad, right, or wrong—are feelings contrary to reason, however improper they may be. Man's feelings do not always follow the dictates of his mind. They arise in man in spite of himself and are difficult to control. In the instance of Prince Genji, his interest in and a rendezvous with Utsusemi, Oborozukiyo, and the consort Fujitsubo are acts of extraordinary iniquity and immorality according to the Confucian and Buddhist points of view. It would be difficult to call Prince Genji a good man, however numerous his other good qualities. But *The Tale of Genji* does not dwell on his iniquitous and immoral acts but, rather, recites over and over again his profound awareness of the sorrow of existence and represents him as a good man who combines in himself all good things in man. . . .

For all that, *The Tale of Genji* does not regard Genji's misdeeds as good. The evil nature of his acts is obvious and need not be restated here. Besides, there is a type of writing whose purpose is the consideration of such evils—in fact, there are quite a few such writings—and an objective story therefore need not be used for such a purpose. The novel is neither like the Buddhist Way, which teaches man how to achieve enlightenment without deviating from the right way, nor like the Confucian Way, which teaches man how to govern the country or to regulate his home or his conduct. It is simply a tale of human life that leaves aside and does not profess to take up at all the questions of good and bad and that dwells only on the goodness of those who are aware of the sorrow of human existence. The purpose of *The Tale of Genji* may be likened to the man who, loving the lotus flower, must collect and store muddy and foul water in order to plant and cultivate it. The impure mud of illicit love affairs described in *The Tale of Genji* is there not for the purpose of being admired but for the purpose of nurturing the flower of the awareness of the sorrow of human existence. Prince Genji's conduct is like the lotus flower, which is happy and fragrant but which has its roots in muddy water. But *The Tale of Genji* does not dwell on the impurity of the water; it dwells only on those who are sympathetically kind and who are aware of the sorrow of human existence, and it holds these feelings to be the basis of the good man. [pp. 486–88]

[*Motoori Norinaga zenshū*, vol. 7, pp. 472–88; RT]

HIRATA ATSUTANE

If we credit Motoori Norinaga with having made National Learning a subject worthy of a great scholar's attention and thereby having given the reconstituted Shinto "tradition" the authority of a sacred canon, it remained for Hirata Atsutane (1776–1843) to popularize Shinto nativism by asserting the singular supremacy of Japan, its culture, Way, and people.

Little is known of Atsutane's early years. He ran away from his home in the north of Japan at the age of nineteen and made his way to Edo, where for several years he apparently eked out a hand-to-mouth existence with menial jobs. In 1801 he became interested in National Learning, although too late to have met Norinaga, who died a few months earlier that year. This, however, did not deter Atsutane from claiming Norinaga's posthumous benediction, which Atsutane insisted the late master had conferred on him in a dream.

Atsutane's focus on Shinto can also be regarded as an extension of trends evident in eighteenth-century Shinto theology. The emphasis in National Learning on the value of an ancient Way in Japan and the dangers of the Chinese sage and his Ways accorded with the theological formulations of such Shinto priests as Yoshimi Yukikazu (1673–1761) and Matsuoka Yūen (1701–1783). The eighteenth century had its own Shinto purist and popularizer in Masuho Zankō (1655–1742), who tried to disentangle the teachings regarding the *kami* from non-Japanese accretions. Indeed, much of what has been understood in modern times as "Shinto" can be traced to Norinaga's imaginative reconstruction of ancient Shinto, which he claimed to have found in the *Kojiki*, and Hirata Atsutane's popularization of this creed. Atsutane was willing to look anywhere for support of his doctrines, which made him more open to foreign ideas than was either Kamo no Mabuchi or Motoori Norinaga. For example, although Atsutane was at pains to revile the nations of the West as, like all nations, inferior to Japan, he also expressed admiration for Western science. He was fascinated by what he knew of Western astronomy, at least partially because of its heliocentric congruence with Shinto cosmogony. No less remarkable was Atsutane's liberal use of Christian theology. Christian writings had been banned in Japan for nearly two centuries, but Atsutane obtained copies of at least three

Chinese works written by Catholic missionaries in Beijing. In one early essay, he adapted arguments advanced by the Jesuit priest Matteo Ricci in support of Christianity against Confucianism in such a way that they became arguments for the supremacy of Shinto. Elsewhere, Atsutane also turned to Confucianism, Daoism, and even Buddhism (which he detested), for ammunition in his battle on behalf of Shinto.

At times, xenophobia and hucksterism can be detected in Atsutane's arguments. For example, he interrogated individuals who claimed to have visited the moon when traveling to the stars or to have lived among mountain elves, noting with satisfaction any instance he could construe as supporting Shinto teachings. He declared that the Japanese had had writing before its introduction from China and produced as evidence a script that later proved to be the fifteenth-century Korean alphabet. The fact that ancient Japanese chronicles made no mention of the Flood, mentioned so prominently in both the Bible and early Chinese writings, led Atsutane to assert that its absence was proof of Japan's having been created first (and thereby highest), unlike the inundated countries.

ON JAPANESE LEARNING

People commonly speak of "learning" as if all learning were one and the same; in fact, however, there are many different kinds of learning, each of which is centered on one particular discipline. Japanese learning itself may be divided into some seven or eight categories, the most important of which is Shinto, the Way of the Gods. We may also mention the study of poetry; the study of the legal code; the study of *The Tales of Ise* or *The Tale of Genji*, to which some scholars devote their chief attention; and the study of history, which deals with the events of the successive reigns of emperors. These various disciplines may in turn be divided into smaller groupings. Chinese studies, to which the Confucian scholars devote themselves, has its schools, and Buddhism is divided into sects. In the study of astronomy and geography known as *rangaku*, which is the learning of Holland, and in medicine there also are schools, both traditional and Dutch. We can see how many types of learning are to be found.

If we asked which of them were the greatest, we must answer, though it may seem slightly presumptuous, that no learning can equal that of Japan. It is easy to see why this is true. The Confucians learn the Four Books and the Five Classics or the Thirteen Classics and similar books. Having once perfunctorily run their eyes over the pages of these works and learned how to compose a bit of poetry and prose in Chinese, they qualify as Confucian scholars. It is really not very difficult to read so limited a number of books and to acquire the rudimentary knowledge of Chinese composition that they possess. And yet this is the general level of those who pass for Confucian scholars.

Compared with these Confucian scholars, the Buddhist monks have a much broader learning, for they are required to read the more than five thousand volumes of the canon, enough books to make at least seven pack loads for a strong horse. Even assuming that they do not read the entire collection but only a tenth of it, this still amounts to at least twice what the Confucian scholars are supposed to read. Moreover, since it is not considered a defect in a Confucian scholar if he neglects to read Buddhist books, he naturally never does, with some very rare exceptions. The Buddhists, however, must study Confucian books from their childhood days in order to learn Chinese characters, and they write Chinese prose and poetry just as Confucian scholars do.

Buddhist learning is thus broader in scope than Confucian, but Japanese learning is even more embracing. All the various types of learning, including Confucianism and Buddhism, are joined in Japanese learning, just as the many rivers flow into the sea where their waters are joined. Because of the diversity and number of the different parts of Japanese learning, people are often bewildered and at a loss to evaluate it. Therefore, unless we can distinguish accurately the elements making up this vast amalgam of learning, the excellence of the true Way will remain obscure. . . . We must be aware of such matters in order to appreciate the pure and righteous Way of Japan. Japanese should study all the different kinds of learning—even if they are foreign—so that they can choose the good features of each and place them at the service of the nation. We may properly speak not only of Chinese but even of Indian and Dutch learning as Japanese learning: this fact should be understood by all Japanese who delve into foreign studies.

[*Hirata Atsutane zenshū*, vol. 1, pp. 5–7; RT]

THE LAND OF THE GODS

People all over the world refer to Japan as the Land of the Gods and call us the descendants of the gods. Indeed, it is exactly as they say: as a special mark of favor from the heavenly gods, they gave birth to our country, and thus there is so immense a difference between Japan and all the other countries of the world as to defy comparison. Ours is a splendid and blessed country, the Land of the Gods beyond any doubt, and we, down to the most humble man and woman, are the descendants of the gods. Nevertheless, unhappily many people do not understand why Japan is the Land of the Gods and we their descendants. . . . Is this not a lamentable state of affairs? Japanese differ completely from and are superior to the peoples of China, India, Russia, Holland, Siam, Cambodia, and all other countries of the world, and for us to have called our country the Land of the Gods was not mere vanity. It was the gods who formed all the lands of the world at the Creation, and these gods were, without exception, born in

Japan. Japan is thus the homeland of the gods, and that is why we call it the Land of the Gods. This is a matter of universal belief and is quite beyond dispute. Even in countries to which our ancient traditions have not been transmitted, the peoples recognize Japan as a divine land because of the majestic influence that emanates from our country. In the olden days when Korea was divided into three kingdoms, we heard reports of how splendid, miraculous, and blessed a land Japan was, and because Japan lies to the east of Korea, they said in awe and reverence, "To the East is a divine land, called the Land of the Rising Sun." Word of this eventually spread all over the world, and now people everywhere refer to Japan as the Land of the Gods, whether or not they know why this is true.

[*Kōdō taii*, in *Hirata Atsutane zenshū*, vol. 1, pp. 22–23; RT]

THE CREATOR GOD

The men of the countries of Europe sail at will around the globe in ships that recognize no frontiers. In Holland, one of the countries of Europe (though a small one), they consider astronomy and geography to be the most important subjects of study because unless a ship's captain is well versed in these sciences, it is impossible for him to sail as he chooses to all parts of the world. Moreover, the Dutch have the excellent national characteristic of investigating matters with great patience until they can get to the very bottom. To help them in such research, they have devised surveying instruments as well as telescopes and helioscopes with which to examine the sun, moon, and stars. They have devised other instruments to ascertain the size and proximity of the heavenly bodies. It may take five or ten years or even a whole lifetime for such research to be completed; when problems cannot be solved in one lifetime, scholars write down their own findings and leave the solution for their children, grandchildren, and disciples to discover, though it may require generations.

With their scientific instruments the Dutch attempt to determine the properties of things. Unlike China, Holland is a splendid country where they do not rely on superficial conjectures. When the Dutch come across matters that they cannot understand, no matter how much they may ponder over them, they say that these are things beyond the knowing of human beings and belong to *Gotto* [God] and that only with divine powers can such matters be comprehended. The Dutch thus never resort to wild conjectures. Their findings, which are the result of the efforts of hundreds of people studying scientific problems for a thousand, even two thousand years, have been incorporated in books that have been presented to Japan. I have seen them, and that is how I happen to be able to write about them.

[*Kōdō taii*, in *Hirata Atsutane zenshū*, vol. 1, p. 53; RT]

ANCIENT JAPANESE ETHICS

Let me present a few of the arguments offered by scholars of Chinese learning. First of all, we may cite Dazai Jun [Shundai], who wrote in *Book on Instruction* (*Bendōsho*),

> In Japan there was originally no such thing as a Way. Proof of this is the fact that no native Japanese words exist for the concepts of humaneness, rightness, decorum, music, filial piety, and fraternal affection. There certainly must have been a Japanese word for everything that originally existed in Japan, and the absence of such terms proves that the concepts were lacking.

This opinion, shocking though it is, is not confined to this particular Confucian scholar. Far from it—the majority of the Confucian pedants and other scholars partial to things Chinese are overjoyed and infatuated with the idea that China possesses the teachings of a Way, and [they] proclaim that in ancient Japan there were no teachings like those of China. But however much they may heap indignation on Japan, all that they assert is utterly in error. Humaneness, rightness, filial piety, and the rest all are principles governing the proper conduct of man. If they are always automatically observed and never violated, it is unnecessary to teach them. If they are the invariable standard of behavior, what need is there for a "Way?". . .

The ancient Japanese all correctly and consciously practiced what the Chinese called humaneness, rightness, the Five Cardinal Virtues, and the rest, without having any need to name them or teach them. There was thus no necessity for anything to be especially constituted as a Way. This is the essentially Japanese quality of Japan, and one in which we may see a magnificent example of Japan's superiority to all other countries of the world. In China, as I already have frequently mentioned, there were evil customs from the very outset, and human behavior, far from being proper, was extremely licentious. That is why so many sages appeared in ancient times to guide and instruct the Chinese. . . . From this we may see that the very fact that in ancient Japan there was no Way is the most praiseworthy feature of the nation and that it is the shame of a country if it had to invent a Way to guide the people.

> [*Hirata Atsutane zenshū*, vol. 1, pp. 96–97; RT]

THE ART OF MEDICINE

The art of medicine, though introduced to Japan from abroad, appears originally to have been taught to foreign countries by our own great gods. Later, because of the special needs it meets, this art came to be widely practiced in

Japan, and although it may be said to have once been of foreign origin, we are not obliged to dislike it for that reason. Nevertheless it is true that the art of medicine developed to such a high degree in China by way of a quite natural reaction to the rampant and pernicious maladies that resulted from the evil character of the country itself. Since middle antiquity, the spread in Japan of Confucianism and Buddhism, both exceedingly troublesome doctrines, has worsened and confused men's minds, and as a result of the attendant increase in the number of things to worry about, various maladies that were unknown in ancient times have become prevalent. The Chinese methods of treatment were perfectly suited to deal with such maladies and are therefore now in general employ. Just as in countries where there are numerous bandits the government enacts strict laws to punish them, when pernicious maladies are first detected, people knowledgeable about medicine appear to combat them. In countries where there are many doctors, there also are many deadly sicknesses, and as the doctors gradually grow more proficient, the sicknesses become proportionately more difficult to cure.

[*Hirata Atsutane zenshū*, vol. 1, p. 22; RT]

ŌKUNI TAKAMASA

Ōkuni Takamasa (1792–1871) shared much with Hirata Atsutane regarding Shinto and a nativist disdain for the foreign, and yet by not turning to the past for his model, Takamasa was able to argue for certain forms of accommodation and to anticipate the language of Emperor Meiji's Charter Oath of April 1868. One can discern in Takamasa's writings an effort to engage the West intellectually and spiritually on terms favorable to Japan. For example, in his *New True International Law (Shinshin kōhōron)* of 1867, Takamasa describes the concept of international law as a seventeenth-century invention of the West to counter cultural and diplomatic Sinocentrism. Just as he intended knowledge of the West to help defend against the West, he argued for opening Japan now in order for it to respond to the West later on Japan's own terms.

THE NEW TRUE INTERNATIONAL LAW
(SHINSHIN KŌHŌRON)

In Holland there was a man by the name of Hugo [Grotius (1583–1645)], who founded a system of learning called international law. It appears that the discipline was developed in various nations of the Western world; there certainly are many there who now teach it. It is my view that it owes its origins to Westerners' dislike for the Chinese practice of dividing the world into "flowering center" and "barbaric periphery," with all its implications for the Chinese revering China alone and despising all other nations. International law was the foreigner's reaction to this practice.

From an early period, there were in China, I hear, Christian scholars who dismissed as "national theorizing" the Chinese practice of calling their ruler the "Son of Heaven." I made a similar point at the end of my essay "Discussion on Shintō" (Shintō yōron). I explained there that in the Fourth Age of the Gods, when the two deities Onamuchi and Sukunahikona were traveling hither and yon, our theories [of nation building] reached China. It was under this [Japanese] influence, I argued, that the Chinese came to call their own kings "Sons of Heaven." Many Japanese today follow Chinese Confucianism. They typically confuse center with periphery, and they are wrong to do so. Some even believe that the Japanese practice of calling the Japanese emperor "Son of Heaven" or "descendant of heaven" is derived from the Chinese. This is not the case, however. It is an ancient tradition in Japan to call our emperor the child of Heaven or a descendant of Heaven. The Chinese practice is derivative and distorted. We know that there is but one true emperor on this earth, and that it is our emperor.

The new Western discipline of international law is not *true* international law, either. We should think of Western international law as a precursor of *true* international law, which will arise in this great nation of Japan and eventually extend to all nations.

In recent years, foreign scholars have been coming to Japan. This is an opportunity for us to toughen our moral fiber; it is surely incumbent on us to bear witness to the [great] ancient words and deeds of our nation. At the same time, however, we must learn about Western nations and engage in discourse with foreigners themselves. In Japanese learning of recent years, scholars have been vying with one another to praise things foreign, but they are at a loss as to what to say when faced with a foreigner. Among those now living in Japan, there are bound to be experts in international law. It is imperative that we prepare to face them. I should thus like to comment now on those aspects of Japan's learning that we should expose in our discourse with foreigners.

Foreigners are bound to say this: "All nations must conform to international law simply because there exists no single ruler over all the nations of the world. I hear that in Japan you have Shinto, but that this is a 'national' teaching confined to Japan. It is not worth listening to. You must have a change of heart and follow the international law."

The Japanese should reply along these lines:

There is none yet in Japan who can expound the truths of Japanese Shinto. We have no response, therefore, to your challenge that it is merely a "national" theory. However, the deity we know as Ame-no-minaka-nushi no kami is precisely the deity you in the West call the Lord of Heaven. The deities we know as Takami-musu-bi no kami and Kamu-musu-bi no kami are what the Chinese refer to as their creator deities. The Lord of Heaven and the Creator instructed Izanagi no mikoto and Izanami no mikoto to give birth to all the nations on earth. Izanagi no mikoto is the spirit of the sun, who temporarily adopted the form of a man and from heaven bestowed the seeds of creation. Izanami no mikoto is the spirit of the earth, who, temporarily adopting the form of a woman, actually gave birth to all the nations and all living things on this earth. She created the other nations first and Japan last. The countries created first were the result of "the woman having spoken first"; they are thus topsy-turvy.[19] Japan, created later once order was restored, was a country of superior birth, however. That is why, while other countries lacked a settled royal lineage, the lineage of Japan has never wavered from the Age of the Gods to the present day. Thus it is that we hold Japan to be the center and noble and other nations, the periphery and base. This is our ancient tradition. The proofs emerge yearly, monthly, and daily.

To assert this is by no means like the Chinese boasting of their country as the center and despising all others. Our ancient tradition is the true international law; we cannot accept as true the international law that has arisen in the West.

I find it unacceptable to say that because there is no overall ruler in the world, all nations should abide by international law. . . . It remains, however, that knowledge of the Japanese imperial line has yet to reach other nations, and they are bound to reject all this as "national theorizing." We have no choice but to wait for the day when all nations acknowledge this truth.

We should not, in any case, countenance attempts by foreigners with whom we have signed treaties to have the emperor communicate directly and on equal terms with the sovereigns of other countries, thus relegating the shogun to a position of imperial vassal. The emperor must be kept apart as the object of veneration. It would be appropriate for [foreign diplomats] to deal on equal terms with the shogun. All this will come to pass, and when it does, it will be due to the subtle workings of the Ruler of Heaven and the Creator. The Japanese must adhere strictly to this idea and brook no compromise. The nobility of our emperor is greater by far; he should not be placed on equal footing with foreign royalty. The fact that people throughout Japan believe this to be true is, by itself, something made possible by the laws of Heaven-and-earth, the "good laws" of Japan. I refer specifically to the Nakatomi Ritual (Nakatomi no

---

19. This is a reference to the creation passage in the *Nihon shoki*, in which, just before the union of Izanami, the female creator deity, and Izanagi, the male creator deity, the former had spoken first (de Bary et al., eds., *Sources of Japanese Tradition*, 2nd ed., vol. 1, pp. 13–15). The product of this first union, according to the *Nihon shoki*, was a leech. Izanami was reprimanded by the deities in heaven for having destroyed the correct order of things, and the two deities "reunited." Ōkuni offers here a thorough reinterpretation of this passage.

harae), which has this to say: "The deities that reside in Takamagahara, with whom the sovereign is 'intimate,' Kamurogi no mikoto and Kamuromi no mikoto. . . ."[20]

This is not merely Japan's "good law;" it is, rather, the true law that will spread to all nations on the earth.

In foreign nations, theories about Heaven are little advanced; in Japan they have been handed down in the most detailed form. Ame-no-minaka-nushi no kami is the supreme object of veneration and so must be left out of consideration. We on this earth should venerate Amaterasu as the "Ruler of Heaven." What is important to realize is that the Ruler of Heaven and the Creator put their minds together, sent Ninigi no mikoto down to Japan, and made him lord of the land. Their plan was that after the people's hearts had been pacified, he and his descendants would be revered as supreme rulers of the world. The people of the distant lands, those lands that we call Western or "barbarian" lands, do not yet know the ancient truths. This, too, is part of the secret heavenly plan of the Ruler of Heaven and the Creator, whose firm intention it is to eventually elevate Japan to the rank of greater imperial nation. Japanese must not lose sight of this truth and must ensure that we do not regard kings of foreign countries as equal to our emperor.

A certain warrior questioned my true international law. He had this to say: Chinese sages are truly deserving of reverence, and barbarians should be attacked. We are falling into the clutches of the barbarians, and we should be weeping and wailing. Instead, you are telling me we should be rejoicing. How can this be? To copy everything from China and to say that a country like ours is superior to China, that it is the supreme nation on earth, has no basis in fact. Rather than flattering Japan, we should have a change of heart and recommend to the powers-that-be a policy of forcefully expelling the barbarians. Each person should sacrifice himself and display unflinching loyalty to the nation.

. . . When it comes to the present issue of expelling barbarians, even great leaders must not act on their instincts. It is crucial to realize just how difficult the barbarian expulsion of the lesser variety would be. In the world there are things that are meant to be and those that are not. It is, of course, noble of a warrior to devote himself with total passion to a cause he knows is doomed. Kusunoki father and son are a case in point.[21] But the issues of today are not like those of that age; nor are they comparable to the age of Yue Fei in Song

---

20. The Nakatomi no harae, a prayer used on the occasion of such major imperial rituals as the Daijōsai, is in volume 8 of the *Engishiki*, a fifty-volume compilation of the laws relating to court ritual dating from the early Heian period (794–1185).

21. Both Kusunoki Masashige (1294–1336) and his son, Masatsura (1326–1348), dedicated themselves to the lost cause of Emperor Go-Daigo (r. 1318–1339).

China.[22] You must know that the court, and Heaven too, permitted trade as the first phase in barbarian expulsion of the greater variety. It would have been useless for someone of my lowly status to have addressed my superiors on this matter. It would have been pointless, too, for me to have sacrificed myself for this. The leader must first be enlightened and distance himself from the Confucians, for whom all foreign nations are inferior; he must thwart Western international law; he must take heed from the ancient tradition of this great nation of Japan and lend his support to the great task of elevating our nation to a position above all others on earth.

You are a bold warrior, and you should understand it is important for you to become a shield for the emperor and his vassals. Be cautious always, look after yourself well, and prepare for self-sacrifice in the event that foreign nations do launch an attack.

All people born in Japan, be they Confucian, Buddhist, or Western scholars, should know that the emperor, being the descendant of the Ruler of Heaven, rules the world for eternity. They must look forward to the time when the whole world is under his sway, and they should rejoice. When that time comes, there will be many surprised to discover belatedly that the words of me, Takamasa, were not incorrect.

[Adapted from Breen, trans., "New True International Law," pp. 233–45]

---

22. Yue Fei (1103–1141) was the great Song general who, when serving Emperor Gaozong (1127–1162), won notable successes against the Jurchen occupying North China. Even so, he was executed as a result of political intrigue at court.

Chapter 31

BUDDHISM IN THE TOKUGAWA PERIOD

No student of Japanese culture and religion can fail to be impressed by the consensus that has prevailed regarding the character of Buddhism in the Tokugawa period (1600–1868). For generations, both Japanese and Western scholars have depicted the religion in these centuries as having entered an era of sharp decline. Although the first expressions of this view can be traced back to the Tokugawa period itself, modern Japanese scholars have generally agreed that while limited activity could be seen in such areas as sectarian scholarship, clerical discipline, and apologetics, Tokugawa Buddhism generally was a formalized, lifeless religion led by a degenerate clergy.

Even though this chapter somewhat contradicts this characterization of Tokugawa Buddhism, it must be acknowledged that the established view is not without some basis in fact. In the Tokugawa period, Buddhism did indeed lose the dominant position it had maintained in Japanese religious and intellectual history shortly after its introduction into the country in the sixth century C.E. Neo-Confucianism now attracted many of the best minds of the age, its political and social theories appealing especially, though by no means exclusively, to the leadership of the ruling samurai, or warrior, class. By the late seventeenth century, Neo-Confucianism, which from the start was opposed to Buddhism, had become the dominant ideology. The revival of interest in Shinto, championed by the National Learning scholars, was hardly less critical of Buddhism. To be sure, most Japanese continued, as they had done for centuries, to embrace a

Buddhist-based syncretism that included elements of Shinto and Confucianism, but never before in Japanese history had Buddhism been placed so broadly on the intellectual defensive.

In addition, Buddhism faced internal problems that eroded its religious integrity, problems of a marked decline in discipline within the clergy and of an entrenched and divisive sectarianism. Neither of these issues was entirely new to Japanese Buddhism. Moral laxity within the clergy had been a problem to one degree or another in every age, and sectarianism—though having no intrinsic relationship to the phenomenon of religious decline—had a history that stretched as far back as the Heian period (794–1185), with the rise of the Shingon and Tendai sects.

Both the laxity in discipline and the sectarianism were accentuated by circumstances unique to the Tokugawa period and, in particular, by policies adopted by the Tokugawa military government (*bukufu*). Having come to power after more than a century of civil war, in which not only great feudal lords but even certain Buddhist institutions had played a prominent role, the Tokugawa shoguns tried to assert their unquestioned authority over every segment of the reunified feudal society they inherited. To prevent interference from without, they expelled the Christian missionaries who had been arriving since the mid-sixteenth century and, in 1641, sealed off the country, leaving only the port of Nagasaki open to a few Chinese and Dutch traders. At the same time, the shoguns adopted a variety of domestic policies that reflect this same desire for tighter control.

Among the measures that contributed to the decline in clerical discipline was the *terauke*, or "temple registration" system. Instituted by the *bakufu* as part of its program to stamp out Christianity, as well as to aid generally in the monitoring of population movements, the *terauke* system eventually required every Japanese family to register at a Buddhist temple as proof that its members had no Christian affiliation. This system dramatically increased the number of Buddhist parishioners—especially in the Pure Land, True Pure Land, Nichiren, and Zen sects—and was the commencement of an era of financial stability and even wealth for numerous Buddhist temples. Despite enjoying both political backing and relative economic security, a significant number of the clergy appear to have lost sight of their religious calling, the worst (as the popular novelist Ihara Saikaku [1642–1693] delighted in pointing out) giving themselves over to the satisfaction of their material and prurient desires.

Government policy also accentuated the already highly sectarian character of Japanese Buddhism. Stimulating this development was the *bakufu*'s decree that each sect organize its temples along strict hierarchical lines. In this arrangement, known as the main temple/branch temple (*honmatsu*) system, each sect had a relatively few main temples (*honji*), under which other temples associated with the sect were ranked as branch temples (*matsuji*). The government recognized the special authority of the main temples in managing the affairs of its branches, and by keeping a close watch over the main temples, it was able to control the entire temple system.

Still further reinforcing Buddhist sectarianism was the government's policy of encouraging the scholarly pursuits of the clergy while forbidding it from advocating heretical doctrines or criticizing the doctrines of rival sects. The intent of these directives was, on the one hand, to put the clergy on notice that scholarship—not politics—was its proper sphere of activity and, on the other, to suppress doctrinal disputes, which had been a major cause of instability in the Buddhist community both before and during the Tokugawa era. These policies did lead to a profusion of Buddhist scholarship during the seventeenth and eighteenth centuries, but on the whole it was a conservative brand of scholarship dominated by narrow sectarian concerns.

Recent scholarship has brought out more positive aspects of Tokugawa-period Buddhism. New interest has been shown in Buddhism's role in the formation of early Tokugawa ideology, in its place in the social history of the period, and in its continuing influence in literature and the arts. Researchers in both Japan and the West have also brought to light leading practitioners of Buddhism who spoke to the new situation in which the religion found itself. In this chapter we give five such examples. We cannot say that they represent a concerted or consistent movement, but together they demonstrate that Buddhism had the resources to regenerate itself, maintain certain vital continuities, and, through self-critical reexamination and reform, renew its own religious life.

SUZUKI SHŌSAN

The teaching and writings of Suzuki Shōsan (1579–1655) constitute an original Buddhist response to the era of peace initiated by the triumph of Tokugawa Ieyasu. Although not an influential thinker, Shōsan represents an age that seemed to offer new opportunities to everyone. He is particularly noted for having recognized merchants' contribution to society.

Shōsan was born into a samurai family in Mikawa, also Ieyasu's home province. His father was a minor vassal of the Tokugawa house, and Shōsan himself fought at the battle of Sekigahara (1600) and the siege of Osaka (1615). In 1621 he became a Zen monk. He seems to have remained fiercely independent of both the Rinzai and the Sōtō school of Zen, although he sympathized with Sōtō.

In a world in which Confucianism, with its emphasis on society and statecraft, was beginning to overshadow Buddhism, Shōsan argued that only Buddhism could give Japan the lasting benefits of peace. The Buddhism that he meant was his own teaching, and his single-mindedness on the issue resembled that of Nichiren. Shōsan's great mission, as he saw it, was to have the shogun proclaim Buddhism (Shōsan's Buddhism) as the faith and, above all, the practice of Japan.

Although Shōsan's teaching had an individual dimension centered on overcoming death, he insisted that practice to this end be carried out in society in accordance with one's inherited station in life, for the good of all. For this reason, he would not ordain anyone (even though he himself was ordained), and he strove to address his message to all social classes as they were then defined. He even described Buddhist monks as "officers" who properly served, in their own way, the interests of society as a whole. It was in this spirit that he addressed samurai, farmers, artisans, and merchants in his best-known work, *Right Action for All (Banmin tokuyō)*.

RIGHT ACTION FOR ALL
(BANMIN TOKUYŌ)

In *Right Action for All*, Buddhism converges with attitudes more commonly associated with general Confucianism, particularly its insistence on the selfless performance of one's duty to society. For samurai, Suzuki Shōsan recommended his own, strenuously energetic practice, and for the other classes he urged the easier and more accessible practice of the *nenbutsu* (calling the name of Amida Buddha). In Japan, the *nenbutsu* does not properly belong to Zen practice, but Shōsan had no interest in making that sort of distinction.

Prayers Regarding Practice

The Buddha-treasure, the Dharma-treasure, and the Sangha-treasure: he is not a monk who accepts these Three Treasures and still practices without the goal of giving generously to the people and making himself a treasure for the whole land. It is my prayer that you should preserve in your practice the aim of the Three Treasures.

The Buddha's teaching is the teaching of the attainment of Buddhahood. However, there [is] a right way and a wrong way to understand "attainment of Buddhahood.". . .

The practice of Buddha's teaching is the way of emancipation from the three worlds. Therefore a monk is said to have "left his home." He has not left his home who does not aim to emancipate himself from the three worlds. . . .

The Buddha's words teach that once one fully enters the world, he cannot leave it because there is nowhere left to go. This statement signifies that it is by the world's teaching that one attains Buddhahood. Thus the world's teaching is the Buddha's teaching. The Avatamsaka Sutra makes the following declaration: "The Buddha's teaching does not differ from the world's teaching.". . . If we do not proceed according to the principle that one achieves Buddhahood by following the world's teaching, we are totally ignorant of the Buddha's intention. . . .

Now, the Buddha's teaching is one that destroys the evilness of men. Shall disciples of the Buddha not take that road? At present, however, practice capable of matching the Buddha's intention is rare. People dwell upon fame and fortune and take wrong paths. This is my prayer, and none other: that the Buddha's disciples should enter the true Way and lead sentient beings out of their bewilderment.

The Benefits of the Three Treasures in Action (Sanbō tokuyō)

The treasures of Buddha and Dharma:

1. to be employed in the exercise of martial courage. . . .
2. to be employed in regard to the laws of the land. . . .
3. to be employed in correctly following the way of the five relationships. . . .
4. to be employed in all the arts. . . .
5. to be employed in one's own profession. . . .
6. to be employed without hindrance from good or evil. . . .
7. to be employed in setting mind and body at ease. . . .
8. to be employed for the greatest good in all things. . . .
9. to cure the sicknesses of the mind. . . .
10. to dwell in the Pure Land of Supreme Bliss. . . .

Buddhist practice is to observe the precepts strictly, never opposing the teaching of the Buddha and of the patriarchs; to banish the mind warped and twisted, and to become of good mind; to clearly distinguish right from wrong, then to let right go; to practice only a morality without morality; and to lead all people, uprightly and with compassion, to enlightenment. This mind is the treasure to use in connection with the law.

Practice of Buddhism is to abandon self-preoccupation; to set the six harmonies in action, making no distinction between self and other; and to achieve integrity of mind, thus requiting, above, the four generosities, and saving, below, sentient beings in the three worlds. This mind is the treasure to use in the correct pursuit of the way of the five relationships.

Practice of Buddhism is to let go the mind of cleverness and discrimination, and thus to leave behind thoughts that cling to form; to reach the mind of selflessness; and to entrust yourself to things without any personal partiality whatever. This mind is the treasure to use in all the arts.

Practice of Buddhism is to erase the mind of evil desire. Here, there is no more arrogance, flattery, covetousness, or seeking after fame and profit. This mind is the treasure to use in the trades and the professions. . . .

The Four Classes

FOR THE WARRIOR'S DAILY GUIDANCE

A warrior said, "You claim that the Buddha's teaching and the world's teaching are like the two wheels of a carriage. Even without the Buddha's teaching, though, the world would still lack nothing. Why then do you use the simile of the two wheels of a carriage?"

"The Buddha's teaching and the world's teaching are not two separate things," I replied. "The Buddha has said that if you fully enter the world, you cannot leave it because there is nowhere left to go. The Buddha's teaching and the world's teaching both establish the right and true, practice morality, and take the way of uprightness; that is all. As far as uprightness is concerned, there are the shallow level and the deep. Worldly uprightness, in my view, is to preserve morality without bending principle, to follow correctly the way of the five relationships, and not to be at odds with things but to have no personal bias at all. This is the road down which to proceed from shallow to deep. From the Buddhist standpoint, true uprightness is to realize that all conditioned things are lies, empty and illusory, and to act at one with the original Law Body (*dharmakaya*), the natural self-nature. . . .

"Methods of practice are infinitely diverse, but the main thing is simply to banish all thought of oneself. The source of suffering is the one thought 'I,' 'I.' To know that this is so, is right. To strive on this basis and to annihilate that one thought, with sincerely fierce courage, is exactly what is meant by moral conduct. . . ."

The very foundations of fierce courage [are]

1. Mounting guard over birth-and-death.
2. Acknowledging generosity.
3. Advancing to the front line of battle.
4. Acknowledging the principle of karma.
5. Perceiving illusion and transience.
6. Perceiving the impurity of this body.
7. Regretting the passing of time.
8. Having faith in the Three Treasures.
9. Offering this body up to one's lord.
10. Guarding oneself.
11. Being always ready to give up one's life.
12. Acknowledging one's own faults.
13. Feeling that one stands before a great personage or before one's lord.
14. Keeping to humanity and morality.
15. Keeping one's eyes upon the words of the Buddha and of the patriarchs.

16. Compassion and uprightness.
17. Keeping in mind the link with the one great matter (birth-and-death).

FOR THE FARMER'S DAILY GUIDANCE

A farmer said, "I do not neglect that great matter, my Rebirth, but I have no time, for work on the farm never lets up. It is a wretched way I have to make my living. This present life of mine is worthless, and suffering will be mine in the future. This distresses me very much. What can I do to attain realization?"

"Farm work is Buddhist practice," I replied. "It is misunderstanding that makes it menial work. When your faith is firm, it is the practice of a Bodhisattva. You are wrong to think you need leisure to pray for Rebirth. Those who insist upon attaining Buddhahood torment both body and mind in their quest, while those who pray for Rebirth will not reach Buddhahood in ten thousand eons. As you labor so painfully hard in burning heat and freezing cold, with spade, hoe, and sickle, take body and mind, where the passions grow so thick, as your enemy. While you hoe and reap, press the attack and press it again upon your mind, as you work. In any period of leisure the passions will grow thicker yet. When you work painfully hard as you assault body and mind, your mind is untroubled. Thus you do your Buddhist practice the year round. Why should a farmer prefer any other practice? A man can enter a monastery and worship all day long, but if he does not give up preoccupation with himself, everything he does will turn to the karma of transmigration, let him be as holy as he likes. To reach Buddhahood or to fall into hell, therefore, depends upon the mind and not upon the work. . . .

"To receive life as a farmer is to be an officer entrusted by heaven with the nourishment of the world. Give your body, therefore, utterly up to heaven, without the least thought for yourself. Work the fields in true service to Heaven's Way and celebrate, as you grow the five grains, the Buddhas and the kami. Make a great vow to give to all, yes, even to the very insects, and say Namu Amida Butsu, Namu Amida Butsu in time with the strokes of the hoe. . . ."

FOR THE ARTISAN'S DAILY GUIDANCE

An artisan said: "Enlightenment in the life to come is certainly important, but my trade leaves me no leisure. Day and night I do nothing but work at my living. How can I possibly reach realization?"

I replied: "All trades whatsoever are Buddhist practice. It is on the basis of men's actual work that Buddhahood is to be attained. Without smiths, carpenters, and all the other trades, the needs of the world would never be met. Without warriors, the world would not be governed. Without farmers it would not be fed, and without merchants nothing in the world would circulate freely. Every other trade, as it comes into being, works for the good of the world. . . ."

FOR THE DAILY GUIDANCE OF MERCHANTS

A merchant said: "I was born into the human realm, it is true, but my work is the sorry business of buying and selling, and there is no instant when my thoughts are not on profit; therefore I cannot advance toward enlightenment. This situation pains me greatly. Please, teach me a remedy."

"He who proposes to engage in trade," I replied, "must first of all develop the right frame of mind for increasing profit. That is the frame of mind for you, that and none other. Give your own life up to heaven and singlemindedly study the way of uprightness. . . . But he who, in his longing for profit, cheats people and makes a difference between himself and others will come under the malediction of heaven. Thus calamities will befall him. He will be hated by all, loved and respected by none, and nothing will ever be the way he wants it. . . .

"Offer this body to the world, and make up your mind that what you do is only for the sake of the land and of the whole people. Vow then that you will transport goods from your own province to others, that you will bring goods from other provinces to your own and trade them in lands and villages yet more distant, and thereby please everyone. . . . When thus you conduct your trading without greed, having given up all clinging, the devas will protect you, the gods will be generous toward you, your profits will be enormous, and you will become a man of the greatest wealth. . . ."

[*Banmin tokuyō*, in *NKBT*, vol. 83; Tyler, trans.,
Selected Writings of Suzuki Shōsan, pp. 53–74]

TAKUAN SŌHŌ

Takuan Sōhō (1573–1645) was a commanding figure in Rinzai Zen at the beginning of the Tokugawa period. In 1628 Takuan, representing a radical group at Daitokuji in Kyoto, where he had received his training, protested the *bakufu's* regulations and the government's intervention in temple affairs in order to enhance its administrative power. As a result, in the following year, Takuan was exiled to the province of Dewa in the northern part of Japan. In 1632 he was released, but for two more years was not permitted to leave Edo to return to Daitokuji. While he was in Kyoto, some of his admirers who were influential in the *bakufu* repeatedly asked him to meet the third shogun, Iemitsu. Finally, Takuan could no longer refuse their urgent requests and reluctantly went to Edo in 1635, staying with Yagyū Tajima no Kami (1571–1646), a great fencing master of that day.

The story has it that Iemitsu once asked Yagyū the secret of his knowledge of swordsmanship. Yagyū replied that he had mastered the art through the practice of Zen under Takuan. At their first meeting, the shogun was very much attracted to Takuan and therefore would not let him leave Edo. The Zen master, however, had no desire to associate with the shogun and other dignitaries of high rank. He complained to his students about his unfortunate circumstances, for his greatest desire was to be free to live out his life, unnoticed by the world, in a quiet mountain spot. In order to keep Takuan near him, therefore, the shogun built the Tōkaiji in Edo and installed him as its head.

MARVELOUS POWER OF IMMOVABLE WISDOM (FUDŌCHI SHINMYŌROKU)

The instructions excerpted here were originally written in a letter addressed to Yagyū Tajima no Kami as Tokugawa Iemitsu's official fencing instructor. Takuan Sōhō's letter explains how several common Buddhist and Confucian concepts might be interpreted in terms of fencing to argue for the importance of cultivating a strong sense of imperturbability, the immovable wisdom that allows the mind to move freely, spontaneously, and flexibly, even in the midst of the most frightening or difficult circumstances. It concludes by stressing that the purpose of all self-cultivation is to enable a person to better serve his lord by living a moral life.

Since it first appeared in print in 1779, entitled *The Marvelous Power of Immovable Wisdom (Fudōchi shinmyōroku)*, Takuan's instructions have been included in innumerable anthologies addressed not only to martial art devotees but to general audiences as well, and thus they have helped promote the popular perception that Zen is an intrinsic element of martial art training. It would perhaps be more accurate to say that success in the martial arts demands mental discipline, a topic about which Zen monks (among others) have much to say.

Where to Focus the Mind

To what ends should the mind be directed? If you focus on your opponent's movements, then his movements will restrict your mind. If you focus on your opponent's sword, then his sword will restrict your mind. If you focus on cutting down your opponent, then the thought of cutting will restrict your mind. If you focus on wielding your own sword, then your own sword will restrict your mind. If you focus on avoiding your opponent's cut, then your intention to not be cut will restrict your mind. If you focus on a person's stance, then that stance will restrict your mind. In short, there is nothing on which you should focus your mind.

Someone might ask, "If focusing on any one object causes that thing to restrict my mind and thereby allows the opponent to defeat me, then wouldn't it be better for me to concentrate my mind in the area below my navel, to prevent it [my mind] from being moved by distractions and merely to respond automatically to the opponent's moves?"

Yes, this sounds reasonable. From the viewpoint of the highest techniques of the Buddha-dharma, however, concentrating your mind below the navel and preventing it from being moved by distractions is an inferior method, not the best one. It corresponds to a beginner's level of training, or to what Confucians refer to as reverent seriousness (*kei*) of purpose. It is no more than what *Mencius*[1] called "finding the lost mind" [of humanity]. It is not a method that leads to the highest realization. . . . If you strive to concentrate your mind below your navel and to prevent it from being moved by distractions elsewhere, then that very striving will restrict your mind; you will lose your ability to lead the encounter; and consequently you will have even less freedom of action than in other cases.

Reverent Seriousness in Neo-Confucianism and Buddhism

Neo-Confucian texts explain the word "seriousness" (J. *kei*, Ch. *jing*) as concentrating on one task without wavering (*shuitsu muteki*).[2] It means that your mind is devoted to one object without other diversions. The essence of seriousness lies in being able to unsheathe your sword and to cut without disturbing your mental composure. When you receive an order from your lord, it is especially important to serve him with this serious composure. The Buddha-dharma also includes this serious composure. For example, Buddhists sound the bell of devotion when they strike a gong three times [and] place the palms of their hands together before addressing the Buddha. The serious composure in Buddhist chanting is the same whether explained in Buddhist terms as being single-minded without disturbance (*isshin furan*) or in Confucian terms as concentrating on one task without wavering.

In Buddhism, however, this sense of seriousness is not the highest teaching. Controlling one's own mind and preventing it from becoming disturbed is the practice of a beginner. Buddhists continue in this kind of training for only as many months or years as is needed to attain imperturbability so that even when the mind is allowed to wander, it retains full freedom. This is what I referred to elsewhere as the free-flowing mind, which is the highest level. According to the Confucian teaching of seriousness, the mind must be kept in check. Because mental wandering is seen as a disturbance, the mind must not be given free reign even for an instant. While this practice is useful as a short-term technique for developing unflappability, if you train in this way constantly, it will result in a

---

1. *Mencius* 6A:11.

2. In Zhu Xi's concept of the "method of the mind" (*xinfa*), self-cultivation involved attending to "oneness." For the Cheng–Zhu school, this cryptic "oneness" generally referred to one's unity with Heaven-and-earth and the myriad things, but some thinkers took it to mean focusing on one thing at a time.

loss of mental freedom. For example, it is like pulling back on a cat's leash to prevent it from pouncing on a baby sparrow. When your mind lacks freedom, like a cat tied to a leash, then it cannot function freely in accordance with its needs. But if a cat is well trained, then it can be released from the leash to go where it may, even right next to the sparrow without pouncing on it. When the free-flowing mind is released and abandoned, like the cat off the leash, it can wander everywhere without distraction and without becoming harried.

Stated in terms of your swordsmanship, you should not think about techniques for striking with a sword. Forget all striking techniques and strike. Cut the other person, but do not dwell on the other person. Both self and other are emptiness. The striking sword also is emptiness. But do not let your mind be restricted by emptiness.

Personal Advice

Because you have mastered swordsmanship to a degree unequaled in the past or present, you now enjoy a good rank, stipend, and reputation. You must not be ungrateful for this good fortune even while sleeping but must always strive to totally repay this benefaction with the finest loyal service to your lord. The finest loyal service requires, first, that you think correctly, maintain your health, and be single-minded in your devotion to your lord. You must never resent or criticize others or neglect your daily duties. In your own family, you should be exceedingly filial toward your father and mother, avoid even the slightest hint of infidelity in your marriage, observe the correct ritual decorum, and not love a mistress or practice pederasty. Do not presume on your father or mother but always observe social norms. In employing underlings, do not be guided by personal feelings. Merely promote good men so that they might admonish you for your shortcomings and correctly implement the government's policies, and demote bad men. When bad men see good men progress day by day, the bad men will naturally be influenced by your delight in the good, and they will abandon the bad and return to being good. In this way, lord and samurai (ruler and minister), superior and inferior, will become good men; their desires will weaken; and they will end their extravagant waste. Then the country's treasury will become full; the people will grow wealthy; children will care for their parents; the strong will be charitable toward the elderly; and the country will rule itself. This is how to practice the finest loyalty.

["Fudōchi shinmyōroku," in *Takuan Oshō zenshū*, vol. 5, pp. 12–27; WB]

BANKEI

Bankei (1622–1693) was the son of a masterless samurai (*rōnin*) who, in the early years of the Tokugawa peace, turned from the arts of war to the art of medicine. When sent to a local Confucian school, Bankei showed his independence early.

He left school, dissatisfied with his teacher's explanation of the *Great Learning*'s "luminous virtue" (in Neo-Confucian terms, generally equated with the moral nature), and struck out on his own. Although he went on to study briefly with Esoteric and Zen Buddhist teachers, from two of whom he received their "seal" (certification), Bankei considered himself essentially self-taught and made no secret of his conviction that what he had discovered for himself went beyond anything he had learned from others.

After a succession of intensive efforts at solitary meditation, which included extreme hardship and severe illness, he emerged self-enlightened and ready to teach his doctrine of the Unborn Buddha Nature. For Bankei, this was an extremely simple and direct teaching, involving a complete and radical deconditioning from all received influences, a stripping away of all parental influences and worldly culture to reveal one's original nature. The following excerpts explain how he taught this to increasingly large audiences and how he related it to other contemporary trends. Most of his teachings pertain to the spiritual life and the direct response to daily experience and very little to contemporary, political, social, or educational issues of a secular kind. Although Bankei sometimes used language suggesting that, as Suzuki Shōsan argued, enlightenment could be attained in the context of everyday life, unlike Shōsan, Bankei retained close ties to Zen monastic institutions.

Bankei was obviously a self-made individualist who had a powerful charismatic influence on his hearers. In his own time, he had a wide reputation as a popular lecturer to crowds of people. This contrasts with the kind of spiritual direction between master and disciple, one on one, that is more typical of Zen training. But it fits the trend in this period toward popular lecturing by both Confucians and Shinto preachers. Taken together, these methods may help explain the strong rise in popular education in the Tokugawa period, drawing on religious evangelism as well as secular developments. We also note that Bankei's emphasis on simplicity, directness, and spontaneity resonates with the concept of *makoto* in other popular lecturers of the time.

Bankei's great reputation as a teacher in his own day eventually brought him imperial recognition as a "national teacher" (*kokushi*). However, this achievement was quite personal, for he left no significant school or movement that outlasted his own charisma. Not until the twentieth century was he resurrected from comparative obscurity.

OPENING OF THE SERMONS

The following are extracts from sermons given in 1690 at the Ryōmonji Temple, Bankei's home temple in Hyōgo Prefecture.

When the Zen Master Bankei Butchi Kōsai, founder of the Ryōmonji at Aboshi in Banshū, was at the Great Training period [held] at the Ryōmonji in the winter of the third year of Genroku, there were 1,683 monks listed in the temple register. Those who attended included not only Sōtō and Rinzai followers but members of the Ritsu, Shingon, Tendai, Pure Land, True Pure Land, and Nichiren schools, with laymen and monks mingled together, thronging round the lecture seat. One sensed the Master was truly the Teacher of Men and Devas for the present age. . . .

The Master addressed the assembly: "Among all you people here today there's not a single one who's an unenlightened being. Everyone here is a Buddha. So listen carefully! What you all have from your parents innately is the Unborn Buddha Mind alone. There's nothing else you have innately. This Buddha Mind you have from your parents innately is truly unborn and marvelously illuminating . . . and, what's more, with this Unborn, everything is perfectly managed. The actual proof of this Unborn which perfectly manages [everything] is that, as you're all turned this way listening to me talk, if out back there's the cawing of crows, the chirping of sparrows, or the rustling of the wind, even though you're not deliberately trying to hear each of these sounds, you recognize and distinguish each one. The voices of the crows and sparrows, the rustling of the wind—you hear them without making any mistake about them, and that's what's called hearing with the Unborn. In this way, all things are perfectly managed with the Unborn. . . .

"Well, then, while you're all turned this way listening to me talk, you don't mistake the chirp of a sparrow out back for the caw of a crow, the sound of a gong for that of a drum, a man's voice for a woman's, an adult's voice for a child's—you clearly recognize and distinguish each sound you hear without making any mistake. That's the marvelously illuminating dynamic function. It's none other than the Buddha Mind, . . . the actual proof of the marvelously illuminating [nature of the Buddha Mind]." [pp. 4–5]

Precepts

What is usually translated as "precepts" in Buddhism might more accurately be rendered as "admonitions," since they mainly have to do with things prohibited (no killing, no lying, no adultery, etc.). This clarification is needed to understand why Bankei speaks of this as "all for wicked monks who broke the rules," not for buddhas.

A certain master of the Precepts school asked: "Doesn't your Reverence observe the precepts?"

The Master said: "Originally, what people call the precepts were all for wicked monks who broke rules; for the man who abides in the Unborn Buddha Mind, there's no need for precepts. The precepts were taught to help sentient beings—they weren't taught to help buddhas! What everyone has from his parents innately is the Unborn Buddha Mind alone, so abide in the Unborn Buddha Mind. When you abide in the Unborn Buddha Mind, you're a living

Buddha here today, and that living Buddha certainly isn't going to concoct anything like taking precepts, so there aren't any precepts for him to take. To concoct anything like taking the precepts is not what's meant by the Unborn Buddha Mind. When you abide in the Unborn Buddha Mind, there's no way you can violate the precepts. From the standpoint of the Unborn, the precepts too are secondary, peripheral concerns; in the place of the Unborn, there's really no such thing as precepts. . . ." [p. 7]

Growing Up Deluded

"What everyone has from his parents innately is the Buddha Mind alone. But since your parents themselves fail to realize this, you become deluded too, and then display this delusion in raising your *own* children. Even the nursemaids and baby-sitters lose their temper, so that the people involved in bringing up children display every sort of deluded behavior, including stupidity, selfish desire, and the [anger of] fighting demons. Growing up with deluded people surrounding them, children develop a first-rate set of bad habits, becoming quite proficient at being deluded themselves and turning into unenlightened beings. Originally, when you're born, you're without delusion. But on account of the faults of the people who raise you, someone abiding in the Buddha Mind is turned into a first-rate unenlightened being. This is something I'm sure you all know from your own experience. . . .

"That which you *didn't* pick up from outside is the Unborn Buddha Mind, and here no delusions exist. Since the Buddha Mind is marvelously illuminating, you're able to learn things, even to the point of thoroughly learning all sorts of deluded behavior. [At the same time,] since it's marvelously illuminating, when you hear this, you'll resolve *not* to be deluded, and from today on cease creating delusion, abiding in the Unborn Buddha Mind as it is. Just as before you applied yourself skillfully to picking up delusions and made yourself deluded, now you'll use the same skill to listen to this and *stop* being deluded — that's what a splendid thing the Buddha Mind is. . . .

"When you hear this, I want you all from today on to abide in the Unborn Buddha Mind just as it is — the Unborn Buddha Mind you have from your parents innately. Then you won't create delusions about anything, and, since no delusions will remain, you'll be living buddhas from today forever after. Nothing could be more direct! You've all got to realize this conclusively." [pp. 17–19]

Everybody Has the Buddha Mind

"When your parents gave you life, there wasn't a trace of selfish desire, bad habits or self-centeredness. But from the age of four or five you picked up the mean things you saw other people do and the bad things you heard them say, so that gradually as you matured, growing up badly, you developed selfish desire, which in turn produced self-centeredness. Deluded by this self-centeredness, you then proceeded to create every sort of evil. If it weren't for being centered on yourself, delusions wouldn't arise. When they don't arise, that's none other than abiding in the Unborn Buddha Mind. . . ." [pp. 31–32]

Samurai

"Nowadays there are lots of people who own high-priced ceramics—flower vases and Korean tea bowls. I don't own anything of this sort myself, but when I see the people who do, they take the ceramics and wrap them round and round with soft cotton and crepe and stick them in a box, which makes good sense. If a costly ceramic strikes against something hard, it's sure to break, so to keep these ceramics from breaking by wrapping them in cotton and crepe is surely a judicious measure. The samurai's mind is just like this. To begin with, samurai always place honor above all else. If there's even a single word of disagreement between them, they can't let it pass without calling it to account—such is the way of the samurai. Once a single word is challenged, there's no going back. So a samurai always keeps the 'hard' parts of his mind under wraps, swathed in cotton and crepe, and from the start takes the greatest care to avoid 'striking against' abrasive people. Everyone would do well always to be careful about this. Once anyone has challenged his words, the samurai is bound to kill him. You'd better grasp this clearly.

"Then there's the sort of killing that occurs when a samurai throws himself before his lord and cuts down an attacker. This serves to destroy evildoers and pacify the realm and constitutes the regular vocation of the samurai, so for a warrior this sort of thing is not considered to be murder. But to kill another simply scheming for your own personal ends, stirring up selfish desires as a result of self-centeredness—this is murder indeed. It shows disloyalty to your lord, unfiliality to your parents, and changes the Buddha Mind for a fighting demon. On the other hand, in circumstances when one must die for one's lord, to fail to die, to run away and behave like a coward, is switching the Buddha Mind for an animal. Birds and beasts don't have the sort of intelligence people do, so they can't understand the proper way to act; they don't know the meaning of honor and simply flee from place to place trying to stay alive. But when a samurai, similarly, fails to understand the meaning of honor and runs away, not even showing shame before his fellow warriors, that's just like being an animal. . . ." [pp. 41–42]

Nothing to Do with Rules

"In my place, I'm always telling everyone, 'Abide in the Unborn Buddha Mind and nothing else!' Other than that, I'm not setting up any special *rules* and making them practice. All the same, since everyone got together and decided to practice for [a period of] twelve sticks of incense every day, I told them, 'Go ahead, do whatever you like'; so I'm letting them practice every day for [a period of] twelve sticks of incense. But the Unborn Buddha Mind isn't a matter of sticks of incense! When you abide in the Buddha Mind and don't become deluded, then, without looking for enlightenment outside, you'll just sit in the Buddha Mind, just stand in the Buddha Mind, just sleep in the Buddha Mind, just get up in the Buddha Mind—just abiding in the Buddha Mind, so that in all your ordinary activities you function as a living Buddha. There's really nothing to it.

"As for *zazen*, since *za* [sitting] is the Buddha Mind's sitting at ease, while *zen* [meditation] is another name for Buddha Mind, the Buddha Mind's sitting at ease is what's meant by *zazen*. So when you're abiding in the Unborn, *all the time* is *zazen*; *zazen* isn't just the time when you're practicing formal meditation. Even when you're sitting in meditation, if there's something you've got to do, it's quite all right to get up and leave. So, in my group, everyone is free to do as he likes. Just always abide at ease in the Buddha Mind. . . ." [pp. 58–59]

Plain Speaking

"As you can see in the records that have been brought to Japan, the true teaching of the Unborn long ago ceased to exist there, so that nowadays, even in China, men of the Unborn are not to be found, and that's why no records that speak of the Unborn Buddha Mind have come to Japan.

"When I was young and trying to uncover the Buddha Mind, I even made a serious effort at taking part in questions-and-answers (*mondō*) [using Chinese expressions]. But later on, having come to a real understanding of things, I gave it up. Japanese are better off asking about things in a manner that's suitable to Japanese, using their ordinary language. Japanese are poor at Chinese, so in dialogues using Chinese [terms], they can't question [teachers] about things as thoroughly as they might wish. When you put your questions in ordinary Japanese, there's no matter you can't ask about. So, instead of taking a roundabout way and knocking yourselves out trying to pose your questions in difficult Chinese words, you're better off freely putting them in easy Japanese, without exhausting yourselves. . . .

"The reason Japanese monks are teaching laymen inept at Chinese using Chinese words that are hard for them to understand is that they *themselves* haven't settled the matter of the Unborn Buddha Mind, and evade people's questions by using Chinese words that are hard for ordinary folk to grasp. On top of which, these [difficult expressions] are nothing but the dregs and slobber of the Chinese patriarchs! . . ." [pp. 60–61]

The Proof

Once I asked the Master: "Is it helpful in studying the Way to read through the Buddhist sutras and the records of the old masters?"

The Master said: "It all depends. If you rely on the principles contained in the sutras and records, when you read them, you'll be blinding your own eyes. On the other hand, when the time comes that you can *dismiss* principles, if you read [such things], you'll find the proof of your own realization." [p. 114]

[*Bankei zenji zenshū*, pp. 3, 6, 21–22, 37–42, 50–57, 34–35, 72–73, 144;
Haskel, trans., and Hakeda, ed., *Bankei Zen*, pp. 4–5, 7, 17,
31–32, 41–42, 58–59, 60–61, 114]

HAKUIN EKAKU

All present-day masters of the Rinzai sect claim descent from Hakuin Ekaku (1686–1769), an extraordinary man who gave all his efforts to reviving Zen Buddhism in eighteenth-century Japan. He rejected formalistic and intellectual Zen, as well as the *nenbutsu* chanting that was popular among some Zen practitioners at the time. Among his followers were all classes of people—farmers, samurai, daimyo, and women as well as men. Like Takuan Sōhō, he taught those who seriously sought after Zen for its own sake, regardless of their social background.

Hakuin is unusual among Zen masters in that he left many writings in colloquial Japanese, as well as in the literary language and in *kanbun*. Most are in the form of letters or essays written to his followers. Hakuin was a versatile master who excelled not only in writing but also in painting, calligraphy, and sculpture. We find in his writings a detailed account of his Zen experience, whereas similar descriptions are seldom to be found in other Zen literature.

In his system of Zen training, Hakuin emphasized focusing all one's energy on penetrating *kōan* stories until the mental exhaustion induced by the conflict between one's great determination and one's great doubt would lead to Zen awakening (*satori*), or seeing true nature (*kenshō*). Zen practitioners must penetrate several series of *kōan*, inducing repeated awakenings. Hakuin rejected formalistic and intellectual Zen, as well as other practices, such as invoking the name of Amida Buddha (*nenbutsu*) or silent reflection (*mokushō*) meditation, which he probably identified with Ōbaku as well as with the Sōtō and Genjū (i.e., Rinzai) Rinka lineages. Hakuin also wrote numerous letters to lay people, encouraging them to practice Zen at home and at work; composed folk songs; and gave away numerous works of Zen calligraphy and drawings.

A final note concerns the present institutionalized forms of Zen, which divided into the two main streams of Sōtō and Rinzai in the mid-Tokugawa period, after the arrival of Yinyuan Longqi (J. Ingen Ryūki, 1592–1673) in 1654 and other Chinese monks who eventually founded the Ōbaku Zen lineage. The Ashikaga period's Five Mountain and Rinka Zen networks[3] each included both Sōtō and Rinzai lineages, and clerics of various Rinzai and Sōtō lineages commonly studied at one another's temples. By the time Yinyuan arrived, however, all the Five Mountain lineages had died out. Differences between the new Chinese-style Ōbaku Zen and the Japanese Rinka traditions, however, awakened among Japanese Zen monks a new sense of anti-Ōbaku sectarian consciousness. In the Rinka lineages, Sōtō monks such as Manzan Dōhaku (1636–1714) and Menzan Zuihō (1683–1769) advocated a return to Dōgen's teachings, especially as expressed in his *True Dharma Eye Treasury*, whereas the Rinzai monk Hakuin Ekaku advocated a vigorous system of *kōan* study based on earlier Japanese Rinka practices, which he identified with the Song-dynasty ancestor of his own Ō-Tō-Kan lineage, Zutang Zhiyu (J. Kidō Chigū, 1185–1269). Thus Japanese Rinka monks, both Sōtō and Rinzai, identified their own traditions with the heritage of the Chinese Song dynasty, in opposition to Ming-dynasty culture of Ōbaku. While the surviving Sōtō and Rinzai lineages have a common Rinka heritage, the differences between them have grown more pronounced since the late Tokugawa period.

MY OLD TEA KETTLE
(ORATEGAMA)

The text excerpted here consists of letters that Hakuin sent to different lay people in 1748 when he was sixty-three years old and that show how he actively sought to popularize Zen practice among lay people. The first letter, addressed to the feudal lord Nabeshima Naotsune (1701–1749), describes how the meditation practice of holding one's vital energy in the lower abdomen—what Hakuin calls the true practice of introspection (*naikan*)—not only nurtures health and maintains youth and vitality but also is essential to success in *kōan* meditation. Finally, an excerpt from the supplement to this work provides Hakuin's Zen interpretation of the Pure Land practice of chanting the name of Amida Buddha (*nenbutsu*). While Hakuin seems to have accepted these other forms of Buddhism, ultimately he insisted that they could be religiously meaningful only if performed as a type of Zen practice directed toward the goal of seeing true nature (*kenshō*, or Zen awakening).

If their motivation is bad, virtually all Zen practitioners [will] find themselves blocked in both the active and quietistic approaches to the practice of *kōan* meditation. They fall into a state of severe depression and distraction; the fire-elemental phase mounts to the heart; the metal-elemental phase in the lungs

---

3. See de Bary et al., eds., *Sources of Japanese Tradition*, 2nd ed., vol. 1, chap. 14.

shrinks painfully; the health generally declines; and quite frequently they develop an illness most difficult to cure. Yet if they polish and perfect themselves in the true practice of introspection (*naikan*), they will conform to the secret methods for the ultimate nourishment; their bodies and minds will become strong; their vitality [will be] great; and they will readily attain to awakening in all things.

Shakyamuni Buddha taught this point in detail in the Agama [Sutras]. Master Zhiyi has culled the import of these teachings, whether examining the principles of the Dharma, whether sitting for long periods without lying down, or whether engaged in walking practices throughout the six divisions of the day, the vital breath (*ki*) must always be made to fill the *cakra* sphere (*seirin*), the lower field of cinnabar (*tanden*), between the navel and the loins. Even though one may be hemmed in by worldly cares or tied down by guests who require elaborate attention, the source of strength two inches below the navel must naturally be filled with the vital breath, and at no time may it be allowed to disperse. This area should be pendulous and well rounded, somewhat like a new ball that has yet to be used. If a person is able to acquire this kind of breath concentration he can sit in meditation all day long without its ever tiring him; he can recite the scriptures from morning to night without becoming worn out; he can write all day long without any trouble; he can talk all day without collapsing from fatigue. Even if he practices good works day after day, there will still be no indications of flagging; in fact, the capacity of his mind will gradually grow larger, and his vitality will always be strong. On the hottest day of summer he will not perspire or need to use a fan; on the snowiest night of deepest winter he need not wear socks or warm himself. Should he live to be a hundred years old, his teeth will remain firm. Provided he does not become lax in his practices, he should attain a great age. If a man becomes accomplished in this method, what Way cannot be perfected, what precepts cannot be maintained, what *samadhi* cannot be practiced, what virtue cannot be fulfilled!

If, however, you do not become proficient in these ancient techniques, if you have not made the essentials of the true practice your own, if by yourself you recklessly seek for your own brand of awakening, you will engage in excessive study and become entangled in inappropriate thoughts. At this time, the chest and breathing mechanism become stopped up; a fire rises in the heart; the legs feel as though they were immersed in ice and snow; [and] the ears are filled with a roaring sound like a torrent sounding in a deep valley. The lungs shrink; the fluids in the body dry up; and in the end you are afflicted with a disease most difficult to cure. Indeed, you will hardly be able to keep yourself alive. All this is only because you do not know the correct road of true practice. A most regrettable thing indeed!

The *Cessation and Insight* speaks of cessation in relation to phenomena (*ke'enshi*) and of cessation in relation to true emptiness (*taishinshi*). The method of introspection that I describe here represents the essential of this cessation in relation to phenomena. When I was young the content of my *kōan* meditation was poor. I was convinced that absolute tranquillity of the source of mind was the Buddha Way. Thus I despised activity and was fond of quietude. I would always seek out some dark and gloomy place and engage in dead sitting. Trivial and mundane matters pressed against my chest, and a fire mounted in my heart. I was unable to enter wholeheartedly into the active practice of Zen. My manner became irascible, and fears assailed me. Both my mind and body felt continually weak; sweat poured ceaselessly from my armpits; and my eyes constantly filled with tears. My mind was in a continual state of depression, and I made not the slightest advance toward gaining the benefits that result from the study of Buddhism.

But later I was most fortunate in receiving the instruction of a good teacher. The secret methods of introspection were handed down to me, and for three years I devoted myself to an assiduous practice of them. The serious disease from which I suffered, that up until then I had found so difficult to cure, gradually cleared up like frost and snow melting beneath the rays of the morning sun. The problems with those vile *kōans—difficult to believe, difficult to pene-trate, difficult to unravel, difficult to enter—kōans* that up to then had been impossible for me to sink my teeth into, now faded away with the passing of my disease.

Even though I am past sixty now, my vitality is ten times as great as it was when I was thirty or forty. My mind and body are strong, and I never have the feeling that I absolutely must lie down to rest. Should I want to, I [would] find no difficulty in refraining from sleep for two, three, or even seven days, without suffering any decline in my mental powers. I am surrounded by three [hundred] to five hundred demanding students, and even though I lecture on the scrip-tures or on the collections of the Zen ancestors' sayings for thirty to fifty days in a row, it does not exhaust me. I am quite convinced that all this is owing to the power gained from practicing this method of introspection.

Initially emphasis must be placed on the care of the body. Then, during your practice of introspection, without your seeking it and quite unconsciously, you will attain, how many times I cannot tell, the power of awakening. It is essential that you neither despise nor grasp for either the realm of activity or that of quietude and that you continue your practice assiduously.

Frequently you may feel that you are getting nowhere with practice in the midst of activity, whereas the quietistic approach brings unexpected results. Yet rest assured that those who use the quietistic approach can never hope to enter into meditation in the midst of activity. Should by chance a person who uses this approach enter into the dusts and confusions of the world of activity, even the power of ordinary understanding that he had seemingly attained will be entirely lost. Drained of all vitality, he will be inferior to any mediocre, talentless person. The most trivial matters will upset him; an inordinate cowardice will afflict his mind; and he will frequently behave in a mean and base manner. What can you call accomplished about a man like this?

[Adapted from *The Zen Master Hakuin*, trans. Yampolsky, pp. 29–33]

Outside the Mind There Is No Lotus Sutra

Outside the mind there is no Lotus Sutra and outside the Lotus Sutra there is no mind. . . . Outside the ten realms of existence there is no mind, and outside the ten realms of existence there is no Lotus Sutra. This is the ultimate teaching. It is not limited to me, but all the Tathagatas of the past, present, and future, and all learned sages everywhere, when they have reached the ultimate understanding, have all preached in the same way. The essential purport of the text of the Lotus Sutra speaks gloriously to this effect. There are eighty-four thousand ways of practicing Buddhism, but they are all provisional teachings and cannot be regarded as other than expediencies. When this ultimate is reached, all living beings and all Tathagatas of the past, present, and future, mountains, rivers, the great earth, and the Lotus Sutra itself all bespeak the Dharma principle that all things are a nondual unity representing the true appearance of all things. This is the fundamental principle of Buddhism.

We have indeed the 5,418 scriptures of the Buddhist canon that detail the limitless mysterious meaning preached by Shakyamuni Buddha. We have the sudden, gradual, esoteric, and indeterminate methods. But their ultimate principle is reduced to the eight fascicles of the Lotus Sutra. The ultimate meaning of the 64,360 odd written words of the Lotus Sutra is reduced to the five words in its title: Lotus Sutra of the Wondrous Law (Myōhō renge kyō). These five words are reduced to the two words Wondrous Law (Myōhō) and the two words (Wondrous Law) return to one word: mind. If one asks to where this one word, mind, returns: "The horned rabbit and the furry turtle cross the nowhere mountain." What is the ultimate meaning? "If you wish to know the mind of a wife who laments in the midst of spring, it is at the time when her sewing needle is stopped and words cannot be spoken."

This One Mind, derived from the two words Wondrous Law mentioned above, when spread out includes all the Dharma worlds of the ten directions and, when contracted, returns to the no-thought and no-mind of self-nature. Therefore the Buddha preached such things as "outside the mind no thing exists," "in the triple world there is One Mind alone," and "the true appearance of all things." Reaching this ultimate place is called the Lotus Sutra, or Amida Buddha of Infinite Life; in Zen it is called the Original Face; in Shingon the Sun Disc of Inherent Nature of the Syllable A; in terms of Buddhist morality it is Basic, Unconditioned Essence of the Precepts. Everyone must realize that these are all different names for the One Mind. . . .

After meditating in the Himalayas the Buddha discovered the nature of the mind that is endowed from the outset. He called in his noble voice: "How marvelous! All living beings are endowed with the wisdom and the virtuous characteristics of the Tathagatas." He preached the sudden and the gradual teachings and the partial and complete doctrines of the various scriptures and became himself the great teacher of the triple world. When he was worshiped by the gods Brahma and Indra, it is as though the lotus blossom had emerged from the mud and opened to its full beauty. Just as the lotus's color and fragrance inhere in it as it lies in the mud, as it emerges, and as it blooms above the surface, so when the Buddha preached the Dharma as numerous as the sands in the Ganges, he referred to nothing that was brought in from the outside. In terms of the common person, he spoke of the appearance of the Buddha-nature itself, with which all are without a doubt endowed; in terms of living beings, once the vow to become a Buddha has been made, the Wondrous Dharma of the One Mind does not increase nor lessen one bit It is just the same as the lotus: at the time that it lies amidst the mud, and after its blossoms are scattered in the summer, it does not undergo any fundamental change whatsoever. Thus he provisionally likened the lotus plant to the Wondrous Law of the One Mind. Is this not irrefutable proof that the Buddha mind, with which all people are endowed, was called the Lotus Sutra of the Wondrous Law? . . .

The True Reality that is the Lotus Sutra cannot be seized by the hands or seen by the eye. How then is one to receive and hold it? What then should one say to the practitioner of the Lotus Sutra who wishes to take it himself? There are three types of capacity. The practitioner of inferior capacity is captivated by the yellow scroll with its red handles, and copies, recites, and makes explanations of it. The practitioner of average capacity illuminates his own mind and so receives and holds to the sutra. The person of superior capacity penetrates this sutra with his wisdom eye, just as though he were viewing the surface of his own mind. That is why the Nirvana Sutra says: "The Tathagata sees Buddha-nature with his wisdom eye." The practitioner of the Lotus Sutra, if he is engaged in the true practice of the ultimate of Mahayana, will not find it an easy thing to do. What is simple is very much so; what is difficult is very, very difficult indeed.

[Adapted from *The Zen Master Hakuin*, trans. Yampolsky, pp. 87–90]

Supplement: Zen Practice and Recalling the Name Amida Buddha Are the Same

Suppose one man is occupied with Zen meditation on the *kōan* of Zhaozhou's *mu* (nothing) and another man devotes himself exclusively to the recalling of the Buddha Amida's name (*nenbutsu*). If the meditation of the former is not pure; if his determination is not firm, even if he devotes himself to the *kōan* for ten or twenty years, he will gain no benefit whatsoever. The man who recalls Amida Buddha's name, on the other hand, should he call it with complete concentration and undiluted purity, should he neither concern himself with the filthy mundane world nor seek the Pure Land, but proceed determinedly without retrogression, he will, before ten days have passed, gain the benefits of *samadhi*, produce the wisdom of the Buddha, and achieve the Great Matter of deliverance in the very place he stands. . . .

Doesn't the [Contemplation] Sutra state: "Amida's brilliance illumines the world in all directions"? But do not understand this to mean that the brilliance and the world are two different things. If you are awakened, the worlds in all directions, grass, trees, lands are perfected and at once are the true body of the pure light of the Tathagata. If you are deluded, the true body of the pure light of the Tathagata is perfected, but in error is made to be the world in all directions, grass, trees, and lands. That is why the [Diamond Perfect Wisdom] Sutra says: "If you see me as form or seek me as sound, you are practicing the ways of the heretic and will never be able to see the Tathagata."

The true practitioner of the Pure Land doctrine is not like this. He does not contemplate birth; he does not contemplate death; his mind does not falter or fall into error. Recalling the name of Amida Buddha constantly, he has reached the state where his mind is undisturbed. The great Matter appears suddenly before him, and his salvation is determined. Such a man can be called one who has really seen true nature. His own body is the limitless body of Amida Buddha, the Pure Land's jeweled trees of seven precious gems, the pond of the eight virtues. His own mind is illumined and radiates before his eyes. He has penetrated to the understanding that mountains, rivers, the great earth, all phenomena are the rare and the mysterious Sea of Adornment. The ultimate, in which there is complete concentration, is recalling the name, in which not an instant of thought is produced and in which the body and life are cast aside, is known as "going" (ō). The place where *samadhi* is perfected and true wisdom makes its appearance is known as "delivered" (*jō*). The welling forth of this absolute principle in all its clarity, the immovable place in which the true practitioner stands, not one fraction of an inch apart from truth, is "the welcoming of Amida" (*raigō*). When the welcoming of Amida and deliverance are then and there not two things—this is the true substance of seeing true nature.

[Adapted from *The Zen Master Hakuin*, trans. Yampolsky, pp. 127–29]

JIUN SONJA

Jiun Sonja (Onkō, 1718–1804) was born in Osaka, the son of a *rōnin* and a devoutly Buddhist mother. As a boy, Jiun received a Confucian education and, for a time, exhibited a disdain for Buddhism and its clergy that reflected his early Confucian sympathies. However, after his father's death in Jiun's thirteenth year, his upbringing was entrusted to a monk affiliated with the Shingon vinaya sect (Shingon risshū), and within two years Jiun had been won over to Buddhism.[4] In his late teens, he was sent by his teacher to Kyoto for further study of Confucianism at the Kogidō, or School of Ancient Meanings, established by Itō Jinsai (1627–1705). Immediately thereafter, Jiun resumed his Buddhist training in Shingon *ritsu* temples in the Osaka area. By his early twenties, he had succeeded his teacher as abbot of Hōrakuji in Osaka, but he soon gave up that post to embark on a period of uninterrupted meditation under the direction of a Sōtō Zen monk. It was during this time that he apparently had his first enlightenment experience.

In his late twenties, troubled by what he judged to be a lack of commitment to practice, as well as by the sectarian character of Tokugawa Buddhism, Jiun commenced a movement to revive what he sometimes called "Buddhism as it was when the Buddha was alive" or, more frequently, the "True Dharma." At the heart of his movement—known as the Shōbōritsu, or "Vinaya of the True Dharma"—was an emphasis on the fundamentals of Buddhist practice and a deemphasis on sectarian concerns. After a long career as a Buddhist scholar, reformer, and apologist, Jiun died in Kyoto.[5]

SERMONS ON THE PRECEPTS AND MONASTIC LIFE

The following three sermons date from the middle period of Jiun Sonja's life, which he passed in retreat in a hut on Mount Ikoma, east of Osaka. For nearly fourteen years before this, Jiun had worked in a variety of ways to spread the "True Dharma"; then, in 1758, he withdrew to the mountain. He spent much of his time there meditating, but he also concentrated on the study of Sanskrit, completing, with the help of a handful of disciples, the bulk of his thousand-fascicle *Guide to Sanskrit Studies* (*Bongaku shinryō*).

The sermons that follow were selected to illustrate the importance that Jiun attached to the precepts and the monastic life. Students of Dōgen (1200–1253) will notice a strong similarity between the Zen master's thought and Jiun's on these subjects. Both viewed the celibate, meditative way of life initiated by the Buddha and established as the norm for all later generations of monks and nuns as simultaneously a means to and a consequence of the enlightenment experience. As Jiun states in one of the sermons translated here, the way of life of one who "leaves home" is "natural to people who follow the great path to liberation from birth and death."

---

4. The Shingon *ritsu* sect, which emphasizes the Buddhist precepts, was originally founded by Eison (1201–1290) and Ninshō (1217–1303) and, after a period of decline, was revived in the late sixteenth and early seventeenth centuries by Shunshō Myōnin (1576–1610).

5. For Jiun's critique of Confucianism, see Watt, "Jiun Sonja," pp. 188–214.

Arouse the Thought of Enlightenment and Observe the Precepts

A wise person should earnestly arouse the thought of enlightenment. The thought of enlightenment is the thought pure in its self-nature. It naturally has no relationship to fame and profit, the desires of the five senses, to self-pride and conceit, and to much talk and many concerns. Rather, it is naturally related to gentleness and harmony, to compassion and forbearance, to loyalty, filial piety, sincerity, and good faith, to humility and respect, to meditation and wisdom. From the Buddhas above to flying and creeping insects below, all are seen as the same in their self-nature, yet their distinctive attributes are not destroyed. Accordingly, one seeks enlightenment above and transforms sentient beings below; one reveres those above and loves those below.

The place where the thought of enlightenment takes form is in the practice of the precepts. That which accompanies the practice of the precepts is the mind of great compassion. Practice of the precepts without the thought of enlightenment leads to the attainment of a pleasant retribution in the conditioned world; this is the lesser karma attained by human beings and devas. A time will come when this retribution is exhausted and, as before, you will fall back into the cycle of birth and death.

Practice of the precepts with the thought of enlightenment extends infinitely into the future and in the end leads to the realization of the retribution of Buddhahood. In the sutras, it is written, "The Buddhas of the three periods of time gained the thought of enlightenment through these precepts." All of you should believe this and receive and observe the precepts in conformity with the Dharma.

[Watt, trans., "Sermons," p. 122]

Leave Home for the Protection of the True Dharma

The Dharma is fundamentally not something that arises and becomes extinct. Even if all sentient beings, at the same time, were to arouse the thought of enlightenment, fulfill the practice of the bodhisattva and realize unsurpassed enlightenment, as regards the Dharma, there would not be the slightest increase. . . . Corruption in the conduct of monks, however, may accurately be referred to as a sign of the Dharma's decline. . . . Seeing the corruption today in the appearance and conduct of the five groups [within the Buddhist clergy],[6] one must arouse a [high] aspiration.

The sutras say that when Shakyamuni was a prince and went forth from the north gate [of his palace], he saw an ascetic, and for the first time, he aroused

---

6. The five groups are monks, nuns, male and female novices, and *siksamana*, a special category of female novice between the ages of eighteen and twenty.

the thought of enlightenment. Thereafter, he followed a hunter and exchanged his garments for a robe, and cutting off his hair with a knife, for the first time [himself] took on the appearance of an ascetic. Then, in the guise of one who had left home, he begged for food in the country of Magadha. . . .

The Buddha, the World-Honored One, was not a person who left home because the position of a Cakravartin king[7] or the governance of the empire had become a burden. . . . It was not that his officials and subjects had become a burden. For the Buddha, the World-Honored one, even when he was among great numbers of people, it was no different than when he was alone in a quiet place with no one around. It was not that the palaces and towers had become a burden. . . . Nor was it that he left home because his three wives . . . had become a burden. . . . Nor was it that he left home because his relatives had become a burden. . . .

Why, then, did he leave home? It is simply that the guise of an ascetic and of one who leaves home is natural to people who follow the great path to liberation from birth and death. Because all of the Buddhas of the three periods of time left home and realized enlightenment, Shakyamuni also, following their [example], left home and realized unsurpassed enlightenment. . . .

Therefore, when illustrious masters of ancient times discoursed on the three Treasures and spoke of the element most important for the transformation of people, [they held that] the merit of the Buddha comes first. For the attainment of liberation, [however,] the merit of the Dharma comes first. Even the Buddha realized enlightenment by taking the Dharma as his teacher, and people today also practice relying upon the Dharma. [Yet] for the maintenance of the Three Treasures, the merit of the Sangha comes first. If the conduct of the Sangha is correct, then the Buddha and the Dharma will survive, and, as a consequence of that, the true Dharma will long abide. . . .

Today, a person who sees the signs of the Dharma's decline and who [still] has a [high] aspiration, cannot pass the days at ease. If, arousing a [high] aspiration, a person wants to protect the Dharma, there is nothing better than leaving home in accord with the Dharma. If one's appearance is correct, one's aspiration will naturally be correct, and if one's aspiration is correct, the Buddha's Dharma will survive. . . .

[Watt, trans., "Sermons," pp. 123–25]

The Merit of Leaving Home

The merits of a person who leaves home are innumerable and without limit. . . .

---

7. A Cakravartin king is a universal monarch, an ideal Buddhist ruler who governs through spiritual power rather than force.

On the one hand, one who leaves home inherits the seeds of Buddhahood and causes them to flourish. . . .

On the other hand, one who leaves home becomes a field of blessing for all sentient beings. This is because one who has left home is the manifest form of compassion. For those human beings and devas who see him, he becomes a cause of virtue. . . . Those who reverence and honor him will surely gain the retribution of being held in high esteem, and those who make offerings to him and sing his praises will surely give rise to all virtue and wisdom. . . .

When a monk walks under the moon in meditation, his mind is emptied of all conditioning. When he sits in meditation beneath a tree, all gates to the Dharma manifest themselves within his mind, and he roams far beyond the three worlds. He is unaware that he is still on earth; yet, at ease, he moves about in one room. He is unaware that he is a person who has left home, or again, that he is a human being. Gain and loss, right and wrong—of what concern are they to him? A ruler cannot make him his subject; his father cannot again make him his child. He has no ties to wife or children; he does not compete for fame or profit. Rather . . . he is like the ruler of a country who becomes the overseer of the four classes of people, causes each to work at this task, and yet himself simply sits with folded arms, having nothing to do.

[For the monk], all sentient beings are his children. There is only compassion; there are no relative degrees of intimacy. To shave off one's hair is to discard all ornamentation. To dye one's clothes is to transcend all distinctions of noble and humble. To take the begging bowl in hand is to become a field of blessing for all sentient beings.

[*Jiun Sonja zenshū*, vol. 14, pp. 378–89, 25–27; Watt, trans., "Sermons," pp. 119–28]

Chapter 32

ORTHODOXY, PROTEST, AND LOCAL REFORM

In its original sense as "right teaching," orthodoxy was by no means a foreign concept in Tokugawa Japan. *Seigaku*, "right teaching" or "correct learning," conveyed the same idea. Nor was the concept of "heterodoxy" unknown. *Igaku* expressed the idea of "different," "divergent," or "deviant" teachings or learning, although it signified more a departure from a "Way" than from a stated creed (as "heresy" does).

Almost a universal feature of established traditions, orthodoxy itself has assumed many forms, depending on the nature of its advocacy or its institutional backing; thus it has more often been a contested issue than an accepted fact. In Japan, as we have seen, orthodoxy as the "right" or "correct" teaching was asserted in different forms by individual leaders, each of whom insisted on his own understanding of the teaching as the original true or correct one. In each case, a new fundamentalism claimed to be the one correct or orthodox teaching.

More often, however, orthodoxy has been associated with institutional sponsorship or enforcement. We saw earlier that official orthodoxy was often identified with sponsorship by the Tokugawa ruling house, although the nature and extent of its sponsorship of the Hayashi school, or of Zhu Xi's teaching, varied from age to age, shogun to shogun, and even minister to minister and scholar to scholar. In other words, it was more like personal patronage than an established state system.

How this worked depended on several systemic factors. The Tokugawa regime has generally been characterized as a centralized feudalism. Because of its dominant position, the *bakufu* (literally, "military headquarters") was looked to for direction or as a model by its subordinates, who tended to "follow the leader." Thus much of what headquarters adopted in Edo was taken as a model by its daimyo, and this was especially true of feudal houses that were branches of or closely associated with the ruling house (and that themselves, in turn, exerted an influence on the center).

Besides the political factors, religious, intellectual, and social factors were operating as well. Because there was no civil service examination system acting as a magnet to draw students into "examination studies," as there was in China and Korea, scholars responded to other needs and influences, among them many of the intellectual challenges common to the intellectual elite of East Asia as a whole.

Moreover, as feudal states, the daimyo domains (or *han*) remained largely autonomous in matters not considered to affect the security of the shogunal regime. Thus within this loose structure, as events developed and education spread, there was a considerable diversity among schools, teachers, and scholars, which was abundantly shown in our earlier reading. Concomitant with rapid social growth and economic change, however, serious problems compelled the attention of both scholars and officials, arousing intense concerns and, indeed, alarm. Among those who responded to these concerns in a decided and determined way was the *bakufu* leader Matsudaira Sadanobu (1758–1829). His education had been in the Zhu Xi school, and he acted in accordance with the fundamental premise of that teaching: that the whole political and social order rested on sound education in public morality sustained by individual moral and intellectual cultivation as expressed by Zhu Xi as "self-discipline [as the key to] the governance of humankind" (*shūko chijin*).

Matsudaira was also much concerned with preparing retainers for public service. He tried to convert the school under the nominal leadership of the Hayashis from one that allowed considerable freedom of intellectual inquiry and discussion open to all classes to a program that was more focused on moral training for public service by Tokugawa retainers. The curriculum that Matsudaira advocated was based on the standard texts of Zhu Xi, especially the Four Books and the *Elementary Learning*. He also instituted examinations to certify retainers for official service. A similar regimen was later ordered for the domain schools.

Thus at the end of the eighteenth century, steps were taken to change the pattern of schooling privately conducted but open to all, to a more official one, with a strong sanction for Zhu Xi's teachings and the proscription of those deemed "deviant" (*igaku*). At the same time, since education at large was expanding in the late Tokugawa period, it is noteworthy that among the many new schools established—whether private, official, or semiofficial (i.e., patronized by local daimyo)—the Zhu Xi curriculum predominated. Although this trend may be partly attributable to the move toward a new orthodoxy, the fact that many of these schools (*terakoya*) were locally sponsored and managed suggests that more was at work here than central direction. Indeed, the Zhu Xi curriculum may well have survived an intellectual attack on its own educational merits in local settings, as it had in quite different systemic conditions in late imperial China and Chosŏn Korea.

Along with the persistence and even the revival of this "orthodox" educational system, or what might be called the ground level of basic literacy, there was an equally significant spread of intellectual activity and a challenging diversity on the higher, more advanced level of scholarship. The Prohibition of Heterodox Studies (or Ban on Deviant Learning) may have set limits on the influence of independent and original thinkers, but its effect was nothing like the repression of modern totalitarian systems.

At the end of the Tokugawa era, education may be roughly characterized as having two levels. The first level, of basic education and literacy, was still very much formed by Neo-Confucian discourse, the language of the Four Books and the Five Classics, the *Elementary Learning*, and the *Classic of Filiality*. The second level showed much greater heterogeneity among the intellectual elite, whose thinking, to the extent that it could be characterized in general terms, opened out onto a much larger horizon while often eclectically trying to reconcile different poles of thought in a loose framework of coexistence or syncretic fusion. Indeed, even the later Hayashi school reflected this syncretic trend.

The selections in this chapter start with the reassertion of the old, and yet systemically new, orthodoxy, followed by examples of challenges to that orthodoxy or established authority, still other forms of advocacy on behalf of local domestic reform, and, finally, bold proposals for national planning and external expansion.

THE PROHIBITION OF HETERODOX STUDIES

THE KANSEI EDICT

The Kansei Edict, issued in 1790 during the administration of Matsudaira Sadanobu, strongly reaffirmed the shogunate's support for the traditional Zhu Xi teaching. In form, however, it was merely a directive to the head of the Hayashi school, hereditarily entrusted with supervising education, to stamp out unorthodox teachings in his own and other official schools. Five years later, another directive called for the enforcement of this ban in the official schools maintained by the other feudal lords. The main effect of these decrees was to discourage the open propagation of heterodox views, but without actually suppressing the schools in which they were privately taught.

The teaching of Zhu Xi has had the full confidence of successive shoguns since the Keichō era [1596–1615; i.e., since the founding of the shogunate], and your family, generation after generation, has been entrusted with the duty of upholding and expounding this teaching. It has been expected, therefore, that orthodox studies would be pursued without remiss and that your students would be trained in accordance with it. Lately, however, various new theories have been put forward; heterodox teachings have become popular; and social standards have been broken down. Indeed, since they [heterodox teachings] point to a complete decline in orthodox studies, we have heard from time to time of those whose thinking is not pure and correct. Consequently in order to tighten discipline at the Confucian college, we are assigning Shibano Hikosuke and Okada Seisuke responsibility in these matters, and you are requested to consult with them on this question, so as strictly to bar your students from heterodox teachings. Not only in your own school, but in all others as well, you are advised to see that the orthodox doctrine alone is taught as the basis for training men for public service.

[Inoue, *Nihon shushi gakuha*, pp. 522–23; WTdB]

THE JUSTIFICATION FOR THE KANSEI EDICT

As the text of the edict indicates, two men were appointed especially to ensure that the new ban would be observed in the official school, probably because the eclectic views of Hayashi Kinpō, then head of the school, did not inspire confidence in his readiness to enforce the new policy wholeheartedly and vigorously. One of these men, Shibano Hikosuke, who was instrumental in having the edict promulgated, had himself been influenced by the views of Nishiyama Sessai, a convert from Ogyū Sorai's school. When a friend of Shibano's sent him a letter protesting this narrow view of Confucian orthodoxy, Nishiyama was eventually entrusted with formulating a reply. This reply clearly shows that the primary targets of the ban were followers of the Ancient Learning propounded by Sorai and Itō Jinsai, as well as those identified with the Wang Yangming school.

Letter from Nishiyama Sessai to Akamatsu Sōshū

After the fall of the Zhou dynasty, the conduct of education declined, and heterodox teachings sprang up. Yang Zhu upheld self-interest and cast doubt on rightness, [and] Mo Di upheld all-embracing love and cast doubt on humaneness and righteousness, but they were mistaken in what they said. Mencius exposed them as perverters who, failing to acknowledge [the claims of the] sovereign and [the special affection due to a] parent, thwarted humaneness and rightness. Han Yu paid tribute to Mencius, saying that his merit [in exposing these heretics] was no less than that of the [sage-king] Yu.

Both Lu Xiangshan with his "sudden enlightenment" and Wang Yangming with his innate knowledge [literally, "good knowing"] talked about sage wisdom but were mistaken about it. Wise men of the Song and Ming dynasties exposed them as "overtly Confucian and covertly Buddhist"[1] and as destroyers of the moral law. . . .

How much more in recent times with Itō and Ogyū, who opposed the tradition of the *Great Learning* and the *Mean* as being contrary to the original [doctrine] of Confucius and slandered Zisi, Mencius, Cheng, and Zhu, saying that they contradicted the Way of the sages! With sophistry and eloquence they seduced their followers; while pretending to speak for the "ancient learning," they simply peddled their own pernicious doctrines. What small men they were! . . . Since their time, second-rate Confucian scholars have imitated them. Arrogant and conceited, each has insisted on his own mistaken interpretation of the classics and slandered the Cheng–Zhu school. Hundreds of them now vie with one another to set up their own schools, in which they propound new teachings under the strange name of "ancient learning."

You have said: "There have been many different methods of reading the texts and studying the Way, but what all alike revere and believe in are the teachings of Confucius. These consist of nothing more than filial piety, duty toward elders, loyalty, fidelity, [the study of] the *Odes* and the *Documents*, rites and music, governing the country, and pacifying the people. If this be so, then why must one take as one's foundation the Song Confucians alone? Those who use the Han and Tang commentaries or follow Wang Yangming or adopt the teachings of [Jinsai's] Horikawa school or of Ogyū Sorai or choose at will from among the interpretations of many different schools do no injury to the Way as a consequence." If it were as you say, however, those who study the Way of the sages would have no need of true guidance, and the art of teaching would have nothing to do with the conduct of ordinary life. Your students, I believe, are well aware that Buddhism and Daoism are deviant and false doctrines, for the followers of Buddhism and Daoism state explicitly what each regards as the Way, and the deviant nature of their doctrines is immediately apparent. But these stupid Confucians appeal to the authority of the classics and commentaries to advance their own false beliefs, so that what is false, yet appears true, utterly contaminates human eyes and ears and greatly confounds the world.

[*Kansei igaku-kin kankei monjo*, vol. 3 of *Nihon jurin sōsho*, p. 6; WTdB]

THE LATER WANG YANGMING (ŌYŌMEI) SCHOOL

In the eighteenth and nineteenth centuries, the so-called learning (or school) of Wang Yangming would have been just another of the many different

---

1. Quoting Chen Jian (1497–1567). See de Bary and Bloom, eds., *Sources of Chinese Tradition*, 2nd ed., vol. 1, pp. 884–87.

Confucian schools had not its intense moral activism extended beyond the school to play an important role for the instigators and leaders of the "Restoration" movement in the 1860s.

SATŌ ISSAI

Satō Issai (1772–1859) stands as an outstanding example, at the very center of late-Tokugawa-period *bakufu* education, of an influential teacher of the ideas of Wang Yangming who synthesized them with those of Zhu Xi. He was born in Edo as the eldest surviving son in a family that had served the lord of Iwamura domain (in Mino Province) as Confucian advisers for three generations. His father had studied for a period under Hattori Nankaku, a famous disciple of Ogyū Sorai, and had had an important part in the government of his domain for more than thirty years. In his childhood, Issai became close friends with a boy named Taira, who—four years his senior—was the third son of the Iwamura daimyo, Matsudaira Norimori. In 1790, the same year as Matsudaira Sadanobu's Prohibition of Heterodox Studies was promulgated,[2] Issai officially entered Norimori's personal retinue. In 1792 he went to Osaka, where he was able to study for a while under the great Kaitokudō scholar Nakai Chikuzan. In 1793 both he and Taira began studying under Hayashi Kanjun, head of the Hayashi college (Shōheikō), but before long Kanjun died without an heir, prompting Sadanobu to order that Taira be adopted into the Hayashi family as heir to Kanjun's position. Taira, henceforth known as Hayashi Jussai, then formally took Issai as a disciple. In 1800, Issai was invited by the lord of Hirado to Nagasaki, where he was able to meet with visiting scholars from Qing China.

In 1805 Issai became professorial head (*jukuchō*) of the Shōheikō, which in 1790 had been converted into the official school for training *bakufu* officials.[3] Under his and Jussai's leadership, the college flourished as never before, attracting superior students from the various domains all over Japan. Although the Shōheikō was supposed to be a bastion of Zhu Xi learning, especially after the Kansei Edict, Issai early on was strongly attracted to Wang Yangming's teachings. Thus it was commonly said that Issai followed "Zhu Xi outwardly, Yangming inwardly (*yōshu in-ō*)." In Issai's case, however, this was not a matter of insincerity but a matter of a distinction between his public functions and his

---

2. As part of the Kansei Reform, Sadanobu prohibited the teaching in the *bakufu* college of the teaching of Itō Jinsai, Ogyū Sorai, Yōmeigaku, and the "poeticists and novelists" who were strongly influenced by Sorai. Five years later, this prohibition was extended to the domainal schools, although in most domains it was not enforced very strictly.

3. It became the training school for the sons of *hatamoto* (bannermen), but later, undervassals (*baishin*) and *rōnin* also were admitted. The new official system of learning was fully established under Jussai's leadership in 1797.

private beliefs. In 1821, when he turned fifty, Issai began to attract major disciples (e.g., Asaka Gonsai), and those who became his students between 1820 and 1836 include many of the leading scholars of the late Tokugawa period.[4]

In 1841, at the age of seventy, Issai built a retreat near his daimyo's residence and thought of retiring from active service. Later in the same year, he was greatly saddened by the death of Jussai and the suicide in exile of his disciple, the artist Watanabe Kazan. Nevertheless, toward the end of the year, Issai was formally appointed a professor of the official Shōheikō, which required him to move into a residence at the college. Here he continued to guide students, give lectures, meet dignitaries, write diplomatic documents, and give policy advice to the government until his death in 1859.

ATTENTIVENESS TO ONE'S INTENTIONS
(SEI-I)

In the following passage from Satō Issai's interpretation of the *Great Learning* (*Daigaku ikka shigen*), he tries to harmonize the views of the Zhu Xi and Wang Yangming schools in his comments on a prime text of both, the *Great Learning*. An influential strain of Zhu Xi thought affirmed the primacy of "reverent seriousness, concentration, or attentiveness (*kei*)," as represented by Yi T'oegye in Korea and Yamazaki Ansai in Japan. The Wang Yangming school emphasized "making one's intention sincere" through reliance on innate knowledge. Issai equates the two, thus circumventing the issue of orthodoxy by minimizing differences and emphasizing common grounds.

Keeping one's intention sincere (*sei-i*) is nothing other than reverent attentiveness (*kei*). To think of sincerity and not let it slip away—if that is not attentiveness, what is? Therefore, [Yangming says that] if one has already spoken of keeping the intention sincere, it is not necessary to speak of attentiveness precisely because there is no attentiveness outside keeping one's intention sincere. The subsequent passage in which he explains making the intentions sincere also begins with vigilance in solitude (*shindoku*) and ends with attentiveness. One can see his meaning. The *Mean*'s concept of making the self sincere (*seishin*) ends in perfect sincerity (*shisei*), and the practice by which it is achieved is clarifying goodness. The *Great Learning*'s "making the intentions sincere" culminates in utmost goodness (*shizen*), and the practice by which it is achieved is extending knowledge (*chichi*) and rectifying affairs (*kakubutsu*).

[Adapted from Ichikawa, *Nihon jukyōshi*, vol. 4, pp. 407–9; BS]

---

4. They are Yoshimura Shūyō (Yōmeigaku), Sakuma Shōzan (principally Shushigaku), Ōhashi Totsuan (Shushigaku after a period of Yōmeigaku), Yamada Hōkoku, Takemura Kaisai, Ikeda Sōan, and Yokoi Shōnan—all of them Yangming school followers.

ARTICULATING ONE'S RESOLVE
(GENSHIROKU)

Among the most famous of Issai's works are his four collections of guidelines for life, called *Articulating One's Resolve*. For the most part, they are simple maxims for daily life, illustrating the importance of conduct that exemplifies one's deepest commitments and high aspirations—in other words, conduct in keeping with the demanding vocation of Confucius's "noble person" (*kunshi*) or the dedicated Japanese samurai. They also purport to serve as the common ethical denominator between the Zhu Xi and Wang Yangming schools. Moreover, since noble ethical conduct cannot be achieved without a firm clarity of mind and a healthy flow of vital energy in the body, many maxims also refer to techniques of training the mind and vital energy, fighting distraction and dissipation, and minimizing the buildup of tension.

Of the many Japanese of the Restoration period who kept these maxims close by for regular self-admonition and encouragement, the best known is Saigō Takamori (1827–1877), the much-celebrated samurai leader of Satsuma who, after his death, lived on as a symbol of the samurai spirit and the Japanese Yangming school (Yōmeigaku).

1. All matters between Heaven and earth, from ancient times to the present, through yin and yang and day and night, through the alternating brightness of the sun and the moon, through the alternation of the four seasons: all are determined in advance by destiny. As for people's conditions of wealth or poverty, high or low station, long or short life, fortune or misfortune, coming together or being separated, all these too are fixed by a predetermined destiny.[5] It is only that we do not know this destiny in advance. It is like a puppet play that has a mechanism behind it all but the observers are not aware of it. People of the world do not realize that this is the case, forever busying themselves searching this way and that in the belief that their own power of knowing is enough to rely on, until finally, exhausted and emaciated, they die. This also is a great delusion.

2. Foremost is to take Heaven as your teacher. Next is to take a person as your teacher. After that is to take the classics as your teacher.

3. In whatever you are doing, the most important thing is to have a mind to serve Heaven. It is not important to think of displaying anything to people.

6. In learning there is nothing more important than establishing your resolve. However, establishing your resolve is not a matter of forcing yourself. It is just a matter of following the natural inclination of your mind-and-heart.

---

5. In a later version of the text, Issai replaced the character *sū* (predetermined order or fate), which he used first for "destiny" in both the natural and the human worlds, with the characters *ri* (order, pattern, principle) and *mei* (command, fate, mandate), respectively. He was evidently somewhat uncomfortable with the fatalistic or non-Confucian nuances of the word *sū*, so he tried replacing it with words that are authentically Confucian.

18. Whenever things go really well for you, it is only because you have grasped the natural flow of things. There is nothing more wondrous than this.

19. Your face needs to be cool; your back needs to be warm; your breast needs to be empty; your belly needs to be full.

20. If the spirit is all in your face, you cannot avoid chasing after things and acting indiscriminately. Only when you draw in the spirit and make it dwell in your back is it possible to forget your body. And only then are you really the possessor of your body.[6]

21. If your heart-mind is obstructed, then all your thoughts will be misled.

22. Miscellaneous idle thoughts arise helter-skelter in your mind because of disturbances caused by external things. If you constantly use your own resolve like a sword to drive out all outside distractions, not allowing them to get inside you, then your mind will naturally feel clean and clear.

24. The correctness or crookedness of your mind and the strength or weakness of your vital energy (*ki*) are inevitably revealed in your writing. Even the mental states of delight, anger, sadness, and fear, as well as the degree of your diligence and inner tranquillity—all are expressed in the characters you write. Accordingly, it will help your practice of self-examination if you write some characters every day and use them to judge the condition of your mind.

26. In reflecting on things, it is necessary to be thorough; in handling affairs it is necessary to be simple.

27. A person who truly has a great aspiration [resolve] is able to be diligent in little things. A person who is truly farsighted does not neglect little things.

30. A person who is strict in reproaching himself will also be strict in reproaching others. A person who is tolerant in pardoning others will also be tolerant in pardoning himself. Everyone tends to lean to one side or the other. The noble person (*kunshi*) is "demanding of himself but sparing in his reproach of others."[7]

31. Most people today say they are very busy, but if you look at what they are doing, about 10 to 20 percent of their time they are taking care of important matters, and the other 80 or 90 percent of their time they are occupied with matters of little consequence.

[Satō Issai, *Genshiroku*, in *NST*, vol. 46, pp. 10–13; BS]

ŌSHIO HEIHACHIRŌ

Ōshio Heihachirō (Chūsai, 1793–1837) was the son of a samurai in line to inherit the family's position of city police captain (*machi yoriki*) in the Osaka

---

6. *Yijing*, hexagram 52.
7. *Analects* 15:15.

city magistrate's office. When he was only seven, however, his father died, and when his mother died the following year, his upbringing was entrusted to his grandparents. At the age of fourteen, Ōshio began his apprenticeship as a *yoriki*, not a high-status position, but one well remunerated and carrying a great deal of actual authority. When reading his family genealogy at the age of fifteen, however, Chūsai discovered that his ancestor at the time of the founding of the Tokugawa order had been a warrior who, in the campaign of Odawara (1590), had impaled an enemy general with his sword right before Ieyasu's very eyes. For this, he was rewarded with a bow that had belonged personally to Ieyasu and was granted a fief in Tsukamoto village in Izu. In an autobiographical letter to Satō Issai in 1833, Ōshio reminisced about this:

> On learning all this I was deeply grieved and felt ashamed at being a petty document writer in the company of jail keepers and municipal officials. It seems that my ambition (*kokorozashi*) at that time was to fulfill the will (*kokorozashi*) of my ancestor by winning fame as a man of great deeds and heroic spirit. Perhaps that is why I constantly felt frustrated and despondent, unable to have any real enjoyment.

Compared with the glorious martial exploits of his ancestor, who had played a part in the heroic founding of the shogunate itself, being a mere civil official in a bureaucratic hierarchy, writing documents and rubbing shoulders with petty clerks, criminals, and jailers, seemed like the height of shame.

The inner moral confusion that this caused Ōshio, combined with his need for a firm ground of moral decision making in carrying out his police work, led him to take up Confucian studies as taught in the Zhu Xi school. At the age of twenty-four, he happened to read a book of moral maxims by the Ming thinker Lü Kun (1536–1618), which impressed him immensely. Searching further, he was led to the study of Wang Yangming and his school. As a result, he gradually learned how to focus the energy of his moral aspiration on the daily tasks of his official position, confident that the mundane duties before him were in themselves the proper field for realizing ethical greatness. This dispelled his earlier sense of shame and frustration regarding these tasks.

The magistrate who took office in 1820 was impressed by Ōshio's character and abilities and promoted him successively to public prosecutor (*meyasuyaku*) and public examiner (*ginmiyaku*). In these capacities, Ōshio won fame through his resolute prosecution of three difficult legal cases: the exposure of a supposed "Kirishitan" cult and the arrest and punishment of its members, the prosecution of a large bribery scandal involving another *yoriki*, and the banishment of Buddhist clergy who had persisted in violating monastic discipline. In 1830, disturbed by the public attention these cases had brought him (and by his patron's retirement), Ōshio suddenly resigned from his position, hoping to devote himself fully to teaching Yangming's thought at the private school, the Grotto[8] for Mind Cleansing (Senshindō), that he had set up in his official residence. In 1833, he privately published his most important philosophical work, *Notes from the Grotto for Mind Cleansing (Senshindō sakki)*, a meticulous yet vehement exposition of the practice of the Confucian Way as understood in the Wang Yangming school, focusing on the intertwined teachings of "the mind itself is Heaven," "returning to the Great Vacuity," and "extending innate knowledge."

In the same year, serious flooding in many regions resulted in a severe famine throughout much of the country. In Osaka, where the price of rice almost doubled, rumors of riots began to fill the air. No longer able to act directly as an official, Ōshio decided to leave his school to give lectures in rural areas. He also stepped up his efforts to get his own writings published and distributed in the hopes of warning officials before it was too late. Unfortunately, the famine did not abate in response to traditional governmental measures for dealing with such crises. Ōshio repeatedly offered policy advice to the new city magistrate through his adopted son, but his advice was angrily rejected. Many people were starving in the streets of Osaka, and even more in the rural districts under Osaka's jurisdiction, but the magistrate's office still issued a decree ordering that Edo be supplied with as much rice as it had ordered. Finally, burning with indignation, Ōshio distributed a fiery manifesto addressed to "the village headman, elders, peasants, and tenant farmers in every village, who were given birth by Heaven."

On the nineteenth day of the second month of 1837, Ōshio led more than twenty of his disciples in a cannon attack on the mansion across the street, after which they set fire to Ōshio's own residence and marched into the city. With cannonballs, flaming arrows, and incendiary bombs, the band set fire to the entire Tenma district, beginning with the residences of the *yoriki* and their underlings. They then headed for the waterfront area of the city, setting fire to the mansions of rich merchants on the other side of the Yodogawa River—including the residences of the Kōnoike, Mitsui, Iwaki, Shimaya, and Yoneya. By noon, the band had grown to more than three hundred people. The *bakufu* authorities were at first thrown into confusion by the disturbance, but by 4:00 P.M. they had dispersed the rebels. Within a few days, almost all the rebels had committed suicide, turned themselves in, or been arrested. More than a month later, the police discovered Ōshio's hiding place. Rather than allow himself to be arrested, he set fire to the house he had been staying in and committed suicide with his adopted son.

---

8. In traditional usage, the word "grotto" was used, often metaphorically, for a quiet spot used for teaching, study, or meditation.

During the anti-*bakufu* movement toward the end of the Tokugawa period, the unselfish intent (*kokorozashi*) of Ōshio's rebellion was widely admired, and his indomitable idealism came to be reinterpreted as a model for radical political action aimed at popular liberation and the preservation of national sovereignty. Radical leaders like Yoshida Shōin pondered the strategic lessons of the failure of Ōshio's rebellion. After the Meiji Restoration as well, the spirit of Japanese Yōmeigaku—symbolized most frequently by Ōshio, Yoshida, and Saigō Takamori—remained very much alive in Japanese political thought. With its exaltation of the absolute moral and spiritual autonomy of the individual, it mingled with French concepts of individual liberty and natural right in the popular rights movement of the 1880s. At that time, it appealed particularly to former members of the samurai class, helping redirect their impulses toward violent protest into a constructive political movement for parliamentary government.

In 1893, after the promulgation of the constitution in 1889 had deflated the popular rights movement, Tokutomi Sohō (1863–1957) and Miyake Setsurei (1860–1945)—advocates of a popular-based nationalism opposed to the authoritarian style of Confucian ethics promoted by Motoda Eifu—published books promoting the spirit of Wang Yangming learning as a means of cultivating the moral autonomy and independence of mind required of the citizens of a modern nation-state. A year later, the nationalist Christian Uchimura Kanzō (1861–1930) published a book entitled *Japan and the Japanese* (later renamed *Representative Men of Japan*), which exalted Nakae Tōju as a Japanese saint and Saigō Takamori as a national hero and praised Yōmeigaku as the Chinese philosophy that came closest to the noble religion of Christianity. When the conservative Tokyo University philosophy professor Inoue Tetsujirō (1855–1944) began promoting a system of "national ethics" (*kokumin dōtoku*) based on Japanese Confucianism, the first in his influential series of books on Tokugawa Confucianism was on Yōmeigaku (1900). The affirmative conception of Wang Yangming learning in the Meiji period was also carried back to China by Chinese nationalists who took refuge in Japan, such as Liang Qichao, Zhang Binglin, Sun Yat-sen, and Chiang Kai-shek.

In Japan, among those who idealized Ōshio and Saigō in the Taishō and early Shōwa periods was the journalist and politician Nakano Seigō (1886–1943), who decried the Meiji oligarchs' betrayal of the ideals of the Restoration and called for a "second restoration" that would unite the emperor and the people into a powerful egalitarian order. In the postwar period, the most prominent promoters of Yangming learning were Yasuoka Masahiro (1898–1983), a prolific writer, scholar, and adviser to several generations of Liberal Democratic Party prime ministers, and Mishima Yukio (1925–1970), the famous novelist, playwright, and aesthete, who wrote an impassioned essay a few months before his suicide promoting Ōshio's samurai philosophy of uncompromising moral commitment—which he presented as a sort of native equivalent of Nietzschean nihilism—as the only way to save Japan from the conformist mediocrity of bureaucratic capitalism and mass-consumer hedonism.

ŌSHIO'S PROTEST
(ŌSHIO HEIHACHIRŌ GEKIBUN)

Ōshio Heihachirō's manifesto for revolt during the great famine of 1837 begins with a reminder to his countrymen that Heaven's blessings would be withdrawn from the ruler if the people were driven to desperation. Appealing to the benevolent founding principles of the government established by Ieyasu, it condemns the self-seeking corruption and immorality that had spread throughout the ranks of the government since the establishment of the Tokugawa peace, claiming that the entire populace now burned with rancor against the government.

Since the time of Ashikaga Takauji, the Son of Heaven has been removed from participating in government and has been deprived of the power to distribute rewards and punishments. Therefore the rancor of the people no longer has a place of appeal and has reached to Heaven itself. In response, Heaven has sent down a long series of calamities. Forgetting the "humaneness that unites all beings as one body," the officials of the Osaka magistrate's office are conducting the government for their own selfish ends. They send tribute rice to Edo, but they send none to Kyoto, where the emperor himself resides. On top of this, in recent years the moneyed merchants of Osaka have accumulated vast profits from interest on loans to the daimyo and appropriated great quantities of rice, living a life of unheard-of luxury. . . . Knowing no want themselves, they have lost all fear of Heaven's punishment and make no attempt to save those who are begging and starving to death on the streets.

[*Nihon keizai taiten*, vol. 45, pp. 673–76; BS]

INNATE KNOWLEDGE AND THE SPIRITUAL RADIANCE OF
THE SUN GODDESS

In the following passages, Ōshio asserts a common spiritual consciousness linking the innate knowledge of Mencius and Wang Yangming with the spiritual radiance of Amaterasu shining in the self.

If one asked the ancient sages of our own country, one would also find [the teaching] that no moral principles, no learning, and no human affairs exist outside one's innate knowledge. How can I say this with such certainty? Lu Xiangshan wrote, "If a sage appears in the Eastern Sea, this mind is the same, and this principle is the same." Who is worthy of being called the Sage of the Eastern Sea, if not the Great Kami Amaterasu herself? . . . The spiritual radiance of the Great Goddess corresponds precisely to the innate knowledge "taught by Confucius, Mencius, and Wang Yangming. . . ." Unfortunately, this statement will certainly offend people. But it will not offend the gods. Therefore, it is enough just to understand this truth secretly in the depths of one's own heart.

Mencius derived the term "innate knowledge" from the *qianzhi* [Heaven rules] of the *Classic of Changes* and the words of Confucius. This *qianzhi* is nothing other than the spiritual radiance of the Great Vacuity. The spiritual radiance of the Great Goddess [Amaterasu] corresponds precisely to the innate knowledge taught by Confucius, Mencius, and Wang Yangming.

[Ōshio Heihachirō, *Hōnō shosekishū batsu* 2, in *Nihon no yōmeigaku*, vol. 1, pp. 410–11; BS]

NOTES ON "CLEANSING THE MIND"
(SENSHINDŌ SAKKI)

The phrase "cleansing the mind," derived from the Xici commentary on the *Classic of Changes*, refers to a method of mind cultivation and control by which all selfish and self-limiting thoughts are dispelled and the mind returns to a state of pure spiritual openness and unobstructedness as expansive as the open sky and as luminous as the Heavens. This openness and receptivity is referred to as the Supreme Vacuity or Emptiness (*taikyo*) in Neo-Confucianism. It is especially emphasized in the Wang Yangming school as the ultimate source of spontaneous innate knowledge (the faculty of knowing), transparent and translucent when undistorted by bad habits, partiality, or selfishness. In this state, the mind clearly reflects both the underlying unity and the moral differences among all things and affairs and responds to them accordingly.

A:1. Heaven does not mean only the vast blue space of the sky above. Even the empty space between stones or the hollow inside a branch of bamboo is also Heaven. If so, how much more is this true of what Laozi calls the "spirit (god) of the valley." The "spirit of the valley" is nothing other than the human mind. Accordingly, the fact that the wondrousness of the human mind is the same as Heaven can be verified in the sage. Because the ordinary person has lost this openness, however, we cannot say that this is the case. [p. 370]

2. The Vacuity outside the body is itself Heaven. What is called "Heaven" is one's own mind. Here one can realize that the mind encompasses all things. For this reason, if we see a living thing, even a plant, a tile, or a stone, killed or broken or destroyed, it causes pain in our hearts. This is because all these things exist originally and essentially in our mind. If beforehand, desires are obstructing the mind, then the mind is no longer empty. If it is no longer empty, then it is only a little insensate thing, not the substance of Heaven. It is already alienated even from our own physical body, not to mention from other things.

Is it not fitting that a person in such a condition be called a "small person"? [p. 370]

6. If we speak from the point of view of physical form, the body envelops the mind, and the mind is inside the body. If we look at it from the point of view of the Way, the mind envelops the body, and the body is inside the mind. A person who takes the view that the mind is inside the body will find himself encumbered by things the moment he abandons the effort of holding on to and preserving it. A person who realizes that the body is inside the mind will always enjoy the wonder of transcendence, and he will always be able to put things to work for himself. The student should know the difference between putting things to work for oneself and being encumbered by things. [p. 371]

7. The reason that [Confucius's disciple] Yan Yuan was spoken of as "empty"[9] is that he often returned to the Supreme Vacuity. But he still had a little way to go. The sage, on the other hand, from beginning to end, is nothing but one Supreme Vacuity. [p. 371]

10. The person who is bound up by things wavers even in ordinary times. How much more will he waver in the face of an emergency? The person who is grounded in the earth does not waver even in the face of an emergency, let alone in ordinary times. For this reason, one must know to abide in that in which it is proper to abide. [p. 372]

11. When you are going to help someone in distress, you should check whether or not there is a ripple of movement in the depths of your spirit. If there is the slightest ripple, then selfish desire is already there, and your mind is no longer [in accord with] Heavenly substance. If your mind is not [in accord with] Heavenly substance [i.e., completely open to perfect goodness], then it is best not to help the person. [p. 372]

13. If in deep sleep you experience chaotic and repugnant dreams, these are nothing but shadows of your own self-deception in that solitary awareness at the core of your waking consciousness. But if you truly reach the realm where you are not self-deceived in that solitary awareness, you will be a realized person. That is why it is said that "the realized person has no dreams." It is not that he has no dreams but that he has no chaotic and repugnant dreams. The cases of King Wuding of the Shang dreaming of the sage Fu Yue and of Confucius dreaming of the Duke of Zhou would not have been possible if they were not realized people. [p. 372]

14. The return of the human mind to the Supreme Vacuity also begins by being vigilant over the mind in solitude (*shindoku*) and working to overcome the self. If one does not enter by vigilance in solitude and the conquering of self, then it will turn into the vacuous and misguided way of Zen. It is a matter of a difference of a hair's breadth that becomes a gulf of a thousand *ri*. Thus

---

9. *Analects* 11:18.

this is a point at which the student of the learning of the mind-and-heart can easily go wrong. [p. 373]

19. "The resolute scholar (*shishi*) and the humane person do not seek life at the expense of humaneness (*jin*)."[10] Life is something that can be extinguished. Humaneness as the virtue of the Supreme Vacuity cannot be extinguished for all time. It is misguided to throw away what can never be extinguished to protect what is extinguishable. Accordingly, it is truly reasonable that the resolute scholar and the humane person should choose the former and give up the latter. This is not something that the ordinary person understands. [p. 374]

26. The *ki* of the blood-force is corrupted and dissipates with death, but the great floodlike *ki* is not corrupted and does not dissipate with death. The moral power and meritorious deeds of the sages, worthies, and heroic personages radiate throughout the universe, and as the years pass, they only shine more brightly. Why is this? This is the great floodlike *ki*. The ordinary person has no trace of this. Bound to the physical *ki*, he always feels impatient or fretful, passing his days sluggishly and irresolutely and ending up rotting away not much differently from an insect or a plant. Is this not a great pity? Is it not a great shame? If one thinks on this, how can one afford to neglect the all-important word "diligence"? [p. 376]

106. The commendable words and virtuous actions of other people are themselves the goodness in my own heart, and the disgraceful words and evil actions of other people are themselves the evil in my own heart. For this reason, the sage is unable to regard these things with indifference. The tasks of ordering one's family, ruling the state, and bringing peace to the realm are nothing but preserving all that is good in one's heart and eliminating all that is evil. . . . [p. 404]

129. Humaneness is the life of the Supreme Vacuity; rightness is the completion of the Supreme Vacuity; ritual decorum is the penetration of the Supreme Vacuity; wisdom is the luminosity of the Supreme Vacuity; [and] trustworthiness is the oneness of the Supreme Vacuity. . . . [p. 413]

162. Ordinary people regard Heaven and earth as infinite and everlasting but regard their own selves as something perishable. Therefore they concern themselves only with giving free rein to their desires while their physical vitality (*kekki*) is still strong. The sages and worthies, on the other hand, regard not only Heaven and earth as infinite but also their own selves as Heaven and earth. Therefore they are not afraid of the death of the body but fear the death of the spirit (*kokoro*). As long as the spirit does not die, one's unendingness can rival that of Heaven-and-earth. Accordingly, one regards one day as the same as a hundred years, bracing oneself with unwavering firmness as if one were standing at the brink of a chasm, unable to let go of oneself for even a moment. For this

---

10. *Analects* 15:8.

reason, one does not let one's resolve be moved by external things and does not seek longevity through the indulgence of desires. One concerns oneself just with eliminating human desires and holding firm to the principles of Heaven. . . . [pp. 430–31]

B:20. In studying the Way of the sages, we entrust everything to our innate knowledge of the good. Therefore we are like someone crazed (*kyōsha*) in our efforts to make public what we perceive to be right and wrong. Accordingly, we have no way of telling how much trouble from other people this will bring upon us. Nevertheless, to end up diminishing our sensitivity to right and wrong just because we are afraid of the trouble it will cause us is something that a man of character (*jōfu*) would consider shameful. And what honor (*menboku*) would we have to be able to meet the sages in the afterlife? Therefore, I concern myself with nothing but following my resolve (*kokorozashi*). [p. 465]

57. Only after the mind has returned to the Supreme Vacuity can real moral principles be maintained. If a person has not returned to the Supreme Vacuity, real principles will [still] lie buried, and there will be nothing to distinguish him from a material thing. There is nothing more shameful than for a human being to be no different from a material thing, something without that spiritual nature (*rei*). If everyone in the world feels no shame about this, then what is going to happen to that spiritual nature? [p. 479]

69. The Supreme Vacuity is filled to the brim with real principles and real vital energy (*ki*). Moreover, things that have form, even when they are not empty within, also all possess perfect vacuity in the core of their being. This can be verified by examining plants and trees. [p. 487]

[Ōshio Heihachirō, "Senshindō sakki," in NST, vol. 46, pp. 370–76, 404, 413, 430–31, 465, 479, 487; BS]

AGRARIAN REFORM AND COOPERATIVE PLANNING

NINOMIYA SONTOKU

Fuji no shirayuki wa	The white snow on Fuji
Asahi ni tokeru	Melts in the morning sun,
Tokete nagarete	Melts and runs down
Mishima ni ochiru	To Mishima,
Mishima jorōshū no	Where Mishima's prostitutes
Keshō no mizu.	Mix it in their makeup.

Ninomiya Sontoku (1787–1856), who grew up within sight of Mount Fuji, must have hummed this popular ballad on occasion and may have mused on what it meant. The white snow is beautiful to look at, but it can be useful to people only when it melts and runs down to the foot of the mountain, where people live. The Japanese often speak of the "underground activity of water" (*chika-suigyō*) as a simile for self-effacing service on the lowest level of human life. Ninomiya's lifelong service was something akin to that of water. He never wanted to be a government official, nor did he offer to serve as a political adviser. Starting life as a farmer, he always remained one. But at the same time, he did much to improve the farmer's life by teaching and practicing a creed that can be summed up in these few articles: first, manual labor is the worthiest of human activities, since it brings to fruition the creative labors of the gods; second, the law of averages in nature requires a sort of planned agrarian economy in which something is set aside from good harvests to tide over bad years; third, agrarian life is essentially communal, and its success depends on unselfish, cooperative activity in an organization through which the savings of some members may be made available for the use of others; and fourth, human life must be conceived as a continuing act of thanksgiving for the providence of Heaven, earth, and man.

This creed and the indefatigable labors of Ninomiya Sontoku to rescue his fellow farmers from the vagaries of nature won for him the affectionate title Peasant Sage of Japan. A popular ivory image of Ninomiya represents him as a hardworking and affable youth with a happy, smiling face. But a wooden portrait kept in his home and a drawing now placed in the Ninomiya Shrine at Odawara represent him as a man of rugged physique and rough features, with a look of unshakable determination. This is the man to whom shrines were built, as to a patron saint in the rural districts around modern Tokyo.

At first glance, it might seem hard to reconcile Ninomiya's deep sense of gratitude to nature with his constant emphasis on the need for planning against the vagaries of nature. But to his mind, the seeming irregularities of nature were in no way arbitrary or capricious. Natural calamities indeed occur without regard to immediate human desires, but they are part of an inexorable natural order that works ultimately for the good of humans, provided that they do their share. People cannot rescue themselves from the miseries of a hazardous livelihood by crying out against nature. Instead, they must be ready to understand the conditions set by nature and take them into account when planning their lives. This requires, above all and before all, the virtue of integrity or honesty (*shisei*),[11] which to Ninomiya meant not only a recognition of law and order in human relationships but also a wholehearted acceptance of the order of nature. The Way of Heaven (*tendō*) and the Way of humankind (*jindō*) should be mutually enhancing, but it is not for people to supersede or dominate Heaven (nature). Humankind succeeds by accepting and following nature, and something that must be accepted as a law of nature is the necessity for human labor.

---

11. The "Absolute Sincerity" of the Confucian classic, the *Mean*.

Hard work is just as much a part of the natural order as is the rising and setting of the sun or the change of the seasons. Every year, every month, every day, and every hour has an incalculable value to advancing human life. Therefore idleness cannot be tolerated. "The root of virtue is found in labor," Ninomiya once said, "and the loss of virtue comes from idleness."

Labor also makes people what they are, for civilization and human advancement are nothing but the cumulative achievements of human labor. The Japanese nation itself is only what generation after generation of forebears have made of it through their loving labors. Ninomiya expresses his idea in a poem that refers to the rising tide of neo-Shintoist concepts in early-nineteenth-century Japan:

Furu michi ni	The beaten path
Tsumoru ko no ha wo	Is covered with fallen leaves;
kakiwakete	Brush them aside
Amaterasu kami no	And see the footprints
Ashiato wo miru	Of the Sun Goddess.

The practical side of Ninomiya's teaching is embodied in his own system of economic planning. Farmers are apt to experience the seeming indifference, or even cruelty, of nature during a year of poor harvest. This will be felt most keenly by those whose existence is most precarious, who are living from day to day or from harvest to harvest at the limit of their resources. The only plan is for them to think and plan in long-range terms. In other words, people must try to see things in somewhat the same way that nature does, and statistics, based on the law of averages, is what enables them to do so. Ninomiya thus urges his fellow farmers to compile their own statistics of crop yields over a ten-year period or longer. With this, they can estimate their annual average income fairly reliably and budget their expenses accordingly. The major portion of Ninomiya's collected works, which run to thirty-six volumes, is devoted to the budgets or formulas (*shioki*) that he worked out for various individuals, village communities, feudal domains, and even the shogunate. They represent probably the most detailed case studies of agrarian problems and the most immediately practical solutions for them attempted in the Tokugawa period.

Ninomiya's system of planning or budgeting, however, was not conceived in terms of immediate personal needs alone. People had to contribute to the welfare of others, especially of posterity. Just as the individual shares in the life of a community and benefits from the contributions of his predecessors, so must he contribute to the general welfare. Since each individual's welfare is bound up with that of the community, the sufferings of some, if unaided in times of distress, will eventually affect the lives of others and hold back the progress of all. The mark of a civilized community is what it provides for mutual aid. In agrarian communities, this should take the form of a voluntary credit union.

Ninomiya gave the societies that he organized the name Society for the Repayment of Virtue. Thus he acknowledged the debt that each man owes to his fellows and to his forebears for their contribution to the general welfare.

Perhaps the only thing original in Ninomiya's teachings is these simple formulations for long-range planning and mutual aid in the agrarian community. These are by no means insignificant contributions, for the depressed condition of agriculture in many Asian countries still urgently called for more of the planning, cooperative enterprise, and short-term farm credit that Ninomiya was promoting. Community cooperation and mutual aid had been prominent features of Neo-Confucian communitarian thought and practice in China and Korea, but few, if any, were applied to commercial enterprise and economic planning to the extent that Ninomiya's cooperatives did.

Nevertheless, his espousal of such techniques alone cannot explain the success of his movement or the lasting impression he made on Japanese farmers. He was as much a religious leader as anything else, although he did not consider himself to have been favored by any special insight or inspiration or by the sort of education that might command respect among the learned. He had no formal instruction, and readers of his life story are impressed that he took from his reading only what he had already learned from life. His thought does not bear the mark of any established tradition, and yet it seems to have absorbed much from existing cults that would contribute to his purpose. Thus he once said that his teaching was one-half Shinto, one-quarter Buddhist, and one-quarter Confucian. That his creed does combine the most practical aspects of these doctrines is not hard to see: the emphasis on honesty or sincerity, which is a cardinal virtue in Confucianism and one that the Neo-Shintoists valued to the exclusion of almost all others in their bare, spare system of thought; the emphasis on thanksgiving, which is important to both Shinto and Pure Land Buddhism; the same insistence on disciplined and devoted service that Nichiren called for in the name of the Lotus and the nation; and, finally, the self-reliance that Zen inculcated in its followers. Above all, Ninomiya must have shown the poor peasant the effectiveness of these ideas in action. While others talked and wrote about them, he worked at them. His accomplishments in rescuing numerous communities from poverty and ruin, starting with nothing more than his native wit and willingness to work hard, became the inspiration for many others after him who joined together to solve their problems in a self-reliant but selfless spirit.

THE REPAYMENT OF VIRTUE
(HŌTOKU)

Ninomiya Sontoku's collected works fill thirty-six volumes; for the most part, they contain his detailed analyses and solutions of the economic problems of various domains. For his more general beliefs, we must refer to the accounts kept by disciples of his conversations with them, or to the simple slogans and formulas that he found so effective in spreading his ideas among people who, like himself, had little formal education.

Through the following refrain runs the theme of man's dependence on nature and society and the cumulative benefits accruing from that inheritance, and everyone's obligation to repay that debt by extending the benefits to others.

The origin of father and mother depends on the will of Heaven-and-earth.
The origin of the human body depends on its being given birth to, and cared for, by father and mother.
The succession onward to children and grandchildren depends on the sincere solicitude of husband and wife.
The wealth and status of parents depend on the labor and achievements of their forebears.
The wealth and status of ourselves depend on the accumulated goodness of father and mother.
The wealth and status enjoyed by children and grandchildren depends on our own labor and effort.
The growth and preservation of our selves depend on three things: food, clothing, and shelter.
The three necessities of food, clothing, and shelter depend on [the products of] field and farm, woods, and forest.
[The products of] field and farm, woods and forest, depend on the labor and cultivation of the people.
This year's food and clothing depend on the production of last year.
Next year's food and clothing depend on the exertions and hardships of this year.
Year in and year out we must be ever mindful of the repayment of virtue.

> [*Hōtoku-kun* 1, in *Seikatsu genri* vol. of *Ninomiya Sontoku zenshū*, p. 544; WTdB]

THE PRACTICE OF REPAYMENT

The teaching of the Repayment of Virtue is a practical teaching. In practicing it, the three most important things are to labor, to be thrifty, and to pass on something to others. To labor means to work hard at one's own occupation; to be thrifty means to keep the family income clearly in mind and to live within that income; [and] to pass something on to others means to practice the five forms of sharing according to one's own means. These are what I call the Three Duties of my school. These duties are like a tripod, which needs each one of its legs and fails to fulfill its function if one is missing. A man may labor hard at his occupation, but if he is not thrifty, it will be labor wasted. A man may be thrifty, but if he is not also hardworking, he will be unable to produce anything, and he will have a sense of guilt toward Heaven and earth. Last, even if a man is both hardworking and thrifty, if he does not pass something on to others, he will be lacking humanity and may become miserly. Industry and thrift are practiced only for the sake of passing something on to others.

[*Hōtokugaku naiki* 7, ed. Fukuzumi, in *Ninomiya Sontoku zenshū*, vol. 36, pp. 864–65; WTdB]

THE WAY OF NATURE

Ninomiya's teaching stressed the maximum utilization of the gifts of nature without suggesting in any way that humans should try to dominate or exploit nature. He does not think in terms of technological progress but, rather, in terms of fulfilling nature's own plan through rational management and human industry. Less of a scientist and an engineer and more of an ethical or a religious reformer, Ninomiya puts his faith in voluntary efforts on the part of the individual instead of state planning or controls.

Here is a man who wants to eat rice to feed his body and sustain life. The best thing for him to do is to cultivate rice. Now rice culture follows the seasons. Seeding starts at the end of spring, and transplanting, hoeing, fertilizing, and other kinds of care are done in the summer. When the rice is ripe in autumn, it is cut and taken in before winter arrives. After threshing, the grain is apportioned so that there will be enough for needs throughout the year, avoiding excess now and deficiency later. This is the quickest way to get rice to eat. Although some people might consider it too long a process, I can assure you that there is no other proper way to obtain rice for the people. If you work hard and faithfully at this great task, you will be free from hunger and starvation from generation to generation. Do not ask for a shortcut. In the final analysis, Heaven has its own natural way of doing things, and in order to obtain rice, the only proper way is to cultivate rice plants. When cultivating rice plants, too, there is a proper procedure, which is sowing the seeds. Remember that rice plants never produce rice plants and that rice seeds never produce rice seeds. First the seeds must grow into plants, and then the plants produce seeds. From the beginning of creation there has always been this endless process of transformation and transmigration.

> So let our labor bring benefits
> Equally to all,
> That all as one may attain the Buddha-mind
> And go on to live in the land of Bliss.

[*Sangyō shizen dan*, in *Ninomiya Sontoku zenshū*, vol. 1, pp. 951–52; WTdB]

THE "PILL" OF THE THREE RELIGIONS

Old Ninomiya once said, "I have long thought about Shinto—what it calls the Way, what its virtues and deficiencies are—and about Confucianism—what its teaching consists of, what its virtues and deficiencies are—and also about Buddhism—what its various sects stand for and what their virtues and deficiencies are. And so I wrote a poem:

Yo no naka wa	The things of this world
Sute ajirogi no	Are like lengths
Take-kurabe	Of bamboo rod
Sore kore tomo ni	For use in fish nets—
Nagashi mijikashi	This one's too long, that one's too short.

"Such was my dissatisfaction with them. Now let me state the strong and weak points of each. Shinto is the Way that provides the foundation of the country; Confucianism is the Way that provides for governing the country; and Buddhism is the Way that provides for governing one's mind. Caring no more for lofty speculation than for humble truth, I have tried simply to extract the essence of each of these teachings. By essence I mean their importance to mankind. Selecting what is important and discarding what is unimportant, I have arrived at the best teaching for mankind, which I call the teaching of Repaying Virtue. I also call it the 'pill containing the essence of Shinto, Confucianism, and Buddhism.'". . .

Kimigasa Hyōdayū asked the proportions of the prescription in this "pill," and the old man replied, "One spoon of Shinto, and a half-spoon each of Confucianism and Buddhism."

Then someone drew a circle, half of which was marked Shinto and two quarter segments were each labeled Confucianism and Buddhism. "Is it like this?" The old man smiled. "You won't find medicine like that anywhere. In a real pill all the ingredients are thoroughly blended so as to be indistinguishable. Otherwise it would taste bad in the mouth and feel bad in the stomach." [pp. 822–23]

The old man said: "The Buddhists say that this life is temporary and that only the life hereafter is important. Nevertheless, we have obligations to our masters, our parents, our wives, and our children. Even if we could renounce this world, leaving behind our masters and wives and children, our bodily life still would go on. And as long as our bodily life goes on, we cannot do without food and clothing. In this world you cannot get across the river or sea without paying the boat fare. So Saigyō says in his poem:

Sute hatete	Having renounced all,
Mi wa naki mono to	I feel myself utterly nonexistent,

Omoedomo   And yet when it snows,
Yuki no furu hi wa   I know
Samuku koso are   How cold I am! [p. 820]

[*Ninomiya ō yawa*, ed. Fukuzumi, in *Ninomiya Sontoku zenshū*,
vol. 36, pp. 820–23; WTdB]

SOCIETY FOR RETURNING VIRTUE
(*HŌTOKUSHA*)

The Society for Returning Virtue was organized by one of Ninomiya's leading disciples, Fukuzumi Masae, to advance the work of his master and eventually spread all over Japan. The following account of its organization and activities was written in 1912.

"Men who wish to render thanks to Heaven by benefiting mankind as much as they can; men who wish to reform villages in order to help the poor; men who wish to sow the seeds of goodness that they may enjoy its lovely flowers and noble fruit; of such men does the 'Hōtokusha' consist." So wrote Fukuzumi Masae, a great disciple of Sontoku.

This Hōtokusha (Society for Returning Virtue) was organized by Fukuzumi according to Sontoku's instructions and consisted of a Central Society and many branches which have since spread all over Japan. The central organization was on the principle of Sontoku's Hōtoku office, or Hōtoku yakusho, as it was called, of which Sontoku said, "The spirit of the Hōtoku office, if pictured, would be like an august deity shedding a holy light and filled with love and compassion for the common people. No other picture would do justice to its subject."

The purpose of the Hōtokusha is to help the poor and to aid them to unite in helping one another, first, by opening their hearts and developing goodness of character among them, and secondly by assisting them to open up wild lands, improve irrigation and roads, repair bridges and river banks, and, in general, by doing all that is of benefit to the poor. It begins by helping the poorest and encouraging and rewarding the good. The function of the Central Society is to give financial help as well as advice to the branches, so its members are well-to-do persons who freely give their money and services in order to show their gratitude to Heaven by helping their fellow men, and they expect no material reward for themselves.

The Branch Societies consist of poorer men who pay a small subscription known as the "Nikka-sen" or "Daily Subscription Money," laying aside from day to day a certain amount of their regular earnings, or the product of extra labor, though it be but a farthing a day, to be paid into the Society monthly. The money thus subscribed by the poor, together with money received from the Central Society, forms a fund from which loans are made to members requiring capital for sound productive enterprises, such as improving their trade or industry. No interest is charged, because the purpose of the Society is to help the needy. . . .

Zenshukin, "Seed-of-Goodness Money," is a fund formed from occasional contributions of members, and is employed in charity and various public benefits. The following extracts from an old cashbook of a branch indicates the source of such contributions:

Contributions to Zenshukin

Yen	Sen	
3	0	Amount saved by economizing expenses on marriage ceremony of donor's sons.
9	50	Proceeds of sale of unnecessary clothing in donor's family.
5	0	Share of profit from keeping pigs.
2	0	Proceeds of sale of three trees planted for the purpose five years ago.
1	25	Amount saved by economizing in traveling expenses.
0	75	Amount saved by giving up drinking saké.
0	37	Amount realized by selling pipes and tobacco, donor having given up smoking.
0	25	Proceeds of nightwork making rope.
0	65	Proceeds of sale of a silver hairpin.

The Hōtokusha is virtually a Cooperative Credit Society founded with a high moral purpose, and it has proved a great boon to the poorer classes of people. Its organization at the present time is not precisely the same as at its inception, having been more or less modified to meet the changing circumstances of the times and the various needs of different localities, but in spirit and in general principles, it remains as it was at its origin.

[Yoshimoto, trans., *Peasant Sage of Japan*, pp. 227–31]

Chapter 33

FORERUNNERS OF THE RESTORATION

RAI SANYŌ AND YAMAGATA DAINI: LOYALISM

RAI SANYŌ'S UNOFFICIAL HISTORY

Rai Sanyō (1781–1832), a major figure in the rise of emperor-centered nationalism at the end of the Tokugawa period, was the son of Rai Shunsui, a well-known Neo-Confucian teacher in Osaka who was enlisted in the service of the Aki domain (Hiroshima) when Sanyō was four years old. Sanyō's mother also was accomplished in the literary arts, and two uncles of his were well-known Confucian scholars, which ensured that he would receive an excellent education from an early age. At the age of sixteen, he accompanied his uncle and teacher Kyōhei to Edo, where he studied for a year at the Shōheikō. There, he is reported to have amazed scholars with his abilities in Chinese poetry and prose. With the permission of domainal leaders, his father had already set out to write a national history, but this permission was abruptly withdrawn four years later, and the manuscript he had been working on was destroyed.

As a child, Sanyō felt his father's disappointment keenly, and this nourished his own aspiration to devote his life to writing history. In order to fulfill his ambition free of external pressures, he decided to free himself from duties in the service of a domain and become an ordinary unattached "grassroots" scholar (*sōmō no sōshi*). Leaving one's domain without special permission, however, was a crime under Tokugawa law. At the age of nineteen, after his father was appointed to teach at the Shōheikō, Rai took the opportunity to flee the Aki domain and make his way to Kyoto. This led to his father's angrily disinheriting him in order to fend off greater punishment and to Sanyō's being placed under house arrest for three years. Later, however, he was allowed to have the books he needed to begin writing his *Unofficial History of Japan* (*Nihon gaishi*).

In 1809, Sanyō was invited to become headmaster of a private school run by a distinguished poet of Song-style Chinese poetry, Kan Sazan (1748–1827), in the neighboring province of Bingo. Although Sazan was hoping to adopt Sanyō as his heir and had arranged a well-paying position for him in the service of the Fukuyama domain, this was hardly a route that would satisfy Sanyō's real ambition, and he carefully explained to Sazan his desire to go to Kyoto. Sazan yielded, and in 1811 Sanyō moved to Kyoto, where he opened a small school of his own. Here he lived for twenty years as an independent man of letters, supporting himself by teaching, writing, and calligraphy; associating regularly at his school with many of the leading literati of Kyoto in his time—poets, literati painters (*bunjinga*), and Confucian scholars—living a rather bohemian lifestyle cut off from officialdom; and engaging in aesthetic pursuits. In this environment, Sanyō was free to express his own views in his writings on history.

Finally, in 1827, Sanyō completed his *Unofficial History*, and in response to an invitation by the senior statesman (*rōjū*) Matsudaira Sadanobu (1758–1829), he presented it to the shogunate. To his own relief, the work was accepted and even praised by Sadanobu, helping give it the wide circulation it later enjoyed. In his late years, Sanyō also presented his *Unofficial History*, through his son, to the daimyo of Hiroshima and, through his disciples, to the daimyo of several other domains. That it truly did present views that might be considered "dangerous" is suggested by the fact that several domains strictly prohibited the public circulation of the book. Famous Confucian scholars like Yokoi Shōnan (1809–1869) had to obtain it surreptitiously and read it in secret. Gradually, however, it was brought to people's attention and came to be widely read.

Sanyō was not only a historian but also an accomplished calligrapher and writer of Chinese-style poetry. What helped make his history famous was the elegant, vigorous, and highly readable style of Chinese in which it was written, which was modeled on the *Zuo Commentary on the Spring and Autumn Annals* and the *Records of the Historian*. In an article on Rai Sanyō published in 1893, the prominent Meiji historian Yamaji Aizan wrote,

Through him, the Japanese came to know the history of their fatherland. The Japanese came to know what the country of Japan was. They came to know why it is that the country of Japan is superior to all other countries. And they came to know of these things not merely in theory but were taught them in language that had the quality of poetry, the quality of song. Subsequently, it came about that the country met with a succession of maritime emergencies. The hearts of the people were suddenly awakened, and the cry of "revere the emperor and expel the barbarians" filled the four seas. Who can say that this was not a result of the lessons he had taught us? Ah! Such is the accomplishment of Rai Noboru (Sanyō)!

UNOFFICIAL HISTORY OF JAPAN
(NIHON GAISHI)

The following passage, giving Rai Sanyō's views on the abortive Kenmu Restoration, includes the key concepts of historical explanation that he used and the values he celebrated of self-sacrificing devotion to the emperor. He speaks of him in the Confucian sense as a true king, thus challenging such claims sometimes made on behalf of the shoguns as kings or princes (ō).

The Unofficial Historian says:

In writing the history of the shogunal houses, whenever I get to the Heiji and Jōkyū periods, I put down my brush and sigh: Ah! Such a decline of morals in the world! Such a lack of correspondence between name and reality! In earlier times, those referred to as military retainers[1] had no concern other than to loyally serve the king [emperor].[2] The Heike and Minamoto clans were no exception. Yet beginning from the Heiji period [1159–1160], they took advantage of the slackened discipline in the court to fulfill their greedy lust for power. Some [people] were totally without scruples in their violence and ferocity, and some were fiercely and unfathomably suspicious of other people.[3] Although their actions were different, they all were the same in their disregard for the kingly laws and in their pursuit of personal gain. However, they could still claim that they had a right to do what they did because they were of royal ancestry and had been royally appointed as military commanders.

When we get to the Hōjō clan, however, even though they were only subordinates of the shogun, they ordered the court around with impudence. From this point, I can hardly bear to speak about the affairs of the realm. Moreover, regarding the Jōkyū incident,[4] all the writings that discuss which side was in

---

1. Literally in Chinese, "military ministers" (bushin), which in Japanese was understood as samurai.

2. The word that Sanyō uses throughout is "king" (ō), not "emperor," emphasizing the Confucian ideal of kingly rule, as opposed to mere power holders with no legitimate claim to rule.

3. Sanyō is referring mainly to Taira no Kiyomori and Minamoto no Yoritomo.

4. After the Jōkyū incident of 1221, in which cloistered emperor Go-Toba attempted by military means to reassert the power of the throne over the newly established shogunate, three cloistered emperors were banished by the shogunal regent, Hōjō Yoshitoki.

the right were by men who lived in the period of Hōjō power, so we have no way to verify their authenticity today. Besides, how can it be acceptable to compare Hōjō rights and wrongs in the relationship between ruler and vassal? Nevertheless, the Hōjō vilified the court and turned their rage on it, subjecting it to the greatest insult, treating the emperor in all his dignity as if he were nothing more than a pig. Oh people of the eight islands,[5] which one of you has not been bathed in the beneficence of the early kings?[6] But all the so-called warriors (*bushi*) of that time were used to being taken care of by the Hōjō, and they were willing to serve them hand and foot. Even if the nominal rank and status of their lineage were much higher than the Hōjō, they were content to take orders from the Hōjō and put themselves at their beck and call. In time, because this state of affairs continued, they came to take it for granted. How can one even bear to talk about this?

As for those known as court nobles (*kōkei*), they ordinarily hung around the court at their pleasure, using the ranks and emoluments they had appropriated from the emperor to lord it over the realm. Even at a time like this, they did not come up with a single strategy to deal with the crisis; they folded their arms and watched on the sidelines while the Hōjō did what ever they wanted. So how can we blame it all on the warriors (*bujin*)? It is true that the trend of the times made some things impossible and the virtue of the ruler was not without blemish, but the occurrence of such a calamity was also the fault of the emperor's ministers. From that point on for the next hundred years, the succession to the throne and the appointment of shoguns and ministers were completely controlled by the Hōjō, and the court shrank in stature as if it were tied and bound. The emperor even had to check the look on the Hōjō regent's face before deciding to feel happy or sad. What a sorry state of affairs!

I have heard that after the ex-emperor Go-Toba was exiled to Oki, he had to build himself a hut leaning against a cave in order to shelter himself from the wind and rain. He lived this way for nineteen years before he died. The three ex-emperors—the father and his two sons—were separated from one another by a thousand *ri*, each living on a remote island in the sea.[7] To the end of their days they were not able to see one another again. How could they have forgotten the Hōjō for even one day? In view of this, the Genkō incident[8] was absolutely inevitable.

As for the merit of loyal service to the emperor in this incident, in my opinion, the first place goes to Kusunoki no Masashige. If it were not for

---

5. Yashima or Ōyashima is a name for Japan that occurs in the *Kojiki* and *Nihon shoki*.

6. In the Japanese context, the "early kings" or "former kings" who founded the nation were the imperial ancestors.

7. Tsuchimikado was exiled to Tosa and then went to Awa. Juntoku was exiled to Sado Island.

8. The Genkō incident was the attack on the Hōjō by Emperor Go-Daigo in 1331 to 1333.

Kusunoki, then as I see it, the royal western progress of Emperor Go-Daigo[9] would have ended up the same way as the Jōkyū incident. Why so? Even though Hōjō Takatoki made some mistakes in his government, his power was greater than ever. He could have relied on the authority the Hōjō had built up over several generations to pressure the long-weakened imperial throne. He had a million warriors as fierce as tigers and wolves following his commands and raging around the country. There was no way anyone could stand up to him. People in the realm had taken the Jōkyū incident as a warning, and they were reluctant to act, waiting with bated breath and not daring to mention the idea of "loyal service to the emperor." But Lord Kusunoki, alone, braced his humble body against all of this, raising the cry of righteousness, marching straight into the ranks of the Hōjō troops, and overcoming Takatoki's bodyguards. Through this he was able to rouse the spirits of righteous warriors in all directions, persuading them to rise up quickly one after another and annihilate the source of evil in one attack, avenging the deep rancor of many generations of emperors and clearing away their great shame. The masses of the people were again able to look up at the light of the sun and moon. Although we can say that the time was ripe for the destiny of the throne (kōun) to open up, if Lord Kusunoki had not raised his voice for the cause, how could it have been achieved? How do we know that Heaven did not deliberately give birth to this person to rectify the way of the world and save it from moral decay? . . .

In sum, Kusunoki's rank was lower than his capacity, so he was not given enough opportunity to fully reveal his talents. Thus in the end he gave his life for his country. Finding peace in righteousness, he dedicated himself in complete sincerity to the ancestors of the imperial line. The merit of his heroic deeds has not only passed down to his descendants. After his time, probably every nobleman or warrior who has taken up bow and arrow in the name of loyalty to the emperor has been inspired by hearing about Kusunoki. Ah! It is men like Kusunoki who can truly be called worthy of the title *samurai*.

[Rai Sanyō, *Nihon gaishi, kan* 5, "Nitta-shi zenki," vol. 1, pp. 280–83; BS]

YAMAGATA DAINI'S NEW THESIS

Early in 1759, a samurai-physician, master tactician, Confucian scholar, and classical Chinese poet completed a polemical tract on sociopolitical reform entitled *Master Ryū's New Thesis* (*Ryūshi shinron*). This man, known to history as Yamagata Daini (1725–1767), never published or widely circulated his

---

9. That is, Hōjō Takatoki's exile of Emperor Go-Daigo to Oki.

polemic because it harshly criticized warrior regimes in Japan since the twelfth century. But eight years later, the Tokugawa *bakufu* in Edo arraigned Yamagata, his student Fujii Umon (1720–1767), and another Confucian scholar named Takenouchi Shikibu (1712–1767) on charges of lèse-majesté in the Meiwa incident of 1767. Yamagata and Fujii were beheaded for their contumely. Takenouchi was ordered into remote exile but died en route.

In the following excerpts from Yamagata's principal work, he does not seem like a loyalist in either the "restorationist" or "revolutionary" sense usually ascribed to him. That is, Yamagata never tried to reinstate direct imperial rule by destroying the *bakufu* and abolishing warrior supremacy and domain ownership, the cardinal principles on which the Edo regime was based. Instead, his loyalism was of another variety. His main thesis, implicitly advanced in *Master Ryū's New Thesis* of 1759, held that the shogun and daimyo were imperial regents or ministers of state who— as long as they took sagely counsel from Confucian scholar-advisers like Master Ryū—should enjoy de facto autonomy in "assisting" (*hohitsu*) political administration under figurehead emperors.

Yamagata Daini was in fact harshly critical of the *bakufu* governments dating from 1185, including the Tokugawa. And since gratuitous—unsolicited—criticism of a regime in power was considered to warrant the death sentence, Edo leaders had ample pretext for executing Yamagata. But this does not make him a "revolutionary" loyalist or a "restorationist" in the sense of wishing to end all forms of warrior rule and domain ownership in order to restore the emperor and court to ruling power. Second, in viewing the imperial court as a "fallen dynasty" barely surviving from the past and in formulating sociopolitical reforms for his own day, Yamagata Daini followed the Ogyū Sorai school far more closely than he did either the Yamazaki Ansai or the National Learning schools. Moreover, Yamagata's proposed reforms called for strengthening and perpetuating—not ending—socioeconomic discrimination based on hereditary class privilege under the existing sociopolitical order. Third, Yamagata held two key implicit assumptions: that although the imperial house would reign forever, emperors were not expected to rule, and so emperors should emulate Chinese exemplars by delegating power to loyal state ministers—the shogun and daimyo—who, in turn, would seek out bold criticism and enlightened counsel from scholar-advisers like Master Ryū. Above all, Yamagata's brand of loyalism lay in the tradition of "imperial assistance" that was inspired by the Fujiwara regents and articulated in medieval histories such as Jien's *Views of an Ignorant Fool* (*Gukanshō*) and Kitabatake Chikafusa's *Chronicle of the Direct Succession of Gods and Sovereigns* (*Jinnō shōtōki*), works that extolled the principle of ministerial autonomy exercised on behalf of figurehead emperors. The main historical significance of Yamagata Daini's political thought is here, not in his anti-*bakufu* criticism or his putative restorationist aims.

MASTER RYŪ'S NEW THESIS
(RYŪSHI SHINRON)

Rather than advancing his views on his own, unsolicited from the authorities, Yamagata Daini attributed them to a Master Ryū in the mid-sixteenth century. The contents, however, bear the marks of Yamagata's own antecedents in the school of Ogyū Sorai and Dazai Shundai (see chap. 29). Yamagata draws heavily on ideal Chinese models, cited from the Confucian classics, as the basis for a critique of the deplorable state of affairs in Japan. Nevertheless, like Jien and Kitabatake Chikafusa earlier,[10] Yamagata accepts the traditional structure of an imperial Japanese house assisted by civil ministers and military shoguns, if only they would live up to their true responsibilities.

I. Making Name and Actuality Conform

Master Ryū said:

Something may have a name but not be actual.[11] But nothing actual ever lacked a name. We cannot do without names; that is why the sages used them in their teachings. In antiquity, the Duke of Zhou made officials perform as their titles dictated, and all states submitted to benevolent rule. Confucius made the conduct of state ritual and music accord with their ceremonial names, and all under Heaven praised its efficacy. The *Daodejing* says, "The myriad things were begotten by the named."[12] The *Zhuangzi* says, "Reality accompanies name as guest does host."[13] Confucians and Legalists have mastered many teachings revealed in names.

The divine emperor Jinmu founded our eastern land [in 660 B.C.E.] and ruled by the dictum "Nourish the people's livelihood and eliminate hardship from their lives."[14] His radiant virtue extended throughout the four quarters for over a thousand years. [Shōtoku Taishi] set up a system of graded court caps and robes [in 603] to distinguish ranks and so enacted ritual and music to teach

---

10. See de Bary et al., eds., *Sources of Japanese Tradition*, 2nd ed., vol. 1, chap. 11.

11. This set of paired opposites, "name and actuality" (*mei/kei*), is crucial to Yamagata's thesis. *Mei* (Ch. *ming*) stands for stated norms or terms as well as names. Here *kei* (Ch. *xing*) does not mean "form." In classical usage, as in the *Zhuangzi* and *Han Feizi*, the homophone *kei*, both "form" and "punishment," means the "true situation" or "reality."

12. *Rōshi jō*, p. 31; Lau, trans., *Tao te ching*, p. 57.

13. *Sōshi naihen*, pp. 44–46.

14. Jinmu, the mythical founder of Japan's imperial dynasty, supposedly ruled from 660 to 585 B.C.E., and the ideal of virtuous government (*riyō kōsei*) was expounded by the sage-king Yu, founder of the Xia dynasty, as described in the (spurious) "Counsels of the Great Yü" chapter in the *Book of Documents*.

proper government.[15] We had counterparts to the Dukes of Zhou and Shao and to the regents Yi Yin and Fu Yue, so our civilizing dynastic powers of moral suasion left no commoner untouched.[16] Later, nobles like Fujiwara no Mototsune [836–891] and Yoshifusa [804–872] made state affairs conform to the Taihō Code and thereby carried on the glorious institutions first established by Shōtoku, the Sharp-Eared Prince.[17] Our long-lived dynasty attained such great heights that its flowering civilization rivaled the Three Dynasties of high antiquity.

Imperial rule deteriorated by Hōgen-Heiji times [1156–1159], and the government fell into the hands of [Minamoto] eastern barbarians, owing to civil strife in the Juei–Bunji eras [1182–1189].[18] After that, the military dictated state affairs. Underlings seized power and installed or deposed sovereigns at will, so the former sages' ritual and music were lost.[19] Later still, when the Ashikaga arose, warrior power increased further; and they waxed impudent toward the throne despite their lowly title of "general in chief."[20] But the illustrious virtue of former sage-emperors had so permeated the peoples' hearts that even these brutal subjects dared not give their presumption free rein. The imperial regalia remained with His Majesty, and the dynastic line survived "like a thread.". . .[21]

Local warlords arose with the passing of generations. They ran amok like tigers and dragons, stealing and killing to no end. Villainous rebels hatched

---

15. Shōtoku Taishi (574–662) patterned his twelve-rank system of court caps and garments on the Chinese models.

16. The Dukes of Zhou and Shao were ministers under King Cheng (r. 1115–1079 B.C.E.) of the Zhou dynasty, who was a grandson of King Wen. Shao administered the western part of the empire, and Zhou, the eastern. Yi Yin and Fu Yue were regents during the Shang dynasty. Yi Yin served under Kings Tang (r. 1766–1753 B.C.E.) and Tai Jia (r. 1753–1720 B.C.E.). The *Book of Documents* stresses that meritorious service by these four ministerial exemplars accounted for the ideal government of those times.

17. Shōtoku Taishi earned the name Toyosatomimi no mikoto because, according to legend, he could understand ten people talking to him at the same time.

18. Yamagata sees the Juei–Bunji eras (1182–1189) as beginning the decline and fall of imperial rule. Thus he ignores Yoritomo's receipt of the title "Barbarian-Quelling Great General" (*seii taishōgun*) in 1192, the Kenkyū era.

19. After the Jōkyū incident in 1221, Hōjō Yoshitoki forced Emperors Juntoku and Chūkyō to abdicate; later he banished the former emperors Tsuchimikado, Go-Toba, and Juntoku.

20. Ashikaga Yoshimitsu (1358–1408) became shogun in 1368 at the age of eleven. In 1381 he became minister of central affairs and minister of the left. His "Palace of Flowers" was about twice the size of the Imperial Palace. In 1394 he became the grand state minister (*dajōdaijin*), then unprecedented for a warrior, when he bequeathed the shogunal post to his son. In 1401 he proclaimed himself "king of Japan" and "vassal" to the Ming emperor in order to obtain lucrative trading rights with China.

21. *Ito no gotoku*, a phrase taken from the *Sorai shū*, in *Ogyū Sorai*, in *NST*, vol. 36, p. 491.

every sort of conspiracy while warrior-barbarians plundered at will. They wore neither cap nor headcloth; their garments lacked collar and sleeves. The arrogant touted their virtue; the violent took pride in their deeds. A few of them truly pitied the masses, but they continued the evils of a Warring States era.[22] How could they know the sages' teachings? And how could lowly commoners remain in their native abodes to enjoy a stable livelihood?

What are the greatest of those evils? First is the grand disarray of state offices. The Way is valid in all times and places: Civil rule maintains order under normal conditions, [and] martial rule deals with emergencies. Now people do not distinguish civil from martial rule. Those who are supposed to deal with emergencies maintain order in normal times. That should not be. . . .

The daimyo are provincial rulers who inherit lands, pass on hereditary titles, and administer states and peoples.[23] They assume the airs of military commanders and issue arbitrary decrees unauthorized by recorded precedent. Even cooks and clerks, who never wield arms, presume to be warriors and oppress the people. That is the first evil inimical to the Way of government. All daimyo, great officials, and others who hold the fifth court rank or above receive the post of provincial governor and are appointed to one of the eight imperial government ministries.[24] But these are in name only; reality differs. . . .

And the discrepancy is even worse below the fifth rank. Why? I do not know. But we cannot avoid duplicity when using one form of government [military] to perform the functions of another [civil]. Here is a second evil: Government offices lacking meaning and order. Generals are masters; court counselors, their servants.[25] Princes of the fifth rank hold posts tied to the fourth. The tail wags

---

22. Yamagata wants us to believe that his tract dates from the age of Oda Nobunaga, when Japan was emerging from the Warring States period toward unification. Modern historians date that period from 1467 to 1568, but evidence in his text shows that Yamagata interpreted it to have begun in 1185, when Minamoto hegemony was established, or in the 1330s. "Imperial rule lasted over two thousand years," he says later, after which the imperial house split into Northern and Southern branches when Ashikaga rule began.

23. Throughout this tract, Yamagata depicts the *bakuhan* system as roughly analogous to the Zhou-era *feng-jian* system. Thus his "realm," or "all under Heaven" (*tenka*), comprises numerous *kokka*, "states" or daimyo domains. Here the words "rulers" and "states" are rendered in the plural, except where Yamagata writes of rulership in the abstract or clearly refers to the shogun or emperor.

24. All daimyo and high-ranking *bakufu* bannermen who held the fifth court rank, more than three hundred in number, theoretically qualified for the post of provincial governor. The eight central-government ministries set up by the ancient imperial law codes were Central Affairs, State Ceremonial, Popular Affairs, Civil Administration, War, Justice, Treasury, and Imperial Household.

25. Strict adherence to the rank-office concordances stipulated by the old imperial law codes would mean that the Tokugawa shogun as a general could hold junior third rank at most. That would place him below a grand counselor (*dainagon*), who held senior third rank. But the

the dog; we wear shoes on our heads and hats on our feet. So power justifies pretension. Here is a third evil: Hierarchy is subverted and the base become exalted. . . .

IV. Main Guidelines

Master Ryū said:

He who would rule all states under heaven must first establish main guidelines; details will work themselves out later. He must promote great benefits and eliminate great evils in the realm. A benevolent ruler, wise ministers, and good men in office make for "great benefits." A violent ruler, foolish ministers, and petty men in office make for "great evils." When great benefits are promoted, great evils disappear; when good men are elevated to office, contemptible men defer to them. . . .

Men in office today cannot devise policies or create ideas on their own. They adhere to the customs of bygone eras without a thought to validity, saying, "That's how it's always been." But if this is so, one cannot question a thing's proper nature or function. Of course there are good customs we should follow— those set down by sages, conveyed by worthies, and proved over time to be harmless in government and helpful in conducting affairs. When a custom does not work, we must examine the original intent behind it and the current circumstances surrounding it. We must amend it so as not to contravene antiquity or contradict the present, and only then, implement it. Why should we stick blindly to a custom just because it exists? . . .[26]

A state has both civil and military officials because neither can perform both functions; in this they are comparable to horses and oxen. By nature, horses can run far and oxen can pull heavy loads. But if we made either do the opposite, neither could bear the task. Men entrusted with civil affairs study classical texts—the *Odes, Documents, Rites,* and *Music.* So they develop warm dispositions that become character traits. The highest are ministers; the lowest, local clerks. But that is the work they can do. If we put them in the ranks and give them armor and weapons, we could never hope for the exploits of a Meng Bin or Xia Yu.[27] By contrast, men entrusted with military affairs wield

---

Tokugawa branch houses of Kii and Owari held the grand counselor title, so they should have outranked the shogun, their patriarch and overlord. Moreover, Tokugawa Ieyasu received junior first rank in 1602, even before being granted the shogunal title.

26. Contrast Yamagata with Motoori Norinaga's rigid adherence to established methods: "In general, affairs in society are beyond human wisdom and manipulation, no matter how wise you may be. So do not implement new methods readily. If you rule by following the times and holding to established ways in all small things, you will make no serious errors, even though some flaws remain" ("Hihon tamakushige," in *Motoori Norinaga zenshū,* vol. 8, p. 331).

27. Yamagata is referring to Sima Qian: "As they say, 'Even though things be of the same

arms—the halberd, shield, hatchet, and battle-ax. So they develop fierce dispositions that become second nature. The highest are generals; the lowest, horsemen or footmen. But that is the work they can do. If we gave them sacrificial implements and dressed them in court garments, we could never expect the capacity for ceremonial of a Ziyou or Zixia.[28] Clearly, then, neither civil nor military officials can perform both tasks. . . .

VII. Exhorting Officials

Master Ryū said:

Farmers, artisans, and merchants are the good peoples—"good" in that they "nourish others and eliminate hardship." They assist and foster one another and thus benefit their states. The former sage-kings loved these peoples as parents do children. They set up teachers to edify them and officials to rule over them. Mutual surveillance groups were instituted, and corvées properly regulated. The sages elevated and grouped these good peoples with state officials. Hence the name "the four peoples" (*shimin*) and its rationale. Performers, entertainers, and their ilk pursue riches and money by dealing in sensual pleasure. They feed only themselves and produce nothing to feed or clothe the realm's peoples. . . .

Petty officials consort with entertainers, frequenting theaters daily. They see alluring sights and hear charming words. They envy these entertainers and come to believe that such talents are unrivaled in the realm. They lose all sense of shame and emulate the ways of actors. They soon become glib and slick and are fully adapted to base ways. Discipline breaks down, and officials popularize vile, lewd customs. . . . As a result, officialdom degenerates to a nadir. No official can manage his affairs without loyalty, faithfulness, and a sense of shame. . . . When the former sage-kings prescribed their tenets, they established state posts for teachers and officials. They sought out, employed, and promoted talented men to those posts, overlooking no one in the realm. Such is not true in later ages. Once a man renowned for some skill is lucky enough to gain a post, it is passed on as a hereditary calling even when the house's head is unqualified.[29] Although he wishes to quit, he cannot; forced to carry on the calling, he feels shackled by it. . . . With no system of civil service examinations,[30] we thwart able men who try to get ahead and make unqualified men do work they dislike. Yet we complain that there are no good men in government. How foolish! We

---

class, abilities differ.' Thus we praise Wu Huo for his power, cite Qing Ji for his swiftness, and emulate Meng Bin and Xia Yu for their valor" (*Shiji*, vol. 3, p. 226).

28. Singled out by Confucius for "culture and learning" (*Analects* 11:3).

29. Yamagata is criticizing hereditary succession to office in service positions, even though his treatise, on the whole, accepts hereditary status.

30. The Chinese, unlike the Japanese, had such a system.

suppress men who would benefit their states and impede those who would serve the realm. Can this be the Way to exhort officials or give repose to the peoples?

XI. The Need to Circulate Goods and Currency

Master Ryū said:

The Way for ensuring enough food is to promote farming; the policy for distributing wealth is to "level" prices. Assess no high taxes, and farming will advance. End merchant profiteering, and prices will level off. . . . [In Japan] of late, taxes run from 50 to 60 percent of the crop, plus levies on goods and demands for corvée. Whatever stays with the farmer does not meet his expenses. So he neglects farming and his fields turn to wasteland. Neglect leads to want, want to desperation, and desperation to flight. For a lack of tillers, fields produce no crops and food supplies decrease.

Merchants are different. They hoard when prices are low, sell when these are high, and so make easy money. . . . They buy up homes and lots, and some come to own a thousand houses. They rent out shops and dwellings, and some become millionaires. They enjoy life to the hilt. At home, they hoard goods without loss. In society, they throw state revenues into chaos by their timely hoarding and selling. No present measures can combat their wily machinations, so they become contemptuous as their wealth rivals that of feudal lords. . . .

Well, what should we do? . . . Create agencies and issue edicts to make them eat the same food as farmers and live on a par with artisans. Confiscate their luxury playthings and stately mansions. Punish anyone who refuses to mend his ways and obey. If sellers are many and buyers few, the goods now hoarded in storerooms will go up for sale everywhere. When many goods go up for sale, they sell poorly and prices fall. Then we can tell the genuine from the fake and the good from the shoddy. We can fine profiteers and confiscate from hoarders. Prices could not but level off; goods and money could not but circulate.

XII. Benefits and Evils

Master Ryū said:

The key to government is striving to promote benefits and eliminating evils in the realm. Benefits are not for oneself alone. All people must partake of the ruler's virtue; all must have enough food, gain wealth, and be relieved of anxiety and suffering. By teaching "equilibrium and harmony" we bring peace to the common masses. . . .

There is no other Way to promote benefits. But commoners are stupid. If they stray from the Way that must be followed—and so create harmful disorder—they must be punished to eliminate evils. Only thus can one chastise them for doing evil and encourage them to do good. When many persons do good and few do evil, the realm benefits. Ritual and music are instruments of cultured adornment in civil rule; laws and punishments are matters of martial rule. Civil rule maintains order under normal circumstances; martial rule brings emergencies under control. Civil rule creates good administration; martial rule suppresses the chaos of war. Civil rule is the norm; martial rule is a last resort. . . .

What must be done? A ruler needs only to find worthy men for office. That is very easy. What is very hard is for those men to make themselves known to him. . . . How much more eager they would be if what he liked were not painful at all. If he only wants something done, endless streams of men will come forth to do it. But if a ruler rejects this dictum and keeps things as they are, it will be clear that he does not want to promote benefits in the realm.

The ancients knew how hard it was to see themselves, so they used mirrors to view their faces; they knew how hard it was to know the limits of wisdom, so they used the Way to rectify their conduct. A ruler's best course of study is not to master the refinements of the Six Arts, not to recite the doctrines of the Hundred Schools [in late Zhou China]. He should just accept the need to believe in the Way. Then those who have mastered it will come forth to serve him. If he but places his trust in them, how could villainous rebels ever arise in his state? All troubles in the realm would then cease.

Yamagata Masasada of Kai Province
Second lunar month of 1759

[Adapted from Wakabayashi, *Japanese Loyalism Reconstrued*, pp. 3–28, 129–71]

HONDA TOSHIAKI: AMBITIONS FOR JAPAN

What is perhaps most significant about the reformers considered here is that their responses to the challenge of a new age reflect their own past. Thus two of them demonstrate a notable willingness to learn from the West, to the extent that this was possible through contact with the Dutch in Nagasaki, combined with the sort of fierce nationalism that had steadily risen in the late Tokugawa period.

A typical example of this man of the future, who would have one foot in the old world and another in the new, was Honda Toshiaki (1744–1822), from the west coast province of Kaga. As a mathematician, ship captain, and scholar, he concerned himself with the economic strengthening of Japan and its survival in a world of expanding imperialism. Another example is Satō Nobuhiro, from Dewa in the north, who had an unusual heritage in that he represented the fifth generation of a family of experts in horticulture and mining in northern Japan. A keen student of Western science and a passionate nationalist, in his later years he designed a program of national reorganization along totalitarian lines.

In view of the shogunate's efforts to channel all thought and discussion within certain prescribed limits, we could understand if the Japanese had shown little awareness of their true situation during the early nineteenth century and little inclination to speak about it. But despite the Prohibition of Heterodox Studies in 1790, the restrictions on intellectual contact with the West, and the penalties for any direct criticism of government policies, there was a surprising degree of intellectual ferment and diversity of opinion in regard to the very problems that the Tokugawa had chosen to ignore or proved incapable of solving. With the more numerous and frequent appearances of the "black ships" of the West in Japanese waters, as well as the worsening economic conditions, as manifested in the impoverishment of both peasants and samurai, expressions of dissatisfaction increased as the new century wore on. This was especially true in the northern regions of Japan, where fears of Russian expansion and economic troubles were most acutely felt.

At the same time, the long reign of peace under the Tokugawa shogunate had been kind to many peaceful intellectual pursuits, among them mathematics. Very early in the eighteenth century, Seki Kōwa (Takakazu, 1642–1708) is said to have arrived simultaneously with Newton and Leibniz at the mathematical problems of integral and differential calculus and their solution. Because the shogunate was concerned at that time with calendar reform and the preparation of new maps of the country, it needed men trained in mathematics. The rising tide of mercantilism, with its emphasis on navigation, likewise helped make this field of study popular. Accordingly, Seki's followers opened schools in important towns and feudal domains. At the age of eighteen, Honda's biographer says, he made his way from the northwest province of Kaga (Echigo) to Edo, in order to study mathematics under a famous master of the time. His progress was such that at the age of twenty-four, he was able to open his own school and became known as a first-rate mathematician in his own right.

Not satisfied with the native Japanese system of mathematics, Honda decided to study Dutch, in the hope that a knowledge of that language would open to him the secrets of Western mathematics. Other Japanese of his day were studying Dutch in order to read books of medicine, astronomy, and military science. Indeed, many of Japan's best minds in the late eighteenth century were turning to the West for new information and guidance as the country's isolation grew increasingly indefensible. That they chose to study Dutch rather than any other Western language was dictated by the fact that since 1639 the Dutch had been the only Europeans permitted to remain in Japan, and it was to their trading station at Nagasaki that many young Japanese looked for knowledge. There were no decent dictionaries, however, and the difficulties besetting the would-be scholar of Dutch were enormous, but with great determination and expense of energy some of them became proficient enough in the language to be able to make significant contributions in many fields.

Honda's interest in Dutch mathematics moved to a study of astronomy and navigation, sciences closely connected with mathematics, and from them to more general considerations of the importance of shipping and trade (which depend on a knowledge of navigation). He was convinced that Japan's economy was at a standstill and that only by breaking out of its self-imposed isolation could it achieve greatness. Honda's books are filled with ambitious programs and suggestions about how to incorporate the new knowledge from the West.

No matter how diverse the subjects he wrote about, Honda used or displayed his knowledge of mathematics wherever possible. In some cases, his penchant for mathematical formulations of economic and social problems, together with his impatient disregard of the niceties of conventional prose, make it difficult for the reader to follow him. And sometimes it is painfully apparent that he likes multiplying statistics, often unnecessarily, merely to magnify his conclusions and stagger the reader. But it also is true that at times his tedious computations produce significant results, such as his conclusions concerning the relation of population growth to food supply, corresponding to those of his English contemporary Thomas Malthus.

It was this combination of circumstances—population growth beyond the limits of the Japanese islands to sustain; increasing impoverishment of a society trapped in a static agrarian economy; and Honda's recognition that Western nations, some of them with even less territory than Japan, had overcome such limits by means of a maritime, mercantilist policy—that led him to turn away from the inward-looking, home- and land-centered view of the Confucians to an expansionist one. Such a view was not unprecedented—sixteenth-century daimyo and merchants had engaged in overseas enterprises, and Hideyoshi had dreamed of an Asian empire—but the Tokugawa had opted for a policy of containment and control, which to Honda was no longer viable.

Honda's chief program of action, as enunciated in *A Secret Plan of Government* (*Keisei hisaku*), was labeled "secret" or "confidential" because public advocacy in matters of state policy was not allowed to anyone not officially responsible for them. The *Plan* centered on Japan's "four imperative needs": gunpowder, metals, shipping, and the acquisition of overseas possessions. Honda was interested in gunpowder primarily for use in blasting new channels for rivers, part of his program for improving transportation in the country, rather than for its use in warfare. By metals, he was referring to both the precious ones, which, in mercantile fashion, he wanted to bring to Japan, and the base metals, whose use he advocated in place of wood, so as to reduce loss to rot and fire. His views on shipping and the acquisition of overseas possessions are given in the readings.

Honda devoted almost equal attention to such matters as the aggrandizement of Japan and the problems of daily living faced by settlers of the proposed colonies. In all things, he tried to regulate himself by what he conceived to be the dictates of practical use. For example, he favored abolishing the use of cumbersome Chinese characters in writing Japanese and adopting instead the more practical Western alphabet. He decried the impressionistic renderings of nameless mountains often found in Japanese paintings and praised instead Dutch realistic painting, which, he thought, was better for pedagogical purposes. He hoped that by taking advantage of the benefits of Western science, Japan could shake off its long somnolence and emerge as the "England of the East":

> How may Japan become the greatest nation in the world? She should profit by the arts of civilization which she has learned during the 1,500 years that have elapsed since the time of the emperor Jinmu. She should move her main capital to the country of Kamchatka. (It is located at 51° N. Lat., the same as London, so the climates must be similar.) She should build a great stronghold on Karafuto [Sakhalin]. . . . Once great cities spring up in Karafuto and Kamchatka, the momentum will carry on to the islands to the south, and the growing prosperity of each of these places will raise the prestige of Edo to great heights. This, in turn, will naturally result in the acquisition of the American islands.[31]

This outspoken imperialism was voiced in 1798, at a time when Japanese were forbidden by law to leave their country and only a few castaways had ever visited foreign shores. Honda's program may at points seem excessively crude, and when he assumes that the climate of Kamchatka must be the same as that of London, he may make us smile. Nevertheless, even in such instances he also compels our admiration by his bold use of Western knowledge—even though it sometimes was misinformation—in his attempt to help Japan out of the economic stagnation that he so deplored. Apart from a brief period of service to the lord of Kaga, however, Honda remained an independent teacher and wrote under pseudonyms. His ideas were known to only a small circle of close friends and students until his works were finally published in the late nineteenth century.

A SECRET PLAN OF GOVERNMENT
(KEISEI HISAKU)

Shipping

By shipping I mean the transport of and trade in the products of the whole country by means of government-owned ships, and the relief of the hunger and cold of all people afforded by these instruments of supplying each region with what it needs. Shipping and foreign trade are the responsibility of the ruler and should not be left to the merchants. If shipping is left entirely in the hands of

---

31. Quoted in Keene, *The Japanese Discovery of Europe*, p. 223.

merchants, they will act as their greed and evil purposes dictate, thereby disturbing commodity prices throughout the country. Prices then fluctuate enormously, and the farmers find it difficult to survive. If this situation is remedied by using government-owned ships for transport and trade, the prices of commodities will be stabilized naturally and the farmers relieved.

As long as there are no government-owned ships and the merchants have complete control over transport and trade, the economic conditions of the samurai and farmers grow steadily worse. In years when the harvest is bad and people die of starvation, the farmers perish in greater numbers than any other class. Fields are abandoned and food production is further reduced. There is then insufficient food for the nation and much suffering. Then the people will grow restive and numerous criminals will have to be punished. In this way citizens will be lost to the state. Since its citizens are a country's most important possession, it cannot afford to lose even one, and it is therefore most unfortunate that any should be sentenced to death. It is entirely the fault of the ruler if the life of even a single subject is thereby lost.

All the many varieties of troubles, disasters, and crimes found among the common people are a product of their unhappiness and anger over fluctuations in commodity prices. Such fluctuations are caused by the inadequacy of sea transport, which in turn is caused by the fact that the ruler controls no ships, and there is no government service. It cannot be estimated how greatly the prerogatives of the ruler are thereby impaired. Shipping and trade are now the business of merchants. Under this system no distinction is made between the interests of the merchants and the duties of the ruler. By developing the techniques of shipping it would become possible to equalize prices throughout the country, thus helping both the samurai and the farmers. Food production would increase steadily, which, in turn, would make the nation prosperous.

It is obviously impossible to feed the thousands of people living in a great city with only the food that can be brought in by coolie labor or on the backs of beasts; unless food is transported in ships the population will go hungry. But when shipping is controlled, as is the case by merchants, it will lead in the end to disaster; this must be changed. . . . [pp. 166–67]

Some daimyo have now ceased to pay their retainers their basic stipends. These men have had half their property confiscated by the daimyo as well and hate them so much that they find it impossible to contain their ever accumulating resentment. They finally leave their clan and become bandits. They wander lawlessly over the entire country, plotting with the natives who live on the shore and thus entering a career of piracy. As they become ever more entrenched in their banditry one sees growing a tendency to revert to olden times.[32]

---

32. Reference to the *bahan,* Japanese pirates who were at their strongest in the fifteenth and sixteenth centuries.

It is because of the danger of such occurrences that in Europe a king governs his subjects with solicitude. It is considered to be the appointed duty of a king to save his people from hunger and cold by shipping and trading. This is the reason why there are no bandits in Europe. Such measures are especially applicable to Japan, which is a maritime nation, and it is obvious that transport and trade are essential functions of the government.

Ships which are at present engaged in transport do not leave coastal waters and put out to sea. They always have to skirt along the shore, and can navigate only by using as landmarks mountains or islands within visible range. Sometimes, as inevitably happens, they are blown out to sea by a storm and lose their way. Then, when they are so far away from their familiar landmarks that they can no longer discern them, they drift about with no knowledge of their location. This is because they are ignorant of astronomy and mathematics, and because they do not possess the rules of navigation. Countless ships are thereby lost every year. Not only does this represent an enormous annual waste of produce, but valuable subjects also perish. If the methods of navigation developed, the loss at sea of rice and other food products would be reduced, thus effecting a great saving. This would not only increase the wealth of the nation, but would help stabilize the prices of rice and other produce throughout Japan. The people, finding that they are treated equally irrespective of occupation and that the methods of government are fair, would no longer harbor any resentment, but would raise their voices in unison to pray for the prosperity of the rulers. By saving the lives of those subjects who would otherwise be lost at sea every year, we shall also be able to make up for our past shame, and will keep foreign nations from learning about weak spots in the institutions of Japan from Japanese sailors shipwrecked on their shores. Because of these and numerous other benefits to be derived from shipping, I have termed it the third imperative need. [pp. 168–70]

If the islands near Japan were colonized, they would make highly desirable places. By such colonization numerous possessions—some sixty or more—would be created, which would serve not only as military outposts for Japan but would also produce abundant metals, grain, and fruit, as well as various other products, thus greatly adding to Japan's strength. I presume that run-of-the-mill officials must be thinking that colonization could be effected only at the expense of the ruler, and the authorities are not in the least inclined to spend any government money on developing farmland. This is the way mediocre minds always react.

The order to be followed in colonizing territories is as follows: First, ships are dispatched to ascertain the location of the islands to be taken and to measure their extent. The natural products of the islands are investigated, and the native population estimated. Then, when it is known about how many provinces the islands would make if colonized, the actual work is begun. If the natives are still living in caves, they are taught about houses. A house should be built for the tribal chief. Those natives without implements or utensils should be supplied with them. By helping the natives and giving them everything they desire, one will inspire a feeling of affection and obedience in them, like the love of children for their parents. This is true because they are moved by the same feelings that pervade the rest of the world, barbarians though they may be considered.

The way to compensate for the expenses involved in colonization lies in taking the natural products of the islands and shipping them to Japan. Trading marks a beginning of compensation for those expenses. Even barbarians do not expect to ask favors and give nothing in return. The products they offer represent a commencement of taxation. Since every island has wooded areas, there will always be some value in the lumber which can be taken from the islands, even after a great many years. The value of other products besides lumber would be too great to calculate. It is the task of the ruler-father to direct and educate the natives in such a manner that there will not be a single one of them who will spend even one unprofitable day. This matter should not be put off for another moment; it is a vital state duty.

At this point we must discuss the foundation of colonization—the sciences of astronomy and mathematics. In Japan these sciences are not as yet fully known, and there are few men who understand their significance. Even in China the principles of astronomy and mathematics have roughly been understood since the arrival of a number of Europeans late in the seventeenth century.[33] If, in connection with colonization projects, ships cross the seas without reference to the principles of astronomy and mathematics, there is no way to tell how much easier sea travel is than land travel. The name of the book in which the natural laws behind these principles are contained is *Schatkamer*, a European work.[34] One may learn from the latitude of a particular island what its climate is like throughout the year. Or, without actually visiting an island, one can predict in this way whether it will prove fertile. This may be done with certainty; false tales need not be believed.

The key to colonization is to establish a system with long-range objectives as to future profit and loss. By encouraging the good customs of the natives and eliminating their bad ones, it is possible to have them maintain human dignity. They should never be permitted to forget the generosity of the Japanese ruler. This is how colonization should be set about, but Japan persists in her bad habit of imitating old Chinese usages. Very few of the government authorities possess any real knowledge of astronomy or mathematics, and it is because of their ignorance that whenever there is talk of colonizing the northern territories, as

---

33. Honda is a century off; the late sixteenth century would be more accurate.

34. Honda possibly is referring to Klaas de Vries's *Schatkamer of te Konst der Stuur-Lieden*, a navigator's handbook frequently reissued in Holland. The book was known in Japan before the country was opened. See Hayashi, "List of Some Dutch Astronomical Works," p. 44.

occasionally happens, the project is never carried through. It is Japan's misfortune that her officials are misled by foolish tales about these great countries, which are actually far superior to Japan, and consequently do not take advantage of great opportunities for profitable ventures. This is a matter of especial regret because there have been Russian officials in the islands inhabited by the Ainu since about 1765. They have displayed such diligence in their colonization efforts that eighteen or nineteen Kurile islands and the great land of Kamchatka have already been occupied. Forts are said to have been built at various places and a central administration established, the staff of which is regularly changed and which rules the natives with benevolence. I have heard that the natives trust them as they would their own parents.

In Japan, on the other hand, this system is as yet not followed. It is forbidden to carry from the country seeds for the five cereals or edged tools for use in building houses. It is forbidden to teach Japanese to any natives. These are supplemented by a host of other prohibitions. It is a most lamentable system which has as its object keeping barbarians forever in their present condition. Since the Russians operate under a system which provides that their own subjects are sent out to live among the natives, it is only to be expected that the Ainu look up to the Russian officials as gods and worship them. . . . [pp. 170–72]

When the Ezo islands are colonised, they will make worthwhile places which will yield several times as much produce as Japan does today. Although there are other islands both to the east and west which should also be Japanese possessions, I shall not discuss them for the moment. At this crucial time when the Ezo islands are being seized by Russia, we are faced with an emergency within an emergency. When, as now, Japan does not have any system for colonizing her island possessions, there is no way of telling whether they will be seized by foreign countries or remain safe. This is not the moment for neglect; such actions by foreign powers may lead to the destruction of our national defense. With the establishment of a system of colonization, a knowledge of navigation will naturally develop among Japanese, but if navigation, shipping, and trade continue to be considered the occupation of merchants, the natives of our island possessions are doomed to an eternal want of civilization. The fact that the Ainu are living in a state of barbarity has been regarded by Russia as affording a fine opportunity for her to devote her energies to the colonization of the islands, a timely undertaking. The lack of a colonization system has kept Japanese rule from the island and has meant that the natives are unaware of the goodness of the ruler of Japan. Because of this ignorance they have been quick to become subject to Russia.

So important is colonization that I have termed it the fourth imperative need. [p. 178]

[Keene, *The Japanese Discovery of Europe*, pp. 166–72, 178]

SATŌ NOBUHIRO: TOTALITARIAN NATIONALISM

Like Honda Toshiaki, Satō Nobuhiro (1769–1850) was a northerner from that side of the country facing the Japan Sea. Dewa was his native province, the same province from which came the militant Neo-Shintoist Hirata Atsutane. Two things appear to have been uppermost in Satō's mind: the economic rehabilitation of the country in order to rescue it from poverty and starvation, and the buildup of Japan's military power in the face of frequent visits by the "black ships" of the West in Japanese waters. For Satō, as for Honda and a few others, a drastic renovation of the national life seemed necessary. And in truth, no other thinker, even in late-nineteenth-century Japan, came forward with a more complete and detailed program of reform than Satō did. His *Confidential Memoir on Social Control* (*Suitō hiroku*) contains a complete program of political, economic, and cultural reconstruction, which was the fruit of a long life of freedom and independent study, of broad learning and special training, such as few men enjoyed in his time.

In the early 1840s, Satō's writings aroused a great deal of interest among high shogunal officials. The chief minister, Mizuno Tadakuni, who wished to transform the shogunate into a more centralized polity, asked for and received from Satō a summary of his ideas. However, Mizuno was driven from office shortly thereafter by those who opposed the direction of his reforms. Besides a solid grounding in Chinese culture, common to the leading thinkers of the later Tokugawa period, Satō could draw on a large store of experience and experimentation in the fields of agriculture, horticulture, forestry, and mining, accumulated by five generations in his own family. Of the five, his father and grandfather in particular had become real specialists, and to them he owed much of his expert knowledge in the development of natural resources, which formed the basis of his economic rehabilitation program. To this family heritage, Satō added his intensive study of the Dutch language, which was for him the gateway to a knowledge of Western mathematics, astronomy, geography, history, navigation, and artillery. His knowledge of Western astronomy was impressive, as is shown in *Essays on Creation and Cultivation* (*Yōzō kaiku ron*), and using Dutch sources he was able to write *Brief History of the Western Powers* (*Seiyō rekkoku-shiryaku*). In addition, he wrote a general survey of the oceans and several handbooks on the use of artillery. Satō also claimed to have conducted experiments on a motor boat propelled by fire and on a new type of explosive. It was studies like these that impelled him to write about military and naval reorganization of the country and to develop his imperialistic program of world union.

Satō was not satisfied with the knowledge gained from books, so he took every opportunity to travel around the country, from the land of the Ainu in the northeast to Kyushu island in the southwest. His personal observations of the feudal domains are contained in *Lands and Climates* (*Shokoku fudoki*), an important source of firsthand geographical information.

Thus Satō may be considered a worthy representative of the rationalistic and empirical strain in Tokugawa thought. He also represents, to an equal or perhaps greater degree, another important trend in this period: nationalism. Free of any feudal allegiance, he tended to think in terms of the nation as a whole and not of the interests of a single domain. Therefore, it is not surprising that in his later years he was influenced by the extreme nationalist and Neo-Shinto leader Hirata Atsutane. With his knowledge of Western astronomy, Satō assumed that the sun was the center of our universe, and so Japan, with the Sun Goddess as its progenitrix, must be the sovereign land of the whole world. Furthermore, he claimed that the oldest annals of Japan, the *Kojiki* (*Record of Ancient Matters*), was the true book of revelation. In it he found the truth concerning the triple godhead: the Sovereign God and Center of Heaven (Amenominaka-nushi), the August Spirit of Vitality (Takami-musubi), and the August Spirit of Fertility (Kami-musubi). According to Satō, the highest truth in the three realms of nature (Heaven, earth, and humankind) was the law of vitality and fertility. And this law of vitality and fertility, personified in two of the three godheads, assumed an enduring form in the Sun Goddess as sovereign of the solar system and forebear of the divine rulers of the divine land. It was this law of vitality and fertility, according to Satō, that must be the basis of all political, economic, and cultural reconstruction of the nation.

Satō's program of reconstruction dwells on what he calls "three essentials and six indispensables." A state that aims at upholding the aforementioned principle must have a Department of Education (Kyōkadai), a Department of Religion (Jingidai), and a Department of Justice (Dajōdai). In regard to the Department of Religion, Satō believed that the gods and goddesses in the national pantheon were those who had made signal contributions to the divine way of vitality and fertility and were installed in the pantheon so that their example could inspire devotion to this principle.

Satō insisted on the importance of education as the basic function of the state. The Department of Education would include a minister of education and a state university, with the right to choose the curriculum, select teachers, and perform other necessary duties without any outside intervention. The university would have ten divisions: philosophy, religion, social institutions, music, law, military defense, medicine, astronomy, geography, and foreign languages. All government officials should be graduates of the university. The department would also have under its jurisdiction provincial schools, one in each district that yields 20,000 *koku* of rice. They would admit all children at the age of eight, regardless of their social status. The provincial school, in turn, would have under its jurisdiction an institute of general relief, four free dispensaries, six asylums for poor children, forty playgrounds, and twenty kindergartens. The benefits of education at the expense of the state must go to every member of society.

Under the three departments come six administrative bureaus: (1) Bureau of Basic Affairs (Honji-fu), and by basic affairs Satō meant agriculture; (2) Bureau for the Development of Natural Resources (Kaimotsu-fu), including forestry and mining; (3) Bureau of Construction and Manufacture (Seizō-fu); (4) Bureau of Commerce and Treasury (Yūzū-fu), which would control the exchange of all commodities through local offices of price control (Heijunkan) and act as the financial agent of the state, providing funds for all state expenses and relief activities (Satō insisted that these functions be in the hands of trained civil servants and not of merchants); (5) Bureau of the Army (Rikugun-fu), with complete control of unskilled labor and offices in important defense districts of the country; and (6) Bureau of the Navy (Suigun-fu), along with sixteen coast defense forces of 3,200 men and seventy-two outer defense forces with 35,000 men. The entire population would come under the jurisdiction of one or another of these government bureaus and would be divided into eight classes along functional lines.

For Satō, the country could never be saved from the menace of poverty as long as the Japanese were limited to their own home islands. That is, the law of vitality and fertility demands that the nation move on and spread all over the world. The world is one and is ruled by the simple principle of production and procreation; it is the destiny of Japan and the duty of all Japanese to produce and procreate so as to become the first nation of the world.

PREFACE TO *THE ESSENCE OF ECONOMICS* (*KEIZAI YŌROKU*)

The empirical strain in Satō Nobuhiro's thought is brought out in this preface, which is largely autobiographical. Although some recent historians have doubted whether Satō's immediate forebears contributed as much to the technological development of agriculture, mining, and manufacturing as he claims here, it is at least clear that he regards advances in these fields as dependent on the steady and systematic accumulation of empirical knowledge. Since Satō places a premium on firsthand observation, much of this account is a travelogue of his and his father's "field trips" throughout Japan, studying the topography and economic geography of different regions. Finally, he talks about his increasing interest and employment in matters of military defense.

My family lived for generations in Okachi County, Dewa Province, where it held an hereditary estate. After losing its estate in the debacle of 1600,[35] it turned

---

35. The defeat of Ieyasu's enemies at Sekigahara.

to medicine as its profession. In later days my grandfather, Fumai-ken, himself saw tens of thousands made homeless by recurring famines, and scores die of starvation. He was grief stricken and thought: "The profession of medicine is of minor importance if it cannot save the masses. I should like to find a way to save the people from the dire afflictions of cold and hunger in times of national poverty and distress." Thus began his interest in the study of economics. Taking precedence in his studies was the management of agriculture, followed by mining, the manufacture of various commodities, and the improvement of methods of manufacturing. In his desire to improve the methods of manufacturing, he traveled widely through the provinces, calling on experts in various fields and seeking advice from stone cutters, jewelers, mine managers, coal workers, kiln owners, brick makers, fishermen, trap setters, paper makers, weavers, dyers, masons, smiths, coppermen, woodcutters, sawyers, arrowhead makers, lacquer artisans, sheath makers, tea masters, brewers, candy experts, and beverage makers. He asked each one about the principles of his trade.

He also traveled to remote mountains and distant valleys, forded rivers and crossed lakes, and explored gold mines and oil wells. After more than forty years of laborious, indefatigable research and leaving his tracks nearly everywhere in the country, he died at the Ani copper mine in Akita County, Dewa, in 1732. Among his works are *New Book on Natural Resources* (*Kaikoku shinsho*) in twelve chapters and *Secret of Tracing Ores* (*Sansō hiroku*) in two chapters. The *New Book on Natural Resources* explains the principles of economics and the secret of developing natural resources, and it constitutes the basis of our family program of study. In a few words, its aim is to discuss how to develop our land, which is in a primeval state, so as to yield products contributing to the enrichment of our country. It is similar to plans proposed for the development of Ainuland [Hokkaido]. It examines minutely the particulars of topography, the taking of measurements, and the marking of boundaries, and it explains their techniques. The *Secret of Tracing Ores* describes the physiognomy of mountains, which should yield gold, silver, copper, iron, tin, lead, cinnabar, mercury, jade, precious stones, verdigris, sulfur, and alum. It also explains how to determine the presence of gold, silver, or other metals in mountains by their shape and the color and quality of their soils and rocks. It further discusses how to find veins of metals and how to determine the logical sequence of veins of various metals. Moreover, because it deals with the kinds and amount of metal deposits, estimating the height or depth at which they may be found and the difficulty expected of their excavation, it enables one to calculate in advance the suitability of a particular mountain for mining and the prospects of success. Consideration of the natural topography the existence of water courses on and under mountains reveals the secret of cutting tunnels to keep the pits dry. Thus, the work has been of incalculable value to mining engineers, who have closely guarded its secrets. Because this study of mountain physiognomy existed in the past only in name and not in fact, many miners have made all kinds of wild claims, deceiving and luring people into bankruptcy. Indignant about this situation, my grandfather spent more than forty years of careful study to write this book, which he then presented to his followers. As a result of his study, mountain physiognomy has become a science, providing a standard for students to rely on. Today, those who study the science of mountain physiognomy in Dewa, Mutsu, Iyo, Tajima, and Iwami are, for the most part, followers of my grandfather.

When Fumai-ken was still alive he ordered my father, Genmei-ka, to develop and improve the science of economics and natural resources, which he did. After my grandfather's death my father also traveled about the country for more than forty years in his study of this subject, and he wrote the *Theory of Developing Resources* and *Lectures on Economics* in thirteen chapters, *Mountain Physiognomy, Illustrated*, in one chapter, and *Management of Miners* in two chapters. In the spring of Tenmei 1 [1781], when my father journeyed to Matsumae, I accompanied him to the land of the Ainu. I spent the year at Matsumae, seeing the land with my own eyes, studying its climate, and inspecting its various products. In the spring of Tenmei 2 [1782] we crossed over from Matsumae to Tsugaru, from where we toured Nanbu, Sendai, Sōma, and the entire seacoast of Mutsu. That fall we reentered the Sendai region via Nihonmatsu and Fukushima, and traversing a by-road called Koyasugoe, at year's end we returned home to Akita, where we observed the New Year. In the spring of Tenmei 3 [1783] we left home to go to the silver mines of Shinjō, and in the summer of that year we toured the province of Dewa, climbing the Chōkai, Gassan, Haguro, and Hayama mountains. We inspected the natural features and products of Shōnai and Mogami fiefs, Yamagata, Kamiyama, and Yonezawa fiefs. That fall we reached Aizu, where we climbed Iide and Bandai and walked around Lake Inashiro. Wherever we went in Aizu, we inspected the soil and the products. In October of that year we passed through Hidama Pass to reach Nasu County in Shimotsuke Province. We climbed Mount Takahara and stopped for several days at the gold mine in its foothills, where my father taught the natives how to grow mushrooms. At year's end we arrived at Nikkō and greeted the New Year at the village of Kujira, where a disciple of my father, Sarubashi Kai-no-kami, lived.

During the early spring of Tenmei 4 [1784] we traveled on foot and examined the natural products of the mountains and valleys of Nikkō, beginning with Kurokami. Then we took leave of Sarubashi and made our way to the copper mine of Ashio, where there were disciples of my father and grandfather. My father visited this place to consider a method of extracting silver from copper, at the invitation of the villagers of Nitamoto, who wished to develop a tin mine. The output of the Ashio copper mine in recent years had been extremely small, and the mines had deteriorated considerably. My father remained there for more than a hundred days. In the heat of the waning summer, he contracted dysentery, and medicines proving ineffective, he died at an inn on the third day of August.

On his deathbed he advised me that if I returned home after his death, I would live out my life exactly like a plant and the scholarship gained by the labors and hardships of my father and grandfather through two generations would be wasted. "Although you are only a youth," he said, "you seem to be intelligent. It is my wish that you go to Edo, study the science of economics and of natural resources under a competent teacher, carry out the cherished wishes of your father and grandfather by succeeding to the family profession, and carry this science to its completion."

I was at the time a mere youth of sixteen, and I did not know what to do. I listened, however, to my father's injunction and went to Edo to become a pupil of the Master Udagawa Genzui, or Kaien. I heard lectures on natural history, both descriptive and functional. I received training in the reading and translation of Dutch. And from Master Inoue Chū, or Bubi-en, and from my friend Kimura Taizō, I learned astronomy, geography, mathematics, and surveying.

Then I picked up my basket and set out on an extensive trip around the country. I visited towns and cities as well as remote mountains and ravines, searching for plants and products, and covering by foot more than sixty provinces. Besides economics and natural resources, I was able to acquire training in such military arts as the making of armor, the making of bows and arrows, and the use of artillery and fireworks. In Bunka 3 [1806] I returned to the Eastern Capital (Edo) and took up residence on Yanagi Street in Kyōbashi.

In 1808 I went to Awa Province, where I devoted my attention largely to fireworks and to inventing numerous devices. It was here also that I wrote *A Historical Survey of Eastern Nations* in two chapters and *My Idea of Real Military Science* in seven chapters (which was enlarged to thirteen chapters in Bunsei 4 [1821] and the title changed to *My Idea of Military Science*). I also studied the mathematical principles of firing by gunpowder and wrote the *Theory of Firearms* in two chapters. It was in Awa too that I experimented with new weapons of my own invention for use in military expeditions, coastal defense, and naval warfare and wrote the book *How to Use Three Types of Firearms* in three chapters. Moreover, after painstaking study of military matters, I perfected a method of applying firepower to offensive action, and I built a ship propelled by firepower as well as two types of miraculous bullets, which I called the New Thunder and the Golden-Purple Bell. In this way I was able to complete my plans for the maritime defense of our nation.

In 1809 I left Awa to return to Edo, but in the following year I again left Edo to retire to Mamezaku village in Shimōsa. I made this move because during my stay in Awa I had suddenly become famous as an inventor of devices relating to maritime defense, and officials in the service of the various fiefs and other curious persons flocked to my residence every day, forming large groups of carriages before my gate. My wife, fearing the unforeseen consequences of such great notoriety for a *rōnin* like me, constantly urged me to retire.

Since my retirement I have become interested in a school of thought called Japan's Ancient Way, which is espoused by a fellow native of Dewa, Hirata Atsutane. As I studied carefully the traditions of our heavenly gods and earthly deities, the purity of our origins, our manifest national purpose, and the principles for the evolutionary improvement of all things on earth, have become clear to me, so that I have been able to perfect and complete my family's program of studies.

Thereupon, using my grandfather's *New Book on Natural Resources* and my father's *Development of Natural Resources* as a foundation and adding to them what I myself had gained through constant study and research, I collected the various principles and theories of my family's studies in the following works: *Essays on Creation and Cultivation* in three chapters, *The Pillar of Heaven* in three chapters, and *Compendium of Economics* in eighty chapters. The drafts of these works are ready now, and after they have been proofread, they will become a family legacy entrusted to the safekeeping of my children.

[Satō Nobuhiro, *Keizai yōroku*, in *Nihon keizai taiten*,
vol. 18, pp. 174–78; RT, WTdB]

QUESTIONS AND ANSWERS CONCERNING RESTORATION OF THE ANCIENT ORDER
(*FUKKO-HŌ MONDŌ-SHO*)

The following passage from *Questions and Answers Concerning Restoration of the Ancient Order* amplifies the preceding account of Satō's activities as an economic, military, and technical adviser to various feudal lords. It illustrates how local daimyo were pursuing their own interests in economic and technological development autonomously, whereas the range of Satō's activities was nationwide, expressed a unified national consciousness, and called for rulership responsible for the national welfare.

In the beginning of the Kansei era [1789–1801], I had an audience with the lord of Tsuyama. I discussed with him methods of making his domain prosperous, and I wrote for him a book in two volumes on the subject of reforms. Later, during my visit to Kazusa Province, I discussed fishing methods with the natives of the coast of Tsukumo and showed them ways of maintaining a fishing economy. Early in the Bunka era [1804–1818] I became adviser to Chief Officer Shūdō of Awa fief, and visiting in the city of Tokushima I participated in discussions on coastal defense and wrote *Theory of Firearms* in two chapters, *How to Use Three Types of Firearms* in three chapters, and a *Brief History of Western Countries* in three chapters. In addition, I discussed the subject of unifying the world, wrote the fifty-chapter book *How to Control the Ocean*, helped cast many cannons, and thus spent three years in Awa. I then went to Owari, where I remained for a year and wrote the *Development of Natural Resources* in seven chapters. The following year I returned to my native village and helped the Satake family open a sea route on the Pacific to transport Akita's products to Edo. The following year I went to Edo and took up residence at Nakabashi. When I wrote *How to Administer Satsuma* for Igai, the chief officer of Satsuma fief, who had enrolled as my student, the lord of Satsuma who read the tract was so pleased he sent me an honorarium in the personal care of Yamamoto Rihei and Tanaka Shichibei. I then went to the lord's residence at Takanawa to pay my respects and stayed for more than ten days at the home of Chief Officer Igai. Because he asked me many questions in great earnestness about agriculture, I later wrote and presented him with a copy of *Agricultural Problems* in ten chapters. The venerable lord was again highly pleased and made me a present of three male and three female pigs. I put them in the care of one of my pupils, Aida Gihei. Their numbers increased many times. Later, I took up residence at Daizudani in southern Shimōsa where I lectured on economics and agriculture and began revising the works on agriculture written by my forebears.

> [Satō Nobuhiro, *Fukko-hō mondō-sho,* in *Nihon keizai taiten,*
> vol. 19, pp. 98–99; RT, WTdB]

THE POPULATION PROBLEM

The great increase in Japan's population during the peaceful years of Tokugawa rule created a problem whose magnitude few of even thinking Japanese appreciated. Satō, feeling that population growth was in accordance with natural law and the divine spirit of creativity, called for fuller employment of Japan's resources and greater food production and opposed limiting the birthrate as well as infanticide. The following passage is from *The Essence of Economics (Keizai yōroku).*

Since the Middle Ages, agricultural guidance in the various provinces has been on the decline because no farm experts were appointed to study and help the people develop natural resources. Thus, despite the beauty of our country and the abundance of fertile land, the exhaustion of the soil and the lack of new attempts at cultivation have led to a scarcity of produce, which is hardly sufficient to feed and clothe the populace of the country. This, in turn, has led to difficulty in rearing children and to the secret practice of infanticide. The practice is particularly widespread in the northeast and in the eastern regions. It also is widespread in the Inland Sea region, Shikoku and Kyushu, but there the children are killed before they are born, so it does not look like infanticide. The one place where infanticide seems to be extremely rare is Echigo, but in its place is the widespread practice of selling girls over seven or eight years of age to other provinces for prostitution. In fact, they are a kind of "special product" of northern Echigo. Some consider this practice inhumane, but to think so is a great mistake. It is far more humane than either abortion or infanticide. I was told that long ago in Central Asia there was a large country whose king killed 3,300 children each year to obtain their livers, with which he made a medicine for the kidneys to be used for sexual purposes. No one who is told of this practice can help but feel a sense of shock and revulsion. When first I heard of it, I too was greatly shocked, but later as I reflected on it deeply, it occurred to me that while the king's act of slaying 3,300 children annually was indeed inhumane, it was not as barbarous as the practice of infanticide that is prevalent today. In Mutsu and Dewa alone, more than sixty thousand or seventy thousand children are killed each year. And I have not yet heard of anyone who deplores this situation. I find it nonetheless an unspeakable state of things. . . . That infanticide is so widespread in the various provinces cannot be attributed to the inhumanity of the parents. In the final analysis, it must be attributed to the ruler who lacks compassion, who is unaware of his duty as a deputy of Heaven to help the people, who does not study the science of developing natural resources, who does not appoint agricultural experts, and who fails to carry out a program of agriculture that would encourage farmers to make their greatest effort. Under such rule agricultural yields are meager and the condition of the land [is] poor. Human beings are the beloved children of Heaven. If rulers fail to teach service to Heaven and permit the slaying of several tens of thousands of children year after year, who knows what Heaven will not do? If this state of affairs continues, divine punishment is inevitable. Therefore the ruler of the land must not fail to adopt methods to achieve natural prosperity.

[Satō Nobuhiro, Keizai yōroku, in Nihon keizai taiten, vol. 18, pp. 433–34; RT, WTdB]

TOTAL GOVERNMENT

Satō's plan for the total utilization and control of natural and human resources, contained in Confidential Memoir on Social Control (Suitō hiroku), seems frighteningly modern and yet owes much to Confucian social ideals and the already well-developed Chinese pattern of centralized government, with the Tang dynasty as his model. Here he extends and adapts it to the complex requirements of his own society in order to exploit the potentialities of technological development. Although Satō anticipated considerable innovation from the West, he characteristically regarded this political reform as the fulfillment of the ancient (Chinese) ideal of a rationally ordered society in a universe governed by natural law (also explained in his Restoration of the Ancient Order [Fukko-hō], 1846). That this would be in accord with divine law and providence, as understood through Shinto traditions, is made clear in other writings to follow.

This passage concerns the chief agencies of government that Satō would put in control of the nation's economic life. Because it would mean completely reorganizing the four-class system and military government of his day, Satō treated this plan as private and confidential rather than appear to be taking issue with established Tokugawa policy.

The six ministries should be the Ministry of Fundamental Affairs,[36] Ministry of Development, Ministry of Manufacture, Ministry of Finance, Ministry of the Army, and Ministry of the Navy. This system is similar to six offices of the Zhou government and the six departments of the Tang dynasty in China. However, the systems of the Zhou and Tang dynasties governed the people by dividing them into four classes: the rulers, the farmers, the artisans, and the merchants. After much thought, I decided that in a four-class system some matters do not come under the effective control of the government, and [so] the possibilities for developing industry cannot be exploited fully. For this reason, we are neglecting some of the great resources that nature has bestowed on us.

In order to promote government "in the service of Heaven,"[37] it should be based on the occupations of all the people, who should be classified into groups with similar functions. The country's industries should be divided into eight groups, namely, plant cultivation, forestry, mining, manufacturing, trading, unskilled occupations, shipping, and fishing. After being classified into these eight groups, the people would be assigned to one occupation and would attend diligently to their respective occupations. The law should strictly prohibit anyone from trying another occupation. Those who cultivate plants should be assigned to the Ministry of Fundamental Affairs, foresters and miners to the Ministry of Development, craftsmen to the Ministry of Manufacture, traders to the Ministry of Finance, unskilled labor to the Ministry of the Army, and boatmen and fisherman to the Ministry of the Navy. Thus, the six ministries will oversee the groups of people assigned to them, encouraging them to study their occupations and making them devote their time constantly and exclusively to performing their occupations without faltering or becoming negligent and to the fullest extent of their energies. In this way, as the months and years pass, each industry will become proficient and perfect itself, providing steadily more benefits for the greater wealth and prosperity of the state.

As in the systems of the Zhou and the Tang, if the people are divided into four classes for purposes of administration, although such a division may be clear and distinct in appearance, its practice will inevitably lead to confusion.

---

36. "Fundamental Affairs" signifies "agriculture," traditionally regarded as the mainstay of the state.

37. This means something much like "in accordance with natural law."

This is because the ruling class concerns itself exclusively with the administration of government and national defense, paying no attention to the production of goods from land or sea, and placing the burden of production for the entire country on the other three groups: the farmers, craftsmen, and merchants. Because a small number of groups must encompass a large number of industries, the merchants must assume some of the functions of the farmers, foresters, artisans, and fishermen. Each trade is left largely uncontrolled and thus is unable to develop any skill and ingenuity. Profits dwindle from year to year, and some people have to turn over their businesses to others, also losing their house and home. The number of homeless people will gradually increase and eventually will lead to the decline of the nation itself. This is a matter of the greatest magnitude, requiring serious thought and investigation.

Moreover, when the people are divided into eight groups, each group should be segregated and not permitted to live together, as in the ancient rule of [the early Chinese statesman] Guan Zhong of Qi. If this system is followed, the people will learn their trades beginning in their adolescence, and even without being formally instructed they will become familiar with their roles. Thus, the number of specialists will naturally increase.

[Satō Nobuhiro, *Suitō hiroku*, in *Nihon keizai taiten*, vol. 18, pp. 635–36; RT, WTdB]

ESSAYS ON CREATION AND CULTIVATION
(*YŌZŌ KAIKU RON*)

Satō pursued his economic and technological studies in a rationalistic and empirical spirit, focusing on increasing the production and utilization of goods. In his later years, under the influence of Hirata Atsutane, Satō's rationalism was joined to Shinto vitalism. He now saw productivity and the technological transformation of nature as implicit in the natural order. Indeed, to Satō, they had a metaphysical basis in the primordial gods, the Spirit of Vitality and Spirit of Fertility.

For rulers, to employ every means in their power for the sake of agriculture— including studying natural law[38] and astronomy, surveying land and sea, determining latitude and longitude, examining climate, distinguishing the nature of soils, reclaiming paddy fields and farms, rectifying boundaries, repairing irrigation ditches, building and repairing embankments, preparing for drought and rain, tilling and harrowing with infinite care, and cultivating with earnestness— is the way to carry out the divine will of creation and to help cultivate nature. These are what we call the thirteen principles of agricultural management.

---

38. Literally, "Heaven's principles."

If the thirteen principles of agricultural management are conscientiously followed, then all things will produce an abundant harvest. These products will then be controlled by a system of allocation and distribution. In this manner the goods and wealth of the land will accumulate, and the way will be opened for civilizing the countries of the world. If we strive to teach service to Heaven, all living people will enjoy the benefits of benevolent rule. To be well versed in agricultural management, to bring all products under a single control, and to endeavor to spread education are what we call the three essentials of economics.

When the head of a nation satisfactorily carries out these three essentials, production will increase greatly, money and wealth will flow, the whole country will prosper, all the people will be rich and happy, and suffering due to poverty will be unknown. Then what harm will there be in having a large family? Then and only then can the teaching of gratitude for divine favors be promoted and the foul practice of infanticide be eradicated. Only in this way can talents be developed, military defense be perfected, and laws be enforced. Therefore if the government is conscientious in this respect, the innate goodness of all men will assert itself. Acts of violence will decrease gradually, moral discipline will gradually improve, and the population will increase greatly. . . .

Let us respectfully examine the annals of the Divine Age. Before the creation of heaven and earth there were three godheads: the Lord of the Center of Heaven, the Spirit of Vitality, and the Spirit of Fertility. These three together were the fountainhead of all creation.

Then, at the beginning of creation, one original energy was revealed in the midst of the great void of fusion and confusion. Because of the divine act of creation, what was heavy was separated from what was light, and what was clear was separated from what was foul. The ethereal essence was condensed in the center, and the upper heaven was completed.

[Satō Nobuhiro, Yōzō kaiku ron, in Nihon keizai taiten,
vol. 18, pp. 106–8; RT, WTdB]

CONFIDENTIAL PLAN OF WORLD UNIFICATION
(*KONDŌ HISAKU*)

As a prelude to his plan of world empire, Satō pursues further the preceding theme: the reconciliation of Shinto creation legends and the naturalistic cosmology of the Chinese, which had already been incorporated into the *Nihon shoki* (*Chronicle of Japan*). Here the pivotal concept is Heaven (*ten*), which embraces both nature and the divine, so that the will of the Shinto gods is readily identified with the natural law (Heaven's principles) of the Chinese and the West.

World rule by Japan would result from (1) divine favor, in the form of natural geographical advantages; (2) a capacity for rational organization of the world's resources; and (3) a divine spirit among the Japanese, such that their superior moral fiber would be sufficient to overcome all obstacles. Echoes of these arguments were heard in the twentieth century from Japanese militarists, who counted heavily on the Japanese "spirit" to offset the West's material superiority.

Our imperial land came into existence at the very beginning of the earth, and it is the root and basis of all other countries of the world. Thus if the root is attended to with proper care, the entire world will become its prefectures and counties,[39] and all the heads and rulers of the various countries will become its ministers and servants. According to the scriptures of the Divine Age, the imperial progenitors, Izanagi and Izanami, instructed Susanoo [the Impetuous Male Deity] that "our rule extends over the eight hundred folds of the blue immense." And thus we learn that to make clear the divine teaching of production and procreation and thereby to set the peoples of the entire world at peace was, from the very beginning, the principal and urgent mission of our heavenly country. My earlier works, the *Compendium of Economics* (*Keizai taiten*) and the *Outline of Heaven's Law* (*Tenkei yōroku*), examined the divine teaching of creation with the purpose of uniting the entire world in peace.

The salvation of the people of the world is an immense task that requires, first of all, a clear knowledge of geography and the state of affairs in the countries of the world. If measures are not taken to harmonize the actual state of affairs with Heaven's will, the principle and teaching of production and procreation cannot be realized. And therefore the study of geography is imperative.

Let us now examine the situation of our country in terms of the geography of the countries of the world. It extends from 30° N latitude to 45° N latitude. Its climate is temperate, its soil [is] fertile, and it has a variety of crops that produce abundant harvests. Facing the ocean on four sides, for convenience of ocean transportation it has no equal among the nations of the world. Its people, living on sacred land, are superior, excelling those of other countries for bravery and resoluteness. In truth they are fully capable of holding the reins of the world. From this position of strength they can majestically command the world in every direction, and by virtue of the awesome prestige of this imperial land they can readily subjugate the puny barbarians and unify the world under their control. Ah, how boundless have been the blessings of the creator on our imperial land!

However, even in our imperial land, since the descent from Heaven of the Imperial Grandson, rulers have disobeyed the laws and teachings of the Divine Age. They have squandered many years in pleasure, idleness, and unbridled

---

39. The process of empire building is described as it had taken place in China, where the feudal states of antiquity were absorbed into the Qin empire as centrally administered prefectures and counties.

dissipation, setting their hearts on beautiful women instead of heroic women, and thus shortening their own lives. . . . The ruler did not act like a ruler, nor the subject like a subject. The providential plan initiated by Ōnamochi and Sukuna-hikona was abandoned, and the national polity remained in a state of decline for a long time. Thus magic and Buddha's teachings came into vogue, and no one remained who knew the true teachings of old. The ignorant masses of this corrupt age, having been informed of the vastness of China and India on the one hand, while seeing the smallness of their Heavenly land and the weakness of its power on the other hand, convulsed with laughter when they heard my arguments for unifying the world, telling me that I lacked a sense of proportion. They are not aware that Heaven ordained our country to command all nations. . . .

In terms of world geography our imperial land appears to be the axis of the other countries of the world, as indeed it is. Natural circumstances favor launching an expedition from our country to conquer others, whereas they do not favor the conquest of our country by an expedition from abroad. The reason why an expedition from our country could be executed more easily than one from abroad is as follows. Among the nations of the world today, no country compares with China in immensity of territorial domain, in richness of products, and in military prestige. Yet even though China is our neighbor and very close to us, there is no way that it can inflict harm on us. . . . If our nation attempted to conquer China, however, with proper spirit and discipline on our part China would crumble and fall like a house of sand within five to seven years. . . . Thus, before Japan attempts to open other countries, it must first absorb China.

As we already noted, despite its great strength, China could not oppose our country. Needless to say, other countries likewise could not oppose us, for by the grace of nature Japan is situated as to be able to unify the other countries of the world. Therefore, I will explain in this work how China can be subjugated. After China is brought within our domain, the Central Asian countries, as well as Thailand, India, and other lands where different languages are spoken and curious costumes are worn, which yearn for our virtues and fear our power, will come to us with bowed heads and on hands and knees to serve us.

[Satō Nobuhiro, *Kondō hisaku,* in *Nihon keizai taiten,*
vol. 18, pp. 567–69; RT, WTdB]

Chapter 34

THE DEBATE OVER SECLUSION AND RESTORATION

After 1739, Russian ships were seen in Japanese waters with increasing frequency. A report was brought home by castaways that the Russians had established a school of navigation at Irkutsk in 1764 and that a Japanese language department had been added in 1768. The Russian government was not alone in its persistent efforts to open Japan's closed door. In 1808 the English ship *Phaeton* humiliated the shogunate by forcing its way into the port of Nagasaki, and the commissioner of the port had to commit suicide as a result of the disgrace. The country was already in turmoil when Commodore Matthew Perry of the United States arrived in 1853 at Uraga Bay near the shogunal capital to demand that Japan be opened to navigation and trade. This was only five years after the United States had annexed California. Literally defenseless, the shogunate had no choice but to accept a treaty stipulating that two ports be opened. This was a complete reversal of the long-established shogunate policy of excluding foreigners and provoked an uproar from one end of the country to the other. The mounting discontent and agitation pointed unmistakably to the downfall of the tottering shogunate.

From the raging debate on the new open-door policy, three main points of view emerged. The Mito schoolmen, headed by Tokugawa Nariaki and eloquently articulated by Fujita Tōko and Aizawa Seishisai, came to be known as the group that advocated "reverence to [eventually meaning "restoration of"] the emperor and repulsion of foreigners" (*sonnō-jōi*). A more conciliatory group advocated "union of the civil authority [Kyoto court] and military authority [Tokugawa shogunate]" (*kōbu gattai*) in order to unify and strengthen the nation politically. In the cultural sphere, it called for the adoption of Western science and art while preserving Eastern ethics. The most important spokesman for this view was Sakuma Shōzan (later assassinated by a political opponent), who proposed the shogunal policy of opening the country in order to learn Western techniques indispensable to the defense of the country. The third group believed that the salvation of the country would come not from the mere adoption of certain techniques or tactics but only from a complete renovation of national life through a system of education based on Western civilization and science. This group had as its predecessors such leaders as Sugita Genpaku and Takano Chōei. In the latter half of the nineteenth century, Fukuzawa Yukichi was its foremost leader and spokesman, with "independence and self-respect" (*dokuritsu jison*) as his slogan.

THE LATER MITO SCHOOL

The Mito school, as we have seen, was inaugurated in the seventeenth century by Tokugawa Mitsukuni, with one of its purposes being to compile an official history of Japan. This work, however, remained in preliminary draft during Mitsukuni's lifetime and was not put into final form until the early years of the twentieth century. Meanwhile, in the eighteenth and early nineteenth centuries, the influence of the Mito branch of the Tokugawa family rose steadily, partly owing to the great prestige acquired through its sponsorship of a project in which many illustrious scholars participated. Its political fortunes improved especially after Nariaki succeeded to leadership of the family and his son became a candidate for the office of shogun in the absence of an heir in the main Tokugawa line. But the rising political power of the Mito was also due in no small measure to the simple and forceful doctrines disseminated by its leading schoolmen. These were dramatized in the slogans "Civil and military [arts] go together" (*bunbu-fugi*) and "Loyalty and filiality are one-in essence" (*chūkō-ippon*).

This was a program designed to conciliate and unite the country's principal religious, intellectual, and political elements against the threat from outside. But what answer did these men have to the great question of the moment: How are the foreigners to be dealt with? To understand their answer, we must review Japanese history as the Mito men themselves were doing in their compilation of the *History of Great Japan* (*Dai Nihon shi*). The office of shogun, which the Tokugawa held, had its inception in the subjugation of the Ainu, then known as the Northern Barbarians. Generals commissioned by the imperial court to lead campaigns of suppression were designated "barbarian-subjugating generalissimos" (*sei-i tai shōgun*), subsequently abbreviated to simply "generalissimo" (*shōgun*). The original function of the shogunate therefore was to cope with "barbarians." But the Tokugawa were obviously unable to discharge this responsibility. By yielding to the demands of the barbarians from America, the shogunate had abandoned its trust and forfeited its authority to rule. In this predicament, the Mito branch of the Tokugawa, one of three specially appointed to guard the interests of the ruling house, was in a logical position to take the lead in salvaging the situation. Its solution, as set forth by Aizawa Seishisai and Fujita Tōko (1806–1855), was to deal with the new barbarians as vigorously and contemptuously as earlier barbarians had been dealt with.

AIZAWA SEISHISAI: "REVERE THE EMPEROR, REPEL THE BARBARIAN"

In his "New Theses" (Shinron), Aizawa Seishisai (1782–1863) explains the issue as follows:

> To defend the state by means of armed preparedness, a policy for peace or for war must be decided on before all else. If there is indecision on this point, the people will be apathetic, not knowing which way to turn. Morale will deteriorate while everyone hopes for a peace that cannot be obtained. The intelligent will be unable to plan; the brave will be unable to stir up their indignation. Thus day after day will be spent allowing the enemy to refine his plans. Waiting until defeat stares us in the face is caused by an inner sense of fear that prevents resolute action. In the days of old when the Mongols were insolent, Hōjō Tokimune stood resolute. Having beheaded the Mongol envoy, he ordered his generals to summon the army for war. Emperor Kameyama, majestic as he was, prayed at the Ise Shrine and offered his life for the salvation of the country. Thereupon the men who were called upon to sacrifice themselves responded by defying death in a body, as if the entire nation were of one mind. Their loyalty and patriotism were such as to bring forth a storm and hurricane that smashed the foe at sea. "Put a man in a position of inevitable death, and he will emerge unscathed," goes the saying. The ancients also said that the nation would be blessed if all in the land lived as if the enemy were right on the border. So, I say, let a policy for peace or for war be decided on first of all, thus putting the entire nation into the position of inevitable death. Then, and only then, can the defense problem be easily worked out.[1]

---

1. Takasu, *Shinron kōwa*, p. 253.

This is what came to be known as the policy of "repelling the barbarians" (*jōi*). But even though he could not openly declare it, Aizawa felt that the shogun lacked the authority to make a final decision in favor of such a policy. The historical studies of the Mito school had already established that the descendants of the Sun Goddess were the ordained rulers of the Land of the Rising Sun. So with Aizawa, as with Nariaki and Tōko, reverence for and loyalty to the sovereign (*sonnō*) had to be the rallying cry for the entire nation in putting up a unified front against the growing threat of the Western barbarians. On this point, the Mito spokesmen joined hands with the promoters of National Learning. Aizawa mentions the special features of Japanese geography and history: that the country was created by Heavenly forebears and was located at the center of the world; that ever since the descent of the Sun Goddess, the country had been ruled by a single line of her descendants; and that in Japan loyalty to the sovereign and filial piety to parents formed the basis of all morality, so that the people would live happily and die happily for the sake of the emperor and their parents.

In this process of joining loyalty and filiality, in that order, Mito spokesmen reversed the normal Neo-Confucian priority, which gave primacy to filiality as the genetic virtue. This was not new to Mito, or to Japanese Confucianism, but it marked a significant escalation of loyalty to the emperor as a component of the rising nationalist ideology identified with the concept of "national substance (both form and essence)" (*kokutai*) promoted by the Mito school.

Because of the introduction of Buddhism in earlier times, Aizawa argues, the people had lost sight of the basic truths of history and had become lax in their observance of the fundamental duties of loyalty and filial piety. Throughout the medieval period, confusion and disorder became almost the rule until Hideyoshi and Ieyasu pacified the country:

> Thus the whole land and the entire population came under a single control, and all as one paid respect to the benevolence of the Heavenly court while at the same time obeying the commands of the shogunate. Peace reigned supreme over the nation. Because of the prolonged peace, however, signs of weakness and sluggishness have appeared: the rulers of fiefs are easygoing; they make no provision for times of need and destitution; reckless people are left to themselves and go unpunished; foreign barbarians stand by off our coasts awaiting their chance. . . . But all the people, high and low, are intent only on their own selfish gain, with no concern for the security of the nation. This is not the way to preserve our national polity. When a great man assumes leadership, he is concerned only that the people be inactive. Mediocre leaders, thinking only of easy peace, are always afraid of the people's restlessness. They see to it that everything appears quiescent. But they let barbarians go unchecked under their very eyes, calling them just "fishing traders." They conspire together

to hide realities, only to aggravate the situation through half-hearted in-action. Standing on high and surveying the scene in order to practice delaying tactics with an intelligent air seems to me a sure way of carrying us all to an inevitable catastrophe. . . . If instead the shogunate issues orders to the entire nation in unmistakable terms to smash the barbarians whenever they come into sight and to treat them openly as our nation's foes, then within one day after the order is issued, everyone high and low will push forward to enforce the order. . . . This is a great opportunity such as comes once in a thousand years. It must not be lost.[2]

Such was the clarion call of Aizawa's "New Theses," which before World War II was acclaimed as one of the two immortal essays on militant loyalty and patriotism, the other being Yamaga Sokō's "Historical Evidence of the Central Kingdom" (Chūchō jijitsu).

In reconciling native tradition with the Neo-Confucianism that had domi-nated intellectual life in the Tokugawa period, Aizawa took an expansive view of the Way, pursuing a theme of the original Mito school expressed in the name of its founding academy as an institute for the expanding of the Way through active human agency (kōdōkan). In Japan's golden age, the natural moral and spiritual values bequeathed by the native gods—implicit in the lives of the Japanese people but numinous and ineffable as befit their divine character— were consciously articulated in the rhetorical teaching and texts of the Way of Yao, Shun, and Confucius, needed to give civilizational values concrete, insti-tutional embodiment through human effort to "expand the Way." Subse-quently, these natural values were subverted by Buddhism, a foreign teaching that in its esoteric form had subordinated the gods to the buddhas and, in the Zen of the Five Monasteries, with its depreciation of textual discourse and education, had kept the people ignorant of the classic texts.

After the consequent disorder of the medieval age, it was the historic mission of the Tokugawa house to reunify the country and promote authentic education through Ieyasu's support of the Hayashi school and Mitsukuni's establishment of the Mito school, which recouped the original synthesis of divine rule and Confucian morality. To support this thesis, Aizawa offered a critique of the leading schools of the Tokugawa period, especially that of Ogyū Sorai, which, in its exaltation of Chinese antiquity, was, like Buddhism, Christianity, and "Dutch learning," too worshipful of things foreign. At the same time, Aizawa criticized the National Learning movement for failing to recognize the contri-bution of Confucian ethics to the national polity.

Thus Aizawa, speaking for the mission of the Mito school and calling for the reform of shogunal rule as led by Tokugawa Nariaki of the Mito house,

---

2. Takasu, *Shinron kōwa*, pp. 71–72.

offered a revival of the ancient Way together with a rejoining of the military and civil cultures represented by the shogunate and imperial house.[3]

"NEW THESES"
(SHINRON)

Aizawa Seishisai's "New Theses," written in 1825, represents the first declaration of the creed of the Mito school, which until that time had confined itself to writing history and avoiding political controversy. The crisis brought on by the appearance of Western ships in Japanese waters and, in particular, the detention of crewmen from a British whaler in the Mito domain (1824), prompted this explicit statement of doctrines that had a powerful impact on their time.

Preface

Our Divine Land is where the sun rises and where the primordial energy originates. The heirs of the Great Sun have occupied the imperial throne from generation to generation without change from time immemorial. Japan's position at the vertex of the earth makes it the standard for the nations of the world. Indeed, it casts its light over the world, and the distance that the resplendent imperial influence reaches knows no limit. Today, the alien barbarians of the West, the lowly organs of the legs and feet of the world, are dashing about across the seas, trampling other countries underfoot, and daring, with their squinting eyes and limping feet, to override the noble nations. What manner of arrogance is this!

The earth in the firmament appears to be perfectly round, without edges or corners. However, everything exists in its natural bodily form, and our Divine Land is situated at the top of the earth. Thus, although it is not an extensive country spatially, it reigns over all quarters of the world, for it has never once changed its dynasty or its form of sovereignty. The various countries of the West correspond to the feet and legs of the body. That is why their ships come from afar to visit Japan. The land amid the seas that the Western barbarians call America occupies the hindmost region of the earth; thus, its people are stupid and simple and are incapable of doing things. These all are according to the dispensation of nature. Thus, it stands to reason that by committing errors and overstepping their bounds, the Westerners are inviting their own eventual downfall. But the vital process of nature waxes and wanes, and Heaven may be overcome by the collective strength of men in great numbers.[4] Unless great

---

3. Aizawa, *Kōdōkanki, Taishoku kanwa,* in NST, vol. 53, pp. 230–57.

4. According to Confucian theory, Heaven, earth, and humankind form a harmonious triad, whose balance may be temporarily upset by the evil actions of men.

men appear who rally to the assistance of Heaven, the whole natural order will fall victim to the predatory barbarians, and that will be all.

If, today, we discussed a farsighted program in the public interest, the public would stare at one another in astonishment and suspicion, for they have been weakened by time-worn tales and become accustomed to outdated ideas. [Sunzi's] *Art of War* says: "Do not rely on their not coming to you; rely on your own preparedness for their coming. Do not depend on their not invading your land; rely on your own defense to forestall their invasion."

Therefore, let our rule extend to the length and breadth of the land, and let our people excel in manners and customs. Let the high as well as the low uphold righteousness [duty]; let the people prosper; and let military defense be adequate. If we proceed accordingly and without committing blunders, we shall fare well no matter how powerful the invasion of a strong enemy is. But if the situation were otherwise and we indulged in leisure and pleasure, then we would be placing our reliance where there is no reliance at all.

Some say that the Westerners are merely foreign barbarians, that their ships are trading vessels or fishing vessels, and that they are not people who would cause serious trouble or great harm. Such people are relying on the enemy's not coming and invading their land. They are relying on others, not on themselves. If I ask such people about the state of their preparedness, about their ability to forestall an invasion, they stare blankly at me and do not know what to say. How can we ever expect them to help save the natural order from subversion at the hands of the Western barbarians?

I have not been able to restrain my indignation and my grief over this state of affairs. Thus, I have dared to propose what the country should rely on. The first section deals with our national polity, in which connection I call attention to the establishment of our nation by the loyalty and filial piety of our divine forebears. I then emphasize the importance of military strength and the welfare of the people. The second section deals with the general situation, in which I discuss the trend in international affairs. The third is on the intentions of the barbarians, in which I describe the circumstances of their designs on us. The fourth is on defense, in which I talk about the essentials of a prosperous and militarily strong nation. The fifth presents a long-range plan in which I map out a method of educating the people and uplifting their customs. I wrote these five essays with the fervent prayer that in the end Heaven would triumph over man. They [the essays] represent the general principles to which I have pledged my life in the service of Heaven-and-earth.

[Takasu, *Shinron kōwa*, pp. 1–10; RT, WTdB]

The National Substance

Aizawa's "New Theses" opens with his central conception of the "national substance" (*kokutai*), probably the most potent concept in modern Japanese nationalism because it so effectively brings together Shinto mythology and Confucian ethics of the *bushidō* variety. Note that from beginning to end, Aizawa identifies the Sun Goddess with Heaven, which presides over the moral order of the Confucian universe; attributes to her the promulgation of moral law and political order among men; and equates the Confucian virtues of loyalty and filial piety with Shinto worship and thanksgiving. For this reason, the "national substance" (*kokutai*) has simultaneous religious, moral, and political overtones. It embraces the "national structure," especially the imperial institution; the "national basis," as found in the divine origins of the country and the dynasty; and the "national character" or essence, as embodied in those moral principles and virtues that were considered indispensable to social unity and order.

The means by which a sovereign protects his empire, preserves peace and order, and keeps the land from unrest is not by holding the world in a tight grip or keeping the people in fearful subjection. His only sure reliance is that the people should be of one mind, that they should cherish their sovereign, and that they should be unable to bear being separated from him. Since Heaven and earth were divided and mankind first appeared, the imperial line has surveyed the Four Seas for generation after generation in the same dynasty. Never has any man dared to have designs on the imperial position. That this has been so right down to our own time could scarcely have been by mere chance.

The duty of subject[5] to sovereign is the supreme duty in Heaven-and-earth. The affection between parent and child is the quintessence of kindness (*on*)[6] in the land. The foremost of duties and the quintessence of kindness pervade everything between Heaven and earth, steadily permeating the hearts of men and enduring forever without change. These are what the sovereign relies on above all in regulating Heaven-and-earth and maintaining order among the people.

In olden times, when the heavenly progenetrix [Amaterasu] established the state on a foundation as broad as Heaven, her position was a heavenly position, and her virtues were heavenly virtues, and with them she accomplished the heavenly task of bringing order into the world. All things great and small were made to conform with Heaven. Her virtue was like that of the jewel; her brightness was like that of the mirror; and her awesome power was like that of the sword.[7] Embodying the benevolence of Heaven, reflecting the radiance of Heaven, and displaying the awesome power of Heaven, she beamed majestically over the whole realm. When she bequeathed the land to her imperial grandson

---

5. In the Confucian context, the word *shin* most often means "minister"; in the Japanese context, it often means "retainer" or "samurai." Here the samurai's extreme sense of duty is being generalized and attributed to all subjects.

6. Implying a strong sense of indebtedness.

7. These are the properties of the three imperial regalia: jewel, mirror, and sword.

and personally bestowed the three [imperial] regalia on him, these were taken to be symbols of the heavenly office, giving form to the heavenly virtue and taking the place of Heaven's own hand in the performance of the heavenly functions. Subsequently, they were handed down to unbroken generations; the sanctity of the imperial line being such that no one dared violate it. The status of sovereign and subject was clearly defined, and the supreme duty [of loyalty to the throne] was thereby made manifest.

When the heavenly progenetrix handed down the divine regalia, she took the treasured mirror and, giving her benediction, said: "Looking at this is like looking at me." Bearing this in mind, countless generations have revered the mirror as the divine embodiment of the heavenly progenetrix. Her holy son and divine grandson looked into the treasured mirror and saw in it a reflection. What they saw was the body bequeathed to them by the heavenly progenetrix, and looking at it was like looking at her. Thus, while reverently worshiping her, they could not help feeling an intimate communion between the gods and men. Consequently, how could they not but revere their ancestors, express their filial devotion, respect their own persons [as something held in trust], and cultivate their own virtue? Even so, as the love between parent and child deepens, the quintessence of kindness becomes fully manifest.

Having thus established human morality on these two principles, the heavenly progenetrix imparted her teachings to endless generations. The obligations of sovereign and subject, parent and child: these are the greatest of Heaven's moral obligations. If the quintessence of kindness is achieved within and the highest duty is manifest without, loyalty and filial piety will be established, and the great Way of Heaven and humankind will brilliantly show forth. By loyalty, honor is done to those worthy of honor; by filial piety, affection is shown to parents. It is truly by these means that the hearts of the people are made one, and high and low are made to cherish one another.

But how is it that these superlative teachings are preserved without being propagated in words, and how is it that the people practice them daily without being conscious of them?[8] Because the heavenly progenetrix resides in Heaven and beams majestically on the earth below, so Heaven's descendant below manifests to the utmost his sincerity and reverence in order to repay his debt to the heavenly ancestor. Religion and government being one,[9] all the heavenly functions that the sovereign undertakes and all the works that he performs as the representative of Heaven are means of serving the heavenly forebear. [By]

---

8. The question implies that these truths have a mysterious power so that they may be perpetuated in the life and experience of the people, even though they have not been committed to writing. The subsequent passage explains how this mysterious power operates.

9. The early Japanese word for "government" (*matsuri-goto*) is a compound based on the words for "religious rite" (*matsuri*) and "affairs" (*goto*), indicating a close association of political and religious functions.

revering the ancestor and reigning over the people, the sovereign becomes one with Heaven. Therefore, that his line should endure as long as Heaven endures is a natural consequence of the order of things. And thus, in expressing their supreme filial piety, successive sovereigns have maintained the imperial tombs and performed ceremonies of worship to their ancestors. They have manifested to the full their sincerity and reverence by observing the whole system of rites and have fulfilled their duty of repaying the debt to their progenetrix and of revering their ancestors by performing the Great Thanksgiving Ceremony. This ceremony consists of the first tasting of the new grain and the offering of it to the heavenly god[s].

[Takasu, *Shinron kōwa*, pp. 13–20; RT, WTdB]

The Danger from the West

The following excerpt from the "New Theses" is preceded by a discussion of the principle known as "retracing the descent and repaying the original debt" (*hanshi hōhon*), which affirms the divine descent of the imperial house and the gratitude of the Japanese people for the blessings of the gods. According to Aizawa, this principle was inculcated by the original Shinto teaching and reinforced by Confucianism from China. Later, however, it declined owing to the spread of superstitious beliefs identified with Shamanism, Buddhism, unorthodox Confucian teachings, and Christianity.

Thus, our ancestral teaching has been muddled by the shamans, altered by the Buddhists, and obscured by pseudo-Confucians and second-rate scholars who have, through their sophistries, confused the minds of men. Moreover, the duties of sovereign and minister and of parent and child have been neglected and left undefined in their teachings. The great Way of Heaven and man are nowhere to be found in them.

In the past, those who have attracted popular attention and confused the thinking of the populace with their improper teaching have been people only of our own realm. But now we must cope with the foreigners of the West, where every country upholds the law of Jesus and attempts therewith to subdue other countries. Everywhere they go, they set fire to shrines and temples, deceive and delude the people, and then invade and seize the country. Their purpose is not realized until the ruler of the land is made a subject and the people of the land [are] subservient. As they have gained momentum, they have attempted to foist themselves on our divine land, as they have already done in Luzon and Java. The damaging effects of their heresies go far beyond anything done by those who attack from within our own land. Fortunately, our rulers were wise and our ministers alert and thus were able to perceive their evil designs. The barbarians were killed and exterminated, and there has been no recurrence of this threat. Thus, for two hundred years, the designing and obstinate fellows have been prevented from sowing their seeds in our soil. That the people have been free from the inflammatory teaching of the barbarians has been due to the great virtue of our government. . . .

Recently, there has appeared what is known as Dutch studies, which had its inception among our official interpreters [at Nagasaki]. It has been concerned primarily with reading and writing Dutch, and there is nothing harmful about it. However, these students, who make a living by passing on whatever they hear, have been taken in by the vaunted theories of the Western foreigners. They enthusiastically extol these theories, some going so far as to publish books about them in the hope of transforming our civilized way of life into that of the barbarians. And the weakness of some for novel gadgets and rare medicines, which delight the eye and enthrall the heart, have led many to admire foreign ways. If someday the treacherous foreigner should take advantage of this situation and lure ignorant people to his ways, our people will adopt such practices as eating dogs and sheep and wearing woolen clothing. And no one will be able to stop it. We must not permit the frost to turn to hard ice. We must become fully aware of its harmful and weakening effects and make an effort to check it. Now the Western foreigners, spurred by the desire to wreak havoc on us, are daily prying into our territorial waters. And within our own domain, evil teachings flourish in a hundred subtle ways. It is like nurturing barbarians within our own country.[10] If confusion reigns in the country, and depravity and obsequiousness among the people, could this land of ours still be called the Central Kingdom? Would it not be more like China, India, or the Occident? After all, what is the "basis" of our nation?[11]

[Takasu, *Shinron kōwa*, pp. 90–95; RT, WTdB]

The Source of Western Unity and Strength

As a Confucian, Aizawa believed that the moral unity of the people in support of the ruler, not coercive means, was the basis of true governance, and he saw the strength of the West as deriving more from its underlying Christian values than from its more apparent military might. Christianity, then, was the real threat from the West, and to counter it, Aizawa tried to rally Japan's religious and moral unity, advancing what became a new, synthetic national ideology, corresponding in many ways to the new nationalisms of Europe and America.

---

10. Literally, the "Central Kingdom," the usual Chinese name for China. For its application to Japan, see chaps. 22 and 24.

11. Reference to the "national polity" (*kokutai*), especially as found in the divine origins of the country and the dynasty and as embodied in those moral values and virtues considered indispensable to social unity and order.

The Western barbarians have independent and mutually contending states, but they all follow the same God. When there is something to be gained by it, they get together in order to achieve their aims and share the benefits. But when trouble is brewing, each stays within his own boundaries for self-protection. So when there is trouble in the West, the East generally enjoys peace. But when the trouble has quieted down, they go out to ravage other lands in all directions, and then the East suffers. Russia, for instance, having subjugated the Western plains, turned eastward to take over Siberia and penetrate the Amur River region. But because the Manchus were still strong in China, the Russians could not attain their objectives and had to turn their aggressive designs toward the land of the Ainu. [p. 215]

As for the Western barbarians who have dominated the seas for nearly three centuries: Do they surpass others in intelligence and bravery? Does their benevolence and mercy overflow their own borders? Are their social institutions and administration of justice perfect in every detail? Or do they have supernatural powers enabling them to accomplish what other men cannot? Not so at all. All they have is Christianity to fall back on in the prosecution of their schemes. . . . When these barbarians plan to subdue a country not their own, they start by opening commerce and watch for a sign of weakness. If an opportunity is presented, they will preach their alien religion to captivate the people's hearts. Once the people's allegiance has been shifted, they can be manipulated, and nothing can be done to stop it. The people will be only too glad to die for the sake of the alien God. They have the courage to give battle; they offer all they own in adoration of the God and devote their resources to the cause of insurrection.[12] The subversion of the people and overthrow of the state are taught as being in accord with the God's will. So in the name of all-embracing love, the land is subjugated. Even though greed is the real motive, it masquerades as a righteous uprising. The absorption of the country and the conquest of its territories all are carried out in this fashion.[13] [p. 198]

[Takasu, *Shinron kōwa*, pp. 198, 215; RT, WTdB]

THE OPENING OF JAPAN FROM WITHIN

In the atmosphere of impending crisis that pervaded Japan in the mid-nineteenth century, the Mito slogan "Revere the Emperor, Repel the Barbarian" proved to be remarkably effective in rallying nationalistic sentiment around a single center: the imperial house. Yet the very simplicity and generality of this appeal rendered it susceptible to conflicting interpretations and left many questions unanswered, which, as events brought nearer the final crisis in foreign

---

12. Reference to the uprising of Christians at Shimabara, near Nagasaki, in 1637/1638.

13. In a later work, dated 1862, according to a recent finding by Donald Keene, Aizawa relented from his virulent espousal of "repelling the barbarians" to support the "opening of the country."

relations, were to be resolved in an unexpected manner. Thus for some of the Mito leaders, themselves prominent members of the Tokugawa family and desirous of strengthening its position rather than abandoning it, the expression "Revere the Emperor" represented a call to national unity, and not what it later became to proponents of the imperial restoration: a call for surrender to the emperor of functions long performed by the shogunate. Similarly, the cry "Repel the Barbarian," which at first gave vent to a xenophobic rejection of all intercourse with the West, was in a few years sufficiently moderated to allow for "opening the country" as the only practicable way of building up Japan's strength against the West. In the rapid evolution of Japanese thinking about these questions, Sakuma Shōzan and his disciple Yoshida Shōin stood as important links between the old order and the new.

SAKUMA SHŌZAN: EASTERN ETHICS AND WESTERN SCIENCE

A samurai from mountainous Shinano Province, Sakuma Shōzan (Zōzan, 1811–1864) completed his Confucian classical studies in Edo under Satō Issai (see chap. 32), a noted scholar and literary stylist who taught under the aegis of the official Hayashi school but was also influenced by the intuitionist philosophy of Wang Yangming. Shōzan's own writings, and those of his disciple Yoshida Shōin, betray this influence in their emphasis on the inseparability of knowledge and action. Shōzan nonetheless felt that his master had gone too far in the direction of subjectivism, to the neglect of Zhu Xi's objective "investigation of things." That he subsequently became interested in Western science and technology, however, was not a purely logical development of this early concern for Zhu Xi's "investigation of things." He devoted himself mainly to teaching classical studies until suddenly thrust into a situation requiring much more practical knowledge than he possessed. In 1841 his lord, Sanada Yukitsura, who had considerable influence in shogunate circles by reason of both his family connections and his personal talents, was appointed to its highest council of advisers and put in charge of Japan's coastal defenses. As a trusted counselor of his lord, Shōzan found himself confronting the most difficult and fateful question of the day: how to deal with the threat of Western naval power in Japanese waters.

Despite being a believer in "revering the emperor and repelling the barbarian," Shōzan was not blinded by this antiforeignism to the realities of the situation but immediately began studying Western gunnery as it was taught by two Japanese pioneers in this field: Takashima Shūhan and Egawa Tan'an. The eight-point program that Shōzan subsequently submitted to Lord Sanada as the

---

Thus, following the arrival of Matthew Perry' ships and Townsend Harris's opening of diplomatic relations in the 1850s, Aizawa underwent a major change in attitude similar to that of many other Japanese in the 1860s.

basis for the shogunate's policy reveals both his firm adherence to the seclusion policy and his espousal of technical developments from the West:

1. Fortifications must be erected at all strategic points on the coast and equipped with adequate artillery.
2. The export of copper through the Dutch must be suspended, and the metal used for casting thousands of guns be distributed to all points.
3. Large merchant ships must be built so as to prevent the loss of rice through the wreck of small coastal vessels, which are all that the exclusion edicts allow.
4. Maritime trade must be supervised by capable officials.
5. Warships of foreign style must be constructed, and a force of trained naval officers be assembled.
6. Schools must be established throughout the country, and modern education provided, so that "even the most stupid men and women may understand loyalty, piety, and chastity."
7. Rewards and punishments must be made clear, and government must be conducted benevolently but firmly, so as to strengthen the popular mind.
8. A system of selecting and employing men of ability in official posts must be established.[14]

While noting Shōzan's bold advocacy of Western military methods, we must not regard his references to Confucian virtues and precepts as mere lip service to tradition. The emphasis in articles 6 and 8 on the need for universal schooling and meritocratic recruitment had been articles of Neo-Confucian reform since the Song period and were echoed frequently by Japanese scholars. Their advocacy in the late Tokugawa period produced an increasing restlessness and resistance to the feudal system of inherited aristocratic position. For Shōzan, at this critical stage, such reforms were urgently needed, since support for such a stupendous national undertaking as he called for could be guaranteed only by intensifying the moral indoctrination of the people and improving the quality of government so as to ensure popular backing.

Shōzan's proposals met with strong opposition, however, and when his lord was finally forced to relinquish his high place in the shogunate councils, Shōzan found himself free to devote his full energies to Western studies. This involved learning Dutch, in order to have direct access to sources of knowledge made available only through the Dutch trading mission at Deshima. For instance, by following an encyclopedia translated from Dutch, he experimented in making glass and refining certain chemicals. By 1848, he had become

---

14. As summarized in Sansom, *The Western World and Japan*, p. 254.

proficient enough to cast cannon and make small arms. These activities, and the steps he also took to improve animal husbandry in his native region, were supported by Lord Sanada to develop and strengthen his own fief of Matsushiro. They also served to make Shōzan more widely known as a leader in adopting Western methods.

Meanwhile, through his lord and others high in the Tokugawa government, Shōzan continued to press for building up land fortifications and a Western-type navy. Unsuccessful in this, he still had the satisfaction of seeing his hopes for a modern navy carried forward by one of his disciples, Katsu Awa (or Kaishū [Sea Vessel]), who later studied naval science and construction in the United States and, as the first minister of the navy in the Meiji regime, became known as "the father of the Japanese navy."

Another disciple of Shōzan during these years was the aforementioned Yoshida Shōin, who met a far different fate in his attempt earlier to go abroad for study. With the encouragement of his teacher, Shōin had tried to stow away on one of Matthew Perry's ships in 1854, only to be turned over to the shogunal authorities and imprisoned for violating the seclusion laws. Shōzan himself would probably have been punished far more severely for his part in this "crime" had not influential persons interceded to reverse the death penalty for both him and his disciple. After less than a year in jail, each was released in the custody of his home domain for domiciliary confinement.

Undeterred and irrepressible, Shōzan continued to take an active part in the debate on political and military questions. His prison diary ended with the following statement, echoing a famous utterance by Confucius:

At twenty I realized I had a part to play in the life of my state.
At thirty I realized I had a part to play in the life of the entire nation.
At forty I realized I had a part to play in the life of the entire world.[15]

In this sequential development, Shōzan speaks as if one stage naturally evolved from the other, his horizons gradually extending outward like the *Great Learning*'s sequence of maturing from self to family to state to the world at large. He thought in this way not because the Neo-Confucian "investigation of things" necessarily led him to the kind of technical learning developed in the West—actually something forced on him by the advance of Western power— but because of his Neo-Confucian conviction that nothing lay beyond the scope of "the unity of principle and its diverse particularizations." In other words, Western technology and scientific principles could be only a particularized expression of underlying universal principles inherent in the Way. Neo-Confucian scholarly learning was limited in its own bookish way and did not exhaust all possible manifestations of principle.

---

15. *Analects* 2:4.

Up to this time, Shōzan's advocacy of Western methods still did not imply that Japan itself should be opened to the West. In 1858, however, the signing of a commercial treaty with the United States ended the shogunate's seclusion policy. Accepting this state of affairs, Shōzan eventually became known as an active proponent of the new policy of "opening the country" (*kaikoku-ron*), to which the Tokugawa were now unavoidably committed. Meanwhile, opposition to the shogunate and to intercourse with the West centered increasingly on the emperor in Kyoto, and Shōzan, fearing the effects of this cleavage on Japan's capacity to resist Western encroachment, devoted his efforts to bridging the gulf between the two courts. In the early 1860s, a compromise party appeared in both Edo and Kyoto, calling for collaboration between the shogunate and the imperial court under the slogan "Union of Civil and Military [Government]" (*kōbu gattai*). The aim of this movement was, on the one hand, to uphold the policy of "opening the country" and, on the other, to grant a greater voice in government to the imperial court and its supporters among the so-called outer daimyo. In the interests of such a compromise, Shōzan offered his services as an emissary from the shogunate to the Kyoto court, convinced that he could persuade the emperor of the necessity of "opening the country." It was on this mission to Kyoto that Shōzan was murdered by assassins from the southwestern fief of Chōshū, who were bitterly opposed to the Tokugawa and any move toward reconciliation.

Besides being identified with the policy of "opening the country" to the West and the movement for "Union of Civil and Military Government," Shōzan's name is remembered especially in connection with a slogan he made famous: "Eastern ethics and Western science" (*tōyō no dōtoku, seiyō no gakugei*). In these few words, Shōzan summed up his belief in the need to defend Japan and preserve its "Eastern" (mainly Confucian) ethical heritage while adopting the new technical knowledge of the West. No doubt, in so acclaiming the respective virtues of East and West, Shōzan failed to anticipate many of the frictions that might develop between them and the difficulty of preserving traditional values in the midst of the technological revolution that lay ahead. Nevertheless, his simple formula was more than just a facile cosmopolitan gesture or the hasty contrivance of a desperate man, hoping, in the face of overwhelming Western superiority, to salvage something from the wreckage of his own civilization. It satisfied at least two of the basic conditions for Japan's survival in the modern world: the need for developing military power sufficient to hold off the West while preserving the unity of national purpose and action that, under the circumstances, could spring only from common and well-established traditions. Thus the formula proved workable enough to serve a whole generation of leaders during the Meiji Restoration and to provide the basis for a modernization program of unparalleled magnitude in the late nineteenth century. What is noteworthy in this is not that the pursuit of these two aims brought them into continual conflict but that Japan's leaders and its people, adhering as much to received values as they were guided by the vision of a modernized nation, managed to limit these contradictions and conflicts sufficiently so as not to disrupt the whole enterprise.

Shōzan was not the only man of this era in world history to discover such an answer to the predicament of Asians suddenly confronted with the power and expanding energy of the West. In China, during the latter half of the nineteenth century, essentially the same solution was advanced under similar slogans, most prominently as "Chinese learning to provide the [moral] basis, Western learning to provide the [technical] means" (*Zhongxue wei ti, xixue wei yong*).[16] This is not the place to compare these two movements that encouraged the adoption of Western technology (especially the production of modern arms) while professing to uphold traditional moral teachings. Although the attempt made in China was far less successful in promoting rapid modernization than it was in Japan, it is significant that in neither case do we find the claims to tradition so incompatible with the requirements of modernization that the one could be advanced only at the direct expense of the other.

REFLECTIONS ON MY ERRORS
(*SEIKEN-ROKU*)

Reflections on My Errors seems to be a record of Sakuma Shōzan's reflections while in prison, although it was not actually written until after he was released. Ostensibly a piece of self-examination, the book is in fact a vigorous self-defense, dealing in turn with his fundamental Confucian beliefs, the need for pursuing Western studies, and the justification for his political activities. Because of his outspoken criticism of the existing regime, it was not published until after Shōzan's death and the fall of the shogunate.

In the summer of Kaei 7, the fourth month [May 1854], I, Taisei, because of an incident, went down into prison. During my seven months of imprisonment I pondered my errors, and as a result, there were things that I should have liked to say concerning them. However, brush and inkstone were forbidden in the prison, and I was therefore unable to keep a manuscript. Over that long period, then, I forgot much. Now that I have come out, I shall record what I remember, deposit the record in a cloth box, and bequeath it to my descendants. As for publicizing what I have to say, I dare do no such thing. [p. 239]

---

16. See de Bary and Lufrano, eds., *Sources of Chinese Tradition*, 2nd ed., vol. 2, chaps. 28 and 30. Wei Yuan (1794–1856) is probably the first exponent of this point of view in China. In *Reflections on My Errors* (*Seiken-roku*), Shōzan mentions having read a work of Wei's on China's defense policies in 1850/1851 and asserts that each of them had arrived at the same general conclusion independently. Sakuma's memorial on Japanese maritime defense was drawn up in the winter of 1842/1843, and Wei completed his *Record of Imperial Military Exploits of the Manchu Dynasty* (*Shengwu-ji*) in the summer of 1842.

2. Take, for example, a man who is grieved by the illness of his lord or his father and who is seeking medicine to cure it. If he is fortunate enough to secure the medicine and is certain that it will be efficacious, then, certainly, without questioning either its cost or the quality of its name, he will beg his lord or father to take it. Should the latter refuse on the grounds that he dislikes the name, does the younger man make various schemes to give the medicine secretly, or does he simply sit by and wait for his master to die? There is no question about it: the feeling of genuine sincerity and heartfelt grief on the part of the subject or son makes it absolutely impossible for him to sit idly and watch his master's anguish; consequently, even if he knows that he will later have to face his master's anger, he cannot help but give the medicine secretly. [p. 239]

16. Although my family branch was poor, I grew up with plenty to eat and with warm clothing to wear. I never underwent the tempering of cold and hardship. I was therefore always afraid that in the event of a national emergency I would have difficulty bearing the attendant difficulties in everyday living, such as privations in food and drink. However, last summer, when the American ships suddenly arrived, and Edo was put on strict guard, I managed military affairs in the mansion belonging to my *han*, and although I got no sleep for seven days and nights, my spirits grew higher and higher. This year, I was condemned and sent to prison. For several weeks I have eaten meager food, licked salt, and received the same treatment as men under heavy punishment. However, I have kept calm and have managed to become content with my lot. Moreover, my spirit is active, and my body is healthy. To have tried myself somewhat on these two points is of no small profit. My ordeal can thus be called a heavenly blessing. [p. 242]

20. The noble man has five pleasures, but wealth and rank are not among them. That his house understands decorum and rightness and remains free from family rifts—this is one pleasure. That exercising care in giving to and taking from others, he provides for himself honestly, free, internally, from shame before his wife and children, and externally, from disgrace before the public—this is the second pleasure. That he expounds and glorifies the learning of the sages, knows in his heart the great Way, and in all situations contents himself with his duty, in adversity as well as in prosperity—this is the third pleasure. That he is born after the opening of the vistas of science by the Westerners and can therefore understand principles not known to the sages and wise men of old—this is the fourth pleasure. That he employs the ethics of the East and the scientific technique of the West, neglecting neither the spiritual nor material aspects of life, combining subjective and objective and thus bringing benefit to the people and serving the nation—this is the fifth pleasure. [p. 244]

27. All learning is cumulative. It is not something that one comes to realize in a morning or an evening. Effective maritime defense is in itself a great field of study. Since no one has yet thoroughly studied its fundamentals, it is not easy to learn rapidly its essential points. Probably this fact explains why even if

you take hold of a man's ear and explain these essential points to him, he does not understand. [pp. 245–46]

30. Of the men who now hold posts as commanders of the army, those who are not dukes or princes or men of noble rank are members of wealthy families. As such, they find their daily pleasure in drinking wine, singing, and dancing; and they are ignorant of military strategy and discipline. Should a national emergency arise, there is no one who could command the respect of the warriors and halt the enemy's attack. This is the great sorrow of our times. For this reason, I have wished to follow in substance the Western principles of armament and, by banding together loyal, valorous, strong men of old, established families not in the military class—men of whom one would be equal to ten ordinary men—to form a voluntary group that would be made to have as its sole aim that of guarding the nation and protecting the people. Anyone wishing to join the society would be tested and his merits examined; and if he did not shrink from hardship, he would then be permitted to join. Men of talent in military strategy, planning, and administration would be advanced to positions of leadership, and then if the day should come when the country must be defended, this group could be gathered together and organized into an army to await official commands. It is to be hoped that they could drive the enemy away and perform greater service than those who now form the military class. [pp. 246–47]

35. Mathematics is the basis for all learning. In the Western world after this science was discovered, military tactics advanced greatly, far outstripping that of former times. This development accords with the statement that "one advanced from basic studies to higher learning." In Sunzi's Art of War, the statement about "estimation, determination of quantity, calculation, judgment, and victory" refers to mathematics. However, since Sunzi's time, neither we nor the Chinese have ceased to read, study, and memorize his teachings, and our art of war remains exactly as it was then. It consequently cannot be compared with that of the West. There is no reason for this other than that we have not devoted ourselves to basic studies. At the present time, if we wish really to complete our military preparations, we must develop this branch of study. [p. 248]

40. What do the so-called Confucian scholars of today actually do? Do they clearly and tacitly understand the way in which the gods and sages established this nation, or the way in which Yao, Shun, and the divine emperors of the three dynasties governed? Do they, after having learned the rites and music, punishment and administration, the classics and governmental system, go on to discuss and learn the elements of the art of war, of military discipline, of the principles of machinery? Do they make exhaustive studies of conditions in foreign countries? Of effective defense methods? Of strategy in setting up strongholds, defense barriers, and reinforcements? Of the knowledge of computation, gravitation, geometry, and mathematics? If they do, I have not heard of it! Therefore I ask, What do the so-called scholars of today actually do? [p. 249]

42. Learning, the possession of which is of no assistance and the lack of which is of no harm, is useless learning. Useful learning, on the other hand, is as indispensable to the meeting of human needs as is the production of the light hemp-woven garment of summer and the heavy outer clothing of winter. [pp. 249–50]

44. We say that this nation has an abundance of gold, rice, and millet. However, our territory is not large, and after the country's internal needs have been met, there is hardly any surplus of the materials produced here. Such things as the need for coastal defense arise from without. To install several hundred defense barriers, to construct several hundred large warships, and to cast several thousand large artillery pieces call for vast expenditures. Again, all these things are not permanent: every ten or twenty years they must be repaired, reconstructed, or improved. Externally, we will need funds to carry on relations with foreign countries and, internally, [to cover] the expense of necessary food supplies for our own country. Where can the money for these sorts of things be obtained? If a family in financial distress receives many guests and frequently prepares feasts for them, its resources will be dissipated to the point that it no longer can continue to carry on these activities. How does the present position of the nation differ from the plight of this poor family? With what tactics can such a situation be overcome? Those who sincerely wish to conduct the affairs of state well must make careful plans in advance. [p. 250]

46. At the time when my former lord assumed office in the government, and later, when he took charge of coastal defense, the English barbarians were invading the Qing empire, and news of the war was sensational. I, greatly lamenting the events of the day, submitted a plan in a memorial. That was, actually, in Tenpō 13, the eleventh month [December 1842–January 1843]. Later I saw the *Shengwu-ji* of the Chinese writer Wei Yuan [1784–1856].[17] Wei had also written out of sorrow over recent events. The preface to the book was composed in the seventh month of the same year [August–September 1842]; and although Wei thus wrote only four months before I submitted my memorial, the two of us, without having had any previous consultation, were often in complete agreement. Ah! Wei and I were born in different places and did not even know each other's name. Isn't it interesting that we both wrote lamenting the times during the same year and that our views were in accord without our having met? We really must be called comrades from separate lands. However, Wei says that from ancient times until the present, China has had a naval defense but has had no naval warfare; therefore as the method of defense against

---

17. Wei Yuan was a scholar and an associate of the commissioner Lin Zexu, whose attempt to suppress the opium trade at Canton led to the war with the British. Wei's book *Shengwu-ji* was finished just after the Treaty of Nanjing was signed, ending the Opium War. See de Bary and Lufrano, eds., *Sources of Chinese Tradition*, 2nd ed., vol. 2, pp. 207–9.

attacks from the sea, it should strengthen fortified towns and clear fields in order to be able to push back the landing invaders. I, on the other hand, wish to promote to the full the teaching of techniques for using armored warships and to form a plan of attack whereby an enemy could be intercepted and destroyed, in order that the death sentence may be given to the plunderers before they have reached the country's shores. That is the only point of difference between Wei and me. [p. 251]

47. In order to master the barbarians, there is nothing so effective as to ascertain in the beginning the conditions among them. To do this, there is no better first step than to be familiar with barbarian tongues. Thus, learning a barbarian language is not only a step toward knowing the barbarians but also the groundwork for mastering them. When the various nations on one pretext or another began sending ships frequently to the territory around Sagami and Awa, I thought it genuinely difficult to find out facts about them. As a result, I felt the desire to compile a lexicon in several volumes, translating other languages into Japanese, in order to teach the tongues of the various European countries. Also, since we have long had trade relations with Holland and since many of us already know how to read the books used in that country, I wished to publish the Dutch section first. Before this, the government had ordered to the effect that all books to be published must be officially inspected. Therefore, in the winter of Kaei 2 [1849–1850], I came to Edo, submitted my manuscript, and requested permission to publish it. The affair dragged on for a year, and I was ultimately unable to obtain permission. During the time I was in the capital, I first secured Wei's book and read it. He also wished to set up schools in his country primarily to translate foreign documents and to promote a clear understanding of conditions among the enemy nations, in order to further the cause of mastering the enemies. In this, too, his opinion concurred with mine. I do not know, however, whether or not his country has put his words into effect. [pp. 251–52]

48. The main requirement for maritime defense are guns and warships, but the more important item is guns. Wei included an article on guns in his *Haiguo tushi* [*sic*].[18] It is for the most part inaccurate and unfounded; it is like the doings of a child at play. No one can learn the essentials of a subject without engaging personally in the study of it. That a man of Wei's talent should fail to understand this is unfortunate. I deeply pity Wei that in the world of today, he, ignorant of artillery, should have unwittingly perpetrated these errors and foisted these mistakes on later generations. [p. 252]

49. Last summer the American barbarians arrived in the Bay of Uraga with four warships, bearing their president's message. Their deportment and manner

---

18. The correct title is *Haiguo tuzhi* (*Illustrated Gazetteer of the Maritime Countries*, 1841), compiled by Lin Zexu and Wei Yuan. See de Bary and Lufrano, eds., *Sources of Chinese Tradition*, 2nd ed., vol. 2, pp. 209–12.

of expression were exceedingly arrogant, and the resulting insult to our national dignity was not small. Those who heard could only gnash their teeth. A certain person on guard in Uraga suffered this insult in silence, and having been ultimately unable to do anything about it, after the barbarians had retired, he drew his knife and slashed to bits a portrait of their leader, which they had left as a gift. Thus, he gave vent to his rage. In former times Cao Wei of Song, having been demoted, was serving as an official in Shensi, and when he heard of the character of Zhao Yuanhao, he had a person skillful in drawing paint Zhao's image. Cao looked at this portrait and knew from its manly appearance that Zhao would doubtless make trouble on the border in the future. Therefore Wei wished to take steps toward preparing the border in advance and toward collecting together and examining men of ability. Afterward, everything turned out as he had predicted. Thus, by looking at the portrait of his enemy, he could see his enemy's abilities and thereby aid himself with his own preparations. It can only be regretted that the Japanese guard did not think of this. Instead of using the portrait, he tore it up. In both cases it was a barbarian; in both cases it was a portrait. But one man, lacking the portrait, sought to obtain it, while the other, having it, destroyed it. Their depth of knowledge and farsightedness in planning were vastly different. [pp. 252–53]

52. Formerly, with one or two friends, I took a trip to Kamakura; at length, we sailed over the sea past Arasaki to Jōgashima; we lodged at Misaki, continued on past Matsuwa, and stopped over at Miyata. Then, having stayed a time at Uraga, we went up to Sarujima, viewed Kanazawa, went out to Honmoku, and returned to Edo. In the course of this trip I stopped at about ten places where barricades had been set up in preparation against an invasion from the sea. However, the arrangement of them made no sense, and none of them could be depended on as a defense fortification. Upon discovering this, I unconsciously looked up to Heaven and sighed deeply; I struck my chest and wept for a long time. Edo is the throat of the nation, and while Futtsu, as its lip, may be called a natural barrier, the mouth opening into the sea is still broad. From the outset, it would be difficult without warships and naval troops to halt an enemy transgression or attack. Now, without any real effort, these foolish walls and mock parapets have been thrown up high above the surface of the sea, only to display to the foreign nations our lack of planning. If during these times the nations to east and west sent ships to pay us a visit, how could they take us seriously? There is no point in criticizing the mediocrity of the lower officials. But what is to be done if even those who ride on golden saddles with ornate saddle cloths, who wear brocade and feast on meat, and who call themselves high class, fail to recognize the great plan for the nation but instead use up the country's wealth on this useless construction work? If barbarian ships arrived in force, how could we either defend against them or defeat them? After my trip, I felt the urge to write a petition discussing the things that should and should not be done in maritime defense, with the hope that I might be of assistance

in this time of emergency. I completed my manuscript and requested my former lord for permission to submit it. He refused, and I gave up my plan. This was in the early summer of Kaei 3 [1850]. Four years later, as I had predicted, the affair of the American barbarians arose. At the time my former lord stopped my memorial, he was probably acting out of the fear that I might be punished for impertinence. His benevolence in protecting me was truly great. If he were in the world today and were informed that I have been imprisoned, his grief would be profound! [pp. 257–58]

> [*Seiken-roku,* in NST, vol. 55, pp. 239–60; trans. adapted from Terry,
> "Sakuma Shōzan," pp. 58–86]

YOKOI SHŌNAN: OPENING THE COUNTRY FOR THE COMMON GOOD

Yokoi Shōnan (1809–1869) illustrates, perhaps even more strikingly than Sakuma Shōzan does, the transition from a committed Confucianism to a wider world of intellectual engagement. From Kumamoto, Shōnan at an early age established himself as a scholar of exceptional brilliance and versatility in his home domain and then in Edo. Early on, he had been among the xenophobes calling for Japan to "repel the barbarians." But like Shōzan, his reading of Wei Yuan,[19] the Chinese Confucian statecraft thinker who responded to the disaster of the Opium War, was a wake-up call.

Now he realized, as Wei had, that there was no way of "repelling the barbarian" without opening up to the West. Latter-day scholarship was inadequate—too much lost in metaphysical speculation, quiet contemplation, bookishness, or belles lettres—to deal with the realities of the threat from the West. Indeed, the more Shōnan studied the West, the more he became convinced that it embodied in many ways the humane values and activism of the early sage-kings Yao, Shun, and Yu, who were directly engaged in meeting the needs of the people rather than in lofty theorizing or in bookish scholarship. The latter vices had alienated both leaders and people from their natural (*shizen*) recognition of and response to the historical changes that had come about through the natural course of Heaven-and-earth (*tenchi no kiun*).

From this new standpoint, Shōnan could view a general like George Washington as more closely resembling the sages who served the common good than the decadent rulers of China who were limited by a narrow vision and corrupted by a self-centered, effete complacency. Even the Confucian value of public discussion, or discourse concerning the common good (*kōgi*), he came to believe, was better served by the political institutions of the United States and England.

---

19. See de Bary and Lufrano, eds., *Sources of Chinese Tradition,* 2nd ed., vol. 2, pp. 184, 206.

By thus invoking the higher authority of the sages in favor of a universal standard transcending immediately received tradition, Shōnan engaged in a kind of Confucian revisionism similar to that of the Ancient Learning thinkers of the seventeenth century (especially Yamaga Sokō and Ogyū Sorai), who likewise emphasized the practical, social applications of early Confucianism. Even Zhu Xi had returned to the ancient sources of Confucianism in this way, so Shōnan was only learning and doing in his own time what Zhu had done in his. If one could call this reinventing tradition, then Confucianism itself was a tradition of continual reinvention in contemporary terms.

The same impulse to "restore the ancient order," however, had earlier inspired Song Neo-Confucian reformers to reject the anodyne, and amoral, influence of Buddhism in order to press for radical political change. Thus it is significant that at this time, Shōnan also was impressed by the strong moral stance and social teachings of Christianity, which he contrasted to Buddhist emptiness and antinomianism.

When Shōnan's views attracted the attention of Mito scholars and Matsudaira Shungaku (lord of the Fukui domain in Echizen), both Tokugawa related, he became associated with the movement to bring the shogunate and the imperial court together (*kōbu-gattai*) in a common cause and strategy for dealing with the West. Later, however, after imperialist forces succeeded with the Meiji Restoration in 1868, Shōnan, as an outspoken exponent of Westernization, met the same fate as Sakuma Shōzan: assassination by die-hard fanatics who still rejected all compromise with the West.

Along with his qualified advocacy of Westernization, Shōnan remained convinced that with its traditional values and native talents, Japan had enough resources to compete with and surpass other nations in the larger world—and even to dream of a world role for Japan. In the process, he formulated and articulated many of the aims that were espoused in the modernization process of the Meiji period. Thinkers in the next generation who were particularly inspired by Shōnan included Motoda Eifu, tutor to the Meiji emperor (see chap. 38), and Tokutomi Roka (1868–1927), an influential writer on liberal and humanitarian themes.

THREE THESES ON STATE POLICY
(KOKUZE SANRON)

The following excerpts are from policy recommendations made to Matsudaira Shungaku, lord of Echizen, in 1860. The focus of the three theses is on economic and military reform and the cultivation of the samurai as a leadership class. Although his recommendations are nominally directed to his lord and local domain, when Yokoi Shōnan speaks of "Enriching the Country" (Fukoku-ron), his first thesis, he is addressing the needs of Japan as a whole. Hence "state" (*koku*) here means not just feudal state but "country," and he sees this in the context of the larger world, so that in the Neo-Confucian paradigm of self-family-state and "all under Heaven," instead of starting his presentation with self-cultivation (as one would with Zhu Xi's formula of "self-cultivation for the governance of men"), he reverses the order—establishing first a larger world context in which to define the state and self. Much of his theses is devoted to opening up this larger perspective, just as Wei Yuan had tried to expand Chinese horizons in the 1840s.

On this basis, Shōnan argues that the common good (the ultimate criterion of Neo-Confucian self-cultivation and governance) can be met only through a policy of "enriching the country" by opening it up to public discourse, to trade, and to economic growth for the benefit of the people as a whole, not just to serve the narrow "selfish" interests of the feudal family domain.

Having established this larger context of "all-under-Heaven," in which economics and military power now play so large a role, Shōnan then returns to the matter of the self-cultivation of the samurai. In the third of his theses, "The Way of the Samurai" (Shidō), he contends that self-cultivation of the mind-and-heart, as developed in Japan by the likes of Yamaga Sokō, combining the feudal military virtues with Confucian civil cultivation, is the key to human governance. Here, however, he emphasizes that they are not two separate Ways; they can be fulfilled only by a unified mind, achieved through moral discipline and practical arts. These enhance a natural human response to the unavoidable situations that arise in the natural course of things.

Enriching the Country

Under the feudal system during the period of national seclusion, the various daimyo isolated their own provinces or counties without considering the harm to others so long as there was gain for themselves. Even though there was not a single regime that did not seek its own profit, it was difficult to supplement the deficiencies for state expenditures. Hence, the stipends of the samurai were inevitably withheld in the form of forced loans; money was squeezed from rich farmers and merchants; and the lifeblood of the common people was sucked. Even with these measures the emergency of the present day could not be remedied. [p. 439]

Today, with all nations navigating freely and trading with one another like neighbors, if Japan alone holds on tightly to its seclusion law, it will be unable to escape the armed might of foreign enemies. When this happens, it is extremely doubtful that the state can be administered, let alone make adequate military preparations, with national power virtually lacking; nor can it rally the samurai and commoners—some resisting, others resentful—into setting up a policy of defense and driving out the foreigners.

These are the evils of seclusion.

The dangers of opening up trade are great, and likewise are those of seclusion. How can these two policies best meet the needs of our economy?

Since the natural course of Heaven-and-earth (*tenchi no kiun*) and the conditions in the various nations are not amenable to change through willful human action, for Japan alone to keep itself isolated is out of the question. Even if trade should be begun while retaining our seclusionist outlook, there are disadvantages to both intercourse and isolation, as shown above, and long-term security is difficult to attain. However, if we work in harmony with the natural course of Heaven-and-earth and adapt to conditions in the various nations, and if we administer the land in the interests of the common public good, the obstacles everywhere will disappear, and the distressful state of affairs of the present will no longer be a problem at all. [pp. 440–41]

We can rule Japan only if we have the ability to inform ourselves broadly about the various nations; only by knowing how to rule Japan can we administer a single province. And only by knowing how to administer a province can we manage one job. This accords with reason. In the pursuit of the common good, the empire and the province should not be treated separately, but if we start our discussion at the level of a province and enlarge it from there, we know it will extend to all-under-Heaven. [p. 441]

Now especially, if trade is opened up, our prestige among foreign countries will be preserved, and our obligations will be fulfilled. We can obtain the profits of trade, and through proper finances the ruler can bring about a humane government and the ministers [can] avoid injuring the people. The logic of this is roughly given below. [p. 442]

Many people wish to produce various goods or to increase their production but lack the resources to do so. If the government lent money and grain so that they could fulfill these wishes, and if it [the government] bought these goods, redeeming the loans but not looking for profit, then the people would greatly benefit. The original stock, food for peasants, fertilizer, and the like all should be bought with loans from the government on a nonprofit basis in order to eliminate the unnecessary expense of high interest rates. All loans from the government should be made without profit but without resulting in a net loss to the government. The government must secure its profit from foreign countries.

In fostering the production of various goods by the people, the government should first try them out to find the best methods and tools and then sympathetically guide the people in using them. A great deal of labor can be saved and conveniences obtained in various production methods, including sericulture, and in the use of various agricultural tools. These the government should try out, and after winning the confidence of the people, it should help them carry out these methods. However, when a new method, even though convenient, is forced on people, generally they will have no faith in it.

Artisans and merchants should be given comparable consideration. Rice and money should be lent and better methods should be taught them in order to ensure them their livelihood. [pp. 442–43]

Because it is important that we make our country economically and militarily strong (*fukoku-kyōhei*) and because each samurai should play his part, each should be paid a stipend in accordance with his ability so that he will not be pressed with immediate needs for food and clothing, and he should be given housing near his place of employment. For example, those who wish to take up seafaring should be permitted to live near the water and should be given the tools of seamanship. Those who desire to go into sericulture should be permitted to dwell near mulberry fields and should be given rooms for raising silkworm cocoons. Each should have his livelihood stabilized in the place he prefers, [and] he should be able to get married and rear children. Those near the sea would eventually be used in the navy. Those near the mulberry fields should be trained for service as soldier-peasants. The requests of all those who wish to serve their country in other capacities, as swordsmiths, gunsmiths, and the like, should be granted.

Governing a country means governing the people, and the samurai are the instruments for governing the people. Although teaching filial piety and brotherly love, trust, and loyalty to both samurai and commoners is the basis of rulership, the sages have explained that teaching these is not possible without material means. Therefore, all the more so in the present period of decline, we should give priority to gaining economic strength. [pp. 443–44]

In recent years because trade has been initiated by foreign countries, the average person believes that this was the start of commercial intercourse, but this is by no means the truth. From the very beginning, commerce with foreign countries has been an important part of a country's trade, and its path has been firmly fixed by principles inherent in Heaven-and-earth. Those who govern others must be nourished by the latter, and those who nourish must be governed. This is the way of trade, and the same applies to government. Nourishing the people is the main work. . . . This is the natural principle (*shizen no jōri*). Yao and Shun's rule of all-under-Heaven was none other than this. [pp. 446–47]

In our country since the Middle Ages, wars have followed in succession; the imperial court has become weak; and various lords have parceled out groups of provinces, each defending his own territory while attacking others in turn. The people were regarded as so much waste, and the severity of forced labor and the arbitrary collection of military rations knew no bounds. Good government was swept away from the land; it was a period in which one who was skilled in warfare became a great lord and one who was clever in strategic planning became a renowned minister.

In the Keichō [1596–1615] and Genna [1615–1624] periods when a period of peace had come, these old ways remained. The great retainers on the war council, including Honda Sado-no-kami [1538–1616], all strove to make the foundation of the Tokugawa household supreme and firm, and not once was consideration given to the people of the realm. Although there are said to have been many outstanding rulers and ministers from that time to the present, all have continued the work of administering the private affairs of one household only. The various lords have followed this pattern, and according to the old ways handed down from their ancestors, they have planned with their ministers for the convenience and security of their own provinces with a barrier between neighboring provinces.

As a result, not all those known as great ministers in the shogunate and in each of the provinces have been able to disentangle themselves from the old ways of national seclusion. They have devoted themselves to their lords and their provinces, while their feelings of love and loyalty for the most part ignore the virtues of the good life and, on the contrary, invite the resentment of the people. All this leads to troubles in ruling the land. Japan has been split up accordingly and lacks a unified system. Therefore we must admit that Envoy Perry's observation in his *Expedition to Japan*[20] about the lack of governmental administration in Japan when he arrived here in 1855 was truly a discerning one. [pp. 447–48]

All systems, including currency, are transmitted and executed throughout the land by the power of the supreme government in the interest of the Tokugawa household, without in any way benefiting the empire or the people. For Perry to call this "lack of government" was indeed correct.

Under the system of national seclusion, Japan sought safety in isolation. Hence it experienced no wars or defeats. However, the world situation has vastly changed. Each country has broadly developed enlightened government.

America has followed three major policies from Washington's presidency on: first, to stop wars in accordance with divine intentions, because nothing is worse than violence and killing among nations; second, to broaden enlightened government by learning from all the countries of the world; and, third, to work with complete devotion for the peace and welfare of the people by entrusting the power of the president of the whole country to the wisest person instead of transmitting it to the son of the president, and by not having ministers bound in service to the ruler, they endeavor to work together with one aim: to achieve peace and serve the common good. All methods of administrative laws and practices and all men who are known as good and wise throughout the world are put into the country's service, and a very beneficial administration—one not solely in the interest of the rulers—is developed. [p. 448]

In England the government is based entirely on the popular will, and all government actions—large and small—are always debated by the people. . . . Furthermore, all countries, including Russia, have established schools and military academies, hospitals, orphanages, and schools for the deaf and dumb. The

---

20. *Nihon kikō*, the Japanese translation of *Narrative of the Expedition of an American Squadron to the China Seas and Japan Under the Command of Commodore M. C. Perry.*

governments are entirely based on moral principles, and they work hard for the benefit of the people, almost as was done in the three ancient periods of sage-rule in China.

Thus when the various countries attempt to open Japan's doors according to the way of international cooperation, who would not call Japan foolish for persisting in its old seclusionist views, for ruling for the benefit of private interests only, and for not knowing the principles of commercial intercourse? [pp. 448–49]

The present Manchu rulers of the Qing empire originated long ago from the northern barbarians, entered China as conquerors of the Ming empire, and changed their national customs. Their early emperors, like Kangxi and Qianlong, were wise and virtuous. Their rule was enlightened; they made innovations in culture and in teachings; and they brought about an effective peace. However during the Daoguang [1821–1851] and Xianfeng [1851–1862] eras, more than a hundred years after the opening of their country, China became weak with the corruption and extravagances of a long peace. It was unaware that countries beyond the seas had been expanding their knowledge by investigating science and logic, had been carrying out benevolent rule out of respect for justice, and had been strengthening their countries economically and militarily (*fukoku-kyōhei*); in other words, they were not like other foreign countries that had long since died out. China continued to hold the same views as it did in ancient days when it looked down with contempt on barbarian peoples.

As a result, during the latter years of the Daoguang era, China was badly defeated by England in the Opium War, which ended in the inevitable peace treaty. . . . Its humiliation was extreme.

Nevertheless the court, lacking men of ability and being refined and elegant but irresolute, did not have the least intention of learning from these costly experiences. [p. 449]

China and Japan are close neighbors. The results of China's debacle are right before our eyes, causing us to shudder so that we cannot calmly sit back and watch. Because of this, in accordance with divine virtue and sage teachings, we must observe today the conditions in all countries, greatly develop the system of our government in promoting the welfare of the people by innovating an enlightened rule, and earnestly make our country strong economically and militarily in order to avoid indignities from other countries. However, this does not mean that Western ways should necessarily be looked up to in all respects. [p. 450]

Military Reform: Strengthening the Military

In discussing arms for the present day, we can continue using the traditional hand-to-hand fighting, or we can stress the fierce Western rifle columns. What are their respective advantages and disadvantages?

In the old days, either way would do for Japan at home, but today we cannot refuse contacts with the overseas countries that have greatly developed their navigation. In the defense of an island country like ours, a navy is of prime importance in strengthening our military. In Japan up to the present, nothing had been heard concerning regulations for a navy. Furthermore, nothing had been observed about Western naval methods, so how could we know how to apply them? Navigation has progressed so much in the world today that we must start our discussion with the importance of a navy. Let us put aside for the time being the problem of Japan.

In Asia there is China, a great country facing the sea in the east. Early on, it developed a high material culture, and everything, including rice, wheat, millet and sorghum, has been plentiful for the livelihood of the people. In addition, there has been nothing lacking within its [China's] borders in regard to knowledge, skills, arts, goods of daily use, and entertainment. [But] from the imperial court down to the masses of the common people, extravagant habits have come to prevail. Although China permits foreigners to come and carry on trade, it has no intention of going out to seek goods. Moreover, it does not know how to obtain knowledge from others. For this reason, its arms are weak, and it must suffer indignities from various countries.

Europe is different from China. Its territory touches Asia on the east and is surrounded by seas on three sides. It is located in the northwest part of the earth, and compared with Asia it is small and is lacking in many things. Hence it was inevitable that it [Europe] should go out in quest of things. It was natural that its nations should develop navigation to carry on trade, to fight one another with warships, and to attempt establishing possessions with monopoly controls. [p. 451]

This year [1860] English and French forces attacked the Manchu empire, taking Tientsin and threatening the capital at Beijing. Russia is watching from the sidelines to take advantage of a stalemate and is like a tiger waiting to pounce on its prey. If Russia has designs of dominating China, then a great force must be mustered to prevent this. England must also be feared.

With the situation beyond the seas like this and growing worse all the time, how can Japan arouse its martial vigor when it alone basks in peace and comfort and drills its indolent troops as though it were child's play? Because there is no navy, a defense policy simply does not exist. . . .

For several decades Russia had been requesting permission for trade in vain. England's requests also had been rejected. Therefore America laid out its plans long and carefully, and in 1853 its warships entered Uraga Bay, and bluffing with its armed might, it eventually unlocked our closed doors. Thereafter in succession, the Russians, English, and French came and instituted procedures for peaceful trade.

Japan has consequently learned some information about conditions beyond the seas. But we still cling to our antiquated views and depend on our skill in hand-to-hand fighting. Some believe that we can quickly learn to fire in rifle formations and thus avoid indignities. Indeed, our outmoded practices are pitiable. [pp. 453–54]

Consider England: it prevents indignities being committed by foreigners, and it rules possessions. . . . In 1848 there were 673 well-known English navy ships, of which 420 were operating. Steamboats are included in these figures. There were about 15,000 cannons, 29,500 sailors, 13,500 marines, and 900 officers. In wartime, France had 1,000 navy ships and 184,000 sailors. Today it has more than 700 steam naval vessels, 88,000 fighting men, and 240 armored warships. Compared with earlier times, it has twice as many fighting men. In 1856 it had more than 200,000 troops.

In our Bunroku era [1592–1595] during the Toyotomi campaign in Korea, Japan had 350,000 troops, not an inconsiderable figure when compared with England's. Moreover, the circumstances of Japan and England are very much alike, and therefore our militarization should be patterned after that of England, with 420 naval vessels ships, 15,000 cannons, 29,500 sailors, 13,500 fighting men, and 900 officers in the navy. Military camps must be set up in the vicinity of our open ports, and warships must be stationed there in preparation for emergencies. They can go to one another's assistance when circumstances require, and they should be adequate to forestall any indignities. England is situated in the northwest, and its land is not good. But with the advantages of a maritime country, it has seized distant territories and today has become a great power.

Better yet, Japan lies in the central part of the earth, and we excel in the advantages of a sea environment. If the shogunate issued a new decree, aroused the characteristic vigor and bravery of the Japanese, and united the hearts of the entire nation with a firmly established military system based on clarified laws, not only would there be no need to fear foreign countries, but we could sail to various lands within a few years. And even if these lands should make armed attacks, we could, with our moral principles and courage, be looked up to for our benevolent ways.

Even though we need a navy, it cannot be built without an order from the shogunate. Nevertheless, if each province were to take action . . . we could, first of all, take those from the samurai class who have the desire to become apprentices in navigation and, in accordance with their ability, give them a moderate salary so that they could take care of their daily needs. They should live near the sea. At first they could sail fishing vessels and catch fish or sail to foreign lands in merchant vessels. Thus they would learn about the wind and waves while on the sea.

In addition, the shogunate should build two or three vessels of the cutter-schooner type. . . . According to this plan, each vessel would engage in trade, whaling, or the like. If it makes a profit from trade, it should be divided among the members of each ship. The original fund would again be put to use. With this experience in seeking profits according to man's normal impulses, impoverished samurai and others would greatly benefit. They could be trained in techniques while enjoying their work.

Furthermore, those with an interest could be taught the skills of surveying or astronomical observation. These can be learned in actual work in the field. The samurai who constantly go back and forth to foreign countries could broaden their knowledge through observation . . . Hence when the shogunate finally issues a new decree, they will most certainly be able to offer their services in the navy.

We have now discussed how navigation must be learned first and how this knowledge can eventually be put to naval use. But how can this [alone] be called strengthening the military (*kyōhei*)? It is said that no military reform surpasses the Way of the warrior (*bushidō*), which is to cultivate that spirit in actual practice. [pp. 454–56]

The Way of the Samurai

Shōnan was still teaching in Kumamoto when Matsudaira Yoshinobu (Shungaku) asked for his advice with regard to educational reform in 1853, a year of crisis with Perry's arrival. Shōnan responded at that time in writing, reviewing the history of schooling in China and Japan and deploring the overemphasis on bookishness and literary skills.[21] This had been a major issue among Neo-Confucians from the Song on down, highlighted by Zhu Xi's advocacy of universal schooling in his preface to the *Great Learning* and Zhu's stress on moral action rather than belles lettres. Shōnan's distinctive synthesis of the civil and military (absent in Zhu Xi) was summed up seven years later in the third of his theses. Here he reaffirms the mental and spiritual discipline, the "method of the mind" (*shinpō*) central to Neo-Confucian cultivation, and decries the influence of Zen in divorcing military arts from moral cultivation. The issue is between *bun*, understood as civil (i.e., civilizing, humanizing) arts, and letters in the sense of belles lettres or proficiency in literary styles. Shōnan argues for "letters" and military arts that are joined as one in serving humane, civilizing purposes, rather than as separate, value-free specializations devoid of any moral value.

Although couched in terms of the familiar "Way of the samurai," Shōnan is defining a new leadership ideal of humane practical action for the world at large, beyond simply "enriching the country (state) and strengthening the military."

Everyone knows that as samurai functions, letters (*bun*) and military arts (*bu*) are essential to the way of rulership. However, today what is known as letters means familiarity with the classics and histories or entering into superficial

---

21. Shōnan, *Questions and Answers on Schooling* (*Gakkō mondōsho*), in NST, vol. 55, pp. 428–33; for similar questions addressed in Kumamoto, see pp. 496–98.

discussions about the arts that have been passed down from ancient times, but it has turned out to be nothing more than memorizing texts and composing Chinese poetry. The military arts include horsemanship and swordplay, but in practice they are nothing more than discussing shades of meaning or lofty mysteries or else admiring the fierceness of swordplay or exaggerating the importance of beating others in combat. Therefore the scholar looks down on the warrior as being stupid, rough, and not of much use. Conversely, the warrior cannot stand the conceit and softness of the scholar. Both groups are unyielding in their disrespect for each other. Consequently a rift has opened up between the two avenues to rulership; this impasse is a general defect throughout Japan resulting from a failure to clarify the basis of the samurai way of life. [p. 458]

The original meaning of *bu* [warrior] lay in the realm of the mind-and-heart and not in techniques. Although we have not heard that the crossed lance (*daijūmonji*) of Lord Katō Kiyomasa [1559–1611] and the art of the spear (*tonbogiri*) of Lord Honda Tadakatsu [1568–1610][22] were transmitted and used in training, nevertheless they began with the disciplining of the whole mind-and-heart. [p. 459]

In the [Tokugawa] period when commanders of the empire could not train in actual warfare, warriors had to find a teacher to obtain this training. But both teachers and pupils stressed the method of the mind-and-heart (*shinpō*) over skill and technique. Consequently, in the old days those who were skilled invariably were masters of the situation. . . . Miyamoto Musashi [1584–1645][23] was a guest teacher for the Hosokawa family and worked on plans for provincial affairs. . . . Musashi's military teachings were based on the principle of the one-directedness of the mind, but he constantly taught moral self-reflection, self-control, regulating the household, and ordering the state [from the *Great Learning*] as the basis of the Way of the samurai. Simply to talk about empty, bare-handed thrusts was too much like the emptiness of Zen meditation and would degenerate into the moral void of the Emptiness principle, to the neglect of practical judgments in both study and military combat. [p. 459]

Generally, it is difficult to rule a state, during peace or war, without the right men, and it is hard to find such men among those who have not mastered both the civil and the military arts. Although it has been known in both past and present that this mastery of civil and military arts is essential to the education of men of ability and character, it is not well understood that its basis rests on the method of the mind-and-heart, without which the attempt to obtain men

---

22. Katō Kiyomasa added a short, slightly curved crosspiece about a foot from the tip of the lance, in order to make it easier to retract the lance after an enemy had been stabbed. *Tombogiri* originally was the name of Honda Tadakatsu's famous spear. He was one of Ieyasu's great generals.

23. Miyamoto Musashi, or Niten, was a master of Zen-style monochrome painting as well as of swordsmanship.

of character through training in today's letters and today's military arts is like trying to cook sand into a meal. We know that as a result, it is difficult to obtain men of both character and ability and thus to rule the state properly. [pp. 460–61]

Through letters to clarify the principles of moral duty as an aid to good government and through the military arts to train for courageous combat so as to strengthen the body for any emergency—these are carried out in those feudal domains known for their realization of the Way, but when the basic meaning of the civil and military arts is lost, the effectiveness of schools in training men of ability and character is lost. [p. 461]

If a person wishes to learn the Way of the warrior based on moral principles, he must study the Way of serving his lord or father on down to the conduct of intercourse with his friends, and [he] must also study the Way of regulating his household and ordering the state. [p. 461]

As can be seen in [Zhu Xi's] preface to the *Great Learning*, the main idea of schools in the three ancient dynasties of China was to teach the Way of "self-discipline for the governance of men," which began with such household duties as "sprinkling and sweeping, and responding to others," all based on the individual's moral nature, with each person exerting himself to fulfill his proper function and without any compulsion whatever being exerted on the others.[24]

By contrast, in schools today the classics and histories are memorized and discussed, and the [separate] military arts are practiced. Rules and systems are established,[25] and all pupils are driven to acquire [the specialized] knowledge to be used in their occupation. Depending on their strong points, some go into letters, [and] some into military training; thus they become divided into opposing factions within the school. As a result, letters lack the [civilizing] function of letters, and the military arts lose their own substantial reality. [pp. 462–63]

All men have parents; all samurai have lords. To serve lords and parents with loyalty and filiality, to know the Way for humans to act like true human beings, is inherent in their Heaven-endowed moral nature and does not require formal instruction. To pursue the underlying principles of the moral nature and correct one's conduct in accordance with the Way is the civilizing function of letters; to control the mind-and-heart and discipline one's impetuosity, and to test these

---

24. The first reference is to Zhu Xi, preface to the *Great Learning*; the second, to Zhu Xi, *Elementary Learning*. See de Bary and Bloom, eds., *Sources of Chinese Tradition*, 2nd ed., vol. 1, pp. 722–24, 803–4. Shōnan does not disagree with Zhu Xi, but only with later Neo-Confucians who fail to fulfill these aims.

25. Contrary to Zhu Xi's recommendations in his postface to *Articles of the White Deer Grotto Academy*, which deplored the use of rules and regulations. See de Bary and Bloom, eds., *Sources of Chinese Tradition*, 2nd ed., vol. 1, pp. 743–44.

in skilled practice so as to perform worthy deeds, is the function of the military arts. Although the method of testing appears to be no different today, the attempt to control the mind through special techniques is indeed fundamentally different. . . . The method of mind control (*shinpō*) used earlier by persons [in Neo-Confucianism], practicing techniques for cleansing impurities from the mind [in quiet sitting] and engaging in lofty [philosophical] discourse about it, is nothing but empty talk. [p. 463]

Teachings on rulership should follow the example of the three ancient dynasties of China, during which there were great sages above and many wise men under them. As a result of these teachings, the school system also aided in rulership and produced men of character and ability. Even if the ability and virtues of rulers and ministers today do not equal those of these earlier dynasties, there is no alternative to using the teachings of the ancients as goals. Hence both rulers and ministers must realize that they cannot depart from the unified way of civil and military arts. The ruler must exercise affection, respect, modesty, justice, and frankness. He must study the practice of these among the ancient sages and worthies, and he must develop them in military exercises. In carrying out these sage teachings based on their natural sentiments and moral relations, he must lead his ministers with the greatest sincerity and compassion in ruling the people.

A high officer must conform to the mind-and-heart of the ruler and establish the principle of concern for his country and love for his prince. He must overcome his own extravagances and practice the virtue of economy; he must strain his resolves and exert his body without yielding to hardships and without dreading dangers, thus building up his strength and perfecting his whole being. The fundamentals of the Way of the samurai are necessarily like these. A man must tread the footsteps of the sages without regret and make himself an example to the people. He must listen to the opinions of others with frankness and self-effacement. He must develop the good practice of taking ideas from the people. He must consult with the various officials in order to carry out the ruler's plans, promote the good, and teach those who are untrained.

The various officers also receive orders from their lord and absolutely must not inject their own wishes. They must perform their respective functions with fidelity and sincerity. They must follow the samurai's Way with disinterestedness and integrity, encourage their colleagues, and govern those below in the service of the common good. Also, they must enlighten those who teach the civil and military arts, thus dispelling ignorance. They must discard persistent and base, antiquated customs. With lord and minister having due regard for each other, and teachers and students listening to each other, the true civil and military arts together will benefit the teachings of rulership.

If it is so done, the teaching of the civil and military arts and the administration of schools will then serve as the foundation of government, and subordinates will naturally turn to the Way. They will naturally resolve to live up to the Way of the samurai. If all the people are of one mind with their lord and ministers, they will grasp the fundamentals of everything when they study the classics and histories and practice with sword and lance. Thus they will not be drawn into empty letters and one-sided military arts. They will be completely able to perform their duties. This is indeed the teaching of the true civil and military arts. Customs will become gentle and genuine. Then will there be any doubt that men of character and ability will arise? [pp. 464–65]

[Yokoi Shōnan, *Kokuze sanron*, in *NST*, vol. 55, pp. 439–65; trans. adapted from Miyauchi, "Kokuze sanron," pp. 156–86; WTdB]

YOSHIDA SHŌIN: DEATH-DEFYING HEROISM

Torajirō	Torajirō—
Nijū-ikkai mōshi	Twenty-one times a death-defier!

Yoshida Torajirō (better known by his pen name, Shōin, 1830–1859), whose heroism drew acclaim like this from young Japanese of the Meiji Restoration and even won admiration abroad through the writings of Robert Louis Stevenson, was born in the southwestern fief of Chōshū and adopted into the family of a samurai in rather humble circumstances. His father, a military instructor, found it necessary to divide his time between teaching and cultivating the soil in order to earn a frugal living, and Shōin, who succeeded to the direction of his father's school at a very young age, always remained a peasant at heart— earnest, unsophisticated, and reflecting the raw energy of the earth. From his father, he also inherited a deep devotion to the precepts of Yamaga Sokō, whose teachings on the Way of the warrior (later known as *bushidō*) had been handed down in the family school. Shōin also acquired a close acquaintance with the principles of military science as explained in the ancient Chinese classic Sunzi's *Art of War*.[26] Perhaps an even more decisive influence on Shōin was the book of *Mencius*, whose idealism, assertion of the inherent worth of the individual, and opposition to arbitrary authority instilled in Shōin a sense of his own mission in the world and impatience with all external restraints.

An avid learner, and impressed by Sunzi's *Art of War* with the importance of military intelligence, Shōin traveled around, picking up what information he could about the West in Nagasaki and from such progressive teachers as Yokoi Shōnan and Sakuma Shōzan. On a trip to northern Japan, he also visited the school at Mito, which was proclaiming Japan's divine mission to turn back the West and to establish a world empire under the legitimate imperial dynasty. After the failure of his ill-planned attempt to stow away on one of Matthew

---

26. See de Bary and Bloom, eds., *Sources of Chinese Tradition*, 2nd ed., vol. 1, pp. 213–23.

Perry's ships, which ended in his being confined to his native fief, Shōin was permitted by his indulgent feudal lord to resume teaching. With *Mencius* as his main text, he stressed Mencius's implicit justification of redress against an unworthy and incompetent ruler and pointed to the shogun's failure to fulfill the function indicated by his title of "barbarian-subduing generalissimo" (*sei-i tai shōgun*). Throughout the ranks of the aristocracy, however, Shōin found a similar incapacity to assume the responsibilities of leadership in the crisis facing Japan. He became convinced that only among those close to the soil and untainted by the corruption of wealth and high office were there men selfless and fearless enough to overthrow the regime. To arouse these stalwarts of the countryside, only dedicated leadership and an inspiring example of the true warrior spirit were needed.

Shōin's call to action contained some of the ingredients of a modern revolution: the overthrow of the hereditary feudal aristocracy and the raising up of the Japanese common man to a role of importance. Here were the seeds of epochal changes that were realized by the Restoration—the abolition of feudalism, the emancipation of the peasants, and the arming of them in modernized forces—changes initiated by such youthful leaders and former disciples of Shōin as Kido Kōin, a key figure in the dismantling of feudalism; Itō Hirobumi, framer of the Meiji constitution; and Yamagata Aritomo, father of the modern Japanese army. But theirs was a revolution aimed more at revitalizing the national leadership than at completely overturning the social order. Shōin's dissatisfaction with the status quo was inspired not by class consciousness or a concern for the rights of any economic group but by disdain for the failure of the aristocracy, and especially the shogunate, to measure up to their responsibilities and a belief in the need for heroic individuals to stand up in their stead.

Typically, therefore, Shōin's mind was not on planning and organizing for political action but on some spectacular act of bravery that would dramatize the need for selfless leadership. Thus he conceived the idea of assassinating the shogun's emissary to the imperial court, whose mission was to secure the emperor's approval for a treaty with the United States. Considering his impetuosity and the previous failure of his ill-considered plans, it is not surprising that this daring plot was detected and quashed. Sent as a prisoner to the shogunate capital at Edo, Shōin was beheaded in 1859 at the age of thirty. But in death, his dreams were fulfilled: he became a hero to a whole generation, and his self-sacrifice was the spark that lit the minds and hearts of Japan's new revolutionary leaders. Reverently his patriotic disciples, including Itō and Kido, took home his remains, and with deep emotion, young Japanese of the new era recited the two poems that were his last testament in prison:

Oya wo omō	The son's solicitude for his mother
Kokoro ni masaru	Is surpassed by
Oyagokoro	Her solicitude for him

Kyō no otozure	When she hears what befell me today,
Ika ni kikuran?	How will she take it?
Kaku sureba	That such an act
Kaku naru mono to	Would have such a result
Shiri nagara	I knew well enough.
Yamu ni yamarenu	What made me do it anyhow
Yamato damashii	Was the spirit of Yamato.

But if this spirit was inspirational to Shōin's followers in the subsequent Restoration movement, it also left a less beneficial, longer-term legacy: the idea that spectacular examples of individual bravery and impetuous, direct action could change the course of history, as in the "government by assassination" of the 1930s.

ON LEADERSHIP

In these passages from Yoshida Shōin's writing, it is not difficult to see the same intense belief in the resoluteness of the individual will as the defining characteristic of the Confucian noble man—that is, in his self-sacrificing samurai incarnation—already noted in the later thinkers of the Zhu Xi, and especially Wang Yangming, schools in early-nineteenth-century Japan (see chaps. 31 and 32).

What is important in a leader is a resolute will and determination. A man may be versatile and learned, but if he lacks resoluteness and determination, of what use will he be? [vol. 8, p. 146]

Once the will is resolved, one's spirit is strengthened. Even a peasant's will is hard to deny, but a samurai of resolute will can sway ten thousand men. [vol. 5, p. 239]

He who aspires to greatness should read and study, pursuing the True Way with such a firm resolve that he is perfectly straightforward and open, rises above the superficialities of conventional behavior, and refuses to be satisfied with the petty or commonplace. [vol. 2, p. 26]

Once a man's will is set, he need no longer rely on others or expect anything from the world. His vision encompasses Heaven and earth, past and present, and the tranquillity of his heart is undisturbed. [vol. 3, p. 145]

Life and death, union and separation, follow closely after each other. Nothing is steadfast but the will; nothing endures but one's achievements. These alone count in life. [vol. 5, p. 334]

To consider oneself different from ordinary men is wrong, but it is right to hope that one will not be like ordinary men. [vol. 2, p. 25]

[*Yoshida Shōin zenshū*, vol. 2, pp. 25–26; vol. 3, p. 145;
vol. 5, pp. 239, 334; vol. 8, p. 146; RT, WTdB]

ON BEING DIRECT

In relations with others, one should express resentment and anger openly and straightforwardly. If one cannot express them openly and straightforwardly, the only thing to do is forget about them. To harbor grievances is to act like a weak and petty man—in truth, it can only be called cowardice. The mind of the noble man is like Heaven. When it is resentful or angry, it thunders forth its indignation. But once having loosed its feelings, it is like a sunny day with a clear sky: within the heart there remains not the trace of a cloud. Such is the beauty of true manliness.

[*Yoshida Shōin zenshū*, vol. 3, p. 239; WTdB]

ARMS AND LEARNING

These next excerpts mark two important stages in Shōin's intellectual development: first, when he was led by his studies in military science to seek a deeper knowledge of classical philosophy and, second, when he realized the importance of firsthand knowledge of the West. It was characteristic of him that he expressed this latter realization in typically Confucian terms.

Those who take up the science of war must not fail to master the [Confucian] classics. The reason is that arms are dangerous instruments and not necessarily forces for good. How can we safely entrust them to any but those who have schooled themselves in the precepts of the classics and use these weapons for the realization of humanity and rightness? To quell violence and disorder, to repulse barbarians and brigands, to rescue living souls from agony and torture, to save the nation from imminent downfall—these are the true ends of humanity and rightness. If, on the contrary, arms are taken up in a selfish struggle to win land, goods, people, and the implements of war, is it not the worst of all evils, the most heinous of all offenses? If, further, the study of offensive and defensive warfare, of the way to certain victory in all encounters, is not based on those principles that should govern their employment, who can say that such a venture will not result in just such a misfortune? Therefore I say that those who take up the science of war must not fail to master the classics. [vol. 2, p. 145]

What I mean by the "pursuit of learning" is not the ability to read classical texts and study ancient history but to be fully acquainted with conditions all over the world and to have a keen awareness of what is going on abroad and around us. Now from what I can see, world trends and conditions are still unsettled, and as long as they remain unsettled, there is still a chance that something can be done. First, therefore, we must rectify conditions in our own domain, after which conditions in other domains can be rectified. This having been done, conditions at court can be rectified, and finally, conditions through-out the whole world can be rectified. First one must set an example oneself, and then it can be extended progressively to others.[27] This is what I mean by the "pursuit of learning." [vol. 4, p. 115]

[*Yoshida Shōin zenshū*, vol. 2, p. 145; vol. 4, p. 115; WTdB]

FACING DEATH

From the beginning of the year to the end, day and night, morning and evening, in action and repose, in speech and in silence, the warrior must keep death constantly before him and always have in mind that the one death [that he has to give] should not be suffered in vain. In other words, [he must have perfect control over his own death], just as if he were holding an intemperate steed in rein. Only he who truly keeps death in mind in this way can understand what is meant by [Yamaga Sokō's maxim of] "preparedness." [vol. 4, p. 238]

If the body dies, it does no harm to the mind, but if the mind dies, one can no longer act as a man, even though the body survives. [vol. 8, p. 299]

If a general and his men fear death and are apprehensive about possible defeat, then they will unavoidably suffer defeat and death. But if they make up their minds, from the general down to the last foot soldier, not to think of living but only of standing in one place and facing death together, then, although they may have no other thought than meeting death, they will instead hold on to life and win victory. [vol. 1, p. 101]

[*Yoshida Shōin zenshū*, vol. 1, p. 101; vol. 4, p. 238; vol. 8, p. 299; WTdB]

SELFISHNESS AND HEROISM

A strong undercurrent of antagonism toward the idle rich, inspired by the traditional disapproval of self-indulgence found in Confucianism and Buddhism, runs through the following passages. Here Shōin stands as a link between the old samurai ideals of frugality and self-sacrificing service and the same virtues as exemplified by peasant soldiers in the service of twentieth-century Japanese nationalism.

The first passage is a commentary on a poem by the Chinese poet Li Bo, who points out that the most beautiful things in the world, the beauties of nature, are no one's private possession and may be enjoyed by all, free of charge.

Nowadays all people live selfishly and seek only the leisure in which to indulge their own desires. They look on all the beauties of nature—the rivers and

---

27. This type of reasoning follows the opening text attributed to Confucius in the *Great Learning* and echoed by Shōin's teacher, Sakuma Shōzan.

mountains, the breeze and the moon—as their own to enjoy, forgetting what the shrine of the Sun Goddess stands for [i.e., that everything is held in trust from Heaven]. The common man thinks of his life as his own and refuses to perform his duty to his lord. The samurai regards his household as his own private possession and refuses to sacrifice his life for his state. The feudal lords regard their domains as their own and refuse to serve king and country. Unwilling to serve king and country, at home they cherish only the objects of desire, and abroad they willingly yield to the foreign barbarians, inviting defeat and destruction. Thus the scenic beauties they enjoy will not long remain in their possession. [vol. 4, p. 175]

As things stand now, the feudal lords are content to look on while the shogunate carries on in a high-handed manner. Neither the lords nor the shogun can be depended on [to save the country], and so our only hope lies in grassroots heroes.[28] [vol. 5, p. 315]

When I consider the state of things in our fief, I find that those who hold official positions and receive official stipends are incapable of the utmost in loyalty and patriotic service. Loyalty of the usual sort, perhaps, but if it is true loyalty and service you seek, then you must abandon this fief and plan a grassroots uprising. [vol. 9, p. 239]

It seems hopeless, hopeless. Those who eat meat [at public expense] are a mean, selfish lot, and so the country is doomed. Our only hope lies in the grassroots folk who eat our traditional food [i.e., rice]. [vol. 6, p. 164]

If Heaven does not completely abandon this land of the gods, there must be an uprising of grassroots heroes. [vol. 9, p. 297]

If the plan [to intercept the shogunate emissary to the Kyoto court] is to be carried out, it can be done only with men from the grass roots. Wearing silk brocades, eating dainty food, hugging beautiful women, and fondling darling children are the only things hereditary officials care about. To revere the emperor and expel the barbarian is no concern of theirs. If this time it is my misfortune to die, may my death inspire at least one or two men of steadfast will to rise up and uphold this principle after my death. [vol. 9, p. 286]

[*Yoshida Shōin zenshū*, vol. 4, p. 175; vol. 5, p. 315; vol. 6, p. 164; vol. 9, pp. 239, 286, 297; RT, WTdB]

FUKUZAWA YUKICHI: PIONEER OF WESTERNIZATION

"Here lies," the epitaph on a monument to Fukuzawa reads, "a man of self-reliance and self-respect with a worldwide vision." It is probably safe to say that

---

28. *Sōmō eiyū* means, literally, "Grass-clump heroes."

no other Japanese in those turbulent pre-Restoration days had such wide vision as Fukuzawa Yukichi (1834–1901), nor in the reconstruction period that followed did any Japanese of his renown and ability live the life of an independent commoner with such native dignity.

Born in the Kyushu province of Bungo, which had produced such progressive thinkers as Miura Baien and Hoashi Banri, Fukuzawa came from the lower levels of the feudal aristocracy. Always alert and energetic, he began studying Dutch very early in life and then became a pioneer student of English. As early as 1860, he took advantage of an opportunity to visit America with a shogunate mission, made a return visit in 1867, and in between traveled to European countries, especially England. When he finally started writing and lecturing about Western civilization and its achievements, it was on the basis of a wider firsthand knowledge of the West than any other Japanese of his time could boast. Hale, handsome, and of a sanguine nature, Fukuzawa radiated a lively enthusiasm that helped convey his ideas to others. Around him in his little school of Keiō, he drew ambitious young Japanese in growing numbers, men who became leaders of the new Japan in its political, economic, and social reconstruction. As a writer, he probably surpassed all his contemporaries in versatility and persuasiveness. His books sold millions of copies, bringing him a fortune and giving him the financial independence that enabled him to live the life of a commoner without having to accept a position in the government. It also provided him with the means to establish a newspaper through which he could freely voice his opinions on current questions.

Because of the practical and popular character of his writings, Fukuzawa's influence was widely felt. He aimed less at converting the scholarly elite to a new philosophy than at conveying to great numbers of Japanese his enthusiasm for the tangible advantages of life in the West. Not all these advantages were of a material sort. Fukuzawa's appreciation of Western civilization was surprisingly broad, and while he lacked any deep knowledge of its background or traditions, he sensed that the meaning of the West was to be found as much in the moral tales told to its children or in the procedure for running meetings as in treatises on natural or political science. If there is any single influence from the West that Fukuzawa most clearly exemplified and fostered, it is British utilitarianism and liberalism, a trend especially strong in the early decades of the Restoration. Linked closely to this was his prevailing belief in human progress through the wider application of the methods of the natural sciences. Increasingly toward the end of his life, however, Fukuzawa expressed the conviction that the moral and religious regeneration of the Japanese was indispensable to their future progress.

Fukuzawa's abilities as a writer, a publicist, and an educator gave him great prominence in Japan's public life in the late nineteenth century. The following excerpts reveal his early reactions to the West and Japan's reactions to him as a proponent of things Western. In subsequent chapters, he also is represented as an advocate of "civilization and enlightenment" (chap. 36) and educational modernization (chap. 38).

THE AUTOBIOGRAPHY OF FUKUZAWA YUKICHI

This book was dictated in 1898 shortly before Fukuzawa's death and was later translated into English by a grandson, Kiyooka Eiichi, under the title *The Autobiography of Fukuzawa Yukichi* (1934). These selections pertain to his first visits to America and Europe and to his founding of a private school for Western studies and of a private newspaper.

I am willing to admit my pride in Japan's accomplishments [in rapid modernization]. The facts are these: It was not until the sixth year of Kaei (1853) that a steamship was seen for the first time; it was only in the second year of Ansei (1855) that we began to study navigation from the Dutch in Nagasaki; by 1860, the science was sufficiently understood to enable us to sail a ship across the Pacific. This means that about seven years after the first sight of a steam ship, after only about five years of practice, the Japanese people made a trans-Pacific crossing without help from foreign experts. I think we can without undue pride boast before the world of this courage and skill. As I have shown, the Japanese officers were to receive no aid from Captain Brooke throughout the voyage. Even in taking observations, our officers and the Americans made them independently of each other. Sometimes they compared their results, but we were never in the least dependent on the Americans.

As I consider all the other peoples of the Orient as they exist today, I feel convinced that there is no other nation which has the ability or the courage to navigate a steamship across the Pacific after a period of five years of experience in navigation and engineering. Not only in the Orient would this feat stand as an act of unprecedented skill and daring. Even Peter the Great of Russia, who went to Holland to study navigation, with all his attainments in the science could not have equaled this feat of the Japanese. Without doubt, the famous Emperor of Russia was a man of exceptional genius, but his people did not respond to his leadership in the practice of science as did our Japanese in this great adventure. [pp. 118–19]

On our part there were many confusing and embarrassing moments [in our travels abroad], for we were quite ignorant of the customs and habits of American life. . . . Things social, political, and economic proved most inexplicable. One day, on a sudden thought, I asked a gentleman where the descendants of George Washington might be. He replied, "I think there is a woman who is directly descended from Washington. I don't know where she is now, but I think I have heard she is married." His answer was so very casual that it shocked me.

Of course, I knew that America was a republic with a new president every four years, but I could not help feeling that the family of Washington should be regarded as apart from all other families. My reasoning was based on the reverence in Japan for the founders of the great lines of rulers—like that for Ieyasu of the Tokugawa family of shoguns, really deified in the popular mind. So I remember the intense astonishment I felt at receiving this indifferent answer about the Washington family. As for scientific inventions and industrial machinery, there was no great novelty in them for me. It was more in matters of life and conventions of social custom and ways of thinking that I found myself at a loss in America. [pp. 121–25]

While we were in London, a certain member of the Parliament sent us a copy of a bill which he said he had proposed in the House under the name of the party to which he belonged. The bill was a protest against the arrogant attitude of the British minister to Japan, Alcock, who had at times acted as if Japan were a country conquered by military force. One of the instances mentioned in the bill was that of Alcock's riding his horse into the sacred temple grounds of Shiba, an unpardonable insult to the Japanese.

On reading the copy of this bill, I felt as if "a load had been lifted from my chest." After all, the foreigners were not all "devils." I had felt that Japan was enduring some pointed affronts on the part of the foreign ministers who presumed on the ignorance of our government. But now that I had actually come to the minister's native land, I found that there were among them some truly impartial and warmhearted human beings. So after this I grew even more determined in my doctrine of free intercourse with the rest of the world. [pp. 138–39]

During this mission in Europe I tried to learn some of the most commonplace details of foreign culture. I did not care to study scientific or technical subjects while on the journey, because I could study them as well from books after I had returned home. But I felt that I had to learn the more common matters of daily life directly from the people, because the Europeans would not describe them in books as being too obvious. Yet to us those common matters were the most difficult to comprehend.

For instance, when I saw a hospital, I wanted to know how it was run—who paid the running expenses; when I visited a bank, I wished to learn how the money was deposited and paid out. By similar firsthand queries, I learned something of the postal system and the military conscription then in force in France but not in England. A perplexing institution was representative government.

When I asked a gentleman what the "election law" was and what kind of institution the Parliament really was, he simply replied with a smile, meaning I suppose that no intelligent person was expected to ask such a question. But these were the things most difficult of all for me to understand. In this connection, I learned that there were different political parties—the Liberal and the Conservative—who were always "fighting" against each other in the government.

For some time it was beyond my comprehension to understand what they were "fighting" for, and what was meant, anyway, by "fighting" in peace time. "This man and that man are 'enemies' in the House," they would tell me. But these "enemies" were to be seen at the same table, eating and drinking with each other. I felt as if I could not make much out of this. It took me a long time, with some tedious thinking, before I could gather a general notion of these separate mysterious facts. In some of the more complicated matters, I might achieve an understanding five or ten days after they were explained to me. But all in all, I learned much from this initial tour of Europe. [pp. 142–44]

In the beginning my reputation in my lord's household was very bad, for I was simply an upstart samurai who had studied some foreign sciences, traveled in strange lands, and was now writing books to advocate very unconventional ideas; moreover I was finding fault with the venerable Chinese culture—a very dangerous heretic. I can imagine the kind of reports made about me to the inner household.

But when years passed and times had changed, the whole country turning inevitably toward the new culture, my class came to find that this Fukuzawa was not so spiteful a person as was thought and that he might really prove useful in some way. A certain chancellor named Shimazu Yutarō was the first to see the situation and speak well of me in the feudal household.

At that time there was a certain lady dowager in the household whom people called Horen-in Sama. She was of very noble lineage, having come from the great house of Hitotsu-bashi, and now at her advanced age she was held in particular respect by the whole household.

In conversing with this lady, Shimazu described much of the medicine and navigation and other sciences of the Western lands; also the customs which were very different from our own. The most remarkable of all the Western customs, he told her, was the relation between men and women; there men and women had equal rights, and monogamy was the strict rule in any class of people—this, at least, might be a merit of the Western customs.

The lady dowager could not help being moved by this conversation, for she had had some unhappy trials in earlier days. As if her eyes were suddenly opened to something new, she expressed a desire to make the acquaintance of Fukuzawa. When I was admitted to her presence, she found that I was quite an ordinary man—though often called a heretic, I had no horns on my head nor tail beneath my formal skirt. So she gradually began to place confidence in me. Many years later Shimazu told me all about this, and then I learned how I was first admitted to the inner household of the lord. [pp. 326–27]

[The Autobiography of Fukuzawa Yukichi, trans. Kiyooka, pp. 118–44, 326–27]

REFORM PROPOSALS OF SAKAMOTO RYŌMA, SAIGŌ TAKAMORI, AND ŌKUBO TOSHIMICHI

In the events leading up to the Restoration, negotiations were conducted among the principal proponents of imperial restoration as to what steps should be taken to replace the Tokugawa shogunate and inaugurate imperial rule. Two proposals by leading players in the process outlined programs on whose basis the transition could be made from shogunal to imperial rule.

One was offered by Sakamoto Ryōma (1835–1867), a Tosa samurai and imperial loyalist, who facilitated a united front between the powerful Satsuma and Chōshū domains. The other was drawn up by Satsuma leaders, including Saigō Takamori (1828–1877) and Ōkubo Toshimichi (1830–1878), who became prominent figures in the early Meiji scene (see chap. 35).

These proposals reflect a shift in emphasis from Sakamoto's moderate stance, emphasizing cooperation between the shogunate and the court to achieve national unity, to the outright replacement of the shogunate by a new political process. Likewise, the early emphasis in the first proposal on the importance of "public consultation" (*kōgi*) or public opinion (*kōron*), assuming a broad consensus among the participants on the basis of which problems could be resolved, gives way in the second document to a call for decisive leadership and direct action, taking the place of what is impatiently dismissed as endless debate on the matter.

SAKAMOTO RYŌMA: EIGHT-POINT PROPOSAL, 1867

1. Political power of the entire country should be returned to the Imperial Court, and all decrees should be issued by the Court.
2. There should be established an Upper and a Lower Legislative House which should participate in making decisions pertaining to all governmental policies. All governmental policies should be decided on the basis of deliberation openly arrived at (*kōgi*).
3. Men of ability among the court nobles, daimyo, and people at large should be appointed as councillors and receive appropriate offices and titles. Those sinecure positions of the past should be abolished.
4. In dealing with foreign countries, appropriate regulations should be newly established which would take into account broadly the deliberation openly arrived at.
5. The laws and regulations (*ritsu-ryō*) of earlier times should be scrutinized [to preserve only those provisions that still are applicable], and a great new code to last forever should be promulgated.
6. The navy should be properly expanded.

7. An Imperial Guard [directly controlled by the imperial court and not dependent on the *bakufu* or various *han*] should be set up to defend the capital.
8. There should be a law established to equalize the value of gold, silver, and goods with those of foreign countries.

The above eight-point program is proposed after due consideration of the present state of affairs in the nation. When this is proclaimed both internally and externally to all the countries, it becomes inconceivable to think of engaging in the urgent talk of alleviating the current crisis outside of this program. If with determination these policies are carried out, the fortunes of His Majesty will be restored, national strength will increase, and it will not be difficult to attain the position of equality with all other nations. We pray that based on the enlightened and righteous reason (*dōri*), the Imperial Government will act decisively to undertake the path of renewal and reform of the country.

[Lu, ed., Japan, pp. 301–2]

LETTER FROM SAIGŌ TAKAMORI AND ŌKUBO TOSHIMICHI ON THE IMPERIAL RESTORATION, 1867

This letter is addressed to Iwakura Tomomi, a leading figure at the Kyoto court.

When with great resolve, a policy of establishing the foundation for the imperial restoration is proclaimed, there is bound to be a great deal of confusion. People have been contaminated by the old habit of settling down into the more than two hundred years of peace. If we decide to resort to arms, it can conversely have the salutary effect of renewing the spirit of all people under Heaven, and pacifying the central regions of the country. Therefore we deem it the most urgent task to decide for war, and to find victory in the most difficult situation.

It is a well-established principle that one must not take up arms because one loves warfare. However, if everything is allowed to proceed as it is, and the great issue of how to govern the country is delegated merely to the hard work of the Imperial Court and to the consensus (*kōron*) reached by the three highest positions within the Council of State (Dajōkan), then war is to be preferred. In the olden days, when great works were begun, how to conserve such great works was hardly decided by debates. Even those [debaters] who were exceptionally well endowed did not escape criticism from later generations of scholars. The situation is even more critical today with the deteriorating conditions. We urge you to think through the matter carefully and consider all the alternatives. It is most important that the first step in the new government is not a mistaken one.

On the important matter of how to deal with the Tokugawa family, we have been informed of the outline of a secret decision. We heartily concur with your decision through a secret edict to order the [former] Lords of Owari (Tokugawa Yoshikatsu, 1824–1883) and Echizen (Matsudaira Yoshinaga, 1828–1890) to become intermediaries in arranging for the shogun's immediate repentance and restitution. This is indeed an appropriate and magnanimous gesture.

The danger which has befallen our imperial country today is due to the great crime committed by the *bakufu*. This fact is very well established, and two months earlier, on the thirteenth day, you did reach a decision to impose certain penalties. At the present time, regardless of whatever arguments may be advanced, it is necessary to demote the shogun to the position of a mere daimyo, reduce his official rank by one degree, let him return his domains, and let him ask for pardon of his sins.[29] Unless these measures are followed, whatever we do will be contrary to the consensus [*kōron* or, broadly, "public opinion"] and there is no way the public can be satisfied. These secret understandings which we reached previously must not be changed in any manner.

If the mediation through the Lords of Owari and Echizen does not succeed, it shows very clearly that the shogun fails to appreciate the magnanimity of the Imperial Court, works against the consensus, and is not truly penitent. In that event an imperial command must be given immediately and resolutely to implement the above measure. . . .

If we fail to take these appropriate measures, we will be acting contrary to principle and to the consensus at the initial phase of the imperial restoration. Then the fortunes of the imperial power will suffer, and the great ills of the past years will resurface. . . . May we beg you to consider the matter carefully, and also consult with the three ministers to arrive at a resolute decision. . . .

> *Eighth day of the twelfth month, 1867*
> *Iwashita Sajiuemon*
> *Saigō Kichinosuke (Takamori)*
> *Ōkubo Ichizō (Toshimichi)*

> [Lu, ed., *Japan*, pp. 302–3]

---

29. Saigō originally favored death for Yoshinobu, but British minister Harry Parkes advised Saigō that in such an event, all foreign powers might side with the *bakufu*.

BIBLIOGRAPHY

SERIES AND COLLECTIONS ABBREVIATIONS

BNB   *Bonaben ershisi shi.* 820 fascs. Shanghai: Commercial Press, 1930–1937.

CSJC   *Congshu jicheng.* 1,384 titles in 2,000 vols. Shanghai, 1935–1937.

NKBT   *Nihon koten bungaku taikei.* 100 vols. Tokyo: Iwanami shoten, 1958–1968.

NKSS   *Nihon kyōiku shi shiryōsho.* 5 vols. Compiled by Nihon kokumin seishin bunka kenkyūjo. Tokyo: Kokumin seishin bunka kenkyūjo, 1937.

NKST   *Nihon kindai shisō taikei.* 24 vols. Tokyo: Iwanami shoten, 1988–1992.

NKZ   *Nihon koten zenshū.* 266 vols. Tokyo: Nihon koten zenshū kankōkai, 1925–1944.

NST   *Nihon shisō taikei.* 67 vols. Tokyo: Iwanami shoten, 1970–1982.

SBBY   *Sibu beiyao.* 537 titles in 1,372 fascs. Shanghai: Zhong guo shuju, 1927–1935.

SKQS   [Wenyuan ge] *Siku quanshu.* 1,500 vols. Taibei: Taiwan shangwu yinshu guan, 1983–1986.

PRIMARY AND SECONDARY SOURCES

Aizawa Seishisai. *Kōdōkanki, Taishoku kanwa.* In NST, vol. 53.

Aizawa Seishisai. "Shinron." In *Sōsho Nihon no shisōka*, vol. 36. Tokyo: Meitoku shuppansha, 1981.

Aoki, Michiko Y., trans. *Izumo no kuni fudoki*. Tokyo: Sophia University Press, 1971.

Aoki, Michiko Y., and Margaret B. Dardess. "The Popularization of Samurai Values: A Sermon by Hosoi Heishū." *Monumenta Nipponica* 31 (1976): 393–413.

Arai Hakuseki. *Arai Hakuseki zenshū*. Edited by Imaizumi Teisuke and Ichijima Kenkichi. 6 vols. Tokyo: Yoshikawa hanshichi, 1905–1907.

Arai Hakuseki. *Oritaku shiba no ki*. Edited by Odaka Toshirō and Matsumura Akira. In *NKBT*, vol. 95.

Arai Hakuseki. *Seiyō kibun*. Edited by Miyazaki Michio. Tokyo: Heibonsha, 1968.

Asaka Tanpaku. *Dai Nihon shi sansō*. Compiled by Matsumoto Sannosuke and Ogura Yoshiko. In *NST*, vol. 48. Tokyo: Iwanami shoten, 1974.

Asaka Tanpaku. *Resso seiseki*. 20 vols. Tokyo: Tokugawa Akitake, 1978.

Asami Kōsai. *Kinsei buke shisō*. In *NST*, vol. 27.

Aston, W. G., trans. *Nihongi*. 2 vols. In *The Transactions and Proceedings of the Japan Society, London*, supplement no. 1. London: Kegan, Paul, Trench, and Trübner, 1896.

Aston, W. G., trans. *Nihongi: Chronicles of Japan from the Earliest Times to A.D. 697*. Rutland, Vt.: Tuttle, 1972.

Baien. *See* Miura Baien.

Baigan. *See* Ishida Baigan.

Ban Gu. *Han shu*. BNB.

Bankei. *Bankei Zen: Translations from the Record of Bankei*. Translated by Peter Haskel. Edited by Yoshito Hakeda. New York: Grove Press, 1984.

Bankei. *Bankei zenji zenshū*. Edited by Akao Ryūji. Tokyo: Daizō shuppan, 1976.

Bodart-Bailey, Beatrice M. *Kaempfer's Japan*. Honolulu: University of Hawai'i Press, 1999.

Brownlee, John S. "The Jeweled Comb Box: Motoori Norinaga's *Tamakushige*." *Monumenta Nipponica* 43 (1988): 35–61.

Camões, Luís de. *The Lusiads*. Translated by Richard Fanshaw. Edited by Geoffrey Bullough. Carbondale: Southern Illinois University Press, 1964.

"Cartas qve os Padres e Irmūos da Companhia de Iesus escreuerūo dos Reynos de Iapūo & China aos da mesma Companhia da India, & Europa, des do anno de 1549. atè o de 1580 . . . Em Euora por manoel de Lyra." Anno de M.D. XCVIII.

Chamberlain, Basil Hall, trans. "Educational Literature of Japanese Women." *Journal of the Asiatic Society of Great Britain and Ireland*, n.s., 10 (1878).

Chan, Wing-tsit. *Reflections on Things at Hand: The Neo-Confucian Anthology*. New York: Columbia University Press, 1967.

Chan, Wing-tsit. *A Source Book in Chinese Philosophy*. Princeton, N.J.: Princeton University Press, 1963.

Chen Beixi. *Neo-Confucian Terms Explained: The Pei-hsi tzu-i*. Translated and edited by Wing-tsit Chan. New York: Columbia University Press, 1986.

Chen Beixi. "Seriousness." In *Xingli ziyi*. In *CSJC*.

Chen Qun. "The Feelings." In *Xingli ziyi*. In *CSJC*.

Chen Qun. "The Way." In *Xingli ziyi*. Collated by Chŏng Ŭngo. Chinju, 1553.

Cheng Hao and Cheng Yi. *Er Cheng yishu*. In *Er Cheng quanshu*. In *SBBY*.

Cheng Yi. *Yichuan wenji*. In *Er Cheng quanshu*. In *SBBY*.

Ch'oe, Yŏngho, Peter H. Lee, and Wm. Theodore de Bary, eds. *Sources of Korean Tradition*. Vol. 2. New York: Columbia University Press, 2000.

Chu Tzu Yü-lei. Taibei: Chengchung, 1970.

Chūsei zenke no shisō. Edited by Ichikawa Hakugen. In *NST*, vol. 16.

Chūshingura (The Treasury of Loyal Retainers): A Puppet Play by Takeda Izumo, Miyoshi Shōraku, and Namiki Senryū. Translated by Donald Keene. New York: Columbia University Press, 1971.

A Concordance to the Hsiao ching [Xiaojing]. Harvard-Yenching Institute Sinological Index Series, supplement no. 23. Taibei: Chinese Materials and Research Aids Service Center, 1966.

A Concordance to Yi ching [Yijing]. Harvard-Yenching Institute Sinological Index Series, supplement no. 10. Taibei: Chinese Materials and Research Aids Service Center, 1973.

Confucius. *Analects of Confucius*. Translated by Arthur Waley. New York: Random House, 1989.

Crawcour, E. S., trans. "Some Observations on Merchants: A Translation of Mitsui Takafusa's *Chōnin kōken roku*." *Transactions of the Asiatic Society of Japan*, 3rd ser., 8 (1961): 9–139.

Dai kanwa jiten. Compiled by Morohashi Tetsuji. 13 vols. Tokyo: Taishūkan shoten, 1960.

Dai Nihon shi. 17 vols. Tokyo: Dai Nihon yūbenkai, 1928.

Dai Nihon shiryō. Edited by Tōkyō daigaku shiryō hensanjo. Tokyo: Tōkyō daigaku shuppankai, 1901–.

Daodejing. *See* Lau, D. C.

Dazai Shundai. *Kinsei buke shisō*. In *NST*, vol. 27.

Dazai Shundai. *Sango*. In *Dazai Shundai shū*. Vol. 4 of *Kinsei shakai keizai gakusetsu taikei*. Tokyo: Seibundō shinkōsha, 1939.

Dazai Shundai. *Seigaku mondō*. In *Dazai Shundai shū*. Vol. 4 of *Kinsei shakai keizai gakusetsu taikei*. Tokyo: Seibundō shinkōsha, 1939.

de Bary, Wm. Theodore, and Irene Bloom, eds. *Sources of Chinese Tradition*. 2nd ed. Vol. 1. New York: Columbia University Press, 1999.

de Bary, Wm. Theodore, Donald Keene, George Tanabe, and Paul Varley, eds. *Sources of Japanese Tradition*. 2nd ed. Vol. 1. New York: Columbia University Press, 2001.

de Bary, Wm. Theodore, and Richard Lufrano, eds. *Sources of Chinese Tradition*. 2nd ed. Vol. 2. New York: Columbia University Press, 2000.

Dore, Ronald P. *Education in Tokugawa Japan*. Berkeley: University of California Press, 1965.

Dumoulin, Heinrich, trans. "Kamo Mabuchi: *Kokuikō*." *Monumenta Nipponica* 2 (1939): 165–92.

Elison, George. *Deus Destroyed: The Image of Christianity in Early Modern Japan*. Cambridge, Mass.: Harvard University Press, 1988.

Fabian Fucan. *Ha Daiusu*. In *NST*, vol. 25.

Fabian Fucan. *Myōtei mondō*. Part 3 of *Kirishitan sho, Hai-Ya sho*. Edited by Ebisawa Arimichi et al. In *NST*, vol. 25.

French, Calvin L. *Shiba Kōkan: Artist, Innovator, and Pioneer in the Westernization of Japan*. Studies of the East Asian Institute. New York: Weatherhill, 1974.

Fróis, Luís, S.J. *Historia de Japam*. Vol. 3. Edited by José Wicki, S.J. Lisbon: Biblioteca Nacional, 1982.

Fróis, Luís, S.J. *Tratado em que se contem muito susinta e abreviadamente algumas contradiões e diferencas de custumes antre a gente de Europa e esta provincia de Japao*. Edited by Josef Franz Schütte, S.J. Tokyo: Sophia University Press, 1955.

Fuchi. "Kōzan sensei jikyōroku." Typescript.

Fujiwara Seika. *Daigaku yōryaku*. In *NST*, vol. 28.

Fujiwara Seika. *Fujiwara Seika shū*. Edited by Ōta Hyōzaburō. 2 vols. 1939. Reprint. Tokyo: Kokumin seishin bunka kenkyūjo, 1991.

Fujiwara Seika. *Kana shōri*. In *NST*, vol. 28.

Fujiwara Seika. *Seika sensei bunshū*. In *NST*, vol. 28.

Fujiwara Seika. Hayashi Razan. In *NST*, vol. 28.

Fukuzawa Yukichi. *The Autobiography of Fukuzawa Yukichi*. Translated by Eiichi Kiyooka. Tokyo: Hokuseido, 1934.

Fukuzawa Yukichi. *An Encouragement of Learning*. Translated by David A. Dilworth and Umeyo Hirano. Tokyo: Sophia University Press, 1969.

Fukuzawa Yukichi. *Fukuzawa Yukichi zenshū*. Compiled by Keiō gijuku. 21 vols. Tokyo: Iwanami shoten, 1958–1964.

Goi Ranshū. *Kinsei buke shisō*. In *NST*, vol. 27.

Goodman, Grant K., trans. "A Translation of Ōtsuki Gentaku's *Ransetsu benwaku*." *Occasional Papers* (Center for Japanese Studies, University of Michigan), no. 3 (1952): 71–99.

Hagakure. See Yamamoto Tsunetomo.

Hakuin. *The Zen Master Hakuin: Selected Writings*. Translated by Philip B. Yampolsky. New York: Columbia University Press, 1971.

Han shu. See Ban Gu.

Hasegawa Nyozekan. *Ushinawareta Nihon: Nihon-teki kyōyō no dentō*. Tokyo: Keiyūsha, 1952.

Hayashi Hōkō. *Hōkō Hayashi gakushi shū*. 105 vols. 1689.

Hayashi Razan. *Hayashi Razan bunshū*. Compiled by Kyōto shisekikai. 2 vols. 1918, 1921. Reprint. Tokyo: Perikansha, 1979.

Hayashi Razan. *Hayashi Razan shishū*. Compiled by Kyōto shisekikai. 2 vols. 1920, 1921. Reprint. Tokyo: Perikansha, 1979.

Hayashi Razan. *Honsaroku*. In *NST*, vol. 28.

Hayashi Razan. *Kama shōri*. In *NST*, vol. 28.

Hayashi Razan. *Razan Hayashi sensei bunshū*. In *NST*, vol. 28.

Hayashi Razan. *Razan Hayashi sensei shū*. Edited by Kyōto shisekikai. 4 vols. Kyoto: Heian kōko gakkai, 1918–1921.

Hayashi Razan. "Santokushō." *In NST*, vol. 28.

Hayashi Razan. *Seiri jigi genkai*. Kyoto: Arakawa Jirouemon, 1659.

Hayashi, T. "A List of Some Dutch Astronomical Works Imported into Japan from Holland." *Nieuw Archief voor Wiskunde*, 2nd ser., 7 (1907).

Hirata Atsutane. *Hirata Atsutane zenshū*. Compiled by Muromatsu Iwao. 15 vols. Tokyo: Itchidō, 1911–1918.

Hirose Tansō. *Ugen*. Edited by Naramoto Tatsuya. In *NST*, vol. 38.

Hosoi Heishū. *Heishū zenshū*. Edited by Takase Daijirō. Tokyo: Heishūkai zōhan, 1921.

Hou Han shu. Beijing: Zhonghua shuju, 1966.

Hsün Tzu (Xunzi). *Basic Writings: Hsün Tzu*. Translated by Burton Watson. New York: Columbia University Press, 1963.

Ichikawa Mototarō. *Nihon jukyōshi*. 5 vols. Tokyo: Kyūkō shoin, 1994.

Ihara Saikaku. *The Japanese Family Storehouse or the Millionaire's Gospel Modernized*. Translated and edited by G. W. Sargent. Cambridge: Cambridge University Press, 1959.

Ihara Saikaku. *Saikaku zenshū*. Edited by Ozaki Kōyō and Watanabe Otowa. Tokyo: Hakubunkan, 1894.

Imanaka Kanshi. *Sorai gaku no kisoteki kenkyū*. Tokyo: Yoshikawa kōbunkan, 1966.

Inoue Tetsujirō. *Nihon rinri ihen*. 10 vols. Tokyo: Ikuseikai, 1901–1903.

Inoue Tetsujirō. *Nihon shushi gakuha no tetsugaku*. Tokyo: Fuzanbō, 1933.

Inoue Tetsujirō. *Nihon yōmei gakuha no tetsugaku*. Tokyo: Fuzanbō, 1932.

Ishida Baigan. *Tohi mondō*. In *NKBT*, vol. 97.

Ishihama Juntarō. *Tominaga Nakamoto*. Osaka: Sōgensha, 1940.

Ishii Kyōdō, ed. *Shōwa shinshū Hōnen Shōnin zenshū*. Kyoto: Heirakuji shoten, 1974.

Ishin Sūden. "Bateren tsuihō no fumi." In *Eiinbon Ikoku nikki: Konchiin Sūden gaikō monjo shūsei*. Edited by Ikoku nikki kankōkai. Tokyo: Tōkyō bijutsu, 1989.

Issai. *See* Satō Issai.

Itō Jinsai. *Gomō jigi*. In *NST*, vol. 33.

Jinsi lu. In *Shushigaku taikei*, vol. 9. Tokyo: Meitoku shuppansha, 1974.

Jiun Sonja. *Jiun Sonja zenshū*. Edited by Hase Hōshū. 19 vols. Kyoto: Shibunkaku, 1974.

Kada no Azumamaro. *Kada zenshū*. Edited by Inari jinja. 7 vols. Tokyo: Yoshikawa kōbunkan, 1928–1932.

Kaempfer, Engelbert. *The History of Japan*. Translated by J. G. Scheuchzer. 3 vols. Glasgow: MacLehose, 1906.

Kaibara Ekken. *Ekken zenshū*. 8 vols. Tokyo: Ekken zenshū kankōbu, 1910–1911.

Kaibara Ekken. *Taigiroku*. In *NST*, vol. 34.

Kaibara Ekken. *Yamato zokkun*. Tokyo: Kiyomizu Kakujirō, 1967.

Kaiho Seiryō. *Kaiho Seiryō shū*. Vol. 9 of *Kinsei shakai keizai gakusetsu taikei*. Tokyo: Seibundō shinkōsha, 1939.

Kaitokudō isho. 15 vols. Osaka: Kaitokudō kinenkai, 1911.

Kaitokudō yōran. Edited by Kaitokudō kinenkai. Osaka: Kaitokudō kinenkai, 1942.

Kamo no Mabuchi. *Sekai daishisō zenshū*. Vol. 54, *Nihon shisōhen*. Edited by Kanda Hōsui. Tokyo: Shunjūsha, 1927.

Karlgren, Bernard. *The Book of Odes*. Stockholm: Museum of Far Eastern Antiquities, 1950.

Karonshū. Edited by Hisamatsu Sen'ichi. Tokyo: Miyai shoten, 1971.

Kassel, Marleen. *Tokugawa Confucian Education: The Kangien Academy of Hirose Tansō (1782–1856)*. Studies of the East Asian Institute of Columbia University. Albany: State University of New York Press, 1996.

Keene, Donald. *Dawn to the West*. 2 vols. New York: Columbia University Press, 1998, 1999.

Keene, Donald. *The Japanese Discovery of Europe: Honda Toshiaki and Other Discoverers, 1720–1798*. 1952. Reprint. Stanford, Calif.: Stanford University Press, 1969.

Keene, Donald. *World Within Walls: Japanese Literature of the Pre-modern Era, 1600–1867*. New York: Holt, Rinehart and Winston, 1976.

Keichū. *Keichū zenshū*. Edited by Hisamatsu Sen'ichi et al. 9 vols. Osaka: Asahi shinbunsha, 1926–1927.

Keichū. *Keichū zenshū, Fu Chōryū zenshū*. Edited by Sasaki Nobutsuna et al. 11 vols. Osaka: Asahi shinbunsha, 1926–1927.

Kinseishi ronshū. Edited by Matsumoto Sannosuke and Ogura Yoshihiko. In *NST*, vol. 48.

Knox, George Wm., trans. "A Japanese Philosopher." *Transactions of the Asiatic Society of Japan* 20, pt. 1 (1892).

Kokubun chūshaku zensho. Edited by Motoori Toyokai et al. 20 vols. Tokyo: Kokugakuin daigaku shuppanbu, 1907–1910.

Konchiin Sūden. *See* Ishin Sūden.

Kumazawa Banzan. *Banzan zenshū*. Edited by Masamune Atsuo. 6 vols. Tokyo: Banzan zenshū kankōkai, 1940–1943.

Kumazawa Banzan. *Zōtei Banzan zenshū*. Edited by Taniguchi Sumio and Masamune Atsuo. 7 vols. Tokyo: Meicho shuppan, 1940, 1978.

Kuwata Tadachika. *Toyotomi Hideyoshi kenkyū*. Tokyo: Kadokawa shoten, 1975.

Kyūki zatsuroku, kōhen. Vol. 4 of *Kagoshimaken shiryō*. Edited by Kagoshimaken ishin shiryō hensanjo. Kagoshima: Kagoshimaken, 1984.

Laozi. In *Sources of Chinese Tradition*, vol. 1. 2nd ed. Edited by Wm. Theodore de Bary and Irene Bloom. New York: Columbia University Press, 1999.

Lau, D. C., trans. *Mencius*. Harmondsworth: Penguin, 1970.

Lau, D. C., trans. *Tao te ching [Daodejing]*. New York: Penguin, 1980.

Legge, James, trans. *Book of Documents*, "The Counsels of Great Yü." In *The Sacred Books of China: The Texts of Confucianism*. Part 1, *The Shu king. The Religious Portions of the Shih king. The Hsiao king*. Sacred Books of the East, vol. 3. Oxford: Clarendon Press, 1879.

Legge, James, trans. *Book of Rites*. In *Confucian Analects, the Great Learning, and the Doctrine of the Mean*. Vol. 1 of *The Chinese Classics*. London: Trübner, 1861–1872.

Legge, James, trans. *The Chinese Classics*. 5 vols. London: Trübner, 1861–1872.

Legge, James, trans. *The Ch'un ts'ew, with the Tso chuen*. Vol. 5 of *The Chinese Classics*. London: Trübner, 1861–1872.

Legge, James, trans. *Confucian Analects, the Great Learning, and the Doctrine of the Mean*. Vol. 1 of *The Chinese Classics*. London: Trübner, 1861–1872.

Legge, James, trans. *I ching*. Edited and introduced by Ch'u Chai, with Winberg Chai. New Hyde Park, N.Y.: University Books, 1964.

Legge, James, trans. *Li Chi: Book of Rites. An Encyclopedia of Ancient Ceremonial Usages, Religious Creeds, and Social Institutions*. 2 vols. Edited and introduced by Ch'u Chai, with Winberg Chai. New Hyde Park, N.Y.: University Books, 1967.

Legge, James, trans. *The Shoo king, or the Book of Historical Documents*. Vol. 3 of *The Chinese Classics*. London: Trübner, 1861–1872.

Li Jingde. *Zhuzi yülei*. Kyoto: Chūbun shuppansha, 1979.

Lu, David J., ed. *Japan: A Documentary History*. Armonk, N.Y.: Sharpe, 1997.

McEwan, J. R. *The Political Writings of Ogyū Sorai*. Cambridge: Cambridge University Press, 1962.

Mean. In *Liji*. In *SBBY*.

Mencius. *See* Lau, D. C.

Minear, Richard H. "Ogyū Sorai's 'Instructions for Students': A Translation and Commentary." *Harvard Journal of Asiatic Studies* 36 (1976): 5–81.

Mitsui Takafusa. "Chōnin kōken roku." In *Nihon keizai sōsho*. Edited by Takimoto Seiichi. Tokyo: Nihon keizai sōsho kankōkai, 1915.

Mitsui Takaharu. "Chōnin's Life Under Feudalism." *Cultural Nippon* 8 (1940).

Miura Baien. *Baien zenshū*. Edited by Baienkai. 2 vols. Tokyo: Kōdōkan, 1912.

Miura Baien. Edited by Shimada Kenji and Taguchi Masaharu. In *NST*, vol. 41.

Miwa Shissai. *Shissai nichiyō shinpō*. Edited by Takase Takejirō. In *Shissai zensho*, vol. 10. Kyoto: Nakada Hikosaburō, 1925 (microfilm).

Miyauchi, D. Y., trans. [Yokoi Shōnan's] "Kokuze sanron: Three Major Problems of State Policy." *Monumenta Nipponica* 23 (1968): 156–86.

Motoori Norinaga. "Hihon tamakushige." In *Motoori Norinaga zenshū*, vol. 8. Compiled by Ōno Susumu and Ōkubo Tadashi. Tokyo: Chikuma shobō, 1972.

Motoori Norinaga. *Motoori Norinaga*. Edited by Motoori Toyokai and Motoori Kiyozō. Revised and enlarged ed. 13 vols. Tokyo: Yoshikawa kōbunkan, 1926–1928.

Motoori Norinaga. *Motoori Norinaga zenshū*. Edited by Motoori Toyokai and Motoori Kiyozō. Revised and enlarged ed. 10 vols. Tokyo: Yoshikawa kōbunkan, 1926–1928.

Motoori Norinaga. *Motoori Norinaga zenshū*. Compiled by Ōno Susumu and Ōkubo Tadashi. 20 vols. Tokyo: Chikuma shobō, 1968–1977.

Motoori Norinaga. *Motoori Norinaga zenshū*. Supplement. 3 vols. Compiled by Ōkubo Tadashi and Ōno Susumu. Tokyo: Chikuma shobō, 1976–1993.

Murasaki Shikibu. *The Tale of Genji*. Translated by Royall Tyler. 2 vols. New York: Viking, 2001.

Muro Kyūsō. *Rikuyu engi taii*. In *Nihon kyōiku bunko, kunkai hen* 2. Edited by Kurokawa Mamichi. Tokyo: Dōbunkan, 1910–1911.

Nakae Tōju. *Nakae Tōju*. Compiled by Yamanoi Yū et al. In *NST*, vol. 29.

Nakae Tōju. *Okina mondō*. In *NST*, vol. 29.

Nakae Tōju. *Tōju sensei zenshū*. Edited by Tōju jinja sōritsu kyōsankai. 5 vols. Shiga-ken Takashima-gun Aoyagi-mura: Tōju shoin, 1928–1929.

Nakae Tōju. *Tōju sensei zenshū*. 5 vols. 1940. Reprint. Tokyo: Kōbundō, 1976.

Nakai, Kate Wildman. *Shogunal Politics: Arai Hakuseki and the Premises of Tokugawa Rule*. Harvard East Asian Monographs. Cambridge, Mass.: Harvard University Press, 1988.

Nihon jurin sōsho. Edited by Seki Giichirō. 6 vols. Tokyo: Tōyō tosho kankōkai, 1927–1929.

Nihon keizai taiten. Edited by Takimoto Seiichi. 54 vols. Tokyo: Shishi shuppansha, 1928–1930.

Nihon no yōmeigaku. Edited by Uno Tetsuto et al. 3 vols. Tokyo: Meitoku shuppansha, 1972–1973.

Nihon shiseki kyōkai sōsho. Edited by Nihon shiseki kyōkai. Tokyo: University of Tokyo Press, 1967.

Nihon shoki. In *NKBT*, vol. 67.

Ninomiya Sontoku. *Kaisetsu Ninomiya Sontoku ō zenshū*. Edited by Yoshiji Shōichi. 6 vols. Tokyo: Kaisetsu Ninomiya Sontoku ō zenshū kankōkai, 1938.

Ninomiya Sontoku. *Ninomiya Sontoku ō zenshū. Seikatsu genri hen*. Tokyo: Kaisetsu Ninomiya Sontoku ō zenshū kankōkai, 1937.

Ninomiya Sontoku. *Ninomiya Sontoku zenshū*. Compiled by Sasai Shintarō. 36 vols. Kakegawa machi: Ninomiya Sontoku igyō sen'yōkai, 1927–1932.

Nishimura Sey. " 'First Steps into the Mountains': Motoori Norinaga's 'Uiyamabumi.' " *Monumenta Nipponica* 42 (1987): 449–93.

Nishimura Tenshū et al., eds. *Kaitokudō isho*. Osaka: Matsumura bunkaidō, 1911.

Nishio Minoru, ed. *Shōbōgenzō zuimonki*. Vol. 14 of *Nihon koten bungaku zenshū*. Tokyo: Chikuma shobō, 1964.

Ogyū Sorai. *Bendō*. Edited by Nishida Taichirō. In *NST*, vol. 36.

Ogyū Sorai. *Benmei*. Edited by Yoshikawa Kōjirō. In *NST*, vol. 36.

Ogyū Sorai. *Benmei*. Translated by John A. Tucker. Leiden: Brill, 1998.

Ogyū Sorai. *Gakusoku*. Edited by Yoshikawa Kōjirō et al. In *NST*, vol. 36.

Ogyū Sorai. *Ogyū Sorai*. Compiled by Yoshikawa Kōjirō et al. In *NST*, vol. 36.

Ogyū Sorai. *Ogyū Sorai [Miura Baien] shū*. In *Kinsei shakai keizai gakusetsu taikei*, vol. 13. Edited by Kokushō Iwao. Tokyo: Seibundō shinkō-sha, 1937.

Ogyū Sorai. *Ogyū Sorai shū*. Vol. 12 of *Nihon no shisō*. Edited by Kanaya Osamu. Tokyo: Chikuma shobō, 1970.

Ogyū Sorai. *Ogyū Sorai zenshū*. Edited by Imanaka Kanshi and Naramoto Tatsuya. 5 vols. Tokyo: Kawade shobō shinsha, 1973–.

Ogyū Sorai. *Ogyū Sorai zenshū*. Edited by Yoshikawa Kōjirō and Maruyama Masao. 21 vols. Tokyo: Misuzu shobō, 1973–1983.

Ogyū Sorai. *Ogyū Sorai's Distinguishing the Way (Bendō)*. Edited by Olof G. Lidin. Tokyo: Sophia University Press, 1970.

Ogyū Sorai. *Shijūshichi Shi ron*. In *NST*, vol. 27.

Okado Denpachirō. *Kinsei buke shisō*. Compiled by Ishii Shironō. In *NST*, vol. 27.

Ōkubo Hikozaemon (Tadataka). *Mikawa monogatari*. Edited by Ōtsuka Mitsunobu. In *NST*, vol. 26.

Ōkuni Takamasa. *Shinshin kōhōron*. In *NST*, vol. 50. ["New True International Law." Translated by John Breen. In *Readings in Tokugawa Thought*. 2nd ed. Edited by Tetsuo Najita. Chicago: Center for East Asian Studies, University of Chicago, 1994.]

Oritaku shiba no ki Rantō kotohajime. Edited by Odaka Toshirō and Matsumura Akira. Vol. 95 of *NKBT*.

Ōshio Heihachirō (Chūsai). *Hōnō shosekishū batsu*. In *Nihon no yōmeigaku*, vol. 1. Edited by Uno Tetsuto et al. Tokyo: Meitoku shuppansha, 1973.

Ōshio Heihachirō. "Senshindō sakki." In *NST*, vol. 46.

Ōtsuki Gentaku. *Ransetsu benwaku*. In *Bansui zonkyō*, vol. 1. Edited by Ōtsuki Shigeo. Tokyo: Ōtsuki Shigeo, 1912.

Perkins, George W., trans. *The Clear Mirror: A Chronicle of the Japanese Court During the Kamakura Period (1185–1333)*. Stanford, Calif.: Stanford University Press, 1995.

Pinto, Fernão Mendes. *Peregrinação*. Introduction by Jose Manuel Garcia. Maia: Castoliva, 1995.

Pye, Michael, trans. *Emerging from Meditation by Tominaga Nakamoto*. Honolulu: University of Hawai'i Press, 1990.

Rai Sanyō. *Nihon gaishi*. Edited by Rai Seiichi and Rai Tsutomu. 3 vols. Tokyo: Iwanami shoten, 1977.

Ramseyer, J. Mark. "Thrift and Diligence: House Codes of Tokugawa Merchant Families." *Monumenta Nipponica* 34 (1979): 209–30.

Rōshi jō. Edited by Fukunaga Mitsuji. Tokyo: Asahi shinbunsha, 1978.

Saikaku. *See* Ihara Saikaku.

Sakuma Shōzan. *Seiken-roku.* In *NST,* vol. 55.

Sansom, George Bailey. *The Western World and Japan: A Study in the Interaction of European and Asiatic Cultures.* New York: Knopf, 1950.

Sargent, G. W., trans. *The Japanese Family Storehouse or the Millionaire's Gospel Modernized.* Cambridge: Cambridge University Press, 1959.

Sasayama Baian. *Terako seikai shikimoku.* In *NKSS.*

Satō, Hiroki. *Legends of the Samurai.* Woodstock, N.Y.: Overlook Press, 1995.

Satō Issai. *Genshiroku.* In *NST,* vol. 46.

Satō Issai, Ōshio Chūsai. Edited by Sagara Tōru et al. In *NST,* vol. 46.

Satō Naokata. *A Discussion on Wang [Yangming] Learning.* In *Satō Naokata zenshū,* vol. 12. Tokyo: Perikansha, 1979.

Satō Naokata. *Kinsei buke shisō.* In *NST,* vol. 27.

Satō Nobuhiro. *Fukko-hō mondō-sho.* In *Nihon keizai taiten,* vol. 19. Edited by Takimoto Seiichi. Tokyo: Shishi shuppansha, 1928–1930.

Satō Nobuhiro. *Keizai yōroku.* In *Nihon keizai taiten,* vol. 18. Edited by Takimoto Seiichi. Tokyo: Shishi shuppansha, 1928–1930.

Satō Nobuhiro. *Kondō hisaku.* In *Nihon keizai taiten,* vol. 18. Edited by Takimoto Seiichi. Tokyo: Shishi shuppansha, 1928–1930.

Satō Nobuhiro. *Suitō hiroku.* In *Nihon keizai taiten,* vol. 18. Edited by Takimoto Seiichi. Tokyo: Shishi shuppansha, 1928–1930.

Satō Nobuhiro. *Yōzō kaiku ron.* In *Nihon keizai taiten,* vol. 18. Edited by Takimoto Seiichi. Tokyo: Shishi shuppansha, 1928–1930.

Sentetsu sōdan. Edited by Hara Nensai, Minamoto Ryōen, and Maeda Tsutomo. Tōyō bunko, vol. 574. Tokyo: Heibonsha, 1994.

Shao Yong. *Yichyuan jirang ji.* In *SKQS.*

Shiba shi lüe. Compiled by Zeng Xianzhi. Edited by Hayashi Hideichi. 2 vols. Tokyo: Meiji shoin, 1967.

Shissai. *See* Miwa Shissai.

Shōnan. *See* Yokoi Shōnan.

Shōsan. *See* Suzuki Shōsan.

Shukke taikō. 1789 woodblock ed. [copy in possession of William Bodiford].

Shundai. *See* Dazai Shundai.

Shushigaku taikei. Edited by Morohashi Tetsuji and Yasuoka Masahiro. Multivolume ed. Tokyo: Meitoku shuppansha, 1974–.

Sima Qian. *Shiji.* Translated by Noguchi Sadao. Vol. 12 of *Chūgoku koten bungaku taikei.* Tokyo: Heibonsha, 1971.

Sorai. *See* Ogyū Sorai.

Sōshi naihen. Edited by Fukunaga Mitsuji. Tokyo: Asahi shinbunsha, 1978.

Sūden. *See* Ishin Sūden.

Sugita Genpaku. *Dawn of Western Science in Japan. Rangaku kotohajime.* Translated by Ryōzō Matsumoto and Eiichi Kiyooka. Supervised by Tomio Ogata, Masafumi Tomita, and Kazuyoshi Nakayama. Tokyo: Hokuseido Press, 1969.

Suzuki Shōsan. *Banmin tokuyō.* In *NKBT,* vol. 83.

Suzuki Shōsan. *Selected Writings of Suzuki Shōsan.* Translated by Royall Tyler. Cornell University East Asia Papers, no. 13. Ithaca, N.Y.: Cornell University Press, 1977.

Taiheiki. Edited by Gotō Tanji and Kamada Kisaburō. 3 vols. In *NKBT*, vols. 34–36.

Taishō shinshū daizōkyō. Edited by Takakusu Junjirō and Watanabe Kaigyoku. 85 vols. Tokyo: Taishō issaikyō kankōkai, 1924–1932.

Takasu Yoshijirō. *Shinron kōwa*. Tokyo: Heibonsha, 1941.

Takuan Sōhō. *Takuan Oshō zenshū* (*Sōhō*). 6 vols. Tokyo: Kōgeisha, 1928–1930.

The Tale of Genji. See Murasaki Shikibu.

Taniguchi Sumio. *Zōtei Shizutani gakkō shi*. Edited by Tokubetsu shiseki Shizutani gakkō kenshō hozonkai. Okayama: Fukutake shoten, 1987.

Terry, Charles. "Sakuma Shōzan and His *Seiken-roku*." Master's thesis, Columbia University, 1957.

Tokugawa jikki. Edited by Kuroita Katsumi. Vols. 38–47 of *Shintei zōho kokushi taikei*. Tokyo: Yoshikawa kōbunkan, 1998–1999.

Tominaga Nakamoto. *Okina no fumi*. In *Nihon jurin sōsho*, vol. 6. Tokyo: Tōyō tosho kankōkai, 1929.

Tominaga Nakamoto. *Shutsujō kōgo*. In *NST*, vol. 43.

Tsunoda, Ryusaku, Wm. Theodore de Bary, and Donald Keene, eds. *Sources of Japanese Tradition*. 1st ed. Vol. 2. New York: Columbia University Press, 1958.

Tucker, Mary Evelyn. *Moral and Spiritual Cultivation in Japanese Neo-Confucianism: The Life and Thought of Kaibara Ekken*. Albany: State University of New York Press, 1989.

Valignano, Alexandro, S.J. *Sumario de las cosas de Japon* [1583]. Edited by José Luis Alvarez-Taladriz. Monumenta Nipponica Monographs, no. 9. Tokyo: Sophia University Press, 1954.

Wakabayashi, Bob Tadashi. *Japanese Loyalism Reconstrued: Yamagata Daini's Ryushi Shinron of 1759*. Honolulu: University of Hawai'i Press, 1995.

Watson, Burton, trans. *The Lotus Sutra*. New York: Columbia University Press, 1993.

Watt, Paul. "Jiun Sonja (1718–1804): A Response to Confucianism Within the Context of Buddhist Reform." In *Confucianism and Tokugawa Culture*. Edited by Peter Nosco. Princeton, N.J.: Princeton University Press, 1984.

Watt, Paul. "Sermons on the Precepts and Monastic Life by the Shingon Vinaya Master Jiun." *Eastern Buddhist* 25 (1992): 119–28.

Wei Zheng et al. *Gunsho shūyō* (Ch. *Chunshu zhiyao*), 50 *kan*.

Wu Jing. *Jōgan seiyō* (Ch. *Zhenguan zhengyao*), 10 *kan*.

Xiaojing. Edited by Kurihara Keisuke. In *Shinshaku kanbun taikei*, vol. 35. Tokyo: Meiji shoin, 1986.

Xiaojing yinde. See *A Concordance to the Hsiao ching*.

Xingli ziyi. Collated by Chŏng Ŭngo. Chinju, 1553.

Xunzi (Hsün Tzu). *Xunzi*. In *SBBY*.

Yamaga Sokō. *Haisho zanpitsu*. In *NST*, vol. 32.

Yamaga Sokō. *Seikyō yōroku*. In *NST*, vol. 32.

Yamaga Sokō. *Yamaga gorui*. 4 vols. Tokyo: Kokusho kankōkai, 1910–1911.

Yamaga Sokō. *Yamaga Sokō bunshū*. Yūhōdō bunko. Tokyo: Yūhōdō shoten, 1926.

Yamaga Sokō. *Yamaga Sokō shū*. Vol. 4 of *Kinsei shakai keizai gakusetsu taikei*. Tokyo: Seibundō shinkōsha, 1935.

Yamaga Sokō. *Yamaga Sokō zenshū: Shisōhen*. Edited by Hirose Yutaka. 15 vols. Tokyo: Iwanami shoten, 1940–1942.

Yamamoto Shinkō. *Shingaku gorinsho no kisoteki kenkyū.* Tokyo: Gakushūin daigaku, 1985.

Yamamoto Tsunetomo. *Hagakure.* In *NST*, vol. 26.

Yamazaki Ansai. *Suika Shintō.* 2 vols. Tokyo: Shintō taikei hensankai, 1978, 1984.

Yamazaki Ansai. *Suika-sō.* In *Yamazaki Ansai zenshū*, vol. 1. Tokyo: Nihon koten gakkai, 1936.

Yamazaki Ansai. *Yamazaki Ansai gakuha.* Compiled by Nishi Junzō, Abe Ryūichi, and Maruyama Masao. In *NST*, vol. 31.

Yamazaki Ansai. *Yamazaki Ansai zenshū.* 2 vols. Tokyo: Nihon koten gakkai, 1936, 1937.

Yamazaki Ansai. *Zoku Yamazaki Ansai zenshū.* 3 vols. 1937. Reprint. Tokyo: Perikansha, 1978.

Yang Xiong, *Fayan.*

Yi T'oegye. *Chŏn-myŏngdo.* In *Ri Taike zenshū*, vol. 2. Tokyo: Yushima seidō, 1975.

Yi T'oegye. "Diagram of the Supreme Ultimate." In *To Become a Sage: The Ten Diagrams on Sage Learning.* Translated and edited by Michael C. Kalton. New York: Columbia University Press, 1988.

Yijing. See A Concordance to Yi ching.

Yokoi Shōnan. *Gakkō mondōsho.* In *NST*, vol. 55.

Yokoi Shōnan. *Kokuze sanron.* In *NST*, vol. 55.

Yōmeigaku taikei. Edited by Uno Tetsuto et al. 13 vols. Tokyo: Meitoku shuppansha, 1971–1974.

Yoshida Shōin. *Yoshida Shōin zenshū.* 12 vols. Edited by Yamaguchi-ken kyōikukai. Tokyo: Iwanami shoten, 1938–1940.

Yoshida Yutaka, ed. *Shōka no kakun.* Tokyo: Tokuma shoten, 1973.

Yoshikawa Kōjirō. "Sorai gakuan." In *NST*, vol. 36.

Yoshimoto Tadasu, trans. *A Peasant Sage of Japan: The Life and Work of Sontoku Ninomiya.* Translated from *The Hōtokuki.* London: Longman's, Green, 1912.

Zhu Xi. *Daxue huowen.* Edited by Kinsei kanseki sōkan. Kyoto: Chūbun shuppansha, 1971.

Zhu Xi. *Daxue zhangju.* In *Shushigaku taikei*, vol. 7. Tokyo: Meitoku shuppansha, 1974.

Zhu Xi. *Lunyu jizhu.* In *Shushigaku taikei*, vol. 7. Tokyo: Meitoku shuppansha, 1974.

Zhu Xi. *Mengzi jizhu.* In *Shushigaku taikei*, vol. 8. Tokyo: Meitoku shuppansha, 1974.

Zhu Xi. Preface to the *Mean.* In *Shushigaku taikei*, vol. 7. Tokyo: Meitoku shuppansha, 1974.

Zhu Xi. *Ren shuo.* In *Huian Zhu wengong wenji.* Kyoto: Chūbun, 1977.

Zhu Xi. *Wenji.* In *Huian Zhu wengong wenji.* Kyoto: Chūbun, 1977.

Zhu Xi. *Zhuzi quanshu.* In *SBBY.*

Zhu Xi. *Zhuzi yulei.* Taibei: Zhengzhong shuju, 1970.

Zuo zhuan. In *SBBY.*

INDEX

Abhasvara, 336
abortion, 143, 511–12
academies, 4–5, 218–54, 235–54; Daigakuryō (Court), 28; Dazaifu, 401; and Hirose Tansō, 250–54; Kaitokudō, 238–46, 257, 331, 342, 343, 377, 464; Kangien, 250; local, 284–88, 460–61; merchants', 238–46; Neo-Confucian, 120, 125–26; and Ogyū Sorai, 246–50; popular, 220, 395; private, 218, 220; Seidō (Hall of Sages), 359; semi-private, 218; Senshindō (Grotto for Mind Cleansing), 469; Shizutani, 121n.37, 235–38; Suzunoya (House of Bells), 397; White Deer Grotto, 41, 219–22, 236, 238, 551n.24. See also Hayashi academy
Account of Tokugawa (Tokugawa jikki), 10, 19–21, 26–27
adoption, 16
Aesop's Fables, 128
Agricultural Problems (Satō Nobuhiro), 511
agriculture: irrigation in, 482; mutual aid in, 475–83; Neo-Confucianists on, 41, 97, 98, 114, 203, 213, 214–16; and population growth, 498; pre-Restoration thinkers on, 495, 496, 504, 506, 511–15; rationalists on,

343–44; reforms in, 475–83, 531, 542, 543. *See also* farmers
Aida Gihei, 511
Ainu, 504, 507, 508, 519; and Russia, 503, 529
Aizawa Seishisai, 518, 520–29
Akamatsu Hiromichi, 32, 35, 36
Akechi Mitsuhide, 9
Akō vendetta, 353, 354–93; dramatization of, 383–87
Alcock, Sir Rutherford, 561
Amaterasu Ōmikami (sun goddess), 67, 69, 72, 81, 93, 430; and Dutch learning, 291; and *kokutai*, 525–26, 527; Motoori Norinaga on, 409–11, 413; and National Learning, 398; Neo-Confucianists on, 174, 471–72, 477; in open-door policy debate, 521, 523, 558; pre-Restoration thinkers on, 505
Amida Buddha, 144, 145; calling on name of, 116, 435, 438, 448, 449, 453–54
Amur River, 529
An Lushan, 358
Analects (Lun-yü; Confucius): and Akō vendetta, 362n.6, 381n.20; in education, 221n.3, 239–43, 249n.41, 259; on food, 335;

OTHER WORKS IN THE

COLUMBIA ASIAN STUDIES SERIES

TRANSLATIONS FROM THE ASIAN CLASSICS

Major Plays of Chikamatsu, tr. Donald Keene 1961

Four Major Plays of Chikamatsu, tr. Donald Keene. Paperback ed. only. 1961; rev. ed. 1997

Records of the Grand Historian of China, translated from the Shih chi of Ssu-ma Ch'ien, tr. Burton Watson, 2 vols. 1961

Instructions for Practical Living and Other Neo-Confucian Writings by Wang Yang-ming, tr. Wing-tsit Chan 1963

Hsün Tzu: Basic Writings, tr. Burton Watson, paperback ed. only. 1963; rev. ed. 1996

Chuang Tzu: Basic Writings, tr. Burton Watson, paperback ed. only. 1964; rev. ed. 1996

The Mahābhārata, tr. Chakravarthi V. Narasimhan. Also in paperback ed. 1965; rev. ed. 1997

The Manyōshū, Nippon Gakujutsu Shinkōkai edition 1965

Su Tung-p'o: Selections from a Sung Dynasty Poet, tr. Burton Watson. Also in paperback ed. 1965

Bhartrihari: Poems, tr. Barbara Stoler Miller. Also in paperback ed. 1967

Basic Writings of Mo Tzu, Hsün Tzu, and Han Fei Tzu, tr. Burton Watson. Also in separate paperback eds. 1967

The Awakening of Faith, Attributed to Aśvaghosha, tr. Yoshito S. Hakeda. Also in paperback ed. 1967

Reflections on Things at Hand: The Neo-Confucian Anthology, comp. Chu Hsi and Lü Tsu-ch'ien, tr. Wing-tsit Chan 1967

The Platform Sutra of the Sixth Patriarch, tr. Philip B. Yampolsky. Also in paperback ed. 1967

Essays in Idleness: The Tsurezuregusa of Kenkō, tr. Donald Keene. Also in paperback ed. 1967

The Pillow Book of Sei Shōnagon, tr. Ivan Morris, 2 vols. 1967

Two Plays of Ancient India: The Little Clay Cart and the Minister's Seal, tr. J. A. B. van Buitenen 1968

The Complete Works of Chuang Tzu, tr. Burton Watson 1968

The Romance of the Western Chamber (Hsi Hsiang chi), tr. S. I. Hsiung. Also in paperback ed. 1968

The Manyōshū, Nippon Gakujutsu Shinkōkai edition. Paperback ed. only. 1969

Records of the Historian: Chapters from the Shih chi of Ssu-ma Ch'ien, tr. Burton Watson. Paperback ed. only. 1969

Cold Mountain: 100 Poems by the T'ang Poet Han-shan, tr. Burton Watson. Also in paperback ed. 1970

Twenty Plays of the Nō Theatre, ed. Donald Keene. Also in paperback ed. 1970

Chūshingura: The Treasury of Loyal Retainers, tr. Donald Keene. Also in paperback ed. 1971; rev. ed. 1997

The Zen Master Hakuin: Selected Writings, tr. Philip B. Yampolsky 1971

Chinese Rhyme-Prose: Poems in the Fu Form from the Han and Six Dynasties Periods, tr. Burton Watson. Also in paperback ed. 1971

Kūkai: Major Works, tr. Yoshito S. Hakeda. Also in paperback ed. 1972

The Old Man Who Does as He Pleases: Selections from the Poetry and Prose of Lu Yu, tr. Burton Watson 1973

The Lion's Roar of Queen Śrīmālā, tr. Alex and Hideko Wayman 1974

Courtier and Commoner in Ancient China: Selections from the History of the Former Han by Pan Ku, tr. Burton Watson. Also in paperback ed. 1974

Japanese Literature in Chinese, vol. 1: Poetry and Prose in Chinese by Japanese Writers of the Early Period, tr. Burton Watson 1975

Japanese Literature in Chinese, vol. 2: Poetry and Prose in Chinese by Japanese Writers of the Later Period, tr. Burton Watson 1976

Scripture of the Lotus Blossom of the Fine Dharma, tr. Leon Hurvitz. Also in paperback ed. 1976

Love Song of the Dark Lord: Jayadeva's Gītagovinda, tr. Barbara Stoler Miller. Also in paperback ed. Cloth ed. includes critical text of the Sanskrit. 1977; rev. ed. 1997

Ryōkan: Zen Monk-Poet of Japan, tr. Burton Watson 1977

Calming the Mind and Discerning the Real: From the Lam rim chen mo of Tsoṇ-kha-pa, tr. Alex Wayman 1978

The Hermit and the Love-Thief: Sanskrit Poems of Bhartrihari and Bilhaṇa, tr. Barbara Stoler Miller 1978

The Lute: Kao Ming's P'i-p'a chi, tr. Jean Mulligan. Also in paperback ed. 1980

A Chronicle of Gods and Sovereigns: Jinnō Shōtōki of Kitabatake Chikafusa, tr. H. Paul Varley 1980

Among the Flowers: The Hua-chien chi, tr. Lois Fusek 1982

Grass Hill: Poems and Prose by the Japanese Monk Gensei, tr. Burton Watson 1983

Doctors, Diviners, and Magicians of Ancient China: Biographies of Fang-shih, tr. Kenneth J. DeWoskin. Also in paperback ed. 1983

Theater of Memory: The Plays of Kālidāsa, ed. Barbara Stoler Miller. Also in paperback ed. 1984

The Columbia Book of Chinese Poetry: From Early Times to the Thirteenth Century, ed. and tr. Burton Watson. Also in paperback ed. 1984

Poems of Love and War: From the Eight Anthologies and the Ten Long Poems of Classical Tamil, tr. A. K. Ramanujan. Also in paperback ed. 1985

The Bhagavad Gita: Krishna's Counsel in Time of War, tr. Barbara Stoler Miller 1986

The Columbia Book of Later Chinese Poetry, ed. and tr. Jonathan Chaves. Also in paperback ed. 1986

The Tso Chuan: Selections from China's Oldest Narrative History, tr. Burton Watson 1989

Waiting for the Wind: Thirty-six Poets of Japan's Late Medieval Age, tr. Steven Carter 1989

Selected Writings of Nichiren, ed. Philip B. Yampolsky 1990

Saigyō, Poems of a Mountain Home, tr. Burton Watson 1990

The Book of Lieh Tzu: A Classic of the Tao, tr. A. C. Graham. Morningside ed. 1990

The Tale of an Anklet: An Epic of South India—The Cilappatikāram of Iḷaṅkō Aṭikaḷ, tr. R. Parthasarathy 1993

Waiting for the Dawn: A Plan for the Prince, tr. and introduction by Wm. Theodore de Bary 1993

Yoshitsune and the Thousand Cherry Trees: A Masterpiece of the Eighteenth-Century Japanese Puppet Theater, tr., annotated, and with introduction by Stanleigh H. Jones, Jr. 1993

The Lotus Sutra, tr. Burton Watson. Also in paperback ed. 1993

The Classic of Changes: A New Translation of the I Ching as Interpreted by Wang Bi, tr. Richard John Lynn 1994

Beyond Spring: Tz'u Poems of the Sung Dynasty, tr. Julie Landau 1994

The Columbia Anthology of Traditional Chinese Literature, ed. Victor H. Mair 1994

Scenes for Mandarins: The Elite Theater of the Ming, tr. Cyril Birch 1995

Letters of Nichiren, ed. Philip B. Yampolsky; tr. Burton Watson et al. 1996

Unforgotten Dreams: Poems by the Zen Monk Shōtetsu, tr. Steven D. Carter 1997

The Vimalakirti Sutra, tr. Burton Watson 1997

Japanese and Chinese Poems to Sing: The Wakan rōei shū, tr. J. Thomas Rimer and Jonathan Chaves 1997

Breeze Through Bamboo: Kanshi of Ema Saikō, tr. Hiroaki Sato 1998

A Tower for the Summer Heat, Li Yu, tr. Patrick Hanan 1998

Traditional Japanese Theater: An Anthology of Plays, Karen Brazell 1998

The Original Analects: Sayings of Confucius and His Successors (0479–0249), E. Bruce Brooks and A. Taeko Brooks 1998

The Classic of the Way and Virtue: A New Translation of the Tao-te ching of Laozi as Interpreted by Wang Bi, tr. Richard John Lynn 1999

The Four Hundred Songs of War and Wisdom: An Anthology of Poems from Classical Tamil, The Puṟanāṉūṟu, ed. and tr. George L. Hart and Hank Heifetz 1999

Original Tao: Inward Training (Nei-yeh) *and the Foundations of Taoist Mysticism*, by Harold D. Roth 1999

Lao Tzu's Tao Te Ching: *A Translation of the Startling New Documents Found at Guodian*, by Robert G. Henricks 2000

The Shorter Columbia Anthology of Traditional Chinese Literature, ed. Victor H. Mair 2000

Mistress and Maid (Jiaohongji), by Meng Chengshun, tr. Cyril Birch 2001

Chikamatsu: Five Late Plays, tr. and ed. C. Andrew Gerstle 2001

The Essential Lotus: Selections from the Lotus Sutra, tr. Burton Watson 2002

Early Modern Japanese Literature: An Anthology, 1600–1900, ed. Haruo Shirane 2002

The Sound of the Kiss, or The Story That Must Never Be Told: Pingali Suranna's Ka-lapurnodayamu, tr. Vecheru Narayana Rao and David Shulman 2003

The Selected Poems of Du Fu, tr. Burton Watson 2003

Far Beyond the Field: Haiku by Japanese Women, tr. Makoto Ueda 2003

Just Living: Poems and Prose by the Japanese Monk Tonna, ed. and tr. Steven D. Carter 2003

Han Feizi: Basic Writings, tr. Burton Watson 2003

Mozi: Basic Writings, tr. Burton Watson 2003

Xunzi: Basic Writings, tr. Burton Watson 2003

Zhuangzi: Basic Writings, tr. Burton Watson 2003

The Awakening of Faith, Attributed to Aśvaghosha, tr. Yoshito S. Hakeda, introduction by Ryuichi Abe 2005

The Tales of the Heike, tr. Burton Watson, ed. Haruo Shirane 2006

Tales of Moonlight and Rain, Ueda Akinari, tr. and introduction by Anthony H. Chambers 2007

MODERN ASIAN LITERATURE

Modern Japanese Drama: An Anthology, ed. and tr. Ted. Takaya. Also in paperback ed. 1979

Mask and Sword: Two Plays for the Contemporary Japanese Theater, by Yamazaki Masakazu, tr. J. Thomas Rimer 1980

Yokomitsu Riichi, Modernist, Dennis Keene 1980

Nepali Visions, Nepali Dreams: The Poetry of Laxmiprasad Devkota, tr. David Rubin 1980

Literature of the Hundred Flowers, vol. 1: Criticism and Polemics, ed. Hualing Nieh 1981

Literature of the Hundred Flowers, vol. 2: Poetry and Fiction, ed. Hualing Nieh 1981

Modern Chinese Stories and Novellas, 1919–1949, ed. Joseph S. M. Lau, C. T. Hsia, and Leo Ou-fan Lee. Also in paperback ed. 1984

A *View by the Sea*, by Yasuoka Shōtarō, tr. Kären Wigen Lewis 1984

Other Worlds: Arishima Takeo and the Bounds of Modern Japanese Fiction, by Paul Anderer 1984

Selected Poems of Sō Chōngju, tr. with introduction by David R. McCann 1989

The Sting of Life: Four Contemporary Japanese Novelists, by Van C. Gessel 1989

Stories of Osaka Life, by Oda Sakunosuke, tr. Burton Watson 1990

The Bodhisattva, or Samantabhadra, by Ishikawa Jun, tr. with introduction by William Jefferson Tyler 1990

The Travels of Lao Ts'an, by Liu T'ieh-yün, tr. Harold Shadick. Morningside ed. 1990

Three Plays by Kōbō Abe, tr. with introduction by Donald Keene 1993

The Columbia Anthology of Modern Chinese Literature, ed. Joseph S. M. Lau and Howard Goldblatt 1995

Modern Japanese Tanka, ed. and tr. Makoto Ueda 1996

Masaoka Shiki: Selected Poems, ed. and tr. Burton Watson 1997

Writing Women in Modern China: An Anthology of Women's Literature from the Early Twentieth Century, ed. and tr. Amy D. Dooling and Kristina M. Torgeson 1998

American Stories, by Nagai Kafū, tr. Mitsuko Iriye 2000

The Paper Door and Other Stories, by Shiga Naoya, tr. Lane Dunlop 2001

Grass for My Pillow, by Saiichi Maruya, tr. Dennis Keene 2002

For All My Walking: Free-Verse Haiku of Taneda Santōka, with Excerpts from His Diaries, tr. Burton Watson 2003

The Columbia Anthology of Modern Japanese Literature, vol. 1: *From Restoration to Occupation, 1868–1945*, ed. J. Thomas Rimer and Van C. Gessel 2005

STUDIES IN ASIAN CULTURE

The Ōnin War: History of Its Origins and Background, with a Selective Translation of the Chronicle of Ōnin, by H. Paul Varley 1967

Chinese Government in Ming Times: Seven Studies, ed. Charles O. Hucker 1969

The Actors' Analects (Yakusha Rongo), ed. and tr. Charles J. Dunn and Bungō Torigoe 1969

Self and Society in Ming Thought, by Wm. Theodore de Bary and the Conference on Ming Thought. Also in paperback ed. 1970

A History of Islamic Philosophy, by Majid Fakhry, 2d ed. 1983

Phantasies of a Love Thief: The Caurapañcāśikā Attributed to Bilhaṇa, by Barbara Stoler Miller 1971

Iqbal: Poet-Philosopher of Pakistan, ed. Hafeez Malik 1971

The Golden Tradition: An Anthology of Urdu Poetry, ed. and tr. Ahmed Ali. Also in paperback ed. 1973

Conquerors and Confucians: Aspects of Political Change in Late Yüan China, by John W. Dardess 1973

The Unfolding of Neo-Confucianism, by Wm. Theodore de Bary and the Conference on Seventeenth-Century Chinese Thought. Also in paperback ed. 1975

To Acquire Wisdom: The Way of Wang Yang-ming, by Julia Ching 1976

Gods, Priests, and Warriors: The Bhṛgus of the Mahābhārata, by Robert P. Goldman 1977

Mei Yao-ch'en and the Development of Early Sung Poetry, by Jonathan Chaves 1976

The Legend of Semimaru, Blind Musician of Japan, by Susan Matisoff 1977

Sir Sayyid Ahmad Khan and Muslim Modernization in India and Pakistan, by Hafeez Malik 1980

The Khilafat Movement: Religious Symbolism and Political Mobilization in India, by Gail Minault 1982

The World of K'ung Shang-jen: A Man of Letters in Early Ch'ing China, by Richard Strassberg 1983

The Lotus Boat: The Origins of Chinese Tz'u Poetry in T'ang Popular Culture, by Marsha L. Wagner 1984

Expressions of Self in Chinese Literature, ed. Robert E. Hegel and Richard C. Hessney 1985

Songs for the Bride: Women's Voices and Wedding Rites of Rural India, by W. G. Archer; ed. Barbara Stoler Miller and Mildred Archer 1986

The Confucian Kingship in Korea: Yŏngjo and the Politics of Sagacity, by JaHyun Kim Haboush 1988

COMPANIONS TO ASIAN STUDIES

Approaches to the Oriental Classics, ed. Wm. Theodore de Bary 1959

Early Chinese Literature, by Burton Watson. Also in paperback ed. 1962

Approaches to Asian Civilizations, ed. Wm. Theodore de Bary and Ainslie T. Embree 1964

The Classic Chinese Novel: A Critical Introduction, by C. T. Hsia. Also in paperback ed. 1968

Chinese Lyricism: Shih Poetry from the Second to the Twelfth Century, tr. Burton Watson. Also in paperback ed. 1971

A Syllabus of Indian Civilization, by Leonard A. Gordon and Barbara Stoler Miller 1971

Twentieth-Century Chinese Stories, ed. C. T. Hsia and Joseph S. M. Lau. Also in paperback ed. 1971

A Syllabus of Chinese Civilization, by J. Mason Gentzler, 2d ed. 1972

A Syllabus of Japanese Civilization, by H. Paul Varley, 2d ed. 1972

An Introduction to Chinese Civilization, ed. John Meskill, with the assistance of J. Mason Gentzler 1973

An Introduction to Japanese Civilization, ed. Arthur E. Tiedemann 1974

Ukifune: Love in the Tale of Genji, ed. Andrew Pekarik 1982

The Pleasures of Japanese Literature, by Donald Keene 1988

A Guide to Oriental Classics, ed. Wm. Theodore de Bary and Ainslie T. Embree; 3d edition ed. Amy Vladeck Heinrich, 2 vols. 1989

INTRODUCTION TO ASIAN CIVILIZATIONS
Wm. Theodore de Bary, General Editor

Sources of Japanese Tradition, 1958; paperback ed., 2 vols., 1964. 2d ed., vol. 1, 2001, compiled by Wm. Theodore de Bary, Donald Keene, George Tanabe, and Paul Varley; vol. 2, 2005, compiled by Wm. Theodore de Bary, Carol Gluck, and Arthur E. Tiedemann

Sources of Indian Tradition, 1958; paperback ed., 2 vols., 1964. 2d ed., 2 vols., 1988

Sources of Chinese Tradition, 1960, paperback ed., 2 vols., 1964. 2d ed., vol. 1, 1999, compiled by Wm. Theodore de Bary and Irene Bloom; vol. 2, 2000, compiled by Wm. Theodore de Bary and Richard Lufrano

Sources of Korean Tradition, 1997; 2 vols., vol. 1, 1997, compiled by Peter H. Lee and Wm. Theodore de Bary; vol. 2, 2001, compiled by Yŏngho Ch'oe, Peter H. Lee, and Wm. Theodore de Bary

NEO-CONFUCIAN STUDIES

Instructions for Practical Living and Other Neo-Confucian Writings by Wang Yang-ming, tr. Wing-tsit Chan 1963

Reflections on Things at Hand: The Neo-Confucian Anthology, comp. Chu Hsi and Lü Tsu-ch'ien, tr. Wing-tsit Chan 1967

Self and Society in Ming Thought, by Wm. Theodore de Bary and the Conference on Ming Thought. Also in paperback ed. 1970

The Unfolding of Neo-Confucianism, by Wm. Theodore de Bary and the Conference on Seventeenth-Century Chinese Thought. Also in paperback ed. 1975

Principle and Practicality: Essays in Neo-Confucianism and Practical Learning, ed. Wm. Theodore de Bary and Irene Bloom. Also in paperback ed. 1979

The Syncretic Religion of Lin Chao-en, by Judith A. Berling 1980

The Renewal of Buddhism in China: Chu-hung and the Late Ming Synthesis, by Chün-fang Yü 1981

Neo-Confucian Orthodoxy and the Learning of the Mind-and-Heart, by Wm. Theodore de Bary 1981

Yüan Thought: Chinese Thought and Religion Under the Mongols, ed. Hok-lam Chan and Wm. Theodore de Bary 1982

The Liberal Tradition in China, by Wm. Theodore de Bary 1983

The Development and Decline of Chinese Cosmology, by John B. Henderson 1984

The Rise of Neo-Confucianism in Korea, by Wm. Theodore de Bary and JaHyun Kim Haboush 1985

Chiao Hung and the Restructuring of Neo-Confucianism in Late Ming, by Edward T. Ch'ien 1985

Neo-Confucian Terms Explained: Pei-hsi tzu-i, by Ch'en Ch'un, ed. and tr. Wing-tsit Chan 1986

Knowledge Painfully Acquired: K'un-chih chi, by Lo Ch'in-shun, ed. and tr. Irene Bloom 1987

To Become a Sage: The Ten Diagrams on Sage Learning, by Yi T'oegye, ed. and tr. Michael C. Kalton 1988

The Message of the Mind in Neo-Confucian Thought, by Wm. Theodore de Bary 1989